Meeting the Psychoeducational
Needs of Minority Students

Meeting the Psychoeducational Needs of Minority Students

Evidence-Based Guidelines for School Psychologists and Other School Personnel

Craig L. Frisby

WILEY

Library of Congress Cataloging-in-Publication Data:

Frisby, Craig L.
    Meeting the psychoeducational needs of minority students : evidence-based guidelines for school psychologists and other school personnel / Craig L. Frisby.
        1 online resource.
    Includes bibliographical references and index.
        Description based on print version record and CIP data provided by publisher; resource not viewed.
    ISBN 978-1-118-28637-1 (ebook) — ISBN 978-1-118-28208-3 (ebook) — ISBN 978-1-118-28259-5 (ebook) — ISBN 978-0-470-94075-4 (print)
        1. School psychologists. 2. Minority students—Counseling of. I. Title.
    LB1027.55
    371.7'13—dc23
                                                                                2012050796

Printed in the United States of America

10 9 8 7 6 5 4 3 2 1

This book is dedicated to Professor Thomas Oakland,
a fine human being and scholar, whose pioneering work
on behalf of serving minority children in schools
established a large footprint
for others to follow.

Contents

Acknowledgments

This author is indebted to numerous individuals who have provided crucial direction, interviews, and materials contributing to the quality of this book and its value to readers.

Serving minority children and youth in schools begins with persons who are on the front lines of some very difficult battles in schools and communities. I extend a very big *thank you* to Dr. Stan Bosch, Lori Hanna, and the Miami-Dade School District Police Department for taking the time to speak with me about your important work.

I am particularly indebted to Professor Thomas Fagan at the University of Memphis, who generously allowed access to historical information on the National Association of School Psychologists (NASP) through *NASP Communiqué* archives. Dr. Randy Schnell is deserving of much appreciation for sharing materials on the fine psychological services work being done in the Memphis Unified School District, as are Drs. Danna Diaz and Michael Parker, who have opened my eyes as to what can be done on behalf of children and youth in the Fort Worth Independent School District.

Marie Concannon (University of Missouri Government Documents Regional Coordinator) and John Blodgett (Sr. Scientific Programmer/Data Analyst, University of Missouri Office of Social & Economic Data Analysis) are to be commended for generously giving of their valuable time to locate national, state, and county data for various tables in this text. I am indebted to Becky Gerhardstein (Data Analyst, Psychological Assessment Resources), Ying Meng (Sr. Statistical Analyst, Clinical Psychometrics, Pearson Assessments), and Professor Steve Osterlind for using their quantitative skills to access and organize helpful test data needed for this text.

I thank Henry Duvall (Director of Communications, Council of the Great City Schools) for compiling a directory of urban schools that assisted in providing key contacts necessary for this research. Special thanks goes to Dr. Kenneth Thomas for sharing materials shedding light on contentious debates within counseling psychology. Your commitment to honest principles is an inspiration.

I am appreciative of those colleagues (Frank Miele, Dr. Linda Gottfredson, and Dr. Rebecca Kopriva) who generously gave of their time to review portions of this text.

Special appreciation goes to the indefatigable Robert Bligh, who has kept me (and others) informed of the latest conversations of interest in the education of minority children.

On a more personal note, many in the world of professional psychology mourn the passing of Professor Nadine Lambert, who was truly one of the giants in our field. I cannot forget Dr. Betty Henry, an early mentor who continues to provide a refreshing oasis of wisdom and common sense in the midst of a crazy world.

Thank you, Marquita Flemming (Wiley Publications), for answering my many questions and shepherding me through the long and arduous process of publishing this book.

Finally, to members of my immediate and extended family: Thank you for your encouragement and support, without which this book would not have been possible.

1

Why the Need for This Book?

In 1977, barely a decade after the creation of the National Association of School Psychologists (NASP), Professor Thomas Oakland published *Psychological and Educational Assessment of Minority Children*. This groundbreaking edited text, developed for a school psychology audience, was the first of its kind to focus the field's attention on minority children and issues related to (what was referred to at that time) "non-discriminatory" psychoeducational assessment.

Although school psychologists are widely viewed as top specialists in the area of individual assessment for diagnosing pupils' psychoeducational problems, the field has pursued additional areas of expertise over the decades that extend beyond individual assessment for placement in special programs. In addition, the world has changed considerably in the 35 years since Prof. Oakland's text was first published. As one example, immigration—barely acknowledged 35 years ago—is an issue that has risen to the forefront of contemporary social, educational, and political discussions. Today, more and better research informs educational practice, generally, and school psychology practice, specifically, about minority children and schooling. Unfortunately, much of what is popularly promoted in school psychology today on these important issues remains stuck in the 1970s. A simple analogy illustrates the nature of this problem.

SCRIPTED KNOWLEDGE

Large commercial theme parks (e.g., Six Flags, DisneyWorld, SeaWorld) use elaborate transportation systems, such as ferry boats, chair lifts, monorails, and bus trams, to give customers a safe, structured, and controlled means of getting from point A to point B within the park. Such rides control how many persons can ride at one time, the speed at which the ride moves, and which areas of the park are covered. Typically, a company tour guide points out carefully selected "areas of interest," about which park officials provide "canned," company-approved stories and descriptions.

Psychoeducational issues and problems involving racial/ethnic/language minority students are choreographed for school psychology audiences in much the same way. That is, the field invents its own terms (e.g., *cultural competence*), as well as its own definitions for them; frames multicultural problems in a prescribed manner that suits particular sociopolitical agendas (e.g., eradicating disproportionalities; promoting "social justice"); dictates how multicultural issues are to be framed, interpreted, and discussed; dictates the "correct" attitudes and feelings (e.g., "tolerance," "sensitivity") that audiences should have toward problems; and carefully arranges structural contingencies that determine how programs are to be rewarded or sanctioned for the extent to which multiculturalism ideology is infused into training.

In contemporary school psychology, multiculturalism ultimately boils down to an "everything-is-biased-against-CLD-children" message. This message has an intuitive appeal, as most students and professionals have a natural affinity for a professional identity that exposes injustices and "fights for the underdog." Although this message may have seemed new and fresh 35 years ago, it has grown increasingly more stale with each passing decade. This is because the field has the benefit of much more high-quality empirical research than it did 35 years ago, which includes clear evaluations of so-called "multicultural" remedies that have been tried (and most of which have failed) in the real world. When it comes to racial/ethnic conflicts in society, careful analyses have shown that there are no simplistic morality plays involving clear saints and clear villains. Hence, facile explanations for minority pupils' school problems that may have been persuasive decades ago are no longer persuasive to better informed researchers and scholars today.

Unfortunately, such insights have not permeated contemporary discussions of multicultural issues in school psychology. For all practical purposes, the field is figuratively held hostage by two primary messages on multicultural issues, which are as scripted and predictable as the rising and setting of the sun every 24 hours. First, racial/ethnic minority groups are viewed as "culturally exotic," which presumably requires nonminority school psychologists to learn about the odd cultural traits of different groups in order to be effective in serving them. Second, minority groups are seen as perpetual "victims" of racism, discrimination, and/or prejudice—which presumably lurks just beneath the surface of polite society, is expressed in countless subtle ways (e.g., "stereotype threat," "micro-aggressions"), and serves as the all-purpose explanation for most problems faced by minority groups in schools. The role of school psychologists, therefore, is to develop a zeal for "social justice"—which then prepares them to parachute into schools to rescue minority children from the harm that most assuredly awaits them at the hands of culturally insensitive educators.

The fundamental message of this book is that these ideas, no matter how appealing they may sound, *have nothing at all to do with actual practices that effectively help vulnerable minority children in schools.* Before discussing the material covered in this text, however, the principle of truth in advertising requires an initial discussion of what this book will *not* cover.

WHAT THIS BOOK IS NOT

There exist many outstanding texts for school psychologists that describe specific academic and behavioral interventions that are effective for helping children, youth, and families in school settings. With the exception of interventions that require non–English language modifications, no credible data-based psychological theory has demonstrated that such interventions cannot also be used with minority children. *First and foremost, minority children and their families are not kitchen appliances that come equipped with a "multicultural instruction manual" for proper care and service.* Hence, this book is not an inventory of scripted how-to recipes designed to magically work with nonwhite or non-English-speaking children. Contrary to current fashions, knowing the racial or ethnic status of students—by itself—provides no useful information on their school adjustment, academic performance, or how they are to be served when they experience problems in educational settings. The reality is that many minority students adjust well and achieve satisfactorily in schools, and many do not. Therefore, knowledge of minority status alone is not sufficient for problem solving. It is the *correlates* of racial/ethnic/language status, and *how these correlated variables interact*, that must be understood before school psychologists (and other school personnel) can appreciate how best to effectively serve vulnerable children in schools.

Second, although special education issues are discussed in various places within this text when necessary, the exclusive focus of this book is not on special education. Many texts attempt to marry special education with multiculturalism, but this hybrid often seems forced and artificial. Many school psychologists were initially motivated to enter the field because of its characterization as a profession that applies psychological knowledge to helping all children in schools. Only after entering the field as graduate students did many begin to realize how special education plays a dominant role in defining school psychology roles and functions. This text departs somewhat from this tradition by addressing problems of minority children throughout all levels of the education system, which is in keeping with a simple definition of the field as the application of psychology to education, defined broadly.

Third, many school psychology students and scholars who are interested in multicultural issues find themselves attracted to ideas and insights drawn from the specialty of counseling psychology. Counseling psychology, compared to other applied psychologies, has a reputation for showcasing prolific writing from "academic superstars" who specialize in multiculturalism. Because school psychology does not produce this same degree of sustained scholarship on multicultural issues, it comes as little surprise that opinions in school psychology are often shaped by ideas that are vigorously promoted within counseling psychology.

This book departs substantially from this tradition, for the following reason: Fundamentally, counseling psychologists who specialize in multiculturalism often place an inordinate emphasis on the deleterious effects of real or imagined "racism" (e.g., see Sidebar 2.2), which in the final analysis reflects group grievance politics and sociopolitical advocacy more than it reflects objective, empirically supported research. Although school psychology roles and functions can overlap somewhat with the roles of school counselors, much in school psychology practice simply is not easily translatable from counseling psychology. This text, in contrast, adopts the view that a better and more empirically supportable understanding of how minority children are served in schools owes much more inspiration from the field of educational psychology than it does from counseling psychology.

CHAPTER CONTENT

Returning to the earlier commercial theme park analogy, the purpose of this book is to permit readers to disembark from the scripted tour and walk freely about the park, drawing one's own conclusions and exploring areas unhindered by "Do Not Enter" signs.

Multiculturalism ideology is currently the primary vehicle through which graduate students in school psychology (and other related applied professions) first learn about issues and problems of minority groups in schools. Toward this end, various facets of multiculturalism ideology are analyzed in detail in **Chapter 2**. Multiculturalism ideology so permeates preservice training that audiences are usually unaware that what are promoted as "truths" are little more than ideological talking points. Audiences simply assume that if their professional organizations or university trainers promote an idea, and repeat it often enough, then it must be true, and it has a prescriptive right not to be questioned or challenged. With rare exceptions (e.g., see Frisby, 2005a, 2005b), multiculturalism ideology is never treated as an object of scrutiny in its own right, nor is it ever examined directly in order to test the validity of its implicit assumptions. When this is done, *the irony is that multiculturalism ideology contributes next to nothing that informs school psychologists (and other school personnel) about practices that are found to actually help minority children in schools.*

Quack Multiculturalism is the name given to a particular brand of multiculturalism that promotes falsehoods and distortions, yet amazingly continues to be promoted as received wisdom in the field. The primary theme of the chapter is that multiculturalism is fundamentally a sociopolitical ideology. It is not—as many would presume—a science, nor does it necessarily represent "best practices" for school psychologists. Quack Multiculturalism is not to be confused with research and practices that have been found to actually help minority children in schools, thus readers are encouraged to keep these two concepts separate.

Minority children are raised in a variety of home and neighborhood environments, some of which include the structure, nurturing, support, and freedom from chaos that is conducive to school learning, and many others that do not. Within every country on the face of the globe, social class is an extremely important scientific variable that has been shown to be empirically related to many social outcome variables. In most (but certainly not all) cases, social class supersedes race/ethnicity as a powerful predictor of schooling outcomes. Yet inexplicably, this variable receives almost no attention in the published literature in contemporary school psychology. The purpose of the material discussed in **Chapter 3** is to showcase the role of social class and home/neighborhood environments in contributing to social and educational outcomes for minority children.

Minority children are not homogeneous in the school settings in which they are educated, which is another variable that is all but ignored in Quack Multiculturalism. Even when home/family environments may not be ideal, variability in the educational philosophies, instructional practices, and curriculum offerings of schools play a crucial role in the quality of educational experiences that minority children receive. The material in **Chapter 4** discusses these important differences in the contexts for school learning, which can help readers better understand the proximal factors that influence psychoeducational outcomes for minority children.

To understand the relationship between classroom instruction and school learning, while pretending to ignore the role of general cognitive ability, is like trying to bake a cake without using flour. School psychologists, more than any other school professionals, should know that individual differences in cognitive ability is the one psychological variable that is most highly predictive of individual achievement in school and beyond. Because of the contentious politics surrounding this issue, however, school psychologists have largely ignored their professional responsibility to apply what research clearly indicates about the relationship of this important variable to instructional practices and school learning. The material in **Chapter 5** explicates these relationships.

School psychologists are also widely considered to possess (at least in principle) more measurement and testing expertise than most other school professionals. As testing and assessment experts, they should not be intimidated by claims that standardized testing is biased against minority groups who are native-born English speakers. The field has given an open forum to this claim in previous decades, which has produced no substantial evidence or valid arguments against the use of standardized testing in education. As shown in **Chapter 6**, however, there is still a role for school psychologists (and other school personnel) in helping minority children in the context of testing and assessment practices in schools. Properly trained school psychologists are uniquely positioned to help schools in accessing and choosing the proper test accommodations for limited English speakers. School psychologists can lend their expertise to schools' efforts to help minority students prepare for, and perform to the best of their abilities on, classroom and schoolwide standardized tests.

Without a basic level of behavioral discipline, students cannot learn in schools. There is no magic formula for disciplining children differently as a function of their racial/ethnic group membership. However, when a critical mass of minority students with poor behavioral socialization skills are present in a school, fundamental structural changes in school organization and school policies are required. The material in **Chapter 7** has shown that good discipline and classroom management can occur in schools where the principal is freed from the kinds of bureaucratic constraints—present in most public schools—that make learning all but impossible.

The presence of organized youth gangs in schools with significantly large minority enrollments has a way of making a mockery of schools' best efforts to promote a safe and orderly academic environment. The serious problems caused by school crime and youth gangs focus discussions on what is most important: the physical safety of students, teachers, and staff. There is nothing overtly "multicultural" about what schools do to combat these problems, because most interventions adopted by schools involve basic protections for students whose learning and development is compromised by the presence of gangs, crime, and delinquency in schools. Most school psychology programs barely acknowledge this problem in discussions of multicultural issues. The material discussed in **Chapter 8** is designed to introduce school psychologists (and other school personnel) to this issue, and to show how schools can effectively respond to this difficult problem.

School districts enrolling large numbers of racial/ethnic minority and immigrant children find that they must devote considerable resources to within-district programs to combat vexing social problems (e.g., criminal activity, teen pregnancy, drug abuse, lack of services for immigrant newcomers) that undermine the ability of students to benefit from their educations. School psychology students may be quite surprised to discover that, rather than minority students being underserved in schools, many school districts are quite intentional and proactive in developing programs specifically targeted to combating these social problems. The material in **Chapter 9** provides a more in-depth discussion of exemplary programs for minority students in select districts around the country.

Chapters 2 through 9, when considered as a whole, generate specific guidelines, principles, and recommendations that need to be carefully considered if school psychology desires to move forward and become a key contributor to national discussions about improving psychoeducational outcomes for minority children. These ideas are discussed at length in **Chapter 10**. This needed direction is two-pronged: (1) the field needs to seriously reconsider, and in some cases abandon, modes of thinking that have consistently proven to result in hopeless dead-ends; and (2) there are new directions to pursue that are more empirically sound, yet are linked more closely to the practices of schools that are successful in educating large numbers of minority children.

Many terms and concepts could have been defined and explained in greater detail, but this would have interrupted the flow of the text if these definitions were included in the chapters. The book concludes with a concise **Glossary**, where key terms are defined and explained in greater detail for readers.

Lastly, the book includes certain features to help readers navigate the text and locate sources more easily. The book makes extensive use of highlighted Sidebars, which are self-contained explanations or illustrations of key concepts that can be read separately from the main flow of the text. In an effort to keep current, a conscious effort was also made to include information sources and examples that can be accessed more easily from the Internet. At the end of most chapters, additional resources are given that supplement the main concepts discussed in the text.

CHAPTER

2

⟨━◆━⟩

The Problem of Quack Multiculturalism

Advocacy is different from science. . . . For the zealous advocate, cause and effect are predetermined to serve one's interests. An advocate need not even believe a cause or effect that she claims; her goal is to persuade others to believe it. An advocate searches not for probable causes and effects but, rather, for merely plausible ones—ones that others are willing to believe. . . . The desired outcome is neither truth nor understanding, but conversion—getting others to view a situation in a manner that serves one's own interests.

—Phelps & Gottfredson, *Correcting Fallacies About Educational and Psychological Testing*, 2009, p. 250
Copyright © 2009 by the American Psychological Association.
Reproduced with permission.

WHAT IS MULTICULTURALISM?

Graduate students in applied psychology and education are typically first exposed to discussions about the school problems of cultural minority children and youth as filtered through the ideological lens of *multiculturalism* (Banks & Banks, 2004; Jones, 2009; MacCluskie, 2010; Pedersen, 1999; Ravitch, 2007; Steinberg, 2009). As a popular term in the applied social sciences, *multiculturalism* has been defined differently in different contexts. For school psychologists, multiculturalism is the name given to a sociopolitical philosophy that, for better or worse, functions as the de facto ideology of the National

Association of School Psychologists (NASP) and the American Psychological Association (APA)—as these pertain to racial/ethnic/language minority issues. If asked to spontaneously define this term, rank-and-file school psychologists would most likely mention phrases that they have heard endlessly repeated in their professional readings—namely, that multiculturalism has something to do with "valuing diversity," "being sensitive to cultural differences," or developing "cultural competence," to name a few.

TYPES OF SUPERFICIAL MULTICULTURALISM

Multiculturalism is a sociopolitical ideology that is fundamentally designed to shape and modify attitudes and perceptions. Before embarking on an in-depth analysis of the central tenets of this ideology, it is necessary to first describe the more superficial manifestations of multiculturalism as they are experienced by the general public and professional educators. These superficial manifestations of multiculturalism, called Boutique, Kumbayah, Light-and-Fluffy, and Bean-Counting Multiculturalism, are briefly described as follows.

Boutique Multiculturalism

An elementary school hosts a Back-to-School Night where parents can visit their child's school, chat with teachers, and see displays of various arts-and-crafts projects that the students have been working on in their home classrooms throughout the school year. This year, the theme is Learning Around the World. Here, parents can visit different classrooms, each of which focuses on a particular country in the world. In one classroom, parents are greeted with the sounds of indigenous Mexican music playing from a CD player. The teacher's aide dresses in a colorful knit poncho, while the head teacher wears a beautiful Jalisco dress. The room is adorned with the Mexican flag and various pictures of Spanish bullfights, flamenco dancers, and Mexican architecture. On tables throughout the room, various string and percussion instruments used in Mexican folk music are displayed. Parents can also sample chile, salsa, fajitas, and other Mexican food dishes that the children have made at home and brought to school. At each table, children (when prompted) will read a paragraph or two on Mexican history and culture that they have practiced. Other classrooms in the school feature similar presentations of Swedish, Nigerian, and Taiwanese cultures.

This is one of many examples of what Fish (1997) labels *Boutique Multiculturalism*, characterized by "the [superficial or cosmetic] multiculturalism of ethnic restaurants [and] weekend festivals" (p. 378). In short, Boutique Multiculturalism touts an appreciation of diversity that is analogous to the *It's a Small World (After All)* boat ride at the Magic Kingdom Disney World theme park. Readers are encouraged to consult Wise and Velayutham (2009) for a more detailed treatment of Boutique Multiculturalism in everyday life.

Kumbayah Multiculturalism

"Kumbayah" is a simple, hymnlike folk song popularized by demonstrators and activists in the civil rights and world peace movements of the 1960s. In more recent times, the word is evoked as a euphemism for a naïve and utopian vision in which all ethnic and cultural groups worldwide cast aside their differences and join hands in celebration of universal peace and brotherhood (e.g., see Stern, 2009; Weiss, 2006). Because Kumbayah Multiculturalism has never existed anywhere on the globe in real life, it must be artificially manufactured in visual images promoted by advertisers. Thus, television commercials often display multiracial/multiethnic groups interacting harmoniously in everyday settings, even if such images are not nearly as common in real life (Associated Press, March, 1, 2009). It has become standard protocol for the covers of National Association of School Psychologists (NASP) publications to feature groups of camera-cute children smiling, hugging, playing, and laughing together, all of whom represent a United Nations visual array of racial and ethnic diversity. In short, Kumbayah Multi-culturalism dreams of a world where every group's cultural values and traditions will be respected by every other group, and intergroup tensions are effortlessly overcome in the service of cross-cultural mutual understanding and unity (for an example of Kumbayah Multiculturalism, see the website for the World Parliament of Religions at http://www .parliamentofreligions.org).

Light-and-Fluffy Multiculturalism

In many professional training programs, multiculturalism is not viewed as an area of investigation that is taken seriously enough to be subject to the normal standards of empirical analysis, scholarly debate, or principled criticism. Rather, multiculturalism is viewed as a philosophy that is so noble and inspirational that it is exempt from the rough-and-tumble intellectual scrutiny commonly afforded to other topics and move-ments in professional school psychology. No effort is made to seriously grapple with the difficult and complex subject matter involved in the intersection of race, ethnicity, and education (or to learn from those disciplines that have done so).

Rather, the primary objective of Light-and-Fluffy Multiculturalism is to promote pithy slogans and catchphrases that sound good to the ears, and for audiences to feel good about themselves for promoting them (e.g., "celebrate multicultural diversity," "teach tolerance," "promote social justice"). Despite their endless repetition in professional newsletters and training materials, the tenets of Light-and-Fluffy Multiculturalism rarely reflect what people really think, what they plainly see or experience with their own senses, or what has been discovered from actual research. Rather, the truths of Light-and-Fluffy Multiculturalism reflect mere repetition of what has been overhead or said by others, ideas that are felt to be right (or ought to be right) to believe "in one's heart," or beliefs that are to be publicly endorsed in order to be accepted by one's professional peers or to be seen as a good person.

Therefore, the ultimate objective of Light-and-Fluffy Multiculturalism is to avoid any penetrating analyses or discussion of harsh realities that might be upsetting to audiences, or at least might cause them to think about things that they would prefer not to think about. Influential political constituency groups must not be angered, and care must be taken to ensure that opinions/viewpoints are monitored and drained of any insights or information that is too controversial for mass consumption. Light-and-Fluffy Multiculturalism sees little need to bore audiences with the specific details of how multicultural principles are actually implemented in school settings, or analyses of whether they actually work as they are supposed to. All that is necessary is to endlessly recite, or at least encourage allegiance to, hackneyed platitudes, soothing bromides, and feel-good pleasantries.

Bean-Counting Multiculturalism

Bean-Counting Multiculturalism is the name given to the manner in which businesses, educational institutions, and government agencies respond to federal and state affirmative action mandates (see Greenhut, 2003; Sowell, 2004). Here, an agency, business, or university training program becomes multicultural simply on the basis of a specified proportion of persons from underrepresented groups that are hired/admitted into the program, business, or agency. In order to document compliance, the employer or training program must quantify the racial/ethnic breakdown of its employees or applicants, displayed in the appropriate tables and/or charts. School psychology training programs that are accredited by the APA or approved by NASP are required to submit such information on a regular basis, where successful numbers supposedly show that the program "recognizes the importance of cultural and individual differences and diversity in the training of psychologists" (Office of Program Consultation and Accreditation, 2010, p. 16).

All of these examples readily come to mind when school professionals encounter the term "multiculturalism." Nevertheless, a deeper and more penetrating analysis is required in order to understand how multiculturalism ideology has influenced the training of psychologists and educators over the decades. In doing so, this discussion begins first with *what multiculturalism is not*. Then, the six essential doctrines that collectively constitute multiculturalism ideology are discussed.

WHAT MULTICULTURALISM IS NOT

A careful understanding of what multiculturalism is requires first a fundamental understanding of what multiculturalism *is not*.

Multiculturalism Is Not a Science

"Science" refers to knowledge describing reliable truths and the operation of general laws, which are discovered and tested through what has come to be known as the scientific method. Here, observation and experimentation are employed to describe and explain the human behavior of individuals and groups in particular contexts. In the social sciences, science begins with the formulation of theories about human behavior, from which a large number of clear, specific hypotheses can subsequently be tested. Hypotheses are tested using a wide variety of experimental designs and the statistical analysis of measurable and observable data. Good theories enable clear hypotheses to be tested, supported, or disconfirmed, which in turn helps researchers to interpret their empirical findings within a meaningful context. Bad theories are stated in a manner that is so vague or imprecise that specific hypotheses cannot be formulated (let alone tested). Even when bad theories are stated in a manner that allows verification, such theories consistently fail to be supported. When scientists living in different continents (or operating from widely different political orientations) arrive at similar conclusions from continuously replicated and well-conducted research studies, then this increases consumers' confidence in that scientific knowledge base.

Scientific research can be distinguished from unscientific methods, which formulate knowledge claims based on appeals to authority, popular opinion, ideological biases, custom and tradition, or wishful thinking (Ruggiero, 2001). In contrast to knowledge gained through the scientific method, much of the so-called knowledge base of multiculturalism is a "received wisdom." That is, multiculturalism begins with a set of propositions handed down from multicultural writers or professional organizations as to how one should view the world, and the correct attitudes, feelings, and opinions that approved professionals should have toward particular multicultural topics. The acceptable role of research within multiculturalism ideology is not to discover objective truth, but to arrive at conclusions that can ultimately support and reinforce the ideology (see Table 10.3). When use of the scientific method yields data that *contradicts* the received wisdom of multiculturalism ideology, the data is summarily dismissed or ignored by multiculturalists, and the methods used to generate the data are denigrated as inherently biased (e.g., see Jensen, 1982, response to Gould, 1981).

Multiculturalism Is Not (Necessarily) "Best Practice"

The term *best practices* suggests that a variety of applied practices have been evaluated in real-life settings, and one or more practices have been shown—through either experience and/or research—to yield the best and most reliable outcomes. Journal articles and best practices chapters on multicultural issues in school psychology texts are replete with variations on the following core claims (see Martines, 2008):

a. School psychologists must be culturally competent in order to effectively serve cultural minority clients.

b. Cultural minority students are best served with culturally sensitive or culturally appropriate interventions.

c. In order to work effectively with culturally different families, the school psychologist should evaluate his or her own cultural biases.

In regards to statement *a*, no published systematic program of research, of which this author is aware, has (1) arrived at a consensus definition of cultural competence that enjoys universal acceptance among school psychologists, (2) identified appropriately standardized and psychometrically sound instruments for measuring cultural competence, or (3) demonstrated that those trained in cultural competence are more effective with English-speaking culturally different clients (or whose practice leads to better outcomes) compared to those who are not (see Frisby, 2009). In regards to statement *b*, no published systematic program of research has demonstrated how interventions discussed in mainstream school psychology texts cannot be effective (when applied in their original form) with English-speaking culturally different children. Conversely, no systematic research demonstrates that all English-speaking children (who experience difficulties in schools) within a particular ethnic/racial group require the same culturally modified interventions. Regarding statement *c*, no systematic program of research supports the assumption that culturally different clients have substantially different values *in all areas* compared to the values held by school psychologists. Furthermore, no well-replicated studies have shown that caregivers with biases different from their clients actually harm them in observable ways. The bottom line is that these claims, like many claims in the multicultural school psychology literature, reflect a received wisdom rather than conclusions that have been verified through rigorous, scientific research studies.

THE DISTINGUISHING FEATURES OF SOCIOPOLITICAL IDEOLOGIES

Multiculturalism shares many features in common with other social or political ideologies. As indicated in the opening quote of this chapter, the overall objective of a sociopolitical ideology is to persuade audiences to do something, believe something, feel something, or develop an attitude in favor of the ideology's pet agendas. The distinguishing features of sociopolitical ideologies are briefly described in the following sections.

An Ideology Must Exaggerate Its Own Importance in Order to Motivate Followers

Committed believers in ideologies believe that they are fighting for lofty, righteous goals, which if obtained have profound consequences for humankind. This fight gives life meaning and purpose for those who are looking for an organizing set of beliefs that would enable them to feel proud about their chosen profession. Thus, it is not unusual for sociopolitical ideologies to be framed as indispensable for fighting injustices (e.g., statistical inequities, racism, poverty, discrimination, prejudice, unfairness, cultural misunderstanding). In reality, these societal problems have existed ever since human beings have existed, and they will continue to exist as long as human beings continue to exist, regardless of what ideologies try to do to "fight" them. Nevertheless, ideologies excite supporters with the hope that these problems can be easily eradicated or solved, if only as many people as possible can be convinced to rally around the righteous cause. This casts supporters of the ideology as "saviors" who will rescue victims from the harm that supposedly will be inflicted on them by those who do not believe in the ideology.

An Ideology Must Oversimplify Life's Complexities

No one scholarly discipline is sufficient by itself to permit learners to fully understand life in all of its nuances and complexities. History, education, psychology, sociology, psychometrics, anthropology, political science, humanities, and economics all contribute in their own specialized manner to understanding a complex and confusing world. Even within any one of these disciplines, numerous subdisciplines war against each other, each with its own arguments as to why its particular way of viewing a set of phenomena is better than another competing viewpoint. Add to this the staggering complexity of human beings, where individuals are uniquely characterized by their own constellation of ability strengths and weaknesses, temperament/personality makeup, unique upbringing, life experiences, and personal convictions that guide them in making life choices. People cannot be persuaded to believe in and follow an ideology if they have to struggle to understand and appreciate all of these complexities. Hence, ideologies must portray the world with the least amount of ambiguity, so that the moral/philosophical battle lines can be drawn more sharply. Stated figuratively, ideologies view life in "black and white." In the ideologue's universe, there are no greys, mauves, crimsons, or pastel colorings. This kind of thinking leads to single-issue politics, where ideologues convince themselves that winning a single issue (e.g., banning IQ tests for special education eligibility determination) will magically revolutionize the world according to their ideals.

Ideologies Have Their Own Unique Lexicon

Ideologies must invent their own unique lexicon, partly to allow members to communicate ideas more parsimoniously, but also to designate who belongs (or does not belong) in the club. New words and concepts are invented out of thin air (e.g., *people of color, tolerance, cultural competence, social justice, homophobia, CLD children*) and then given their own specialized meaning by supporters of the ideology. If these new concepts are repeated often enough, they become so entrenched in the thinking of ideologues that it is difficult to believe there was a time when these words or concepts did not exist. Loaded words then lead to bumper sticker sloganeering, which reminds followers of the correct thinking required by the ideology (e.g., "Practice Tolerance," "Celebrate Diversity," "Equity with Excellence," "Differences are not Deficits," etc.).

Ideologies Must Enforce Conformity

In order for an ideology to accrue political power, its followers must be numerous, and all of them must think the same way and hold the same attitudes. Nonconformity threatens the cohesiveness of a movement, and may encourage others within the ideological movement to criticize its views or to defect to the other side. In various ways, some more subtle than others, the ideology must communicate the message that conformity will be rewarded and nonconformity will be punished. The potential threat of nonconformity to the ideology is increased if followers are allowed to think for themselves and arrive at their own conclusions. Therefore, the ideology must ensure that this does not happen. This can be accomplished in many ways. Ideologues will often promote the inherent virtue of the ideology, while demonizing those who either disagree with, do not follow, or engage in activities that threaten the ideology (e.g., see Sidebar 10.7). Followers must be kept from accessing research or other outlets that present cogent arguments for opposing viewpoints. More often, such opposing viewpoints are simply ignored by promoters of the ideology as if they do not exist. In other situations, reality must be continually reinterpreted for followers in order to model the correct way to perceive events. If followers see something plainly with their own eyes that undermines the ideology, supporters must spin and/or re interpret what is plainly seen in ways that support the ideology.

SIX ESSENTIAL DOCTRINES THAT CONSTITUTE MULTICULTURALISM IDEOLOGY

Sidebar 2.1 summarizes the standard "party line" promoted in school psychology concerning multiculturalism issues. Each talking point within the multicultural party line includes a set of implicit assumptions. These, in turn, lead to philosophies of training that are also fraught with implicit assumptions. Such assumptions are rooted in implicit doctrines that characterize multiculturalism ideology. These six interlocking implicit doctrines are described as follows (for an extended discussion and critique of these doctrines, consult Frisby, 2005a, 2005b).

🖎 Sidebar 2.1   The Multicultural "Party Line" in School Psychology Training

U.S. society, for a variety of reasons, is becoming more culturally diverse (operationalized by racial/ethnic/language differences) with each passing decade.[1–3] Cultural differences, and schools'/educators' inability to adapt to or understand them, are largely responsible for disproportionate psychoeducational problems, school underachievement, and disproportionate rates of special education placement among certain racial, ethnic, and language groups in U.S. schools.[4,5] In order to be properly prepared for these changes, school psychologists are obligated to immerse themselves in new training that leads to *cultural competence*.[2,6,7] Cultural competence, as defined by national and state school psychology professional associations and multicultural experts, will presumably lead to new knowledge, greater insight and sensitivity toward cultural differences, better interpersonal skills, the more frequent use of culturally sensitive assessments, and new attitudes in serving the psychoeducational needs of CLD (culturally and linguistically diverse) children in schools.[8,9] When integrated into existing school psychology training and practice, training for cultural competence will result in the reduction of inappropriate practices and improved outcomes for CLD students in schools.[9–12]

SUPPORTING REFERENCES

1. Miranda, A. H. (2008). Best practices in increasing cross-cultural competence. In A. Thomas & J. Grimes (Eds.), *Best practices in school psychology V: Volume 5* (pp. 1739–1750). Bethesda, MD: National Association of School Psychologists.
2. Crockett, D., & Brown, J. (2009). Multicultural practices and response to Intervention. In J. Jones (Ed.), *The psychology of multiculturalism in the schools: A primer for practice, training, and research* (pp. 117–137). Bethesda, MD: National Association of School Psychologists.
3. Ortiz, S., Flanagan, D. P., & Dynda, A. (2008). Best practices in working with culturally diverse children and families. In A. Thomas & J. Grimes (Eds.), *Best practices in school psychology V: Volume 5* (pp. 1721–1738). Bethesda, MD: National Association of School Psychologists.
4. Elizalde-Utnick, G. (2008, November). Using Response to Intervention framework with English language learners. *NASP Communiqué, 37*(3), 18–21.
5. Green, T., & Ingraham, C. (2005). Multicultural education. In S. Lee (Ed.), *Encyclopedia of school psychology* (pp. 338–342). Thousand Oaks, CA: Sage.
6. Carroll, D. (2009). Toward multiculturalism competence: A practical model for implementation in the schools. In J. M. Jones (Ed.), *The psychology of multiculturalism in the schools* (pp. 1–15). Bethesda, MD: National Association of School Psychologists.

7. Palacios, E. D., & Trivedi, P. (2009). Increasing cultural literacy: Historical perspectives and cultural characteristics of minority groups. In J. Jones (Ed.), *The psychology of multiculturalism in the schools: A primer for practice, training, and research* (pp. 17–48). Bethesda, MD: National Association of School Psychologists.

8. Clare, M. (2009). Thinking diversity: A habit of mind for school psychology. In T. B. Gutkin & C. R. Reynolds (Eds.), *The handbook of school psychology* (4th ed., pp. 840–854). Hoboken, NJ: Wiley.

9. Martines, D. (2008). *Multicultural school psychology competencies: A practical guide.* Thousand Oaks, CA: Sage.

10. Rogers, M. R., Ingraham, C. L., Bursztyne, A., Cajigas-Segredo, N., Esquivel, G., Hess, R., . . . Lopez, E. C. (1999). Providing psychological services to racially, ethnically, culturally, and linguistically diverse individuals in the schools. *School Psychology International, 20*(3), 243–264.

11. Rogers, M. R., & Lopez, E. C. (2002). Identifying critical cross-cultural school psychology competencies. *Journal of School Psychology, 40*(2), 115–141.

12. Green, T., Cook-Morales, V., Robinson-Zañartu, C., & Ingraham, C. (2009). Pathways on a journey of *Getting It*: Multicultural competence training and continuing professional development. In J. Jones (Ed.), *The psychology of multiculturalism in the schools: A primer for practice, training, and research* (pp. 83–113). Bethesda, MD: National Association of School Psychologists.

The Group Identity Doctrine

According to this doctrine, schoolchildren are seen as little more than members of identity groups typically defined by race, ethnicity, social class, and/or language. Each group has a prescribed role in Marxist-inspired morality plays (e.g., ongoing conflicts between the "advantaged" against the "disadvantaged," the "victims" against the "victimizers," the "oppressed" against the "oppressors," the "dominant culture" against the "subordinate culture"; see *Marxism* in Glossary). Under multiculturalism ideology, school psychologists are led to believe that promoting certain generalizations about these groups presumably prepares school psychologists to understand or have greater insight into the psychology of individuals who belong to such groups (e.g., see White, 1984). This doctrine assumes implicitly that whatever characteristics define the group (e.g., race, ethnicity, social class, or language) are valuable for explaining the psychoeducational problems of, or providing the appropriate interventions for, individuals who belong to these groups (Jones, 2009).

The Difference Doctrine

According to this doctrine, differences among racial/ethnic/language groups are presumed to be so profound and mutually exclusive that a proper understanding of, and service to, these groups requires "different" culturally specific assessment instruments, "different" culturally specific classroom instructional methods, and "different" culturally specific counseling and intervention techniques (e.g., see Bernal, Trimble, Burlew, & Leong, 2003). This reflects a belief in *Culture × Treatment Interactions* (see Sidebar 2.9 and Glossary). Based on such ideas, training programs operate under the unchallenged assumption that whatever is culturally different about groups is presumed to be more important and necessary to learn compared to what is culturally similar about groups. This doctrine either ignores or explicitly discourages research that compares groups on a common/universal standard, or even may go so far as to deny that such common/universal standards exist.

The Equity Doctrine

"Equity" has become a near-sacred word in multiculturalism ideology, and as such, there are two applications of its meaning. In the noncontroversial application, equity is viewed as a *process* where children from all groups are treated equally and fairly in the context of schooling and psychoeducational services. In the controversial application, equity is viewed as a *product*—brought to fruition only when children from different groups achieve equal outcomes (e.g., in academic attainment, special/gifted education placement rates, test scores, or discipline referrals). Here, it is implicitly assumed that the lack of equity (i.e., equal outcomes) is *prima facie* (on its face) evidence of the presence of bad testing/teaching practices, mistreatment, misunderstanding, or discrimination (Harry, 2006). Some training programs frame this problem as an issue of "social justice" (see Trainers of School Psychologists, *Trainer's Forum Newsletter*, Vol. 28, No. 4). Under this doctrine, school psychologists are socialized to consider advocacy for "outcomes equity" to be a moral imperative for the profession.

The Inclusion Doctrine

This doctrine is best known by its ubiquitous buzzword *diversity*. Here, it is assumed that the highest value to which school psychologists should subscribe is for educational outcomes to be sufficiently diverse—where racial/ethnic/language groups are "included" in outcomes according to their proportional representation in broader society. Training programs and professional organizations for educators thus encourage this doctrine by constantly reminding students that they must "celebrate," "value," or "embrace" diversity in order to have the proper mindset toward personal and professional growth in their field. The word *diversity* has come to imply *a particular type of diversity*—that is, one that emphasizes outward physical racial/ethnic characteristics (e.g., see O'Connor, 2010). Thus, a collection of physically identifiable Hispanic, Black, White, Asian, and disabled individuals are viewed as a prime example of diversity, whereas a group of white fiscal conservatives, white independents, white communists, white libertarians, and white liberal Democrats would not be considered as an example of diversity. If an outcome does not display a sufficient degree of racial/ethnic diversity, then the outcome is vulnerable to charges that it is practicing "exclusion" rather than "inclusion" (e.g., see Ford, Grantham, & Whiting, 2008; Wallace & Eriksson, 2006).

The Sensitivity Doctrine

According to this doctrine, members of the "majority" or "dominant" cultural group are morally obligated to avoid using any language, entertaining certain beliefs/ideas, or pursuing any research that has the potential to inadvertently offend or upset members of minority or nondominant groups (or those who style themselves as their spokespersons). In the research arena, the Sensitivity Doctrine exerts pressure on researchers to avoid findings that are critical of minority group behavior, attitudes, or abilities, or that portrays them in an unflattering light. In the words of one writer, "the need for free and unfettered scientific exchange must be balanced against the need that no group in society feels threatened by such exchange" (Gottfredson, 2007, paraphrasing Estes, 1992).

The Sensitivity Doctrine encourages a perception of the problems faced by minority groups as fundamentally attributable to their status as perpetual victims of historical or current mistreatment and misunderstanding (which is a perspective that harmonizes with multiculturalism ideology). Students, practitioners, trainers, and professional organizations allow themselves to be cowed into silence from the Sensitivity Doctrine by studiously avoiding discussion of certain relevant but politically "radioactive" topics. These sensitive topics cause professionals to modify their speech or interpretation of research results in order to conform to the dictates of current multicultural orthodoxy—for fear that not doing so would invite accusations of "bigotry," "Eurocentrism," "cultural incompetence," or "cultural insensitivity." In the words of one writer, "[o]ne can feel the gradient of collective alarm and disapproval like a deepening chill as one approaches the forbidden area" (Gottfredson, 1994, p. 56). Militant multicultural advocates capitalize on these fears by adopting a professional identity as "enforcers" of politically correct multiculturalism in university training, journal editorial boards, and state professional organizations.

The Sovereignty Doctrine

According to this doctrine, racial/ethnic minority psychologists, educators, or organizations—simply by virtue of their minority status—are assumed to have automatic and unquestioned expertise in all matters related to serving or understanding racial/ethnic minority children in schools. As a corollary, white middle-class professionals—by virtue of their "outsider" status—are expected to defer to the opinions of racial/ethnic minority individuals without regard to their training, experience, or knowledge in serving cultural minority children (e.g., see Swisher, 1998). According to Hale-Benson (1986, p. 4), for example, it is the singular task of the "black community" of psychological scholars to pool their scholarly talents so that black children can succeed educationally. Similarly, Swisher (1998) argues that only Native American educators can significantly improve education for Native American children.

The following section describes how these six doctrines are blended together in supporting various models of multicultural advocacy in the context of preservice training for school professionals. Many training programs in school psychology, counselor education, and teacher training are under an often self-imposed pressure to (a) admit students who fit specified "diversity goals," (b) integrate multicultural content into courses and practica in order to secure or retain accreditation status, or (c) generally arrange training experiences to win students over to the goals and values of multiculturalism. As indicated in the quote at the beginning of this chapter, the primary goal of multiculturalism ideology is *conversion*. Three major models for changing hearts and minds to embrace multiculturalism can be identified in most university training programs, which are labeled *The Moral Model, The Culture Model,* and *The Social Engineering Model* (adapted from Fein, 2001). The central tenets of each model are summarized, followed by a description of how each model typically responds to criticism, concluding with a critical evaluation of the serious flaws that are inherent within each model.

MODELS OF MULTICULTURAL ADVOCACY WITHIN PROFESSIONAL TRAINING

The Moral Model

Under the *Moral Model*, multiculturalism advocacy is framed as a fundamental battle between good versus evil. Counseling psychology and multicultural education are two disciplines that are well known for characterizing racism, racial/ethnic prejudice, and discrimination as the preeminent moral evils presumed to be responsible for minority group misery (see Sidebar 2.2). According to the *Moral Model*, properly trained multiculturalists (who represent the forces of good) should be socialized to aggressively fight these evils as advocates for fairness and "social justice" (Briggs, 2009; Shriberg, 2009).

Under the *Moral Model*, minority group status is viewed as synonymous with "victimhood." That is to say, victimhood becomes the lens through which majority groups are encouraged to view minority group identity in U.S. society. Members of nonwhite and/or non-English-speaking groups are assumed to be automatic victims of racism, prejudice, and discrimination simply on the basis of their minority status—with only the most superficial observations being required as corroborating evidence. Such "victim narratives" are well known to anyone with even a cursory exposure to contemporary racial/ethnic politics in the United States. That is, audiences are constantly reminded that African Americans used to be slaves in the United States, faced legally sanctioned discrimination in the past (particularly in Southern states), and are poorer and incarcerated at greater rates than whites on average (Healey, 2010; Sue & Sue, 2003).

Likewise, audiences are constantly reminded that American Indians were swindled in the past by the U.S. government from broken treaties, had their land forcibly taken away from them, had their cultural traditions disrupted by forced resettlement efforts, and suffer disproportionately from a variety of health problems (Healey, 2010; Sue & Sue, 2003). Hispanics are likewise presumably victimized by pressures to acculturate to English-speaking U.S. society, as well as political efforts to crack down on illegal immigration (Healey, 2010; Sue & Sue, 2003). Although Asian Americans have typically fared better than other groups on income, education, and social achievement variables, the *Moral Model* portrays them as victims on the grounds that their model minority status subjects them to unfair perceptions and stereotypes (Sue & Sue, 2003). Arab Americans are seen as victims of U.S. stereotypes and unfair perceptions (e.g., racial profiling), particularly in the aftermath of the 9/11 attacks on the World Trade Center and the Pentagon (Sue & Sue, 2003). Under the *Moral Model*, any persons belonging to these groups automatically share the victim status of their ancestors.

⟲ Sidebar 2.2   The Ubiquity of Racism as Perceived By Counseling Psychology and Multicultural Education Texts

- "... all racial and ethnic minority groups in the United States share experiences of oppression as a result of living in the dominant White American culture." (Sodowsky, Kuo-Jackson, & Loya, 1997, p. 13)
- "White therapists and counselors are the major purveyors of power because of their disproportionate representation among the mental health professionals. This also means they are the greatest perpetrators of racism. . . . Although they may be well meaning, they often behave as unintentional racists." (Ridley, Espelage, & Rubinstein, 1997, p. 139)
- "(R)acism is what people do, regardless of what they think or feel." (Ridley, 1995, quoted in Fong & Lease, 1997, p. 389)
- "... what may have worked previously to combat racism in the 1960s may need to be reorganized to meet the new challenges of racism's protean [changeable] manifestations." (Liu & Pope-Davis, 2003, p. 99)

- "Over the past 500 years in U.S. history, racism has reflected many forms, including blatant racism, enlightened racism, symbolic racism, paternalistic racism, liberal racism, and unintentional racism. . . . Although many of the laws that perpetuated and maintained racism have been abolished, racism continues in contemporary U.S. society in numerous individual and institutionalized forms." (Coleman & Hau, 2003, p. 174)

- ". . . issues related to race and racism are among the causes of discrepancies in student achievement among students of color and their white peers." (Holcomb-McCoy, 2003, p. 416)

- "Others . . . have also noted the presence of racist practices in schools such as tracking ethnic minority students in low-performing classes, excluding students of a particular ethnic/cultural group from school programs, and disproportionately referring ethnic minority students for special education services. Multiculturally competent school counselors have not only a clear understanding of systemic racism but also the ability to effectively challenge racist practices that occur in their schools." (Holcomb-McCoy, 2003, p. 416)

- ". . . racism as a social force influencing access to and the delivery of health services, as well as the manner in which research is conducted, is clearly evident in the United States as it is in other countries." (Merluzzi & Hegde, 2003, p. 423)

- "The exposure to acute and chronic stress due to racism is considered to be a significant and possibly unique risk for African Americans compared to other ethnic groups." (Merluzzi & Hegde, 2003, p. 423–424)

- "Institutional racism and discrimination do not have to be intentional for them to have psychological and physical consequences." (Root, 2003, p. 481)

- "Institutional racism is characterized by practices or policies that systematically limit opportunities for people who historically have been characterized as psychologically, intellectually, or physically deficient." (Root, 2003, p. 481)

- "White children are socialized into a society that, despite strides in civil rights legislation, continues to be racist in many of its social institutions, not the least of which are schools." (Taylor & Quintana, 2003, p. 512)

- "Although so-called 'old-fashioned racism' is, arguably, less prevalent today than it was 40 years ago, other forms of racism are alive and well in U.S. society." (Taylor & Quintana, 2003, p. 512)

- ". . . the challenge of the multicultural movement in the 21st century is to ameliorate more sophisticated and insidious forms of cultural-racial discrimination, oppression, and injustice that are deeply embedded in the institutions and organizations that constitute the infrastructure of our society." (D'Andrea & Daniels, 2001, p. 227)

- "Racism is a critical component in the organization of modern American society characterized most critically by the superior position of whites and the institutions—ideological as well as structural—which maintain it." (Wellman, 1993, pp. 54–55; quoted in Neville, Worthington, & Spanierman, 2001, p. 260)

- "We believe that White racism represents one of the most important moral problems our nation faces in the 21st century." (D'Andrea & Daniels, 2001, p. 290)

- ". . . structural racism is deeply embedded in our societal institutions, resulting in a broad range of negative consequences for the overall health and well-being of millions of persons of color in the United States." (D'Andrea & Daniels, 2001, p. 290)

- ". . . White persons commonly exhibit certain behaviors and emotional dispositions and fail to exhibit other types of behaviors and emotional reactions that effectively help perpetuate [racism]." (D'Andrea & Daniels, 2001, p. 294)

- "White racism is a pervasive force in our society that is deeply embedded in our societal structures and entrenched in the ideological and epistemological paradigms used by the dominant cultural-racial group in the United States to construct meaning of reality." (D'Andrea & Daniels, 2001, p. 294)

- ". . . the economic-educational-social-political realities of our society provide overwhelming evidence that underscores how White racism continues to thrive in our society." (D'Andrea & Daniels, 2001, p. 294)

- "White racism remains a major societal problem that will not disappear without concerted effort by all justice-loving persons in this country. . . . It is vital for all White persons . . . to become more knowledgeable of the complex ways that this serious problem is manifested in our nation and work to ameliorate this pervasive form of social pathology." (D'Andrea & Daniels, 2001, p. 295)

- "Because racism is such an integral part of our society, it looks ordinary and natural to persons in the culture." (Delgado, 1995; as quoted in Ladson-Billings, 2004, p. 58)

- "Cultural racism refers to the elevation of the White Anglo-Saxon Protestant cultural heritage to a position of superiority over the cultural experiences of ethnic minority groups." (Gay, 1973; quoted in Bennett, 2004, p. 857)

- "Racism can enter the school curriculum through written texts which depict minorities negatively or ignore them altogether. Intelligence tests may be considered a form of racism, since they measure one's knowledge of middle class culture." (Madrid, 1986; quoted in Bennett, 2004, p. 858)
- ". . . one can view the clock as a tool of racism that the monochromic dominant society uses to regulate subordinate groups." (Sleeter & Bernal, 2004, p. 253)
- "Racist structures and processes [in schools] can include institutionalizing better instruction for White children than for children of color; using tracking, special education, and gifted programs to differentiate instruction along racial lines; using racially biased tests and other assessment processes; employing mainly White professionals; and so forth." (Sleeter & Bernal, 2004, p. 251)

As overt, egregious examples of racism become increasingly difficult to identify in contemporary U.S. society, multiculturalism redefines racism as petty slings and slights occasionally experienced during the hustle and bustle of everyday life. These incidents, some of which are invisible to the naked eye, nevertheless are presumed to be responsible for the "oppression" of minorities on a regular basis. At the time of this writing, for example, the concept of racial "microaggressions" is in vogue among multiculturalists in counseling psychology, which has subsequently spread to school psychology as well (Sue, 2003).

The *Moral Model* depends on two related categories of evidence to rally support for the "minorities-as-victims" narrative: (1) observed social inequalities and disproportionate outcomes between groups, and (2) accusations of racism by minorities and their advocates. The practice of putting observed inequalities between racial/ethnic groups front and center in educational debates is a favorite tactic of *civil rights moralism* (see Glossary). Civil rights moralism compels school professionals to view equality (currently referred to as *equity*) among groups as the preeminent moral mandate. In short, equality is prized, whereas inequality is viewed as inherently evil.

The quantification of *disproportionate outcomes* constitutes key evidence used in multicultural advocacy within school psychology and special education (Coutinho, Oswald, & Best, 2002; Figueroa, 1999; Losen & Orfield, 2002; Sullivan, 2010). Conti and Stetson (1997) pinpoint the heart of this issue as follows:

Under the contemporary regime of "proportionalism," in many venues, from education to government contracts to the professions, all that is necessary to establish a presumption of discrimination and unfairness is to show that women and minorities are not distributed in a given area in exact proportion to their distribution in the population. (p. 71)

Disproportionate outcomes between racial/ethnic groups—whether they exist in special education eligibility, discipline referrals, suspension rates, or high school graduation statistics—are viewed as inherently unjust and evidence that something sinister is at work "beneath the surface" that is ultimately responsible for these "wrong numbers" (e.g., see Blanchett, 2010). Therefore, under the *Moral Model*, the appropriately trained school psychologist accepts the moral obligation to lend his or her services to correcting these disproportionalities, so that egalitarian outcomes can hopefully result. At the time of this writing, one school psychology training program website describes this moral obligation as follows (under the heading "Commitment to Social Justice"):

. . . faculty and students have a strong commitment to social justice as an integral part of our training. Longstanding patterns of oppression and discrimination have left our nation with inequities that continue to plague our schools and society. We believe that school psychologists have a responsibility to develop an identity that incorporates a commitment to social justice. This dedication to equity cannot be an add-on or a single course in diversity. Rather, the commitment to cultural responsiveness and advocacy must be an integral part of the training and role of the school psychologist, as central as our commitment to evidence-based practice and effective collaboration. Thus, we train our students . . . to act as an advocate and systems change agent, actively monitoring the quality of the educational experience and outcomes for students from groups who have been under-represented or marginalized. (accessed January 2011 from http://site.educ.indiana.edu/Default.aspx?alias=site.educ .indiana.edu/schpsy)

Testimonials that document injustices are another favorite tactic used by the *Moral Model* to generate sympathy for the "minorities-as-victims" narrative. Jonathan Kozol is an education writer who is well known in teacher education programs for his books that chronicle, in heart-rending detail, educational inequalities that particularly affect some racial minorities in urban schools (e.g., see *Savage Inequalities, Death at an Early Age, The Shame of the Nation*). One such example reads as follows:

In one make-shift elementary school housed in a former skating rink next to a funeral parlor in another nearly all-black-and-Hispanic section of the Bronx, class size rose to 34 and more; four kindergarten classes and a sixth grade class were packed into a single room that had no windows. Airlessness was stifling in many rooms; and recess was impossible because there was no outdoor playground and no indoor gym, so the children had no place to play. In another elementary school, which had been built to hold 1,000 children but was packed to bursting with some 1,500 boys and girls, the principal poured out his feelings to me in a room in which a plastic garbage bag had been attached somehow to cover part of the collapsing ceiling. "This," he told me, pointing to the garbage bag, then gesturing around him at the other indications of decay and disrepair one sees in ghetto schools much like it elsewhere, "would not happen to white children." (Kozol, 2005, p. 41)

As graduate students and school professionals are continually marinated in these and other examples of *civil rights moralism*, they are expected to feel sorry for cultural minority groups, further cementing a perception of these groups as perpetual victims of a perpetually unjust society. Under the *Moral Model* framework, the ultimate goal of multicultural training is for school psychologists in training to come to the place where they suddenly experience an epiphany (called *getting it*; see Green, Cook-Morales, Robinson-Zañartu, & Ingraham, 2009). Once school psychologists "get it," a noble passion will presumably ignite in their hearts, which then begins a process of internalizing an identity as protectors of, and advocates for, "the oppressed." Newly emboldened by this righteous cause, the school psychologist is then expected to expose injustices wherever they may be found, and to use one's cultural sensitivity/awareness to fight the racism, prejudice, and discrimination that most assuredly lies at the root of the problems experienced by minority groups in schools. Green et al. (2009) articulate this emotional epiphany as follows:

"Getting it" emotionally allows that tear to run down our cheek when we witness injustice, and it elicits a cringe of outrage when we hear a racist remark. . . . Emotional knowing is experienced in the essence of our beings and felt in our hearts, in our bellies, and in our blood. (pp. 91–92)

There is virtually no limit to the various ways that minorities are thought to be victimized by schools, according to the *Moral Model*. As examples, minorities are said to be victimized by biased tests that are insensitive to their cultures (Helms, 1992); they score lower on standardized achievement tests because of "stereotype threat"(see Glossary) and economic disadvantages in the home (Jones, 2007); they are disciplined at more frequent rates in schools because teachers misunderstand their cultural traits (Osher et al., 2004); and they are referred more frequently to certain special education classes presumably from inappropriate referral practices (U.S. Commission on Civil Rights, 2009).

How Does the Moral Model Philosophy Respond to Its Critics?

Because passion for social justice is the engine that drives the *Moral Model* of multiculturalism advocacy, it comes as no surprise that its proponents' responses to critics are also fundamentally *visceral*, appealing to the emotions rather than to evidence, data, or reason. *Moral Model* multiculturalists respond to their critics in one or more of the following ways.

Opposing Arguments Are Simply Ignored.

Criticisms cannot hurt multiculturalism if they are not even acknowledged to exist. The implicit worth and virtue of multiculturalism is seen as so profound that critics' appeal to data, logic, and evidence is largely irrelevant—and not worthy of the effort required to respond seriously. When multicultural activists surround themselves only with like-minded individuals, and insulate themselves socially and professionally against exposure to legitimate criticism, then it becomes easier to simply convince themselves that their positions have no fatal weaknesses. The problem, instead, is reinterpreted as originating in the character flaws of their critics.

Deflect Attention Away From the Empirical Weaknesses of Multiculturalism Ideology and Toward an Emphasis on Its Superior Moral Virtue.

Because all debates under the *Moral Model* are reduced to a fundamental conflict between good versus evil, multicultural advocacy requires no independent justification other than an admiration of its own moral goodness. The ideologue couldn't care less about persuasive research that contradicts or undermines cherished beliefs. What ultimately matters is the satisfaction that results from a reputation of being an unwavering advocate for a righteous cause. Sympathetic audiences are expected to overlook the empirical bankruptcy of multiculturalism and sympathize with the fact that its defenders are sincere in fighting a noble cause.

Twisting Logic and Common Sense to Defend the Position at All Costs.

Those who follow the *Moral Model* of multicultural advocacy often are committed to twisting logic to incomprehensible lengths in order to protect and defend the moral sanctity of their positions. As an example, consider a report entitled "Suspended Education: Urban Middle Schools in Crisis" (Losen & Skiba, 2010), published by the Southern Poverty Law Center (SPLC). The SPLC™ describes itself as "a nonprofit civil rights organization dedicated to fighting hate and bigotry, and to seeking justice for the most vulnerable members of society" (Southern Poverty Law Center, 2012). According to its website, the SPLC tracks and exposes the activities of organized "hate groups" nationally, publishes and distributes "Teaching Tolerance" instructional materials to schools and interested organizations, and retains a cadre of civil rights lawyers to litigate discrimination cases, some of which have resulted in high-profile judgments netting multimillion-dollar settlements for SPLC and their clients. The NASP website on diversity resources (http://www.nasponline.org/resources/culturalcompetence/diversity websites.aspx) prominently features links to various projects sponsored by the SPLC, ostensibly designed to assist school psychologists in helping educators "reduce prejudice," "teach tolerance," and respond appropriately to bigotry. On the surface, there appears to be no other organization that "does the work of the angels" as nobly as the SPLC.

However, as with any ideology that is fundamentally driven by moral passions (as opposed to the careful analysis of research), the temptation for corruption, greed, and recklessness is apparently too seductive to resist. A Spring 2010 special issue of *The Social Contract* journal (Volume 20, No. 3) is exclusively devoted to articles detailing how the SPLC has grown rich and corrupt by, among other things, exaggerating what does (and does not) qualify as a "hate group" and concomitant hate crimes. According to the SPLC, any organization that opposes illegal immigration, criticizes affirmative action, has an explicitly conservative political bent, or opposes homosexual behavior on religious grounds is morally equivalent to the neo-Nazis and the Ku Klux Klan (Colson, 2010; Gemma, 2010; Menzies, 2010).

Of particular concern here is how supposedly data-based publications suspend logic and common sense in the service of *Moral Model* advocacy. The SPLC-sponsored "Suspended Education" document (Losen & Skiba, 2010) appropriately begins with a careful documentation of middle school suspension rates, disaggregated by race, sex, and ethnicity, since the 1970s. The report analyzed data from 18 large urban school districts in Florida, Wisconsin, Indiana, Texas, North Carolina, Washington, Georgia, California, Connecticut, Rhode Island, Massachusettes, and Maryland. The authors found that racial gaps in suspension rates have grown considerably since 1973 in all districts and states studied. In particular, suspension rates for some racial/ethnic groups significantly exceeded average suspension rates of the general population, especially for African American males.

These data certainly present a legitimate cause for alarm, but what is most alarming is the authors' *interpretation* of this data and their recommendations for future action. Fantastically, the authors make the claim that, despite this data, "[r]esearch on student behavior, race, and discipline has found no evidence that African-American over-representation in school suspension is due to higher rates of misbehavior" (p. 10). Suspending for a moment legitimate challenges over the factual accuracy of this claim, this response illustrates an all-too-common reflexive tendency of *Moral Model* advocacy.

That is, instead of facing squarely the problem of minority overrepresentation in school misbehavior, *Moral Model* advocacy spins painful facts into an opportunity to reconfigure them as examples of minority victimhood (by implying that a widespread and sinister agenda impels school districts nationwide to unfairly discriminate against racial/cultural minority students). In the context of their review of school desegregation research, Caldas & Bankston (2005) write:

> But can we discount some or even most of these suspensions and expulsions of minority students as reflections of biased teachers and administrators? It seems we cannot. Major research studies find no evidence to support the so-called prejudiced teacher hypothesis as an explanation for overall differences in ethnic grades or disciplinary actions. Indeed, substantial evidence confirms that misbehavior on the part of minority students is actually greater than indicated by most statistics. A recent study of the issue has concluded, "In many school systems black students are less likely to be suspended for the same offense as a white student. Moreover, the greater the discretion given administrators in suspension decisions, the fewer the black students suspended." It does indeed look very unlikely that the high suspension and expulsion rates of minority students are produced by biased enforcement. (p. 92)

Engaging in Anger, Sanctimony, Name Calling, and Character Assassination.

Those who identify with multiculturalism ideology come in all shapes, sizes, backgrounds, and personality styles. However, those who are most vocal and militant about multiculturalism see it as an integral feature of their personal and professional identities. Some become angry simply over the perception that others do not take multiculturalism as seriously as they do. To illustrate, Green et al. (2009) write:

> "They just don't get it!" I shouted these words in my mind at a meeting of national leaders charged with charting the future of our profession. No one (else) seemed outraged that schools were still failing our diverse youth and that our role in righting that wrong would be critical. Where was our depth of concern and our plan for action? Why did I have to call across the country to find a colleague who shared my passionate concern and check my reality? Here was a conference filled with brilliant minds, but the journey of the heart and spirit to linking those minds to meaningful actions for our diverse children, conceptualizing the problem with multifaceted depth, seemed to be a place we dare not go. (p. 108)

The *Moral Model* assumes that those who criticize any aspect of multiculturalism (on either empirical or philosophical grounds)—or who fail to behave in ways expected by multiculturalists—do so not because of any legitimate or principled reasons, but because of fundamental moral or character flaws that require sanctimonious condemnation and correction (Fein, 2001). Thus, those who take issue with any aspect of multiculturalism are viewed as morally compromised by their inherent "Eurocentrism" (Helms, 1989; Richardson, 1993), their sense of "white privilege" or "white supremacy" (D'Andrea & Daniels, 2003), their latent or overt racism (D'Andrea & Daniels, 2003; Mio & Awakuni, 2000), or "[the loss of the] desire to be considered serious scholars" (Parham, 2002, p. 31). One writer even claimed that the failure of whites to enroll their children in lavishly funded minority schools (for the purposes of promoting racial integration) reflects "something very evil about America" (Jordan, 1992). A particularly telling example of this mindset can be seen in "white privilege" conferences that are currently in vogue among militant multicultural educators (an example of which is shown in Sidebar 2.3).

Sidebar 2.3   *Moral Model* Multiculturalism Training: "White Privilege" Workshops

Approximately 1,500 teachers, students, activists, artists, social workers, and counselors from more than 35 states attended the 12th annual White Privilege Conference held from April 13–16, 2011, in Minneapolis, Minnesota. The conference was sponsored by the Matrix Center for the Advancement of Social Equity & Inclusion at the University of Colorado at Colorado Springs. According to the White Privilege Conference (WPC) website (www.whiteprivilegeconference.com/wpc.html), the WPC is not designed to "attack, degrade or beat up on white folks," but nevertheless is "built on the premise that the U.S. was started by white people, for white people." As such, the purpose of the conference is to provide a comprehensive examination of the concepts of "privilege and oppression" involving race, gender, sexuality, class, and disability, as well as "the ways we all experience some form of privilege, and how we're all affected by that privilege." Select titles from the more than 150 workshops offered during the conference are listed as follows:

- "Making Your School or Classroom a Force for Eliminating Racism"
- "Helping Non-White Students Survive Academia—The Pinnacle of White Dominance"

- "How Queer Stays White: Interrupting White and Male Supremacy in Queer Struggle"
- "The Joy of Unlearning Racism: How White People Experience the Journey Toward Liberation and Healing"
- "This is Your Brain on Racism: Understanding and Transforming the Neurophysiology of White Privilege and Internalized Racism"
- "Uprooting Christian Hegemony"
- "Whose Hip Hop Is It? How White Supremacist Ideology Commoditized a Movement"
- "Beyond Jerry Springer: Correcting the Myths and Misconceptions of Transsexuality"
- "Building Political Consciousness for Social Transformation: Land, Labor and the end of Whiteness as Property"
- "'ESPN's Rap Sheet': How Sports Media Promotes White Male Supremacy"

As quoted directly from workshop descriptions, attendees learned how "black inferiority and white superiority still impact many institutions in American life, such as education"; how white privilege "can keep some of our students from experiencing academic success"; and how "social justice educators" can use "strategic organizational change efforts" to create "systemic, long-term culture change" in organizations. One workshop purported to teach "essential qualities and skills required for white people to avoid acting from a 'savior' or 'superiority' complex when working in community organizations and educational settings." In another workshop, attendees participated in an "interactive performance event" based on real testimonials from migrants who have attempted to cross the U.S.–Mexico border.

(adapted from Kersten, 2011)

Fatal Flaws of the Moral Model

Passionate emotions may provide an immediate sense of inspiration, motivation for action, and self-satisfaction, but they are unacceptable as a foundation on which to build a knowledge base that guides an applied profession. Emotions may ignite action, but they cannot sustain it over time (Fein, 2001).

Conflicts Rooted in Opposing Moral Positions Are Resistant to Resolution.

Debates in which two or more sides are each driven by the *Moral Model* are extremely resistant to resolution, because sides often disagree on which moral principle should drive policy decisions. In debates over affirmative action, for example, one side feels that it is profoundly immoral for groups who have experienced discrimination in the past to be denied special help in the present. Similarly, those on the opposing side feel just as strongly that it is profoundly immoral to extend special privileges unequally to certain groups simply on the basis of race or ethnicity. In the same way, those who support gay rights feel that it is profoundly immoral for persons to be denied public and social affirmation because of naturally occurring sexual tendencies that are largely beyond their control. Yet those who oppose gay rights feel just as strongly that homosexual behavior is deviant and immoral (on the basis of deeply held religious or nonreligious beliefs), and equally as immoral to publicly affirm the legitimacy and mainstreaming of such behavior.

The point here is that when two or more sides argue over opposing positions rooted in deeply held moral convictions, *they are unlikely to persuade the opposing side*. Instead, advocates become unhinged in defense of favored ideologies, with name calling and character assassination becoming the preferred modes of debate. This creates winners and losers in organizational policy decisions (Schein, 1998), where the losers are prone to resist initiatives of the winning side. Instead, the losing side is much more likely to build resistance movements of like-minded individuals within the organization (e.g., Cummings, 2008) or to break away from the organization with the goal of forming a new one. The point is, viscera is never a reliable foundation on which to build training models in school psychology or any other field.

Clear, Objective Thinking Is Compromised.

The emotional intensity with which moral positions are held tend to create pervasive blind spots in other intellectual or moral areas (Fein, 2001). This causes otherwise careful scholars and professionals to become quite sloppy and/or careless in how they apply (or do not apply) research to practice. Here, professional objectivity is compromised, and there is a tendency to distort priorities. For example, while "color-blind merit" and "representative diversity" may both be noble goals, they often lead to opposite outcomes in policy decisions. The ideologues' tendency to elevate representative diversity over color-blind merit in all instances leads to what one writer refers to as the "dictatorship of virtue" (Bernstein, 1994). Ideological rigidity manages only to inspire like-minded followers. For others, rigid moralism invites only alienation, opposition, and backlash.

The Moral Model *Creates Moral Confusion Rather Than Moral Clarity*.

By portraying educational problems as a good guy/bad guy dichotomy, the *Moral Model* encourages professionals in training to become more acutely race conscious at the same time that they are receiving opposing messages to be color-blind in dealings with others. In many multicultural advocacy movements, the ideal of "color-blindness" is openly held up to ridicule (Kunjufu, 2002; Schofield, 2004). The *Moral Model* encourages professionals to view the world through the prism of racial/ethnic identity politics. That is to say, all minority problems are perceived as attributable to the long-term effects of whites' mistreatment of minorities in the distant past, or to something whites are currently doing (or not doing) to minorities in the present. This, in turn, creates an inducement for teachers, counselors, and school psychologists to cease being appropriately judgmental toward any legitimate faults or wrongdoing on the part of minorities—since they are viewed as little more than hapless victims of circumstances beyond their control. Such double standards in expectations rarely escape public notice. Here, militant multiculturalists make themselves vulnerable to the charge of *liberal racism* (see Glossary), defined as patronizing attitudes toward minority groups that in essence absolves them from any personal responsibility or accountability for life outcomes. According to Ahlert (2008), for individuals who subscribe to the *Moral Model* of race relations:

> . . . the color of a man's skin . . . determines everything, but in this case being non-white confers a sense of permanent victimhood coupled with permanent entitlement. Non-whites can never accomplish anything without government set-asides, affirmative action, quotas, etc., all of which were/are provided by the enlightened segment of the white population. Any white who does not subscribe to such a worldview gets tossed into the dedicated racist category. Nothing will convince them otherwise . . .

Although some whites may be particularly susceptible to this form of emotional manipulation, many are not. When exposed to multicultural advocacy and indoctrination rooted in the *Moral Model*, such persons will either tune out such messages, superficially pretend to "go along to get along," or actively resist being unfairly stereotyped and demonized (for a more detailed discussion, see Chapter 10).

The Culture Model

Although the *Moral Model* of training reduces multicultural issues to an essential conflict between good versus evil, the *Culture Model* of training reduces multicultural issues to an essential conflict between "enlightenment versus ignorance."

The *Culture Model* approach to multicultural training is modeled after the training students receive in introductory human exceptionalities classes. In such classes, students learn that certain diagnosable conditions (e.g., autism, deafness, blindness, mental retardation, learning disabilities, emotional disturbances) have specific identifiable characteristics in schoolchildren that can undermine normal academic and social functioning. Thus, if a preservice teacher, school counselor, or school psychologist plans to work with autistic children in the future, they must first learn specialized terms and concepts that are specific to the unique social, language, cognitive, and developmental characteristics of autistic children. In the same way, the *Culture Model* views "culture" and "cultural differences" as all-purpose explanations that presumably help preservice professionals understand the peculiarities of children from different racial, ethnic, social class, or language groups.

As in the *Moral Model*, minorities are still essentially viewed as perpetual victims of the society around them. Unlike the *Moral Model*, however, the *Culture Model* emphasizes the role of "cultural misunderstanding" as the primary ingredient responsible for school problems. In the *Culture Model* worldview, minority groups are seen as growing up in an insular cultural environment that, for all practical purposes, is largely unknown to citizens belonging to the majority culture. The task of training, therefore, is threefold. First, the *Culture Model* seeks to identify the "clinical disorder" in majority groups that presumably causes them to be insensitive to the needs of minorities in schools. Predictably, these disorders are framed in cultural terms using a variety of names, such as "Eurocentrism" (Helms, 1989), "cultural blindness" (Cross, Bazron, Dennis, & Issacs, 1989), or "ethnocentrism" (Pope-Davis, Coleman, Liu, & Toporek, 2003). Second, students trained under the *Culture Model* are socialized to view cultural differences as the primary explanation for different educational outcomes among racial/ethnic groups. Third, the *Culture Model* encourages students to seek and use so-called "culturally sensitive" interventions that presumably work better with cultural minority students (compared to interventions that are not culturally sensitive).

Whereas the fundamental message of the *Moral Model* is that minorities are victims, the fundamental message of the *Culture Model* is that minorities are exotic. Minorities-are-exotic messages are designed to control the *image* of how minority groups are portrayed in the social science literature. These images, as applied to different groups, are depicted in Sidebars 2.4, 2.5, 2.6, and 2.7.

🖎 Sidebar 2.4   "Minorities-as-Exotic" Perspective in Psychoeducational Literature: African Americans

Worldview (Boykin, 1986; Hale-Benson, 1986; Huber & Pewewardy, 1990)

- Emphasizes spiritualism and harmony with nature
- Values affect and interconnectedness with people
- Flexible orientation toward being on time
- Orientation toward people rather than objects
- Emphasis on oral rather than print-based communication

Preferred Learning Style (Allen & Boykin, 1992; Hale-Benson, 1986; Huber & Pewewardy, 1990; Kunjufu, 2002; Turner, 1986)

- Learns better under cooperative rather than competitive learning situations
- Learning is enhanced (particularly for young children) when opportunities for movement are incorporated into lessons
- Learning is enhanced when test questions are read orally rather than read as text
- Learns more easily from materials that have social, rather than abstract, content

Preferred Style in Language, Interpersonal Communication, and Helping Contexts (Hale-Benson, 1986; Kochman, 1981; Martines, 2008; Orr, 1997)

- Frequent use of context-specific word meanings, "colorful" and idiomatic expressions
- Language syntax is restricted and grammatically simple; rigid and limited use of adjectives and adverbs
- Language patterns interfere with standard English necessary for understanding math problems
- Males may use "brother's" handshake
- In interacting with others, 36 to 42 inches of space preferred
- Relating style is animated and confrontational
- May look away when helper is speaking; can show disrespect in same manner
- Expressive; nods and facial expressions common

⬡ Sidebar 2.5   "Minorities-as-Exotic" Perspective in Psychoeducational Literature: Asian Americans

General Cultural Values (Morrow, 1989)

- Geared toward spiritualism
- Mankind is supposed to live in harmony with, rather than dominate, nature

Child-Rearing/Family Practices (Chan, 1986; Morrow, 1989)

- Family, rather than the individual, is the basis of society
- Family members must develop a sense of moral obligation and primary loyalty to family
- Child behaviors that maintain and enhance the family name are considered valuable

- Negative child behaviors (e.g., disobedience, disrespect) bring collective shame on the family
- Traditionally, teachers are more respected than parents
- Children are not allowed much independence
- Parents control child's behavior by appealing to child's sense of obligation to others
- Children often sleep with their parents
- Greets the head of a family or an older person first
- Sons are valued more than daughters

Special Education Issues *(Chan-sew, 1980; Morrow, 1989)*

- Child's handicap thought to be punishment for moral transgressions committed by parents and/or ancestors
- Handicapped children are thought to be possessed by demons, ghosts, or evil spirits

Preferred Style in Helping Contexts (Martines, 2008)

- Soft and pliable handshake
- Prefer respectful distance, 36 to 42 inches okay
- Indirect eye contact
- Few smiles; head nods may be used to signal respect
- Categorized as East (Chinese, Japanese, Korean) and Southeast (Vietnamese, Cambodian, Laotian) Asians

---

Sidebar 2.6 "Minorities-as-Exotic" Perspective in Psychoeducational Literature: Hispanics

Cultural Values (Dunn & Griggs, 1995)

- Loyalty to the family; adolescents more inclined than Anglos to adopt parents' religious and political beliefs
- Males are more authority oriented; females are more peer oriented

Cognitive/Learning Style (Dunn & Griggs, 1995; Tileston & Darling, 2008)

- Field dependent; perceive stimuli globally and experience new information holistically
- Learn best when material to be learned has social content
- Internalize criticism from teachers
- Greater preferences for a cooler (temperature) learning environment

Communication/Language (Tileston & Darling, 2008)[*]

- Values diplomacy and tact in communication with others

Social Interaction Style (Tileston & Darling, 2008)[*]

- Hispanics (particularly Mexican Americans) work well together in co-operative or collective efforts, as opposed to competitive individualism
- Predominant response style is "experiencing life to its fullest"
- Role definitions between males and females must be respected

Preferred Style in Helping Contexts (Martines, 2008)

- Firm handshake for males; soft and pliable handshake for unacculturated females
- Contact 24 to 36 inches with no barriers
- Indirect eye contact, at least initially
- Initially reserved; smiles and head nods may occur frequently later

---

*Primarily Mexican Americans

🖎 Sidebar 2.7   "Minorities-as-Exotic" Perspective in Psychoeducational Literature: Native Americans

Group Values/Behaviors (Dunn & Griggs, 1995)

- God is viewed as positive, benevolent, and integral to daily living
- Bravery, patience, honesty, respect for others, controlled emotions, and self-respect are admired personality traits
- Everyone knows their geneaology and has a strong sense of community and tribal identity

Preferred Style as Clients in Helping Contexts (Martines, 2008)

- Soft and pliable handshake
- Respectful distance initially; later, much closer distances are okay
- Indirect eye contact
- Few smiles and head nods

Preferred Learning Style (Dunn & Griggs, 1995; Kaulback, 1995)

- Learns primarily through observation and imitation, rather than through listening to verbal instructions

- Group-oriented, and prefer to work in small groups or on team projects

Communication Style (Lomawaima, 2004; Kaulback, 1995)

- Asking questions is not found in day-to-day speech habits outside of schools
- Highly skilled in nonverbal communication
- In the classroom, may use silence to exercise control over the teacher

Cognitive Abilities (Dunn & Griggs, 1995; Kaulback, 1995)

- Possess highly defined visuoperceptual skills developed from hunting/trapping experiences
- Score higher on simultaneous processing measures and lower on sequential processing measures compared to Caucasian students
- More highly skilled in holistic processing (i.e., seeing the whole versus the parts)

Instructional Implications (Kaulback, 1997; Smith & Shade, 1995)

- Learns best from visual instructional materials (e.g., films, diagrams, pictures, drawings)
- Children should be allowed freedom of movement in learning situations
- Due to cultural background, children may not understand how and why a certain succession of printed letters corresponds to certain phonetic sounds (necessary in learning how to read)
- Learn better when instruction moves from practice to theory, rather than from theory to practice
- Instruction should provide opportunities for a high percentage of group projects and a low percentage of oral questions and answers
- Instruction should incorporate manipulative devices and activities that allow students to feel and touch
- Use artwork that illustrates people and animals, cartoons, wood-carving, model building, miniature displays, and map-making
- Encourage opinionated expression of viewpoints in social studies and other subjects where controversy can be found
- Use metaphors, images, analogies, and symbols rather than dictionary-type definitions
- Adolescents feel uncomfortable in competitively structured situations
- Prefer to learn in a cool (temperature) environment
- Afternoons are the worst time of the day for concentrating on new and difficult material

In these portrayals, multiculturalism lectures audiences that "differences are not deficiencies" (e.g., see Hale-Benson, 1986; Tucker & Herman, 2002; Wright, 2008). Here, audiences are told that behavioral and cognitive standards for children in schools are little more than a manifestation of a Eurocentric middle-class worldview, and such standards should not be applied to culturally different children (e.g., Hale-Benson, 1986). According to this thinking, a more enlightened view requires modification in educational practices and standards that recognizes the role of culture and cultural differences in understanding cognition and behavior. The *Culture Model* assumes that once teachers, administrators, and psychologists are educated in the norms, folkways, and values of a particular culture, they will develop the necessary sensitivities and competencies to serve these groups "correctly," which presumably will lead to improved outcomes.

Following this model, training programs will infuse multicultural content into their coursework; professional organizations will provide a plethora of workshops, seminars, and training videos on multiculturalism; and publishing houses will flood the market with textbooks on multiculturalism—all in an effort to prepare professional educators and psychologists for an increasingly "diverse" world. This mindset has spawned an entirely new lexicon in education and psychology that promotes culture as the central construct that the majority group must understand in order to be properly enlightened. A wide variety of culture buzzwords commonly found in the multicultural education and multicultural psychology literature are listed in Sidebar 2.8.

Sidebar 2.8   Culture Buzzwords Commonly Found in Education, Counseling, and School Psychology Literature

cross-cultural	cultural deprivation
culture brokers	cultural determinism
culture-centered knowledge	cultural differences
culture conflict	cultural discontinuity
culture shock	cultural diversity
cultural affiliation	cultural empathy
cultural ambassadors	cultural encapsulation
cultural ambience	cultural entrenchment
cultural backgrounds	cultural equivalence
cultural bias	cultural hegemony
cultural competence	cultural identity
cultural congruence	cultural integrity

cultural matching   cultural relevance
cultural mistrust   cultural sensitivity
cultural pluralism   culturally appropriate practice
cultural proficiency   culturally consistent practice
cultural racism   culturally specific counseling

How Does the Culture Model Respond to Its Critics?

Contradictory Research Is Simply Ignored.

Similar to the *Moral Model*, the *Culture Model* must completely ignore contradictory empirical research in order to protect its integrity. For example, White (1984) claims that the average lower scores achieved by black students on individually administered intelligence tests are largely a result of "culturally inappropriate" test items (pp. 109–112). Such statements are quite surprising, given that they were made four years *after* the landmark text *Bias in Mental Testing* exhaustively examined such claims and found them to be false (Jensen, 1980). Similarly, Helms (1992) urges psychometricians to develop more "culturally appropriate" cognitive tests for lower-scoring minority groups, despite the fact that contemporary research finds no evidence of statistical test bias in well-developed standardized instruments (Reynolds & Lowe, 2009).

Treating the Concept of Culture as Mysterious.

By its very nature, the *Culture Model* of training sets up a politically useful antagonism between "insiders" versus "outsiders." In this approach, culture represents a mysterious black box containing secrets that are presumably beyond the experiential understanding of outsiders (see Swisher, 1998, for this view as applied to Native American education). Insiders—typically academics/educators who belong to the minority group under discussion—are assumed to possess unassailable expertise in all matters related to the cultural group of which they are members. In contrast, outsiders are portrayed as possessing

> . . . a structurally imposed incapacity to comprehend alien groups, statuses, cultures, and societies. Unlike the Insider, the Outsider has neither been socialized in the group nor has engaged in the run of experience that makes up its life, and therefore cannot have the direct, intuitive sensibility that alone makes empathic understanding possible. (Merton, 1973, p. 106)

Outsiders are expected to be deferential toward any belief or theory that presumes to have inside knowledge of the culture that is different from his or her own culture.

Outsiders are socialized by enlightened multiculturalism to avoid any appearance of criticizing the culture theories of insiders, for to do so is interpreted—particularly within politically contentious climates—as acts of disrespect and cultural arrogance (e.g., see Sue, Capodilupo, Nadal, & Torino, 2008, response to Thomas, 2008).

Whenever educational problems are politically embarrassing to multiculturalism, the *Culture Model* takes refuge in the "secret mysteries of culture" as a means to explain away the difficulty. Thus, if a given minority group routinely displays lower average scores on cognitive tests, then the issue is attributed to test developers' failure to incorporate culture into the design of tests (Helms, 1992). If a minority group displays discipline and behavioral problems at a consistently greater rate than other groups, then the problem is blamed on teachers' lack of understanding of students' cultural backgrounds (Osher et al., 2004). The self-esteem of minority children is seen as so fragile, that if the school curriculum fails to include a sufficient proportion of "cultural" content, it is believed that students will fail to achieve adequately (see discussion in Roth, 2005). Only a select group of expert multiculturalists are presumed to have access to special cultural insights that will magically transform how professionals serve minority children.

Use of Obfuscation in Communicating Ideas.

Obfuscation is another method used by adherents of the *Culture Model* in responding to critics. If culture is assumed to be fundamentally mysterious, then obfuscation can make culture seem even more mysterious. When used as a verb, synonyms for *obfuscation* are to *confuse, bewilder, muddle, perplex, baffle,* or *confound.* As a noun, synonyms for *obfuscation* are *blurriness, fuzziness, unclarity, vagueness,* and *murkiness.* Obfuscation is rampant in academic writing, where communicating ideas using "50-dollar words" is preferred over communicating ideas using simpler language that the lay public can easily understand. This allows the writer to hide half-baked ideas behind pompous-sounding verbiage. Such language may indeed impress the gullible, but in the final analysis it is so incomprehensible as to make not the slightest bit of sense. As examples, consider the following excerpt from the second edition of the *Handbook of Research on Multicultural Education*:

> In addition to using race as an analytical tool, critical race theorists challenge the separate discourses on race, class, and gender and focus on the intersectionality of subordination. . . . These types of analyses could contribute to multicultural education by interrogating the racialized context of teaching, and connecting race with multiple forms of oppression. Multicultural research conducted within a [critical race theory] framework might offer a way to understand and analyze the multiple identities and knowledges of people of color without essentializing their various experiences. A second potential contribution of [critical race theory] is the way that it challenges Eurocentric

epistemology and questions dominant discursive notions of meritocracy, objectivity, knowledge, and individualism. . . . Critical race theorists ground their research in these systems of knowledge and "integrate their experiential knowledge, drawn from a shared history as 'other' with their ongoing struggles to transform." (Sleeter & Bernal, 2004, p. 246)

Ferguson (2000) adds the following insights:

> In this contemporary racial formation the category of race has increasingly been defined through cultural rather than biological difference. Relations of power and inequality are explained as the demonstrated consequence of superior or pathological cultural characteristics. Attitudes, values, behaviors, familial and community practices become the field from which social distinctions derive. . . . Since a good part of the ideological work on race is to fix meanings and relationships as natural and durable, the racialization of cultural forms and practices not only extracts behaviors and attitudes from the social matrix in which they are embedded but transforms them into immutable racially linked characteristics that produce poverty and bad citizens. (p. 20)

Such writing is, unfortunately, all too frequent in multicultural education texts enamored by Marxist thought (for an extended discussion, see Sokal & Bricmont, 1998).

Fatal Flaws of the Culture Model

The *Culture Model* has several fatal flaws, not the least of which is the superficial manner in which culture is conceptualized and promoted under this approach. The practice of equating race/ethnicity as synonymous with culture is quite understandable, given that outwardly observable differences in physical traits are the easiest and most expedient method for classifying human beings. In reality, however, culture includes variables that are not easily visible to the naked eye, which are associated with socioeconomic status, the child-rearing philosophy of parents and caregivers, as well as a host of other religious, regional, subcultural, and school context variables (see Frisby, 2005b).

Multiculturalism Degenerates Into Racialism.

For all practical purposes, politicized multiculturalism equates culture with racial/ethnic group membership. As an example, consider the case of a second-generation Japanese American child from a hard-working Christian fishing family who grows up in the Pacific Northwest. When the child starts public school, how is his or her elementary teacher (following the dictates of current thinking in multicultural education) supposed to expose the child to cultural role models in history lessons? Should the child's role models be successful fishermen from the past? Should the child's role models be successful Christians throughout U.S. history? Or, should the appropriate role models be famous Japanese Americans? It comes as no surprise to many that multiculturalism ideology overwhelmingly supports the last answer—simply because culture, for all practical purposes, is reflexively treated as a proxy for race and ethnicity. Thus, multiculturalism is merely a more socially acceptable form of *racialism* (see Glossary). Here, multiculturalism allows the academic community to discuss race covertly "in stealth mode," but without the appearance of discussing it overtly.

Lazy Stereotypes Have Minimal Scientific Value.

Legitimizing the cultural stereotypes displayed in Sidebars 2.4–2.7 is fundamentally unscientific. The breezy descriptions in Sidebars 2.4–2.7 cannot be construed as independently verifiable facts, because there is no objective, scientific method for operationalizing such statements. The authors of such statements provide no quantifiable data to support these stereotypes, which in essence consist of authors' personal opinions or interpretations of group traits. Furthermore, basic common sense acknowledges the wide variability among human beings (even within the same racial/ethnic group), as well as the considerable overlap in traits among groups (see *Star Trek Fallacy* in the Glossary). This view presents a threat to multiculturalism ideology, because acknowledging intragroup variability or the overlapping of traits across groups undermines simplistic cultural explanations for educational problems.

Lazy Stereotypes Justify Blame-Shifting.

The real purpose of the stereotypes in Sidebars 2.4–2.7 are well known to anyone who is savvy in the multicultural politics that are played out all too often in academic and applied settings. A simple hypothetical scenario illustrates how this political gamesmanship operates. Suppose a mother from a nonwhite low-SES minority group has a chronic tendency to show up late for school appointments, if she shows up at all. The school psychologist knows that the mother has no competing demands on her time, and quite naturally concludes that this mother is irresponsible or unreliable. However, a recent multicultural article claims that such behavior simply reflects "a different or more flexible concept of time" that is indicative of that particular cultural group (e.g., see Sue & Sue, 2003, p. 169). Thus, with facile words, irresponsibility is magically transformed into a legitimate cultural trait that is to be accepted as normal. Thus, the *blame has shifted* from the mother's behavior to the "Eurocentric" attitudes of the school psychologist, who can now be criticized as woefully ignorant and insensitive to the mother's culture. It is therefore incumbent on the school psychologist to be sensitized and "enlightened" so that he or she will cease being "judgmental." As will be shown in Chapter 7, effective interventions for improving student and family behaviors in at-risk minority communities have no qualms about being judgmental of nonproductive behavior.

Culture as "Bad Genetics."

As stated in the previous discussion of the *Group Identity Doctrine*, multiculturalism ideology views individuals as little more than representatives of their racial/ethnic group. Militant multiculturalists essentially argue that unrelated individuals (bound by culture) have similar behaviors and cognitive patterns simply on the basis of shared skin color, language, or ethnicity. In reality, the more complex organisms (i.e., human beings) are, the more complex are the determinants of phenotypic traits and day-to-day behaviors (e.g., see Petrill, Plomin, DeFries, & Hewitt, 2003). Lobo and Shaw (2008) articulate this complexity as follows:

> Each individual *organism* is exactly that—an individual. . . . Even laboratory organisms, which have a high degree of genetic similarity because they have been inbred for many generations, behave differently under the same conditions. . . . Similarly, among humans, even "identical" twins who are raised together in nearly the same *environment* are never truly identical. . . . Even though such twins are indeed the same at the genetic sequence level, people who know them can easily tell them apart. This is because the individuality and variation we observe in each *organism* is generated through a complex *interaction* between the *organism*'s "complete genetic endowment" and its *environment* from conception onward.

Because multiculturalism is fundamentally an ideology (and not a science), it leapfrogs over these simple truths to indoctrinate audiences with the notion that culture is a fixed, all-powerful, quasi-genetic force that determines and standardizes the behavior and psychological traits of all persons belonging to the same racial/ethnic or language group. No properly trained geneticist would dare suggest such a principle, as this would ignore a host of environmental factors, such as parental upbringing, socioecomic status, and differences in schooling contexts.

Successful educators—who have real-world experience studying effective educational practices with at-risk minority student populations—conceptualize culture in a more concrete, practical sense. To illustrate, Thernstrom and Thernstrom (2003) write:

> In arguing that the cultures of racial and ethnic groups strongly influence the educational performance of youths, we are simply saying that children first develop values, attitudes, and skills as a result of their experience in the families that raised them. But those values, attitudes, and skills continue to be shaped by

children's interaction with their peers, teachers, neighbors, and other aspects of their environment. . . . Good schools can become an enormously important element in that environment. (p. 66)

Human Universals Are Ignored.

An important question that is rarely discussed seriously in debates on multiculturalism is: Are human beings (regardless of their racial/ethnic/language differences) more similar than they are different? The open acknowledgement of social and behavioral universals shared by all groups is virtually ignored in multicultural psychology, primarily because it yields no political advantages for advocacy groups. Multiculturalism is built on the fundamental premise that different racial/ethnic groups have little to nothing in common, and they cannot (or should not) be compared on a similar standard (for numerous examples of this view, see Taylor, 2011, Chapters 5, 6, and 7). In short, militant multiculturalism argues that comparing different racial and ethnic groups is akin to comparing apples and oranges. As an illustration, Boykin (1986) writes:

> To characterize Afro-Americans as culturally different from Euro-Americans is not graphic enough. To the extent that the Black experience reflects a traditional West African cultural ethos, the two frames of reference are non-commensurable. There are fundamental incompatibilities between them; they are not quite polar opposites, but they are almost dialectically related. . . . This incommensurability makes it difficult to put black cultural reality in the service of attainment in Euro-American cultural institutions, such as schools. The ideology that informs those institutions is a profound negation of the most central attributes of African culture. (p. 63)

This is utter nonsense. Although it is true that cultural differences certainly exist (both within and across groups), are these differences so profound as to reflect "fundamental incompatibilities" as Boykin and others suggest? As an illustration, what can be more culturally identifiable than musical styles and genres? Yet, at one point in time, arguably the world's greatest classical trumpet player and female opera singer (musical genres considered European) were African Americans (e.g., Wynton Marsalis and Jessye Norman, respectively). Similarly, many of the world's most accomplished jazz musicians (a musical genre originating with African Americans) are whites (e.g., Bill Evans, Benny Goodman, Gerry Mulligan, to name a few).

To understand different-cultures-are-like-apples-and-oranges thinking, one must understand the *political advantages* of promulgating such views. Multiculturalism avoids any emphasis on human universals, because these imply common standards along which groups can be compared and evaluated (e.g., see Sidebar 10.6). In comparing different groups on the same standard, the fear is that one group may be unfavorably compared to other groups, which is politically embarrassing to multicultural advocacy efforts.

The Empirical and Philosophical Bankruptcy of "Culture × Treatment Interaction" Theorizing.

Multiculturalism's fundamental sales pitch to school psychology is through the assumed validity of *culture × treatment interactions* (see Glossary). In a nutshell, multiculturalism implies that unique treatments that are particularly effective for racial/ethnic minorities differ from treatments shown to be effective for nonminorities—simply on the basis of some as-yet-unspecified cultural modifications. Examples of culture × treatment advocacy in psychology and education are given in Sidebar 2.9.

Some multicultural advocates attempt to argue that the poor academic performance of minority groups in schools simply reflects culturally different modes of interacting with material, and they are not to be interpreted as "deficient" relative to the majority culture (e.g., see Hale-Benson, 1986). "Differences-are-not-deficits" theorizing provides an emotionally satisfying way for multiculturalists to airbrush the image of minority groups (e.g., see Kunjufu, 2005, 2011). However, this fools no one—least of all minority educators who are laboring in the front lines of minority school failure (e.g., Carter, 2000; Stern, 2009; Whitman, 2008). These hard-working professionals know that low academic performance, intractable behavior problems, and anti-intellectual attitudes are patently unacceptable, and they pursue plain, common-sense prescriptions for reversing such problems against tremendous odds (see Chapter 7).

⌨ Sidebar 2.9   Examples of "Culture × Treatment Interaction" Advocacy in Psychoeducational Literature

- "Unfortunately, many teachers, both minority and mainstream, are unable to identify traits among ethnic minority youths that require a unique set of instructional strategies for a positive learning environment. Equally disturbing is that, once such cultural traits have been identified, teachers have no idea how to adapt classroom instruction to these traits." (Vasquez, 1998, p. 1)
- "When instructional processes are consistent with the cultural orientations, experiences, and learning styles of marginalized African, Latino, Native, and Asian American students, their school achievement improves significantly. . . . Culturally responsive practices unveil some solutions to the seemingly unsolvable mystery of the perpetual underachievement of

marginalized students of color. They are not being taught in school as they learn in their cultural communities. This discontinuity interrupts their mental schemata and makes academic learning harder to achieve." (Gay, 2000, pp. 181–182)

- "Black children grow up in a distinct culture. Black children therefore need an educational system that recognizes their strengths, their abilities, and their culture and that incorporates them into the learning process." (Hale-Benson, 1986, p. 4)

- ". . . [A] multicultural approach to consultation is one that considers the influence of the culture of each member of the triad in every step of the process. Multicultural consultation also allows for adjusting services to address the culturally related needs that arise. When members of the consultation triad differ culturally from one another, this . . . adds complexity to the process. . . . . The consultant's role is to make hidden cultural aspects explicit to consultation participants and to generate hypotheses informed by cultural knowledge. The resulting information allows one to either appropriately intervene on problems created by ignoring cultural variables or to find appropriate methods to incorporate the information obtained." (Booker, 2009, p. 176)

- ". . . [M]ost educational agencies function between cultural incapacity and cultural blindness. It is common to hear, 'We treat everyone here the same.' Although those espousing this view may be well intentioned, this cultural blindness paradigm negates children's lived experiences and translates to a 'one size fits all' model. . . . [C]ulturally responsive education recognizes and addresses students' learning styles, their different modes of reflective learning, the role of group collaboration, and the function of nonverbal behavior." (Crockett & Brown, 2009, p. 120)

Cultural immersion schools (see Chapter 4) are built on the premise that minority children must be educated comprehensively in their group's culture in order to do well in school. However, not a speck of solid, replicable research evidence shows that cultural immersion schools, *because of their culturally specific curricula*, result in significantly higher levels of school achievement compared to non-culturally specific schools (all other variables being equal).

In reality, the only culture × treatment interactions that have face validity involve bilingual programs (see Chapter 4) and other non-English-language interventions (e.g., Baker & Good, 1995; Baker, Plasencia-Peinado, & Lezcano-Lytle, 1998; de Ramirez & Shapiro, 2006)—as these must be delivered (in full or in part) in a language that non-English-speaking clients can understand.

Cultural Role Models.

It is customary for professional organizations to complain about the shortage of minority professionals (i.e., teachers, counselors, school psychologists) presumably needed to serve as "role models" for minority children and youth. One educator puts the matter bluntly (reported in Kane, 2010):

> Black people are the only ones who can teach black children, it's as simple as that. . . . Throughout history, people have always stayed with their own kind. . . . The bottom line is we are not all the same. Black children are not going to grow up and be white.

Although school psychology organizations do not frame the issue in terms as crude as this, many believe that minority professionals share a deep cultural bond with their minority clients that ultimately is advantageous for facilitating positive outcomes. Although common sense dictates that bilingual school psychologists are needed to serve non-English-speaking children, audiences assume that racial/ethnic status alone offers a distinct advantage in working with racially/ethnically similar clients. Such ideas appear intuitive to most, so they are rarely challenged publicly.

Nevertheless, the "cultural matching hypothesis" can be empirically tested like any other topic in the social sciences. Maylor (2009) reviewed the empirical data on the "black teachers–are-role-models-for–black kids" hypothesis, as well as conducting thorough qualitative interviews with black teachers in Great Britain. His conclusions are summarized as follows:

> Being a role model is not an "ethnic skill" Black teachers should be presumed to "naturally" possess. Moreover, just because a teacher is Black . . . does not mean that her/his ethnicity would enable her/him to serve as a role model to Black pupils or improve Black male attainment. The findings in this study demonstrate that the recruitment of Black teachers does not automatically convert into those teachers either desiring to serve as role models or feeling comfortable in such a role, or indeed being accepted or acknowledged as appropriate role models by all Black pupils. This suggests that ethnic (and gender) "matching" in teaching is too simplistic an approach as it does not take into account Black pupils' perception of or reaction to Black teachers, and/or Black teachers' perception of the concept of role modeling and their experience of role modeling with Black

pupils. This research provides further evidence that ethnic (and gender) "matching" in role modeling discourse is not only misguided, but that where it is applied it is likely to flounder where pupils do not recognize the Black teacher standing in front of them as a role model. (pp. 17–18)

Similar research has never been conducted in the field of school psychology. In the absence of hard research, the burden of proof is on professional organizations representing school psychology to justify the advantages of ethnic matching with more than simple platitudes and bromides.

The Educational Failure of All-Minority Schools.

In the absence of more direct tests of the ethnic matching hypothesis, indirect tests are available for all to see, and they do not bode well for the *Culture Model.* Recall that the *Cultural Model* implies that cultural conflicts are fundamentally responsible for the various problems faced by minority children and youth in schools (e.g., see Kunjufu, 2002). Teachers, pupil personnel service professionals, and test developers are inundated with the message that they need to learn an entirely new set of cultural skills in order to properly serve minority clients. *This philosophy predicts that all-minority environments should represent a veritable paradise of top-notch educational practices and student success, particularly when the majority of professionals in the school belong to the same culture.* Unfortunately, such predictions are flatly contradicted by cold reality. Many (but not all) predominantly minority schools are notorious for being among the worst schools in the country (see Edelman, 2011; MacDonald, 2004; Maeroff, 1988). In such schools, academic failure, gang violence, teenage pregnancies, anti-achievement attitudes, low parental involvement, bureaucratic incompetence, and corruption are pervasive.

The *Social Engineering* Model

In order for the *Moral Model* of training to be credible, it is assumed that racism and prejudice must be thoroughly expunged from the hearts and minds of those who teach or interact with cultural minority children in schools, in order for said children to succeed educationally. In order for the *Culture Model* of training to be credible, it is assumed that professionals must attain a high level of cultural enlightenment in order to properly teach, counsel, or serve minority children in schools. Multiculturalists nevertheless find themselves frustrated at the slow pace in which these goals are realized, if they can be realized at all. As a result, multicultural advocacy sees a need to aggressively promote progressive change through the process of "social engineering."

Social engineering is a term used to describe efforts by federal and state governments and professional organizations to deliberately change behavior and social mores, or modify attitudes on a large scale. This is accomplished by a variety of means, which can include

(a) building incentives and disincentives into institutional policy decisions and practices; (b) issuing court orders and/or passing laws to impel or prohibit certain behaviors; or (c) facilitating the internalization of "acceptable" versus "unacceptable" multicultural attitudes through the social media. In summary, "social engineers wish to reconfigure entire systems to produce a desired result" (Fein, 2001, p. 215).

The *Social Engineering Model* begins with the assumption that the world can be likened to a giant chessboard, in which the pieces can be manipulated by those in power to meet specified sociopolitical objectives. Whereas the *Moral Model* and *Culture Model* both rely on some form of verbal and/or emotional persuasion to manipulate behavior and attitudes, the cornerstone of the *Social Engineering Model* is that individuals or groups *must comply* or face the threat of tangible sanctions for noncompliance. The hope here is that the desired multicultural attitudes, behaviors, and statistical outcomes will naturally follow.

In the government policy arena, the move toward explicitly race-conscious preferential policies began with frustration that color-blind policies for business hiring and college admissions were not achieving the desired racial proportions originally hoped for (see D'Souza, 1995, p. 218). Gradually, quietly, and under the radar of public debate, the period of the 1960s witnessed the creation of federal civil rights agencies such as the Equal Employment Opportunity Commission (EEOC), the Office of Federal Contract Compliance Programs (OFCCP), and the Office of Civil Rights (OCR), all of which are designed to promote racial preferences.

The results of social science research are often used as justification for massive social engineering efforts, particularly as these relate to schooling. For example, the *Brown v. Board of Education* Supreme Court decision of 1954 (that declared state laws establishing separate public schools for black and white students as unconstitutional) was influenced in part by Kenneth and Mamie Clark's famous "doll studies," which purportedly documented the psychological damage visited on black students as a result of segregation (Clark & Clark, 1939). The school busing movement of the 1960s and 1970s was sparked, in part, by findings from the influential Coleman Report (see Glossary), which suggested that school achievement for black students would be maximized by racially integrated learning contexts.

At other times, social engineering is justified simply on the basis of a writer's personal opinion as to its supposed benefits. As examples, Sandhu and Aspy (1997) argue that the isolation of white children from nonwhite children is to be avoided, because "this situation might lead to a false sense of self-esteem due in part to a false notion of racial superiority" in white children (p. 62). They further state that "the overemphasis on a Eurocentric curriculum so influences . . . children's thought patterns that they cannot value the life-style contributions of other cultures" (p. 62). According to these authors, "exposure to cultural contributions from other ethnic groups will forever change children's thinking such that racism and sexism will be reduced in our society" (p. 62). Other examples of multicultural social engineering efforts, particularly those designed to close the racial achievement gap, are listed in Sidebar 4.6.

How Does the Social Engineering Model Respond to Its Critics?

Resistance Is to Be Met With Force.

In a nutshell, social engineering battles are fought through the use of power and coercion; by engaging in internecine political battles within organizations; legal battles fought within the context of the courts; or by outright fraud and/or deception. Such efforts "attempt to bully their way to success over the objections of individuals prepared to resist" (Fein, 2001, p. 207). For example, with respect to forcing programs to infuse multiculturalism in training, Mio and Awakuni (2000) state "if one has a large enough stick, resistance can be overcome" (p. 3). In addition, Mio and Awakuni (2000) opine that "political pressure on the power structure of APA" was largely responsible for pressuring the APA to adopt multicultural requirements for training programs. They describe the politicking and coalition building by the Association of Black Psychologists, the Asian American Psychological Association, the Hispanic Psychological Association, the Committee on Ethnic Minority Affairs, and Divisions 17 and 45 of the APA in order to accomplish these political goals (pp. 3–4).

Sometimes when social engineering schemes fail, they are met with the argument that not enough money was spent, or that participants simply didn't try hard enough. As one among numerous examples, a local chapter of the National Association for the Advancement of Colored People (NAACP) has threatened to sue one school district for failing to rectify ongoing racial segregation patterns and academic achievement inequities, although schools have virtually no control over such outcomes (see Banaszak, 2011).

The Fatal Flaws of the Social Engineering Model

The flaws of the *Social Engineering Model* can be seen most clearly when its underlying assumptions are made explicit. The *Social Engineering Model* rests on three bedrock tenets, each of which is implicitly accepted on faith: (1) the problem under consideration is sufficiently understood, or in common vernacular, and clever people know what is wrong and how problems need to be fixed; (2) the solution to identified problems can always be found; and (3) the identified solutions can easily and readily be implemented as conceived (see Fein, 2001). The shortcomings of these three tenets of the *Social Engineering Model* can be readily seen in several high-profile social engineering attempts that have spectacularly failed in U.S. society.

The Failure of Head Start.

For example, Head Start (see Glossary) began with much fanfare in the Spring of 1965 as a program designed to raise the IQ and academic achievement levels of primarily poor minority students by exposing them to a focused preschool curriculum in the months before most children begin kindergarten. The program is rooted philosophically in a naïve environmentalism (see Glossary) that was in vogue during these times, epitomized in such books as James McVicker Hunt's *Intelligence and Experience* (1961), Martin Deutsch's *The Disadvantaged Child* (1967), and Frank Reissman's *The Culturally Deprived Child* (1962). In this view, the academic performance of poor and minority children is hindered by the absence of social and economic advantages enjoyed by more affluent middle-class children. By beginning their school experience earlier, this "head start" will enable them to catch up to their more-affluent peers.

In the famous (or some would say infamous) 1969 Harvard Educational Review article "How Much Can We Boost IQ and Scholastic Achievement?", educational psychologist Arthur Jensen's opening salvo generated shockwaves throughout the psychological community that still reverberate today: "compensatory education has been tried, and it apparently has failed" (Jensen, 1969, p. 2). Since that time, numerous large-scale evaluations of Head Start have yielded findings that have fallen far short of its lofty predictions (see Thernstrom & Thernstrom, 2003, pp. 221–226 for a summary and overview). Although early evaluation efforts did reveal seemingly dramatic increases in IQ scores immediately after six to eight weeks of the program, better-designed studies soon dampened this optimism. The Westinghouse Evaluation (Westinghouse Learning Corporation and Ohio University, 1969) found that students who had made gains did not maintain them throughout the early grades of regular school. On average, students who participated in Head Start performed no better than controls from similar backgrounds who had not attended Head Start.

Currie and Thomas (1995) compared children who had attended Head Start with siblings who had not. Although they found modest test score gains for white children, African American children showed no gains, and they were equally as likely to be held back a grade in school as black children from similar socioeconomic backgrounds. Garces, Thomas, and Currie (2002) examined the economic and social success of adults under age 30 who had attended Head Start as preschoolers. Although whites showed greater high school graduation and college attendance rates, African Americans showed no substantial benefits in these areas. African Americans who attended Head Start as preschoolers were less likely to have been charged with criminal offenses later in life, but the authors never investigated selection bias as a possible explanation (i.e., Head Start parents display better parenting skills than similar parents of children not enrolled in Head Start).

In response to these disappointing results, contemporary defenders of Head Start began to change the perceived benefits of the program from "improving academic and cognitive skills" to "promoting social/emotional growth and development." As part of former president Lyndon Johnson's War on Poverty, more than $120 billion has been spent on the Head Start program since 1965, with "virtually nothing to show for it" (see Thernstrom & Thernstrom, 2003, p. 226; see also Coulson, 2010; U.S. Department of Health and Human Services, 2010).

The Failure of Money to Buy Academic Achievement.

Social engineers have traditionally believed that economic inequities between majority and minority schools appeared to be an intuitively obvious explanation for inequalities in achievement outcomes. However, more careful research has shown this to be a popular but false assertion.

In one of the earliest major studies on the relationship between resources and school outcomes, Christopher Jencks and a team of researchers from the Center for Educational Policy Research at the Harvard Graduate School of Education conducted a large-scale study in the late 1960s/early 1970s designed to collect data on the extent to which differences among schools and schooling contribute to inequalities in later adult economic attainments, occupational achievements, and social status. Among their most provocative discoveries was the finding that school expenditures and resources (controlling for the initial characteristics of students) showed quite small and inconsistent effects on school achievement outcomes (Jencks, 1972).

The cold facts are that educational spending per pupil has been growing steadily since the 1950s (Greene, 2005). Although inequities among school resources are obvious, the accumulation and synthesis of decades of research shows little to no relationship between schools' monetary expenditures and student achievement outcomes (Greene, 2005; Hanushek, 1997). Many schools with relatively lower monetary resources show higher-than-expected student achievement, and conversely many schools with high monetary resources show lower-than-expected student achievement (e.g., see Sidebar 2.10). Greene (2005) concludes:

> . . . [R]egardless of whether there is a gap between urban spending and suburban spending, the existence of such a gap would not prove that giving urban schools more money would result in improvement. It may be that other problems would prevent urban schools from making good use of the additional funds. . . . [S]ome may believe that it is just inherently wrong for some schools to have more money than others do. This, however, is an entirely separate issue. . . . No doubt there is plenty of room for debate on how best to reform our school system. However, that debate can't happen in a constructive way until

Americans realize that schools are not inadequately funded—they would not perform substantially better if they had more money. The empirical evidence simply doesn't allow for this to be the case. (pp. 18–19)

The Failure of Court-Ordered Busing.

As explained in Thernstrom and Thernstrom (2003, p. 173), ethnic groups choose to cluster together in neighborhood residential patterns for a combination of both personal and economic reasons. Whites have traditionally tended to migrate from cities to the suburbs over many decades. Although more affluent nonwhites have done so as well, nonwhites tend to be strongly concentrated in inner-city neighborhoods, which in turn affects the racial composition of nearby schools. The aggressive integration of schools, made possible by the practice of court-ordered busing (see Busing, in Glossary), was another social engineering experiment that was supposed to inaugurate a new era of increased academic achievement for poor minority children and increased racial harmony and understanding in schools, specifically, and in society, generally (see Wolters, 1984, 2008)

◁ Sidebar 2.10   Does More Money Lead to Increased Minority Student Achievement? The Kansas City Fiasco

In 1986, federal judge Russell Clark issued a desegregation ruling that resulted in $1.4 billion being spent (over 10 years) to rebuild (primarily black) Kansas City urban schools to attract suburban whites and raise black achievement test scores. This effort resulted in the construction of a minimum of 12 brand-new schools, which included the following world-class resources and equipment:

- Planetariums
- Olympic-sized swimming pools with underwater observation windows
- A mock United Nations room wired for simultaneous language interpretation headphones
- Radio and television studios with real broadcasting capabilities
- Video editing and animation laboratories
- Mock moot courts equipped with jury rooms and judges' chambers
- A model Greek village for teaching participatory democracy
- Elementary schools equipped with one personal computer for every two children
- $900 million for hiring special staff to operate new equipment

- Funding for hiring teachers fluent in French and German
- Funding for hiring the former coach of the Soviet Olympic fencing team
- Doubling of the school superintendent's yearly salary
- Instructional costs rose from $3,094 per pupil per year to $8,000 per pupil per year (while the state average rose from $2,470 to $3,760 per pupil per year)
- The number of district school librarians increased from 13 to 56
- 53 new counselors were added

What were the results of this experiment, in which money was no object? Some white students returned to the Kansas City schools, but in numbers that were far below what was originally estimated before the desegregation plan took effect. The new facilities were built to accommodate 5,000 to 10,000 white suburban students, but no more than 1,500 white students enrolled in the Kansas City schools at the desegregation plan's peak. Those white students who did return to the Kansas City schools rarely stayed longer than a year before eventually returning to either parochial or suburban public schools.

The massive increase in the Kansas City district's budget proved overwhelming, which eventually led to massive waste and corruption. As examples, money was used to buy $700 light fixtures in one school and a $40,000 trophy case in another school. Parents in Missouri's other 529 districts became infuriated at the cuts in the budget resulting from the massive funding of the Kansas City desegregation plan. After three years on the job, the superintendent was fired amid corruption charges. Instead of dropout rates declining during the massive spending, these rates actually *increased*, while the average daily high school senior attendance rate *dropped*. The black/white racial gap in achievement test results (i.e., several months in first grade to two to three years by high school graduation) remained unchanged throughout all the years of massive funding.

(Anonymous, 1993; Ciotti, 1998a, 1998b; Evans, 1995; Ross, 2011)

In reality, however, court-ordered busing has proven to be a disaster in most instances in which it was attempted. Early efforts to use busing to integrate schools has resulted in an explosion of discipline and behavior problems for which suburban schools were unprepared, virulent animosity and hostility to forced busing from both white and minority parents, and increased violence and inflamed racial tensions in select major cities impacted by busing (see Thernstrom & Thernstrom, 1997; Wolters, 1984, 2008). Most damaging is the observation that court-ordered busing for racial integration in schools has resulted in massive *white flight* (see Glossary) to private schools, which has ironically resulted in even higher levels of school racial resegregation (Caldas & Bankston, 2005; Taylor, 2011; Wolters, 2008). In addition, forced integration has not resulted in significant increases in minority academic achievement, with some studies even showing detrimental effects on white students (Caldas & Bankston, 2005).

WHAT IS QUACK MULTICULTURALISM, AND WHY IS IT PROBLEMATIC?

Ideally, the goal of any applied psychology professional preparation program is to identify the most reliable findings from rigorous, well-conducted, and replicated research relevant to one's field of study, as well as to distill effective practices from case studies in the field. Unfortunately, most students, trainers, and practitioners are privately uncomfortable openly discussing issues involving race and ethnicity, particularly if such issues have a reputation for being controversial or the least bit embarrassing to a particular group. It is far easier for these issues to be avoided and not openly discussed at all. This, in turn, creates a yawning vacuum of silence on issues that are directly pertinent to experiences that future school psychologists, teachers, and counselors will surely face in real-life settings. In university training programs for school professionals, multiculturalism is a highly scripted ideology that is aggressively promoted to fill this vacuum. Unfortunately, much of what is promoted under the guise of multiculturalism is outright *quackery* (see Glossary).

It needs to be said clearly at the outset that *not all multiculturalism is Quack Multiculturalism.* Multiculturalism serves as a broad umbrella term for a heterogeneous mixture of approaches that differ substantially in both quality and intent. Multiculturalism is a heterogeneous entity that includes one part high-quality rigorous research, one part inconsequential or mediocre research, one part highly effective practices, one part shameless sociopolitical advocacy, and one part pure ideological gibberish. All of these elements are mixed together into one large gumbo called "multiculturalism." Unfortunately, it becomes increasingly difficult to separate the wheat from the chaff. Lynch (1997) echoes this observation and writes: "The diversity machine indiscriminately blends social science and ideology, serious substance with silly platitudes. Often it is easy to tell the difference; sometimes it is not. Therein lies one of many dangers" (pp. 17–18).

The phrase *Quack Multiculturalism* will be used throughout the remainder of this text to refer to that subset of ideas—promoted under the banner of multiculturalism—that is aggressively sold to audiences despite having no serious research support, or in some cases is *blatantly contradicted by quality research*. As the previous material has shown, and subsequent material will show, Quack Multiculturalism can be characterized by the following observations.

Quack Multiculturalism Is Logically Incoherent

Attempts to make coherent sense out of an ideology that is essentially incoherent is an exercise in futility. When Quack Multiculturalism is critically evaluated as to what it actually says (as opposed to how it makes one feel), a troubling array of double standards, paradoxes, and hopeless contradictions becomes readily apparent. Examples of the many basic contradictions inherent in Quack Multiculturalism, as promulgated in applied psychology and education, are given in Table 2.1.

Table 2.1   Paradoxes, Double Standards, and Unintended Ironies of Quack Multiculturalism in Education and Psychology

Majority groups and organizations are told that they must actively foster, promote, or "celebrate" diversity.	Yet, at the same time . . .	Minority groups and organizations are under no obligation to foster, promote, or "celebrate" diversity.
Multiculturalism teaches that it is wrong to promote stereotypes.	Yet, at the same time . . .	In order to promote the belief in culture × treatment interactions (see Glossary), multiculturalism must, by necessity, promote stereotypes.
Multiculturalism teaches that the difficulties of minority children are the direct result of their being unfairly evaluated in the context of the "majority" standards and/or culture.	Yet, at the same time . . .	Often, the same (or worse) problems of minority children are found *to an even greater degree* in all-minority educational settings.
Open discussion of racial and ethnic differences is viewed as necessary for multicultural enlightenment.	Yet, at the same time . . .	Open discussion of *politically embarrassing* racial and ethnic differences is viewed as racism, insensitivity, or stereotyping.
"Traditional" racism is vigorously condemned.	Yet, at the same time . . .	"Liberal racism" (see Glossary) flourishes and is repackaged as "compassion" or "sensitivity."
Extreme multiculturalism asserts that "There are no universal values."	Yet, at the same time . . .	The statement "there are no universal values" is itself a universal value
As an abstract principle, multiculturalism abhors discrimination.	Yet, at the same time . . .	In practice, discrimination *in favor* of certain groups is viewed as illustrative of "social justice" or fairness.
Multiculturalism teaches that the beliefs and practices of all cultures should be respected and tolerated.	Yet, at the same time . . .	Some cultures holding beliefs and practices that are intolerant of the beliefs and practices of other cultures *are not* respected or tolerated by multiculturalism.

Table 2.1   (Continued)

Some cultures holding beliefs and practices that are intolerant of the beliefs and practices of other cultures are not to be respected or tolerated by multiculturalism.	Yet, at the same time . . .	Multiculturalism ignores or overlooks the intolerance of certain favored "victim groups."
Multiculturalism implies that the solution to difficult educational problems involving cultural minorities would be helped through racial/ethnic matching (i.e., teachers/students; counselors/counselees).	Yet, at the same time . . .	With the exception of non-English-language matching, there is no systematic research showing that ethnic matching, in itself, results in significantly greater outcomes for cultural minority students.
Negative attitudes and actions expressed by majority group members against minority group members are to be vigorously condemned.	Yet, at the same time . . .	Negative attitudes and actions expressed by minority group members against majority group members are viewed as an understandable byproduct of their victim status.
Multiculturalism is promoted as the antidote to intergroup conflicts.	Yet, at the same time . . .	The aggressive promotion of multiculturalism is the *source* of many intergroup conflicts.
The aggressive promotion of multiculturalism is the source of many intergroup conflicts.	Yet, at the same time . . .	When intergroup conflicts occur, *more multiculturalism* is viewed as the necessary remedy.
Multiculturalism ideology counsels audiences to visit other countries abroad as a means of developing cultural sensitivity and cultural competence in working with cultural minorities at home.	Yet, at the same time . . .	Although cultural minorities at home have spent their entire lives surrounded by the dominant culture, multiculturalism views it as morally objectionable to require minorities to be culturally sensitive or culturally competent in mainstream culture.
The lack of attention to, and infusion of, multiculturalism ideology in schools and training programs is often given as a reason for disproportionate psychoeducational problems of minority groups.	Yet, at the same time . . .	At least in the past two decades, multiculturalism ideology has been pervasive in the popular media; has been infused to a considerable degree in school curriculum materials; has been a legally sanctioned condition for employee hiring; and is a strictly enforced litmus test for the new and continuing accreditation of training programs.

Quack Multiculturalism Is Empirically Inadequate

New movies advertised through the mass media often include a "tagline," which is a pithy phrase, slogan, or idea designed to hook audiences into paying to see the movie. If Quack Multiculturalism were a movie, its tagline would be "never let facts get in the way of a good ideology." Quack multiculturalism, being fundamentally a sociopolitical ideology, promotes trendy jargon, vague terminology, and oversimplification of complex issues in order to rally followers in emotional support of favored agendas. As an example, the term "CLD children" (shorthand for Culturally and Linguistically Diverse children) is frequently used in school psychology as a shorthand term that supposedly designates all children who are nonwhite or non-English speakers (e.g., see Sidebar 2.1). It certainly is understandable that the use of this term helps writers to avoid having to list every conceivable subgroup that may fall under this category. Unfortunately, such nonspecific terminology actually undermines clear thinking by inadvertently communicating that whites cannot be "diverse," or that persons who come from widely different racial, ethnic, and language groups somehow share some profound commonality by virtue of their nonwhite or non-English-speaking status. Even persons who belong to the same broad racial/ethnic group do not necessarily share the same cultural characteristics (see Sidebar 2.11).

Similar confusion is engendered by such trendy (but essentially vapid) terms as *tolerance, cultural competence*, and *social justice*. Such phrases have no specific meaning other than what a writer subjectively wants these terms to convey. These terms cannot be refuted, because their primary purpose is to activate emotional responses, not thinking. In the words of one writer, attempts to debate these terms "would be like trying to punch the fog" (Sowell, Sept. 8, 2010).

⚖ Sidebar 2.11   The Complexity of Cultural Differences

- "Attributes such as nationality, religion, race, or occupation are not appropriate criteria for defining cultures. The use of a single criterion is likely to lead to confusion, as would happen if all people who eat pizza were placed in one category. Culture is a complex whole, and it is best to use many criteria to discriminate between one culture and another." (Triandis, 2007, p. 65)
- "The label 'Asian' . . . lumps together the immigrant hotel manager from Gujarat State in Western India, the Japanese-American business executive, and the Khmer-American fisherman. The label combines into one category people who speak completely unrelated languages. . . . And the label further makes a spurious unity out of people who take their

cultural and historical bearings from completely unrelated traditions. Western India, Japan and Cambodia were never joined in a single empire, never shared a single culture, and never even experienced similar forms of colonialism or Western contact. . . . The term 'Asian' . . . lumps together far more than Gujaratis, Japanese and Khmers; it encompasses hundreds of cultures, some related, some not." (Wood, 2003, pp. 24–25).

- "Hispanics of my acquaintance include a distinctly Anglophobic Andean professor, a Jewish Brazilian who works in banking, an Argentine poet, an aspiring screen writer whose parentage is part Puerto Rican and part French-Canadian, an Azorian janitor, a lawyer and school superin-tendent born in Cuba who is a dedicated opponent of bilingual education, and another Castro refugee who went crazy and lives on the streets of Boston. . . . The term 'Hispanic' clearly doesn't describe common social background; it doesn't designate a common language; and it doesn't, for that matter, describe gross physical appearance. Some 'Hispanics' look like Europeans; some show Native-American ancestry; some have African fea-tures." (Wood, 2003, p. 25)

- "Many people who trace their roots to the African continent are not even black. Americans of Egyptian, Libyan, or Algerian descent find their ancestral home on the African continent. Would it be appropriate to call these Americans 'African Americans'? Would we call a person African-American who is an American citizen of Afrikaner descent, who traces his ancestry back to 1620 when the Dutch settled Cape Town? . . . In other words, what cultural characteristics do black Americans, Egyptians, Libyans, Algerians, and Afrikaners share in common even though each can trace his roots to Africa?" (Williams, 1990, p. 4)

- "One of the most popular misconceptions about American Indians is that they are all the same—one homogeneous group of people who look alike, speak the same language, and share the same customs and history. Nothing could be further from the truth. . . . Today there are about 500 American Indian tribes, each with its own language and cultural tradi-tions. . . . Sadly, these differences are not appreciated by most non-Native Americans. . . . Toy manufacturers typically misrepresent American Indians by creating toys that, for example, mix the tipi from the Plains culture or the totem pole from the Northwest Pacific Coast groups with the Navajo rug, loom, or desert plants from the Southwest groups." (Michaelis, 1997, p. 36)

Quack Multiculturalism Is Experientially Invalid

Quack Multiculturalism leads to certain predictions about the relationship between school practices and student outcomes. Colleges of Education teach that multiculturalism, if taught correctly in schools, leads to wonderful, harmonious outcomes both within and between racial and ethnic groups in schools (Green & Ingraham, 2005). School psychologists are constantly told that if they develop "cultural competence," they will be most effective in appropriately serving cultural minority children (Carroll, 2009). The cornerstone of this thinking rests on the notion that there is a body of special, "culturally specific" information that, if infused in school practice, should facilitate significant positive outcomes for minority children in educational settings. These are, of course, very pretty words, *but pretty words are not the appropriate basis on which to train future practitioners and scholars.* The stark disconnect between pretty words and ugly realities are listed in Table 2.2.

Table 2.2   Pretty Words vs. Ugly Realities in Multiculturalism Ideology

Guiding Doctrine (for definitions, see Glossary)	Pretty Words	Ugly Realities
Multiculturalism	"Multiculturalism is a worldview that recognizes and values the uniqueness of diverse learners, cultural backgrounds, and identities. . . . [Multiculturalism] promotes the development of attitudes, knowledge, and skills needed to function effectively in a pluralistic society." (Carroll, 2009, p. 3) "The major goal of multicultural education . . . is to [promote] an understanding and appreciation of cultural diversity." (Green & Ingraham, 2005)	Multiculturalism, in practice, typically degenerates into *racialism* (see Glossary), leading to increased strife in schools, specifically (Hacker & Hobbs, 2010; Medrano, 2010; Mohr, 2010), and entire countries, generally (France-Presse, 2011; Jalali & Lipset, 1992; Shweder, Minow, & Markus, 2002; Tyrell, 2011).
Group Identity Doctrine	"Multiculturalism [recognizes] broad dimensions of individual identity, including race, ethnicity, language, sexual orientation, gender, age, disability, class status, education, religious/spiritual orientation, and other cultural dimensions . . . [it] is a framework for understanding groups of individuals." (Carroll, 2009, p. 3)	Racial/ethnic conflicts in schools are increased and exacerbated by identity "tribalism" (Helms & Frazier, 2010; Rolland, 2010)

Table 2.2   (Continued)

Guiding Doctrine (for definitions, see Glossary)	Pretty Words	Ugly Realities
Difference Doctrine	"The diverse needs of multinational, multilingual, and multiracial students, coupled with multiple intelligences and the intersection of cultural identities, present new and challenging demands for learning and service delivery for today's schools." (Carroll, 2009, p. 2)	Cultural differences are politicized in order for advocacy groups to wield power and/or influence (KTVU.com, 2010; WorldNetDaily.com, 2005).
Equity Doctrine	"Creating equitable classrooms for multicultural school populations is a fundamental educational goal . . . despite wide variation in previous academic achievement, the instruction in an equitable classroom does not produce comparable variation in learning outcomes among the students . . . [t]hus there is a higher mean and a lower variance of achievement scores in a more equitable classroom than in a less equitable classroom." (Cohen & Lotan, 2004, p. 737)	Because groups are not equal in many important schooling outcomes, requiring equal outcomes fuels a never-ending wellspring of frustration, resentment, tension, and conflict between groups (Tucker, 2010; Wolters, 2008).
Inclusion Doctrine	"[Multicultural education] is the structuring of educational priorities, commitments, and processes to reflect the reality of cultural pluralism as a fact of life in the United States . . . [and is] a mode of experience and learning to be infused and integrated throughout the curriculum and throughout the school program." (Gay, 2004, p. 34)	This doctrine obliterates the notion of any objectively determined standards of quality, as these are sacrificed on the altar of group representation (Long, 2010; Rado, 2010).
Sensitivity Doctrine	"[C]ulturally sensitive programs incorporate relevant historical, environmental, and social forces into the design, implementation, and evaluation of materials and programs. Incorporating culture from this deeper level involves considering how group members perceive issues. . . . A culturally sensitive approach would assess needs to belong and group affiliation and consider alternatives for incorporating these social elements into the school context." (Booker, 2009, p. 187)	Leads to the enforcement of arbitrary rules of speech and/or behavior; causes fear and skittishness (i.e., "walking on eggshells") whenever "radioactive" multicultural issues and problems are discussed in integrated settings (Associated Press, 2010; KSBW.com, 2010; Thomas, 2010).

(continued)

Table 2.2   (*Continued*)

Guiding Doctrine (for definitions, see Glossary)	Pretty Words	Ugly Realities
Sovereignty Doctrine	"Ethnic Psychologies are those which intentionally emanate from the cultural and scholarly history of those to be studied. These ethnicity-centered psychologies explicitly ask and answer questions of priority to the indigenous group, they employ methods that are congruent with the cultural traditions, apply their findings in the service of the indigenous group and employ methods of application which embody the cultural idiom of the group. They are noncomparative. Their scholarly mission is conducted as orthogonal, independent of the missions of other psychologies." (Monteiro, 1996, p. 10)	Encourages the conviction that only in-group members can teach, understand, and work with other in-group members; the opinions and/or overtures of outgroup members are denigrated, ignored, or held in suspicion (Kane, 2010; Sue et al., 2008).

Basic research has shown that, contrary to the claims of Quack Multiculturalism, well-developed standardized intelligence tests are not psychometrically biased against English-speaking, U.S.-born minorities (Jensen, 1980; Neisser et al., 1996; Reynolds & Lowe, 2009), and showering millions of dollars on minority schools, compensatory education, and bilingual education programs does not reliably lead to significant, sustained increases in academic outcomes (Ciotti, 1998a, 1998b; Greene, 2005; Hanushek, 1997; Rossell & Baker, 1996). Contrary to the enthusiastic claims of commited "multicultural educators" (Banks & Banks, 2004), there is not one scintilla of consistent, replicable empirical evidence showing that the infusion of a multicultural curriculum in schools, or attendance in cultural immersion schools (see Chapter 4), is the key variable that reliably increases social-emotional or academic outcomes for minority children, or even narrows the achievement gap to any significant degree.

Quack Multiculturalism Is an Elaborately Built Castle With Its Foundation Firmly Planted in Midair

When the *Star Wars* films first came to movie theaters in the late 1970s and early 1980s, audiences were thrilled by the special effects showing what life is like in faraway galaxies. In the final action sequences in the movie *The Empire Strikes Back*, audiences were introduced to an elaborate cloud city suspended in midair and floating above the planet Bespin. In the same way, Quack Multiculturalism can be likened to an elaborately constructed castle floating in midair. That is, its central tenets are not based on a solid foundation of systematic empirical research or the accumulation of findings from successful educational practices in previous decades. *Instead, its foundation is built on a wholly arbitrary system of unchallenged assumptions that reflect whatever ideologues want audiences to accept and believe.*

Here, audiences are simply given an elaborate system that dictates the "correct" method of perceiving racial/ethnic/language groups, the "correct" method for framing and interpreting educational problems involving minority groups, and the "correct" attitudes and feelings one should internalize in response to diversity issues.

When audiences are kept ignorant of important information from the past, they can be convinced to believe anything they are told by authority organizations and figures. When the time is taken to investigate what has been learned from prior research, one is immediately struck by the realization that much of what Quack Multiculturalism advocates in the present has already been tried in the past—*and has consistently failed.* Multiculturalism ideology rarely uses these failures as critical opportunities to self-reflect on the validity of its fundamental assumptions. Instead, interventions that have shown consistent evidence of success in the past are routinely ignored by present-day Quack Multiculturalism, for no other reason than the fact that such evidence does not harmonize with (or in many cases blatantly contradicts) its ideologically inspired talking points.

Quack Multiculturalism Is Big Business

Despite these failures, Quack Multiculturalism is "big business" in the applied social sciences. Seductive ideologies quickly capture the public's imagination, and they spread like wildfire among devotees who are eager for social change. No student entering a training program in teacher education, educational administration, or any branch of the applied pupil personnel services can escape from being routinely exposed to stand-alone courses, or at least units within courses, that address multicultural issues. The catalogues for book publishing houses are bursting at the seams with multicultural textbooks that are required readings for almost every university training program in social work, nursing, teacher education, and counseling/school psychology (e.g., see http://teachpsych.org/diversity/ptde/race.php). In fact, publishers often counsel new textbook authors to include at least one multicultural chapter in their book proposals in order to presumably increase book sales.

In the last decade, school psychologists in practice and training have ready access to a plethora of handbooks on multicultural issues (e.g., Clauss-Ehlers, 2010; Esquivel, Lopez, & Nahari, 2007; Frisby & Reynolds, 2005; Jackson, 2006; Kitayama & Cohen, 2007). Visit the NASP website, and access to articles, books, interest groups, committees, sample course syllabi, and video resources on multicultural issues is readily available at anyone's fingertips. Visit any academic library, and every major ethnic group has at least one psychology journal that is devoted exclusively to that group's "psychology."

As far back as the past 50 years, federal and state courts have aggressively legislated and enforced school desegregation and mandated integration schemes to mix racial/ethnic groups in schools, presumably to increase multicultural understanding and raise anemic minority school achievement. As far back as 50 years ago, hundreds of millions of dollars have been poured into federal intervention initiatives such as Head Start and Title I programs to boost academic achievement of minority schoolchildren.

Sensitivity to minorities' feelings is uppermost in educators' practices. Curriculum textbook publishers are required to promote optimal representation of previously neglected groups in U.S. history, as well as to promote a variety of multicultural special interests in order to combat "Eurocentrism." Test developers spend inordinate amounts of time and resources ensuring that test batteries show no evidence of cultural test bias before they are marketed to the general public. Similarly, pictures in test booklets routinely show an array of minority faces and characters.

On college campuses throughout the nation, organizational entities with names such as the *Center for Multicultural Education*, *Center for Equity and Excellence in Education*, *Center for Equity and Diversity*, and *Center for Equity and Inclusion* dot the academic landscape. Lucrative high-level administrative positions in colleges and universities across the nation are a common fixture, with important-sounding titles such as "Chief Diversity Officer" and "Vice Provost for Multicultural Affairs," the purpose of which is to oversee and guide diversity agendas on college campuses (e.g., see Williams & Wade-Golden, 2006).

With all of this massive effort on behalf of cultural minority groups, *one would expect minority children to be the most high-achieving and well-adjusted human beings on the planet.* Yet it is well known that this is obviously not the case. Serious social problems, family collapse, huge gaps in academic achievement, educational apathy, and massive behavior problems remain largely unchanged over the decades—and in some instances, *have gotten worse.* When confronted with the stark contrast between the massive push for multiculturalism versus these dismal outcomes, the typical but misguided response is to promote even more infusion of multiculturalism as the solution. This is reminiscent of a famous quote attributed to Albert Einstein, who defined insanity as doing the same thing over and over again and expecting different results.

Quack Multiculturalism Is a Protest Movement

It bears repeating that the fundamental motivation of multiculturalism ideology is sociopolitical advocacy, not science. The common theme that runs through the *Moral Model*, the *Culture Model*, and the *Social Engineering Model* of training is a protest against research results or real-world conditions that multiculturalism finds objectionable or embarrassing. The purpose of Quack Multiculturalism is to provide alternative explanations or practices that are more politically palatable for maintaining the integrity of, or defending against challenges to, the ideology.

Quack Multiculturalism Encourages Intellectual Laziness

All human beings struggle to fight the temptation to succumb to intellectual laziness. All persons must constantly fight the temptation to try to make complex reality fit smoothly into simple, preconceived notions of how the world works. Reality is extremely complex and is full of a myriad of variables that interact differently under different conditions. Many of these variables are still not completely understood by even the best researchers. Sociopolitical ideologies seek to simplify reality in a manner that reduces life's complexities to a smaller handful of simpler talking points. Quack Multiculturalism is no different. Although it may be emotionally satisfying to believe that minorities disproportionately fail in school because "teachers are racist" (the *Moral Model*), or "teachers don't properly understand minority culture" (the *Culture Model*), or "schools don't infuse enough multiculturalism into the curriculum" (the *Social Engineering Model*), these glib explanations discourage the kind of thoughtful, penetrating analyses needed to properly understand complex issues. Unfortunately, Quack Multiculturalism declares large areas of analytical research as summarily off-limits, thereby discouraging audiences from developing the thinking and reasoning skills necessary for carefully weighing evidence and arguments (see Sidebar 10.2, Table 10.2).

Quack Multiculturalism Requires a Belief in Magic

When a magician performs a magic act on stage, audiences are dazzled by an amazing visual outcome and are not expected to think too deeply about what goes on behind the scenes in order to create the effect. Similarly, many training programs simply prefer to live in the safe and antiseptic world of abstract theory, rather than come to grips with the gritty and often painful realities of the real world. Living in the theoretical world allows Quack Multiculturalism to fashion an interpretation of reality in which hoped-for outcomes can literally appear by magic.

Professional organizations cannot explain how requiring applied psychology programs to incorporate multiculturalism into their training (typically involving little more than talking therapies) will *magically* overcome the deeply rooted and pervasive effects of family breakdown, poverty, low cognitive skills, substance abuse, government dependency, and gang violence that is endemic to many minority communities.

Training programs cannot explain how requiring students to learn generalizations regarding one narrow aspect of human beings (e.g., their race/ethnicity) *magically* gives students profound knowledge and insight into how to serve the entire human being, despite the infinite variety of traits and educational/familial contexts that makes each human being simultaneously complex and unique. Similarly, training programs cannot articulate with any degree of specificity how requiring students to work in a particular racially/ethnically diverse practicum and internship site *magically* translates into concrete skills that help students *generalize* how to more effectively serve any individual minority student in any other applied setting.

Graduate students are presumed to be so impressionable that simple exposure to multicultural homilies in university coursework is all that is needed to *magically* (and permanently) alter their attitudes and perceptions in favor of a "multicultural worldview."

Finally, researchers cannot articulate with any degree of specificity how a single intervention study that demonstrates effectiveness with a certain minority group should *magically* translate with equal effectiveness to any other setting and with any other group who just happens to share the same race, language, or ethnicity.

In Quack Multiculturalism, There Are No Consequences for Being Wrong

If an engineer makes wrong calculations in a blueprint for building a bridge, the bridge will collapse and people will die. If a surgeon uses the wrong procedure during a major operation, the patient may be permanently damaged, and the surgeon will most likely be sued. Quack ideas commonly populate the academic landscape in the soft sciences, but they rarely suffer any significant consequences for being wrong. The fundamental problem is not that audiences are occasionally exposed to incorrect ideas. When sound science is allowed to run its natural course, incorrect theories and ideas are readily abandoned once they consistently fail to withstand empirical scrutiny, or when it becomes obvious that they fail to work in the real world as advertised.

The *real problem* is the proliferation of academic environments that socialize students to *see no need to use their analytical skills to critically evaluate bad ideas*, particularly if such ideas are made to sound socially noble, personally inspirational, and professionally virtuous. In Quack Multiculturalism, incorrect ideas are actually *celebrated* and *encouraged*, particularly if they harmonize smoothly with current sociopolitical fashions (e.g., see Maranto, Redding, & Hess, 2009). Some training programs are little more than echo chambers for Quack Multiculturalism, where not only are incorrect ideas celebrated, but correct (but painful) truths are actively denigrated as "dangerous." Weissberg (2010) articulates how academics can be seduced into spending their entire professional careers promoting multicultural quackery that makes absolutely no impact on minority education in the real world:

> One can spend an entire career advocating multiculturalism as "the cure" for dismal [minority] academic attainment, receive countless honors, build a hefty vita, and otherwise enjoy the good academic life, including a handsome salary, without ever having to defend this failed nostrum before outraged disappointed parents. . . . All and all, better to be published in the right journals and get it wrong versus getting it right and remaining unpublished. . . . [It is] wiser to play

it safe, honor the local ideological gods and just be "professional." If driven to speak the disconcerting truth, do it privately. (p. 152)

Graduate students who are subjected to sustained multicultural advocacy in their training programs quickly find that high-quality research and writing that threatens Quack Multiculturalism is treated as a form of "academic pornography" (i.e., material that is consumed in private, but not acknowledged publicly). Only after entering the real world of public schools do some students see that they have been seriously mislead in their training programs. As they slowly realize that much of what was taught to them about multiculturalism bears little relationship to the reality that they plainly see (or that reality *blatantly contradicts* what they have been taught), they fall silent—terrified of openly articulating their perceptions for fear that this would brand them as traitors to the cause. As this process is allowed to unfold across decades, multiculturalism begins to gain the reputation as being a well-intentioned but somewhat dishonest movement that plays fast and loose with truth and facts.

Quack Multiculturalism and Red Herrings

In mystery novels, *red herrings* (see Glossary) are literary devices that lead audiences to focus on one character as the possible murderer, when in fact a completely different (and unexpected) character is revealed to be the true murderer at the end of the story. In the same way, Quack Multiculturalism is obsessed with focusing audiences' attention on a handful of favored panaceas for educational problems, many of which have been shown to be dead-ends. *This illustrates a fundamental truism that the goals of multiculturalism ideology and the investigation of practices that have been empirically and experientially shown to best serve minority children in schools are not one and the same.* On rare occasions, these two areas may by chance overlap, but they are based on a fundamentally different set of assumptions (e.g., see Table 10.3).

A simple illustration brings this issue into sharper focus. Suppose it is conclusively proven that black children's academic achievement performance rises (and is sustained) significantly as a result of being exposed to courses in Shakespeare and Latin in school. *The "multicultural community" in academia would not have the slightest interest in such a finding* (e.g., see Sowell, 1986). In contrast, now suppose that it is conclusively proven that black children's academic achievement performance rises (and is sustained) significantly as a result of being exposed to courses in East African Swahili language, values, and culture. Anyone familiar with the current multicultural scene would know that if such were the case, this would be front-page news shouted from the rooftops of every multicultural and "Afrocentric" journal/conference outlet in academia.

In reality, one can find both modest successes and failures in schools that offer a wide variety of cultural content to black children. The obvious and unavoidable conclusion, then, is that the cultural content of courses bears no reliable relationship to the academic achievement of black children. If black children show significant academic improvements from being exposed to both Shakespeare and Swahili, then the active ingredients responsible for success must involve more subtle variables that are not immediately obvious *but nevertheless are shared in common* in both instructional environments (e.g., caring teachers, high-quality instruction, use of rewards).

The point to be made here is that multiculturalism, being an ideology, directs all attention to cultural differences (and to a lesser extent racism, prejudice, and discrimination) as the favored explanations for nearly all educational problems involving racial/ethnic minority groups—*regardless of whether or not they actually are*. Explanations that do not traffic in these red herrings are largely ignored by Quack Multiculturalism, thus distorting reality for students in training programs (see Frisby, 2005b).

Quack Multiculturalism's Artificial Preservatives

Nearly everyone has had the unfortunate experience of retrieving leftovers from the refrigerator, only to find that the delicious meal they looked forward to eating is now covered in a sickening, furry mold. The predictable response, of course, is to discard the leftovers immediately into the nearest garbage disposal or trashcan. Unfortunately, this cannot be done with ideas that have long outlived their expiration date.

In modern times, foods can be injected with artificial preservatives, designed to keep them looking and tasting fresh long after they would have literally decomposed without them. In the world of multiculturalism, quack ideas are protected by artificial preservatives that guarantee they will continue to be promoted into perpetuity, despite little or no empirical support (or even in the face of blatantly contradictory evidence).

Each of the three multiculturalism training models discussed previously has its own unique brand of artificial preservatives that keep bankrupt ideas sounding as if they are fresh solutions for solving contemporary problems, despite evidence to the contrary.

Under the *Moral Model* of training, people are viewed as falling into one of only two categories: Either one is a true believer in multiculturalism ideology or one suffers from unconscious/hidden racism or "white privilege" that prevents him or her from seeing the light (see Sidebar 2.3). Because human prejudice, conflict, and envy among and between subgroups has always been, and always will be, a characteristic of peoples on every continent on earth, there will always be golden opportunities for race provocateurs and militant multicultural activists to manipulate real or imagined guilt in audiences for sociopolitical gains.

Under the *Culture Model* of training, audiences are constantly reminded that racial and ethnic minority groups possess an exotic and mysterious culture that outsiders cannot possibly understand. Because most school psychologists are fair-minded people who are sincerely willing to learn about groups who are different from themselves, they are prone to give the benefit of the doubt to self-styled "experts" who presume to have special insights, rare inside knowledge, or an intuitive understanding about such groups. To these audiences, it represents the height of rudeness and presumption to overtly challenge the validity of experts' ideas, particularly when the critic does not belong to the racial/ethnic group under discussion. Hence, naïve graduate students can be easily led with the belief that blithely following the Yellow Brick Road of Quack Multiculturalism will eventually result in the Wizard granting them "cultural competence." Because no human being can ever fully or completely understand what life is like for another human being, such ideas are endlessly perpetuated in training programs absent any clear consensus as to how cultural competence is measured, achieved, or even if it exists at all (see discussion in Frisby, 2009).

Under the *Social Engineering Model* of training, audiences can plainly observe with their own eyes the utter failure of many schemes to promote various "social justice" initiatives. Because of a dogged belief in Quack Multiculturalism, these failures are simply forgotten with the passage of time by successive generations—only to be recycled later with new initiatives repackaged under new labels.

Conversations about multiculturalism and multicultural issues in school psychology are characterized by an unspoken contract, which for all practical purposes remains unverbalized, yet is no less real. Here, audiences agree not to look too closely at the conceptual and empirical flaws in Quack Multiculturalism, and in exchange multicultural activists agree not to accuse them of racism (the *Moral Model*), cultural insensitivity (the *Culture Model*), or of being an impediment to progressive social change (the *Social Engineering Model*). This agreement enables things to run smoothly until somebody breaks the agreement, at which time all h*** breaks loose (e.g., see discussion of controversial publications in Chapter 10).

Because of these artificial preservatives, Quack Multiculturalism is guaranteed to last into perpetuity in the applied social sciences, unencumbered by the need to justify itself with the most basic standards of logic, evidence, or even common sense.

PURPOSE OF REMAINING CHAPTERS

The purpose of the remaining chapters of this text is to return readers to the basic research relevant to effectively addressing the psychoeducational problems of minority children in schools, freed from the obligation to pander to Quack Multiculturalism. That is, the purpose of this text is to showcase what is being done, and what has been learned, in schools' efforts to support and improve psychoeducational outcomes for minority children, regardless of whether or not it harmonizes with current multicultural fashions.

Minority group status, by itself, is not a harbinger of poor school outcomes, for the simple reason that all minority subpopulations are not the same, and wide differences exist *within* each subpopulation. Minority group children experience different degrees of school success, which can be attributable to differences in inborn abilities, home upbringing, quality of their schooling experiences, or availability of district resources. If minority children are observed to experience disproportionate degrees of school failure, audiences must not flinch from facing squarely what is known concerning the empirically derived reasons for these vexing problems.

A special effort is made to highlight programs, conditions, and practices that exist in the real world, in terms of what school systems currently have in place to serve minority populations, as well as identifying examples of schools and/or school systems that have experienced success in facilitating academic outcomes. Occasionally, the text will highlight glaring discrepancies between what Quack Multiculturalism espouses versus contradictory evidence culled from research on effective practices in schools. Toward this end, we now turn our attention to a discussion of the home and family environment as these impact schooling.

ADDITIONAL RESOURCES

Supplemental Readings

Bernstein, R. (1994). *Dictatorship of virtue: Multiculturalism and the battle for America's future*. New York, NY: Knopf.

Frisby, C. L. (2005a). The politics of multiculturalism in school psychology: Part I. In C. L. Frisby & C. R. Reynolds (Eds.), *Comprehensive handbook of multicultural school psychology* (pp. 45–80). Hoboken, NJ: Wiley.

Frisby, C. L. (2005b). The politics of multiculturalism in school psychology: Part II. In C. L. Frisby & C. R. Reynolds (Eds.), *Comprehensive handbook of multicultural school psychology* (pp. 81–136). Hoboken, NJ: Wiley.

Hancock, R. S. (2005). *The wrong direction: An educator speaks out* (Chapter 4). Victoria, British Columbia, Canada: Trafford.

Journal of Mental Health Counseling. (2004), Vol. 26, No. 1. (See entire series of articles on the multicultural counseling competencies debate.)

Sowell, T. (1993). *Inside American education: The decline, the deception, the dogmas* (Chapter 4). New York, NY: Free Press.

Thomas, K. R., & Wubbolding, R. E. (2009). Social justice, multicultural counseling, and counseling psychology research: A politically incorrect perspective. In A. M. Columbus (Ed.), *Advances in psychology research* (Vol. 59, pp. 279–287). New York, NY: Nova Science.

Webster, Y. O. (1997). *Against the multicultural agenda*. Westport, CT: Praeger.

Wood, P. (2003). *Diversity: The invention of a concept*. San Francisco, CA: Encounter Books.

3

Home and Family

In almost every public school nationwide, teachers notice stark differences in students' classroom behaviors, academic performance, and school attitudes that vary as a function of students' home backgrounds.

In her in-depth ethnographic study of a multi-ethnic California public elementary school, Ferguson (2000) provides a rich description of these differences. At one end of this spectrum are students who are well-behaved, score high on standardized achievement tests, and tend to be placed in programs for Gifted and Talented children. Teachers describe such children as coming to school "ready to work." These children "know what they're there for," meaning that "when it's time for them to listen, they listen, they raise their hand, they wait their turn" (p. 45). Such children display age-appropriate self-control in the classroom, and are capable of appropriately regulating their school behavior in order to listen to, and learn from, their teachers. Although many of these children are racial/ethnic minorities, they are predominantly white, live in "nice" neighborhoods, and "come from homes that have separate, quiet places for them to do their homework" (p. 45). Children in this group may occasionally get into trouble for school misbehaviors, but such incidents involve relatively minor offenses.

When teachers share their perceptions of the factors that are responsible for these children's good behaviors, they frequently mention parents who "care about their education" and take the time to monitor their children's schoolwork at home. These parents not only have a strong desire for their children to succeed, but they serve as role models for their children's academic success. Teachers note that parents of high-achieving children spend "quality time" with them, listen to their children, and are "emotionally available" to their children in ways that encourage them to develop their abilities and talents to the fullest potential. Such parents tend to be more likely to help in fundraising for special school programs, attend parent/teacher meetings at school, help chaperone children on school field trips, and, most importantly, have a strong home presence that ensures that homework gets done.

In contrast, children at the opposite end of this spectrum are those whom teachers find to be the worst-behaved children in the school. In multi-ethnic schools, African American boys tend to be overrepresented in this group, although significant numbers of African American girls display similar behaviors. These poorly behaved students tend not to perform well on standardized achievement tests and other classroom academic tasks. According to Ferguson (2000), teachers report that these students eat candy in class when they are not supposed to, and "refuse to work, [and are prone to] fight, gamble, chase, hit, instigate, cut class, cut school, [and] cut hair." These (particularly male) students are described as "defiant, disruptive, disrespectful, [and] profane. . . . [They] fondle girls, draw obscene pictures, make lewd comments, intimidate others, and call teachers names" (p. 46). These students are regularly in suspension rooms or in the principal's office for misbehavior. The neighborhoods in which such children live are dangerous and are often populated by drug dealers. These students are rarely, if at all, enrolled in Gifted and Talented school programs. Instead, they are overrepresented in compensatory education or special education classes.

These students are described by teachers as having poor impulse control and attentional problems in the classroom. Teachers describe their home lives as chaotic. Many live in foster care or with their grandparents or other relatives, and most children who are disruptive in school do not have stable fathers living in the home. Most parents don't bother showing up at parent/teacher conferences, even when strenuous efforts are made to schedule these meetings for parents' convenience. Teachers report that, at times, alcohol can be smelled on the breath of mothers who come to school for teacher conferences. When phone calls are made to the homes of these children, the adults are often belligerent and rude to teachers. According to Ferguson (2000), some adults may "talk a good line" about helping their children at home, but most never follow through on their empty promises. When these parents are confronted about their child's misbehavior at school, parents are quick to blame others and deny responsibility for their own actions.

These observations are all too common among teachers and other school personnel in school settings that serve racially and socioeconomically diverse communities nationwide. Obviously, students' home backgrounds play an important role in understanding variability in what professionals observe in the school setting. In the school psychology consultation literature, however, those adopting a strict behavioral perspective may argue that students' home backgrounds are largely irrelevant for working with teachers in modifying classroom behavior (e.g., Gresham, 1982). Although this perspective certainly has some merit across many classroom applications, there are numerous instances where school psychologists and other professionals must routinely interact with students' home/ family environments in the course of their work. As examples, school psychologists often gather developmental history information directly from parents, solicit parents' assistance in working with their child at home, lead or help facilitate parent groups at school, interact with parents in Individual Education Plan (IEP)/child study team meetings and parent/teacher conferences, and may occasionally be called upon to make home visits.

The purpose of this chapter is to discuss home background and family factors that research has shown to be significantly associated with school readiness and performance, with a particular emphasis on issues related to racial/ethnic/language minority populations. The chapter begins with an overview of geographic settling patterns of racial/ethnic groups. This is followed by a discussion of the importance of the socioeconomic status (SES) construct as this relates to variation in family life and how such variation differentially supports children's schooling. Issues unique to immigrant populations are then discussed. The chapter concludes with a discussion of empirically supported "brand-name" intervention programs that are noted for including a significant home/family intervention component.

SETTLEMENT PATTERNS OF U.S. RACIAL/ETHNIC GROUPS

According to the most recent data from the 2010 Census (Humes, Jones, & Ramirez, 2011), 47 percent of persons living in the Western region of the United States are nonwhite minorities (approximately 33.9 million persons), 40 percent of persons living in the South are nonwhite minorities (approximately 45.8 million persons), 31 percent of persons living in the Northeast are nonwhite minorities (approximately 17.3 million persons), and 22 percent of persons living in the Midwest are nonwhite minorities (approximately 14.8 million persons). The 13 states that are home to the largest percentage of nonwhite minorities (excluding Puerto Rico, and in decreasing order) are Hawaii (77.3 percent), District of Columbia (65.2 percent), California (59.9 percent), New Mexico (59.5 percent), Texas (54.7 percent), Nevada (45.9 percent), Maryland (45.3 percent), Georgia (44.1 percent), Arizona (42.2 percent), Florida (42.1 percent), Mississippi (42 percent), New York (41.7 percent), and New Jersey (40.7 percent).

According to recent 2010 Census figures (U.S. Census Bureau, 2010a), states that are home to more than 90 percent of whites include Iowa, Maine, New Hampshire, Vermont, West Virginia, and Wyoming. The top 30 counties (with populations greater than 30,000) in the United States that are home to the largest percentages of whites are listed in Table 3.1 (U.S. Census Bureau, 2009a). At the county level, the number of counties nationwide with varying percentages of racial/ethnic minority populations (for year 2009) is provided in Table 3.2.

African Americans

According to BlackDemographics.com (www.blackdemographics.com/population.html), approximately 13.5 percent of the U.S. population are African American. This translates

Table 3.1   Top 30 U.S. Counties (With Total Population > 30,000) With Highest Percentage of Non-Hispanic Whites (2009 Estimates)

County, State	Total Population	Percentage Non-Hispanic White
Holmes, Ohio	41,854	98.5
Elk, Pennsylvania	32,011	98.4
Jefferson, Pennsylvania	44,634	98.4
Preston, West Virginia	30,247	98.3
Warren, Pennsylvania	40,638	98.3
Wayne, West Virginia	41,119	98.3
Perry, Ohio	35,359	98.1
Bedford, Pennsylvania	49,579	98.1
Armstrong, Pennsylvania	67,851	98.0
Lincoln, Maine	34,576	98.0
Mifflin, Pennsylvania	45,937	97.9
Marshall, West Virginia	32,556	97.9
Pike, Kentucky	65,446	97.8
Douglas, Minnesota	36,390	97.8
Preble, Ohio	41,422	97.8
Morrison, Minnesota	32,883	97.7
Waldo, Maine	38,287	97.7
Carroll, New Hampshire	47,860	97.7
Franklin, Illinois	39,312	97.7
Whitley, Kentucky	38,813	97.7
Somerset, Maine	50,947	97.7
Greene, Indiana	32,463	97.7
Greenup, Kentucky	38,020	97.6
Brown, Ohio	44,003	97.6
Susquehanna, Pennsylvania	40,646	97.6
Knox, Maine	40,801	97.6
Coos, New Hampshire	31,487	97.6
Clarion, Pennsylvania	39,479	97.5
Tioga, Pennsylvania	40,875	97.5
Perry, Pennsylvania	45,502	97.5

to approximately 42 million African Americans who live in the United States, with the African American population exceeding 500,000 persons in 15 states. Although Hispanics constitute the largest minority group in 20 states, African Americans are the largest minority group in 24 states. According to the 2010 Census (Rastogi, Johnson, Hoeffel, & Drewery, 2011), of all respondents who self-identified as black alone (or black

Table 3.2 U.S. Counties (N = 3,143) Disaggregated by Percentage of White, Black, Nonwhite Hispanic, Asian American, and American Indian/Alaskan Native/Aleut Residents (2009 American Community Survey Data)

	Percentage of Racial/Ethnic Group Within County*									
Racial/Ethnic Group	90–99.7%	80–89.9%	70–79.9%	60–69.9%	50–59.9%	40–49.9%	30–39.9%	20–29.9%	10–19.9%	0–9.9%
White	1345(42.7)	590(18.7)	383(12.1)	292(9.2)	223(7.0)	147(4.6)	84(2.6)	36(1.1)	33(1.0)	9(0.2)
Black	0(0)	3 (0.09)	15(0.4)	29(0.9)	47(1.4)	94(2.9)	136(4.3)	192(6.1)	327(10.4)	2293(72.9)
Hispanic (Nonwhite)	4(0.1)	11(0.3)	11(0.3)	12(0.3)	39(1.2)	56(1.7)	72(2.2)	118(3.7)	324(10.3)	2491(79.2)
Asian	0(0)	0(0)	0(0)	2(0.06)	3(0.09)	0(0)	3(0.09)	4(0.1)	26(0.8)	3104(98.7)
American Indian/Alaskan Native/Aleut	1(0.03)	7(0.2)	10(0.3)	5(0.1)	7(0.2)	6(0.1)	10(0.3)	20(0.6)	71(2.2)	3004(95.5)

*Within each cell, number of counties and percentage of total number of counties (N = 3,143) is reported.

in combination with another group), 55 percent lived in the South, 18 percent in the Midwest, 17 percent in the Northeast, and 10 percent in the West. Although the city of New York is home to the largest population of African Americans (as of 2010, more than 3 million), the five cities hosting the largest percentage of African Americans are Jackson, Mississippi (48%), Memphis, Tennessee (46%), Montgomery, Alabama (43%), Macon, Georgia (43%), and Columbus, Georgia (40%). The top 30 counties (with populations greater than 30,000) that are home to the largest percentage of African Americans are listed in Table 3.3 (U.S. Census Bureau, 2009b).

The states that are home to less than 1 percent of African Americans are Montana, Idaho, Vermont, Maine, North Dakota, Wyoming, Utah, South Dakota, and New Hampshire (Rastogi et al., 2011).

Hispanic Americans

According to recent 2010 Census figures, Hispanic or Latino persons make up approximately 16.3 percent of the U.S. population. Of those persons self-identifying as Hispanic or Latino, 53 percent identified their race as "White," followed by 36.7 percent indicating "some other race." According to the Pew Hispanic Center (2011b), the largest percentage of all Hispanics currently living in the United States (both legally and illegally), who were initially born in a non-U.S. country, were born in Mexico (approximately 30 percent). According to the Pew Hispanic Center, the seven states that are home to the highest percentage of Hispanics—in addition to the percentage of Hispanics or Latinos in that state over 5 years of age who reported speaking only English at home—are New Mexico (46 percent; 39 percent of Hispanics are English speaking), Texas (37 percent; 22 percent of Hispanics are English speaking), California (37 percent; 23 percent of Hispanics are English speaking), Arizona (31 percent; 31 percent of Hispanics are English speaking), Nevada (26 percent; 25 percent of Hispanics are English speaking), Florida (22 percent; 14 percent of Hispanics are English speaking), and Colorado (20 percent; 44 percent of Hispanics are English speaking). The top 30 counties (with populations greater than 30,000) in the United States that are home to the largest percentage of Hispanics are listed in Table 3.4 (Pew Hispanic Center, 2011b).

The 12 states that are home to less than 4 percent of Hispanics are Alabama, Kentucky, Maine, Mississippi, Missouri, Montana, New Hampshire, North Dakota, Ohio, South Dakota, Vermont, and West Virginia (Ennis, Ríos-Vargas, & Albert, 2011).

Asian Americans

According to the 2010 Census (Humes et al., 2011), approximately 5.6 percent of the U.S. population self-identify as being of Asian descent (for a more detailed and disaggregated discussion of Asian American subgroups, see Thao, 2005; Yoon & Cheng, 2005). This translates to approximately 17.3 million Asian Americans (both Asian alone and in combination with one or more additional racial groups) who live in the United States. Hawaii is

Table 3.3   Top 30 U.S. Counties (With Total Population > 30,000) With Highest Percentage of Blacks (2009 Estimates)

County, State	Total Population	Percentage Black
Petersburg City, Virginia	32,986	78.7
Leflore, Mississippi	34,563	71.9
Washington, Mississippi	54,616	68.3
Dallas, Alabama	41,925	68.1
Hinds, Mississippi	247,631	66.9
Prince Georges, Maryland	834,560	66.7
Bolivar, Mississippi	36,766	66.0
Dougherty, Georgia	95,859	65.8
Baltimore City, Maryland	637,418	63.9
Clayton, Georgia	275,772	63.1
Orleans Parish, Louisiana	354,850	62.9
Orangeburg, South Carolina	90,112	62.4
Edgecombe, North Carolina	51,853	57.1
Adams, Mississippi	30,722	56.8
Marion, South Carolina	33,468	55.4
Gadsen, Florida	47,474	55.3
District of Columbia	599,657	55.0
Montgomery, Alabama	224,119	54.8
DeKalb, Georgia	747,274	54.4
Halifax, North Carolina	54,582	54.2
Portsmouth City, Virginia	99,321	53.9
Richmond, Georgia	199,768	53.9
Jefferson, Arkansas	78,705	53.9
Richmond City, Virginia	204,451	52.6
Shelby, Tennessee	920,232	52.4
Bibb, Georgia	156,060	51.6
St. John the Baptist Parish, Louisiana	47,086	50.6
Sumter, Georgia	32,084	50.2
Clarendon, South Carolina	32,988	50.1
Vance, North Carolina	43,056	49.8

the only state in which Asians are the majority (by a slim margin of 57 percent). According to the U.S. Census Bureau (2010a), the states that are home to the largest percentages of Asian Americans (including Native Hawaiian and Pacific Islander) are California (13.4%), New Jersey (8.3%), Washington state (7.8%), Nevada (7.8%), and New York (7.3%). According to the 2010 Census (Hoeffel, Rastogi, Kim, & Shahid, 2012), of the top ten U.S.

Table 3.4   Top 30 U.S. Counties (With Total Population > 30,000)
With Highest Percentage of Hispanics (2009 Estimates)

County, State	Total Population	Percentage Hispanic
Starr, Texas	62,671	97.2
Webb, Texas	241, 438	94.5
Maverick, Texas	53,203	94.2
Hidalgo, Texas	741,152	89.8
Cameron, Texas	396,371	86.6
El Paso, Texas	751,296	81.8
Santa Cruz, Arizona	43,771	80.0
Val Verde, Texas	48,165	78.6
Jim Wells, Texas	41,001	77.4
Imperial, California	166,874	77.3
Rio Arriba, New Mexico	40,678	72.0
Kleberg, Texas	30,647	69.0
Dona Ana, New Mexico	206,419	65.2
Miami-Dade, Florida	2,500,625	62.5
Atascosa, Texas	44,633	61.0
Nueces, Texas	323,046	60.0
Bexar, Texas	1,651,448	58.3
Tulare, California	429,668	58.3
Yuma, Arizona	196,972	57.0
Valencia, New Mexico	72,913	56.1
Bee, Texas	32,487	56.0
Taos, New Mexico	31,507	55.0
San Benito, California	55,058	54.1
Hale, Texas	35,408	54.0
Monterey, California	410,370	53.9
San Patricio, Texas	68,223	53.6
Merced, California	245,321	53.1
Bronx, New York	1,397,287	52.0
Ector, Texas	134,625	51.9
Madera, California	148,632	51.7

cities (over 100,000 persons) with the largest percentage of Asian Americans, 9 were
California cities. The top 30 U.S. counties (with populations greater than 30,000) with the
highest percentage of Asian Americans are listed in Table 3.5 (U.S. Census Bureau, 2009c).
According to 2010 estimates, Mississippi, Montana, South Dakota, West Virginia, and
Wyoming are home to less than 1 percent of Asian Americans (U.S. Census Bureau, 2010a).

Table 3.5   Top 30 U.S. Counties (With Total Population > 30,000) With Highest Percentage of Asians (2009 Estimates)

County, State	Total Population	Percentage Asian
Honolulu, Hawaii	907,574	65.1
Kauai, Hawaii	64,529	57.4
Hawaii, Hawaii	177,835	54.5
Maui, Hawaii	145,157	53.3
Santa Clara, California	1,784,642	33.0
San Francisco, California	815,358	32.8
San Mateo, California	718,989	27.8
Alameda, California	1,491,482	27.4
Queens, New York	2,306,712	23.0
Middlesex, New Jersey	157,387	19.9
Orange, California	3,026,786	17.5
Fairfax, Virginia	1,037,605	17.4
Solano, California	407,234	16.8
Contra Costa, California	1,041,274	15.7
Fort Bend, Texas	556,870	15.7
Sacramento, California	1,400,949	15.5
San Joaquin, California	674,860	15.4
King, Washington	1,916,441	15.4
Bergen, New Jersey	895,250	15.2
Montgomery, Maryland	971,600	14.6
Sutter, California	92,614	14.2
Los Angeles, California	9,848,011	14.2
Loudoun, Virginia	301,171	13.8
Somerset, New Jersey	326,869	13.5
Yolo, California	199,407	13.4
Howard, Maryland	281,884	12.9
Hudson, New Jersey	597,924	12.3
San Diego, California	3,053,793	11.7
New York, New York	1,629,054	11.3
Collin, Texas	791,631	10.7

Native Americans

Native Americans constitute approximately 0.8–1 percent of the U.S. population (see Glossary). Native Americans are often referred to as "indigenous peoples" of the United States, because they were the original occupants of American land before the arrival of European settlers. The term "Native American" includes a variety of people who self-identify as American Indians or Alaska Natives generally, but more specifically identify themselves by tribal affiliation (Berry, Grossman, & Pawiki, 2007).

As of 2000, roughly one-third of all Native Americans lived on reservations (see Glossary), off-reservation federal trust lands, or state-designated American Indian statistical areas (Berry, Grossman, & Pawiki, 2007). Nearly two-thirds of all Native Americans live in locations other than on reservations or tribal lands. These include large metropolitan areas and cities/towns that are adjacent to reservations. Depending on family or employment obligations, many Native Americans split their time traveling back and forth between reservations and adjacent living areas. More recent data on the top 25 counties (with populations greater than 30,000) with the largest percentages of Native American, Eskimo, or Aleut groups is listed in Table 3.6.

Table 3.6   Top 25 U.S. Counties (With Total Population > 30,000) With Highest Percentage American Indian, Eskimo, or Aleut Populations (2009 Estimates)

County, State	Total Population	Percentage American Indian, Eskimo, Aleut
Apache, Arizona	70,591	73.4
Navajo, Arizona	112,975	46.8
Robeson, North Carolina	129,559	38.6
San Juan, New Mexico	124,131	38.2
Cherokee, Oklahoma	46,029	34.5
Coconino, Arizona	129,849	31.0
Caddo, Oklahoma	30,393	26.7
Delaware, Oklahoma	40,555	24.0
Mayes, Oklahoma	40,065	23.0
Sequoyah, Oklahoma	41,433	21.8
Beltrami, Minnesota	44,350	21.4
Fremont, Wyoming	38,719	21.1
Ottawa, Oklahoma	31,629	19.5
Pontotoc, Oklahoma	37,422	18.9
Muskogee, Oklahoma	71,412	18.0
Rio Arriba, New Mexico	40,678	17.0
Okmulgee, Oklahoma	39,292	16.6
Osage, Oklahoma	45,051	16.3
McCurtain, Oklahoma	33,370	16.1
Gila, Arizona	52,199	15.7
Graham, Arizona	37,045	15.6

Table 3.6   *(Continued)*

County, State	Total Population	Percentage American Indian, Eskimo, Aleut
Pittsburg, Oklahoma	45,211	15.3
Juneau Borough, Alaska	30,796	15.0
Neshoba, Mississippi	30,302	15.0
Bryan, Oklahoma	40,783	14.1
Sandoval, New Mexico	125,988	14.0
Chippewa, Michigan	38,731	13.8
Pottawatomie, Oklahoma	70,274	13.2
Rogers, Oklahoma	85,654	13.2
Le Flore, Oklahoma	49,915	12.6

Tribal Sovereignty

Native Americans are unique in their political relationship to the larger United States, in that many Native Americans seek status as sovereign nations (see Sidebar 3.1) that are distinct from U.S. society, while simultaneously participating in it. Among Native Americans, there is tremendous diversity with respect to tribal languages, as well as tremendous variability in how Native American culture adapts to local environmental circumstances. Most Native Americans live in urban areas. However, other Native American tribal groups have adapted over the decades to river life in the northern California coast, the Arctic tundra, subarctic northern forests and northeastern woodlands, the semiarid areas in the Southwest, and the Great Plains that consist of the vast prairies extending south from Alberta, Saskatchewan, and Manitoba in Canada through the west-central United States into Texas. Settling in these different areas led to the development over time of different forms of economic subsistence (e.g., hunting, fishing, farming).

⌦ Sidebar 3.1   Native American Tribal Sovereignty

Currently, approximately 562 federally recognized Indian communities exist that are called *tribes, bands, nations, pueblos, rancherias, communities,* and *Native villages* in the United States. These communities (hereafter referred to as *tribes*), are ethnically, culturally, and linguistically diverse—and consist of American Indians, Alaska Natives, and Native Hawaiians. Approximately 40 percent of these groups are located in Alaska, while the rest are located in 33 other U.S. states.

WHAT IS TRIBAL SOVEREIGNTY?

Sovereignty begins with an official acknowledgement by the U.S. federal government of the political status of that tribe as a government (see National Congress of American Indians, n.d., for an overview of the complex historical relationship between Indian Nations and the federal government). The essence of the word *sovereignty*, as applied to Native American communities, refers to the right of tribes to be self-determining and govern their own affairs. This includes the right to regulate tribal land, taxes, zoning, resources, and the conduct of tribal members. By virtue of their sovereignty, individual tribes sustain their own unique political relationship with the federal government. Both the U.S. Senate and the House of Representatives have established specific internal committees to handle legislation pertaining to American Indians. Members of federally recognized tribes are eligible for several unique federal programs.

TRIBAL GOVERNMENT

Because of tribal sovereignty, tribes have the inherent power to govern all matters involving their members, as well as a range of matters in "Indian Country" (the area over which the federal government and tribes exercise primary jurisdiction). Tribes form their governments either by election of members to a governing council as provided in each tribe's constitution, or by tribal elders choosing leaders through some traditional process. Typically, each tribe generally has one elected chairperson, president, chief, or governor who is the recognized leader of the tribe. States do not have any civil or criminal jurisdiction over Indian Country except what Congress or federal courts may delegate or determine. The federal government funds public safety (i.e., police officers) and criminal justice systems, and has jurisdiction over most major crimes committed in Indian Country. However, individual tribes prosecute all criminal misdemeanors committed by Indians on Indian lands. Tribal courts have jurisdiction over most civil matters that arise within Indian Country. Because tribal governments are considered to be sovereign governments, they are not subject to taxation by the federal government (however, individual American Indians and Alaska Natives pay federal income taxes just like every other U.S. citizen). Tribal governments use their revenues to provide essential services for their citizens. Unlike state governments, tribal governments are generally not in a position to levy property or income taxes. Income from tribal businesses (e.g., the gaming industry) is the only nonfederal revenue source for most tribes.

TRIBAL IDENTITY

Individual Natives view themselves as citizens of three sovereign entities: the United States, the state in which they reside, and their tribe. As their own sovereign government, individual tribes are free to determine their own criteria for citizenship. Citizenship is typically determined through blood proportion requirements or a requirement of lineal descendency from a tribal citizen.

INDIAN EDUCATION

According to some estimates, there are approximately 600,000 American Indian and Alaskan pupils attending K–12 educational programs in the United States. Approximately three-quarters of these pupils attend public schools, while approximately 8 percent attend schools funded by the Bureau of Indian Affairs (BIA; see Glossary). Funding for BIA schools is the sole responsibility of the federal government. Although Local Education Agencies (LEAs) and surrounding communities can pass bond initiatives that provide funds for public school needs (e.g., school repair), tribal and BIA schools must rely exclusively on funds from the federal government. However, tribes can use revenues from gaming as a tax base to fund education (as well as law enforcement, tribal courts, health care, social services, and infrastructure improvement).

(Adapted from Harvard Project on American Indian Economic Development, 2008; National Congress of American Indians, n.d.)

The Impact of Gaming

Economic conditions on many reservations have changed with the introduction of tribal gaming on reservation lands. As defined by federal law, Indian gaming is defined as gaming conducted by an Indian tribe on Indian lands (i.e., a "federally recognized tribal government on a federal reservation or on trust lands," see Light & Rand, 2005). According to the Native American Rights Fund (see http://www.narf.org/pubs/misc/gaming.html), approximately 40 percent of all Native American tribal groups are involved in the gaming industry. As of 2003, Native American gaming generated nearly $17 billion in revenue. However, tribal gaming accounts for less than one-quarter of gambling industry revenues nationwide (Light & Rand, 2005). Although economic conditions on Native American reservations still lag significantly behind the general population, gaming revenue has brought significant improvements for many Native American communities (Light & Rand, 2005).

It is a falsehood that any Native American, by virtue of his or her ethnicity, has the right to open a casino. Only federally recognized tribal governments may initiate casino-style gaming, but only after a protracted negotiation process with a state government (Light & Rand, 2005). The tribe's decision to open a casino involves some inherent compromising of sovereignty rights. That is, while the opening of a casino represents an allowable exercise of a tribe's sovereign authority, federal law nevertheless requires tribal casinos to submit to federal and state regulations (Light & Rand, 2005).

There also exists considerable variation among tribes in their experiences with the gaming industry, making stereotypes and generalizations difficult. For example, it is a falsehood that all Native American tribes participate in gaming. Gaming is simply not an option for tribes living in states that prohibit gambling. Other tribes are located in remote geographic areas that would undermine commercial success. Other tribes prefer not to pursue gaming because of their tribal values and beliefs.

It is also a falsehood that all members of gaming tribes are wealthy. Of those tribes involved in gaming, tribes that game do so with varying profitability. Some tribes have difficulty breaking even, other tribes are only marginally profitable, and other tribes (e.g., the Mashantucket Pequots in Connecticut and the Shakopee Mdewakanton Sioux community in Minnesota) have experienced spectacular financial success.

Native American Poverty

Historically, Native Americans (particularly those living on reservations) are the most impoverished of U.S. citizens. Compared to the rest of the United States, Native Americans have higher rates of chronic unemployment, substance abuse, infant mortality, mental health problems, and domestic violence. The overall economic effects of gaming on tribal nations shows mixed results in addressing these problems (see Harvard Project on American Indian Economic Development, 2008; Light & Rand, 2005). On the positive side, revenue from gaming has been credited with marked improvements in the standard of living for many tribal communities in providing better healthcare, educational services, employment opportunities, and many essential government services. On the negative side, revenue from gaming is cited as being responsible for huge increases in personal wealth only for select individuals, increased drug/alcohol abuse that is linked to increased prosperity, political infighting among tribal members, a compromise in tribal values, and the unintended consequences of greed (for an in-depth discussion, see Light & Rand, 2005).

THE INFLUENCE OF SOCIOECONOMIC STATUS

"Preppy." "Free and reduced lunch kids." "Black American Princess." "White-bread." "Beaner." "Gangsta." "Limousine liberals." "Country." "Trailer trash." "Yuppie." "Bougie." "Hoochie mama." "Old money." "Redneck." "Ghetto fabulous."

These and other terms, nearly all of which are considered to be somewhat pejorative, are slang words typically used (at the time of this writing) by children and youth in schools when referring to behavioral and personality traits that signify awareness of social class differences among peers. Studies have shown that school-aged children are well aware of social class distinctions, however these conceptions begin as a dim awareness and evolve into increasingly more sophisticated concepts of class distinctions as children get older (Leahy, 1983; Simmons & Rosenberg, 1971; Stendler, 1949; Tutor, 1991). Adults are just as keenly aware of these differences, although most have learned to mask this awareness when speaking publicly or professionally.

According to Bornstein and Bradley (2003), "[i]n the long history of research on child well-being, few constructs have received greater attention than socioeconomic status" (p. 1). Unfortunately, the serious acknowledgement of the role of social class stratification in psychoeducational issues is virtually nonexistent in the school psychology literature, except when using bland descriptors such as "high income" or "low income." All too often, Quack Multiculturalism encourages a myopic focus on racial/ethnic group status alone as the key variable that should inform school psychologists about important variation in psychoeducational characteristics of children and youth in schools. Yet, a case can be made that *variation in socioeconomic status*—in a significant number of instances—can play a *much more important role* in helping school personnel to understand the influence of home and family variation on school outcomes. For example, Lareau (2003) studied both black and white families belonging to the middle classes, working classes, and the poor. Her observations showed the power of *social class* in shaping the daily experiences of children, particularly on the key dimensions of daily life, use of language, and relationships with institutions such as schools. She found that black parents differed little from white parents of the same class in their general approach to child-rearing.

A warning against the tendency to ignore within-group SES differences (here called "alpha bias") is forcefully articulated by Pedersen (1999), who writes:

> "Alpha bias" involves an exaggeration of the differences existing between two cultures. . . . This would mean seeing the differences in behavior, values, and mores between the two cultures as being so great that finding a common ground would be difficult. . . . Emphasis on differences classifies people in such a way that variability within each group is obscured, especially those due to social class. For example, an educated urban Turk will have more in common with an urban German than with a rural Turk in some ways, but this is obscured by classifying all Turks as being similar and different from all Germans. (p. 84)

Pedersen's hypothesis was tested empirically with a series of studies described in Frisby (Frisby, 1999; Frisby & Lorenzo-Luaces, 2000; see Sidebar 3.2).

☙ Sidebar 3.2   An Empirical Investigation of Cultural Difference Judgments

What criteria do people use when they make cultural difference judgments—and what is the relative salience of these criteria? Frisby (Frisby, 1999; Frisby & Lorenzo-Luaces, 2000) investigated these questions in a series of empirical studies. In one study, a collection of fictional child portraits was developed, each of which included a 10-year-old male child's picture, as well as factual information pertaining to his ethnic/racial group membership (e.g., Caucasian, Black, or Hispanic), a picture of his home, the occupations of his parents, his geographic place of residence (e.g., a state within the United States or a region abroad), and his primary language spoken. A large group of college students of various ethnicities simply rated all possible portrait pairs quantitatively on a Likert scale of cultural similarity/dissimilarity. All pairwise ratings were then subjected to a multidimensional scaling analysis, to extract the underlying latent dimensions on which subjects made their judgments of cultural similarity/dissimilarity.

The author found that socioeconomic status (SES) differences among the fictional portraits (i.e., the extent to which the children came from rich versus poor families) explained 50 percent of the variance in cultural similarity/dissimilarity ratings, followed by 14 percent of the variance explained by geographic differences (i.e, the extent to which the children lived in the United States versus abroad), followed by 3 percent of the variance in cultural similarity/dissimilarity ratings explained by simple racial/ethnic differences among the portraits. Thus, a tentative hypothesis from this study clearly indicates that SES differences play the largest role in the manner in which individuals cognitively configure the concept of cultural differences.

However, an argument can be made that persons belonging to different racial/ethnic groups think differently when judging cultural differences among individuals. That is, racial/ethnic minority persons may conceivably put more emphasis on racial/ethnic differences in judging degrees of cultural similarity/dissimilarity compared to individuals who are not ethnic/racial minorities. To investigate this hypothesis, Frisby (1999) analyzed this data separately for only the African American subset of college students in the sample, and essentially found the same results.

In a follow-up study, Frisby and Lorenzo-Luaces (2000) developed a new set of portraits, all of which reflected various degrees of Anglo/Spanish heritage, or primarily Spanish heritage (i.e., Mexican, Cuban, Dominican, or Latin American). The sample who rated the portraits for degrees of cultural similarity/dissimilarity were all Cuban American. Using a slightly different rating procedure (but the same multidimensional scaling procedure for analyzing the data), the study found that 42 percent of the variance in cultural similarity/dissimilarity judgments was attributed to the extent to which the fictional portraits spoke Spanish or English. Twenty-eight percent of the variance in cultural similarity/dissimilarity judgments was attributed to social class (i.e., rich versus poor) differences. This tentatively suggests that, at least among Cuban Americans specifically (and perhaps among Hispanics generally), the ability to speak Spanish is perceived as more influential than socioeconomic status in binding economically disparate individuals together culturally.

What Is Social Class?

Gilbert (2011) defines *social classes* as "groups of families, more or less equal in rank and differentiated from other families above or below them with regard to characteristics such as occupation, income, wealth, and prestige" (p. 11). Measures of socioeconomic status (SES) typically consist of a composite of a person's occupation, income, and place of residence. Children are typically assigned the SES of their parents. However, adult SES can be subdivided into "SES of origin" (meaning the SES of the parents who raised the person) versus "attained SES" (the SES that the person has attained in adulthood). This distinction raises the issue of *social mobility*, where individuals can move to lower or higher SES levels as they develop into adulthood. Currently, a person's IQ and the level of educational attainments associated with IQ are the best predictors of social mobility in U.S. society (Jensen, 1998b). Therefore, SES tends to function as an *effect* of IQ and educational achievements, rather than the *cause* of IQ and educational achievements (Jensen, 1998b).

Different sociological frameworks arrive at a different number of social classes, depending on the particulars of the underlying theory. Most theoretical models of social class hierarchies posit anywhere between five to six social class subdivisions (e.g., see http://en.wikipedia.org/wiki/Social_class). However, there is a considerable degree of overlapping of subdivisions across different social class taxonomies.

Persons belonging to similar social classes have similar incomes and a tendency to live in the same neighborhood types, to socialize with each other, and to be similar in lifestyles, social attitudes, and behaviors. Recent data on the percentages of families earning yearly salaries in specific ranges, disaggregated by race and Hispanic origin, is listed in Table 3.7.

Social classes are not to be thought of as rigidly defined categories, however. Many exceptions exist and enter into the complexity that is inherent within diverse societies. For example, families headed by married couples often depend on two incomes. Here, each individual's occupational and economic circumstance may represent a working-class designation, yet the *combined* family income produces a comfortable middle-class lifestyle. Levels of education and income are also often linked in unexpected ways. For example, a gifted athlete who barely finished high school may be drafted into a professional sports team and subsequently earn millions of dollars per year (despite having no substantive college education). Conversely, a Ph.D. graduate may decide to devote his or her life to working as an overseas missionary and earn a salary barely above subsistence levels. College students, for example, work for relatively low pay as graduate and teaching assistants during the earlier years of their degree programs. Once obtaining their degrees and beginning appropriately compensated work, their social class status may rise sharply in a relatively short period.

As a final note, readers must be aware of the widespread tendency to distort impressions of social class labels in the United States in the service of personal and/or political agendas. It is easy to generate sympathy for, and political activism on behalf of "the poor"—as if persons in this category are barely one meal away from starving to death. Here, the concept of being poor is a conceptually relative, and not an absolute, term. This is why statistics such as those reported in Table 3.7 are not reported in terms of family incomes relative to a somewhat arbitrarily defined "poverty level" (as defined by the U.S. government). As Saunders (2005) observes, "'poverty' in Africa is very different

Table 3.7 Annual Income of U.S. Families—Percentage and Distribution by Race and Hispanic Origin, 2009 (Adapted from U.S. Census Bureau, 2010b)

Yearly Income Interval	Percentage All Groups	Percentage White Alone	Percentage Black Alone	Percentage Asian Alone	Percentage Hispanic Alone
< $10,000	5.2	4.2	11.3	4.3	8.8
$10,000–$14,999	3.5	3.0	6.6	2.6	6.5
$15,000–$19,999	4.1	3.7	7.3	3.5	7.2
$20,000–$24,999	5.0	4.7	7.1	3.5	7.5
$25,000–$29,999	5.1	4.8	7.1	4.0	7.2
$30,000–$34,999	4.9	4.8	6.2	3.8	7.0
$35,000–$39,999	5.0	4.9	5.8	3.8	6.1
$40,000–$44,999	4.7	4.7	4.9	3.1	5.1
$45,000–$49,999	4.2	4.1	4.5	3.6	4.9
$50,000–$59,999	8.3	8.5	7.9	7.9	8.2
$60,000–$74,999	11.0	11.4	8.6	9.8	9.7
$75,000–$84,999	6.2	6.5	5.4	5.5	4.6
$85,000–$99,999	7.3	7.6	5.2	6.9	4.9
$100,000–$149,000	14.9	15.7	8.1	19.4	8.2
$150,000–$199,000	5.7	6.0	2.4	8.9	2.3
$200,000–$249,999	2.4	2.5	0.7	4.4	0.9
≥ $250,000	2.6	2.8	0.9	5.0	1.0

Includes persons who did not additionally report any other race but the race designated.

from 'poverty' in Australia. To be poor in Africa means you are starving: to be poor in Australia means you cannot afford to eat out at a restaurant."

These various subtleties involved in efforts to define and understand poverty in the United States are discussed in Sidebar 3.3. The economic, occupational, educational, and behavioral characteristics associated with differences in families' socioeconomic status are described in Sidebar 3.4.

Sidebar 3.3   How Poor Is Poor?

In determining who is or is not "poor," consider the following scenarios:

- A single mother of two children, with only a high school education, works as a waitress for $9 per hour plus tips. She supplements her income by working as a part-time cashier in a local department store. Her combined annual income per year is approximately $20,000.
- An unemployed young woman lives with her wealthy elderly aunt in a beautiful home, and receives free room and board. The young woman accompanies her aunt to the theater and helps her aunt by doing various household chores (e.g., shopping, cleaning, cooking). When she needs money, her aunt gives it to her. On average, her aunt gives her approximately $4,000 per year.
- A former businessman has recently divorced from his wife, partly because of the ravages of schizophrenia. He has no close friends to care for him. He has $500,000 in his bank account, but he lives on the street and subsists off the money he receives for collecting bottles that he finds after returning them for the deposit.
- A young man attends graduate school at a state university. He is studying to be an engineer. He lives in a one-room efficiency apartment in a rundown neighborhood that costs $300 per month in rent. The cost of his books and tuition are paid for by the university. Through stipends from graduate teaching and research assistantships, he lives on $16,000 per year.

Are these people poor? Why or why not? The first case is the most financially well off of the four cases, but comes closest to what many consider to be "the poor." Based on yearly income alone, the last three cases would clearly be classified as "living in poverty" by government income threshold standards. Yet the last three cases would *not* fit the profile of what most people imagine when they think of what it means to be poor in the United States. These examples illustrate the nuances inherent in, and the difficulty of, defining who is poor.

One way of determining who is or is not poor is to examine how organizations describe what poverty looks like. For example, the World Bank defines poverty as pronounced deprivation in well-being, which includes a low income, low levels of health and education, poor access to clean water and sanitation, inadequate physical security, the inability to acquire the basic goods and services necessary for survival "with dignity," and insufficient capacity and opportunity to better one's life. Although this definition may provide more detail in describing poverty, it actually raises more difficult questions than it answers.

U.S. school psychologists and other school professionals typically describe poor families as "low income," which satisfies one portion of the World Bank's definition. Yet with just a little deeper analysis, it can readily be seen how inadequate this descriptor is. The schizophrenic former businessman certainly lives from day-to-day at an economic level that most would consider to be indicative of abject poverty. Yet most observers would salivate at the prospect of having $500,000 in the bank. This highlights the difficult issue of weighing a person's assets against daily lifestyle choices in defining poverty. If a "person on the street" were asked if an income of $4,000 per year is sufficient, most would readily agree that persons who would try to live on this amount are indeed poor. Nevertheless, the young woman living with her elderly aunt enjoys a lifestyle that is far removed from what most would consider to be poor. The graduate student studying to be an engineer has a low income in the technical sense, but he does not fit the profile of the stereotypical low-income person, as euphemistically described by educators. The graduate student's circumstances are *temporary*, and in fact it may be safe to say that after a few years of employment in a job for which he has been trained, he will be considered "rich" by contemporary standards.

That leaves the waitress. Certainly her circumstances do not include the inconsistencies and contradictions that make defining poverty difficult. She, compared to the other hypothetical cases, most assuredly characterizes what most people would think of as poor.

Think again.

In nearly all countries outside of the United States, "poverty" reflects conditions with which a majority of U.S. citizens have no direct experience (see http://en.wikipedia.org/wiki/Poverty). In some third world countries, thousands of women die in childbirth each year, and their children are so malnourished that many die before their fifth birthday. People experiencing poverty in third world countries must contend with high rates of infectious diseases such as malaria, tuberculosis, and AIDS. Rural communities in some countries do not enjoy basic services that U.S. citizens take for granted, such as running water in households, toilet and sanitation systems, and refuse removal systems. According to the

United Nations Educational, Scientific, and Cultural Organization (UNESCO), approximately 100 million children worldwide are homeless and live on the street. In many third world countries, the ability of governments to supply citizens' basic needs is severely restricted by huge debts owed to other countries, endemic graft and corruption among government officials, and a significant "brain drain" of the country's best and brightest education and healthcare professionals to other parts of the world.

Every year, the U.S. Census Bureau reports that more than 30 million U.S. citizens live in poverty. However, the average poor person in the United States enjoys a standard of living that by no stretch of the imagination would make them poor if they lived in another country. According to a 2005 study, the typical U.S. household defined as poor by the government owns at least one car, has household air-conditioning, an average of two color television sets, cable or satellite TV, a DVD player, a VCR, an electronic game system (e.g., Xbox or PlayStation), a refrigerator, stove, microwave oven, clothes dryer, ceiling fans, a cordless phone, and a coffee maker. In fact, appliances and electronic items that were considered unaffordable middle-class luxuries a few decades ago have become commonplace in "poor" U.S. households.

The typical U.S. citizen classified as poor has more household living space than the average European. Compared to what constitutes poverty in third world countries, the average poor U.S. citizen has access to medical care whenever it is needed, does not go hungry for extended periods, and has sufficient funds to meet essential needs. In fact, most contemporary poor children in the United States are well nourished and grow up to be, on average, 1 inch taller and 10 pounds heavier than the GIs who stormed the beaches of Normandy in World War II.

According to 2009 data, only 1 out of 70 U.S. citizens with incomes below the poverty level was homeless. Of these homeless individuals, *two-thirds* actually reside in emergency shelters or transitional housing, with the remaining individuals living in cars, abandoned buildings, alleyways, or public parks.

The concluding lesson here is that government poverty statistics can be misleading, unless it is clearly understood how such statistics have been derived. In addition, researchers and applied psychologists must understand the difference between the dual concepts of "relative poverty" (how an individual's economic situation compares to another's economic situation) versus "absolute poverty" (how an individual's situation compares to an absolute standard of basic unmet needs). Here, additional information about the actual living conditions of persons identified as poor must be carefully considered.

🖎 Sidebar 3.4   Characteristics of Children, Youth, and Families Associated With Broad Socioeconomic Categories*

UPPER CLASSES (APPROX. 15%)

Some Overlap With: Capitalist classes, the "working rich," upper middle classes

Family Occupations: Investors, heirs, high-level executives or managers, business owners, lawyers, physicians, dentists

Adult Education: Selective colleges/universities; often postgraduate degrees

Family Yearly Income (2011 estimates): $150,000 to millions per year. Many possess income-producing assets (real estate, stocks, bonds). There is ample money in the family budget for vacations, domestic help, quality furniture, new cars, multiple homes. Wealth is typically passed from one generation to the next (e.g., family fortunes).

Demographic Characteristics: Accomplished persons have an influence on local, national, and international economies far beyond their number in the general population (i.e., via investments, contributions to political parties/campaigns/ causes, donations to colleges/universities, influence in media outlets; membership in local chamber of commerce).

Behavioral Characteristics: Children spend much of their time involved in highly structured activities with and/or organized by adults (e.g., soccer practice, piano/ violin lessons, swim team, church choir, school play rehearsals, boy/girl scouts, gymnastics).

Educational Characteristics: Parents engage in continual conversation with their children when together. Children are taught to express their views and to believe that their opinions matter. Children are encouraged to ask questions of adults in authority. Parents attempt to reason with children in the context of discipline. When issuing directives, parents supplant these commands with reasons. Children learn to negotiate with parents for wants.

Parents are more likely to be more involved in cultivating their children's academic lives. Parents help with children and/or make sure children complete their home-work. They send their children to private schools; move to neighborhoods with "better" public schools; encourage their children to take Advanced Placement (AP) courses in high school; have high expectations of their children attending college; pay for children's college entrance test preparation courses; take trips to visit colleges the summer before their children's senior year in high school; know how and when to interact with school guidance counselors to assist in selecting schools and preparing college applications; bear the responsibility of paying for their children's college.

High SES students are overrepresented at highly selective colleges and uni-versities. High SES youth are more likely to be in the upper 10 percent of their high school class and/or earn the highest average SAT scores compared to youth in other social classes.

MIDDLE CLASSES (APPROX. 30%)

Some Overlap With: Upper middle classes, lower middle classes

Family Occupations: Combination of white-collar and highly paid blue-collar occupations: public school teachers, social workers, lower managers, craftspeople, foremen, non-retail sales. There is room in the family budget for annual vacations and savings accounts.

Adult Education: At least high school graduation; some college to bachelor's and master's degrees

Family Yearly Income (2011 estimates): $70,000–$150,000

Demographic Characteristics: Very diverse; represents bulk of the U.S. population (lower and upper middle classes included)

Behavioral Characteristics: Children, by imitation and/or observation, learn "the rules of the game" in interacting with adults in institutional settings to pursue their unique goals/preferences and manage interactions (called "sense of entitlement").

Educational Characteristics: Parents are more likely to be more involved in cultivating their children's academic lives; move to neighborhoods with "better" public schools; have high expectations of their children attending college; take trips to visit colleges the summer before their children's senior year in high school; and know how and when to interact with school guidance counselors to assist in selecting schools and preparing college applications.

WORKING CLASSES (APPROX. 30%)

Some Overlap With: Lower middle classes, lower classes

Family Occupations: Semi-skilled or low-skilled manual labor; construction workers; truck drivers; hotel/restaurant work; clerical; retail sales

Adult Education: At least high school graduation

Family Yearly Income (2011 estimates): $40,000–$70,000

Demographic Characteristics: Tendency to have less stable work histories; many are young workers who will be able to move up in the class hierarchy with further training and/or experience.

Behavioral Characteristics: Parents and children are often silent when in the company of each other. Children are disciplined at home with short, clear directives, which are sometimes coupled with physical punishment. Parents expect children to obey directives without further verbal justification.

Children lead slower, less structured lives compared to children in the upper classes, primarily because of the low value parents place on such activities—as well as the lack of requisite time, financial, and transportation resources needed to support such activities. Instead, there is a high frequency of informal, neighborhood play and activities with peers. Children display a "sense of constraint" in institutional settings by not questioning the actions of adults in positions of authority, and they are less likely to know how institutional rules can be managed in their favor.

Educational Characteristics: Parents tend to feel intimidated by school professionals, as parents may not understand the words professionals use and do not feel competent in challenging their expertise. School values that require restraint in child-to-child altercations may conflict with parent values that encourage children to physically defend themselves. Parents are likely to be more uninvolved, passive, and reactive toward their children's college admissions process; rely on the guidance counselor to inform them of their children's college options; and/or need their children to perform childcare and housework in order to make ends meet. Parents are not as likely to help with and/or make sure children complete homework, or to have high expectations of their children attending college.

Children are more likely to consider financial costs in deciding colleges to which they will apply, as well as consider the cost of college as their own responsibility. Guidance counselors serving high schools with large lower-SES populations are concerned more with ensuring that students graduate from high school, as opposed to grooming students for college. Youth are more likely to earn the lowest average SAT scores compared to youth in other social classes. Youth are less likely to receive awards or participate in leadership positions in high school.

THE WORKING POOR (APPROX. 13%)

Some Overlap With: Lower classes

Family Occupations: Low-pay manual labor; low-skilled blue-collar jobs (e.g., assembly-line workers); service workers (e.g., dishwashers, drivers, sales clerks, janitors, low-level secretaries, restaurant servers)

Adult Education: At least some high school

Family Yearly Income (2011 estimates): $25,000–$40,000. Family budget spent on food, housing, utilities, and taxes; little money available for discretionary or leisure purchases; a few weeks of unemployment or a large unexpected bill can significantly disrupt or threaten standard of living.

Demographic Characteristics: Overrepresentation of single women (i.e., single by choice, divorced, or separated female heads of families; elderly widows living alone)

Behavioral Characteristics: Higher incidence of domestic violence involving boyfriends or spouses, particularly during periods of unemployment; higher incidence of child custody issues stemming from personal social problems.

Educational Characteristics: Parents often intimidated by educators and highly defensive/oppositional when confronted with their child's classroom/school behavior problems; low parent turnout at parent/teacher school functions. Children in poor neighborhoods are more likely to have teachers who are overwhelmed or "burned out"; students often do not fully understand the classroom material taught; young children may have high career aspirations, but they have no working knowledge of how to get there; high attraction to sports stars, movie stars, and music entertainers as employment role models; higher incidence of kids being unsupervised in homework activities.

THE UNDERCLASS (APPROX. 12%)

Family Occupations: Unemployed; menial labor; public assistance; "underground" criminal activity

Family Yearly Income (2011 estimates): ≤$15,000 per year (may be an underestimate, as unreported income may be supplemented by involvement with illegal criminal activity)

Adult Education: At least some high school; high frequency of school dropouts

Demographic Characteristics: Living in neighborhoods characterized by a high degree of physical deterioration (e.g., homeless persons sleeping on the streets; buildings abandoned and/or covered in graffiti) and social disorganization (e.g., families impacted by mental illness, prostitution, drug trafficking and addiction); high frequency of income from public assistance (e.g., food stamps, Social Security, disability payments, or veterans benefits); disproportionate black and Hispanic representation.

Behavioral Characteristics: High proportion of children growing up without the nurture and presence of fathers. High rates of unemployment, where large numbers of young men are not in school, not employed, and are not actively seeking employment. Higher unemployment rates are correlated with higher rates of chronic criminality. Higher rates of reported child abuse and neglect in families. Parents are more likely to hold attitudes that condone physical punishment of children. Among young women, out-of-wedlock births become the norm rather than the exception.

Educational Characteristics: Few educationally successful adult role models for young people to emulate; schools have poor resources and offer a chaotic, often dangerous learning environment; low to nonexistent rates of serious school engagement; low high school graduation rates.

See Beeghley (2004); Espenshade & Radford (2009); Gilbert (2011); Lareau (2011); Murray (1999); Shipler (2005); Thompson & Hickey (2005)

(adapted from Lang, 2007; Rector & Sheffield, 2011)

CORRELATES OF SOCIAL CLASS STATUS

Like most psychological and sociological variables, the social class status of U.S. families is distributed as a negatively skewed bell-shaped curve (e.g., see Gilbert, 2011, Chapter 4), with extreme wealth and poverty situated at the less frequent extremes and middle-class groups situated at the more frequent center. Professionals working with lower-class "families of color" in schools find that these families have disproportionately higher rates of involvement in the social services bureaucracy. That is, poor racial/ethnic minority children are disproportionately represented in the U.S. child welfare system, have the highest rates of foster care placements, and are more likely to remain in the child welfare system for extended periods compared to other children (Eddy & Poehlmann, 2010). Some social scientists point out that the explosive growth of welfare policies beginning in the 1960s encouraged poorer persons to become dependent on government assistance and to view this assistance as an expected entitlement rather than as a source of shame (e.g., see Murray, 1994). Many critics argue that dependence on such programs subsidizes irresponsibility and saps personal initiative for positive growth within poor families (Funiciello, 1993; Parker, 2003).

In stark contrast, families represented in the high middle and upper classes are those who can afford private schooling, or at least afford living in exclusive neighborhoods that serve better public schools. In this group, there is typically little difficulty in accessing support services that would facilitate success in children's educational pursuits. Due to parents' economic resources and professional contacts, children growing up in upper social class environments are sensitized to the necessary pathways for applying to the better colleges and universities, and they are knowledgeable about the steps needed to prepare for lucrative professions. A description of the educational socialization of children from upper-class black families —a group that only a few school professionals have knowledge of or exposure to—is described in Sidebar 3.5.

The majority of children and youth that school psychologists and other professionals will have contact with in the public schools belong to the middle classes, working classes, working poor, and the underclasses. There is a significant, but far from perfect, correlation between school achievement, cognitive ability, and academic achievements of school children as these interact with social class status (e.g., see Herrnstein & Murray, 1994). The school climate and the prevalence of behavioral and social problems experienced by schools has been observed to vary considerably as a function of the social class of students (e.g., see Bankston & Caldas, 2002; Rothstein, 2004; Shipler, 2005; Weissberg, 2010).

There are numerous variables, relevant to the home and family life of schoolchildren, that are significantly associated with social class status, which in turn exert a profound influence on individual differences in the quality of minority children's school experiences and the effectiveness with which they are served by teachers and school support professionals. Some of these variables are briefly discussed as follows.

✎ Sidebar 3.5   The Rarefied World of Upper-Class Black Families

Writer, business consultant, and law school graduate Lawrence Otis Graham arrived at the idea to write a book about upper-class black families after a candid conversation with late Harvard businessman Reginald Lewis (see http://www .blackhistory4ever.com/bh5_Reginald_F_Lewis.htm). Mr. Lewis, a black multimillionaire estimated to be personally worth $400 million before his death, complained that his children have little interaction with working and middle-class black children, and he feared that they would not be readily accepted by white children.

Spurred by this revelation, as well as the need to chronicle his own background growing up black and "well-to-do," Mr. Graham began his in-depth research early in 1993 with more than 350 interviews and extensive library research of books, manuscript collections, and newspaper archives.

The title of Graham's book, *Our Kind of People*, refers to a mindset among affluent black families that began in the early days of U.S. segregation. This mindset, handed down through generations, observes rigid distinctions among affluent blacks based on having graduated from the "right" college, having the "correct" familial geneology, being members of the "right" elite social clubs, vacationing in the "right" vacation spots, having the "proper" hair texture, "proper" skin complexion, and of course, having a high enough social status based on occupation and income.

One well-known nonprofit organization for affluent blacks, which still exists today, is the exclusive Jack and Jill of America (JJA) organization. Founded in 1938, JJA has been a defining organization whose membership includes the most wealthy and prominent families nationwide from the black professional classes (membership of which includes bankers, college/university presidents, college deans, CEOs, and top-level business executives of Fortune 500 companies, high-level politicians, prominent surgeons, and top-level corporate lawyers). As of 1999 (the publication of Graham's book), the JJA was reported to have 218 chapters throughout the United States and Germany, with a membership of more than 30,000 parents and children.

Its *advertised purpose* is to bring together children, aged 2–19, for the goals of "achieving excellence," "inspiring greatness," and "motivating youth to lead and serve" through community service projects and fundraising for worthy causes (see http://jackandjillinc.org). Its *implicit purpose* is to provide for children of wealthy black parents a network of friends with similar backgrounds for companionship, dating relationships, and ultimately for the provision of suitable marriage partners. JJA also provides an environment for children of wealthy black families (many of whom own multiple vacation homes, yachts, and country club memberships) to interact with same-aged peers and professional adult role models that they would not have an opportunity to meet otherwise in all-white private schools.

Parents and JJA officers chaperone monthly excursions to museums, theater performances, sporting events, and overnight trips to historic locations both in the United States and abroad. A consistent theme that runs through these activities is a focus on learning about the best and brightest contributors to the pantheon of American black history.

JJA members are admitted by invitation only. Children of JJA members begin participation in the group's activities as young as age two. From "day one," so to speak, JJA children attend the most exclusive private schools and elite public schools. Early on, JJA children are encouraged to begin thinking about their future chosen profession. Whereas less-advantaged children may dream of acquiring money in professional sports or entertainment (fields that have traditionally provided more open opportunities historically for blacks to acquire wealth), these fields are typically discouraged by the families of JJA children. It is customary for JJA children to attend elaborate career day events, where JJA alumni representing the most elite and lucrative professions talk about their jobs. At specified times during this function, JJA teenagers freely question, interview, and collect business cards from JJA alumni, many of whom give students pointers on how to prepare for difficult college entrance exams, and what informal apprenticeship opportunities can be pursued while in high school in order to build a competitive college application. Students are encouraged to attend only the best Ivy League schools, as well as the most elite Historically Black colleges and universities (HBCUs). Although their popularity has waned with the times, some society groups still encourage young girls to "come out" and "be presented" to upper-class society through attending debutante cotillions (see Graham, 1999, for details; see also Casimir, 2004).

Predictably, organizations like JJA, as well as the black bourgeois in general, have been attacked with charges of snobbery and elitism. Few would deny, however, that Graham's book offers a glimpse into a world that few of any background ever knew existed—whose numbers are growing with each passing decade.

(adapted from Graham, 1999)

Social Class and Neighborhood Climate

In a study of the effects of neighborhood variables on parenting behaviors, Pinderhughes, Nix, Foster, and Jones (2001) characterized residents' perceptions of the quality of their neighborhoods with five variables: (1) *poverty* (i.e., the percentage of families in the

Census Bureau tract living below the federal poverty limit), (2) *residential stability* (i.e., the percentage of residents from Census Bureau data who resided in the same location for at least five years and who owned their own homes), (3) *resident dissatisfaction with public services* (i.e., residents' evaluation of the quality of police protection, garbage collection, schools, and public transportation), (4) *presence of social networks* (i.e., frequency of informal socializing among residents, existence of formal community groups), and (5) *neighborhood danger* (i.e., ratings of the frequency of muggings, burglaries, and assaults in the neighborhood). Researchers found that poor urban African American families in their sample reported scores that were worse on all neighborhood variables compared to poor urban and rural white families. Kay (2011) describes the physical conditions characteristic of poor underclass black neighborhoods as follows:

> The tip-offs are litter and graffiti everywhere, vacant stores, small markets typically run by Arabs or Koreans with iron bars on the windows, abandoned buildings with broken windows, trash-filled empty lots, the absence of national chain stores, vandalized parks and schools, run-down housing, tricked-out old cars, and the like. Not visible but equally part of the neighborhood are high food stamp usage, single-parent families, corrupt politics, high unemployment, widespread drug use, and violent crime.

Nevertheless, lower economic status is not necessarily perfectly correlated with dysfunctional neighborhoods. Kay (2011) adds:

> New York City's Chinatown is among the city's poorest, most congested neighborhoods, but it overflows with thriving small businesses (many on sidewalks), crowded cheap restaurants, and high-performing though often ancient schools with graduates going on to prestigious colleges. It is also completely safe for visitors even late at night. My recollection of San Francisco's Chinatown is identical, and I suspect that Chinatowns worldwide are similar.

Marriage, Out-of-Wedlock Births, and Single Parenthood

Attitudes Toward Marriage

The institution of marriage is a "human universal" (e.g., see Sidebar 10.6), meaning that it exists in every known society on the face of the globe regardless of race, ethnicity, language, or economic status. It has been widely acknowledged among both social scientists and the popular press that there is a marked shortage of marriageable black men relative to black women, and that this shortage has been particularly acute in large urban areas (Austin, 2011). Scholars opine that the short supply but high demand of marriageable black men contributes to higher rates of irresponsible sexual behavior of single black men—and their reluctance to marry (i.e., the "why-buy-the-cow-when-you-can-get-the-milk-for-free" theory). Black women—who would prefer to be married—therefore resign themselves to the temptations of having children out of wedlock (see reviews by Hymowitz, 2006; Roth, 1994).

In some communities, there is an economic incentive to avoid marriage, if doing so creates a barrier to receiving federal assistance (which is viewed as a reliable source of income). In more privileged communities, a young girl who bears a child out-of-wedlock is viewed as engaging in behavior that is damaging to her future aspirations for educational, occupational, or social advancement. White and/or middle-class women, while not necessarily refraining from sexual activity, are nevertheless more prone to postpone marriage and maternity until suitable mates are found. In contrast, many young minority girls in ghetto communities view motherhood with a sense of personal accomplishment and as a symbol of emerging womanhood (Roth, 1994). Because of intractable problems related to the unsuitability of potential marriage partners (as disproportionate numbers of minority males are involved with the criminal justice system, have low educational skills, or have no steady employment), young females in minority ghetto communities come to believe that no adequate marriage partner will ever materialize. One black female writer expressed surprise when a 12-year-old black male student told her that, although he sees himself as eventually being a good father to his children, he doesn't see himself getting married because "marriage is for white people" (Jones, 2006).

As the cumulative effects of such environments multiply over decades and across generations, social scientists (whose work involves chronicling the attitudes of young adolescents) begin to notice stark differences between the attitudes of young people in the middle versus lower social classes. As discussed in Hymowitz (2006), sociologists have coined the term *life script*, in referring to individuals' internal sense of the timing and progression of the major events that they expect to happen as their lives unfold. For each individual, this life script is modeled by family and community. For most middle-class young people, the life script involves a protracted period of adolescence and young adulthood that involves preparation for future employment. One is expected to begin a job and career, after which persons are expected to get married and then bear children. According to the middle-class life script, one expects to be financially ready and self-supporting before marriage and children. According to Hymowitz (2006), higher-educated and higher-income mothers (socialized by a "marriage-before-children" culture) buy into the conviction that marriage is fundamentally a necessary institution for properly raising children. Children who grow up in a stable two-parent family are imbued with a life script that guides their attitudes toward the family as they progress from childhood to adolescence, from college to the workplace, and from their own marriages to child-rearing. According to Hymowitz (2006), an orientation toward "marriage-before-children" requires young women to carefully consider what kind of man will become her husband and the father of her children. This orientation requires that she be "future oriented," which requires conscious deliberation and self-discipline, particularly as this relates to her sexual behavior.

In contrast, females growing up in home and neighborhood environments where the message is "marriage is optional" are deprived of crucial life information that teaches them what is optimal for the raising of children (Hymowitz, 2006). In these often chaotic environments, a good education is sporadic, and "sex and babies simply happen" (Hymowitz, 2006). Such women do not grow up with the breezy view that single motherhood is simply a "different lifestyle choice," as even these women dream of marriage (even though their life circumstances and dismal marriage prospects makes this highly unlikely; see Edin & Kefalas, 2005).

Out-of-Wedlock Births and Single Parenthood

The "decline of the family" is a generic term that typically refers to one or more of two separate issues: the frequency of out-of-wedlock births and/or fatherless families—issues that may or may not coexist concurrently. There is a significant association between social class and various indicators of family breakdown, including out-of-wedlock births (see Herrnstein & Murray, 1994). In this regard, Hymowitz's (2006) comments hit the proverbial nail squarely on its head:

> . . . it has become clear that family breakdown lies at the heart of our nation's most obstinate social problems, especially poverty and inequality. . . . Most people assume that divorce, unmarried motherhood, fatherlessness, and [child] custody battles are all equal opportunity domestic misfortunes, affecting the denizens of West Virginia trailer parks or Bronx housing projects just as they do those of Malibu beach homes or Park Avenue co-ops. . . . [However] the assumption that Americans are all in the same boat when it comes to marriage collapse is dead wrong. (pp. 3–4)

According to the most recent U.S. Census data for 2010 (U.S. Census Bureau, 2011), the percentage within each major U.S. racial/ethnic group of births to unmarried mothers between 1980–2007 is depicted in Figure 3.1. The percentage of families within each major U.S. ethnic/racial group who report one-parent households (containing children under 18) is depicted in Figure 3.2.

Single parenthood is a complex phenomenon that results from divorce, widowhood, and unwed motherhood. Simply put, it is much more difficult for single-parent, one-earner families to achieve the same degree of economic well-being, on average, as more

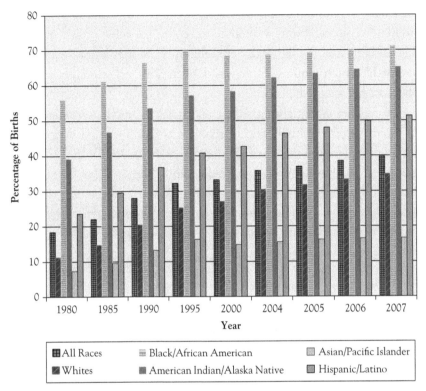

Figure 3.1   Percentage of Live Births to Unmarried Mothers, by Race/Ethnicity: 1980–2007
U.S. Census Bureau, 2011

conventional two-parent, two-earner families (Roth, 1994). In addition, neighborhoods in which biological fathers are routinely present and contribute to the upbringing and care of children rarely exhibit the social pathology that is so common and widespread in neighborhoods in which fathers are routinely absent.

Even when race, education, and income are controlled, children of single mothers are less successful on just about every measure than are children growing up with their married parents (Hymowitz, 2006). Children born to single mothers are more prone to alcohol and drug abuse, crime, and school failure. They are less likely to graduate from college, and they are more likely to have children at a young age while unmarried. This cycle perpetuates itself down through generations. Poor or working-class single mothers with minimal education tend to have children who will themselves become low-income single parents with little education. The same is true for the other end of the social spectrum. That is to say, college-educated and middle-class married mothers tend to raise children who go to college and who get married before having children.

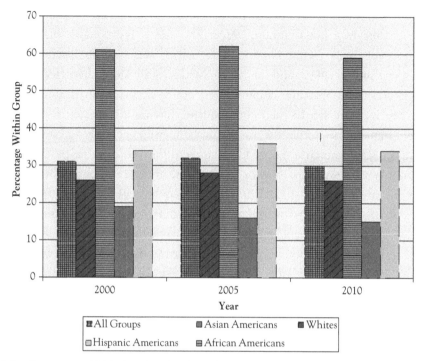

Figure 3.2   Percentage of U.S. Families (With Children Under 18 Years) Reporting One-Parent Households: Years 2000, 2005, and 2010
U.S. Census Bureau, 2011

Many poor minority children who are born to single mothers bear the additional burden of having their biological mothers abandon them through drug addiction or mental illness. As reported in Roth (1994), some inner-city schools serve a clientele in which approximately one-half of the children live in homes without a biological mother or father. One news story describes such children as follows:

> Scarred by years of abuse and neglect, many of these children are angry and disruptive, even after they settle in loving foster homes or with doting grand-mothers. They are distrustful of adults, greedy for attention and convinced that they must be worthless. . . . They are unresponsive to threats that their mis-behavior will land them into trouble, because things already seem as bad as they can get. (Gross, 1992, as quoted from Roth, 1994, p. 300)

The fact that family breakdown is a major contributor to economic and social pro-blems, particularly among blacks and Hispanics, is no longer in serious dispute by a wide variety of social scientists. The popular notion among some quarters that higher rates of black family instability is an outgrowth of "the legacy of slavery" has been empirically shown to be false (e.g., see Gutman, 1976). The rate of (particularly black) family dissolution is a relatively recent phenomenon, which was first discussed openly in the national scene in the 1960s, and has accelerated steadily since then (see Sidebar 3.6).

In some black and Hispanic communities, out-of-wedlock births and single parenthood are nearly universal. In such communities, having a child out-of-wedlock is not considered shameful or disgraceful—as would be considered in other communities with more traditional or conventional middle-class sensibilities (e.g., see Sidebar 3.7).

For minority young people growing up in poor, underclass communities, a coherent life script is virtually nonexistent. These young people have few stable role models and minimal responsible adult involvement in important life decisions. Here, the middle-class rituals of high school graduation, college attendance/graduation, first apartment, first job, and meeting a potential marriage partner hold little emotional meaning (Hymowitz, 2006). Many underclass high school teens see glamorous jobs/careers on TV or in the movies, and they may express a desire to one day become a lawyer or doctor, but they have no serious understanding of what it takes to get there. For many underclass female teens, having a baby is seen as an accomplishment that symbolizes maturity. For many of these young women, it is hoped that having a baby will bring unconditional love and meaning to their lives. Some young girls who do not as yet have children—but see many of their high school friends having children—come to believe that they are "odd" or "weird" for not having children.

🖎 Sidebar 3.6   The Moynihan Report and Beyond

In the 1950s and 1960s, barriers erected by legal discrimination throughout the United States were falling at a rapid speed (e.g., *Brown v. Board of Education* decision of 1954, Civil Rights Act of 1964). Nevertheless, these times witnessed extensive racial rioting in northern ghettos, and alarming numbers of black women were going on welfare despite the increasing access of blacks to a middle-class standard of living.

The *Moynihan Report* is the moniker given to the results of a government study, completed in 1965, originally entitled "The Negro Family: The Case for National Action." The report was written by then-sociologist, Assistant Secretary of Labor, and later U.S. Senator Daniel Patrick Moynihan. It focused on the deep roots of black poverty in the United States, and concluded that the growing absence of nuclear (i.e., husband-wife) families would greatly hinder blacks' further progress toward economic and political equality.

In describing the alarming state of urban ghettos, Moynihan coined the phrase "tangle of pathology" in describing high rates of juvenile delinquency, joblessness, school failure, crime, and fatherlessness in families that were increasingly being evident in these communities. Moynihan blamed the growing economic, educational, and social problems evident among blacks at the time on a "family structure [that had become] highly unstable, and in many urban centers [was] approaching complete breakdown" (Rainwater & Yancey, 1967, p. 51). Among other things, Moynihan concluded that "a national effort towards the problems of Negro Americans must be directed towards the question of family structure."

Because Moynihan served as the Assistant Secretary in the Department of Labor at the time, his recommendations for national action reflected this background. Moynihan felt that the key to curtailing the alarming rise in black family instability was an aggressive effort to provide jobs for black men, which, in his view, would provide an employment bedrock on which family stability could be restored. Largely as a result of the Moynihan Report, then President Lyndon Johnson, in what he called his "greatest civil rights speech" at Howard University, said that "when the family collapses, it is the children that are usually damaged . . . when it happens on a massive scale, the community itself is crippled."

Although the Moynihan Report was designed to be a strictly internal government document that Massey and Sampson (2009) described as "the most famous piece of social scientific analysis never published" (p. 6), an unnamed source leaked the document to journalists. The firestorm of criticism that immediately followed this leaking of the Moynihan Report established the template for the corrosive racial politics and culture wars that continue to the present day.

Moynihan was promptly accused of "racism," as critics took offense that a white man would dare publicly criticize black family life as deviant from a perceived "white norm" (e.g., see Harris, 2010). A new catchphrase was invented, known as "blaming the victim" (Ryan, 1971), a moniker that evaluates any criticism of negative minority behavior as unfair and insensitive to minorities' persecution by an unjust society. Critics charged that Moynihan ignored the strengths of the black family, as well as being insensitive to their unique cultural norms. Some academic critiques from feminist and gay rights movements even began to question the legitimacy of the advantages of the nuclear family. The critics of the Moynihan Report and its author were so hostile, that discussion of its primary conclusions largely disappeared from both public and academic discourse for decades (see review by Hymowitz, 2005). In Massey and Sampson's (2009) words, "Moynihan's report had been consigned to the netherworld of the "politically incorrect," where it would remain for decades" (p. 9).

As the years went by, and the dust was beginning to settle, there began to emerge a dawning, if not grudging, realization that Moynihan was correct in his warnings. By 1980 (15 years after the Moynihan Report was published), the out-of-wedlock birthrate among blacks had more than doubled. Welfare dependency skyrocketed from 2 million families in 1970 to 5 million families in 1995. By 1990, 65 percent of all black children were being born to unmarried women (at present, this figure is approximately 70 percent, and in some communities this figure is closer to 80 percent). Particularly alarming is the entrenched *attitudes* observed among young girls in black communities of childbearing age. Despite increased reproductive services, access to birth control, and sex education in schools, many young unmarried teenagers in ghetto communities *actually want and seek to get pregnant.*

As the 1980s wore on, a change in attitudes toward the Moynihan Report began to materialize, as academics and scholars began to acknowledge the prescience of Moynihan's early conclusions. Ken Auletta, in his 1982 book *The Underclass,* declared Moynihan as "prophetic." Mark Starr and Jerry Buckley wrote an April 1985 *Newsweek* magazine article vindicating the report, which was entitled "Moynihan: I Told You So." Bill Moyers produced a highly regarded CBS-TV documentary in 1986 called "The Vanishing Black Family," which confirmed how the collapse of family life significantly contributed to the cycle of poverty among many black Americans. In 1987, the distinguished black social scientist William Julius Wilson wrote the seminal work *The Truly Disadvantaged,* where he chastises critics of the Moynihan Report for being "confused and defensive" in their failure to confront the social pathologies of the ghetto.

The alarming increase in out-of-wedlock births in all racial groups since 1980 (see Figure 3.1) has literally created two separate classes of families, with widely different outcomes for the children born into them (see Hymowitz, 2006). In a piece written for the online journal *The Family in America,* Bryce Christensen (2004) concluded with the following words:

> . . . the fight against American family disintegration finally has nothing to do with whether the families in peril are white or black. But that fight has everything to do with social health. If the next generation of Americans is watching a television documentary in 2025 called the *Vanishing White Family—Crisis in White America,* that social health will be long gone. And no amount of belated praise for Moynihan's 21st-century epigones will bring it back.

✎ Sidebar 3.7   Birth Rates Among Unwed Hispanics

Unless the life chances of children raised by single mothers suddenly improve, the explosive growth of the U.S. Hispanic population over the next couple of decades does not bode well for American social stability. . . . By 2050, the Latino population will have tripled, the Census Bureau projects. One in four Americans will be Hispanic by midcentury, twice the current ratio. It's the fertility surge among unwed Hispanics that should worry policymakers. Hispanic women have the highest unmarried birthrate in the country—over three times that of whites and Asians, and nearly 1½ times that of black women, according to the Centers for Disease Control and Prevention. . . . Forty-five percent of all Hispanic births occur outside of marriage, compared with 24 percent for whites and 15 percent for Asians. Only the percentage for blacks—68 percent—is higher. But the black population is not going to triple over the next few decades. . . .

To grasp the reality behind those numbers, one need only talk to people working on the front lines of family breakdown. Social workers in Southern California, the national epicenter for illegal Hispanic immigrants, are in despair over the epidemic of single parenting. Not only has illegitimacy become perfectly acceptable, they say, but so has the resort to welfare and social services to cope with it.

Dr. Ana Sanchez delivers babies at St. Joseph's Hospital in the city of Orange, Calif., many of them to Hispanic teenagers. To her dismay, they view having a child at their age as normal. But what is "most alarming," Dr. Sanchez says, is that the "teens' parents view having babies outside of marriage as normal, too. A lot of the grandmothers are single as well; they never married, or they had successive partners. So the mom sends the message to her daughter that it's OK to have children out of wedlock." Dr. Sanchez feels almost personally involved in the problem: "I'm Hispanic myself. I wish I could find out what the Asians are doing right." She guesses that Asian parents' passion for education inoculates their children against the underclass trap. "Hispanics are not picking that up like the Asian kids," she says with a sigh. . . .

"It's considered almost a badge of honor for a young girl to have a baby," says Peggy Schulze of Chrysalis House, an adoption agency in Fresno. It is almost impossible to persuade young Hispanic mothers to give up a child for adoption, Ms. Schulze says. "The attitude is: 'How could you give away your baby?' I don't know how to break through."

The most powerful Hispanic family value—the tight-knit extended family—facilitates unwed child rearing. Relatives often step in to make up for the absence of the baby's father. I asked Mona, a 19-year-old parishioner at St. Joseph's Church in Santa Ana, Calif., if she knew any single mothers. She laughed: "There are so many I can't even name them." Two of her cousins, 25 and 19, have children without having husbands. The situation didn't seem to trouble this churchgoer too much. "They'll be strong enough to raise them. It's totally OK with us," she said. "We're very close; we're there to support them. They'll do just fine."

As Mona's family suggests, out-of-wedlock child rearing among Hispanics is by no means confined to the underclass. The St. Joseph's parishioners are precisely the churchgoing, blue-collar workers whom open-borders conservatives celebrate. Yet they are as susceptible as others to illegitimacy.

Fifty-year-old Irma and her husband, Rafael, came legally from Mexico in the early 1970s. Rafael works in a meatpacking plant in Brea; they have raised five husky boys who attend church with them. Yet Irma's sister—a homemaker like herself, also married to a factory hand—is now the grandmother of two illegitimate children, one by each daughter. "I saw nothing in the way my sister and her husband raised her children to explain it," Irma says. "She gave them everything." One of the fathers of Irma's young nieces has four other children by a variety of different mothers. His construction wages are being garnished for child support, but he is otherwise not involved in raising his children. . . .

But though older men continue to take advantage of younger women, the age gap between the mother and the father of an illegitimate child is quickly closing. Planned Parenthood of Orange and San Bernardino counties tries to teach young fathers to take responsibility for their children. "We're seeing a lot more 13- and 14-year-old fathers," says Kathleen Collins, vice president of health education. Normally, the fathers, of whatever age, take off. "The father may already be married or in prison or doing drugs," says Amanda Gan, director of operations for Toby's House, a maternity home in Dana Point, Calif. Mona, the 19-year-old parishioner at St. Joseph's, says the boys who impregnated her two cousins are "nowhere to be found." Her family knows them but doesn't know if they are working or in jail.

Despite the strong family support, the prevalence of single parenting among Hispanics is producing the inevitable slide into the welfare system. "The girls aren't marrying the guys, so they are married to the state," Dr. Sanchez observes. Hispanics now dominate the federal Women, Infants and Children free food program; Hispanic enrollment grew more than 25 percent from 1996 to 2002, while black enrollment dropped 12 percent and white enrollment dropped 6.5 percent. Illegal immigrants can get welfare programs for their American-born children. Amy Braun works for Mary's Shelter, a home for young single mothers who are homeless or in crisis, in Orange County, Calif. It has become "culturally OK" for the Hispanic population to use the shelter and welfare system, Ms. Braun says.

A case manager at a program for pregnant homeless women in the city of Orange observes the same acculturation to the social services sector, with its grievance mongering and sense of victimhood. "I'll have women in my office on their fifth child, when the others have already been placed in foster care," says Anita Berry of Casa Teresa. "There's nothing shameful about having multiple children that you can't care for and to be pregnant again, because then you can blame the system."

The consequences of family breakdown are now being passed down from one generation to the next. "The problems are deeper and wider," says Ms. Berry. "Now you're getting the second generation of foster care and group home residents. The dysfunction is multigenerational." . . . How these two value systems—a lingering work ethic and underclass mating norms—will interact in the future is anyone's guess. From an intellectual standpoint, this is a fascinating social experiment, one that academicians are—predictably—not attuned to. But the consequences will be more than intellectual: They may severely strain the social fabric. Nevertheless, it is an experiment that we seem destined to see to its end.

Excerpt from: MacDonald, H. (August, 2006), Surge in birth rate among unwed Hispanics creating new U.S. underclass. Accessed October 2011 from *City Journal*, http://www .city-journal.org/html/16_4_hispanic_family_values.html. Reprinted with permission from City Journal

---

For many underclass male teens, fathering babies with multiple girls is viewed as a sign of virility and manhood. These girls, in turn, may have children by different men. As Hymowitz (2006) states, "the end result is a maelstrom of confusion, jealousy, rage, abandonment, and violence" (p. 9). If a young man has a steady job, he is in a better position to marry the girlfriends that he has impregnated. When they remain chronically unemployed or are incarcerated, they are incapable of supporting themselves fully, let alone a new family. In a few instances, some mothers of adolescent males actually want their sons to have children out of wedlock in hopes that fatherhood will impel them to settle down (Hymowitz, 2006).

Some have even gone so far to say that if marriage and childbearing patterns of black and Hispanic groups could be significantly reversed, perhaps even returning to levels that are better than the national average, many social problems experienced by these groups would greatly diminish (Roth, 1994). William Galston, former Deputy Assistant to President Bill Clinton for Domestic Policy, is most well-known from his famous quote: "You need only do three things in this country to avoid poverty—finish high school, marry before having a child, and marry after the age of 20" (quoted from Wilson, 2002). At the time Galston made these comments, only 8 percent of the families who do this are poor, while an astonishing 79 percent of those who fail to do this are poor (Wilson, 2002).

Child-Rearing/Parenting Behaviors

On the basis of results from intensive observations and interviews with 12 families, Lareau (2011) studied how social class shapes parenting styles and behaviors in lower- and middle-class black and white families. Poor and middle-class families (regardless of race/ethnicity) raise children differently, primarily because they view their role as parents in different ways (Hymowitz, 2006). Stated differently, families belonging to different social classes have their own culture of child-rearing. Researchers divide parenting behavior into categories, which include, but are certainly not limited to, nurturance, discipline, teaching, language, monitoring, management, and materials (Brooks-Gunn & Markman, 2005). In summarizing the parenting literature, readers must be careful to note that SES and race/ethnicity are often quite confounded, making it difficult to disentangle issues of race/ethnicity from issues of lower versus higher SES parenting (Hoff, Laursen, & Tardiff, 2002). Therefore, readers must exercise caution whenever they encounter research studies claiming to uncover racial/ethnic differences in parenting.

Nurturance

Nurturing behaviors involve how parents express love, sensitivity, affection, and care (as opposed to detachment, harshness, or directiveness) in daily interactions with their children. According to Brooks-Gunn and Markman (2005), mothers diagnosed with clinical depression tend to engage in less nurturance in interacting with their children. In addition, black mothers tended to be rated as demonstrating lower levels of important aspects of nurturance than white mothers.

Discipline

Discipline generally encompasses the manner in which parents respond to child behaviors that they consider to be inappropriate. One method for understanding differences in the use of parental discipline is to categorize parenting styles into *authoritative* parenting (characterized by warm, firm, and fair control), *permissive* parenting (characterized by leniency, few demands on children), *authoritarian* parenting (characterized by emphasis on control, unquestioned obedience, and punishment), and *uninvolved* parenting (characterized by little or no parental demands or communication and child neglect). Lower SES families tend to use more authoritarian styles than do higher SES families. Black mothers are more likely than white mothers to spank their children.

Children who display antisocial behavior early in life tend to come from home backgrounds characterized by poor parental management, inconsistent discipline practices, and limited supervision (Patterson, DeBaryshe, & Ramsey, 1989). First, ineffective parents often do not even recognize inappropriate behavior. Second, even if bad behavior is recognized, poor parenting practices fail to make punishment contingent on the child's bad behavior. Third, even if the child is punished for bad behavior, the punishment does not occur consistently. In some cases, poor parenting inadvertently reinforces antisocial behavior. This occurs when the level of conflict in the home reaches such a fever pitch, where parents inadvertently begin to redefine bad behavior and begin to overlook continued inappropriate behavior from the child.

When poorly home-socialized children start school, classroom teachers are the first to feel its effects. Veteran teachers who find their school population changing demographically (resulting from an influx of illegal immigration, court-ordered desegregation, or neighborhood/school rezoning changes) can often be heard complaining about increasing difficulties in teaching lower SES minority children. Such teachers often complain that sudden increases in defiance to authority, troublesome classroom behavior, and anti-learning attitudes makes teaching more difficult compared to when the school population was "less diverse" (see also Shipler, 2005). As a result of this poor early socialization, antisocial children are not equipped to handle the rules and social expectations found in most school settings. If the child has a lower IQ, is rejected by higher-performing school-socialized peers, and is attracted to other deviant peers, then the child is set along a path to additional behavioral problems, further school failure, and delinquency (Lynam, Moffitt, & Stouthamer-Loeber, 1993).

Teaching

Parents use didactic strategies for conveying information or skills to their children. High SES parents generally provide greater and more advanced language opportunities, engage in more frequent teaching interactions, and use more instructional materials—all of which help support and develop children's cognitive growth (Brooks-Gunn & Markman, 2005).

Language

This refers to the sheer amount of language heard by and directed to the child, the number of different words that parents use, the length of sentences used, questions asked, how parents may or may not elaborate on their child's speech, and the events discussed with the child. There are significant differences in home language usage between high versus low SES families. Highly educated parents with higher incomes are much more likely to talk a lot and read to their children, ask children more questions, use a wider variety of different words, and have more extended discussions of events (Brooks-Gunn & Markman, 2005). As these differences accumulate over the first few years of a child's life, the children in high SES families have engaged in virtually thousands more parent–child conversations compared to children from lower SES backgrounds (Brooks-Gunn & Markman, 2005). By age three, the vocabularies of low SES children are about half the size of high SES children and two-thirds the size of middle SES children. Given black/white racial disparities in SES status, simple black/white comparisons of children's vocabularies are equally as pronounced (Brooks-Gunn & Markman, 2005).

Materials

This refers to the extent to which cognitively and/or linguistically stimulating materials (e.g., books, magazines, toys, drawing materials) are provided to the child in the home. Research shows that black and Hispanic families have fewer reading and other educational materials in the home (Brooks-Gunn & Markman, 2005).

Monitoring

This refers to the extent to which parents watch or keep track of their child's whereabouts or activities when they are in or outside of the home. The research on SES and parental monitoring is sparse, and what effects have been observed in the few studies in which SES measures have been included have been weak (Hoff, Laursen, & Tardif, 2002).

Management

Management involves the quality with which parents schedule events, complete scheduled events, and how they manage the "rhythm" of the household (e.g., the regularity of bedtimes and/or bedtime routines, or how many meals the family eats together). Middle-class mothers participate in community activities (e.g., clubs, private lessons, sports teams, church-related activities) as volunteers more than working-class mothers, as well as involve their children in more of these activities than do working-class mothers (Hoff, Laursen, & Tardif, 2002). A brief summary of the most salient child-rearing differences associated with social class differences is provided in Table 3.8.

A Brief Comment on the Role of Genetics

Human behavior is multidimensional and complex, and is influenced by biological, genetic, and environmental factors. The previous discussion should not be misinterpreted to mean that economic and environmental factors constitute the sole cause of variation in educational outcomes for children in schools. To interpret a correlation

Table 3.8   Child-Rearing Differences Associated With Social Class Differences

Child-Rearing Issue	Lower-Class Families	Middle-Class Families
Overall Child-Rearing Philosophy ("The Mission")	Parenting is viewed as providing basic child needs for love, food, and safety. If done successfully, then children's development will naturally unfold.	The child's social, emotional, and cognitive development takes center stage as the number-one priority, hence home activities revolve around this objective.
Behaviors Supportive of Cognitive Development	Fewer books and educational materials in the home	More books and educational materials in the home
Behaviors Supportive of Academic Development	Little to no home routines for reinforcing schoolwork; homework completion; school learning is viewed as the teacher/school's responsibility	Enforce home routines that reinforce the notion that school comes first; homework completion and school learning viewed as both the parent and teacher/school's responsibility
Behaviors Supportive of Language Development	Families speak less to children; families read less to children; use more restricted vocabularies in interacting with children	Families speak more to children; families read more to children; use larger vocabularies in interacting with children
Discipline	Tendency for more authoritarian style; more likely to use spanking and/or hitting as a form of discipline; less likely to give positive feedback	Tendency for more authoritative style; less likely to use spanking and/or hitting as a form of discipline; more likely to give positive feedback
Parent–Child Communication	More likely to give commands and/or prohibitions (e.g., "Put that fork down!"); less likely to verbally communicate in ways that elicit responses from children	More likely to give commands containing logical justifications (e.g., "Why don't you give me that fork so that you won't get hurt?"); more likely to verbally communicate in ways that elicit responses from children (e.g., "That's a horse. What does a horsie say?")
Involving Children in Outside Activities	Less likely to involve children in outside community activities (clubs, private lessons, sports teams, or church-related activities)	More likely to involve children in outside community activities (clubs, private lessons, sports teams, or church-related activities)

(Adapted from Hoff, Laursen, & Tardif, 2002; Hymowitz, 2006; Lareau, 2011)

between a social variable (e.g., variables related to SES) and a phenotype (e.g., behavior or test performance) as *causal*, without considering that genetics could mediate this relationship, is to commit the *sociologist's fallacy* (see Glossary). Genetic variation within subpopulations is significantly correlated with SES variables, and parents pass their genes to their biological children just as they play a significant role in fashioning their home environments. For example, high IQ parents are predisposed to talk frequently and have larger vocabularies. The observation that their offspring also have large vocabularies may be caused by a *combination* of both modeling and the fact that high IQ parents are more likely to have higher IQ children who are predisposed toward understanding and using more advanced language.

At the same time, the home, family, neighborhood, and other environmental contexts create both risk and protective factors that can modify the role played by genes in human development. Although genetic influences play an important role in human development, there are also important limitations of genetic influences, as even identical twins are not 100 percent identical in every behavioral trait. Genetic influences are not constant over time, as constancy is often interrupted by environmental influences (Wright, Tibbetts, & Daigle, 2008). Key foundational principles that describe the complex interrelationship between genetic and environmental influences are briefly summarized in Sidebar 3.8.

Sidebar 3.8   Basic Principles for Understanding Genetic and Environmental Influences on Human Behavior

- Individual differences in genetic factors explain a large proportion of variation in human phenotypic traits and behaviors.
- Genetic factors, by themselves, cannot totally explain all causes of complex human behavior, temperament, and cognition. Although monozygotic (identical) twins are very similar on many traits, they also differ in some traits in surprising ways.
- Heritability estimates, and the influence of genetically based characteristics, change over an individual's lifetime and vary according to the environment in which they function. That is, the extent to which genetic variability explains outcomes fluctuates with particular behaviors at particular developmental stages. For example, heritability estimates for IQ increase from about 15 percent during infancy to 40 percent during childhood to 90 percent in adulthood. In addition, heritability estimates for adult criminality are stronger than those for juvenile delinquency.
- The greater degree to which environments are made to be more uniform (e.g., through egalitarian advocacy movements in society), the more that observed differences in phenotypes are better explained by genetic factors (i.e., heritability increases).
- Differences among individuals in their genetic composition produce differences in the manner in which individuals respond to changes in their environment.

- Heritability estimates for a given population can be affected by whatever range of factors are specific to a population, such as sample size, age, gender, sample location, and the outcome variable of interest. In regards to this last factor, relatively common developmental behaviors (e.g., non-serious juvenile mischief) will have low heritability estimates, whereas more rare behaviors (e.g., serious criminal conduct) will yield higher heritability estimates.
- If a population is studied within a context that has little environmental variation, then heritability estimates will be higher for that population compared to populations that exist within highly variable environments. For example, genetic factors will be a stronger explanation for criminal behaviors in a population of middle-class college students, because the degree of environmental variation is restricted in this population.
- The influence of genes is stronger in some environments and weaker in others. For example, environments containing extremely noxious and harmful conditions may suppress or limit genetic predispositions for expression of some behaviors, compared to what would be the case in more advantageous environments.

(Adapted from Plomin, DeFries, McClearn, & McGuffin, 2008; Rutter, 2006; Wright, Tibbetts, & Daigle, 2008)

THE IMPACT OF CRIME ON NEIGHBORHOODS AND FAMILIES

Sampson (2011) coined the term *concentrated disadvantage* (p. 211) in referring to neighborhoods in which poverty, unemployment, family disruption, racial minority status, crime, and violence are clustered in the same neighborhoods. Most middle-class families (of all races/ethnicities) live in neighborhoods in which crime is relatively rare. Aside from occasional property crime pranks by juveniles, middle-class families by and large do not have to worry about their personal safety when walking in the neighborhood at night, or that their homes would be burglarized during the day while they are at work. The same cannot be said for citizens living in poorer neighborhoods, particularly those in the nation's inner cities. Roth (1994) adds his observation on the impact of crime on the business health of poor inner-city neighborhoods:

Crime has a devastating impact on business health in inner city neighborhoods. Here, businesses that were once thriving find that they must leave urban neighborhoods due to the inconvenience and added costs of crime (i.e., losses from theft, vandalism, arson, and the cost of insurance). In addition, middle class patrons understandably avoid doing business in high crime neighborhoods. As a result, businesses are forced to close, taking with them many jobs that could provide at minimum entry level employment for inner-city adolescents. This, in turn, removes opportunities for young people to develop the work skills and attendant attitudes that would enable them to rise to higher management positions in businesses. (p. 248)

Neighborhoods differ considerably in the extent to which personal anonymity and adult supervision exert a deterring effect on crime. *Anonymity* refers to the extent to which youth and their families are known by name by others in the neighborhood. *Adult supervision* refers to the extent to which adults closely monitor, reward, and/or sanction juvenile behavior. In smaller towns in rural and suburban America, adult supervision of children and youth is an integral component of family life. Delinquent-prone youth avoid vandalizing property or stealing from neighbors, as this would run the risk of personal identification and police arrest, as well as exposure to family members (most importantly, fathers) whom perpetrators fear and respect. In urban neighborhoods where adult supervision is more lax, many children and youth are often truant from school and can create mayhem in communities with little fear of identification and arrest. Even if arrested, a growing criminal record means little to youth who have no desire for college or future employment in a prestige occupation. Roth (1994) offers an interesting perspective on the link between the absence of stable fathers and community crime:

> As men became less essential to their families for support, their influence upon and commitment to their families declined, and desertion by fathers became commonplace. This had an important impact on the orderliness of inner-city neighborhoods, for one reason in particular which is rarely acknowledged. . . . In the often lawless . . . conditions of inner-city neighborhoods, the threat of personal retaliation may be a powerful deterrent to predatory delinquents. Such fear of retaliation can prevent a great deal of minor crime like vandalism and petty theft that can in time demoralize a community. When strong adult men are not around, predatory adolescents are given an open season . . . to prey on the weaker members of their communities. (pp. 246–247)

Large housing projects in major cities magnify the problem of crime found in larger metropolitan urban communities. In the seminal text *The Truly Disadvantaged*, published in 1987, sociologist William Julius Wilson describes in detail life in the Robert Taylor Homes, a large Chicago public housing project that was eventually demolished completely in 2007. Wilson reported that this single housing project, which was home to less than 1 percent of the approximately 3 million persons living in Chicago at the time, accounted for approximately 10 percent of the murders, rapes, and aggravated assaults in the city.

Children's Exposure to Crime

Ceballo, Dahl, Aretakis, and Ramirez (2001) summarize the results of numerous investigations on the effect of children's exposure to crime and violence in poor urban neighborhoods. In one study, for example, more than 80 percent of a sample of fifth- and sixth-graders attending a metropolitan school system reported regularly hearing the sounds of gunfire in their neighborhoods, and one in every six of these children reported having witnessed a homicide. In another study, 9 percent of a sample of inner-city adolescents reported that they had been assaulted with a weapon, whereas this figure was only 2 percent in a sample of upper-middle-class youths. In the inner-city sample, 22 percent reported that their lives had been threatened, compared to 12 percent in the upper-middle-class sample. In another study, 39 percent of students in the sample reported witnessing a shooting, and 50 percent of the shooting victims were known to the children as friends, classmates, neighbors, or family members.

According to Ceballo et al. (2001), inner-city children with disproportionately high exposure to community crime and violence experience an increased susceptibility to externalizing behavior problems, general anxiety and distress, and posttraumatic stress disorder (PTSD) symptoms (e.g., sleep disturbances, constricted affect, loss of interest in previously pleasurable activities, and avoidance behaviors). Complicating matters is the fact that many parents generally *underestimate* their children's exposure to violence, which may subsequently impair their ability to effectively monitor and supervise their children.

Effects of Parental Incarceration

Crime can also affect families in more personal ways. The overrepresentation of racial/ethnic minorities in U.S. state and federal prison system is well documented (Eddy & Poehlmann, 2010). Consequently, African American, Hispanic, and American Indian/Alaskan Natives are similarly overrepresented (compared to their representation in the general population) among children of incarcerated parents (Eddy & Poehlmann, 2010). Caucasian children are roughly 57 percent of the general U.S. population, but only 28 percent of children with an imprisoned parent. Hispanic/Latino children make up about 21 percent of both the general population and children with an imprisoned parent. African American/black children account for only 15 percent of the general population, but they represent 45 percent of children of incarcerated parents (Glaze & Maruschak, 2008).

Obviously, parental incarceration disrupts parent–child interaction, but the nature of its effects on children vary as a function of the developmental period in which parental incarceration occurs. Forming attachments to important parent figures is a key developmental task of infancy and early childhood (Bowlby, 1982). When close parents who have cared for a young child go to jail or prison, the children experience acute anxiety and distress, sadness, fear, anger, and confusion (Eddy & Poehlmann, 2010).

Newborns and young infants are not even aware that a parent has left the home for incarceration. For slightly older children, however, common reactive behaviors include excessive worrying, acting out, feelings of loneliness, manifestations of developmental regressions, and sleep problems—to name a few. Complicating matters is the fact that very young children do not possess the language and communication skills to understand why their mother or father is leaving them, as they are not yet able to fully comprehend the concept of incarceration. Only as children get older are they able to cognitively process and articulate distinctions between right and wrong, abstractions related to rules and laws, and the potential consequences of wrong actions.

Children of incarcerated parents between the ages of 5 and 9 often face a different set of problems. For these children, parental incarceration can interfere with the development of age-appropriate social and academic competencies (Eddy & Poehlmann, 2010). For example, these students must face the risk of stigmatization in the school context. Such students are also at-risk for being attracted to, and associating with, delinquent peers.

Many different factors influence the quality of how children cope with a disrupted relationship resulting from a parent's incarceration (see extensive discussion in Eddy & Poehlmann, 2010). For example, children who actually witness the parent's arrest (i.e., see the parent handcuffed and/or driven away in the back of a police car) may experience trauma related to this event. Many children of incarcerated mothers live with their grandparents during maternal imprisonment, whereas a large majority of children of incarcerated fathers continue to live with their biological mothers. Different correctional facilities have different policies concerning contact with outside family members. In some prisons, inmates can only place collect calls to outside family members, and only at specified times. Visitation times for family members are also rigorously monitored. Very young children may feel extremely frightened or upset, depending on the degree to which the prison visitation environment is hospitable.

The social stigma associated with parental incarceration often causes secrecy and distorted communications within families. This stigma transfers to school settings, where children of incarcerated parents may avoid talking to friends about their home situation, for fear of teasing or unwanted attention. Unfortunately, it also needs to be said that the pervasiveness of parental incarceration in some underclass minority communities has made this a somewhat normative life experience for many children (Swisher & Waller, 2008; Western & Wildeman, 2009). Eddy and Poehlmann (2010) review research that has found that adolescents of incarcerated parents are more likely to develop antisocial behaviors, to have failed a class, to be truant or suspended from school, or even to drop out of school. One cannot assume that persons with incarcerated parents will automatically grow up to be criminal offenders themselves, however, as numerous factors influence developmental outcomes.

Eddy and Poehlmann (2010) discuss methods that psychologists and counselors can use for assessing thoughts and feelings related to attachment issues in children of incarcerated parents. For example, Lopez and Bhat (2007) discuss efforts to initiate a support group for fostering resilience in elementary school-age children of incarcerated parents. In summary, intervention efforts for children of incarcerated parents must also be sensitive to the following issues: (a) helping children of incarcerated parents to connect with trustworthy adults at school who can both respect confidentiality and provide reliable social/academic support; (b) helping caregivers develop the skills to assist particularly younger children in labeling and organizing their feelings and thoughts before, during, and following visits with incarcerated parents.

IMMIGRATION STATUS

The laws that regulate who can legally immigrate to the United States, as well as the duration of their stay, have been both restrictive and expansive for different people at different times throughout U.S. history. Some immigrants are granted a status that allows them to live in the United States permanently, whereas others have a status that allows them to be in the United States only temporarily.

There are four main categories through which people may gain a lawful permanent resident status in the United States. A person can become a permanent U.S. citizen through (a) having a close family member who is a U.S. citizen or lawful permanent resident; (b) having a special skill or knowledge that is useful to an U.S. employer; (c) winning a spot in a special lottery of extra visas; or (d) being a member of a special category for protected classes of people (e.g., refugees seeking asylum).

Even if someone does fit into one of these existing categories to obtain permanent status, the person may still not be allowed to enter or stay in the United States for various reasons. These reasons may include having convictions for crimes; being a threat to national security; participating in the persecution of others; the inability to show they can support themselves without receipt of government assistance; having falsely declared oneself to be a U.S. citizen; having immigration violations; and being in the United States without permission for extended periods.

There are a variety of reasons why individuals living in a non-American country choose to immigrate to the United States. Persons who migrate to the United States do so for three primary reasons:

1. *Reunification with family.* The presence of one or more family members in the United States enables the rest of the family (spouses, children, parents) to

immigrate to the United States under family reunification laws (which require demonstration of proof of the relationship and the capacity to support the relative). However, family reunification laws try to balance the right of a family to live together with the U.S. right to control immigration. Many sociologists refer to the concept of a "chain immigration" effect. Here, the first person who immigrates to the United States sends optimistic information to loved ones back home, which in turn motivates them to immigrate to the United States. After these family members migrate to the United States, they in turn send optimistic information to other relatives in the home country, which in turn feeds more interest in coming to the United States to live.

2. *Better financial opportunities.* Many persons migrate to the United States in order to take advantage of higher wages and the perception of a higher standard of living that is associated with working in the United States. For poor families in the Mexican economy, for example, the pay for low-level jobs is very low, and is insufficient for feeding families and providing children with adequate health care (e.g., see Dougherty, 2005). Although U.S. businesses—motivated to hire inexpensive labor from abroad—pay wages that are too low to attract U.S. workers, they are a huge incentive for immigrants seeking better living and educational opportunities for their children in the United States.

   Some parents of older children will send their offspring abroad in hopes that they will attain a better lifestyle than the parents have acquired. To many non-Americans, the United States offers a huge range of high-quality educational opportunities (e.g., top-tier universities and colleges, elite high schools, professional training institutes) that lay the foundation for a better life for graduates.

3. *Freedom and safety from persecution.* When a person seeks the *right of asylum,* or *political asylum,* it means that a person persecuted for political opinions or religious beliefs in his or her own country may be protected by another sovereign authority or a foreign country. *Refugees* are persons admitted to the United States based on a well-founded indication that they have cause to fear persecution in their home country. In the period from 1975 to 2005, the United States has resettled more than 2 million refugees, with approximately one-half having arrived as children (Center for Mental Health in Schools, 2010).

Requirements for American Citizenship

Immigrants must first be lawful permanent residents before they may apply to become a U.S. citizen. No one can apply to be a U.S. citizen without first being a lawful permanent resident. To qualify to apply for citizenship, lawful permanent residents must show that (a) they have been permanent residents at least 5 years (in some cases 3 years) and that half of that time they have been physically in the United States; (b) they have not abandoned their residency or committed an act for which they could lose their permanent residency; (c) they are persons of good moral character; (d) they speak, read, and write English; (e) they can pass a U.S. civics test; and (f) they will take an oath of loyalty to the United States.

According to 2009 Census data (Grieco & Trevelyan, 2010), more than half of all foreign-born persons living in the United States were from Latin America. The largest number of foreign-born persons living in the United States were from the country of Mexico (i.e., 29.8 percent of the total foreign-born population). The largest percentage of the total foreign-born population living in the United States settled in California (25.8%), followed by New York (10.8%), Texas (10.3%), and Florida (9%). Many immigrants come to the United States without degrees from and/or training in higher education. Therefore, other avenues for economic advancement are pursued. Many immigrants thrive in small business ventures (e.g., shops, restaurants, stores in inner-city neighborhoods) that require extremely long hours and help from their children and other immigrant relatives in order to achieve success. Many immigrants find prime opportunities to take over businesses that indigenous Americans have little interest in, because these businesses are located in poorer neighborhoods in major cities (e.g., Korean-owned shops in inner-city black neighborhoods).

Illegal Status

An illegal immigrant in the United States is an alien (noncitizen) who has entered the United States without government permission or stayed beyond the termination date of a visa. As of March 2010, approximately 11.2 million unauthorized immigrants (approximately 3–4 percent of the nation's population) were living in the United States (Pew Hispanic Center, 2011c). Approximately 350,000 children were born to at least one unauthorized-immigrant parent in the year 2009 (Pew Hispanic Center, 2011c).

Illegal immigrants continue to outpace the number of legal immigrants in the United States, which is a trend that has held steady since the 1990s. The majority of illegal immigrants continue to concentrate in U.S. communities with large numbers of Hispanics, but increasing numbers of undocumented immigrants are settling throughout the rest of the country (Pew Hispanic Center, 2011c).

The 10 states with the highest number of illegal immigrants (as of 2010), and the associated change in those states' percentages of illegal immigrants between 2000 to 2010, are depicted in Table 3.9. The countries of origin from which illegal immigrants have come, and the associated change in each country's representation between 2000 and 2010, are depicted in Table 3.10.

Cities in the United States that follow practices that protect illegal immigrants—either by law (*de jure*) or by habit (*de facto*)—are called *sanctuary cities*. These cities do

Table 3.9 State of Residence of the Unauthorized Immigrant Population: January 2000 to January 2011

State of Residence	Estimated Population in January of:		Percentage Change 2000 to 2011
	2000	2011	
All States	8,460,000	11,510,000	+36
California	2,510,000	2,830,000	+12
Texas	1,090,000	1,790,000	+64
Florida	800,000	740,000	−8
New York	540,000	630,000	+18
Illinois	440,000	550,000	+26
Georgia	220,000	440,000	+95
New Jersey	350,000	420,000	+19
North Carolina	260,000	400,000	+53
Arizona	330,000	360,000	+9
Washington (state)	170,000	260,000	+51
Other States	1,750,000	3,100,000	+77

(Adapted from Hoefer, Rytina, & Baker, 2012)

Table 3.10 Country of Birth of the Unauthorized Immigrant Population in the United States: January 2000 to January 2011

Country of Birth	Estimated Numbers in January of:		Percentage Change 2000 to 2011
	2000	2011	
All Countries	8,460,000	11,510,000	+36
Mexico	4,680,000	6,800,000	+45
El Salvador	430,000	660,000	+55
Guatemala	290,000	520,000	+82
Honduras	160,000	380,000	+132
China	190,000	280,000	+43
Philippines	200,000	270,000	+35
India	120,000	240,000	+94
Korea	180,000	230,000	+31
Ecuador	110,000	210,000	+83
Vietnam	160,000	170,000	+10
Other Countries	1,940,000	1,750,000	−10

(Adapted from Hoefer, Rytina, & Baker, 2012)

not allow municipal funds or resources to be used to enforce federal immigration laws, typically by not allowing police or municipal employees to inquire about a person's immigration status.

Unauthorized migrants are much more likely to be in broad occupation groups that require little education or do not have strict licensing requirements. The percentages of workers in farming, fishing, and forestry occupations; building cleaning/maintenance occupations; construction, food preparation, and production occupations; and transportation and material-moving occupations who are undocumented immigrants exceeds the overall proportion of all workers in the United States who are of undocumented status. A brief description of the life of an illegal immigrant, as adapted from an actual news article, is depicted in Sidebar 3.9.

Sidebar 3.9   The Life of an Undocumented Worker in the United States

In Mexico, Alfredo (not his real name) had worked on a fishing boat since he was 12 years old, earning the equivalent of 10 U.S. dollars per day. Because his family could not afford to buy him books and school supplies, he never attended school. Thus, he cannot speak English or read and write in any language. In 2008, Alfredo paid a smuggler, popularly known as *el coyote*, $2,700 that he and his family had saved over the years to lead Alfredo across the U.S. border into Tucson, Arizona. For three days during this journey, with inadequate food and water, he persevered across a brutal desert landscape during hot days and cold nights. He slept in the dirt and attempted to do most of his traveling at night in order to escape detection.

Upon his arrival in Tucson, he was herded into a van with 10 other illegal immigrants, and three days later arrived in Scranton, Pennsylvania, where a cousin lives. Today, Alfredo holds down two jobs—one at a landscaping company and another at a restaurant washing dishes—just to make ends meet. After putting in six long days a week, his take-home pay is approximately $300 per week. He goes to church every week and faithfully pays his taxes. He shares a small, three-bedroom apartment with four other undocumented workers, and he chips in $150 per month toward rent. He tries to send $200 home to his wife and four children in Mexico each week, which leaves him with a net profit of $250 per month for his personal expenses.

Unfortunately, his employers know all too well that, as an illegal immigrant, Alfredo is entitled to nothing. By U.S. standards, he is paid a very low hourly wage, and sometimes he is not paid at all. In one instance, his pay was a month overdue and $120 less than he expected. On another occasion, after finishing work one day, Alfredo asked his boss for a ride home. His boss told him that because he walked three days to get into the country, he could walk another few miles to get home. Alfredo feels he has no choice but to accept these and other indignities as an unavoidable by-product of the position he chose to put himself in. He and his fellow undocumented brethren would never think of filing grievances against their employers for fear of deportation. Alfredo resigns himself to doing whatever his boss tells him to do, because he is just happy to be working and getting paid.

Ironically, Alfredo and his undocumented brethren live in an area of Scranton that is less safe than where he lived in Mexico, which in itself is known as a region notorious for poverty and violent crime. He often fears for his safety, and he vividly recalls how a friend of his was recently robbed at gunpoint for $200. Because of his friend's undocumented status, the crime was never reported. For these reasons, Alfredo now carries a .22-caliber pistol for protection.

Alfredo knows that he is breaking U.S. immigration laws, but he candidly admits that he does not feel like he is a criminal. Given the cold realities of having a large family to support in Mexico, he feels that he has little choice. Alfredo states that "America is good. There is more opportunity here than back home. If you want to work, you can."

For Alfredo and many others like him, he feels that the risk is worth the hardship. As a result of his efforts so far, all four of his children are now able to attend school in Mexico. The downside is that he doesn't know when he will see his wife and family again.

Many immigrants such as Alfredo have been popularly described as "living life in the shadows." In posing for the picture that accompanied this article, Alfredo covers his face with his hands in order not to be identified by authorities.

(Adapted from Campeau, 2010)

Under the Citizenship Clause of the 14th Amendment to the United States Constitution, all persons born or naturalized in the United States are citizens of the United States and of the state wherein they reside. Although the Supreme Court has never explicitly ruled on whether children born in the United States to illegal-immigrant parents are entitled to birthright citizenship via the 14th Amendment (Heritage Foundation, 2005), it has generally been assumed that they are (Erler, West, & Marini, 2007).

Schooling is particularly important for immigrant youth, as "it is the first sustained, meaningful, and enduring participation in an institution of the new society" (Suárez-Orozco, Suárez-Orozco, & Todorova, 2008). In the material that follows, the challenges faced by immigrant youth and families, as they adapt to U.S. schooling, are discussed.

Longitudinal Immigrant Student Adaptation (LISA) Study

One of the best and most recent sources of data on the challenges that school-aged immigrant children face when coming to the United States is provided by the Longitudinal Immigrant Student Adaptation (LISA) study reported in Suárez-Orozco, Suárez-Orozco, and Todorova (2008). In the LISA study (spanning the years between 1997–2002), approximately 309 school-aged students from Central America (e.g., Nicaragua, El Salvador, Honduras, Guatemala), China, the Dominican Republic, Haiti, and Mexico were recruited for participation. Once in the United States, these students enrolled in 100 public schools in seven Boston and San Francisco school districts known for having high densities of newly arrived immigrants. According to the principal investigators, all participants in the study were born abroad, had parents who were also born in the same country, and "had developed a clear sense of identity rooted in their national origin prior to migration to the United States" (p. 6). LISA participants represented roughly equal proportions of girls and boys between the ages of 9 and 14 (mean age 11.8) during the first year of the study.

At the beginning of the study, participants had already spent at least two-thirds of their lives in the countries of origin and spoke a native language other than English upon arrival in the United States. On average, the mothers (or maternal figures) of LISA participants had 9.2 years of schooling in their countries of origin, ranging from a low of no formal schooling to a high of 21 years of schooling. On average, the fathers (or paternal figures) of LISA participants had 8.8 years of schooling in their countries of origin, ranging from a low of no formal schooling to a high of 26 years of schooling. Twenty-six percent of the LISA families had household incomes of less than $20,000 per year. Approximately half had household incomes between $20,000–$40,000 per year. A very small number of LISA families reported incomes greater than $80,000 per year. A majority of LISA families could be described as belonging to the "working poor," with parental occupations representing restaurant and janitorial services, production work, lower-level medical service work, and construction. Some of the parents were unemployed at the time of the study.

The living arrangements of LISA families ranged from households with as little as two persons (one child and one parent) to as many as 17 persons living under one roof (including extended family members of grandparents, cousins, aunts, and uncles). Most of the LISA families migrated from cities (rather than rural areas) in their countries of origin. Principal investigators, along with their team of bilingual and culturally diverse team of research assistants, used a variety of data collection methods (e.g., ethnographic participant observations, structured participant interviews, projective testing, parent and teacher interviews, individually administered academic achievement testing, school educational outcome data). The following five themes emerged from the LISA study:

1. *The emotional turmoil of migration.* Migration from one country to another can occur as a result of catastrophic economic, political, or natural conditions in the country

of origin, or from catastrophic life changes (e.g., loss of a marriage partner). Migration can occur in one of three ways. In the ideal circumstance, the entire family migrates together to the United States. In other circumstances, the parents must leave their children in the country of origin, come to the United States, then send for their children to join them in the United States at a later time. In a third circumstance, the parents may remain in the country of origin but send their children to the United States—with the intention of coming to the United States to join their children at a later time. Students who migrate to the United States from another country often have to leave the only family members they have ever known (e.g., siblings or parents from their country of origin) to live with other family members in the United States that they have barely known (e.g., cousins, aunts, uncles, grandparents). In some cases, migrant children are promised that reunification with their family after migration would occur quickly once they are settled in the United States. Unfortunately, it is much more common for financial obstacles, difficulties with legalizing immigration status, or sometimes parental separation/divorce to slow down family reunification, if it occurs at all. LISA researchers found that migrant children who were separated from their parents during the migration process were much more likely to report depression symptoms than migrant children who were not separated from their parents.

2. *Settling challenges once in the United States.* LISA researchers found that even after reunification with parents in the United States, strained family dynamics may still occur. During the temporary separation from parents during migration, the American family configuration may have adapted so well to the absence of the missing family member that when he or she rejoins the family, close relationships may need to be renegotiated. When children have been separated from their parents at a very young age, and for long periods of time, rebuilding the relationship is more difficult and complicated. Some migrant children may feel ambivalent or even angry about rejoining their parents. Reunified parents may have trouble reasserting their authority over their children, which may result in inconsistent or overindulgent parenting.

3. *Variation in within-family cultural dissonance.* Much has been written about the tensions that occur within families confronted with acculturation issues, particularly between children and their parents (Sam & Berry, 2006). Not surprisingly, the LISA researchers found that the immigrant youth they studied learned the unspoken rules of U.S. cultural expectations more quickly than did their parents. That is, the immigrant children moved with "increasing ease" between their schools into workplaces, shopping malls, movie theaters, and other recreational spaces. One would legitimately expect that children born and raised in U.S. society would develop values that clash with the more traditional values of their parents who, although living in the United States, were born in a

different country. However, the LISA researchers found that the intensity of this issue varied according to family history and ethnicity.

Nearly half of the Chinese and Dominican students reported that home "cultural clashes" were never an issue in their families. However, more than one-third of the Haitian students reported that such tensions occurred often or all the time. Although approximately 40 percent of the entire sample acknowledged that cultural clashes happened at home occasionally, approximately 38 percent of the entire sample reported no problems in this area. Roughly half of their sample reported that their parents followed child-rearing rules from the country of origin, and an equivalent portion of the sample reported that their parents had adapted to using a mix of child-rearing expectations and rules from both their country of origin and the United States.

Despite these cultural challenges, LISA researchers found that many immigrant youth often spoke of the complex combination of love, affection, appreciation, gratitude, responsibility, and sense of duty that characterized their family relationships. They exhibited a keen understanding and appreciation of their parents' sacrifices and struggles on their behalf to succeed academically (Suárez-Orozco et al., 2008).

4. *Higher academic motivation.* Many teachers who were interviewed appreciate the work ethic and attitudes of immigrant students and rated them *more favorably* than native-born students. Such teachers felt that immigrant students highly value education, have a well-developed desire to learn and take advantage of American U.S. opportunities, are more respectful of teachers, and are more disciplined. Researchers discovered that there is a strong press in immigrant homes for parents—many of whom have limited or no education—to encourage their children to do well academically to make up for what their parents lacked. Immigrant children had a clear and focused conviction that doing well academically is crucial for later success in life.

5. *Ethnic patterns in achievement decline.* It has been generally acknowledged that academic motivation, engagement, and grades decline the longer students remain in school. For immigrant children in the LISA study, all students showed a downward trajectory that began in the fourth year of the study, with the exception of the Chinese students. However, across all groups, girls were more likely than boys to be high achievers and to improve academically somewhat as they progressed through school.

FACTORS THAT INFLUENCE ENGLISH-LANGUAGE LEARNING

The most important variable responsible for the maintenance of sharp distinctions among ethnic groups is language. Groups who may be culturally different in many ways can at least find common ground and a minimum degree of mutual cooperation if they speak the same language. When groups do not speak the same language, the implications for civic life reverberate in where one chooses to live, how one is educated, where one finds a suitable job, and the extent to which one can comfortably function in the larger society.

Like all children, many non-English speakers acquire their first language in their families and communities. However, when children who speak a language other than English arrive at school without understanding English, they must simultaneously learn English itself and learn other school subjects through English (Valdés, Capitelli, & Alvarez, 2011). Children and youth who do not possess age-appropriate English-language fluency can be of two basic types: (1) children and youth who were born in another country and are immigrants to the United States, or (2) children and youth who were born in the United States, yet were raised in a non-English-speaking home environment that includes parents/caregivers who are immigrants.

The factors that influence how quickly and easily school-aged non-English speakers learn English are multifaceted, interactive, and complex. School-related factors that influence the quality and speed of English-language learning are discussed in Chapter 4. Home and family factors are discussed in the material that follows.

Immigrant Students Want to Learn English

As mentioned in the previous section, most of the immigrant school-aged children in the LISA study (Suárez-Orozco et al., 2008) came from families belonging to the working poor, with parental occupations represented by restaurant, janitorial, medical service, production, and construction work. When students were asked their opinions on the importance of learning English, the overwhelming majority of students expressed the following opinions: (1) they liked learning English, and they felt that (2) English is important for being successful in school; (3) English is important for getting a good job; and (4) English is important for getting ahead, getting opportunities, and succeeding in the United States. Approximately 90 percent of the sample cited the learning of English as a significant challenge that they needed to overcome in order to get ahead in the United States. At the same time, however, immigrant students' feelings about the importance of learning English exists in harmony with complementary feelings of loyalty toward, and valuing of, their native language.

Varieties of Bilingualism

At its most superficial level of understanding, *bilingualism* can be defined as competence in speaking two languages with at least a minimum level of proficiency in each language (Suárez-Orozco et al., 2008). In reality, however, there are qualitatively different manifestations of bilingualism competence, which are affected by a variety of developmental and experiential factors. A basic distinction made by most texts in bilingualism is between *basic interpersonal communication skills* versus *cognitive/academic language skills*. Basic interpersonal communication skills are those survival skills necessary for carrying out basic life transactions (e.g., interacting with shopkeepers, ordering food in a restaurant, socializing with friends). These language skills can be learned within a year or two with adequate exposure (Cummins, 1991). In contrast, cognitive/academic language skills are needed in the academic arena for formal learning in specific academic subjects, as well as understanding and producing scholarly products such as those required in schools. These skills require an average of approximately seven to ten years of intentional, systematic training and consistent exposure for their development (Cummins, 1991).

A bilingual individual who is equally as proficient in two languages may be an ideal, but is rare in reality (Suárez-Orozco et al., 2008). For example, a person may be a fluent writer and speaker of his or her native language, but may only be able to carry on very basic and simple speaking and writing tasks in a second language. Conversely, another person may be capable of quite sophisticated speaking and writing skills in a second language, but may only be capable of very simple reading and writing tasks in his or her native language. Some bilinguals may develop proficient speaking and writing skills in a new language, but they find that they are better able to verbally express heartfelt, deep emotions and feelings only in their native language.

The circumstances in which bilingual skills are demonstrated can also be quite varied across different individuals. Sometimes such differences are a function of the perceived status of one language relative to the other. If the native language is perceived as a lower-status language, then some individuals may grow up being actively discouraged from using their native language in a new country. These individuals view native language usage as something that is to be done only with close friends and family. Others learn that having proficiency in their native language (in addition to a second language of the host country) offers certain social and/or occupational advantages from developing and using native-language skills.

Factors That Shape the Development of English Learning

Recent figures on the percentage of Americans over the age of 5 who report speaking English versus a non-English language at home (as of 2009) are given in Table 3.11. A breakdown of states that are home to low, middle, and high percentages of persons who speak a non-English language at home as of 2009 (including those who report also speaking English at home) is given in Table 3.12.

The relationship between the effects of a learner's age on language learning is complex. On the one hand, the younger a child is when they arrive in a new country, the more exposure they have to the new language to be learned (August & Shanahan, 2006). On the other hand, older children have a better handle on the rules of literacy in

Table 3.11   Proportion of U.S. Population (Aged 5 and Older) Speaking the Top 15 Most Frequent Languages at Home: 2009

Total Sample (N = 285,797,349)	Percentage of Total (100.00%)
Speak only English	80.00
Spanish or Spanish Creole	12.40
Chinese	0.90
Tagalog	0.52
French (including Patois, Cajun)	0.45
Vietnamese	0.43
German	0.38
Korean	0.36
Russian	0.30
Arabic	0.29
Other Asian languages	0.27
African languages	0.27
Italian	0.26
Portuguese or Portuguese Creole	0.25
French Creole	0.23

(adapted from U.S. Census Bureau, 2009d)

their native language, which helps them learn the rules of a second language more efficiently. Parental education in general, and the mother's education in particular, facilitates second-language learning (Gass & Selinker, 2001), primarily because children hear more academically oriented language and are read to more frequently at home. When students are grounded in at least basic reading and writing skills in their native language, the learning of a second language—with appropriate instructional supports— proceeds in a more efficient manner (August & Shanahan, 2006). In general, variation in cognitive ability (operationalized by an IQ score) is significantly correlated with general learning ability (Jensen, 1998a). It naturally follows that individual differences in general cognitive ability are also correlated positively with the speed and depth of second language learning (Genesee, 1976; Littlewood, 1984; Skehan, 1998).

The frequency and quality of exposure to English-language speakers influences English learning, where the axiom "less contact, less learning" applies (Suárez-Orozco et al., 2008). Here, the more contact English-language learners have with peers and a social environment in which high-quality English is spoken, the higher the quality of English-language learning (the quality of English exposure in the school environment is addressed in Chapter 4). In the home environment, however, wide differences can be observed. As an example, Suárez-Orozco et al. (2008) found that Spanish-speaking

Table 3.12   States With Low, Middle, and High Percentages of Persons
Aged 5 and Older Who Speak a Language Other Than English at Home

States With < 8% Speaking Language Other Than English at Home	States With 8–18% Speaking Language Other Than English at Home	States With > 18% Speaking Language Other Than English at Home
Alabama	Alaska	Arizona
Arkansas	Delaware	California
Indiana	District of Columbia	Connecticut
Iowa	Georgia	Florida
Kentucky	Idaho	Hawaii
Maine	Kansas	Illinois
Mississippi	Louisiana	Massachusetts
Missouri	Maryland	Nevada
Montana	Michigan	New Jersey
North Dakota	Minnesota	New Mexico
Ohio	Nebraska	New York
South Carolina	New Hampshire	Rhode Island
South Dakota	North Carolina	Texas
Tennessee	Oklahoma	
Vermont	Oregon	
West Virginia	Pennsylvania	
Wyoming	Utah	
	Virginia	
	Washington	
	Wisconsin	

Includes persons who report speaking a language *in addition to English* at home.
(U.S. Census Bureau, 2009d)

immigrant children tended to spend more than half of their radio-listening and
television-watching time tuned into the Spanish media, which is a booming industry in
many parts of America (Louie, 2003). In contrast, approximately one-fifth of Chinese
participants in their sample watched television in Cantonese or Mandarin, and no
Haitian students watched Haitian local television programs.

PARENTING INTERVENTIONS

Parent education is one intervention method for helping families make positive changes
for the benefit of their children. As quoted from Einzig (1996) in Smith, Perou, and
Lesesne (2002), parent education generally describes a range of teaching and support
programs that focus on the skills, feelings, knowledge, and tasks of being a parent. There is
no cookie-cutter template for parent education programs, obviously; because the nature of
family needs differ, different programs have different instructional goals, and the methods
for delivering instruction vary considerably. In a general sense, the target population for

parent education programs align themselves along a continuum from all parent groups to narrowly defined groups who are targeted as having very specific family issues.

For example, any family can benefit from education on issues that all families must face (e.g., child discipline). Other programs focus on stressful family events, such as what occurs when new parents are faced with the birth of their first child. Some programs focus on common transition points that need to be negotiated smoothly (e.g., children starting school for the first time, or children transitioning from junior high to high school). Some programs focus on parenting issues involving particular groups of children, such as parenting children with disabilities. Other programs are geared toward vulnerable populations, such as parents who are low income, poorly educated, young and unwed, living in impoverished communities, or who have a higher vulnerability to mental health problems. Given disproportionalities in racial/ethnic representation of families experiencing these challenges, interventions designed to serve poor families end up serving a greater share of minority than nonminority families (see Brooks-Gunn & Markman, 2005).

Parent education programs also differ in their ultimate objectives and goals. At the very minimum, parent education programs are designed to impart knowledge (e.g., sequence of childhood developmental stages). Many programs are designed to simply modify the general child-rearing behavior of parents that are thought to be most helpful to child development (e.g., sensitizing parents on the importance of talking with their children frequently). Other programs focus on introducing and developing specific skills (e.g., how to read to children, or how to enforce bedtime rules). Some programs focus on improving the functioning of the adults in the family, with the hope that general positive changes will benefit children at least indirectly. For example, some programs focus on improving the quality of interactions between the husband and wife, or improving the quality of family economic planning and budgeting. Finally, some programs target issues that directly help adult parents personally, such as imparting knowledge that helps parents to pursue educational opportunities leading to a GED or a college degree.

The contexts in which parent education is delivered to target audiences also differ considerably. For example, interventions designed to modify the behavior of parents of young children (i.e., ages 0–4) can be home-based (i.e., involve a home-visiting component) or center- (or school-) based (Brooks-Gunn & Markman, 2005). It naturally follows that the nature of content delivery would also differ whenever parent education programs are held in different contexts. Instructional objectives are not always delivered by means of didactic lectures. As an example, in center and family literacy programs, age-appropriate activities are provided for both the parent and child to do together. In this context, parents are given instruction or watch role models demonstrate how to interact with young children in problem-solving activities. Family literacy programs attempt to modify how parents read to their children by teaching parents how to ask their children questions, provide feedback to child responses, initiate conversations that go beyond the immediate reading material, and delve deeper into assessing children's understanding of concepts (Brooks-Gunn & Markman, 2005). In parent training for child behavior problems, parents are shown videotaped vignettes of typical discipline situations experienced in the home, which include showing several ways to handle a particular situation.

Although many parent education programs produce demonstrable positive results, Hymowitz (2006) articulates some caveats that are important for interventionists to keep in mind:

> . . . such programs treat the parent not as a human being with a mind, a worldview, and values, but as a subject who performs a set of behaviors. They teach procedural parenting . . . [b]ut it should be clear by now that being a middle-class or an upwardly mobile immigrant mother or father does not mean simply performing a checklist of proper behaviors. It does not mean merely following procedures. It means believing on some intuitive level in "The Mission" and its larger framework of personal growth and fulfillment. In the case of poor parents, that means imagining a better life, if not for you, then for your kids. That's what makes the difference. . . . This is a self that procedural parenting ignores. (pp. 87–88)

BRAND-NAME INTERVENTIONS

School psychologists and other educators may feel overwhelmed that home and family problems observed in their places of employment are too pervasive and entrenched for one professional to handle alone. For this reason, enlisting interest in *brand-name interventions* (see Glossary) among a wide range of professionals is one avenue for initiating systemic change in school and other organizations. Select brand-name interventions, particularly relevant to home and family issues, are briefly summarized in the material that follows. Contact information for each program is provided in the Additional Resources at the end of this chapter.

Nurse Family Partnership

The Nurse Family Partnership (NFP) is the name given to a voluntary, free maternal and childhood health program that provides first-time moms with valuable knowledge and support throughout pregnancy and until their babies reach two years of age. Low-income first-time moms are partnered with nurse home visitors to receive the care and support necessary to have a healthy pregnancy, provide responsible and competent care for their children, and become more economically self-sufficient.

Home-care nurses assist new mothers to improve pregnancy outcomes by helping them to obtain quality prenatal care, improve nutritional/dietary behaviors, and reduce their use of cigarette, alcohol, and illegal substances. Home-care nurses also assist mothers to develop a plan for future personal development (e.g., helping mothers continue their education and/or find gainful employment).

The standard NFP implementation model is for eight nurse home visitors to serve a maximum of 25 families each (totaling 200 families). The activities of the eight home visitors are directed by a full-time nurse supervisor. The NFP program is administered through a central organization (NFP National Service Office), whose fundamental goal is to sustain existing sources and develop new sources of state and federal funding for the NFP program. The first step in becoming a local NFP implementing agency is to contact the local National Service Office Regional Program Developer, who in turn will work closely with interested parties to determine feasibility. Once feasibility is determined, the local agencies sign contracts to become official NFP implementing agencies. Local NFP implementing agencies are administered by a range of non- and for-profit entities, which include state and county health departments, community-based health centers, nursing associations, and hospitals, generally through maternal and child health services. In addition, the National Service Office ensures that local communities implement the NFP model with fidelity. The National Service Office provides consultation and assistance to local community NFP implementers to use the appropriate assessments and collect data necessary for ensuring program effectiveness, build community support for the program, and engage in sustainability efforts. The National Service Office helps communities to effectively advertise the NFP program to a broad range of community stakeholders in order that the volume of referrals can be maintained or increased. The NFP logic model can be viewed online at http://www.nursefamilypartnership.org/assets/PDF/Communities/ Implementation_Logic_Model. NFP profiles in each of 28 states can be viewed at http:// www.nursefamilypartnership.org/Communities/State-Profiles. Partnership locations within each state can be accessed at http://www.nursefamilypartnership.org/Locations

Extensive research documenting the effectiveness of the NFP model has been conducted over the past three decades, much of this research utilizing the "gold standard" of randomized, controlled trials across diverse population groups. Changes in outcome variables that have occurred as a result of the program include, but are not limited to, improved prenatal health, fewer childhood injuries, fewer subsequent pregnancies, increased time intervals between subsequent births, increased frequencies of maternal employment, and children's improved school readiness. Published effectiveness research can be accessed at http://www.nursefamilypartnership.org/proven-results/published-research

Functional Family Therapy

Functional Family Therapy (FFT) is the name given to an evidence-based, short-term intervention program where a therapist works with families of at-risk youth between the ages of 10 to 18 whose problems range from acting out to conduct disorders to alcohol and/or substance abuse. FFT targets the most vulnerable families, whose lives are characterized by limited resources, histories of failure, and frequent exposure to other social service systems. Treatment occurs within the context of approximately 12 sessions (on average) over a three- to four-month time period in a variety of settings (e.g., schools, child welfare facilities, probation and parole offices, mental health facilities).

FFT is described as an intervention that focuses on the assessment of risk and protective factors that impact the adolescent and his or her environment, with specific attention paid to both intrafamilial and extrafamilial factors, and how these present within and influence the therapeutic process. FFT works first to develop family members' inner strengths and sense of being able to improve their situations—even if modestly at first. These characteristics provide the family with a platform for change and future functioning that extends beyond the direct support of the therapist and other social systems (for a more detailed description of the FFT model, see Sexton, 2011).

FFT is implemented within many contexts that involve at-risk youth. The FFT model has been successfully replicated across the continuum of juvenile justice, mental health settings, child welfare systems, prevention and diversion type programs, after-care and parole programs, and traditional drug and alcohol and school-based programs.

FFT Inc. was formed in 1998 to train, consult with, and provide quality assurance for more than 220 local, state, national, and international organizations for implementing FFT. FFT Inc. has training programs in 44 U.S. states, as well as internationally (e.g., Norway, the Netherlands, Belgium, New Zealand, and Great Britain). FFT Inc. employs more than 20 staff members who train and consult with FFT training sites, provide FFT quality assurance, and coordinate numerous research initiatives. FFT Inc. has developed therapist and supervisor training manuals, specific assessments, as well as extensive video and presentation training materials and protocols. Books and videos on FFT are available through the American Psychological Association.

Research documenting the effectiveness of FFT includes studies that use highly controlled efficacy trials, quasi-experimental designs, and meta-analyses that compare effect sizes in FFT to other interventions for adolescent substance abusers. Examples of such studies can be accessed at http://www.fftinc.com/about_effect.html FFT has demonstrated positive program outcomes, which have included significant reductions in youth re-offending and violent behavior, reductions in sibling entry into high-risk behaviors, reductions in high school dropout rates, reduction in family conflicts, and improvements in family communication patterns.

To become an official certified FFT site, a general information packet is requested that provides important information on training fees and guidelines for assessing and preparing potential sites for supporting FFT. Completed applications are submitted to the national FFT Communications Director, after which the completed application is reviewed by an FFT steering committee. If approved, the FFT Communications Director and FFT CEO contact the potential site to discuss program design issues. FFT training dates are arranged, necessary training materials are purchased, and FFT therapists are hired by the site. FFT therapists receive intensive training and may gradually build caseloads as the model is learned. If the site is successful, then two additional phases prior to site certification occur, where site team supervisors are selected and trained, program data is reviewed, and any issues related to staff development, interagency linkage, and program expansion are discussed.

Multidimensional Treatment Foster Care

Multidimensional Treatment Foster Care (MTFC) is the name given to a program that advertises itself as a cost-effective alternative to regular foster care, group/residential treatment, or incarceration for chronically behaviorally disruptive youth. The program was originally developed at the Oregon Social Learning Center in its efforts to treat chronic juvenile delinquency. The goal of the MTFC program is to decrease problem behavior and to increase developmentally appropriate normative and pro-social behavior in children and adolescents who are in need of out-of-home placement. Any juvenile justice, foster care, and mental health system can initiate youth referrals to MTFC, and the MTFC treatment model can be implemented by any organization or agency that provides services to children/youth with serious behavior problems and their families.

The MTFC program accomplishes treatment goals by incorporating close supervision for target youth, fair and consistent limits, predictable consequences for rule breaking, a supportive relationship with at least one mentoring adult, and reduced exposure to peers with similar problems. The intervention is multifaceted and occurs in multiple settings. The intervention components include behavioral parent training and support for MTFC foster parents, family therapy for biological parents (or other after-care resources), skills training and supportive therapy for youth, school-based behavioral interventions and academic support, and psychiatric consultation and medication management when needed.

Three versions of MTFC are specifically designed to serve three age groupings:

- The Multidimensional Treatment Foster Care for Preschoolers (MTFC-P) program is designed to serve children between the ages of 3 to 6 years, and is delivered through a treatment team approach in which foster parents receive training and ongoing consultation/support from program staff. Children receive individual skills training and therapeutic playgroup, and birth parents (or other permanent placement resources) receive family therapy. The MTFC-P intervention employs a developmental framework in which the challenges of foster preschoolers are viewed from the perspective of delayed maturation (rather than strictly behavioral and emotional problems).

- The Multidimensional Treatment Foster Care for Middle Childhood (MTFC-C) program is designed to serve children between the ages of 7 to 11 years, who are in need of an out-of-home placement. Referred children may have been placed numerous times in foster care and may have complex co-morbid conditions. Most of these children have been involved in numerous treatment efforts prior to their referral to MTFC-C, and most have experienced at least one, if not multiple, failed out-of-home placements prior to referral. The treatment plan should entail having children participate exclusively in MTFC-C as the sole comprehensive treatment service. Referrals to MTFC-C programs are most appropriate after in-home family preservation programs or placements in regular foster care have been tried or when children are returning from highly restrictive institutional or group care placements.
- The Multidimensional Treatment Foster Care for Adolescents (MTFC-A) program serves adolescents between the ages of 12 to 17. The two major goals of the MTFC-A program are to create opportunities so that youth are able to successfully live in families rather than in group or institutional settings, and to simultaneously prepare their parents, relatives, or other after-care resources to provide youth with effective parenting so that the positive changes made while the youth are placed in MTFC-A are long-term.

  Four key elements of treatment are targeted during placement and after-care: (1) providing youth with a consistent reinforcing environment, where the adolescent is mentored and encouraged to develop academic and positive living skills, (2) providing daily structure with clear expectations and limits, with well-specified consequences delivered in a teaching-oriented manner, (3) providing close supervision of the youth's whereabouts, and (4) helping youth to avoid deviant peer associations while providing them with the support and assistance needed to establish prosocial peer relationships. Referred youth should not have an IQ score less than 70 and are required to participate exclusively in MTFC-A as the sole comprehensive treatment service. Youth exhibiting acutely suicidal, homicidal, or psychotic behavior, or who are in need of treatment for sex offenses or substance abuse, will not be placed in the MTFC-A program. Referrals to MTFC-A programs are most appropriate after in-home family preservation programs have been tried or when youth are returning from highly restrictive institutional or group care placements. Families of the MTFC-A youth participate in the family therapy component of treatment and engage in services immediately upon placement in the program.

TFC Consultants, Inc., founded in 2002, is the organization that is dedicated to the implementation of model-adherent MTFC programs. TFC Consultants provides consultation, training, and technical assistance to new and existing MTFC programs and helps service providers, policy makers, and community leaders resolve issues related to the implementation of evidence-based practices. A description of these activities is available by accessing http://www.mtfc.com/implementation.html Use of the model name Multidimensional Treatment Foster Care and its abbreviation, MTFC, are both registered service marks of OSLC Community Programs (http://www.oslccp.org/ocp/index.cfm), and are restricted to programs that are certified or are receiving clinical supervision from TFC Consultants, Inc. Through TFC Consultants, MTFC is being implemented in six counties in California and in more than 40 other locations throughout the United States. MTFC also has an international presence in Sweden, Norway, the Netherlands, and the United Kingdom. Published evaluation studies of MTFC can be accessed at http://www.mtfc.com/journal_articles.html

Multisystemic Therapy

Multisystemic Therapy (MST) is described by its developers as an intensive family- and community-based treatment program that focuses on the "entire world of chronic and violent juvenile offenders" (i.e., their homes and families, schools and teachers, neighborhoods and friends; see Henggeler, Schoenwald, Borduin, Rowland, & Cunningham, 2009). Philosophically, MST strives to change how youth function in their natural home, school, and neighborhood settings in ways that promote pro-social behavior while decreasing antisocial behavior. MST works with both male and female offenders between the ages of 12 and 17 who have very long arrest histories. Therapists work with family members daily or weekly to achieve behavior changes that can be observed and measured. The effectiveness of these therapeutic efforts is evaluated continuously from multiple perspectives (e.g., caregivers, identified youth, and school teachers).

An important hallmark of the MST model is that MST-trained clinicians go to where the child is (home, neighborhood) and are on call 24 hours a day, seven days a week. Clinicians work intensively with parents and caregivers to help them gain control of difficult problem situations involving the adolescent. As examples, the therapist works with caregivers to help the adolescent maintain his or her focus on school and gaining job skills, and encourages interest in constructive sports and recreational activities as an alternative to "hanging out."

MST blends the best elements from a variety of clinical treatment models, which include cognitive-behavioral therapy, behavior management training, and other family therapy and community psychology treatments. MST has been extensively researched over nearly 30 years, and has demonstrated effectiveness with white, African American, and Latino populations in reducing adolescents' out-of-home placements, reducing school dropout rates, reducing re-arrest rates, improving family relationships, decreasing psychiatric symptoms, and decreasing drug and alcohol abuses.

As the effectiveness of MST in treating serious juvenile offenders became known to the larger practice and research communities in the 1990s, several groups of investigators are currently using standard MST as a platform to adapt MST for use with other challenging clinical populations (e.g., psychiatric problems, child abuse and neglect, substance abuse, problem sexual behaviors, and healthcare conditions such as diabetes, HIV infection, and obesity), and ultimately transport MST methods to other community-based programs.

Medical University of South Carolina licensed MST Services in 1996 to train therapists in MST and provide them and their supervisors with support, resources, and ongoing coaching. In addition to training, MST services also provides assistance in budgeting and business planning, hiring, record-keeping, reducing staff attrition, quality assurance, marketing, and public relations. MST offers both full and provisional licenses to organizations that comply with all of the policies and procedures in the MST Manuals in connection with the training of staff in licensed MST programs. Licensure also indicates an agreement to ensure that all of its employees involved with the MST System are competent and fully trained in the use of the MST System. According to the MST website, MST teams currently operate in 34 states, the District of Columbia, and in 13 countries outside of the United States. Communities interested in becoming a licensed provider of MST services can access an online description of what is involved by accessing http://mstservices.com/programdesign.pdf

The Incredible Years

According to its developers, The Incredible Years (IY) is a parent training, teacher training, and child social skills training program designed to reduce children's aggression, reduce behavior problems, and increase social competence at home and at school. The IY program was introduced in the early 1980s as a video and group-based parent training method for reducing behavioral problems and promoting social and emotional competence in young children between the ages of 3 to 8 (Webster-Stratton & Herman, 2010). Since then, IY interventions and materials have been translated into many languages and are being used in more than 15 countries.

The IY program is designed to reduce the multiple risk factors associated with poor parenting and classroom management practices, early-onset conduct problems, and emotional difficulties in young children. To facilitate this goal, the IY Training Series includes three complementary curricula for parents, teachers, and children, all of which include similar training methods and processes.

The IY program is grounded in a comprehensive theoretical model, which conceptualizes specific risk and protective factors (associated with child antisocial behaviors) as being associated with three domains (Webster-Stratton & Herman, 2010). In the school/teacher domain, the transition to elementary school represents a critical developmental milestone that is a challenge for children exhibiting aggressive and/or disruptive behaviors. The IY teaching training (IY-TT) program is a six-day program for teachers, school counselors, and school psychologists that is designed to improve teachers' classroom management strategies for dealing with class misbehavior; promote positive teacher–student relationships with difficult children; strengthen students' social skills and emotional regulation in the classroom and lunchroom, on the playground and the bus; and facilitate improved communication with parents of difficult children (see Webster-Stratton, 2000).

In the children/peers domain, the roots of child difficulties revolve around problems with inattentiveness, impulsivity, high rates of aggression, delays in social and cognitive skills, and poor emotional regulation skills. As a result, such children enter school with poor school readiness skills, cognitive deficits, and language/developmental delays. There are two versions of the IY child program (Webster-Stratton & Herman, 2010). In the selective prevention classroom version, teachers deliver 60 social-emotional lessons and small-group activities twice a week, with separate lesson plans for preschool, kindergarten, and first- and second-grade classrooms. The second version is a small-group therapeutic "Dinosaur School" where accredited IY group leaders work with groups of four to six children in one- to two-hour therapy sessions. The program can be offered as a pull-out therapy program twice a week for an hour in schools, or can be offered in two-hour sessions while the parents participate in the parent group. This 22-week program consists of a series of DVD programs (more than 180 vignettes) that teach children appropriate classroom behavior, problem-solving strategies, social skills, feelings literacy, and emotional self-regulation skills.

The parents/family component of IY is rooted in the empirically supported conclusion that serious antisocial behavior is linked to specific parenting practices during the toddler years when parents fail to bond with their children or to provide effective parenting. Specific parent interpersonal characteristics put parents and children at risk for developing these maladaptive interactions (e.g., parent psychopathology, inter-parental conflict and divorce, maternal insularity, and lack of support). In addition, many parents are vulnerable to specific risk factors, such as low income, unemployment, low education, and crowded living conditions. Poor parenting risk factors interact with biological and developmental child risk factors noted earlier, resulting in toxic parent–child interactions where the parent acquiesces to children's defiance and escalating demands. In turn, the parent is at greater risk for responding with harsh or abusive discipline practices when the child escalates to severe misbehavior.

The BASIC parent programs target four separate age groups: baby (0–1 year), toddler (1–3 years), preschool (3–6 years), and school age (6–12 years). Each of these programs includes age-appropriate examples of culturally diverse families dealing with the social, behavioral, and emotional problems of children with varying temperaments (Webster-

Stratton & Herman, 2010). The baby program is eight to nine weekly, two-hour sessions with parents and babies present. The BASIC toddler parent-training program is usually completed in 12 weekly, two-hour sessions, whereas the preschool and school-age programs are 18 to 20 weekly sessions. The cornerstone of the program involves the use of video vignettes of modeled parenting skills (more than 300 vignettes, each lasting approximately one to three minutes) shown by two trained group leaders to groups of approximately 8 to 12 parents. The videos demonstrate social learning and child development principles and serve as the stimulus for focused parent group discussions, problem solving, and collaborative learning. The intentional involvement of parent groups serves to reduce the parent isolation risk factor by building parent support networks.

In addition to the BASIC parenting programs, there are also three supplemental or adjunct parenting programs to be used with particular populations: the ADVANCE parenting program, which addresses parents' interpersonal risk factors, and two SCHOOL Readiness Programs, which focus on reading interactions, ways to coach children's homework, after-school monitoring, and collaboration with teachers. The content of the BASIC, ADVANCE, and SCHOOL programs is also provided in the text that parents use for the program, titled *The Incredible Years: A Trouble-shooting Guide for Parents of Children Ages 3–8 Years* (Webster-Stratton, 2006).

The Incredible Years is a generic name given to many component programs, each of which involve different interventionists and qualitatively different levels of intervention according to the age range and risk-characteristics of the populations served. *Level 1* represents a series of programs that are offered universally to all parents of young children. Level 1 programs include a baby program for new parents in the first year of their child's life (6 weeks to 1 year), toddler programs for parents of children ages 1 to 3 years, and a school readiness program for parents of children ages 3 to 5 years. Parents can access IY information from self-learning modules through libraries, schools, or pediatrician offices, as an alternative to attending groups.

Level 2 also fosters universal prevention by offering appropriate IY programs to all parents and teachers of children ages 3 to 6 years, the purpose of which is to enhance the capacity of adults at home and school to provide structured, warm, and predictable environments. The IY Parent BASIC and IY-TT programs have self-administered manuals so that parents and teachers can access the information through self-learning modules (thus lessening the need to attend groups).

Level 3 targets populations that are socioeconomically disadvantaged and highly stressed because of increased family risk factors related to poverty. Such families would benefit from a continuum of services offered as children develop from infancy to school age, including more intensive parent and teacher training as well as access to the classroom Dinosaur social and emotional skills curriculum.

Level 4 is targeted at children or parents who are already showing symptoms of more serious problems (e.g., parents referred to Child Protective Services because of abuse or neglect, foster parents caring for children who have been neglected or removed from their homes, or children who are highly aggressive but not yet diagnosed as having oppositional defiant or conduct disorders). This level of intervention is offered to fewer families and offers a longer and more intensive parenting program by a higher level of trained professionals. In addition, children with symptoms of externalizing or internalizing problems might be pulled out of class twice a week for the small-group therapeutic Dinosaur Social Skills, Emotion, and Problem-Solving therapeutic interventions delivered by school psychologists or counselors or specially trained social workers or special education teachers.

Level 5 is the most comprehensive intervention, as it addresses multiple risk factors. Level 5 services are usually offered in mental health clinics by IY group leaders with graduate-level education in psychology, social work, or counseling. One of the goals of each of the prior levels is to maximize resources and minimize the number of children who will need these time- and cost-intensive interventions at Level 5. In addition to the parent group-based programs, if parents need individual coaching, this can be provided in supplemental home visits. Trained home visitor IY coaches also have protocols for working with parents at home to reinforce the skills that they are learning in their groups. Successful interventions at this level are marked by an integrated team approach with clear communication among all the providers and adult caregivers in the various settings where these children spend their time (Webster-Stratton & Herman, 2010).

Webster-Stratton and Herman (2010) recommend that each agency or school prepare a minimum of two group leaders or teachers for training in the IY program. After the initial training workshop, group leaders and teachers first need release time to study the manuals and DVDs, to practice and prepare their sessions and materials, and to arrange logistics (e.g., food or day care, handouts, classroom materials, transportation). Webster-Stratton and Herman (2010) recommend that IY-accredited mentors provide support, encouragement, and consultation regularly for the group leaders during their first two to three sets of groups. Ideally, new leaders should have three to four 1-hour consultations during delivery of their first program and ongoing consultation as needed.

For sites that are implementing the IY program for the first time, group leader or teacher consultation and coaching is arranged through IY headquarters (in Seattle) via regular telephone consultations with IY-accredited trainers. Group leaders are also encouraged to submit a DVD of a group session or lesson from their first group for detailed feedback. After group leaders or teachers have had experience delivering the program, approximately six to nine months after training, it is recommended that they participate in an in-person group consultation training with IY trainers or mentors either on-site at the agency or school or at the IY headquarters. In these consultation workshops, group leaders or teachers come together to share selected portions of their videos regarding their delivery of the program.

Peer sharing and feedback, along with IY mentor coaching regarding videotaped sessions, is advantageous for helping group leaders and teachers gain new ways to handle problems that were particularly difficult for them. Once group leaders receive this initial training, ongoing supervision, and support, they will be ready to submit their application for accreditation as group leader. IY program policies require that teachers or group leaders are trained from the same agency so that they can participate in the peer-review process. Individuals are trained not to work without a peer support network. Here, group leaders are encouraged to videotape their groups and meet weekly with peers for video review.

The IY program has been widely endorsed by various review groups, including the Office for Juvenile Justice and Delinquency Prevention (OJJDP) as one of eleven blueprint model violence-prevention, evidence-based programs for treating and preventing disruptive behavior disorders. For further information on the empirical support for the IY program, readers are encourage to consult Webster-Stratton and Herman (2010), as well as the websites in the Additional Resources at the end of this chapter.

ADDITIONAL RESOURCES

Supplemental Readings

Chao, R., & Tseng, V. (2002). Parenting of Asians. In M. H. Bornstein (Ed.), *Handbook of parenting, Vol. 4: Social conditions and applied parenting* (2nd ed., pp. 59–94). Mahwah, NJ: Erlbaum.

Harwood, R., Leyendecker, B., Carlson, V., Asencio, M., & Miller, A. (2002). Parenting among Latino families in the U.S. In M. H. Bornstein (Ed.), *Handbook of parenting, Vol. 4: Social conditions and applied parenting* (2nd ed., pp. 21–46). Mahwah, NJ: Erlbaum.

McAdoo, H. P. (2002). African American parenting. In M. H. Bornstein (Ed.), *Handbook of parenting, Vol. 4: Social conditions and applied parenting* (2nd ed., pp. 47–58). Mahwah, NJ: Erlbaum.

McGoldrick, M., Giordano, J., & Garcia-Preto, N. (Eds.). (2005). *Ethnicity and family therapy.* New York, NY: Guilford Press.

Taus-Bolstad, S. (2006). *Pakistanis in America.* Minneapolis, MN: Lerner.

Films

People Like Us: Social Class in America (2001). This two-hour documentary, created by filmmakers Louis Alvarez and Andrew Kolker, examines American life through the prism of class structure. The material revolves around the question: How do income, family background, education, attitudes, aspirations, and even appearance mark someone as a member of a particular social class? Specifically, the film shows how social class plays a role in the lives of all Americans, whether they live in Park Avenue penthouses, Appalachian trailer parks, bayou houseboats, or suburban gated communities. The documentary travels across the country, presenting stories of family traditions, class mobility, and different lifestyle choices. These various stories are designed to resonate with viewers regardless of where they see themselves on the social spectrum.

Reel Injun (2009). This movie, by Cree filmmaker Neil Diamond, is an entertaining and informative film that explores how North American Native peoples have been portrayed (either accurately or inaccurately) throughout the history of Hollywood cinema, beginning in the silent film era to contemporary times. The film includes interviews with various directors, writers, actors, and activists, including Clint Eastwood, Jim Jarmusch, Robbie Robertson, Sacheen Littlefeather, John Trudell, and Russell Means.

Contact Information for Brand-Name Intervention Programs

Nurse Family Partnership (http://www.nursefamilypartnership.org)
   Nurse Family Partnership National Service Office
   1900 Grant Street, Suite 400
   Denver, CO 80203
   Direct: 303-327-4240
   Toll-free: 866-864-5226
   Fax: 303-327-4260
Functional Family Therapy (http://www.fftinc.com)
   FFT Communications Director
   1251 NW Elford Dr.
   Seattle, WA 98177
   Phone: 206-369-5894
   Fax: 206-453-3631
Multidimensional Treatment Foster Care (http://www.mtfc.com)
   TFC Consultants, Inc.
   1163 Olive St.
   Eugene, OR 97401
   Phone: 541-343-2388 ext. 204
   Cell: 541-954-7431
   Fax: 541-343-2764

Multisystemic Therapy (http://mstservices.com)
    MST General Office
    710 J. Dodds Blvd., Suite 200
    Mount Pleasant, SC 29464
    Phone: 843-856-8226
    Fax: 843-856-8227
The Incredible Years (http://www.incredibleyears.com)
    1411 8th Ave. West
    Seattle, WA 98119
    Phone: 206-285-7565
    Toll-free: 888-506-3562
    FAX: 888-506-3562

CHAPTER

4

❖❖❖

Contexts for School Learning

The practice of categorizing individuals into mutually exclusive groups based on their racial/ethnic/language status, then assigning glib generalizations and stereotypes to such groups (see Sidebars 2.4–2.7), represents a convenient (but lazy) system for organizing multicultural content in applied school psychology and teacher training. As discussed in Chapter 2, Quack Multiculturalism promotes the simplistic notion that knowledge of a student's ethnic, racial, or language group membership—by itself—is all that is needed to help school practitioners understand how to better serve a student's psychoeducational needs (Dunn & Griggs, 1995, Hale-Benson, 1986; Shade, 1995; Sue & Sue, 2003). According to this viewpoint, culture is viewed as a tangible entity that is deeply and stubbornly entrenched in the psychological DNA of individuals. As such, the unspoken assumption is that individuals "carry their culture" with them at all times, and they are wired to think and behave "according to their culture," no matter what environmental contingencies are in place.

This tradition, no matter how pervasive it appears in the multicultural literature, is plagued by two fundamental flaws. First, to assume that individuals who belong to the same ethnic/racial group are influenced in the same way by their reference culture, or to assume that all individuals in a specific group adopt the same cultural norms in all environments in the same manner, is to commit the *ecologic fallacy* (see discussion in Dreher & McNaughton, 2002). Second, it is simply erroneous to assume that all behavior originates from within-the-child variables (i.e., from his or her "culture"), while ignoring influences on behavior that are triggered by immediate environmental and situational contexts. For example, how is the school experience of a 10-year-old boy attending an academically rigorous parochial school the same as a similar-aged boy attending a failing ghetto school whose principal is about to be fired due to incompetence—simply because both children are African American? How is the education of a third-generation bilingual child enrolled in an English immersion program similar to a recent immigrant child enrolled in a bilingual education program—simply because both children are Hispanic? How are the learning attitudes and behaviors of a girl attending a poor reservation school the same as a U.S. Senator's daughter attending an exclusive college prep private school—simply because both children are Native American? Stated differently, the prospects of Johnny receiving a high-quality educational experience are greater if he goes to a good school, with instructionally skilled and dedicated teachers, with a high-quality curriculum, and surrounded by academically motivated peers. If one or more of these variables is significantly compromised, Johnny's chances for receiving a high-quality educational experience lessens accordingly—having relatively little to do with his "culture."

The bottom line is that simple knowledge of a student's group membership, by itself, is extremely limited in providing information that is useful to school psychologists or any other school support personnel. The *contexts for learning*—namely, the type of school attended, the characteristics of other students in the school, its climate and instructional quality, its discipline policies and practices—play a significant role in understanding the quality of a child's educational experience, regardless of his or her cultural background.

If school psychologists, counselors, and teachers are to help minority children regardless of where they attend school, they need to be aware of important learning context variables that are not under their direct control, but nevertheless play a significant role in shaping a child's school experience. In the material that follows, a discussion of these important learning context variables is organized by school type; varieties of bilingual education; salient features of urban, suburban, and rural schooling; select school climate variables; and the influence of principal leadership on school functioning.

SCHOOL TYPE

Public Schools

Federal Control

The U.S. Constitution does not specifically refer to education as the responsibility and duty of the federal government. Under the 10th Amendment of the U.S. Constitution, state governments have assumed the duty to educate their citizens, the authority to tax citizens of the state to finance education, and the power to compel school attendance for all (Jacob & Hartshorne, 2007). Public schools are required by law to admit any student, and each local school district is responsible for providing free public education for all school-aged children residing within its jurisdiction. Any school and/or agency receiving federal funds must comply with Title VI of the 1964 Civil Rights Act, which requires the mandatory withholding of federal funds from institutions practicing racial, religious, or ethnic discrimination. As such, public schooling is the educational context that is most familiar to working school psychologists.

State Control

State control of public education occurs through numerous avenues. States can determine their own academic standards and testing programs. State academic standards determine what is taught in local public school classrooms, and it follows that high-stakes state-standardized tests are constructed around the state's academic standards in content areas. By means of categorical aid (i.e., federal funds targeted for specific programs) provided by the No Child Left Behind Act of 2001, the federal government can require states to report yearly test scores, and identify and improve schools failing to meet adequate yearly progress (AYP; see Glossary). NCLB also specifies that states must make reasonable adaptations and accommodations for limited-English-proficient students and those with disabilities.

States exercise control over schools in other ways, which include licensing teachers and other school service personnel, testing these potential professionals as part of the licensing procedure, enacting state laws that affect the content of public school instruction (e.g., patriotism, human rights, driver's education), and providing grant funds to local school districts.

Local Control

The primary financial support for public schools comes from public funds (usually local property taxes and federal/state funds). This does not mean, however, that every public school is funded at comparable levels. The authority for management of public schools rests in the hands of local school boards. Local communities exercise their control over public schools by electing representatives to local school boards. School boards appoint the Superintendent of Schools, who functions as the chief executive officer of the school district (Spring, 2010) and typically works out of the central office of the school district. Each school principal reports directly to the district central office and to the Superintendent.

Parental Control

In the public school arena, parents do not fundamentally determine what they want their children to learn or how they want their children to be taught. However, they do have some degree of informal influence over these variables (typically exercised on a case-by-case basis). Parents can influence these issues somewhat through local political activities, or by the simple exercise of their voting privileges (e.g., school board elections).

School Structure

Public schools typically have one or more grade groupings (e.g., pre-kindergarten through grade 12), and some configurations allow for ungraded groupings. Public school districts have jurisdiction over multiple school buildings that are organized by preschool, elementary school, middle school, junior high school, and high school groupings (some districts may not have middle schools). Each public school within a school district typically employs one or more teachers per grade to provide instruction, who are supervised by an assigned administrator, who in turn is supported by an administrative staff.

Varieties of Public Schools

Public school districts provide a variety of school types for particular student needs. Some public elementary/secondary schools focus primarily on special education, including instruction for any of the following students with autism, deaf-blindness, developmental delay, hearing impairment, mental retardation, multiple disabilities, orthopedic impairment, serious emotional disturbance, specific learning disability, speech or language impairment, traumatic brain injury, visual impairment, and other health impairments. These schools adapt curriculum, materials, or instruction for the special needs of students served. Some schools in public school districts are generally called *vocational education schools*. These schools focus primarily on providing formal preparation for semiskilled, skilled, technical, or professional occupations for high-school-age students who have opted to develop or expand their employment opportunities, often in lieu of preparing for college entry.

Alternative schools address the needs of students that typically cannot be met in a regular school (e.g., disciplinary needs for students with behavior problems). Such schools function as an adjunct to a regular school, but they fall outside the categories of regular, special education, or vocational education schools. *Magnet schools* are unique schools designed to attract students of different racial/ethnic backgrounds for the purpose of reducing, preventing, or eliminating racial isolation (which in turn may be spurred by court-ordered desegregation rulings). Magnet school programs provide an academic or social focus centered around a particular theme (e.g., science/math, performing arts, gifted/talented education, or foreign language instruction).

According to a 2008–2009 statistical report from the National Center for Education Statistics (Sable, Plotts, Mitchell, & Chen, 2010), the 100 largest public school districts (representing less than 1 percent of all school districts in the United States) were responsible for the education of 22 percent of all public school students in the United States. The majority of students in the 100 largest school districts were Hispanic or black (approximately 63 percent), compared to a baseline of 17 percent of (black or Hispanic) students in all U.S. school districts. As late as the 2008–2009 school year, 27 states each had at least one of the 100 largest public school districts in the United States. The state of Texas had 19 districts among the 100 largest, followed by Florida with 14 districts, and California with 12 districts.

Criticisms of Public Schools

Inherent in public schooling is a myriad of contentious issues, many of which set the stage for the advocacy of alternative forms of schooling. Compared to private schools, classrooms are usually larger in public schools, which may or may not have direct implications for the level of individualized attention that students get from teachers. The huge and unwieldy bureaucracy of public school district central offices is routinely criticized as being a barrier to making any meaningful positive changes on behalf of children (Spring, 2010). Tensions between individual school districts, state education superintendents, and the federal government arise over the lack of state tests in non-English languages, or the requirement to include the test scores of English-language learners in determining a state's Adequate Yearly Progress (Spring, 2010). Some have argued that the quality of academic programs in public schools is not as high as that of private schools. Although this may be accurate in some cases, this is certainly not true in all cases. There are wide differences in the quality of public education as a function of variation in local property values and neighborhood quality (see Chapter 3).

Most public school teachers (who elect not to take advantage of state right-to-work laws) belong to strong teachers' unions (e.g., National Education Association or American Federation of Teachers). Teachers' unions have been on the receiving end of extensive criticisms, which have centered around the following five themes: (1) entrenched union hostility to parental school choice; (2) unions promoting trendy fads and slogans that are rooted in sociopolitical advocacy rather than the desire for substantive improvements in teaching and children's learning; (3) unions' reflexive tendency to oppose any efforts to establish and strengthen teacher accountability for student academic performance; (4) the near impossibility of efforts to efficiently fire incompetent and/or low-performing teachers; and (5) an unwillingness of teachers to "go the extra mile" on behalf of students if such behaviors violate union contract rules (see Moe, 2011; Paige, 2007; Sorokin, 2002; Stern, 1997).

Charter Schools

Broadly defined, charter schools are "publicly funded schools that are granted significant autonomy in curriculum and governance in return for greater accountability" (Buckley & Schneider, 2007, p. 1; see also Glossary). A *charter* is essentially a performance contract that specifies the school's mission, goals, population served, and procedures for assessing the extent to which goals are met. A local agency essentially applies to the state to receive a charter to operate as a school at public expense. Thus, a direct governmental relationship is established between a charter school and the state agency responsible for granting charters, which allows the school to operate outside of the control of the state's educational bureaucracy and the local school board and its bureaucracy (Springer, 2010). Charters are granted for fixed lengths of time (typically three to five years), after which the authorizing body reviews school performance data and makes a decision whether to renew the school's charter. From a philosophical perspective, charter schools are characterized by the following six concepts: competition, autonomy, choice, community, accountability, and achievement.

Competition

Philosophically, charter schools are expected to generate competition among schools, the outcome of which will hopefully result in poorly performing schools getting better or closing down, and good schools continuing to thrive (Buckley & Schneider, 2007).

Autonomy

Charter schools are considered to be autonomous legal entities, and as such they are exempt from most of the regulations that govern traditional public schools. Although public charter schools are afforded some level of exemption from state or local laws or requirements, they must conform to all federal laws and regulations, including the Individuals with Disabilities Education Act (IDEA), Section 504 of the Rehabilitation Act, and the Americans with Disabilities Act (ADA). When charter schools are released from bureaucratic regulations and controls that hamstring public schools, it is hoped that charter schools are then freed to develop more innovative and creative services that better serve their constituencies. This creativity results in many policies and practices that are unheard of in many public schools, which include, but are not limited to, the ability to hire teachers who fit philosophically with the mission of the charter school, lengthening the school day and/or school year, combining grade levels for instructional purposes, requiring a dress code, or requiring parent participation. Charter schools are governed by their own board of trustees, who are responsible for determining the school's fiscal, administrative, personnel, and instructional policies.

Choice

All residents of a school district are eligible to apply to a charter school, and admission is granted on the basis of space availability (Buckley & Schneider, 2007). Applicants are not required to pay entrance fees, nor are they selected based on test scores. Once charter school enrollment has reached capacity, applicants are placed on waiting lists. As space becomes available, a lottery system is often employed to then select students to fill open slots. Although charter schools are expressly forbidden to discriminate in selecting applicants, they do have some leeway in extending preferences to siblings of students who have attended the school previously, or to de-enrolled students who attended the charter school previously. The concept of "choice" means that there is a match between what parents and students want educationally and what they get from their schools. Supporters of charter schools hope that giving schools greater choice in the selection of curriculum and delivery of instruction, as a means of being responsive to consumer preferences, will improve efficiency, academic outcomes, and consumer satisfaction.

Community

Charter schools are more responsive to the needs of parents, students, and the community at large. In addition, by allowing parents and students to choose schools that deliver the type of education that they feel best meets their needs, charter schools can improve the match between what schools offer and what parents/consumers prefer (Buckley & Schneider, 2007). Buckley and Schneider (2007) articulate this issue as follows:

> Charter schools can provide a means for parents and students who perceive themselves as marginalized or disenfranchised to seek shelter from an indifferent or even hostile public school system. Groups as diverse as right-wing Christians in California . . . to Afrocentrists in Michigan . . . have taken advantage of charter-school laws to create schools catering to their particular interests. (p. 5)

Accountability

In exchange for the ability to operate relatively unencumbered by the policies of the local school district, charter schools are held accountable for improving the academic performance of their students.

Achievement

Buckley and Schneider (2007) opine that "for many involved in the school-choice debate, the ultimate test of a reform is whether or not the academic achievement of students improves" (p. 77). In evaluating this research question, investigators attempt to measure school achievement using different research designs. One ideal design requires investigators to compare the school achievement of charter and noncharter schools that serve roughly similar student populations. Using a different approach, investigators attempt to measure school achievement of a group before they are assigned to charter schools, and then measure school achievement in the same group after random assignment to charter schools.

Because all charter schools are not monolithic, it comes as no surprise that evaluations of the effects of charter schools on student achievement can often show conflicting results (e.g., see Gleason, Clark, Tuttle, Dwoyer, & Silverberg, 2010). In the fierce political battles waged between pro-school-choice versus anti-school-choice advocates, partisan explanations for conflicting research results are plentiful. For example, in defending why some charter schools may not show better achievement results compared to public schools, charter school advocates argue that the population of students who attend charter schools are more difficult to educate given their pre-existing school difficulties. In contrast, in trivializing reasons for why some charter schools show better achievement results than public schools, critics argue that charter schools skim "the cream off the top" of better students and more involved parents.

According to the most recent data from the U.S. National Center for Education Statistics, the percentage of students enrolled in public charter schools compared to traditional schools (broken down by race/ethnicity) for the end of the 2008 school year is listed in Table 4.1.

Criticisms of Charter Schools

Given the pressure to produce results as a condition of their autonomy from local school board control, charter school leaders face increased temptation to become lax in documenting and advertising to consumers their school performance data (Buckley & Schneider, 2007). When a charter school is shut down (some estimates arrive at a 15 percent failure rate; see Buckley & Schneider, 2007), critics cite these figures as a failure of the charter school movement as a whole. However, proponents of charter schools argue that the identification of failing charter schools actually supports the charter school philosophy of accountability as working. Here, well-performing individual schools thrive, while poorly performing individual schools are weeded out. For a readable account of various opinions (pro and con) related to charter schools, readers are encouraged to read an online debate that can be accessed at http://roomfordebate.blogs.nytimes.com/2010/03/14/the-push-back-on-charter-schools/

Table 4.1   Percentage Student Enrollment in Traditional vs. Public Charter Schools by Race/Ethnicity, 2008

Student Race/Ethnicity	Percentage Enrolled in Traditional Schools (N = 47,432,000)	Percentage Enrolled in Public Charter Schools (N = 1,047,000)
White, non-Hispanic	58.2	41.0
Black, non-Hispanic	15.7	29.0
Hispanic	20.3	23.8
Asian/Pacific Islander	4.4	3.8
American Indian/Alaska Native	1.4	2.3

(U.S. Center for Education Statistics, 2008)

Private/Parochial Schools

Private schools are not administered by local, state, or national governments. Parochial schools are a subset of private schools. A *parochial school* provides religious education in addition to conventional education and most typically refers to a Christian (often Catholic) grammar school or high school that is part of, and run by, a parish.

Freed from government control, private/parochial schools retain the right to select their students and are funded in whole or in part by charging their students tuition (rather than relying on revenue from mandatory taxes, as is the case with public schools). Private school students can obtain scholarships for private schooling as a function of a special ability or talent (e.g., sport scholarship, art scholarship, academic scholarship). Additional sources of funding for private/parochial schools come from endowments, voucher funds, and donations/grants from religious organizations or private individuals. Since these schools receive no taxpayer funding, they are not required to abide by the policies of a democratically elected local school board.

Private/parochial schools have the freedom to hire teachers who are uncertified and/or non-union. The disadvantage for teachers is that the pay scale for teachers in private schools is typically lower. The advantage for teachers is that they can gain teaching experience before making any long-term career decisions, and they can work while earning teaching certification.

Whereas the curriculum taught in public schools is determined by state regulatory standards and limited in scope by court rulings (e.g., religion), private/parochial schools have the freedom to teach whatever they want and present the material in whatever manner they see fit. Parents can then choose to send their children to a private/parochial school that has a curricular program and educational philosophy that suits their needs.

Parent Perspectives on Reasons for Choosing Private Schools

Obviously, parents who send their children to private/parochial schools can most afford to do so, although scholarships and vouchers can fund students who come from less-affluent families. If a family is very wealthy, the expense required to send their children to private schools does not create a substantial financial hardship. For less-affluent families, however, the choice to send their children to private schools involves significant personal struggles in weighing substantial financial costs against the ultimate benefits for their children.

Students who attend private schools can be more academically challenged. Private schools tend to provide a more academically rigorous curriculum than public schools—in the sense that private school students must submit a higher quality of classwork and homework, meet more demanding graduation requirements, and complete more coursework within the same period of time compared to public school students. Some private schools require students to complete community service requirements or require mandatory participation in Fine Arts classes. For all years in which National Assessment of Educational Progress (NAEP) data is available, the average scores, in all subject areas, obtained by private schools exceed those of public schools (e.g., see http://nces.ed.gov/nationsreportcard/about/private_school_quick_data.asp). However, these results should be interpreted in light of student selection differences between public and private schools.

Many private schools explicitly instill in their students an expectation of applying to and attending college after high school graduation. When college is an explicit focus, then students develop a college goal orientation, and many elements of the private school curriculum can be tailored toward preparing students to be competitive for college admissions. This college orientation is supplemented by the provision of better access to information about different college options and the requirements that must be fulfilled in order to qualify for admission to a specific college and/or university.

Students who attend private schools are exposed to a clearer and more explicit value system. Parents are often offended by the values taught in the public schools, particularly those that do not align with what they feel they would want their children to internalize. If they can afford the tuition (or receive a scholarship), parents can select a private or parochial school that incorporates their values into the curriculum. In addition, some private schools have honor codes and strict behavior standards that are designed to encourage maturity toward responsible adulthood.

Students who attend private schools have potentially greater access to teachers. This is because private schools, on average, have smaller class sizes than do public schools. When classes are smaller, teachers potentially can get a better sense of the child's academic strengths and weaknesses. It is not as likely for students to be able to "hide" in smaller classrooms, because students have more opportunities to speak up in class and participate in class discussions.

Many parents prefer the protections for student safety that private schools provide. It is widely known that public schools suffer from a greater degree of discipline problems, crime incidents, and drug/weapons violations (see Figures 4.2, 4.3, and 4.4 later in the chapter). It is easier for private schools to set and enforce their own discipline standards, as disruptive students can be expelled more easily. When discipline problems and/or disruptive behavior does occur, they can be eradicated more quickly in private school settings.

As an example of the convergence of these advantages in the opinions of private school parents, the appeal of private schooling compared to public schooling is succinctly articulated by one African American parent:

> [For this parent], the emphasis on achievement meshed with an overall sense of safety. She had worried that her two bookish sons would be "used like mops" by bullies in her neighborhood public school. At [this private school], nobody

mocks them for doing their homework, participating in class or speaking in standard English rather than street slang. "The whole environment," she said, "is conducive to study." (Freedman, 2004)

According to figures from the Parent and Family Involvement Survey of the National Household Education Survey Program (U.S. Center for Education Statistics, 2009), the percentage of students enrolled in public versus private schools as of 2007 (broken down by race/ethnicity) is provided in Table 4.2. In some communities, the steady rise of minority enrollment in private schools is a sign that racial divisions no longer have the potency they once had in earlier, more socially turbulent times. According to one professor of education, as quoted in an article on the subject (Dent, 1996):

> Instead of race or ethnicity being the basic division, the divisions are between orthodoxy and progressivism. . . . So, in terms of the fundamentalist Christian movement, it's no surprise that orthodox whites and orthodox blacks are attracted to the same kinds of schools.

Criticisms of Private Schools

Given the very nature of private schooling, such schools are open to charges of elitism—given that more-affluent families can afford private schooling. In the early decades following the *Brown v. Board of Education* Supreme Court decision of 1954, all-white private schools flourished in the wake of efforts to avoid court-ordered desegregation. This has led to a perception, still held by some people, that private schools are more

Table 4.2   Percentage of Students (Broken Down by Race/Ethnicity) Attending Public and Private Schools (Grades 1–12): 2007

Student Race/Ethnicity	Public Assigned	Public Chosen	Private Church-Related	Private Not Church-Related
White, Non-Hispanic	73.6	12.5	10.8	3.1
Black, Non-Hispanic	68.9	23.7	5.5	1.8
Other, Non-Hispanic	72.7	17.4	6.4	3.5
Hispanic	75.8	17.4	5.6	1.2

Public (Assigned): N = 34,700,000; students attending public schools assigned to them by neighborhood zoning patterns
Public (Chosen): N = 7,400,000; students attending public schools chosen by parents
Private (Church-Related): N = 4,100,000; students attending private schools affiliated with a major religious denomination
Private (Not Church-Related): N = 1,200,000; students attending secular private schools not affiliated with a religious denomination
(U.S. Center for Education Statistics, 2009)

racially segregated than are public schools. Although this may have been true immediately following the Brown decision, the fact is that steadily increasing numbers of
racial/ethnic minority families are enrolling their children in private schools (e.g., see
Dent, 1996). Furthermore, the private-schools-are-more-segregated argument is undermined by contrary empirical evidence (see Greene, 2005).

Legitimate concerns have been raised about whether the needs of special populations
are served by private schools. Private schools do not have to accept children with special
needs, and many choose not to (although a small number of private schools are designed
for special-needs children). As a result, most private schools do not have special education programs or teachers trained to work with special populations. Some private
schools recommend that children with learning disabilities look elsewhere for a school.
Other private schools may admit students according to their normal criteria, but when
special education needs are discovered, they contract with nearby public schools to
provide assessment and instructional services.

Cultural Immersion Schools

Cultural immersion schools (see Glossary) emphasize a curriculum that concentrates
exclusively on the history, religious/cultural practices and traditions, and/or language of a
particular cultural group. Cultural immersion programs can be implemented in specific
classrooms within schools that are not necessarily explicitly cultural immersion in focus,
or entire schools can be converted to a cultural immersion model.

Although there is an implicit understanding that cultural immersion education exists
solely for specific groups, such an understanding is not accurate in all circumstances. For
example, although the Boston Chinese Immersion charter school advertises itself as
emphasizing a curriculum that relies heavily on instruction in Mandarin Chinese and
learning about Mandarin Chinese culture, admission is explicitly advertised as being
open to students from diverse racial and ethnic backgrounds (see http://bostonchinese
immersion.org/about/).

Other schools are clearly designed for students belonging to one and only one narrowly defined cultural group. For instance, the Arapaho Language Lodge immersion
school in Riverton, Wyoming, was implemented in response to a strong conviction
among Native American community leaders of the importance of maintaining the
Arapaho Native language throughout successive generations. Such cultural immersion
language schools for indigenous peoples have been started in Oklahoma as well among
the Comanche (see Harris, 2009).

Some Native American schools are not necessarily cultural immersion by design, but
are so by default because of their extreme social isolation and ethnic homogeneity.
Compared to public schools, reservation schools for Native American children and
youth are impacted in various ways by the endemic poverty in the surrounding

communities. It is generally acknowledged that children attending such schools are exposed to a quality of education that is considerably less than children attending the surrounding public schools. Of the 562 federally recognized Indian nations, only 222 have Head Start programs as of 2008 (Harvard Project on American Indian Economic Development, 2008). Bureau of Indian Affairs (BIA) schools are seriously underfunded, spending less than half as much per student compared to public school students in surrounding areas. BIA schools are more likely to have substandard physical facilities that are in poor condition and less likely to support computer and telecommunications technologies (Harvard Project on American Indian Economic Development, 2008).

Perhaps the best-known example of cultural immersion schools are *Afrocentric schools* (see Afrocentrism, in Glossary) that have started primarily in big American cities but have spread as far as Toronto, Canada (e.g., see MacDonald, 2010). Such schools are identified by names such as Afrikan Peoples Action School (Trenton, NJ), Malcolm X Academy (Detroit, MI; San Francisco, CA), Nubian Village Academy (Richmond, VA), and the Ijoba Shule ("school"; Philadelphia, PA). Most Afrocentric schools are founded on, and operate from, the desire to reverse the disastrous achievement trends of black students in predominantly white educational systems (McNeil, 2011). Afrocentric schools share a fundamental conviction that pupils' personal self-esteem, as well as their academic self-confidence/performance, would be greatly enhanced if they were educated in an all-black classroom/school environment. Such schools are represented by alternative schools within the public school system, private schools, or charter schools. How each school interprets its Afrocentric mission also varies from school to school. For some schools, Afrocentric education is interpreted as providing an all-black environment in which black pride, black self-esteem, and American black history is front and center in children's learning experiences. At the other end of the spectrum, Afrocentric education means couching all learning within (usually) Swahili language and cultural concepts.

Criticisms of Cultural Immersion Schools

Many educators generally become nervous at the thought of culturally exclusive education, as this seems contrary to philosophical preferences for racially/ethically integrated education. For example, some have criticized Islamic cultural immersion schools on the grounds that the curriculum fosters anti-Western, anti-Jewish, or anti-Christian sentiments in impressionable children (see Elshinnawi, 2010). By far, the cultural immersion philosophy that has received the greatest amount of critical attention has been Afrocentric education. Some object to Afrocentric schools on legal grounds, claiming that limiting schools (or classes within schools) only to African American males or even to only black students constitutes gender/racial discrimination (K. Brown, 1993, 2000; Crouch, 2011). Others object to the substantive authenticity of history interpreted from the Afrocentric perspective, on the grounds that Afrocentric scholarship is sloppy at best and perpetuates outright falsehoods at its worst (e.g., see D'Souza, 1995; Howe, 1998; Lefkowitz, 1996; Walker, 2001). Still others criticize Afrocentrism on the grounds that efforts to boost black children's self-esteem—through what is perceived to be a distorted interpretation of history and culture—is ultimately a shaky foundation on which to improve academic performance (Decter, 1991; Roth, 2005; Shokraii-Rees, 2007).

Homeschooling

The term *homeschooling* refers to students who stay at home to be taught by one or both parents in lieu of attending a public or private school. According to the latest National Center for Education Statistics (2010) data, the percentage breakdown by race/ethnicity of homeschooled students aged 5 to 17 (compared to all students in public school, private school, and homeschooled) for year 2007 was 3.9 percent white, .8 percent black, 1.5 percent Hispanic, and 3.3 percent other. Among the reasons listed as most important for influencing parents' decisions to homeschool their children are (in descending order of importance): (1) a desire to provide religious or moral instruction; (2) a concern about the environment of other schools; (3) a dissatisfaction with academic instruction at other schools; (4) constraints on family time, finances, travel, and/or distance; (5) a desire to provide a nontraditional approach to the child's education; (6) the need to provide appropriate education for children with special needs; and (7) the need to provide appropriate education for a child who has a physical or mental health problem.

Whitaker (2005) lists five qualitatively distinct approaches to homeschooling, each of which involves different sources for obtaining, and ways of using, curriculum materials. Generally, homeschooled students have been found to exceed public school students on achievement tests (Ray, 1997; Ray & Weller, 2003), and achievement gaps between black and white racial groups have been found to be smaller among homeschooled students.

Criticisms of Homeschooling

Several criticisms have been leveled at homeschooling. One primarily philosophical/ideological criticism is rooted in a fear that many homeschooled children are exposed to a one-sided view of life that may reduce their sense of civic engagement with the broader community (Reich, 2002). Others criticize homeschooling on grounds that (a) homeschooling parents harbor real or imagined feelings of inadequacy and a lack of efficacy in teaching their children, particularly as the subject matter becomes more difficult, and (b) homeschooled children may lack opportunities to develop socialization skills if they are not regularly exposed to same-aged peers outside of the family. In response to these two criticisms, homeschooling families can join *homeschool cooperatives*. A homeschool cooperative is a group of families who homeschool their children together, usually for similar reasons, for educational support. Homeschool cooperatives provide an opportunity for children to learn from other parents who possess more specialized expertise in certain areas or subjects. These cooperatives also provide social interaction for homeschooled children, as they may take lessons or go on field trips together. Some cooperatives may also offer events such as prom and graduation for homeschoolers.

VARIETIES OF BILINGUAL EDUCATION

For students who do not speak English, or have limited English-speaking skills, educational opportunities for learning English vary considerably in both quality and design. Brisk (2006, p. 31), quoting from Nieto (2000), defined bilingual education broadly as "any educational program that involves the use of two languages of instruction at some point in a student's school career." Under the broad moniker *bilingual education*, several different contexts exist for delivering instruction.

Variables That Distinguish Bilingual Education Programs

Brisk (2006) identifies three variables that differentiate among various models for delivering bilingual instruction in schools: (1) the *goal* variable typically encompasses whether the major end goal of these programs is proficiency in two languages versus proficiency in English; (2) the *target population* variable refers to the intended beneficiaries of the program, be they students who speak only one language, two languages, and/or have an identifiable disability (e.g., deaf or hard-of-hearing); and (3) the *instructional design* variable describes how and when one or both languages are integrated and taught to students over the course of their years in school.

Dual-Language Programs/Schools

In dual-language programs, the goal of the curriculum is to develop proficiency in two languages, with half of the day devoted to instruction in one language and the other half devoted to instruction in the other language. The primary difference between dual-language programs and two-way bilingual programs is that the former programs are not purposely created to serve language minority students, but primarily are designed for parents who intentionally want their English-speaking children to develop bilingual skills. An example of this type of program is the Yujin Gakuen Elementary Japanese Immersion School in Eugene, Oregon. The immersion curriculum in Japanese continues from this elementary school on through the local middle and high school. The student body advertises itself as ethnically diverse, according to the school's website (http://schools.4j.lane.edu/yujingakuen/Site/About_YG.html). A majority of the students enrolled in the Yujin Gakuen School are originally English-speaking children whose parents value the learning of Japanese, while a minority of families send their children to the school because it is a neighborhood school (Brisk, 2006). According to the school's website, by the end of the fifth grade, students are expected to attain state-determined benchmarks in English, but they are also expected to meet oral and written skills in Japanese through group and individual class projects, plays, individual assignments, and assessment tests.

Many schools specifically designed to deliver a dual-language curriculum are private schools that cater to families typically headed by primary breadwinners working in international businesses, organizations, and/or embassies. Such schools include native speakers of two languages, native speakers of English only, or native speakers of a non-English language (e.g., see website for the United Nations International School in New York City at http://www.unis.org/about_unis/directors_welcome/index.aspx).

Two-Way Bilingual Education

Two-way bilingual education programs serve English-speaking and language minority children simultaneously, the goal being for each group to maintain its native language but also learn a second language. Two-way programs vary in the amount of each language used, the subjects taught in each language, and the instructional emphases of each language. In some two-way programs, instruction in English increases with each grade until half of the instruction is given in each language. The majority of two-way programs in the United States are conducted in Spanish and English, but there are also programs in Cantonese, Korean, Navajo, Japanese, Russian, Portugese, and French (see review by Brisk, 2006).

Maintenance Bilingual Education

The distinguishing feature of maintenance bilingual programs, sometimes referred to as *developmental bilingual education* or *one-way dual-language programs*, is that they exclusively serve language minority students. The overall goal of such programs is to develop and maintain the native language skills of non-English speakers, and to develop positive attitudes toward native culture while achieving proficiency in English. The linkages between language of instruction and specific courses vary over grades and across different types of maintenance programs.

Because the spirit of maintenance bilingual programs involves some degree of ethnic exclusivity, entire maintenance bilingual schools are difficult to sustain within the context of federal/state desegregation mandates (Brisk, 2006). However, some culturally insular ethnic enclaves are so isolated geographically that entire maintenance bilingual schools that exclusively serve one ethnic group exist without violating the law. To illustrate, the Rough Rock Community School, in Chinle, Arizona, is designed to "educate, enlighten, motivate, challenge, and assist in the proper cultural rearing of . . . Navajo children so they can be self-respecting, respectful of others, speak and practice their language and culture, and be totally functional in the Anglo society," according to its website (http://www.roughrock.k12.az.us/About_Us.htm). At this school, according to Brisk (2006), Navajo students first learn to read in the Navajo language and then continue Navajo language instruction up through the second grade. Beginning in third grade, approximately half of the instruction is in Navajo and half is in English. The state of Arizona's required courses are typically taught in English, and non-required courses are taught in Navajo. The school is designed to socialize students in Navajo community leadership knowledge and awareness. Hence in grades 7 through 12, students study Navajo history, Navajo social problems, Navajo government, and Navajo economic development (Brisk, 2006).

Transitional Bilingual Education

Transitional bilingual education (TBE) can also be referred to as remedial bilingual education (see Thomas & Collier, 2002). The overall goal of TBE programs is for students to learn English by beginning with most instruction in the native language, gradually taking a higher percentage of subjects in English, and then to be eventually mainstreamed into traditional English instructional programs. In order to do this successfully, however, such programs are built on the assumption that literacy in the native (non-English) language serves as the proper foundation for English reading and writing. According to Thomas and Collier (2002), two types of TBE programs are common. One type begins with 90 percent of the instruction in the native non-English language, and gradually increasing English instruction until students can be mainstreamed into English-only instruction in the fifth grade. Another program type exposes students to 50-50 native and English instruction for three to four years before transitioning students to the mainstream.

Early-exit TBE programs offer a third possibility, where students begin native-language literacy instruction in the early grades, but all other subjects are delivered in English. At the end of first or second grade, most students are mainstreamed into English-only instruction (Ramirez, 1992). A modified version of TBE for schools, called pull-out TBE programs, has non-English-speaking students placed in English-only mainstream classrooms, but pulls them out daily for native language and English as a Second Language (ESL) instruction. The overall goal of pull-out TBE programs is to help students with their work in mainstream English-only classes. The role of the pull-out bilingual or ESL teacher is to use the native language to reinforce English-language/literacy development in the mainstream class, as well as to help mainstream teachers communicate with non-English-speaking families.

ESL (English as a Second Language) Programs

ESL programs, also called *remedial English-only programs*, are designed to deliver special classes in the English language for students who are not proficient in English. Typically, students spend most of the school day in mainstream classrooms, but they also attend daily ESL classes. Students are either pulled out of mainstream classes for ESL instruction, or ESL teachers assist mainstream teachers in their classrooms with students who are not yet proficient in English. At the high school level, ESL classes can be offered at the beginning, intermediate, or advanced level (Brisk, 2006).

Structured Immersion Programs

Structured immersion programs, sometimes referred to as sheltered immersion programs, can deliver instruction in two ways. In one method, language minority students are segregated within a school for instruction in English only. Here, teachers simplify the language of instruction, develop highly structured lessons, and use pictures, objects, hands-on activities, and films to present lessons. A second method shares all characteristics of the first method, with the only difference being that teachers have some knowledge of the students' native language, which is necessary to understand the students and occasionally (but rarely) use the students' native language for clarification (Brisk, 2006).

URBAN, SUBURBAN, AND RURAL SCHOOLING

The relative percentage of students (nationally) within four racial/ethnic groups enrolled in city, suburban, and rural school districts (for year 2006–2007) is provided in Figure 4.1.

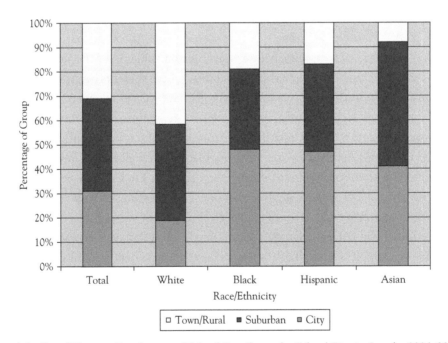

Figure 4.1 Race/Ethnicity Distribution of School Enrollment by School District Locale, 2006–2007 (Adapted from Fry, 2009)

There are tremendous differences in the contexts of urban, suburban, and rural schooling that are related to district resources, student characteristics, and the working conditions for teachers—all of which impact student learning in varying degrees. A comprehensive discussion of these factors is beyond the scope of this chapter, but readers can consult several excellent sources for a more thorough discussion of these issues (e.g., see Monk, 2007; Truscott & Truscott, 2005; Weiner, 2006).

Teach for America

Inner-city schools plagued by high levels of violence, low teacher/staff morale, and low levels of academic achievement find that they struggle considerably with finding appropriately trained teachers to teach at these schools. These schools have turned to the *Teach for America* (TFA) program for potential teaching applicants. The TFA program prepares young, highly motivated teaching candidates who have degrees from non-education fields but who are pursuing alternative modes of certification to work in public schools (see description in Sidebar 4.1).

Sidebar 4.1   Teach for America

Teach for America (TFA) is a privately funded program that sends college graduates from disciplines outside of education into America's poorest urban and rural school districts to teach for two years. The current CEO of TFA is Wendy Kopp, who founded TFA shortly after she graduated from the Woodrow Wilson School of Public and International Affairs at Princeton University in 1989. The genesis of the TFA concept can be traced to her undergraduate thesis, in which she proposed the creation of an elite teacher corps that would make a tangible difference in the lives of America's neediest schools and students.

During a conversation with her fellow college students in 1988, a novel idea struck her to create a national teaching corps (modeled after the Peace Corps) of talented recent college graduates, who would commit two years to teach in urban or rural schools, without having a formal degree in education. After securing commitments from major corporate investors, the first TFA Institute was held in June 1990 at the University of Southern California, with 500 new recruits as the first inaugural class. Ten years later, the TFA movement had grown to approximately 1,500 members teaching in the nation's low-income schools.

The problems in such schools come as no surprise to veteran educators. Nationwide, an estimated 14 percent of teachers leave the classroom in the first year of teaching, and nearly half leave the profession by their fifth year. These dismal rates

(continued)

are particularly pronounced in low-performing, high-poverty urban schools. In the 2005–2006 school year of one urban school profiled by Foote (2008), approximately one-third of the faculty was new and three-fourths had been teaching at the school less than five years. To make matters worse, school districts are unable to fire incompetent teachers, who are protected by tenure and strong teachers' unions. Thus, incompetent teachers are routinely transferred to the less-attractive positions within districts. With rare exceptions, union laws bind principals to accept any tenured transfer teacher regardless of past performance. Without a large pool of applicants seeking positions in difficult inner-city schools, principals have no choice but to accept less-experienced and less-effective teachers. Thus, TFA graduates become some schools' primary hiring source.

The selection process for admission to TFA mirrors its core value of selecting the "best and the brightest." In 2005, 17,000 students applied for only 2,000 open spots—among them 12 percent of the Yale University senior class, 11 percent of the Dartmouth and Amherst College graduating classes, and 8 percent from Princeton and Harvard (Foote, 2008, p. 27). Those who were eventually accepted had average GPA and SAT scores of 3.5 and 1310, respectively. In 2009, the application pool rose to 35,000 applications (Kopp, 2009).

The missionary zeal of the TFA movement is its most distinguishing characteristic. "Closing the achievement gap" (between low-income minority students and higher-income white students) is the single most pervasive rallying cry of the TFA movement.

TFA training has been described as resembling an army bootcamp rather than a teaching preparation program. Once a selected candidate agrees to become a part of TFA, he or she is mailed notebooks covering crash courses in diversity, classroom management, literacy, learning theory, and leadership (Foote, 2008). These notebooks, in addition to teacher observation assignments, are expected to be completed before the intensive five-week summer training session that TFA recruits are required to attend before beginning their first year of teaching. As described by Foote (2008), new recruits move to college dorms in early July, where they will spend the next five weeks in 16-hour-a-day intensive training. The first week of training begins with breakfast served at 5:45 A.M. each day, followed by classroom training from 8 A.M. to 4 P.M. After dinner, evening training sessions begin with three-hour classes starting at 6:30 P.M., after which students are expected to prepare lesson plans for the following day.

By the second week of training, students are required to spend time working in actual urban or rural classrooms with summer school students. Here, TFA students are expected to teach actual classroom lessons while being observed by veteran teachers. By the fourth training week, TFA recruits are expected to function as the main teacher in the classroom for an entire day. Interspersed throughout this rigorous training regimen are large pep rally assemblies in which recruits hear uplifting motivational speeches from TFA alumni, trainers, and its CEO (founder Wendy Kopp) when available.

TFA has formed strategic alliances with state credentialing bodies. All TFA corps members must receive a state teaching credential before they're hired by a school, and they must be considered "highly qualified" according to state-specific requirements. This may include passing a content-knowledge test and/or completing specific college courses as part of a major or minor related to the subject they will teach. Because most TFA members haven't completed a traditional course of study in education before teaching, they are considered "non-traditional" teachers in most states. The credentials they receive are often referred to as "alternative" certificates or licenses. If they choose, TFA members may elect to complete coursework through a local college/university while they are teaching, as a means of achieving advanced levels of certification or licensure (for further information, see http://www.teachforamerica.org/our-organization).

As with any successful organization, TFA has its detractors. Linda Darling-Hammond, currently Professor of Education at Stanford University and former President of the American Educational Research Association, has argued that TFA is harmful to vulnerable students who are most in need of qualified teachers. More pointedly, she criticizes the program as little more than providing a convenient "pit stop" for ambitious students on the way to more lucrative careers in business, medicine, or law. Politically, opposition from teachers' unions is so strong that TFA is allotted approximately 3,800 teaching slots nationwide (as of 2009; see Kopp, 2009), as districts are required to place a cap on the number of TFA teachers who will be accepted. Disgruntled former TFA teachers (or those who have worked for similar organizations) complain that rotating relatively inexperienced teachers in and out of the most challenging classrooms for a short two years does nothing to close the achievement gap (see http://www.feministe.us/blog/archives/2008/08/23/why-i-hate-teach-for-america/).

However, TFA also has its ardent supporters. Many will point to the fact that traditional teacher education programs attract a disproportionately high number of students from the lower end of the distribution of academic ability (Sowell, 1993, 1996, 2002), and traditional teacher education courses have been ridiculed as practically worthless (Kramer, 2000). In contrast, TFA recruits have highly competitive SAT scores, and they are not required to take any preparation courses that are far removed from the central goal of doing whatever it takes to raise students' achievement test scores. This characteristic makes TFA recruits particularly attractive for employment in charter schools, which are not bound by teacher union regulations (e.g., see Whitman, 2008).

(continued)

In 2007, Ms. Kopp founded *Teach For All*, billed as an organization that applies the methods of TFA to countries around the world. Today, TFA has grown into a large, nonprofit organization with more than 8,000 members (who taught during the 2010–2011 school year) and a network of more than 20,000 TFA alumni. Ms. Kopp's experiences are chronicled in two books published by PublicAffairs: *One Day, All Children . . . The Unlikely Triumph of Teach for America and What I Learned Along the Way* (2003) and *A Chance to Make History: What Works and What Doesn't in Providing an Excellent Education for All* (2011).

(adapted from Foote, 2008)

Urban/Suburban School Psychology Practice

The working conditions experienced by school psychologists are often influenced by wide variation in the demographic characteristics of children and communities served by school districts. Empirical surveys that collect data on various aspects of school psychologists' working conditions, practices, and roles/functions have been fairly commonplace (e.g., see Bramlett, Murphy, Johnson, Wallingsford, & Hall, 2002; Brown, Holcombe, Bolen, & Thomson, 2006). However, studies that incorporate more in-depth qualitative and ethnographic methodologies and approaches (for studying school psychology practice) are not. Published material that compares and contrasts professional practices and working conditions for school psychologists across urban, suburban, and rural settings is quite rare (Fagan & Wise, 2007). The only well-known ethnographic study of school psychology practice that comes closest to comparing working conditions across urban and suburban contexts is represented in research conducted in the late 1970s, but published in 1989, in a book entitled *Testers and Testing* (Milofsky, 1989).

Milofsky (1989) observed and interviewed 33 school psychologists employed in the Chicago Public School system and in several suburban school districts outside of Chicago in the late 1970s. This occurred during the period of intense scrutiny of IQ test bias and the Larry P. trial in California (e.g., see Elliott, 1987).

Milofsky interprets his data by making a fundamental distinction between what he calls *profession-oriented* school psychologists versus *school-oriented* school psychologists. School-oriented school psychologists tend to be concentrated in urban schools, particularly those within the city of Chicago. These professionals tend to view themselves primarily as educators, because most of these professionals are former teachers. These professionals tend to see their job as providing support to the regular education system, and they do not seek to actively change the status quo. That is to say, if they are asked to test *x* number of students, they take seriously the obligation to do so cooperatively and efficiently. School-oriented school psychologists accept the bureaucratic job requirements (i.e., paperwork) and interact with students in a professional but somewhat distant and impersonal manner. Many of these professionals work in relative isolation from the schools, teachers, and children they serve. School-oriented school psychologists see standardized testing as providing highly objective information that is far superior to the potential bias that is inherent in having too much background knowledge of the student's personal or family life.

In contrast, profession-oriented school psychologists tend to be concentrated in suburban schools. These professionals tend to view themselves as clinical or community psychologists who happen to work in schools. These school psychologists are more prone to be sensitized to external factors that may contribute to school difficulties (e.g., child's family, poor relationship between student and teacher, or systemic group conflicts in the school environment). In short, profession-oriented school psychologists tend to avoid blaming student failure only on hypothetical problems that are "contained inside the child's head" (Milofsky, 1989, p. 11). Profession-oriented psychologists view standardized testing as having limited usefulness in diagnosing school problems, and they seek more complete non-test information that can shed light on the roots of problems and what kinds of interventions may be most appropriate.

Although these differences provide a fascinating template for understanding the professional identities of school psychologists, the most interesting finding from Milofsky's research is the correlation of these differences with district demographics. Milofsky found that school psychologists with the highest volume and rate of testing tended to work in urban school districts serving the highest proportions of low-income minority (particularly black or Hispanic) students. Milofsky describes urban school psychology as "narrow, formalized, routine, and dull," involving little more than testing children for most of the day (p. 11). When this happens, the sheer repetitiveness of the job "allows the [school psychologist] to practice without thinking creatively, innovatively, or critically" (p. 72). The role of the urban school psychologist is defined primarily by the expectations of the regular school staff. Urban school psychologists have learned how to streamline assessments so as to complete the maximum number of assessments in the shortest period of time. Urban school psychologists find that they have little time to speculate as to why children are failing in schools, or to seek insights from other members of the multidisciplinary team. According to Milofsky, school psychologists who go beyond test scores to understand children, or who view their work as "creative and political" (as in being sensitive to do whatever is needed to effect positive change in schools), tend to serve primarily white children in suburban schools.

There are obvious limitations in generalizing to the broader field of school psychology from Milofsky's conclusions (see also Fagan, 1990; Harris, 1991), not the least of which is that the study is more than 30 years old. It would be interesting to speculate how this research would be conducted in the era of Response to Intervention (RtI), or in other large urban, suburban, or rural school systems in different areas of the country.

LEVELS OF SCHOOL RACIAL/ETHNIC INTEGRATION

The quality of a minority student's school experience is influenced, in part, by the levels of racial/ethnic school integration in the school contexts in which his or her education takes place. The level of school integration is determined by complex factors related to national demographic trends, local neighborhood residential patterns, as well as parental choice of schools for their children. Some minority students, for whatever reasons, find themselves as the "only black," "only Hispanic," or "only Asian" in their classrooms throughout most of their schooling experiences. At the other extreme, many minority students find that they rarely encounter any whites throughout their schooling experiences, as most of their peers, teachers, and building administrators are from their own ethnic/racial group.

According to Fry (2009), the typical white suburban student in 2006–2007 attended a school whose student body was 75 percent white. In contrast, typical black, Hispanic, and Asian suburban students in 2006–2007 attended schools that were only 34 percent, 31 percent, and 48 percent white, respectively. When compared to similar trends 13 years earlier, more racial/ethnic minority students are enrolling in suburban schools.

When this same national data set is analyzed from the perspective of attending school with same-race/ethnicity peers, interesting results emerge for Hispanics. In 2006–2007, the typical suburban Hispanic student attended a school that was 49 percent Latino, which has increased slightly over the previous 13 years. In 2006–2007, typical suburban black and Asian students attended schools that were 44 percent Black and 23 percent Asian, respectively.

The Dissimilarity Index

The *dissimilarity index* is widely used by researchers to assess the racial/ethnic segregation in schools. The dissimilarity index is intended to assess the evenness of the spread of students across schools in a school district by measuring the proportion of a student group that would have to change schools in order for all schools in the district to have the same proportion of the group as the districtwide average (Fry, 2009). For example, a dissimilarity index of 0.0 means that students are spread evenly within schools according to their proportions across the school district. Thus, a district that has 30 percent minorities overall would have 30 percent of minority students represented within each school in the district. At the other extreme, a dissimilarity index of 1.0 reflects complete segregation of a racial/ethnic group within the district. A dissimilarity index of .6 for Group A means that 60 percent of the Group A students in the district would need to change schools in order for all schools within the district to reflect the percentage of Group A in the school district overall (Fry, 2009).

According to the most recent data for the 2006–2007 school year, the top 10 suburban education agencies with the highest segregation levels for blacks, Hispanics, and Asians (as measured by the dissimilarity index) are represented in Tables 4.3, 4.4, and 4.5, respectively.

Table 4.3   Top 10 Suburban Education Agencies (With at Least 1,000 Black Students) With Highest Levels of Black Segregation, 2006–2007

Suburban Education Agency	Metro Area	Dissimilarity Index*
Maywood-Melrose Park-Broadview 89	Chicago-Naperville-Joliet, IL-IN-WI	0.79
East Allen County Schools	Fort Wayne, IN	0.77
DeKalb County	Atlanta-Sandy Springs-Marietta, GA	0.74
East St. Louis SD 189	St. Louis, MO-IL	0.72
Fulton County	Atlanta-Sandy Springs-Marietta, GA	0.70
West Memphis School District	Memphis, TN-MS-AR	0.66
Dade	Miami-Fort Lauderdale-Pompano Beach, FL	0.66
Bremen Chsd 228	Chicago-Naperville-Joliet, IL-IN-WI	0.65
Sewanhaka Central High School District	New York Northern New Jersey Long Island, NY-NJ-PA	0.64
Ouachita Parish School Board	Monroe, LA	0.62

*See Explanation in Text
(Adapted from Fry, 2009)

Table 4.4   Top 10 Suburban Education Agencies (With at Least 1,000 Hispanic Students) With Highest Levels of Hispanic Segregation, 2006–2007

Suburban Education Agency	Metro Area	Dissimilarity Index*
Maywood-Melrose Park-Broadview 89	Chicago-Naperville-Joliet, IL-IN-WI	0.74
DeKalb County	Atlanta-Sandy Springs-Marietta, GA	0.67
Lennox Elementary	Los Angeles-Long Beach-Santa Ana, CA	0.59
Washingtonville Central School District	Poughkeepsie-Newburgh-Middletown, NY	0.57
Prince George's County Public Schools	Washington-Arlington-Alexandria, DC-VA-MD-WV	0.57
Dade	Miami-Fort Lauderdale-Pompano Beach, FL	0.54
Placentia-Yorba Linda Unified	Los Angeles-Long Beach-Santa Ana, CA	0.54
Newhall Elementary	Los Angeles-Long Beach-Santa Ana, CA	0.53
CUSD 300	Chicago-Naperville-Joliet, IL-IN-WI	0.53
Berkeley SD 87	Chicago-Naperville-Joliet, IL-IN-WI	0.52

*See explanation in text
(Adapted from Fry, 2009)

Table 4.5   Top 10 Suburban Education Agencies (With at Least 1,000 Asian Students) With Highest Levels of Asian Segregation, 2006–2007

Suburban Education Agency	Metro Area	Dissimilarity Index*
Montebello Unified	Los Angeles-Long Beach-Santa Ana, CA	0.67
DeKalb County	Atlanta-Sandy Springs-Marietta, GA	0.56
Pasadena ISD	Houston-Sugarland-Baytown, TX	0.55
Fulton County	Atlanta-Sandy Springs-Marietta, GA	0.53
Hacienda La Puente Unified	Los Angeles-Long Beach-Santa Ana, CA	0.52
Rowland Unified	Los Angeles-Long Beach-Santa Ana, CA	0.50
Fort Bend ISD	Houston-Sugarland-Baytown, TX	0.42
Chino Valley Unified	Riverside-San Bernardino-Ontario, CA	0.42
Knox County School District	Knoxville, TN	0.41
Lodi Unified	Stockton, CA	0.40

*See explanation in text
(Adapted from Fry, 2009)

SCHOOL CLIMATE

School climate is typically viewed as a complex construct that includes the following variables (see Lehr, 2005, p. 471): (a) the quality of interpersonal relations between students and teachers; (b) the extent to which the school is perceived as a safe and caring place; (c) the degree to which students, parents, and staff are involved in collaborative decision making; and (d) the degree to which there are high expectations for student learning. According to Lehr (2005), a school can be said to foster a positive climate when the school is (a) clean, well-maintained, and inviting to outsiders; (b) students are positively motivated to achieve to the best of their abilities, and they internalize the importance of hard work in the service of school learning; and (c) interactions among school professionals, and between school professionals and students, can be characterized as respectful and cooperative. To the extent that one or more of these indicators is significantly compromised, the school climate is negatively characterized by contentious relationships among administrators and teachers; both teachers and students develop negative attitudes toward the school; the school is characterized by low academic expectations and apathy; students become alienated and disengaged from school and learning (e.g., see Sidebar 4.2); and pervasive discipline problems demoralize students, teachers, and staff. For example, Roth (1994) opines:

> If the social climate of the school is determined by children from lower-class backgrounds, as is often the case in urban schools, education is likely to

deteriorate, and middle-class parents . . . will desert such schools. . . . An effective school climate can be achieved for lower-class children, but . . . it has to be implemented from above. (p. 280)

Given the demographics of race/ethnicity, socioeconomic status, and difficult challenges in urban schooling, nonwhite and immigrant children and youth attend troubled schools in greater proportion than does the general population (e.g., see Foote, 2008; Suárez-Orozco et al., 2008), and they are more likely to attend schools characterized by negative school climates.

Sidebar 4.2   One Author's Observations of High School Climate

Commenting on research findings from Steinberg, Brown, and Dornbusch (1996), Weissberg describes many high schools as follows:

> An extremely high proportion of students fail to take school seriously—they spend countless hours "goofing off" with friends, often cheat on tests or rely on the homework of others. For many, attending classes is just a nuisance—between a third and 40 percent admit they are not paying attention or not trying hard. Teachers routinely report having classes where half the students seem "checked out." Furthermore, little non-classroom time is devoted to academically-related activities. Homework, even when minimal, is clearly secondary to athletics, socializing, or employment. Academic achievement is not highly valued, and is often demeaned. Less than 20 percent believe that good grades bestow social prestige . . . and a reputation as "a brain" appealed to only one in ten. . . . Students frequently said that low grades failed to bring parental rebuke and one third indicated that parents had scant idea of their school progress.
>
> Student indifference and outside distractions create a downward spiral of low achievement. Faced with bored students, many tired from [outside-of-school] work, teachers stop making the extra effort to inspire, even just to impart the basics, and this, in turn, confirms to students that schooling is just a waste of time. Meanwhile, professional pedagogues who sense the disengagement attempt to make learning "exciting" with bedazzling textbooks and ancillaries, films and other attention-grabber "fun" stunts to jump-start enthusiasm. Though students might welcome the vacation from "dry" academics, these novelties totally fail to address deeper defects, notably a lack of discipline or an ability to concentrate. And without these

(continued)

essential "grind" qualities, subjects like math and science are "too hard" and academic motivation further wilts. . . . [S]chools abandon their traditional and inescapably tedious educational role though administrators can readily defend themselves as "trying to be relevant in today's attention-deficit disorder culture." If juicing things up fail, just keep reducing the assigned readings and homework to make schooling more palatable, just as a TV producer might dumb-down a TV sitcom and add a few sex jokes to sustain a dwindling audience.

Excerpt from Weissberg, R. (2010). *Bad students, not bad schools* (pp. 37–38). New Brunswick, NJ: Transaction Publishers. Copyright 2010 by Transaction Publishers. Reprinted by permission of the publisher.

School Fighting

National data reinforces this perception. According to 2009 statistics from the U.S. Bureau of Justice, the percentage of students (broken down by race/ethnicity) in grades 9 to 12 who report having been in a physical fight (at least one time during the 12 months prior to being surveyed) is reported in Figure 4.2.

Particularly noteworthy about these statistics is the observation that the two groups who report the highest percentage of physical fights anywhere (including outside of school property) also report the highest percentage of participating in fights on school property (i.e., American Indian/Alaska Natives and African Americans).

In related 2007 data, the percentage of students aged 12 to 18 who report being fearful of being harmed at school is shown in Figure 4.3. Although percentages of students reporting fearfulness of attack are relatively small within each racial/ethnic group, African Americans report the highest percentages, which is a theme that is consistent with other negative school climate data.

School Violence

The degree of school violence that is present in the day-to-day functioning of schools plays a big role in the quality of education that students receive. This problem is so pervasive, that many students in violent schools have reported (in the context of survey research) that they feel safer in their homes and neighborhoods and least safe at school (e.g., see Laub & Lauritsen, 1998; Steinberg, Allensworth, & Johnson, 2011). Smith and Smith (2006) conducted extensive interviews with 12 elementary, middle, or high school teachers who quit their jobs at violent urban schools within five years after being hired. The omnipresent threat or actual occurrence of violence was a common feature of

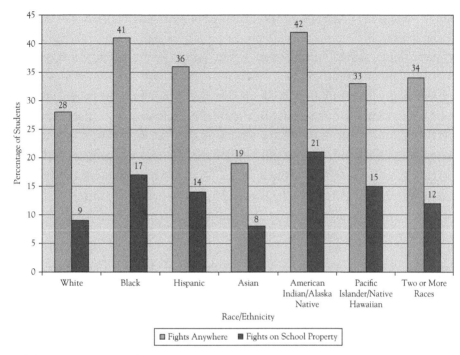

Figure 4.2   Percentage of Students in Grades 9–12 Who Reported Having Been in a Physical Fight at Least One Time During the Previous 12 Months by Location and Race/Ethnicity, 2009 (Robers, Zhang & Truman, 2010)

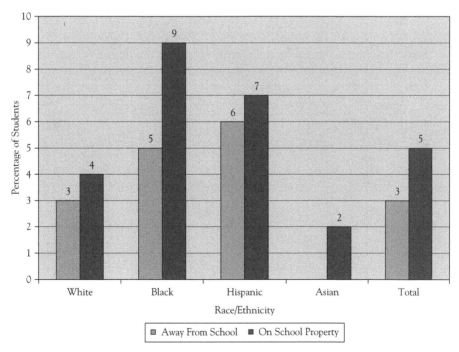

Figure 4.3   Percentage of Students Ages 12–18 Who Reported Being Afraid of Attack or Harm During the School Year by Race/Ethnicity and Location, 2007 (Robers, Zhang & Truman, 2010)

all of these teachers' reasons for quitting their jobs, and in some cases leaving the profession altogether.

Not surprisingly, school teachers in urban school settings (in contrast to those teaching in suburban, rural, or small town settings) report the highest percentages of being threatened with injury from students during the year prior to being surveyed (see Figure 4.4). As examples, one teacher reported fights that would inevitably escalate into full-blown "race wars" between groups, which in turn required classrooms to be under lock-down status for hours on end, and police in full riot gear being called in to use pepper spray to disperse unruly crowds. One teacher, who was pregnant at the time, reported being pinned against the blackboard by an unusually large fifth grader. Another male teacher reported being knocked to the ground and mugged by a student. Smith and Smith (2006) report the following statements made by interviewees:

> This [school] was in the middle of the ghetto. Your life wasn't worth ten cents outside the door; I didn't even like driving there during the day and I bought a cell phone just to feel a little safer; it spooked me out to sit alone in my classroom after hours in that neighborhood and I'd practically run to my car if it were dark out and no one could walk me out; they found bodies in the park next door to the school; I had to drive past this place where a bunch of vagrants hung out and drug dealers were selling. (p. 39)

Such threats of violence in the school atmosphere made teachers unwilling to break up fights between students on school grounds, for fear that they would be beaten up by students. Some teachers reported being unwilling to take students outside of the school

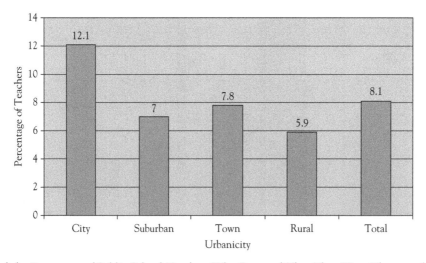

Figure 4.4   Percentage of Public School Teachers Who Reported That They Were Threatened With Injury by a Student From School During the Previous 12 Months, by Urbanicity, 2007–2008 (Robers, Zhang & Truman, 2010)

grounds for field trips (for safety concerns). Some teachers reported being unwilling to be involved in educational projects held on the school site after school hours, because they were fearful of what might happen, and parents were afraid of coming into the community (surrounding the school) at night (Smith & Smith, 2006).

Racial/Ethnic Conflicts

One issue that is rarely, if at all, discussed in school psychology journals and newsletters is the increased level of conflicts among students, teachers, and administrators observed in schools that have significant numbers of pupils from two or more distinct racial/ethnic groups, particularly at secondary school levels. Such conflicts make a mockery of the notion that mere exposure to persons from different racial/ethnic groups should magically foster racial/ethnic "harmony" and "understanding." In many districts, the exact opposite appears to be the case.

Beginning in 1975, Janet Schofield (1982) spent three years studying the impact of integration on student relationships in a middle school in the industrial northeast. One-quarter of the school's population was African American, and the majority of the student body was white. Early in the study, Schofield discovered that the key variable at the root of all subsequent problems was the wide gap in academic skills between whites and blacks. Black students, on average, fell approximately one standard deviation below whites on standardized ability tests, which was subsequently reflected in their average grades received in schoolwork. These obvious disparities in academic performance were noticed by students in both groups, which fostered the belief (again, among both groups) that whites were brighter and more interested in learning than blacks. In interviews, Schofield found that black students perceived white students as arrogant and conceited, but rule abiding and physically restrained. Black students were perceived by both white and black students as being more disruptive in class and more inclined to use toughness in the service of defending themselves and dominating others. Over time, more than 80 percent of suspensions at the school involved black students. As culled from interviews, white students developed the habit of avoiding areas of the school that were unsupervised by adults, as a means for avoiding altercations with black students. When social integration did occur, it usually occurred in the context of team sports at the school, but rarely in non-sports contexts. Over time, white students who did not previously hold negative attitudes toward blacks gradually developed negative attitudes (Schofield, 1982).

Although many districts are ethnically diverse by all superficial appearances, there is little social integration of students. The following excerpt represents intergroup interaction patterns that are all-too-common in racially and ethnically diverse schools:

At [a northern California] Middle School, more than three quarters of the students are either Latino or African American: specifically, 45 percent are Latino,

31 percent are African American, 15 percent are Asian, 7 percent are white, 1.5 percent are Filipino, 0.3 percent are Pacific Islander, and 0.2 percent are Native American. Mexicans make up by far the largest immigrant group in the school: nearly 90 percent of all immigrant students there are Mexican. . . . Inside the cafeteria, we cannot find a single racially mixed group. The segregation here is absolute: Asians sit with Asians, blacks with blacks, Latinos with Latinos, whites with whites. The seating arrangement is a near perfect reflection of the school's social organization. In our two years at the school, we seldom saw students from different ethnic groups working together on projects. When groups come together, it is usually to fight. (Suárez-Orozco et al., 2008, pp. 97, 99)

In many instances, the more racially/ethnically heterogeneous schools are, the *greater* the potential for conflicts. Select examples of such conflicts are described in Sidebar 4.3.

⌦ Sidebar 4.3   The Strengths of School Diversity?

- One author describes everyday life in a contemporary inner-city Los Angeles high school:

  Most teachers made an effort to "integrate" the races in their classrooms. But outside, on the quad and the scruffy playing fields, the cultural turf was clearly demarcated. The handball courts belonged to the Latinos. The football field and basketball courts were all-black terrain. . . . The cafeteria divided pretty much the same way: as you entered, it was blacks in the left-hand corner, Spanish speakers in the first few benches, special ed students tucked away in the right-hand corner. The area just outside the cafeteria—the eastern edge of the quad—was a kind of demilitarized zone bounded by two trees. The African American football players sat under one. Under the other was a group of Latinos, some of them athletes, too. The understanding was that between the trees there would always be peace. The treaty has yet to be broken. (Foote, 2008, p. 22)

- The student body at Jefferson Elementary School (a pseudonym) is 86 percent black and 85 percent of them are poor, according to school district data. The school has been plagued by racial tensions between administrators and teachers, among the teaching staff, and between the community and the school. In 2008, for example, vandals defaced a mural on the side of the school with anti-Semitic graffiti. According to news reports, one angry black parent accused a former school administrator of saying that Muslim students looked like "flying nuns." Four white teachers at the school have filed federal race-bias lawsuits alleging that the current black school principal created a hostile work environment by suggesting that they were unfit to teach black children. According to their lawsuits, the principal allowed black teachers to ignore certain school rules but required white teachers to adhere to them. In addition, the lawsuit accuses the principal of forcing them to read an article which said that "white teachers do not have the ability to teach African-American students" (Associated Press, 2011).

- West City High School (a pseudonym) is 70 percent African American and only 18 percent Asian. Three Asian immigrant students, who are recipients of the "Freedom From Fear" award (designed to recognize students who are committed to protecting immigrants from abuse), have become vocal activists after directly experiencing or witnessing anti-Asian violence in the school they attend. One Asian student relates how he was twice attacked both in school and in his neighborhood during his very first week of school, which thereafter was followed by a steady barrage of verbal taunts and physical attacks. Other Asian students report that food is thrown at them during lunchtime, accompanied by being punched and kicked in the hallways and bathrooms and assaulted while walking back from school. Tensions came to a head when 26 Asian students were targeted in a series of attacks at the school by a group of mostly African American students. Seven of the victims had to be rushed to the emergency room to treat their wounds. According to these Asian students, police and school officials frequently turned a deaf ear to their complaints. According to the students most victimized by these attacks, an "institutional acceptance" of violence as a norm is the root cause of their problems (Sundaram, 2011).

- Raza studies (race studies) have been taught in the Tucson Unified School District (TUSD) for about a dozen years. One of the textbooks used in the Raza studies curriculum is titled *Occupied America*, in which the author advocates the need for Mexico to retake seven states in the American Southwest and "kill gringos" so that the Southwest would become a Chicano nation. Recently, however, the Tucson School Board convened to vote on a proposal to make Mexican American Studies an elective rather than a requirement in the district. Before the vote could be taken, a mob of largely Hispanic students and adults stormed into the meeting room, chanting slogans and chaining themselves to chairs. As a result of this

(*continued*)

disturbance, the school board meeting was cancelled. According to a news report of the incident, the TUSC is waiting for the results of a state audit to determine if the ethnic studies program complies with an Arizona state law that has recently outlawed ethnic studies programs in public schools (Gibson, 2011). According to one writer, the state law represents an "attack on the right of oppressed people to learn their own history . . . [as well as an attempt] to whip up a racist frenzy against Indigenous and Latino/a peoples and blame them for the misery and suffering imposed by the capitalist system itself" (Teitelbaum, 2011).

- An African American young woman has initiated a class-action lawsuit against her predominantly white former high school for racial discrimination after students there celebrated "Wednesday Wigger Day" during the school's annual school spirit week. *Wigger* is a slang term for a white person who emulates the mannerisms, language, and fashions associated with black ghetto culture. In celebration of the event, participating students wear oversized sports jerseys, low-slung pants, baseball hats cocked to the side, and doo-rags on their heads, as well as displaying gang signs. Although the schoolwide event was not officially sanctioned by school administrators, they nevertheless were aware of it but are alleged to have done nothing to stop it. The student who brought the lawsuit against the school district reported that she suffered from depression, loss of sleep, and was forced to quit several school activities as a result of the "hostile environment" created by the school event (Goodyear, 2011).

- A researcher reports on observations from an ethnically diverse American middle school with a large immigrant enrollment (Suárez-Orozco et al., 2008):

The large concentration of Mexican-origin students created a special dynamic, and Mexican culture dominated the ethos of the school. ESL teachers consistently drew from Mexican culture and not from the cultural backgrounds of students of other nationalities, including Salvadorian, Guatemalan, Peruvian, and Vietnamese. . . . [A] Mexican girl and a Salvadorian girl started school on the same day. The teacher asked them to introduce themselves to the class. The Mexican girl got a cheer from the crowd when she said she was from Guadalajara, Mexico. Nobody said anything when the Salvadorian girl introduced herself as being from San Vicente, El Salvador. This reaction was typical whenever new children came into a classroom. During recess, the Mexican newcomer was already talking with a group of five Mexican girls while the Salvadorian girl sat alone on a bench. . . . Newcomer Mexican immigrants had their own grievances about their more acculturated Mexican-American peers. . . . [A] twelve-year old new immigrant . . . explained her dislike of Mexican-American girls: "Chicanas are stuck-up. I don't like them because they feel they are from here and not Mexicans, even if they are as dark as we are. They speak Spanish, but they pretend they speak only English and they don't talk to you if you are Mexican." (p. 101–102)

- A study conducted in the Irving Independent School District (Texas) interviewed 124 black elementary school students over a three-year period (beginning in the third grade), who attended 20 elementary schools in a majority Hispanic (71 percent) district. Among many findings, the study concluded that African American students feel lonely, isolated, and "inferior" because of the large numbers of Hispanic children in their classes whose "Brown mannerisms, style, and language form the dominant culture of Irving's elementary classrooms" (Hines, 2011, p. 4). The principal investigator of the study reports asking African American students if there were a lot of Hispanic students at their schools. The researcher reports:

Looking at me with an angry demeanor, all of the students said "YES!" In a very derisive tone, one of the African American female students exclaimed, "Mexicans are everywhere!" Another African American student followed with "And we don't get along with them!" . . . They also indicated that Hispanic students almost always attempted to control African American students. For example, one African American student said, "The Mexicans are very mean to us." He continued, "They try to fight us over everything!" (Hines, 2011, p. 47)

Fear of "Acting White"

When significant numbers of two or more distinct racial/ethnic groups are represented in a school, and these groups display stark differences in mean levels of cognitive aptitude for more demanding schoolwork, then academic achievement becomes "color-coded" (e.g., see Gottfredson, 2005; see also Sidebar 4.4).

Sidebar 4.4   King of the Blacks

My wife and I have big dreams for our children. We want nothing for them but health, happiness and success and we recognize that a good education can be a step towards realizing that goal. We also demand that our children perform up to their potential. The skills one learns in school—study habits, attention to detail, and meeting deadlines—are essential for success in the work world. In this we are like every other parent in America. . . .

His [7th grade] mid-term report card arrived in the mail. His mother and I were underwhelmed. The comments on my son's report card indicated that he is under the mistaken impression that school is for socializing and his grades reflect a rather lackluster effort at best. . . . There are many black students at my son's middle school, but he is 1 of only 3 in the highly-gifted magnet program within the school. The HGM is a program restricted to students that score 99.9% on an intellectual assessment test. One of three! That doesn't leave much wiggle room to be the black kid that can't cut it, that clowns in class or that falls behind.

Last year I attended the honor roll ceremony and the vast majority of the students receiving certificates were Asian. I didn't enter the auditorium prepared to count heads, but it was hard to miss the fact that every other child walking across the stage had an Asian surname. Nor was it difficult to miss the 3 black faces sitting amongst the rows of eager and happy students.

Conventional wisdom says that black parents are less actively involved in their children's education; that there exists an anti-intellectualism in the black community such that academic achievement is seen as acting white; that black students do not read or write as well as their white and Asian counterparts and that the middle class achievement gap is due to racism as opposed to a gap in work habits. In addition, convention says black boys are angry, prone to violence and better athletes than they are academics. . . .

My son told us about a Korean girl in his class whose opinions command influence among the other Asian girls in the school, or at least she thinks they do. According to him the students refer to her as the "queen of the Asians." She is a straight A student.

My son's little brother asked if there was a "queen of the blacks" at the school.

"Well," my son replied, "there is a king of the blacks."

"Who is that?" his little brother asked.

My son responded, "He is this boy that got held back last year."

I cringed.

My wife cringed.

No doubt there is more to the story but on its face it is damning. How is it that the "queen of the Asians" is a straight A student while the "king of the blacks" is the kid that flunked 8th grade?

This . . . is the paradigm concerned black parents are battling. This is what distinguishes us as parents from the parents of our son's non-black friends. This is why his mother and I feel a tremendous pressure that our son NOT be the black kid that can't make the grade; why we have no patience for shucking and jiving—why we are not satisfied with a B average. We cheat him if we do not push him to be better—if we do not demand that he achieve. If he does not reach his fullest potential he cheats us. . . . My son has been tremendously blessed and he is now charged with carrying the banner of the people. It may not be fair, but that is the way of the world.

Reprinted in part from "King of the Blacks" by Joseph C. Phillips. Reprinted and adapted with permission from the author. Accessed September 2010 from http://www.josephc phillips.com/html/Essays2009.asp?Essay=410

When students are tracked in classes according to their academic ability, higher-achieving members of the lower-achieving group find themselves severely underrepresented and surrounded by peers belonging to the higher-achieving group. Higher-achieving blacks and Hispanics in integrated schools often find themselves having more in common academically with their white peers, and their developing social relationships often reflect these interracial friendships.

When this occurs in integrated settings, higher-achieving students of color find that they are often teased and ostracized by their minority group peers for "acting white." Scholars have investigated this phenomenon over the years, and some have argued that the fear of being accused of "acting white" exerts a negative influence on the school achievement of bright minority students in integrated school settings. This phenomenon is described in greater detail in Sidebar 4.5.

⌨ Sidebar 4.5   The "Burden of Acting White"

The phrase "burden of acting white" was popularized in the academic world by Signithia Fordham and John Ogbu's (1986) study entitled "Coping with the burden of 'acting White'," published in *The Urban Review*. The burden of "acting white" describes a phenomenon—observed to occur in racially integrated school settings—where nonwhite (particularly black) schoolchildren who display studious school behaviors (e.g., speaking standard English, studying hard for good grades, demonstrating a liking for difficult academic subjects, displaying intellectual curiosity) and/or who avoid non-studious characteristics (e.g., class/school disruptive behavior, disrespect to teachers, emphasizing their social life over academic achievement)—are teased, harassed, or ostracized by their nonwhite peers for trying to "act like white people."

Empirical evidence for the "acting white" thesis comes from a study by Harvard economist Roland Fryer (Fryer, 2006), who analyzed National Longitudinal Study of Adolescent Health data consisting of 90,000 students nationwide who entered high school in the mid-1990s. Students were asked to provide a list of their closest male and female friends. Controlling for parental education, occupation, and participation in extracurricular activities, Fryer counted how often each student's name appeared on peers' lists. Whereas white students' popularity steadily increased as a function of increases in their grade-point average, black and Hispanic students experienced a reduction in popularity as their grade-point averages rose. As quoted in Buck (2010), "a black student with straight As is no more popular than a black student with a 2.9 GPA, but high-achieving whites are at the top of the popularity pyramid" (p. 11). Furthermore, Fryer found that high-achieving black students tend to be criticized for "acting white" in integrated schools, whereas no evidence exists for this phenomenon in all-black schools.

Many blacks who participated in the public school desegregation wars of the 1960s, who are now middle-aged, tell similar stories about how they first experienced this negative peer pressure from fellow blacks. The conditions that set the stage for this phenomenon first began to be written about seriously in the academic literature in Janet Schofield's (1982) book *Black and White in school: Trust, tension, or tolerance?* From her extensive interviews with children at one newly desegregated middle school, she writes:

> The children were sensitive to the fact that, in most classrooms, doing well meant doing *better* than others. Thus the whites' generally high level of academic performance became a potential source of friction between

blacks and whites. Interviews with students suggested that black children were more likely than whites to believe that students worked for good grades primarily in order to look better than their peers. Thus, lacking disconfirming information, black children often perceived white students' performance as an arrogant display designed to impress or humiliate others. (p. 94)

Dr. John McWhorter, a black linguistics professor at the University of California (Berkeley), a writer, and a nationally recognized commentator on social issues, writes of a painful childhood memory:

I spent most of my childhood living in one of the first deliberately integrated neighborhoods in the country, West Mount Airy in Philadelphia. As it happens, the very first memory of my life is an afternoon in 1968 when a group of black kids, none older than eight, asked me how to spell *concrete*. I spelled it, only to have the eight-year-old bring his little sister to me and have her smack me repeatedly as the rest of the kids laughed and egged her on. From then on, I was often teased in the neighborhood for being "smart." Importantly, however, none of the white kids ever challenged me like this (on the contrary, most of them knew how to spell *concrete* and were proud of it), nor did they tease any white child this way. . . . My story is not unique; in telling it I join legions of other black people who have reported in myriad articles and books that they were teased for being "smart." Reports of the strong tendency for young African Americans to discourage one another from doing well in school are numbingly common both on paper and in oral anecdote from blacks. (McWhorter, 2000, p. 122–123)

Testimonials from other famous high-profile blacks validate McWhorter's observations. As reported in a May 2009 *Newsweek* article, Michelle Obama—First Lady of the United States at the time of this writing—described the ridicule she faced from neighborhood kids for "acting white" when she got good grades as a child.

The problem of negative peer pressure on academic achievement has always been around, involving students of all racial/ethnic groups and occurring in almost all (particularly secondary) school contexts. However, this issue is exacerbated for high-achieving racial/ethnic minority students in integrated school settings, where

(*continued*)

racial disparities in academic achievement outcomes are obvious and stark. In such settings, minority (particularly black) students are identified as commonly low-achieving, so high-achieving minority students "stand out from the pack" and are accused of not being "authentic" minorities (see Glossary).

The "burden of acting white" phenomenon is by no means universally accepted among all scholars. Cook and Ludwig (1997) reanalyzed data from the National Education Longitudinal Study of 1988 and concluded, among other things, that black students by and large do not experience greater alienation from school compared to non-Hispanic whites. From their interviews with students from eight secondary public schools in North Carolina, Tyson, Darity, and Castellino (2005) argue that black adolescents are by and large just as achievement-oriented as whites, and a racialized peer pressure was not found to be prevalent in all schools studied.

One factor that energizes this debate is the claim that minority students' fear of being accused of "acting white" may contribute to the persistent academic achievement gap among racial groups (particularly blacks and whites). Unfortunately, this hypothesis confuses causes and effects. That is, some researchers argue that the "fear of acting white" comes first, which leads to racial group differences in academic achievement. Others argue that racial differences in academic achievement come first, which sets the stage for minority group high achievers to experience the "burden of acting white." Demonstrating that the "burden of acting white" fails to explain racial group differences in academic achievement is a separate issue from the question of whether it exists in some integrated contexts.

Some have argued that the remedy for neutralizing this phenomenon is to recognize that some black students would thrive academically if they were allowed to choose an all-black academic environment that includes a majority of black students, teachers, and administrators. Others argue that recruiting more black teachers to work in integrated settings may have a positive effect on some minority students, although some research disputes this claim (see discussion of minority role models in Chapter 2). Others argue that integrated schools need to set up special "minorities-only" programs (geared toward academic achievement and attitudes) within the school to counteract negative peer pressure (see Buck, 2010, p. 156).

The bottom line is that school psychologists, teachers, and school counselors would do well to be sensitive to this phenomenon, and to be available to support racial/ethnic minority students and their families as they strive to negotiate these difficult and often painful issues.

(adapted from Buck, 2010)

How School Districts Handle Disproportionalities

One of the most fundamental facts in all of the social sciences is that racial, ethnic, and language groups—in every country on the face of the earth—show average differences in talents, abilities, interests, behaviors, and accomplishments. This simple fact is ideologically unacceptable to Quack Multiculturalism, as well as being unacceptable to contemporary civil rights dogmas. Stated in its simplest form, if population subgroups fail to show statistical equality in certain outcomes, then this is viewed as *prima facie* (on its face) evidence of unfairness or discrimination—as it is assumed that there cannot be any real differences among groups in the skills, talents, abilities, or efforts that influence differential outcomes. Sowell (2010) states:

> That notion is the grand dogma of our time—an idea for which no evidence is asked or given, and an idea that no amount of contradictory evidence can change in the minds of the true believers, or in the rhetoric of ideologues and opportunists. . . . The dogma survives because it is politically useful, not because it has met any test of facts. Innumerable facts against it can be found around the world and down through history. (p. 319)

Large school districts with significant numbers of two or more racially or ethnically distinct groups find that they are constantly vulnerable to sanctions by outside advocacy groups or federal/state civil rights enforcement agencies (e.g., see Pollock, 2008) if their racial/ethnic proportionality statistics "don't look right" (e.g., see Banaszak, 2011; Giunca, 2011; Matteucci, 2010; Scott, 2011). Under the pervasive threat of lawsuits, sanctions, or simply from the desire to avoid public embarrassment, district administrators frantically initiate often drastic proposals to make the problem go away. These district remedies have ranged from the thoughtful to the truly bizarre.

In order to combat racial gaps in academic achievement, one large urban school district moved the most effective principals in the district to chronically failing schools in the district, as well as giving top teachers financial incentives to relocate their teaching service to such schools (Paulson, 2011).

Another large, ethnically diverse metropolitan school district in a southeastern city spent considerable time and effort crafting a large document purporting to outline "strategies for improving instruction for Black and Hispanic male students" (Orange County Public Schools, 2008). Although the statistics documenting disproportionate academic failure of black and Hispanic students are well known, the document predictably recycles the standard litany of "underlying causes" that are presumed to be responsible for these statistics. It comes as no surprise that these "underlying causes" are drawn from the "minorities-are-victims" and "minorities-are-exotic" themes that are so common in Quack

Multiculturalism (see Chapter 2). According to this document, disproportionate academic/behavior problems of black and Hispanic males can be attributed to "strong self-hatred" and "self-disrespect" caused by a lack of "knowledge of self" and a lack of "positive role models"; a school culture that results in "low expectations" and "ineffective instruction"; or a "European-centered curriculum" that fails to be sensitive to students' "diverse learning styles."

The solutions generated by the document reads like a grab-bag of proposals regularly found in trendy multicultural education textbooks: more "culturally responsive instruction"; "building better relationships" between teachers and students; "empowering parents"; "dispelling cultural myths", creating "culturally sensitive environments"; using "unbiased curriculum resources"; and "focusing on student strengths, not their deficits," and so on. The resources cited as support for these solutions are generally not drawn from rigorous empirical research in educational psychology or psychometrics, but instead are drawn mostly from academic writing for popular audiences.

Some districts pin their hopes on racial sensitivity training for white teachers in school districts that are experiencing rapid transitions from being all-white to predominantly minority schools. When teachers in such schools are required to attend such workshops, Kunjufu (2002) has observed that resistance is so thick that "you could cut the tension with a knife" (p. 21). In his experience, he opines:

> The predominantly white teaching staff had been there for more than twenty years and spoke about the good old days when almost all the children were White. . . . The problem was that the teachers viewed the students as "these children" and felt that I needed to fix the children and their parents. They felt nothing needed modification on their part, and the proof was that in the good old days of White teachers and White students everything was fine—the children were disciplined and academically above the national average. . . . Teachers [are] annoyed at having to attend another workshop on multiculturalism and race relations. (pp. 20–21)

Another ethnically and racially diverse school district, dismayed by the wide racial disparities in student attendance in high school advanced placement (AP) classes, were reported to be seriously considering shutting down their school science labs solely because the classes were attended by too many white students (i.e., minority students were not showing up). Shutting these classes down was thought to facilitate "closing the achievement gap" (Hedgecock, 2010).

One source of embarrassment among administrators in racially/diverse districts nationwide is the relative lack of proportionate representation of nonwhites in programs for gifted students (e.g., see Sieff, 2011). Typical district responses to this issue involve attempts to redefine the construct of *giftedness*, usually by adding noncognitive criteria, lowering cutoff criteria for gifted identification on group achievement and/or individually administered intelligence tests, or creating special classes for higher-achieving minority students whose scores do not qualify for gifted education identification (see also Gottfredson, 2004b).

Some districts find that they must resort to outright fraud and cheating in order to give the appearance of "closing the achievement gap." As one of many examples, the state of California recently threw out the test scores of a top-performing Los Angeles school and another charter school (both of which serve a predominantly low-income Latino population) after cheating was uncovered (i.e., several teachers changing answers and inappropriately coaching students). Other questionable social engineering schemes used by school districts to artificially close the achievement gap among subgroups are briefly described in Sidebar 4.6.

Sidebar 4.6   Social Engineering Schemes for Closing the Achievement Gap in Schools

- McCaskey East High School in Lancaster, Pennsylvania, separates black students from the rest of the school's pupils for six minutes each day and 20 minutes twice a month. The principal defends the policy with the observation that black students were not performing as well as other students, and that "research" shows that same-race classes with strong same-race role models may boost the minority students' academic results and self-esteem. The school's instructional coach said that only one-third of the school's African American students scored "proficient" or "advanced" in reading on the previous year's Pennsylvania System of School Assessment tests, compared to 60 percent of white students and 42 percent of students overall (*Daily Mail Reporter*, 2011).

- In 2009, 69 percent of Detroit's fourth graders scored "below basic" on math testing. According to a Michigan State University Education Policy Center study in 2008, only 31.9 percent of Detroit's majority-black public school ninth-grade students graduate in four years. According to recent high school Michigan Merit Exam scores, roughly 14 percent of 4,386 students were proficient or above in math, 34 percent were proficient or above in reading, and 17 percent were proficient or above in writing. Nevertheless, $49 million of taxpayer money was procured by the Detroit public schools to buy laptops for students and teachers. One reporter asks why this money was spent "when too many Detroit kids can't successfully use old-fashioned

(continued)

pencils and paper to write simple words and sentences and do basic math."
One Detroit teacher was caught and suspended for trying to pawn her
district-owned laptop at a Detroit pawnshop (Bouffard, 2008; Smith, 2011;
Wolfram, 2011).

- Teachers and administrators at Township High School in Evanston, Illinois,
  are bothered by the lack of diversity in advanced honors courses. Despite the
  racially mixed student body, such courses are dominated by white students, a
  condition that is common not only in Illinois but across the nation. The
  Evanston Township High School is considering a proposal to completely
  eliminate its honors English courses (which tend to be predominantly white) so
  that students of all ethnic/racial backgrounds can enroll in the same English
  courses. The content of these courses would be upgraded to the "honors" level,
  so that "all students would have the opportunity to earn honors credit
  depending on their grades on assignments." If the board approves this proposal,
  the same plan would be applied to biology classes (Rado, 2010).
- A cheating investigation in the Atlanta Public Schools (APS) system has
  concluded that as many as 100 employees at 12 schools violated proper
  testing protocols on state-standardized tests. The scandal occurred in the
  midst of national attention that APS has recently received for its efforts
  in closing the achievement gap, by posting double-digit gains in reading on
  the National Assessment of Education Progress (NAEP) tests. An audit
  on Criterion-Referenced Compentency Test results, taken in the summer of
  2008, named four APS schools showing evidence of an abnormal number
  of erasures in which the wrong answer often was replaced by the right
  answer. Results of a second investigation revealed 12 APS schools housing
  students who previously were among the bottom performers statewide to
  being among the best in the course of only a single year. According to the
  investigation, the odds of making such a leap were less than one in a billion.
  As the investigation continued, state officials announced that they had
  found suspicious erasures on answer sheets for a year's worth of tests in
  hundreds of classrooms at Atlanta elementary and middle schools. Numerous
  APS teachers and administrators have confessed to changing students' test
  papers, providing answers to students, or watching others manipulate tests
  results (Rankin, Vogell, & Judd, 2010; Torres, 2010).
- Urban Strategies, a nonprofit organization based in St. Louis, is offering
  cash incentives to parents to enroll their children at Jefferson Elementary
  (a predominantly black school). The cash incentives are in response to
  Jefferson Elementary parents receiving letters informing them that the
  school fell short of annual progress goals in the Missouri Assessment

Program, where less than 15 percent of students passed the reading and math sections on the previous year's statewide test. Jefferson parents were offered the option of transferring to other schools in the district. The cash incentive is targeted specifically to students who did not attend the school last year. To receive up to $300 per child, kids must finish the semester with near-perfect attendance, receive no out-of-school suspensions, and parents must attend three parent-teacher meetings (Crouch, 2010).

- Teachers in some Detroit elementary schools have complained to the press that students who had been given failing grades on school report cards have had their grades changed to C's without the teachers' consent. Teachers and union officials in the Detroit Public Schools have admitted that they are indeed aware that illegal grade-fixing exists, particularly in low-performing schools that are under pressure to show academic progress. Under the federal No Child Left Behind law, as well as an additional state reform law passed in 2009, districts can remove principals or restructure/close schools that do not meet state and federal standards. In 2009, nearly one-quarter of Detroit Public Schools were assigned new principals after 33 were fired from low-performing schools. Some teachers have argued that illegal grade-fixing, and promoting failing students to the next grade, are reasons why the Detroit Public Schools show a 59 percent graduation rate and some of the nation's lowest test scores. One angry parent stated that her grandson was socially promoted to the next grade even though he missed most of the previous spring semester of school (Dawsey, 2011).

The Los Angeles Unified School District (LAUSD; which is the second largest school district in America) was the recent target of a federal civil rights investigation by the U.S. Department of Education (see Blume, 2011). Approximately 29 percent of the district's enrollment is composed of limited English speakers, most of whom are Latino. Although federal authorities did not accuse the LAUSD of intentional discrimination, the LAUSD was charged with failing to properly educate its limited-English-speaking and black subpopulations (on the basis of disproportionately poor performance on a variety of educational criteria, as well as disparities in educational resources). As a result of this investigation, the LAUSD has agreed to provide black and limited-English-speaking students with "more effective teachers," better technology, and more library resources (Blume, 2011). The effectiveness of these efforts will be judged by student performance data, and federal funds will be withheld or withdrawn if improvements are not made or are not effective. From her observations of what is happening in the LAUSD, one writer expresses frustration in trying to generate enthusiasm for these initiatives:

> The campaign to raise the achievement of black, Latino and low-income students has been bumping along in this school system for so many years, it's begun to seem like smoke and mirrors. The achievement gap was an issue when I moved to L.A. in 1979. Then, integration was going to be the solution. Then more money for inner-city schools. Then "culturally relevant" instruction for minority students. Now . . . it's fundamentals: better teachers, libraries and technology. Raise your hand if you see that happening soon. . . . Can you say dog-and-pony show? I know I sound cynical. Maybe I've been watching and writing about this struggling school district for too long. (Banks, 2011)

In the school psychology community, perhaps the most well-known example of efforts to respond to embarrassing disproportionalities can be observed in the ban on IQ testing for black students that was implemented in the wake of the *Larry P. v. Riles* decision in the state of California (for a brief summary, see Riverside County Special Education Local Plan Area, 2010).

In the late 1970s, the *Larry P. v. Riles* case was filed against the state of California on behalf of African American parents who argued that the administration of "culturally biased" standardized IQ tests resulted in disproportionate numbers of African American children being identified and placed inappropriately in special education classes for (what was called at that time) the Educable Mentally Retarded (EMR). In 1979, Judge Peckham prohibited the use of IQ tests for placing African American students in classes for EMR or "their substantial equivalent" after concluding that IQ tests were racially and culturally biased. In 1986, Judge Peckham expanded his 1979 order and prohibited the use of IQ tests for African American students for any special education program. Even with parental consent, IQ tests may not be given to African American students, nor may IQ scores from any other source become part of the pupil's school record. In 1986, the California Department of Education (CDE) issued a directive to state special educators regarding the Larry P. litigation, which confirmed that school districts were not to use intelligence tests in the assessment of African American students who have been referred for special education services. In lieu of IQ tests, districts were directed to use alternative means of assessment to determine identification and placement—a prohibition that has lasted to the present day.

There is much variation and struggle among California school psychologists in determining what assessments are or are not acceptable for black students according to state directives (e.g., see Powers, Hagans-Murillo, & Restori, 2004). The bottom line, however, is that the problem of overidentification of Black students for special education programs in California has not been solved. According to Powers et al. (2004), the overrepresentation of Black students has merely shifted disability categories over time from mentally handicapped classes to classes for the emotionally disturbed or learning disabled.

PRINCIPAL LEADERSHIP

Schools in the same district often show wide differences in school climate that can be indirectly attributed to the quality of the school's administrative governance—despite serving the same student population demographically. In some schools, the relationship between the principal and his or her staff is strained, making it difficult for staff to be motivated to buy into the principal's new initiatives. Teachers may not feel supported in their efforts to discipline students, and rampant student misbehavior makes it difficult for students, teachers, and staff to take pride in working at the school. In contrast, the school across town, which serves the same demographic mix of students, has a radically different "feel." In such schools, serious discipline problems are rare, and if such problems do occasionally occur, they are dealt with swiftly and decisively. Teachers in these schools have a strong, shared faith in the principal's leadership, and individual teachers feel supported in their efforts to maintain classroom instructional and discipline standards. From the moment students arrive at school, they get a sense that, in this school, academic achievement is the number-one priority, and off-task behavior will not be tolerated. These scenarios occur in numerous districts throughout the country, and such differences can often be traced to one variable—principal leadership.

Kathleen Cotton (2003) published the findings of her narrative review of the literature on the relationship between principal behaviors and student achievement. Focusing on studies from 1985 until the present, Cotton reviewed 81 reports and identified 25 categories of principal behavior that positively affect the dependent variables of student achievement, student attitudes, student behavior, teacher attitudes, teacher behaviors, and dropout rates. Twenty-one of these categories are described in Table 4.6. Given that she performed a narrative review of the literature, Cotton did not quantitatively estimate the effect of principal leadership on student achievement. However, her conclusions were fairly straightforward: She noted that principal leadership does have an effect on student outcomes, albeit an indirect one.

Marzano, Waters, and McNulty (2005) examined 69 studies involving 2,802 schools, approximately 1.4 million students, and 14,000 teachers. These researchers used the research methodology of meta-analysis, which employs quantitative techniques to synthesize studies of school leadership as practiced by principals. In conducting their meta-analysis, Marzano et al. (2005) considered any and all available studies from 1970

Table 4.6   Research-Based Characteristics of Effective School Principal Leadership

Principal Characteristics	Description
1. Affirmation	The extent to which the principal fairly and systematically recognizes school accomplishments and acknowledges failures of faculty and students
2. Change Agent	The principal's disposition to change the "status quo" and/or upset a school's "equilibrium," which has the effect of energizing the commitment of the school's students/faculty/staff and encouraging them to experiment and take positive risks
3. Contingent Rewards	The extent to which the principal proactively recognizes and rewards hard work and individual accomplishments that the school wants to encourage
4. Communication	The extent to which the principal establishes strong lines of communication and accessibility with and between teachers and students
5. Culture	The extent to which the principal creates a school culture that positively influences teachers, who, in turn, positively influence students
6. Discipline	The extent to which the principal "buffers" and protects teachers from internal or external issues and influences that detract from their instructional time and teaching focus
7. Flexibility	The extent to which the principal adapts leadership behavior to the needs of the current situation and is comfortable with dissent
8. Focus	The extent to which the principal ensures that school change efforts are not fragmented, but aimed at clear and concrete goals that are kept at the forefront of the school's attention
9. Ideals/Beliefs	Effective principals possess well-defined beliefs about schools, teaching, and learning; they share these beliefs with the school staff; and they demonstrate behaviors that are consistent with their beliefs
10. Input	The extent to which the principal involves teachers in the design and implementation of important decisions and policies
11. Intellectual Stimulation	The extent to which the principal ensures that faculty and staff are aware of the most current theories and practices regarding effective schooling, and makes discussions of such information a regular, integrated aspect of the school's culture
12. Involvement in Curriculum, Instruction, and Assessment	The extent to which the principal has a "hands-on" direct involvement in the design and implementation of curriculum, instruction, and assessment activities at the classroom level
13. Knowledge of Curriculum, Instruction, and Assessment	The extent to which the principal is aware of "best practices" in the domains of curriculum, instruction, and assessment, which provide guidance for teachers on the day-to-day tasks of teaching and learning

Table 4.6   (*Continued*)

Principal Characteristics	Description
14. Monitoring/Evaluating	The extent to which the principal monitors the effectiveness of school practices in terms of their impact on student achievement, creating a school culture in which constant evaluation is a norm
15. Optimizer	The extent to which the principal inspires others with positive attitudes and optimism, and is the "driving force" when implementing challenging innovations.
16. Order	The extent to which the principal establishes a set of standard operating principles and routines that set clear boundaries and rules for both students and faculty
17. Outreach	The extent to which the principal is an advocate and a spokesperson for the school to all stakeholders, which includes a willingness and the ability to effectively communicate to individuals both inside and outside the school
18. Relationships	The extent to which the principal demonstrates an awareness of the personal lives of teachers and staff, forging emotional bonds with and among teachers that help staff and administrators stay aligned and focused during times of uncertainty
19. Resources	The extent to which the principal provides teachers with materials, equipment, and professional development necessary for the successful execution of their duties
20. Situational Awareness	The extent to which the principal is aware of the details, "undercurrents," and "brewing issues" regarding school functioning, and uses this information to address current and potential problems
21. Visibility	The extent to which the principal has contact and interacts with teachers, students, and parents—which communicates the message that the principal is interested and engaged in the daily operations of the school

(Adapted from Marzano, Waters, & McNulty, 2005)

to the present that met the following conditions: (a) the study involved K–12 students; (b) the study involved schools in the United States or situations that closely mirrored the culture of U.S. schools; (c) the study directly or indirectly examined the relationship between the leadership of the building principal and student academic achievement; (d) academic achievement was measured by a standardized achievement test or a state test, or a composite index based on one or both of these; and (e) effect sizes in correlation form were reported or could be computed.

The typical study in their meta-analysis used some type of questionnaire asking teachers about their perceptions of the principal's leadership behaviors. Teacher ratings of principal leadership were used, instead of ratings by the principals or their supervisors. Teachers are thought to provide the most valid information because they are closest to the day-to-day operations of the school and the behaviors of the principal. In such studies, the average score for the teachers' responses within each school was then correlated with the average achievement of students in that school.

Marzano et al. (2005) concluded that principals can have a profound effect on the achievement of students in their schools. They found that the studies included in their meta-analysis reported different size correlations between principal leadership and student achievement—some very large and positive, some low and negative. From this meta-analysis, they computed the average correlation between the leadership behavior of the principal in the school and the average academic achievement of students in the school, which yielded an average correlation of .25.

FINAL THOUGHTS

From the material reviewed in this chapter, readers are shown that ethnic/racial/language minority students are educated in a wide variety of contexts, making it difficult to rely on lazy stereotypes and facile generalizations. Many minority children perform quite well in school, and have educational experiences characterized by school climates that support safe school environments, effective instruction, and a clear focus on academic achievement. Unfortunately, many of the educational problems experienced by minority children are exacerbated by school contexts that can undermine school adjustment and achievement. In working with teachers and administrators to address student difficulties, school psychologists are encouraged to consider these context variables in their consultative efforts, as this can (a) give school psychologists realistic expectations as to what can be reasonably accomplished, and (b) give school psychologists direction as to system variables that must be improved in order for minority children and youth to succeed.

In the chapter that follows, the focus is shifted from system variables to the most important individual difference variable that is related to academic achievement: general cognitive ability and its implications for classroom instruction.

ADDITIONAL RESOURCES

Supplemental Reading

Baker, C. (2011). *Foundations of bilingual education and bilingualism* (5th ed.). Bristol, UK: Multilingual Matters.

Leader, G. C. (2008). *Real leaders, real schools: Stories of success against enormous odds.* Cambridge, MA: Harvard Education Press.

Thomas, W. P., & Collier, V. P. (2002). *A national study of school effectiveness for language minority students' long-term academic achievement.* Berkeley, CA: Center for Research on Education, Diversity and Excellence.

Valdés, G., Capitelli, S., & Alvarez, L. (2010). *Latino children learning English: Steps in the journey.* New York, NY: Teachers College Press.

Walberg, H. J. (2007). *School choice: The findings.* Washington, DC: CATO Institute.

Whitman, D. (2008). *Sweating the small stuff: Inner-city schools and the new paternalism.* Washington, DC: Thomas D. Fordham Institute.

Films

The Cartel (2009). This documentary, by television producer Bob Bowden, is a critique of public education in New Jersey specifically, and the nation generally. The documentary poses the question (paraphrased): "How has the richest country on the globe lost its ability to teach its children at a level that most other modern countries would consider to be 'basic'?" The documentary includes interviews with school administrators, teachers, parents, students, and various education advocates—and in doing so presents a point of view that favors charter schools and vouchers, while criticizing teacher unions.

Little Rock Central: 50 Years Later (2007). This documentary, directed by Brent and Craig Renaud, examines the 50-year anniversary of the integration of Little Rock Central High School in Arkansas in 1957. At that time, federal troops were dispatched to help nine African American students integrate the school, as they were prevented from entering the building by angry mobs of whites outside of the school. After 50 years, the filmmaker interviews Arkansas community leaders, school personnel, and some of the original "Little Rock Nine" students. The film documents stark racial disparities in academic achievement and tracking placements within the school that continue to exist despite massive efforts to equalize outcomes.

The Lottery (2010). This documentary, by filmmaker Madeleine Sackler, follows four African American families in the weeks leading up to a charter school lottery for the Harlem Success Academy in Harlem, New York. The documentary includes interviews with Geoffrey Canada (President and CEO of Harlem Children's Zone), Cory Booker (mayor of Newark, New Jersey), Candice Fryer (teacher at Harlem Success Academy 2), Eva Moskowitz (founder and CEO of Success Charter Network), teacher union representatives, as well as the parents of children enrolled in the lottery.

Prom Night in Mississippi (2008). This documentary chronicles the events of Charleston High School, situated in one of the poorest counties in the state of Mississippi, as they prepare for the end-of-year senior prom—where black and white students traditionally hold separate proms, even though their classrooms have been integrated for decades. In 1997, Academy Award–winning actor Morgan Freeman offered to pay for the senior prom at Charleston High School in Mississippi under one condition: The prom had to be racially integrated. His offer was ignored until 2008, at which time the school board accepted and history was made. Canadian filmmaker Paul Saltzman follows students, teachers, and parents in the lead-up to the big day.

The Providence Effect (2009). This documentary, by Rollin Binzer, captures how one charter school in the inner city of Chicago's West Side, named Providence St. Mel, has created a method and environment where children learn to think and to overcome social barriers, family circumstances, and financial pressures to become high-achieving students. At the time of this filming, the school boasted a 100 percent acceptance rate to college for its students, with many being accepted into elite educational institutions.

Waiting for Superman (2010). This documentary, by filmmaker Davis Guggenheim, chronicles the shortcomings of the American public school system within the context of following several students and their families as they hope to be selected in a lottery for acceptance into high-performing charter schools. The documentary also features comments from journalists and educators as they discuss how families can escape failing public schools for a brighter future in charter schools.

Websites

Charter Schools: http://www.uscharterschools.org/pub/uscs_docs/index.htm
Home School Legal Defense Association: http://www.hslda.org
National Alliance of Black School Educators: http://www.nabse.org
National Association for Bilingual Education: http://www.nabe.org
National Association of Independent Schools: http://www.nais.org
National Indian Education Association: http://www.niea.org
National Parochial Schools Association: http://www.parochial.com

⬥━◆━⬥

5

General Cognitive Ability, Learning, and Instruction

George Orwell (1903–1949) was a prolific writer who was well known for his insights into how political movements use language to shape perceptions of reality. As quoted in Sowell (2009), George Orwell once remarked that "some ideas are so foolish that only an intellectual could believe them" (p. 2). When it comes to the issue of the relationship between measured general cognitive ability and classroom learning, one can modify this saying only slightly as "some ideas are so obvious, that only an intellectual would deny them."

The obvious idea referred to here is that individual differences in general cognitive ability is the single most important variable for understanding how well students (belonging to any racial, ethnic, or language group) learn academic material. General cognitive ability is a powerful predictor for understanding not only how well students learn in response to academic instruction, but also the rate and depth of what is learned from instruction, and how learning can be facilitated through modifications of, and improvements in, classroom instruction.

Unfortunately, the very concept of general cognitive ability (or "intelligence") is portrayed as "controversial" in academic, political, and public policy circles (e.g., Jacoby & Glauberman, 1995), primarily because these concepts create tension in society between the *opposing ideals of meritocracy versus equality* (Gottfredson, 2004a). All human beings can relate to being in competitive situations with other human beings, in which it becomes readily obvious that some seem to have an ability to do certain things better, faster, and easier than others—and that those who are better will reap the fruits of their higher ability. In a nutshell, a person who can run the 100-yard dash in less than 10 seconds will (and should) secure a coveted spot on the school track team compared to a person who cannot. This represents the *principle of meritocracy*, which even a young child can understand.

At the same time, schools are viewed as "the nation's best hope to level the playing field" (Gottfredson, 2004a, p. 35), so that persons from all backgrounds will have an equal chance to secure the best that society has to offer. This ideal undergirds such popular phrases as "college for all," "closing the achievement gap," and "no child left behind." When easily identifiable racial and ethnic groups show disproportionate rates of academic failure relative to other groups, the *principle of equality* creates an opposing movement that seeks proportional representation of identifiable groups in highly coveted school academic outcomes.

Due to these tensions, it comes as no surprise that the scientific concept of intelligence (as well as its measurement, interpretation, and implications) has been ferociously attacked ever since its entrance into the psychological literature. These attacks come from a variety of sources within academia, the courts, and civil rights organizations. However, they all share in common a Marxist-inspired view of the world in which the serious study of general intelligence is viewed as a political weapon for denying population subgroups access to limited societal resources (see Marxism, in Glossary). The most common anti-intelligence criticisms are hierarchically organized in Sidebar 5.1.

◭ Sidebar 5.1   Criticisms of "Intelligence," Its Measurement, and Interpretation in the Social Sciences

1. Intelligence is a politicized concept, and it does not really exist.
2. Even if intelligence does exist, it cannot be measured adequately.
3. Even if intelligence can be adequately measured, it cannot be measured fairly in certain population subgroups.
4. Even if intelligence can be measured fairly, it is not that important or consequential.
5. Even if intelligence is important, there exist "multiple intelligences" (e.g., social, kinesthetic, musical) that are equally important.
6. Even if intelligence is singular and important, it is mostly the product of social privilege and one's environment, and is not substantially heritable.
7. Even if intelligence is substantially heritable, it is quite malleable (substantially modifiable through intervention).

(Adapted from Gottfredson, 2005)

Within the discipline of school psychology, it comes as no surprise that Quack Multiculturalism has jumped on the anti-intelligence bandwagon, focusing its criticism particularly on point 3 (and to a lesser extent, point 7) from Sidebar 5.1. The truth, however, is that all students (regardless of their group membership) confront the reality and consequences of individual differences in general cognitive ability in their school experiences. Established principles from decades of research on the nature of intelligence and its measurement are summarized in Sidebar 5.2.

Sidebar 5.2   Established Findings from Intelligence Research

a. Since the turn of the 20th century, *intelligence* has been defined by various scholars as judgment, comprehension, and reasoning; the ability to learn, think abstractly, adapt to changing environmental circumstances, and successfully solve difficult/complex mental problems; skill in mental concentration and planning; and creative and/or original thinking (Sattler, 2008).

b. An objective, empirical definition of *intelligence* was advanced by Charles Spearman (1904), who identified the g (general mental ability) factor as a source of shared variance that is measured, in varying degrees, by all mental tests, regardless of their content. The g factor accounts for one-third to one-half of the variance in scores on any broad battery of mental tests (Jensen, 1998b).

c. Although human variation in mental abilities is caused by several broad and specific abilities (see Gottfredson, 2005), the most fundamental source of variance in human mental abilities is represented by g, the general intelligence factor (Jensen, 1998b).

d. Although g is primarily identified through the factor analysis of mental test scores (e.g., see Carroll, 1993), biological correlates of g include electro-chemical brain activity (e.g., recorded via electroencephalography), cerebral glucose metabolism positron emission tomography (PET) scans during mental activity, and brain nerve conduction velocity (see Jensen, 1998b, for an overview).

e. Despite relatively minor imperfections, commonly used individually administered intelligence (IQ) tests are very good measures of the g factor. The average g loading of IQ scores derived from a variety of standardized IQ tests is in the .80s (Gottfredson, 2005; Jensen, 1998b).

(continued)

Subgroup Differences in IQ

    f. All racial and ethnic groups display the full range of variation in IQ, from mental retardation to intellectual giftedness (Gottfredson, 2005). Members of every racial/ethnic group can be found at all points of the IQ distribution.

    g. However, the mean (average) IQ score of various racial/ethnic groups— both within and outside of the United States—differs significantly. Subgroup differences in the central tendency of IQ score distributions are the rule, not the exception, worldwide (Gottfredson, 2005). Worldwide, the average IQ score obtained by East Asians converges at around 106, for whites around 100, and for American blacks around 85. Hispanic and Native Americans obtain IQ scores that average at around 90, although there is less data for these groups relative to data comparing American blacks and whites. Approximately 22 percent of whites, 59 percent of blacks, 47 percent of Hispanics, and 14 percent of Asians will obtain IQ test scores below 90. Approximately 18 percent of whites, 2 percent of blacks, 6 percent of Hispanics, and 27 percent of Asians will obtain IQ test scores above 115 (Gottfredson, 2005, p. 541).

    h. Average mean differences in IQ can also be identified between subgroups *within* broad racial groups (see reviews by Gottfredson, 2005; Rushton, 2003; Rushton & Jensen, 2005).

    i. Differences between subgroups in social class are *not* a sufficient explanation, exclusively, for explaining average subgroup differences in IQ scores. Black/white differences in mean IQ scores are *widest at the highest income levels*, and groups of African American children at the highest SES levels obtain no higher mean intelligence test scores than do groups of whites at the lowest SES levels (see Gottfredson, 2005, p. 533; Herrnstein & Murray, 1994, pp. 286–288; Jensen, 1998b, pp. 491–494). In a wide variety of socioeconomic (e.g., parental education, income, and employment) and health (e.g., nutrition) indicators, American Indians rank far below American blacks. Yet, the American Indian population obtains higher mean scores on IQ tests compared to the American black population (Coleman, 1966; Roth, Bevier, Bobko, Switzer, & Tyler, 2001).

Bias in Mental Testing

    j. The observation of different means and standard deviations in the distribution of mental test scores across two or more identifiable subgroups is *not*, by itself, a sufficient basis for concluding that a test is "biased" or unfair (Jensen, 1980).

k. Several decades of psychometric research show that, when subjected to the appropriate statistical procedures, well developed individually administered U.S. IQ tests do not show statistically significant levels of predictive or construct bias (see also Test Bias, in Glossary) against American born, English speaking examinees (Jensen, 1980; Reynolds & Carson, 2005; Reynolds & Lowe, 2009). IQ scores predict equally well for all U.S. English-speaking schoolchildren, regardless of race or social class.

l. The cognitive and academic abilities of schoolchildren who speak a primary language other than English can be reasonably assessed using nonverbal tests (Braden & Athanasiou, 2005; McCallum, 2003), or tests appropriately translated, standardized, and normed on non-English-speaking groups (see Georgas, Weiss, Van de Vijver, & Saklofske, 2003; Martines & Rodriguez-Srednicki, 2007). The administration of tests standardized and normed on English-speaking groups can be given to non-English speakers using a non-English-speaking translator, however there are a host of psychometric problems that are associated with this practice (Lopez, 1997).

m. When variance in the IQ scores of random samples of black and white children are partitioned using analysis of variance statistical procedures, approximately 65 percent of the true-score variance in IQ scores can be attributed to differences *within* racial and social class groups, which contradicts the falsehood that IQ scores discriminate unfairly along racial lines (see Jensen, 1998b, pp. 356–357).

Correlates of IQ

n. Whenever there is a significant positive correlation between IQ and socially significant external variables in society, and there exists a specific IQ threshold for selection into certain placement/opportunity outcomes (e.g., special/gifted education, college, occupational, or specialized training selection), subgroup differences in the distribution of IQ scores *will result* in unequal representation in the selection outcome (Gottfredson, 2003b, 2004b; Herrnstein & Murray, 1994; Losen & Orfield, 2002; Ree, Carretta, & Green, 2003).

o. IQ tests have a high degree of predictive validity for a variety of educational criteria, such as the learning rate for new information, time needed to learn new information, performance on standardized or individually administered achievement tests, classroom grades, grade retention and school dropout/graduation rates, the probability of attending college, the selected major in college, and the terminal college degree (Jensen, 1998b; Gottfredson, 2005).

Obviously, school psychologists apply their knowledge of individual differences in general cognitive ability in the context of their assessment activities in schools. However, they often find themselves at a loss when confronted with opportunities to apply what they know about individual differences in general cognitive ability to instruction and classroom learning. The material in this chapter is built on the assumption that the construct of general cognitive ability (or "intelligence") is real, is important, and needs to be integrated into the diagnosis and remediation of school learning problems. The purpose of this chapter is to describe (a) the implications of individual differences in general cognitive ability for learning outcomes, (b) how this knowledge may inform students' success or failure in profiting from instruction, and (c) instructional principles that school psychologists may find helpful to consider when consulting with parents/ teachers and working individually with failing students.

ACADEMIC CHARACTERISTICS OF STUDENTS WITHIN DIFFERENT IQ RANGES

School/educational psychologists, educational diagnosticians, and clinical psychologists rely on an IQ score from an individually or group-administered test as the most reliable and valid estimate of a student's general cognitive ability. Individuals representing the full range of ability levels can be found enrolled in the public schools. The following sections describe the academic and behavioral correlates of students' measured IQ scores falling within the full range of general cognitive ability levels.

IQs Lower Than 70

Under the Individuals With Disabilities Education Improvement Act (IDEIA), an IQ of 70 or below—along with associated deficits in adaptive functioning—is commonly used to justify special education services for individuals with mental retardation (or "intellectual disabilities," see Pierangelo & Giuliani, 2007). Clinically and educationally, mental retardation can be partitioned into the following subcategories based on severity level (see Mental Retardation, in Glossary): *Mild Mental Retardation* (IQs of approximately 55–70), *Moderate Mental Retardation* (IQs of approximately 40–55), *Severe Mental Retardation* (IQs of approximately 25–40), and *Profound Mental Retardation* (IQs below 25).

Persons at extremely low IQ levels usually have concomitant physical problems and genetic anomalies (e.g., Down syndrome, spina bifida, cerebral palsy), and they are typically identified early in development and targeted for special training programs outside of the public schools. Occasionally, however, pupils with milder manifestations of mental delays will participate in public schooling until they are identified as eligible for special services early in their school careers. For pupils in this circumstance, the educational implications are observed as follows.

Developmental Delays

Persons with IQs below 70 move through the same stages of development as those with average IQs, but they move through these stages more slowly than average-IQ children. In addition, their highest level of cognitive functioning falls well below the highest level of cognitive functioning of children with average IQs. Beginning at birth, individuals with IQs less than 70 develop more slowly than average-IQ students in areas related to communication skills, social skills, motor skills, self-help skills, and learning skills. When evaluated with the appropriate rating scales and checklists, these pupils will achieve scores that are significantly lower than those of their cognitively average peers (American Association on Mental Retardation, 2002).

Significant Academic (Rather Than Social) Markers in Early Grades

In the early grades, pupils with milder forms of intellectual disability will not appear significantly different from their peers in social markers (i.e., ability to get along with peers, configuration of social friendships). If they possess exceptional personal attractiveness and a winning personality, they even may be more popular than their average-IQ peers. Whenever such children are confronted with academic tasks in a classroom setting, however, their intellectual limitations become most apparent to teachers. As these students mature into adolescence, similarities in intellectual ability will play a more significant role in the configuration of social friendships.

Significant Memory Deficits

Students with mild intellectual deficits have significant difficulty retaining information in short-term and/or working memory, which in essence is the ability to use information that was encountered just a few minutes or hours earlier. This problem is compounded when the information to be remembered is in amounts that are too large for the pupil to handle. Teachers find that they must teach information to be remembered in smaller chunks, aided by metacognitive strategies that help students rehearse and organize information sufficiently before committing it to long-term memory. Although students without mild mental retardation can use such strategies spontaneously, students with mild mental retardation need to be explicitly taught to do so (Bebko & Luhaorg, 1998).

Significant Attentional Difficulties

Learning situations require students to attend to critical rather than noncritical features of tasks for effective problem solving. For example, in solving a simple math word problem, learners must attend to the key words that indicate the correct mathematical operation required and ignore words that are irrelevant to the task. In learning geometric shape concepts, for example, learners must understand that two rectangles that may be different in size and color are still exemplars of the concept "rectangle." In both of these examples, learners must accurately *attend* to the relevant (rather than irrelevant) features of problems to be solved (Feuerstein, Feuerstein, & Falik, 2010). Students with mild mental retardation often have difficulty attending to relevant features of learning tasks and also have difficulty sustaining attention on tasks, particularly in the presence of distracting stimuli (Zeaman & House, 1979; for a dissenting view, see Iarocci & Burack, 1998).

Significantly Slower Learning Rate

Individuals with IQs under 70 take considerably longer to learn the same material compared to their average-IQ peers—if indeed the material can be learned at all. Although slow learners (pupils with IQs between 70–85) lag behind their average-IQ peers in grade-level attainment, pupils with mild mental retardation lag behind their average-IQ peers in grade-level attainment *to a significant degree*. While slow learners find themselves one to one and one-half years behind their average-IQ peers in the early grades, pupils with mild mental retardation are two to three years behind their average-IQ peers in academic skill attainment in the early grades. Because of this slow learning rate, teachers find that significant learning problems occur if these students do not receive some kind of special education placement by the time they reach the fourth grade. Even with 12 years of formal schooling, individuals with IQs under 70 can, at the very best, achieve a level of academic learning up to the sixth grade.

IQs Between 70–85

Students with IQs falling between 70–85 are estimated to constitute at least 14 percent of the American school population, which is more than all students in all special education categories combined. Nevertheless, a significant portion of these students may receive special education services through the channels of a specific learning disability or emotional disturbance label (MacMillan, Gresham, Bocian, & Lambros, 1998; MacMillan, Gresham, Siperstein, & Bocian, 1996). Such students have been called "slow learners" (S. Shaw, 2008). Slow learners are generally considered to be vulnerable for falling into the gap between special and regular education, and as such, they are most at risk for school failure (S. Shaw, 2008). The following descriptors generally characterize the behavior, school learning, and academic performance of children within this IQ range.

Greater Than Average Difficulty With Multistep or Cognitively Complex Tasks

Slow learners have an easier time learning simpler cognitive associations (e.g., "When did Columbus discover America?") than solving problems that involve more complex mental manipulation (e.g., "After giving the salesclerk $5, how much change would you receive from purchasing two pieces of fruit costing 75 cents each?"). Slow learners have greater difficulty holding multiple segments of information in their working memory when solving problems. Thus, in teaching slow learners, instructors find that they need to break down multiple-step tasks into single steps in order to be properly understood by students. For example, the direction: "When you finish your seatwork, put away your notebooks under the desk but only after you have turned in last night's homework assignment at the front of the room" may be too difficult for the slower student to understand. A better strategy would be to wait until students finish their seatwork, *then* instruct them to turn in last night's homework at the front of the room, *then* instruct them to put away their notebooks under the desk.

Preference for Concrete Over Abstract Learning

When learning is described as *concrete*, it means that concepts and skills are learned through the manipulation of tangible objects. When learning is described as *abstract*, it means that learning is removed from tangible objects (perceived through the physical senses) and occurs through the use of representational symbols. For example, most students clearly understand what a spoon is because they can pick up a spoon, show it to you, and describe its function. In contrast, students have difficulty defining what *freedom* is, because it is a more abstract word that has no stable physical referent. The meaning of *freedom* is more difficult to define, and its meaning can shift in subtle ways depending on the context in which it is used (e.g., personal freedom from financial obligations versus countries fighting for political freedom in wars). It is much more difficult to grasp the essence of what freedom is and to articulate this verbally than it is to understand what a spoon is. This is why the answer to an IQ test item such as "How are a pencil and a pen alike?" is far easier to articulate than the item "How are responsibility and commitment alike?"

Nowhere is the concrete/abstract learning continuum more applicable than in the domain of mathematics. Early math learning in the primary grades necessarily involves helping students learn the properties of numbers through the concrete manipulation of objects (e.g., pattern blocks, cubes, number lines, and/or Cuisenaire rods) or semi-concrete representations of math concepts (e.g., drawings). As students get older, math concepts are taught almost exclusively through written numerals and symbols. At this stage, students must be comfortable with knowing their computational facts and operations and solving problems depicted on worksheets. As students progress through middle, junior, and senior high school, math concepts become increasingly more abstract in domains such as algebra, geometry, trigonometry, and calculus. In the higher grades, the wide discrepancies between what slow learners and average/above-average-IQ students can achieve in mathematics becomes stark and undeniable. While average/

above-average-IQ students in the higher grades are struggling to master trigonometry, slow learners are still struggling with understanding computations using elementary fractions.

Difficulty With Generalizing Learned Material to New Situations

In a learning context, generalization refers to the ability to solve a new problem (to which one has not been previously exposed) that belongs to the same class of a problem that has previously been learned. Thus, when a student learns the proper phonetic pronunciation of the "ei" digraph in the words *reign* and *neighbor* (pronounced "ay"), the child has generalized this learning if he or she can properly pronounce similar words that he or she has never seen before (e.g., *weigh* and *sleigh*). If he or she cannot do this, and perceives these new words as brand new, then generalization has not occurred. Generalization can occur both within and outside of the classroom learning environment.

Generalization is the single most important construct that demonstrates the effectiveness of learning (McKeough, Lupart, & Marini, 1995). Bright children are more able than children who are not as bright to generalize learning to a wider class of novel problems. Slow learners require more explicit instruction to do what brighter children can do spontaneously. *This explains why, no matter how effective a teacher is in preparing all of his or her students for a standardized achievement test, there will still be a wide range of individual differences in the test results.* Standardized achievement tests include novel problems that are similar to what has been reviewed in class, but are not exactly the same as what has been reviewed in class. If slower students have difficulty generalizing from previous learning, they will not perform as well on a test, despite the teacher's best efforts at thorough test preparation (see Sidebar 5.5).

Restricted Fund of General Knowledge

Slow learners have a restricted breadth of knowledge of information generally acquired through focused reading and being alert to one's daily environment. Jensen (1981b, p. 65) offers an interesting example that effectively illustrates this issue. Here, a young man with an IQ in the mid-70s, who was also very much interested in baseball, was questioned on how much he knew about his favorite subject of interest. Although he knew the names of a handful of famous baseball players, he could not correctly name the various baseball playing positions, was vague and incorrect on his knowledge of baseball rules, and did not know the names of any major league teams. In contrast, a high-IQ professor, who incidentally had no interest in baseball, was also questioned about the sport. Although this professor claimed never to have seen a baseball game in person in his life, he was able to name some famous baseball players, as well as numerous major league teams.

Similarly, many years ago this author had an occasion to administer an IQ test on the same day to two black students—one an 11th grader enrolled in special education and the other a gifted kindergarten student. Both were asked what the opposite of *hot* was, and who the president of the United States was (at that time). Whereas the gifted kindergarten student easily answered these questions, the 11th grader could not.

Both of these examples illustrate that lower-IQ persons, although adequately exposed to a wide variety of information in daily life, do not effectively absorb and retain this knowledge as well as brighter students. Higher-IQ students accumulate knowledge at a faster rate compared to lower-IQ students, which results in gaps in absolute levels of knowledge that widen further at each successive grade (Gottfredson, 2005).

Short Attention Span/Poor Concentration

Brighter students are able to focus and concentrate for longer periods of time on academic material during learning tasks. In contrast, slow learners must apply greater effort to the same mental tasks that are easier for brighter students. Because this effort is more tiring, slow learners are more prone to lose interest, and their minds are more prone to wander. Therefore, teachers find that lessons for slow learners need to be broken up into smaller segments (Shaw, Grimes, & Bulman, 2005). Difficulties with sustaining attention for longer periods of time is the factor that often lies at the root of classroom behavioral problems and disruptions.

Need for Additional Practice for Mastery

Slower learners, compared to their brighter peers, need more opportunities to practice learned skills before it can be objectively determined that such skills have been sufficiently mastered. Such skills need to be practiced in a variety of settings, in order to explicitly develop generalization to new contexts. Whenever essential skills have not been mastered, then newer and more advanced skills do not have a sufficient foundation on which to build, so to speak. As a result of this poor foundation, more advanced skills do not consolidate in the learner's skill set, which leads to increased frustration and failure.

Requires a Longer Amount of Time to Learn

Slow learners will always lag behind their brighter peers in academic work, and they will never catch up. This is why political rhetoric that expects all children to attain grade-level skills will always meet with failure, despite the best efforts of school districts and teachers (see Sidebar 5.3).

✍ Sidebar 5.3   Individual Differences, Group Differences, and "Closing the Achievement Gap"

Never before has the chasm between established scientific research and political wishful thinking been so wide as in the contemporary rhetoric on "closing the achievement gap." At the time of this writing, "closing the achievement gap" is the rallying cry of education reformers, politicians, high-level school administrators, and activist civil rights groups who believe that equalizing educational outcomes among income groups (e.g., the rich vs. the poor), racial/ethnic groups (e.g., blacks vs. whites), and educational settings (e.g., suburban schools vs. urban schools) is both desirable and fully attainable with only the right amount of public goodwill and, of course, boatloads of dollars.

"Closing the achievement gap" has become a popular catchphrase that has literally taken on a life of its own in education circles. Despite the consistent record of expensive past failures, granting agencies continue to hope that closing the achievement gap is easily achievable if only backed by a famous researcher and a generous string of zeros added to a program's price tag (e.g., see McNamara, 2011). At the time of this writing, journal articles and books have a greater chance of being published if they include at least some explicit reference for how a favored intervention method or program will contribute to closing the gap, regardless of the absence of any solid evidence that documents such a claim.

Educational and school psychologists, more than any other applied professionals, should know better when faced with the invitation to jump on such fashionable bandwagons. Unfortunately, psychologists—as well as the professional organizations to which they belong—are equally as susceptible to being seduced and/or swept away by "closing the gap" rhetoric. As Adlai Stevenson (Democratic presidential candidate in the 1950s) is quoted as saying: "When given a choice between a disagreeable fact and an agreeable fantasy, Americans will choose the agreeable fantasy every time."

Said another way, why should anyone listen to disagreeable facts from the boring world of academia when there is a flawed world to socially engineer toward perfection? The answer here is that disagreeable facts nevertheless reflect a stubborn reality. And, stubborn reality will always manifest itself despite our best efforts to deny it (see Chapter 10). Among the stubborn facts that will not be denied include the following:

1. *The call to close the achievement gap denies the reality of individual differences.* Suppose for a moment that all human beings belong to the same racial/ethnic group and that no such subgroups exist. Even under this

hypothetical scenario, individual differences in cognitive ability remain and are an inescapable fact of life. Now assume that one wants to compare the achievement outcomes of a group of slow learners (those with IQs between 70–85) with a higher-ability group (say, those with IQs between 115–130). As discussed in this chapter, the ability differences between these two groups are huge and have enormous consequences for academic and life achievements. Interventions for the slow learning group can never *erase* the consequences of slow learning ability, but they can only help teachers and students *cope* by adapting instruction to slow learning capabilities. No one would seriously believe that the achievement gap can be truly closed between these two groups—any more than a 400-pound person can run the 100-yard dash in the same time as an Olympic sprinter.

When what is known about the distribution of cognitive ability within racial/ethnic groups is added to the discussion (e.g., see Gottfredson, 2005), politicized rhetoric and grandstanding slowly begin to cloud the issue. Although all population subgroups display the full range of cognitive capabilities, it is also a well-established fact that racial/ethnic groups display different group averages, leading to the inevitability that some groups are disproportionately over- or underrepresented at different segments of the ability continuum (see Sidebar 5.2). Although this is a well-established finding in the scientific literature, this is *politically unacceptable*—the open discussion of which is studiously avoided in polite society. It is much more palatable for the problem to be reframed and openly discussed as a "civil rights" issue—and civil rights issues are fought primarily through *political* means. Subgroup differences in measured cognitive outcomes *ultimately boil down to individual differences* in measured cognitive outcomes. These intractable truths about individual differences now become inconvenient roadblocks to the quest for "social justice."

2. **No researcher has discovered how to permanently raise IQ.** IQ differences play the most significant (but certainly not the only) role in academic achievement differences. Thus, it comes as no surprise that early attempts to equalize achievement differences among individuals and groups focused attention on efforts to permanently raise the IQ, which have met with a consistent record of disappointment and failure (see discussions of Head Start and other early intervention efforts in Jensen, 1998a; Spitz, 1986; Thernstrom & Thernstrom, 2003). Thus, absent any method for permanently raising the IQ, individual differences in academic achievement levels are an unavoidable fact of life.

(continued)

3. **Continuous-outcome variables manifest themselves in distributions, not uniform levels.** Whether the outcome variables of interest are scores on intelligence and achievement tests or school grades, subgroups (however defined) manifest these outcomes in (usually bell-shaped) *distributions*. The concept of "closing a gap" between two individuals in some outcome variable is relatively straightforward to understand. In contrast, closing the gap *between groups* on a *continuous variable* (particularly when such groups manifest different means in their respective distributions) makes not the slightest bit of sense either conceptually or practically. Thus, when politicians speak of closing the achievement gap, they are in essence advocating that *subgroup distributions have the same mean*. Given what has previously been discussed in the last two points, this would mean that students with mental retardation in the lower scoring group would be raised to achievement levels of persons without mental retardation in the higher scoring group, and high average achievers in the lower-scoring group would need to be raised to levels commensurate with those labeled as "gifted" in the higher-scoring group.

4. **The application of educational interventions that improve achievement for all children will increase individual and group differences, not decrease them.** In closing-the-achievement-gap rhetoric, the impression is given that efforts and/or resources will be aggressively poured into the education of low achievers until they "catch up" to what high achievers can do. Advocates never address what will (or should) be done with high achievers (for exceptions to this rule, see Murray, 2008). The unspoken implication is that high achievers will be "put on hold" and ignored until low achievers catch up to them. This, of course, has no basis in reality. Higher achievers will also be exposed to any innovations in instruction or curriculum used by classrooms, schools, and districts. Unfortunately, one of the fundamental laws of individual differences is that, when exposed to the same interventions, higher-ability persons will improve at steeper rates than will lower-ability persons. This essentially *widens* individual differences in achievement outcomes rather than decreases them (Bereiter, 1987; Gottfredson, 2004b; Jensen, 2003; Rushton & Jensen, 2005).

These converging truths inescapably lead to the conclusion that political movements to close the achievement gap are dead on arrival (e.g., see Hood, 2011). This does not mean, however, that applied professionals who are familiar with the scientific literature cannot play a useful role in assisting vulnerable learners in school settings. What is different here is that the phrase "closing the achievement gap" must be brought in line with reality (e.g., see Gottfredson, 2005).

If this phrase must be used at all, it is much more fruitful to think not in terms of closing a gap among population subgroups, but of *closing the achievement gap within individuals*. Many observers of the educational scene, representing a variety of political viewpoints, all agree that the typical student (regardless of cultural background) rarely works to his or her potential in school. Some students are so unmotivated that nothing will help them to succeed according to their potential. Other students are intrinsically motivated, but they find themselves in academic environments that are simply not conducive to learning. Other students are intrinsically motivated and are in optimal educational environments, but they find themselves in need of highly individualized guidance in finding specific opportunities for success in school. There is much that school psychologists, counselors, and teachers can do to help students narrow the gap between their present levels of performance versus what can be achieved with the right opportunities, effort, and instruction—*commensurate with their own abilities*. In doing so, however, they must fundamentally respect the established empirical findings that inform the professional practice to which they are called.

Poor Reading Comprehension Skills

Starting in the first grade through the third grade, the U.S. school curriculum concentrates on pupils *learning to read* (which emphasizes mastery of word recognition and decoding skills). Beginning in grade four and beyond, the emphasis shifts to *reading to learn* (Joseph, 2006). It is here that reading comprehension (skills in understanding what is read at deeper levels) becomes central to academic progress. Reading comprehension tasks are highly g loaded, and reading comprehension tests are well known in the psychometric community as being highly correlated with the g factor (Jensen, 1998a).

Slow learners have greater-than-average difficulty understanding at deeper levels what they read (assuming that a reading disability that impairs word decoding skills is not the cause of the difficulty). Whereas the brighter student is able to read a passage once and quickly grasp its meaning, the slower student must read the same passage several times in order to comprehend its meaning. If the slow learner has not successfully made the transition from word decoding skills to reading comprehension skills, then reading tasks (particularly those related to schoolwork) are perceived as burdensome and noxious. This is experienced disproportionately by students with low IQs (Jensen, 1998a).

Low Academic Motivation

Although most American students begin to lose their enthusiasm for school at around the third grade, this problem is particularly acute for slow learners. For this group, disproportionate rates of academic failure and frustration have an ongoing presence in their school lives. The cumulative effect of these experiences results in extremely low levels of motivation for schoolwork and academic achievement in general (Shaw, 2010). Slow learners are most commonly known as C and D students by teachers, parents, and peers. Such students will attempt to avoid homework or at least will need high levels of coercion and/or prompting in order to keep abreast of school tasks.

Shaw (2001) examined teacher opinions of slow learners. Teachers were asked to give five words that described slow learners. Ninety-seven percent of teachers described slow learners as being unmotivated; 56 percent described them as being the most difficult to teach, 80 percent reported that they spend less time engaging slow learners than high-functioning students in their classrooms; and 72 percent reported that working with high achievers is more rewarding than working with slow learners. This study showed that not only are slow learners having trouble socially with their peers, but teachers have a generally more negative perception of them as well.

Slow learners display little intellectual curiosity about the world (called *cognitive indifference* by Masi, Marcheschi, & Pfanner, 1998). However, if they have highly developed skills or interests in noncognitive areas (e.g., sports, music), they can be highly motivated or interested in achieving or learning within these domains.

As such students matriculate through the secondary school years, they tend to elect less academically demanding courses and will avoid more difficult material, such as what is commonly found in advanced mathematics and science courses (e.g., algebra, trigonometry, calculus, chemistry, physics) or foreign languages. By the time these students reach high school, they are disproportionately represented in students who drop out of school (Herrnstein & Murray, 1994; Vitaro, Brendgen, & Tremblay, 1999).

Higher Incidence of Correlated Social Problems

Lower IQ is associated with a host of negative personal/social outcome variables in adults (e.g., being a chronic welfare recipient, having a child out-of-wedlock, divorced within first five years of marriage, dropping out of high school, higher rates of incarceration; Herrnstein & Murray, 1994).

For school-aged students, lower IQ has also been shown to be significantly associated with higher rates of grade retention in school (Blair, 2001; Shaw, 2001) and promiscuous sexual behavior (Halpern, Joyner, Udry, & Suchindran, 2000). Many studies showing a negative monotonic relationship between IQ and juvenile delinquency (lower IQ is associated with higher delinquency rates) have been reported in the literature (e.g., Koenen, Caspi, Moffitt,

Rijskijk, & Taylor, 2006; Koolhof, Loeber, Wei, & Pardini, 2007; Lynam et al., 1993; Moffitt, Caspi, Silva, & Stouthamer-Loeber, 1995). Although it would be a mistake to interpret this data as suggesting that lower IQ levels *cause* delinquency (as statistically significant correlations have many underlying explanations other than direct causality), some scholars have offered conjectures as to why lower IQ is significantly associated with delinquency. For example, Levin (1997) suggests that persons with criminal tendencies (who also have deficits in empathy and impulsivity) have difficulty conceptualizing the remote consequences of delinquent actions, both for themselves and for their victims.

IQs Between 90–110

Barring serious learning or emotional disabilities, students within this IQ range—assuming adequate exposure to good instruction, coupled with individual motivation and effort—are able to master grade-level academic material (assuming a reasonable definition of grade level). For obvious reasons, the unique characteristics of students with IQs between 90–110 are the most difficult to describe, for the simple reason that the largest proportion of students (approximately 45 percent) drawn from the general population falls within this range.

The only situations where students within this IQ range come to the attention of their teachers is when they are *outliers* compared to the average IQs of most other pupils in their classrooms. Some schools and classrooms, for example, are filled with a preponderance of pupils representing the borderline/low-average range of the IQ distribution (i.e., IQs between 75–90). Pupils within such classrooms who have IQs between 100–115 will stand out and be perceived by their teachers as "bright." Similarly, highly selective private schools may educate a preponderance of students in the high-average/superior range (i.e., IQs between 115–130). Here, pupils with average IQs will also stand out and may come to the attention of their teachers as being slower than their peers. These examples illustrate why psychometrically sound and properly administered IQ tests are crucial for helping educators distinguish between absolute versus relative impressions of students' general cognitive ability.

IQs Between 115–130

Students whose IQs fall within the range of 115–130 enjoy several advantages in the context of schools, many of which are briefly described as follows.

General Liking for and Motivation to Read

Barring serious dyslexic problems that hamper word decoding, students between the IQ ranges of 115–130 are good readers from an early age. That is, they show a greater-than-average proficiency with developing word decoding skills, and they seem to comprehend text with ease. Whereas slow learners generally display very little motivation for independent reading, pupils with IQs between 115–130 have a natural interest in learning new information gained from independent reading. They generally enjoy visiting the library and checking out books to read at home on their own. They will be frequent customers at school book fairs, and they will eagerly await the publication of new books in fiction or nonfiction series that interest them. They often have their own public library cards and frequently visit libraries to learn new information in areas in which they share a keen interest.

General Liking for and Success in School

Students with IQs between 115–130 have qualitatively different school-related experiences compared to slow learners. Whereas slow learners generally experience repeated academic failure leading to a profound dislike of school, pupils with IQs between 115–130 generally (but certainly not always) take a liking to school as a whole, and they are motivated to excel in particular subject areas of their competence and liking. Students in this IQ range are generally considered to be the A and B students of their classrooms. When these students begin high school, they generally select more cognitively advanced classes, such as algebra, trigonometry, calculus, chemistry, physics, and advanced foreign languages. As such, they populate Advanced Placement (AP) classes in high school, which is a necessary requirement for being competitive for admittance to highly selective colleges and universities.

IQs Higher Than 130

Persons who obtain IQ scores of 130 and above on standardized intelligence tests are very rare in the general population, as shown in Sidebar 5.4.

▧ Sidebar 5.4   Probabilities Associated With IQ Scores of 100 and Above in the General Population*

IQ Threshold	Probabilities (Approximate)
100 and above	1 out of every 2 persons
115 and above	16 out of every 100 persons
130 and above	2 out of every 100 persons
150 and above	1 out of every 1,100 persons
160 and above	1 out of every 11,000 persons
170 and above	1 out of every 160,000 persons
180 and above	1 out of every 3.5 million persons
190 and above	1 out of every 110 million persons
200 and above	1 out of every 5 billion persons

*Figures are approximate. See also http://hiqnews.megafoundation.org/Definition_of_IQ.html

Before describing the general characteristics of pupils with IQs over 130, some confusing issues must first be identified and put to rest. It needs to be clearly acknowledged that IQ scores exist on a continuum, and that any cut-off scores that separate one qualitatively distinct cognitive category from another are somewhat arbitrary. In public schools, an IQ score of 130 on an individually administered IQ test is generally designated as the cut score for determining whether a child receives a label as "gifted," which in turn may lead to placement in an advanced class or series of classes. However, there is no significant qualitative difference in observed cognitive functioning between persons with an IQ of 129 and persons with an IQ of 131. For a variety of reasons, a school district can use whatever subjective criteria it wants to qualify a student as gifted.

From a *social perspective*, the gifted label is a highly coveted moniker in many districts. For many families, a child who is labeled gifted is a status symbol suggesting that one's offspring is special, exceptional, or "a cut above" the rest. Because of the palpable social pressures to democratize education (see Gottfredson, 2003b), the gifted education movement historically has slowly expanded the definition of what it means to be gifted (i.e., beyond high IQ alone) to also include "potential" for high performance (as opposed to *actual* high performance); task commitment in a specific performance area; outstanding talent in academic, artistic, athletic, or social areas; leadership; and creative thinking (Callahan, 2005; Johnsen, 2011).

The egalitarian need to democratize giftedness dovetails with the related desire to promote equity in how giftedness is conceptualized and identified across racial/ethnic groups. Because mean subgroup differences in IQ scores will be most noticeable at extreme ends of the bell curve distribution, some minority groups will predictably be underrepresented (and other minority groups will be overrepresented) in classes for the gifted when IQ scores are used as the sole criterion for selection. This, in turn, sets the stage for Quack Multiculturalism to provide its own unique "explanations" and "solutions" for the problems of minority underrepresentation in gifted programs.

According to Quack Multiculturalism (see Chapter 2), minority (particularly African American) students are underrepresented in gifted identification in schools because (a) teachers and schools have a narrow conception of intelligence that fails to appreciate different kinds of giftedness; (b) traditional IQ tests are culturally biased against non-whites; (c) teachers do not understand minority students' different learning styles in the classroom; and (d) minority students express their giftedness in ways that are different from the European norm that is promoted in schools (Ford, 1996; Ford & Grantham, 2003; Ford, Grantham, & Milner, 2004).

As with many ideas promoted by Quack Multiculturalism, not a speck of solid empirical evidence supports any of these ideas. Knowledgeable readers recognize these explanations as attempts to manipulate the perception of reality simply by manipulating words. According to Quack Multiculturalism, the presumed remedy for these ills is to "expand the thinking" of educators and psychologists to appreciate different kinds of giftedness—where the bottom line ultimately leads to the promotion of different (i.e., lower) admissions standards to gifted programs for non-white groups (see extensive discussion in Gottfredson, 2004b).

As stated in Chapter 2, this text rejects such thinking as empirically unsupportable. Stated bluntly, there is no such animal as "multicultural giftedness." The material that follows rests on the truism that IQ test scores, whether they are in the gifted range or otherwise, have the same educational and real-life implications for all people regardless of their race, language, or ethnicity. Thus, the characteristics of pupils with IQs of 130 or above can be described as follows (adapted from Goldsmith, 1999; Jensen, 1996; Johnsen, 2011; Renzulli, Reis, Gavin, Siegle, & Sytsma, 2003; Sisk, 1977; Winner, 1996).

The Ability to Display Complex Thinking and to Easily Understand Abstract Concepts

Learning any new subject matter area begins with instruction that is concrete (in the early grades) and ends with instruction that is both concrete and abstract (in higher grades). Teachers notice that extremely bright students are able to cognitively grasp abstract concepts quicker and easier than their peers and to generalize knowledge gained to a wider class of new applications. Nowhere is this more evident than in mathematics, where the subject matter must increasingly rely on abstract symbols and abstract concepts that are represented by those symbols. Whereas most cognitively average high schoolers must put forth much mental effort to master intermediate algebra, brighter students easily master this material and find that their intellectual capabilities begin to be palpably challenged with trigonometry and precalculus. High school students with IQs several standard deviations above the mean are able to master intermediate calculus while in high school, and some may find themselves cognitively "at home" with advanced college-level math courses.

Early Use of Advanced Vocabulary That Is Unusual for the Child's Chronological Age

In general, the language development of intellectually gifted children proceeds more quickly compared to similar-aged peers with average IQs. Whereas the average child begins to speak in short and simple sentences at approximately two years of age, extremely bright children begin to do so a little more than six months earlier. The high-IQ child is able to listen to conversations at home and in school and more quickly understand how advanced words are used in the context of conversations. Parents particularly notice that their high-IQ child is able to expressively use vocabulary words and more complex ideas that are atypical and unusual compared to the language usage of similar-aged peers. For example, a typical two-year-old may point to a dog and say "There's a doggie." In contrast, under the same circumstances, an extremely bright child may say "There's a brown doggie in the backyard and he's sniffing our flowers" (Sisk, 1977). An acquaintance related the story of her gifted six-year-old grandson's answer when asked the question, "Why do you think God made the sky blue?" The six-year-old responded: "The fact that God made the sky blue is a given. Bad weather makes the sky different colors." The interesting observation here concerns how words are used in relation to this child's chronological age. The phrase "is a given" reflects a relatively sophisticated concept in formal logic that most six-year-olds do not have the cognitive maturity to understand, let alone use in their everyday conversation. Gifted children not only understand more complex concepts that are beyond the understanding of their same-aged peers, but they are able to translate and communicate this understanding through the occasional use of advanced vocabulary that surprises adults.

Heightened Curiosity and Keen Observation Skills

The high-IQ child is intensely curious about the world. He or she observes details, discrepancies, or problems in the environment that average-IQ children would routinely overlook. For example, a gifted child may enter his or her room at home and immediately notice that the toys on the shelf have been arranged in a slightly different pattern (after his mom cleaned his room). However, this new toy arrangement is so subtle as to go unnoticed by most other children. Because their minds are continually active and inquisitive, intellectually gifted children are curious about finding answers to problems that would put their thoughts to rest. Thus, gifted children have a habit of spontaneously asking many questions, and continually probing answers they receive until an answer is given that satisfies their restless minds—at least for the time being.

For example, a gifted child may ask why Scotch tape is sticky on one side and smooth on the other side. The parent may respond to this question with an answer that satisfies average-IQ children, but this simply raises more troubling questions for the gifted child. The gifted child may respond to the parent's answer with a follow-up question: "How can they make a machine that puts on the sticky part without getting the machine all gummed up?" As the adult fumbles for an answer, the gifted child already has formulated another question that needs to be answered: "Why doesn't the sticky side stay stuck to the other side when you unroll the tape?" (adapted from Sisk, 1977). Many parents of gifted children can relate to moments where their child responds with an endless series of follow-up "why" questions whenever they are given (what was presumed to be) reasonable answers to the last question asked. The gifted child is not satisfied with superficial answers to questions, and seeks to get to the bottom of why things work the way they do. It comes as no surprise, therefore, that gifted persons with IQs that equal or exceed 200 often gravitate toward intellectually demanding fields such as astrophysics, which can provide explanations for phenomenon observed in the universe (e.g., see Goldsmith, 1999).

The Ability to Retain a Wide Variety of Information

Intellectually advanced children and youth literally amaze adults with their ability to recall minute details of past experiences that most average persons have long since forgotten. Some highly intelligent children may show evidence of having "photographic memories." For example, a four-year-old child may be able to look at a series of 50 pictured Christmas cards with signatures and be able to perfectly match each picture with the proper signature (see http://www3.bc.sympatico.ca/giftedcanada/develop.html). A gifted young child with concomitant artistic ability may accurately reproduce a drawing of a space rocket seen in a museum six months ago.

The Ability to Concentrate on Intellectual Tasks for Long Periods

Most individuals have no difficulty sitting in front of a TV screen for hours absorbed in mindless entertainment. In contrast, it is much more difficult for most persons to sustain intense and focused concentration on intellectual tasks for extended periods. Intellectually advanced children and youth can sustain focused concentration on intellectual tasks that interest them for unusually long periods of time (that are age appropriate). For example, a two-year-old gifted child may sit for 10 minutes or more listening attentively to a story being read to him or her by a parent. A 10-year-old gifted boy may concentrate for two hours on building a model airplane. A 17-year-old gifted young woman may be totally absorbed in reading an entire novel in four hours.

A Broad and Changing Spectrum of Intellectual Interests

As they grow in curiosity about the world, gifted children and youth often show an intense interest in a particular subject, and they literally devour everything there is to know about it in order to feed their curiosity. However, once this interest is taken to its limit, the gifted child may develop just as intense an interest in a totally different subject, and manifest the same focused interest in this new area. A few months or years later, this interest may shift yet again to a totally different area. For example, an elementary-aged child may manifest an intense interest in dinosaurs—collecting toy dinosaur figures, cutting out pictures in magazines, and endlessly watching and rewatching videos about dinosaurs. Then, just as quickly, this interest may suddenly shift to model trains. Here the child saves his money to build an elaborate electric model train set and collects as many model trains as he possibly can. As the child matures, this interest may shift to planets in the solar system, where the youth visits space museums and checks out as many books on astronomy as he can from the local library.

As gifted youths mature, peers notice that these individuals show superior achievement in a wide variety of endeavors and often excel academically in a wide variety of subject areas. For example, this author was acquainted in his college years with an American friend who was a German-language instructor for undergraduates, an accomplished euphonium player, a leading officer in a local ham radio club, and an avid collector of baseball cards and baseball player statistics.

Strong Critical Thinking and Self-Criticism Skills

Intellectually advanced children and youth are able to intuitively understand the basic rules that underlie formal and informal critical thinking skills. With explicit training in these competencies, gifted children and youth are formidable adversaries in argumentation and debate. One unfortunate byproduct of this tendency may be highly developed (some may say unreasonable) standards of self-criticism. For example, an A student may achieve an A– on a school exam and mentally "beat him- or herself up" for incorrectly answering questions that missed an A grade. Or, a gifted child who just won a gold medal in a swimming relay race may still become depressed because she did not beat her last time in practice.

Advanced/Accelerated Grade Placements

All of these previous characteristics of gifted children lead to one practical observation, which is that, given the same basic learning opportunities, intellectually superior children are roughly one to two years (at minimum) ahead of their average peers in most subject areas. Pupils with IQs nearing (or exceeding) the 200 mark show levels of advancement that literally defy human understanding. For example, some extremely high-IQ individuals are ready for college at age 11, and others easily graduate from college with their PhD degrees in the most intellectually demanding subjects before they are out of their teens (see http://www.eoht.info/page/IQ%3A+200%2B).

PRACTICAL IMPLICATIONS OF LARGE IQ DIFFERENCES IN SCHOOLS

Practical Implications for Achievement Test Performance

One indirect method that can be used to understand the practical implications of large IQ differences in classrooms is to look at data from academic achievement and IQ tests administered to the same subjects, and then examine the level of mastered academic skills that correspond to various IQ standard score thresholds. The Wechsler Individual Achievement Test—Second Edition (WIAT-II), Wechsler Individual Achievement

Test—Third Edition (WIAT-III), and Woodcock-Johnson Psychoeducational Battery (Achievement)—Third Edition (WJ-III ACH) composite score ranges that are associated with the Wechsler Intelligence Scale for Children—Fourth Edition or Woodcock-Johnson Psychoeducational Battery (Cognitive)—Third Edition (WJ-III COG) composite IQ score ranges (i.e., IQ < 70, 70–79, 80–89, 90–99, 100–109, 110–119, 120–129, 130–139, and 140–149) are listed in Tables 5.1, 5.2, 5.3, and 5.4.

Some significant observations are noted in this data. First, and not surprisingly, the mean achievement test standard score steadily climbs as the level of IQ ranges climbs. This relationship holds for all ethnic groups for which sufficient data is available. Although there is some overlap in achievement composite score ranges among adjacent IQ score ranges (because of extreme outliers), there is virtually no overlap in achievement composite score ranges between many nonadjacent IQ score ranges at the extreme high or low ends of the spectrum.

The extent of these differences are brought into sharper focus when the actual academic skills associated with standard score thresholds are examined. This question was examined using the software scoring program for the Woodcock Johnson Psychoeducational Battery—Third Edition Tests of Academic Achievement (abbreviated WJ-III ACH). The WJ-III ACH, published in 2001, boasts a national standardization sample of approximately 8,000 persons ranging in age from 2 to 90 years old (Woodcock, McGrew, & Mather, 2001). The Woodcock-Johnson III NU (Normative Update) Compuscore and Profiles computer scoring program (Schrank & Woodcock, 2001) allows users to enter raw scores from administration of the 12 achievement subtests from the standard battery. The Compuscore program then calculates standard scores (mean = 100, standard deviation [SD] = 15) for each subtest, as well as for the multisubtest clusters of Broad Reading, Broad Math, Broad Written Language, and Oral Language. Finally, a Total Achievement Composite score can be obtained.

It is possible for users to enter hypothetical raw scores for each achievement subtest into the WJ-III Compuscore program, and to choose any configuration of scores that would eventually yield a Total Achievement Composite score of one's choosing. Before entering data into a students' WJ-III Achievement profile, a current grade level must first be specified. Four grade levels were specified (i.e., grades 2.0, 4.0, 8.0, and 12.0), then raw data was entered to yield five fictional score reports within each grade level (i.e., corresponding to Total Achievement standard scores of 70, 85, 100, 115, and 130). Raw data was manipulated such that all subtests within each fictional score report yielded a standard score within ±5 points of each other.

When raw scores were assigned to each subtest, full credit was given to all items (beginning with the first item) in sequential order until an arbitrarily determined ceiling was reached. This was done for all subtests, making sure to equalize (within ±5 points) the arbitrarily derived standard scores across all subtests. For example, suppose a subtest

Table 5.1 Wechsler Individual Achievement Test—Second Edition (WIAT-II) Total Standard Score Mean and Ranges for Wechsler Intelligence Scale for Children—Fourth Edition (WISC-IV) Full Scale IQ Ranges: Breakdown by Racial/Ethnic Group

WISC-IV FSIQ Score Range	Whites (N = 314) WIAT-II			Blacks (N = 68) WIAT-II			Hispanics (N = 93) WIAT-II			Total (N = 475)* WIAT-II		
	N	%	Range (Mean)	N	%	Range (Mean)	N	%	Range (Mean)	N	%	Range (Mean)
<70	0	0.0	—	3	4.4	55–70 (60)	6	6.5	56–70 (61)	9	0.01	55–70 (60)
70–79	16	5.1	71–99 (83)	10	14.7	68–86 (75)	14	15.1	61–92 (75)	40	0.08	61–99 (78)
80–89	37	11.8	70–107 (88)	15	22.1	63–103 (81)	24	25.7	78–99 (87)	76	0.16	63–107 (86)
90–99	53	16.9	80–127 (96)	17	25.0	77–110 (95)	25	26.8	81–110 (97)	95	0.20	77–127 (96)
100–109	104	33.1	86–129 (105)	12	17.6	89–111 (101)	18	19.4	95–123 (106)	134	0.28	86–129 (105)
110–119	67	21.3	89–128 (114)	8	11.8	101–129 (117)	3	3.2	110–113 (111)	78	0.16	89–129 (114)
120–129	31	9.9	99–139 (122)	3	4.4	108–131 (123)	2	2.2	120–122 (121)	36	0.07	99–139 (122)
130–139	5	1.6	124–136 (129)	—	—	—	1	1.1	130 (130)	6	0.01	124–136 (130)
140–149	1	0.3	135 (135)	—	—	—	—	—	—	1	0.03	135 (135)

*Total N includes only examinees reporting membership in white, black, and Hispanic racial/ethnic groups.
(Data tables courtesy of Ms. Ying Meng, Sr. Statistical Analyst, Clinical Psychometrics, Pearson Assessments)

Table 5.2 Wechsler Individual Achievement Test—Second Edition (WIAT-II) Total Standard Score Mean and Ranges for Wechsler Intelligence Scale for Children—Fourth Edition (WISC-IV) Full Scale IQ Ranges: Breakdown by Age Group

WISC-IV FSIQ Score Range	6–8 Yrs (N = 146) WIAT-II			9–12 Years (N = 160) WIAT-II			13–16 Years (N = 194) WIAT-II			Total (N = 500) WIAT-II		
	N	%	Range (Mean)	N	%	Range (Mean)	N	%	Range (Mean)	N	%	Range (Mean)
<70	2	1.4	70 (70)	3	1.9	55–70 (60)	4	2.1	56 (56)	9	1	55–70 (60)
70–79	15	10.3	68–97 (79)	11	6.9	61–99 (78)	14	7.2	68–85 (77)	40	8	61–99 (78)
80–89	15	10.3	63–103 (86)	31	19.3	70–107 (88)	32	16.5	73–97 (85)	78	15	63–107 (86)
90–99	37	25.2	77–112 (94)	25	15.6	82–110 (98)	35	18.0	81–127 (96)	97	19	77–127 (96)
100–109	35	24.0	91–129 (104)	54	33.7	86–129 (106)	53	27.3	86–125 (104)	142	28	86–129 (105)
110–119	28	19.2	98–130 (113)	22	13.8	98–129 (116)	34	17.5	89–125 (114)	84	16	89–130 (114)
120–129	12	8.2	99–139 (128)	10	6.3	108–134 (124)	19	9.8	110–130 (119)	41	8	99–139 (123)
130–139	2	1.4	129–136 (133)	3	1.9	124–130 (127)	3	1.6	124–130 (126)	8	1	124–136(128)
140–149	0	0	—	1	0.6	135 (135)	0	0.0	—	1	.04	135 (135)

(Data tables courtesy of Ms. Ying Meng, Sr. Statistical Analyst, Clinical Psychometrics, Pearson Assessments)

Table 5.3   Wechsler Individual Achievement Test—Second Edition (WIAT-III) Total Standard Score Mean and Ranges for Wechsler Intelligence Scale for Children–Fourth Edition (WISC-IV) Full Scale IQ Ranges*

WISC-IV FSIQ Score Range	N	%	WIAT–III Total Score Range (Mean)
< 70	—	—	—
70–79	6	5	72–90 (81)
80–89	19	16	75–96 (86)
90–99	26	22	89–104 (97)
100–109	38	33	94–111 (103)
110–119	16	14	102–119 (110)
120–129	10	9	110–131 (121)
130–139	1	1	128 (128)

*Total N = 116; ethnic breakdown: Asian (n = 3; 2.59%), black (n = 19; 16.38%), Hispanic (n = 17; 14.66%), white (n = 75; 64.66%), and other (n = 2; 1.72%). Sex breakdown is 50% male, 50% female. (Data table courtesy of Ms. Ying Meng, Sr. Statistical Analyst, Clinical Psychometrics, Pearson Assessments)

Table 5.4   Woodcock–Johnson Psychoeducational Battery Achievement (WJ-III ACH) Total Standard Score Mean and Ranges for Woodcock–Johnson Psychoeducational Battery Cognitive (WJ-III COG) Full Scale IQ Ranges: Breakdown by Racial/Ethnic Group

WJ-III COG FSIQ Score Range	Race/Ethnicity	N	WJ-III ACH Range*	WJ-III ACH Mean
< 70	White	15	39–84	70.8
	Black	7	46–79	62.5
	Hispanic**	5	69–84	76.2
	Asian/Pacific Islander	2	57–84	70.5
	Native American	—	—	—
70–79	White	24	58–98	77.9
	Black	12	70–79	75.6
	Hispanic	11	63–103	80.0
	Asian/Pacific Islander	—	—	—
	Native American	3	55–83	73.6
80–89	White	102	65–117	89.6
	Black	61	72–105	88.1
	Hispanic	22	75–98	86.5

(continued)

Table 5.4   (Continued)

WJ-III COG FSIQ Score Range	Race/Ethnicity	N	WJ-III ACH Range*	WJ-III ACH Mean
	Asian/Pacific Islander	7	84–107	93.8
	Native American	5	83–95	88.8
90–99	White	363	63–122	98.0
	Black	71	75–121	95.5
	Hispanic	43	67–120	97.1
	Asian/Pacific Islander	18	85–116	99.8
	Native American	14	79–107	95.2
100–109	White	444	78–127	104.5
	Black	43	80–123	101.1
	Hispanic	25	86–124	102.6
	Asian/Pacific Islander	16	96–123	108.5
	Native American	15	87–117	99.6
110–119	White	343	87–135	111.2
	Black	19	96–127	111.1
	Hispanic	21	99–127	109.4
	Asian/Pacific Islander	23	103–137	118.3
	Native American	10	101–122	107.0
120–129	White	187	88–148	117.7
	Black	7	101–128	117.1
	Hispanic	11	103–136	116.9
	Asian/Pacific Islander	11	103–131	122.6
	Native American	2	95–136	115.5
130–139	White	39	106–147	125.4
	Black	1	110	110.0
	Hispanic	2	125–127	126.0
	Asian/Pacific Islander	7	120–155	133.8
	Native American	—	—	—
140–149	White	6	118–141	133.0
	Black	—	—	—
	Hispanic	—	—	—
	Asian/Pacific Islander	2	136–140	138
	Native American	—	—	—

*Score based on standard (rather than extended) achievement battery.
**Hispanics can also report membership in another racial group.
(Data tables courtesy of Dr. Steven Osterlind from data provided by Mr. Fred Schrank and Dr. Kevin McGrew)

includes 30 items. This means that raw scores have to be assigned to the subtest to eventually yield an arbitrary Total Achievement composite score (i.e., 70, 85, 100, 115, or 130). If the Total Achievement Composite standard score was set to 70 (within a specified grade level), then this may translate to awarding full credit to the first four items of the subtest (with all subsequent items within the subtest receiving no credit). Keeping the grade level constant, a Total Achievement composite standard score set to 85 may translate to awarding full credit to the first seven items of the subtest. A Total Achievement composite standard score set to 100 may translate to awarding full credit to the first 10 items of the subtest—and so on.

From an examination of which subtest items were passed and failed within each grade level (i.e., 2, 4, 8, or 12) and Total Achievement composite score (i.e., 70, 85, 100, 115, or 130), the upper limits of general academic skill levels achieved within a given domain (e.g., reading, math, spelling) can be inferred (see Table 5.5). As shown in Table 5.5, an individual of any grade who achieves a Total Achievement composite standard score of approximately 85 will be behind grade-level performing peers. This roughly corresponds to a mean total achievement score obtained by individuals with WJ-III COG IQ scores between 80–89 (see Table 5.4). This means that while second graders on grade level can read simple four-letter words, slow learners are most proficient at reading only three-letter words. While fourth graders on grade level can add two double-digit numbers involving regrouping, slow learners are most proficient in single-digit calculations. While 12th graders on grade level can spell, from oral dictation, words with complex letter/sound digraphs, slow learners are proficient at spelling—with much effort—words at the sixth-grade level. The deficiencies in mental problem-solving skills that hinder slow learners are discussed in Sidebar 5.5.

Similarly, gifted students with truly exceptional IQs (i.e., 130 or higher), who achieve Total Achievement composite standard scores of 130 or above on average, clearly stand out in stark ways compared to their grade-level peers. While grade-level second graders can correctly compute single-digit subtraction problems, gifted students can correctly compute double-digit subtraction problems. Compared to their grade-level peers, gifted fourth graders can spell words appropriate for children at least two grades older than them.

While grade-level eighth graders are mastering simple computations with single-digit fractions, gifted students are comfortable with algebra equations. While average 12th graders are mastering algebra equations, gifted students are easily mastering trigonometry and calculus.

Practical Implications for the Complexity of Content to Be Learned

The content of what students must learn in school is hierarchically arranged, from easy subject matter in the early grades to more difficult subject matter in higher grades. To

Table 5.5 Estimated Academic Skills Corresponding to Total Achievement Standard Scores on the Woodcock-Johnson-III Tests of Achievement Scale for Grades 2, 4, 8, and 12

Grade Level	Total Achievement Standard Score = 70	Total Achievement Standard Score = 85	Total Achievement Standard Score = 100	Total Achievement Standard Score = 115	Total Achievement Standard Score = 130
2.0	Can identify letters such as *d, n*, and correctly read words such as *can* and *is*. Can correctly write the number 4 when asked, knows $1 + 1$. From oral dictation, can correctly write upper and lower case *h, i,* and *d*	Can correctly read words such as *let, pan,* and *log*. Can correctly calculate $6 + 2$ and $5+1$ in horizontal format. From oral dictation, can correctly spell *seed, she,* and *on*	Can correctly read words such as *park, mist,* and *then*. Can correctly calculate $6 - 1$ and $5 - 3$ in both vertical and horizontal format. From oral dictation, can correctly spell *mouse, has,* and *fix*	Can correctly read words such as *decent, grown,* and *about*. Can correctly calculate $8 + 7$. From oral dictation, can correctly spell *pain, why,* and *brook*	Can correctly read words such as *achievement, weird,* and *experiment*. Can correctly calculate $67 - 23$, $14 - 5$, and 3×4. From oral dictation, can correctly spell *return, door,* and *easy*
4.0	Can correctly read words such as *know, then,* and *tart*. Can correctly write the number 5 when asked, calculate $3 + 4$, and $5 - 1$. From oral dictation, can correctly spell *cash, has,* and *list*	Can correctly read words such as *again, distant,* and *before*. Can correctly calculate 2×3, $8 + 6$, and $16 - 9$. From oral dictation, can correctly spell *soap, move,* and *gift*	Can correctly read words such as *achievement, weird,* and *experiment*. Can correctly calculate $6 \div 3$, 4×5, and $45 + 67$. From oral dictation, can correctly spell *return, door,* and *easy*	Can correctly read words such as *peculiar, fantastic,* and *systematize*. Can correctly calculate 13×6, $47 - 28$, and $9 \div 3$. From oral dictation, can correctly spell *hundred, promise,* and *jewel*	Can correctly read words such as *providential, tourniquet,* and *conscientious*. Can correctly calculate $141 \div 47$, $4/5 - 2/5$, and $38 - 19$. From oral dictation, can correctly spell *exposure, mystery,* and *admiration*

8.0	Can correctly read words such as *achievement*, *weird*, and *experiment* Can correctly calculate 7×5, $8 \div 4$, and $78 + 63$ From oral dictation, can correctly spell *below*, *truth*, and *proud*	Can correctly read words such as *peculiar*, *fantastic*, and *systematize* Can correctly calculate $\frac{3}{4} - \frac{1}{4}$, 15×6, and $37 - 26$ From oral dictation, can correctly spell *surprise*, *laugh*, and *breeze*	Can correctly read words such as *providential*, *tourniquet*, and *conscientious* Can correctly calculate $3225 \div 25$, $\frac{7}{8} - \frac{3}{8}$, and $52 - 19$ From oral dictation, can correctly spell *detain*, *committee*, and *bachelor*	Can correctly read words such as *contemptuous*, *disproportionate*, and *pugnacious* Can correctly calculate -5×9, $-56 + 25$, and $2\frac{1}{8} + 5\frac{1}{3}$ From oral dictation, can correctly spell *calculator*, *atrocious*, and *hallucination*	Can correctly read words such as *gustatory*, *quotidian*, and *munificence* Can correctly solve for X in the equation $X^2 + 3x - 8 = 10$, can find the cube root of 64, can solve for $\frac{5}{7} \div \frac{1}{3}$ From oral dictation, can correctly spell *marriage*, *souvenir*, and *technique*
12.0	Can correctly read words such as *agony*, *factor*, and *literal* Can correctly calculate 9×5, $9 \div 3$, and $68 - 44$ From oral dictation, can correctly spell *freight*, *observe*, and *sketch*	Can correctly read words such as *panorama*, *assimilate*, and *contagious* Can correctly calculate $190 \div 38$, 13×8, and $52 - 19$ From oral dictation, can correctly spell *criminal*, *embarrass*, and *mortgage*	Can correctly read words such as *fractions*, *obstinate*, and *hypothetical* Can correctly calculate -5×9, $-56 + 25$, and $2\frac{1}{8} + 5\frac{1}{3}$ From oral dictation, can correctly spell *hoax*, *convenient*, and *knowledge*	Can correctly read words such as *demagogue*, *corpulence*, and *prosaic* Can correctly solve for X in the equation $X^2 + 3x - 8 = 10$, can find the cube root of 64, can solve for $\frac{5}{7} \div \frac{1}{3}$ From oral dictation, can correctly spell *pedagogy*, *glacier*, and *discernible*	Can correctly read words such as *evanescent*, *perfidious*, and *querulous* Can correctly solve and find solutions for the trigonometric equation $2 \cos x + 1 = 0$, find the square root of .0064, and solve for $7\frac{1}{3} \div 6\frac{3}{4}$ From oral dictation, can correctly spell *cuisine*, *reconnaissance*, and *ecclesiastical*

◔ Sidebar 5.5   Sample Achievement Test Items and Below-Average General Cognitive Ability

Consider the following four items similar to those found on the National Assessment of Educational Progress (NAEP) test for eighth graders (correct answers are preceded by an asterisk):

Passage: The ancient Aztec people built elaborate canal systems to irrigate farmland, and are known for their advanced poetry and artwork carved out of wood and stone. They lived by hunting and growing avocados, beans, squashes, sweet potatoes, tomatoes, and corn. The Aztecs were a busy and peaceful people for several hundred years. Then around 1520, an outbreak of smallpox swept through the Aztec population and contributed to the eventual decline of the Aztec people.

Item A: The life of the Aztec people before 1520 was portrayed by the author
    as being _____
    A. Violent and full of conflicts
    B. Thrilling and exciting
    C. Difficult and dreary
    *D. Productive and peaceful

Item B: There were 30 students in Miss Brown's class last year. This year the
    number of students increased by 10 percent. How many students are in
    Miss Brown's class this year?
    (A) 3 (B) 10 *(C) 33 (D) 40

TWO DAYS ABSOLUTELY FREE!

Do you want to grow your business? Simply place an ad with the Daily Gazette newspaper (items must be $20 or less) and get the first two days for free. After the second day, the cost is $10 per day to advertise with us.

Item C: If you want to place a free ad, your goods to be sold must be
    A. Sold within 10 days
    *B. Priced at $20 or less
    C. In excellent condition
    D. Inspected by the newspaper editor

Item D: What is 6 hundredths written in decimal notation?
    (A) 0.006 *(B) 0.06 (C) 0.600 (D) 6.00 (E) 600.0

For each test item, large test publishing companies routinely plot the probability of correctly answering the item (for a given group) against the test's total achievement test score (in the case of individually or group-administered achievement tests) or Full Scale IQ score (in the case of individually administered intelligence tests). Before an item is included in the final test, the plot must show an "S" shape. Beginning at the lowest IQ or total achievement score range, the probability of answering the item correctly is extremely low. As the total IQ or total achievement score rises, a point is reached where the probability of answering the item correctly rises sharply. Finally, a point is reached where nearly all examinees with scores higher than a particular Full Scale IQ or total achievement score pass the item. A test item is considered to be relatively free of cultural bias when the "S" curves for all subgroups overlap to a specified degree (see Reynolds & Carson, 2005).

On items similar to the ones shown above, a significant percentage of eighth graders from a large nationally representative American sample failed to successfully pass these items (Murray, 2008). Critics of testing and intelligence theory have offered every conceivable excuse for explaining away these results (e.g., see Helms, 1992, 1997), while intentionally avoiding the one explanation that *does* explain these results—*low general cognitive ability* (see also Jensen, 1984).

Item A. This item includes a number of easy clues as to the correct answer. For example, the item stem directs the examinee's attention to the year 1520, which is explicitly mentioned in the opening passage. The sentence immediately preceding the year 1520 sentence in the passage explicitly includes the word "peaceful" (which is also included in the correct answer). Finally, the first two sentences in the passage explicitly describe the Aztecs as being busy with activity, which is a synonym for the word *productive* in the correct answer choice. Yet, in order to put these clues together, the examinee must draw out inferences and implications using linguistic knowledge (e.g., to know that to make and build things is related to being productive) and use knowledge of the temporal ordering of events (e.g., knowing where in the passage to look for events that happened prior to 1520). These steps are difficult for the examinee with low average general cognitive ability.

Item B. While most eighth graders would be able to calculate 10 percent of 30, and are able to add 30 plus 3, many students in the lower half of the general ability distribution are unable to spontaneously and correctly put these steps together in the context of a word problem. Classroom teachers can certainly provide students with sufficient pretest practice for handling these types of problems. However, low-ability students are crippled by the *generalizability issue.* That is, while low-ability students can be taught to solve specific test problems of this type, they are lost when confronted with an entirely new and different problem that requires the same general operations but is presented in a new context or puts a slightly different twist on the problem (e.g., when the test taker is asked to calculate a percentage reduction instead of a percentage increase).

(*continued*)

Item C. It is safe to assume that nearly all eighth graders are able to read the words *absolutely, free, grow, business, days, newspaper,* and *advertise*—as well as understanding the numerical symbols 2, $10, and $20. Students with below-average general cognitive ability did not miss this item because they were unable to decode these words and symbols, but because they were unable to properly interpret how the question in the item stem relates to information in the headline.

Item D. Eighth-grade students who are below average in logical-mathematical ability have encountered classroom teaching on decimal notation and terminology, but their teachers find that it takes longer for these students (compared to average/above-average-ability learners) to fully grasp the concept. Even after the concept is grasped, teachers find that the same concept must be repeatedly re-explained because the conceptual understanding does not "stick." When presented with novel decimal notation problems that were not part of the original instruction, the new problems are missed because the concept of decimal notation is beyond the student's capacity to absorb and retain (at least in the time frame allowed for students to prepare for the test).

(Adapted from Murray, 2008)

---

illustrate, students must first learn basic letter/sound correspondences before they can learn to decode three- and four-letter words. Students must learn basic arithmetic and multiplication facts before they can learn to solve word problems whose correct solutions require facility with such facts. Scope and sequence charts within teacher lesson guides specify the entire range of material (i.e., the scope) to be covered in a semester or year, as well as the order of topics, objectives, lessons, or units (i.e., the sequence) to be covered within a particular timeframe. This material is organized in a hierarchical fashion, in the sense that the learning of later objectives, units, topics, or lessons depends on mastery of earlier objectives, units, topics, or lessons.

Within any particular instructional lesson, the knowledge to be learned by students varies according to its degree of cognitive depth and complexity. Regardless of the grade level in which new knowledge is first introduced, knowledge at its simplest and least complex form does not require extensive internal mental manipulation in order to be learned. For example, a lesson that requires students to know that Columbus discovered America in 1492 only requires the learner to associate "Columbus" with "1492" and to remember this association. In contrast, the lesson knowledge involved in giving a coherent answer to the question "What are some factors that would have prevented

Columbus from discovering America?" involves a deeper understanding of historical and political events, as well as an understanding of the navigational obstacles and limited scientific knowledge of the time. The point is, both lessons may be about Christopher Columbus (and both lessons may be introduced in the same grade), but the first type of knowledge is simpler to digest, whereas the second type of knowledge requires a deeper and more complex understanding of the subject matter.

For the process of student learning, four conceptually distinct categories for organizing different forms of knowledge have been identified and explicated by numerous researchers (Kame'enui & Simmons, 1990, 1999; Kozloff, 2002). These forms of knowledge, ranging from simplest to most complex, are (1) verbal associations, (2) concepts, (3) rule relationships, and (4) cognitive strategies.

In a general sense, *verbal associations* involve learning by connecting specific responses to specific stimuli. This form of knowledge includes learning discrete facts (e.g., $3 + 4 = 7$; the letter c is the third letter of the alphabet; the hydrogen atom has one proton and one electron; the Declaration of Independence was signed in 1776); learning verbal chains (e.g., recite in order the months of the year, days of the week, letter alphabet); and learning simple discriminations (e.g., How are men physically different from women? What is the difference between a p and a q?).

Learning *concepts* is a more complex form of knowledge compared to learning verbal associations. A concept can be defined as an object, event, action, or situation that is part of a class of objects, events, actions, or situations, all of which share a feature or set of features that are the same (e.g., all shades of blue are examples of the concept "blue"; all mammals are warm blooded and bear live young; all liquids conform to the shape of their containers; all democracies allow citizens to vote in elections). In order to properly teach students to understand concepts, the teacher must emphasize the essential and nonessential features of the concept and provide students with sufficient practice in learning examples and nonexamples of the concept.

Learning *rule relationships* is a more complex form of knowledge compared to learning concepts. Rule relationships can be defined as propositions that specify a connection between at least two facts, discriminations, or concepts. Examples of knowledge forms that illustrate rule relationships include having students learn that as rates of unemployment rise, rates of mental hospitalization in urban areas also tend to rise; having students discover that the same amount of liquid poured into increasingly taller and thinner containers causes the liquid level to rise; or having students learn that the relationship between test anxiety and test performance is curvilinear. From this knowledge, students learn to predict values on one variable from knowledge of values on a correlated variable.

Finally, the learning of *cognitive strategies* is the most complex form of knowledge compared to the previous three forms of knowledge. Cognitive strategies can be defined as a series of multistep associations and procedures that may involve facts, verbal chains, discriminations, concepts, and rules, which can be combined to bring about a response or a set of responses to a specified problem. Examples of cognitive strategies include learning how to analyze a political speech in order to identify its logical soundness or critical thinking errors; learning how to apply a mathematical strategy or algorithm in solving for an unknown variable in an algebraic equation; learning the scientific strategy needed for isolating the cause-and-effect relationship among variables in a science experiment. Additional examples of these forms of knowledge, as applied to four different subject areas crossed with early, intermediate, and high grade levels, are depicted in Table 5.6.

Each successive level in the knowledge hierarchy can include one or more levels under it. That is, learning at the Concept level often includes learning at the Verbal

Table 5.6   Four Forms of Knowledge With Sample Student Competencies in Four Subject Areas

	Form of Knowledge: Verbal Associations (Simplest)			
	Language Arts	Science	Mathematics	Social Studies
Early Grades	When shown a consonant letter, students can say its sound.	Students can recite the seasons of the year in order.	Starting with the number 2, students can count to 20 by 2s.	Students can name the first five presidents of the United States.
Intermediate Grades	Students can correctly pronounce non-phonetically spelled sight words.	Students can recall the number of pints in a quart, the number of quarts in a gallon, and the number of pounds in a ton.	When given the name of a mathematical operation (e.g., add, subtract, divide, square root), students can write the symbol for the operation.	Students can name the capital of each American state and each country.
Higher Grades	Students can name (and give verbal definitions for) literary elements of a story (e.g., plot, characters, setting, theme)	When presented with names of elements from the periodic table, students can give the abbreviation or the atomic number for each element	Students can give the verbal definition for advanced math terms (e.g., integer, prime number, cube root)	Students can correctly recite the steps in correct sequence for how a bill becomes a law

Table 5.6   (*Continued*)

| Form of Knowledge: Concepts | | | |
Language Arts	Science	Mathematics	Social Studies
Early Grades When they see letters or hear letter sounds, students know which letters represent consonants and which letters represent vowels.	Students are shown different shades of red and blue objects, and can correctly assign the objects to either red or blue color categories.	Students can discriminate between which numbers are odd vs. even numbers.	Students understand how different families can be alike and different.
Intermediate Grades When given a sentence, the students know which words are nouns, verbs, and adverbs.	Students know how to discriminate between similar physical features of the earth (i.e., understand differences between rivers, lakes, streams, oceans).	Students know the essential difference between numbers that are and are not prime numbers.	Students understand the essential characteristics that differentiate the legislative, executive, and judicial branches of U.S. government.
Higher Grades Students know the essential features that distinguish between satire, parody, and allegory.	Students know the properties that distinguish between different types of stars in the universe.	Students know the essential difference between linear vs. nonlinear mathematical equations.	When given descriptions of different and complex societies, students know which societies illustrate democracies, dictatorships, or monarchies—and which societies do not.

| Form of Knowledge: Rule Relationships | | | |
Language Arts	Science	Mathematics	Social Studies
Early Grades Students use knowledge of phonetic rules (e.g., word families, patterns, syllabication, common letter combinations) to spell new words.	Students explain why the apparent size of an object depends on its distance from the observer.	Students understand the commutative, associative, and distributive properties of addition and multiplication.	Through use of case studies and stories, students understand the relationship between increasing migration to the United States and resulting changes in American culture.

(*continued*)

Table 5.6   (*Continued*)

	Form of Knowledge: Rule Relationships			
	Language Arts	**Science**	**Mathematics**	**Social Studies**
Intermediate Grades	Students are able to identify and determine the meaning of unknown words, based on rules that govern the interpretation of Latin and Greek roots.	Using an activity with a plastic resealable bag half filled with water, a straw, a ruler, and a pencil, students discover that the volume of the earth's oceans expands and contracts as its temperature changes, although the amount of water remains constant.	Students understand how formulas for surface area change in relation to whether the object in question is a cube, rectangular prism, or cylinder.	Students describe the factors that led to the founding and settlement of the American colonies (e.g., religious persecution, economic opportunity, adventure, forced migration).
Higher Grades	Students can understand and use writing conventions and rules that characterize written work as facts vs. opinion-based, through use of emotional persuasion vs. logical argumentation writing techniques.	Given two adjacent tubes filled with water and connected by a thin tube at the bottom, students can describe what would happen to the water in the second tube when water in the first tube is heated (using what is known about the concept of pressure).	Students understand the meaning of arithmetic and geometric mathematical sequences, and can construct and apply formulas to predict specific terms in a sequence.	Students are able to understand and articulate how the U.S. government has changed over time to adapt to the changing needs of society.

	Form of Knowledge: Cognitive Strategies (Most Complex)			
	Language Arts	**Science**	**Mathematics**	**Social Studies**
Early Grades	Students will break down words to identify prefixes and suffixes, and use previous knowledge to	Students will analyze and predict weather changes by integrating readings from a thermometer,	Students will add and subtract fractions with nonequivalent numerators and denominators	Students understand the distinctions between deltas, straits, channels, plateaus, prairies, mesas, isthmuses,

Table 5.6   (*Continued*)

	Form of Knowledge: Cognitive Strategies (Most Complex)			
	Language Arts	Science	Mathematics	Social Studies
	determine the correct meaning of words from analysis of how words are used in the context of a given passage.	anemometer, barometer, and hygrometer.	using both drawings and mathematical algorithms.	and peninsulas, and locate novel examples of each on a physical map.
Intermediate Grades	Given an incorrectly written passage, students edit the passage for correct spelling, grammar, sentence structure, punctuation conventions, and sentence clarity.	Using what is known about the interaction of species and environments, students compare and contrast the advantages and disadvantages of both hybrid and pure-bred species of plants and animals.	When given a math word problem, students will think about the given facts stated in the problem, analyze its words, and draw pictures to formulate a mathematical equation to solve for an unknown.	Students will study current and/or recent presidential political campaigns and analyze the strategic and/or political factors in these campaigns that were responsible for the eventual outcome.
Higher Grades	Students evaluate the influence of historical setting and context in excerpts from well-known literary works.	Students conduct a systematic analysis of an unknown chemical, using a flowchart and experimental procedures, including flame tests and precipitation reactions, to determine the presence of metal ions.	When given a probability problem (e.g., "If two dice are tossed, what are the chances of rolling a 7?"), students will understand how to set up a generic probability formula, understand the numerical elements embedded in the problem, and substitute the appropriate elements in the formula to obtain a correct answer.	When given brief quotations from William J. Brennan, Calvin Coolidge, and Albert Einstein, students will study the quotations and write an essay that discusses their meanings in light of what is known about the power of laws and the extent to which laws govern various aspects of American life.

(Adapted from Kozloff, 2002)

Associations level. Learning at the Cognitive Strategy level often includes learning at the Rule Relationship, Concept, and Verbal Associations level. For example, the cognitive strategy for multiplying two three-digit numbers involves steps in a routine (e.g., "begin by multiplying numbers in the ones column," etc.). Each step is governed by rule relationships (e.g., how to carry numbers after multiplying). Rules involve concepts (e.g, concepts of multiplication, carrying). Concepts involve collections of simple verbal associations (e.g., ability to count in a series, knowledge of addition/multiplication facts; see Kozloff, 2002).

The extent to which these forms of knowledge interrelate in classroom instructional lessons varies as a function of grade level. That is, learning in the early grades almost exclusively consists of learning at the *Verbal Associations* level, with a relatively smaller proportion of learning occurring at the *Concept* level. As students get older and mature cognitively, more instruction incorporates learning at the *Rule Relationships* and *Cognitive Strategy* levels. Nevertheless, it needs to be reiterated that within any particular unit of instruction, learning at more complex levels assumes mastery of learning at lower levels.

Researchers have observed that students who are low in abstract/conceptual forms of thinking nevertheless show average or above-average skills in rote memorization and simpler associational thinking (e.g., see Jensen, 1993, 1998b). For these students, lower levels of general cognitive ability (as long as these levels are not lower than a given threshold) need not provide a significant handicap for school learning—as long as the curriculum remains at the verbal associations level. With each successive grade—as the curriculum becomes more abstract, conceptual, and cognitive—students in the slow-learner category begin to struggle with academic material. Because of their slower learning rates compared to cognitively average peers, these learners absorb, consolidate, and generalize material to be learned at slower rates over time. Some subject areas have a modest correlation between learning and IQ. As examples, high performance in subjects that depend on the development of special abilities (e.g., music, art, physical education) or narrow perceptual-motor abilities (e.g., typing) are not as predictive from higher IQ levels (Jensen, 1980). In contrast, other subject area classes (particularly those in the higher grades) cover knowledge that is almost exclusively at the *Rule Relationships* and *Cognitive Strategy* levels, and higher performance levels are most predictive from higher IQs in these classes. This explains why average-ability and slow-learner students tend to avoid them.

INTERVENTIONS FOR VULNERABLE LEARNERS

Understanding individual differences in general cognitive ability is central to having a realistic perspective on the nature and limits of instructional interventions for facilitating learning goals in schools. Unfortunately, school psychologists in real-life school settings find themselves easily seduced by popular bandwagons that may sound good but have no basis in any empirical reality, as revealed by decades of psychological research.

John B. Carroll (1963, 1989) proposed a simple model of school learning that has been highly influential to educational researchers in subsequent decades. The Carroll model establishes a *psychological* (as opposed to an ideological or sociopolitical) framework for understanding how important factors interact in influencing school learning. The reality of what actually transpires in schools' efforts to accommodate individual differences in general cognitive ability can be clearly understood in light of the Carroll model. The Carroll model involves the following component elements, as shown in Figure 5.1 and briefly described in the following sections.

Academic Achievement

Academic achievement is a broad term that has too often been operationalized exclusively as scores on standardized achievement tests. This approach is unfortunate and is responsible for much frustration in school settings. Teachers find themselves

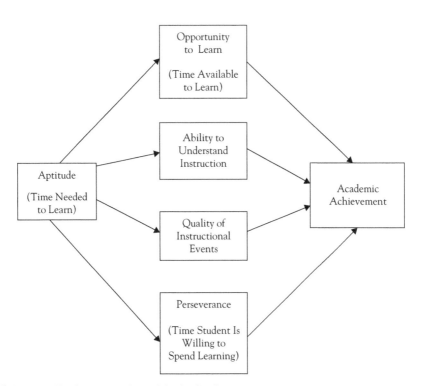

Figure 5.1 Carroll's (1963, 1989) Model of School Learning

under tremendous pressures to raise achievement test scores in competition with other schools—often in response to federal/state political initiatives (e.g., see Sidebar 4.5). Teachers are often unfairly blamed and held responsible for students' low performance on group-administered achievement tests, when in fact a basic understanding of individual differences more than adequately explains such facts.

Academic achievement tests, like all other mental tests, are g *loaded* to some degree (see Sidebar 5.2). Even when a teacher has taught the same material to the same group of students, all students will not achieve the same score on an achievement test that assesses what students have learned. Instead, students will display a range of achievement test scores despite being exposed to the same instruction, simply by virtue of preexisting individual differences in general cognitive ability. Bright students are better able to apply and generalize what has been learned to the solution of novel problems never seen before. Cognitively slower students are not as skilled in this regard, and they will often forget what has previously been learned or will have difficulty understanding the necessary steps required to solve novel problems. Because of this natural variation in students' general cognitive abilities, brighter students often do well on group achievement tests *despite* mediocre instruction, and slower students often perform poorly on achievement tests *despite* exemplary instruction.

As a result of these realities, the term *high achiever* is frequently used as a polite euphemism for referring to students with high general cognitive ability. This begs an interesting conceptual question: Can students with average or below-average general cognitive ability be high achievers?

The position of this chapter is that the answer is yes, but the construct of academic achievement must be considerably broadened in order to accommodate this position. Some students' academic efforts can be captured more accurately in nontest indicators. Other students display positive attitudinal and behavioral traits that may not necessarily be reflected in high test scores, but nevertheless impress teachers as crucial ingredients for later life success. For example, the degree of improvement over time is one important (but overlooked) variable that captures the essence of what most educators look for in their students (see also Stronge & Grant, 2009). A bright student may put forth minimal effort in his or her studies and still manage to perform above C level in classes. In contrast, a slower student who began the semester with failing grades may work extremely hard to bring his or her final course grade up to a C—and be *overjoyed* at this progress. Which of these two students is the high achiever? Obviously, the brighter student receives higher course grades, yet the slower student has put in a greater degree of personal effort in his or her studies. In order to enrich the meaning of "high achiever," one must therefore consider outcome variables that can account for these changes over time.

The variety of outcome indicators that can be considered under the moniker of "academic achievement" are listed in Sidebar 5.6.

Sidebar 5.6   Academic Achievement Outcome Variables

Scores on Standardized Achievement Tests

- Comparing school or grade-level mean scores at Time 1 against school or grade-level mean scores at Time 2
- Comparing school or grade-level mean scores against mean scores of demographically similar schools
- Comparing school or grade-level mean scores against state/national averages

Scores and Rate of Improvement on Informal Classroom Achievement Measures

- Daily/weekly curriculum-based assessments/measurements
- Daily/weekly homework assignments
- Rates of homework completion
- End-of-unit tests/quizzes
- Daily seatwork assignments/worksheets
- Group oral/written projects

Behavioral Correlates

- Enrollment in academically rigorous required/elective classes (e.g., Advanced Placement or College Prep classes)
- School attendance/dropout rates
- High school completion rates

Other Academic Indicators

- End-of-semester/year course grades
- Cumulative grade point average
- Academic honors/awards
- Quality of college to which one has been accepted

Opportunity to Learn

If relatively little or no class time is spent on productive instruction and practice on necessary academic skills, learning does not (nor cannot) occur. In many inner-city schools, this is a significant challenge. Jensen (1993) effectively articulates this point as follows:

[A]pplications of cognitive research are rendered impossible where educational aims are flagrantly obstructed, for example, by the growing social pathology that threatens many inner-city schools—behavior problems, drugs, teen pregnancy, parental indifference, truancy, school dropout, vandalism, gang intimidation, violence, and crime. Such misfortunes spell an altogether different order of school problems from those that stem directly from the inherent difficulty of the material to be learned or the considerable differences in aptitude reflected by psychometric tests. . . . In certain schools discipline is undoubtedly the first order of business. No intrinsic educational improvement can possibly take place without it . . . all seem to agree . . . that discipline is the sine qua non for pupils' standing a chance to benefit from their time in the classroom. (pp. 119–120)

This principle applies not only to conditions that occur within the classroom, but to conditions that occur outside of the classroom as well. If parents do not spend time assisting their children with homework, or at least make intentional efforts to provide the quiet and orderly conditions at home that are conducive for focusing on schoolwork, significant learning does not occur.

Ability to Understand Instruction

Much has already been written in this chapter that highlights the importance of this variable. When a teacher introduces a new lesson, she or he must present a sequence of new concepts at a pace that would allow most students to consolidate new material. As students learn, they form mental structures that permit them to retrieve, generalize, and transfer information to new learning situations. When instructional material is presented to slower-learning students at a pace or complexity that is overwhelming, students cannot properly organize learning structures that would facilitate new learning.

Quality of Instructional Events

Many excellent texts have been published for school psychologists, teachers, and resource specialists that describe the most effective instructional principles for helping vulnerable learners (including those with learning disabilities) to succeed in effectively learning school tasks. Many of these resources are listed in the Additional Resources at the end of this chapter.

Space limitations do not permit a thorough discussion of all instructional principles revealed by high-quality research to help vulnerable learners. The most well known of these principles are summarized in Sidebar 5.7.

🖎 Sidebar 5.7   Sixteen Elements of Effective Instruction

1. Focus instruction on critical content
2. Sequence skills logically
3. Break down complex skills and strategies into smaller instructional units
4. Design organized and focused lessons
5. Begin lessons with a clear statement of the goals and your expectations
6. Review prior skills and knowledge before beginning instruction
7. Provide step-by-step demonstrations
8. Use clear and concise language
9. Provide an adequate range of examples and nonexamples
10. Provide guided and supported practice
11. Require frequent responses
12. Monitor student performance closely
13. Provide immediate affirmative and corrective feedback
14. Deliver the lesson at a brisk pace
15. Help students organize knowledge
16. Provide distributed and cumulative practice

(from Archer & Hughes, 2011, pp. 2–3)

It needs to be emphasized, however, that such principles are both universal and timeless. That is to say, these principles apply to all learners, of any age, regardless of country of origin, race, ethnicity, social class, or language. Following these principles underlies and facilitates effective learning across any curriculum, regardless of its ideological bent. In addition, these principles stand the test of time. Although technological innovations (e.g., audiovisual equipment, the Internet, distance learning) may help instruction to be more efficiently delivered, the principles that underlie effective teaching are the same regardless of whether one is using an abacus in the fifth century BC or a modern high-speed computer.

These principles are particularly important to follow in teaching vulnerable (including slow) learners, and can be briefly consolidated as follows.

Effective Instruction for Vulnerable Learners Is Explicit

Even when instruction is less than perfect, brighter students are able to spontaneously make accurate inferences and generalizations in academic content even when such skills have not been explicitly taught (e.g., correctly pronouncing the new word *snap* although only being previously exposed to *nap* and *snow*). In contrast, slow learners have greater difficulty making spontaneous inferences and generalizations in novel tasks (see Sidebar 5.5), and therefore generalization and inferencing skills need to be taught more intentionally and explicitly. According to Archer and Hughes (2011), explicit instruction is

> characterized by a series of supports or scaffolds, whereby students are guided through the learning process with clear statements about the purpose and rationale for learning the new skills, clear explanations and demonstrations of the instructional target, and supported practice with feedback until independent mastery has been achieved. (p. 1)

These authors then quote Rosenshine (1987), who defined explicit instruction as "a systematic method of teaching with emphasis on proceeding in small steps, checking for student understanding, and achieving active and successful participation by all students" (p. 34).

Not only academics, but also the proper *behaviors* that support academic excellence, are explicitly taught in effective schools for vulnerable (particularly minority) learners. In the first day of school for new fifth-grade students at the Amistad Middle School Academy, for example, students are required to sign contracts agreeing that they will show up at school on time (i.e., 7:30 A.M. each weekday), complete their homework and reading every night, wear their school uniform every day, display maximum effort on school tasks, raise their hand when asking for help, and make every effort to live up to the school's values of Respect, Enthusiasm, Achievement, Citizenship, and Hard Work (REACH; Whitman, 2008). As described by Whitman (2008), new Amistad students are required to learn a plethora of guidelines, rules, regulations, and procedures for how to record homework assignments, organize subject area binders, participate in class discussions, and pay attention to the instructor. For example, Amistad's teachers can be seen frequently telling students to "correct their SLANT," which is an acronym that stands for Sit up. Listen. Ask and answer questions. Nod your head so people know you are listening and understanding. Track the speaker by keeping your eyes on whoever is talking (Whitman, 2008).

Effective Instruction for Vulnerable Learners Is Highly Structured and Includes Frequent Repetition

One model of instructional design stands head and shoulders above all other methods for its demonstrated effectiveness with low-income, minority populations that have higher concentrations of slower learners in educational settings (see Sidebar 5.8). Direct Instruction (DI) refers to a set of effective instructional design principles and teaching behaviors that are integrated into a set of published instructional programs, although effective instructional design principles can certainly be manifested in other published materials that are not labeled as DI (e.g., see Saxon Math, Scholastic Guided Reading, Waterford Early Reading, and Core Knowledge instructional programs/materials).

🔖 Sidebar 5.8   Direct Instruction

Direct Instruction (DI) is the moniker given to a general set of "instructional design principles and teaching behaviors incorporated into a set of published instructional programs" (Marchand-Martella, Slocum, & Martella, 2004, p. 16). DI is an approach to teaching that emphasizes the use of small-group, face-to-face instruction by teachers and aides using carefully scripted lessons in which cognitive skills are broken down into smaller units, sequenced carefully and deliberately, and taught explicitly (Carnine, Silbert, Kame'enui, & Tarver, 2009).

During the 1960s, when the Civil Rights Act of 1964 was passed, the basic principles that underlie Direct Instruction were developed by Dr. Siegfried Engelmann at the University of Illinois Institute for Research on Exceptional Children. According to Dr. Engelmann, DI methods are built on the assumptive foundation that all children would learn if they were taught effectively. The unspoken implication of this principle is that if children are not learning, then teachers are not teaching them in appropriate ways. This deceptively simple principle underlies the development of DI materials and is also the source of political conflicts between DI critics and supporters that have ensued over the succeeding decades of its implementation. Dr. Engelmann developed DI teaching methods meticulously through careful experimentation, application to real-life classrooms, and extensive retooling and refinement of the smallest details of the program. DI methods have been developed with all kinds of students who manifest the full range of normal development and specific disabilities (e.g., autism, brain injuries). However, the DI program is most well known by its proven success with racial/ethnic minority children characterized as "educationally disadvantaged." Nowhere else has this been more effectively demonstrated than in the largest educational experiment ever attempted—Project Follow Through.

Project Follow Through was originally conceived as a comprehensive, large-scale service program for economically disadvantaged children that extends Head Start programs (for preschoolers) to the early primary grades. Because funds needed for this program were not appropriated by the government, the U.S. Office of Education (now the U.S. Department of Education) modified Project Follow Through as an evaluation/research program (Marchand-Martella et al., 2004). Specifically, Project Follow Through's primary objective was to compare the effectiveness of different educational approaches used in Head Start curricula. By all estimates, Project Follow Through cost close to $1 billion and involved nearly 100,000 children from approximately 170 communities throughout the United States.

(continued)

Nine curricula (including DI) were compared, which included *Parent Education* (which emphasized motivating and training parents to serve as teaching aides in the classroom), *Behavior Analysis* (which emphasized the use of a token economy for teaching academic skills), the *Tuscon Early Educational Model* (which emphasized broad intellectual skills and positive attitudes toward school), the *Bank Street Curriculum* (which emphasized the development of a positive self-image, creativity, and coping skills), *Responsive Education* (which emphasized the development of problem-solving skills, sensory discrimination, and self confidence), the *Language Development Approach* (which emphasized language development in Spanish-speaking children), the *High Scope Cognitive Curriculum* (which emphasized the development of reasoning abilities based on Piagetian theory), and *Open Education* (which emphasized self-respect, imagination, and openness to change).

Students exposed to each of these curricula (including DI) were compared to the performance of children in a control group in the same communities with similar economic and social circumstances. The DI model was the only model to demonstrate the most significant positive outcomes on basic skills measures, cognitive/conceptual measures, and affective measures. Seven of the non-DI programs actually showed *worse outcomes* compared to the control group (ABT Associates, 1977; Haney, 1977; Marchand-Martella et al., 2004). Readers may consult Adams and Engelmann (1996) for more recent evaluations of DI.

In order to maximize instruction for vulnerable learners, DI instructional materials are organized around the following principles:

1. Children are encouraged to respond to the teacher as a group (i.e., choral responding). When this occurs, teachers receive immediate feedback at a far faster rate than from questioning individual students sequentially.

2. Teaching materials are scripted so that teachers provide short, concise explanations rather than lengthy explanations. Direct Instruction researchers note that this helps teachers to both learn the lessons faster and deliver instruction with high quality and fidelity.

3. Children are required to produce a very high rate of responses per minute (sometimes up to 20 responses per minute).

4. Lessons are streamlined to include only the basic information needed to learn the instructional objective, and includes no fluff material that is not necessary for learning the immediate instructional objective.

These principles, considered in tandem, are designed to drastically reduce the potential for miscommunication/misinterpretation errors.

In the DI approach, children are assessed to determine where they need to begin in an instructional sequence. From this point on, instruction is parceled in small steps and organized progressively in highly scripted and sequenced lessons to resemble an "instructional staircase." That is, vulnerable learners can only learn so much new information at one time. This new information needs to be explicitly taught, with copious amounts of repetition and opportunities for practice. Once this material is mastered, then they are ready for the next step in learning. This process is repeated at each level of the instructional staircase until instructional goals are met.

For example, if a child cannot follow directions that instruct him or her to "touch the top of their paper," then a beginning lesson needs to focus on the skill needed to accurately discriminate "top of the paper" versus "not top of the paper." If the child was unable to say the sentence "I touched the top of my paper," then the sentence is explicitly taught. In a nutshell, all of the information and skills needed for subsequent lessons are explicitly taught in current lessons (see Foreword by S. Engelmann, in Marchand-Martella et al., 2004). In addition to curriculum lesson development in the areas of reading, English-language learning, mathematics, spelling, and handwriting, DI researchers have developed behavior management techniques as well as detailed procedures for helping teachers monitor and collect learning data.

For further information on Direct Instruction professional groups, training opportunities, and materials, readers may consult the Association for Direct Instruction (ADI; see links below), a nonprofit organization dedicated to promoting and supporting the use of Direct Instruction programs. That support includes conferences, publications, online networking and assistance, and two semiannual publications entitled *Direct Instruction News* and *The Journal of Direct Instruction*. Local ADI member chapters are forming nationwide and in Canada to offer local support, workshops, discussion groups, and newsletters.

Links Related to Direct Instruction

    Association for Direct Instruction (www.adihome.org)

    Dr. Ziegfried Englemann Homepage (http://www.zigsite.com)

    Educational Resources, Inc. (www.erigroup.us)

    J/P Associates (School Improvement Specialists) (www.jponline.com)

    McGraw-Hill Education Direct Instruction Programs (https://www.mheonline
        .com/discipline/tags/1/3)

    National Institute for Direct Instruction (www.nifdi.org)

DI programs have been tried, and shown to be successful, in managing learning of vulnerable students in some of the most impoverished and "at-risk" communities in America (e.g., see Engelmann, 2007). The cornerstone of the DI method begins with a thorough analysis of academic content in a variety of areas (including, but not limited to, reading, spelling, writing, mathematics, history, and science) and identifying key concepts, rules, strategies, and "big ideas" that are commonly taught in these areas. This content is then carefully broken down into a large number of smaller (and very specific) instructional objectives. These objectives are very carefully sequenced, such that mastery of earlier objectives is a necessary precursor for beginning a subsequent objective.

Each DI lesson is highly structured, such that the possibility of unintentional teaching errors and/or student learning errors is reduced. Every verbalization and activity is highly scripted, which provides teachers with a clear, field-tested template for how each lesson is to be delivered. Most lessons, where appropriate, typically follow an "I do/We do/You do" format, where the teacher first models the skill (I do), then both the teacher and students perform the skill together (We do), and finally the students perform the skill independently (You do). Even the nature of the interaction between the teacher and students is highly structured in DI lessons. DI maximizes student engagement by giving students frequent opportunities to respond to (scripted) teacher questions, since more interaction and feedback results in better learning.

In order to increase efficiency of learning, students engage in short choral responding to teacher questions (i.e., the entire class responds in unison), which gives all students opportunities to practice responding to every question posed by the teacher. In order to enable all students to initiate group answers at the same time, teachers use pauses (to give students an opportunity to think) and some kind of auditory/visual signal (e.g., a snap, clap, tapping on nearby furniture) in order to enable all students to initiate their answers at exactly the same time. Each lesson includes effective error-correction procedures that may or may not be used depending on the progress observed in each learning situation. Steps within lessons are repeated as many times as is necessary to guide all students to mastery of the task. Slow-learning students, in particular, require frequent repetition of newly learned concepts (compared to average/above-average ability students) in order to more fully absorb the material. Excerpts from sample DI lessons are provided in Sidebar 5.9.

Sidebar 5.9   Excerpts From Sample Direct Instruction Lessons

Phonetic Word Decoding Lesson

a. (Teacher says:) "My turn to say a word slowly. First, I'll say (pause) 'sss'.
   Then I'll say (pause) 'at'. Listen again. First I'll say (pause) 'sss'. Then I'll say

(pause) 'at'. Here I go. (Teacher holds up one finger, then says:) 'sss'. (Teacher holds up second finger, then says:) 'at'."

b. (Teacher says:) "Do it with me. (Teacher holds up one finger.) First you'll say (pause) 'sss'. (Teacher holds up second finger.) Then you'll say (pause) 'at'. Get ready." (Teacher says 'sssat' with the children as the teacher holds up a finger for each part.)

c. (Teacher says:) "Again. (Teacher holds up one finger.) First you'll say (pause) 'sss'. (Teacher holds up second finger.) Then you'll say (pause) 'at'. Get ready." (Teacher says 'sssat' with the children as the teacher holds up a finger for each part.)

d. Teacher repeats step c until children's responses are firm.

e. (Teacher says:) "All by yourself. (Teacher holds up one finger.) First you'll say (pause) 'sss'. (Teacher holds up second finger.) Then you'll say (pause) 'at'. Get ready." (Teacher holds up one finger, then second finger as the children say 'sssat'.)

f. (Teacher says:) "Again." Teacher repeats step e until children's responses are firm.

*Vocabulary Lesson**

a. (Teacher says:) "Look at word number three on the board. (Signal.) The word is 'honest'."

b. (Teacher says:) "When you tell the truth about something, you are being honest. Here's another way of saying 'She told the truth about her situation: She was honest about her situation'."

c. (Teacher says:) "Your turn. What's another way of saying 'She told the truth about her situation'? (Signal.) **She was honest about her situation.**"

d. Teacher repeats steps b and c until children's responses are firm.

*Spelling Patterns Lesson**

a. (Teacher says:) "Get ready to spell short words that end in the /ll/ sound."

b. (Teacher says:) "Mall. What word"? (Signal.) **Mall.**

c. (Teacher says:) "Spell 'mall'. Get ready." (Signal.) **M-a-l-l.**

d. (Teacher says:) "Fill. What word"? (Signal.) **F-i-l-l.**

e. (Teacher repeats steps c and d for 'ball' and 'still'.)

f. (Teacher says:) "Get ready to write those words on Part A of your worksheet."

g. (Teacher says:) "Word 1 is 'fill'. What word"? (Signal.) **Fill.** (Teacher says:) "Write it."

(continued)

h. (Teacher repeats step g for 'mall', 'still', and 'ball'.)

i. (Teacher says:) "Check the words as we spell them together. Put an X by any word that is spelled wrong and write it correctly."

j. (Teacher says:) "Spell 'fill'. Get ready. (Signal.) *F-i-l-l*. (The teacher writes the word on the board as the students spell it.)

k. (The teacher repeats step j for 'mall', 'still', and 'ball'.)

*Elementary Pre-Algebra Lesson**

a. Teacher writes $3 + \square = 7$ on the board.

b. (Teacher says:) "This is a tough problem. I'll touch and you read." (Pause) "Get ready." (Teacher touches each symbol as the children read:) *3 plus how many equals 7?*

c. (Teacher says:) "There's a box in this problem, so what do we have to do?" (Signal) *Start counting on the other side.*

d. (Teacher says:) "Who can find the box for me?" (Call on a child to go to the board and touch.)

e. (Teacher points to $\square$, then says:) "Everybody, why can't we start counting on the side with a box?" (Signal.) *The box doesn't tell you what number goes inside of it.* "Right. We don't know the number that goes inside the box. That's why we have to start counting on the other side."

f. (Teacher points to $\square$, and says:) "Everybody, I want to draw a ring around the side we start counting on. Read everything on the side we start counting on. Get ready." (Signal.) *7*

g. (Teacher says:) "We start counting on the side with seven, so I'll draw a ring around that side." (Teacher draws ring around the 7 with the chalk.)
$3 + \square = \textcircled{7}$

h. (Teacher points to 7, and says:) "What number do we end up with on this side?" (Signal.) *7*. "Yes, seven."

i. (Teacher points to 3, and says:) "Everybody, do we end up with seven in the first group? (Signal.) *No*. "So we'll have to count until we end up with seven."

j. (Teacher says:) "How many are in the first group"? (Signal.) *3*. "Get it going." (Teacher raises his/her hand. When the response "three" is firm, drop your hand. The teacher draws check—or slash—marks under the ? as children count) *. . . 4,5,6,7, Stop*. ([Correction Procedure] If the children do not indicate correctly when to stop counting, the teacher continues to draw lines, then says:) "You didn't tell me when to stop. What number must we end up with on the side with three plus how many?" (Signal.) *7*. (Teacher repeats steps i and j.)

k. (When students grasp that four check—or slash—marks go under the $\square$, then say:) "Everybody, the lines under a box always tell me what number

goes in that box. Get ready to tell me what number goes in the box."
(Teacher pauses for two seconds.) "What number?" (Signal.) **4**. (Teacher
writes the number 4 in □ .)

$$3 + \underline{\square} = 7$$

1. (Teacher says:) "Everybody, three plus how many equals seven? (Signal.) **4**.
"Say the statement." (Signal.) *3 plus 4 equals 7*. (Teacher repeats step 1
until the response from the class is firm.)

*Words and phrases in bold italics represent unison responses expected from the class.

(Adapted from Marchand-Martella et al., 2004)

Perseverance

Instilling a thirst for learning within students is perhaps the most formidable obstacle
facing today's educators (Weissberg, 2010, p. 53). The best instruction in the world is of
little to no consequence if learners harbor negative attitudes toward learning or are not
willing to engage in the basic learning behaviors necessary to effectively absorb classroom
material. In the Carroll model, this variable is called *perseverance*, and refers to the time
that students are willing to spend learning. A more commonly understood name for this
variable is *motivation*. Motivation is a necessary prerequisite that all students must possess
in order to put forth the effort needed to master complex and challenging academic
subjects in which they may not necessarily have a natural interest (Weissberg, 2010).
According to Weissberg (2010):

> Successful [motivational] strategies undoubtedly must be fine-tuned according to
> age, culture, subject matter, teacher and school characteristics, family life, and
> just about every other factor instigating achievement. What suffices with . . .
> students from backgrounds drilled to obey authority would probably fail with
> unruly confrontational youngsters. (p. 54)

As a variable that contributes to high academic achievement, the origins of motivation can be attributed to two broad sources, generally referred to as *extrinsic* versus
intrinsic motivation. Extrinsic motivation can be defined as motivational factors that
originate from outside of an individual that impel desired behavior, which may or may
not be intentionally imposed by other persons. Within the broad category of extrinsic
motivators that are imposed by the educational system, two subcategories are euphemistically referred to as "carrots" versus "sticks." Carrots are positive motivators such as

awards, good grades, activities, social praise/recognition, scholarships, or other material incentives. Sticks are aversive motivators such as the threat of punishment (e.g., school detentions), bad grades, scorn from peers, failure to be accepted into a good college, or social humiliation.

Intrinsic motivation can be defined as motivation that originates from inside an individual (e.g., taking pleasure in an activity for its own sake) rather than being imposed from the outside. The factors that work together to develop intrinsic motivation in learners are idiosyncratic, nuanced, and complex.

Dismal school dropout, high school graduation, and college attendance rates of minority students from low-income inner-city schools is well known (e.g., Chapman, Laird, Ifill, & Kewal-Ramani, 2011). Charter college preparatory schools for minority inner-city students attack this problem head on, and with a vengeance. As described in Whitman (2008), students attending Amistad Middle School Academy are exposed to a palpable college-going culture from the first moment they step foot in the school. The school is labeled as a college preparatory institution, hence the curriculum is unabashedly college-prep. However, this is just the tip of the iceberg in the college-saturated culture at Amistad. As examples, each class at Amistad is named after a college, and all students are made aware of the exact year in which they are expected to graduate from a four-year college. Banners from a wide variety of colleges and universities adorn the hallways, and the school's eighth graders visit nearby colleges for practice interviews in the college admissions offices. Whitman (2008) writes:

> After a couple of years at Amistad, the vast majority of students buy into the school's system of high expectations, support, and accountability. Slowly . . . they even become excited and proud of doing well academically. . . . [E]xcelling is cool, instead of a lonely pastime for nerdy eggheads. . . . [T]he strong academic commitment of both students and teachers is evident to visitors as soon as they enter the school. . . . One consultant who works for an education venture capital firm was so moved by a recent visit to Amistad that she [retreated] to the bathroom at the end of the day—to weep in private. (p. 107)

Ability: Time Needed for Learning

Scores on rigorously developed psychometric tests are the most efficient and familiar means by which researchers and educators measure individual differences in cognitive ability. In the Carroll model, ability is reconceptualized as the time needed to learn specified content to a particular level of mastery under optimal instructional and motivational conditions. In other words, given the same material to be learned, brighter pupils will learn such material in shorter periods of time (all other components in the model being equal) compared to pupils who are considerably lower in cognitive ability. Conversely, cognitively slower pupils require more time to learn the same material compared to brighter pupils.

Innovative schools that must educate low-income minority students find that creative ways to increase instructional time is one among many ingredients for raising achievement levels (both psychometrically and attitudinally) in students. Some of these methods are briefly described as follows.

Intervention via Cutting Back on Nonessentials

As reported in Whitman (2008), the American Indian Public Charter School requires students to attend three additional weeks of summer school, which lengthens the school year from 180 days to 200 days. The Oakland Charter Academy (for middle-school students) increases instructional time by cutting the lunch period to only 20 minutes per day and reducing course electives. The predominantly Hispanic Cristo Rey Jesuit High School requires an academically rigorous curriculum that requires students to take four years of English, Spanish, Religion, and a work study program, as well as three years of Math, Science, and Social Studies. This curriculum drastically reduces the amount of nonacademic electives that students take, which forces students to focus on the core subjects necessary for competitive colleges (Whitman, 2008).

Intervention via Motivation for Consistent Attendance

Academically vulnerable students cannot benefit from instruction if they are not present for class. Teachers often complain that students' spotty attendance creates an impediment to academic learning, as teachers must constantly retrace instructional steps for students who miss class (Whitman, 2008). The pervasive academics-first culture of the American Indian Public Charter School rewards students for consistent attendance (see also Sidebar 7.4), to the point where motivation for consistent school attendance becomes intrinsic. As an example, one student was pondering whether to take a planned trip with her parents to Mexico, which would have broken her class's astounding record of 125 consecutive days in which every student in the class maintained perfect attendance with no absences. As a result of the girl's sense of responsibility to her class, she elected not to take the trip. In recognition of this action, the school principal personally paid for the student to change the date of her plane ticket so she would not miss school. The class went on to record 180 consecutive days of perfect attendance, breaking school records in the process. As recognition for this sacrifice, the principal arranged to have 10 billboards placed around the city with a photo featuring the class (as reported in Whitman, 2008).

Intervention via Consistent Teacher/Peer Recognition for Academic Achievement

Public and charter schools, faced with the task of instilling an academic achievement ethos in minority children for whom such an ethos has no significant role models, find that an academic achievement orientation must be the single dominant gene in the DNA of the school environment.

Whitman (2008) describes a weekly activity called "The Morning Circle" at Amistad Academy middle school, a college preparatory charter school in New Haven, Connecticut. The ritual begins with all students in the entire school (over 250) standing in a circle in the school gymnasium:

> Led by their teachers and school director . . . the students then start to chant, sometimes with hand gestures or in a call-and-response format reminiscent of boot camp training. . . . [Next] the school-wide meeting proceeds to recognize students who have distinguished themselves academically or shown outstanding character. Teachers step forward to acknowledge students, and the entire school cheers them with a series of chants, stomps, and claps. One student gets two hand claps, two foot stomps, and a round of hands raised to the roof. Another student gets a "home run"—the students collectively pretend to take a swing with a bat and click their tongues to simulate the noise of the bat hitting a home run. A third student gets the "roller coaster" recognition as the students go "woo-woo," simulating the wave of arms held aloft during an up-and-down roller coaster ride. (Whitman, 2008, p. 97)

Intervention via Institutionalized Tutoring Opportunities

As reported by Whitman (2008), most of the new seventh graders at the SEED school (see Glossary) have math and reading skills commensurate with average fifth graders. In addition to small classes that provide focused individual attention, students receive assistance on a daily basis through after school individual tutoring.

Students at the American Indian Public Charter School who do not keep up with their academics are required to log in two to four additional hours per week in tutoring time, some of which can be completed after school but also can be completed during students' Physical Education classes (Whitman, 2008).

Intervention via Rejection of Social Promotion

According to Whitman (2008), SEED schools reject the practice of social promotion, where students are routinely promoted to the next higher grade despite not having mastered necessary academic skills. At the crucial ninth grade gate, SEED students are required to demonstrate proficiency in each component strand within English and Math by earning at least a C grade in each strand. If a student is not proficient in even one strand within an academic domain area, they are required to repeat eighth grade unless the necessary work can be made up in the summer before ninth grade. Whitman (2008) reports that approximately 30 percent of SEED students fail to advance to ninth grade during their first attempt at passing the eighth-grade curriculum, and many drop out of school altogether rather than repeat a grade. Although this uncompromising policy results in high attrition rates before students reach ninth grade, SEED founders feel that the climate of academic focus and seriousness at this juncture in students' academic careers is absolutely necessary in order for students to be competitive for college admissions.

Intervention via Extended School Days/Years

Educators with extensive experience teaching low-performing inner-city minority students have discovered the principle of increasing time for learning as a means for improving achievement outcomes. Whitman (2008) studied several inner-city charter schools that are noted for their unusually positive academic and behavioral outcomes with black, Hispanic, and Native American students. A common theme of these schools is the requirement of an extended day and/or school year, periodic classes held on Saturdays, and mandatory summer school attendance.

For example, daily school hours for the Achievement First college-preparatory charter schools (see http://www.achievementfirst.org/schools/network-overview) begin at 7:30 A.M. and end at 4:00 P.M., which exceeds traditional public school hours. Whitman (2008) estimates that students in the KIPP (Knowledge is Power Program, see Glossary) schools spend approximately 300 minutes per day engaged in core academic instruction, compared to students in typical urban schools who spend approximately 185 minutes per day engaged in core academic instruction. According to the Achievement First website, the extra hours that high-achieving charter schools spend on instruction—in addition to the availability of tutoring both *before and after* school hours and a mandatory three-week Summer Academy—amounts to approximately one extra year of instruction (when compared to traditional public schools).

CONCLUSION

The implications of the material in this chapter are both conceptual and practical in nature. When the issue is general cognitive ability and its relationship to educational performance, the school psychologist—perhaps more than any other applied professional—finds him- or herself torn between what the best empirical literature clearly says versus feel-good platitudes held by the lay public. The fundamental empirical reality of the psychological literature is that there are individual differences in children's general intellectual abilities, and schools must account for these differences in how they deliver instruction. Murray (2008) states the matter bluntly:

> The educational system is living a lie. The lie is that every child can be anything he or she wants to be. No one really believes it, but we approach education's problems as if we did. We are phobic about saying out loud that children differ in their ability to learn the things that schools teach. Not only do we hate to say it, we get angry with people who do. . . . The silence about differences in intellectual ability on educational topics that scream for their discussion is astonishing. . . . The nine-year-old who has trouble sounding out simple words and his classmate who is reading A Tale of Two Cities for fun sit in the same classroom day after miserable day, the one so frustrated by tasks he cannot do and the other so bored that both are near tears. (pp. 11–12)

The properly trained school psychologist knows that children and youth display a range of general cognitive ability levels, and he or she is vigilant for instances in which schools inadvertently undermine the effectiveness of students' education by ignoring this basic truth.

This chapter rejects the notion that minority children—simply by virtue of their racial/ethnic status—display an exotic form of intellectual giftedness that is routinely overlooked by schools or misdiagnosed by supposedly culturally biased cognitive ability tests (see Sidebar 5.10). Despite the popularity of these claims in multiculturalism ideology, no solid empirical evidence supports such notions.

◔ Sidebar 5.10   Examples From the Life Trajectory of Gifted Minorities

Peruse contemporary writing on multicultural issues in education, and one sees no lack of excuses purporting to explain why the intellectual talents of gifted minority (particularly black) students supposedly fail to be properly identified in schools. Writers are quick to blame culturally biased tests (Ford, 2008; Helms, 1992, 1997), the cultural mismatch between the home and the school (Tyler et al., 2008), and "Eurocentric" teachers' failure to understand minority students' unique cultural learning/behavioral styles (Ford & Grantham, 2003; Ford, Grantham, & Milner, 2004; Ford, Grantham, & Whiting, 2008; Hale-Benson, 1986) as responsible for low identification rates.

Readers of a certain age can scarcely imagine what life was like in U.S. schools before school psychology began as a profession, before so-called socially enlightened thinking on multiculturalism in schools became fashionable, and before state-sanctioned racial segregation and discrimination were permanently banished from civic life. Given these so-called "backward" and "unenlightened" times, how in the world could the talents of intellectually gifted minority students be appropriately recognized in schools?

The Answer: *The same as would be the case with intellectually gifted students of any race/ethnicity.*

What is the justification for this politically incorrect conclusion? Simply examine the life trajectories, in their own words, of prominent contemporary intellectuals—who happen to be black. The life stories of Dr. Ben Carson and Dr. Thomas Sowell provide two illustrative examples.

In the summer of 1930, Thomas Sowell was born in poverty in the Jim Crow South during the Great Depression. The house in which he grew up in North Carolina had no electricity, central heating, or even hot running water. Most of the streets in black neighborhoods were unpaved. His biological father had died shortly before Thomas's birth. His biological mother, who was a housemaid, was unable to raise him, so instead he was raised by his great-aunt and her two daughters. None of his immediate family had ever successfully completed public education past the seventh grade.

Ben Carson was born in 1951 in Detroit, Michigan, to a mother who had dropped out of school in the third grade. When Ben was only eight, his parents divorced, leaving Mrs. Carson with the responsibility of taking on up to three jobs to raise Ben and his older brother. Sometimes life became so rough for Mrs. Carson that she would occasionally check herself into a mental hospital to be treated for depression and emotional stress.

In his memoirs, Thomas Sowell recalls how he already learned at home how to read and count before attending school for the first time. Although he was too young to understand its significance, he reports being administratively promoted to the third grade shortly after starting second grade, and shortly thereafter he was always at or near the top of his classes academically.

In the public schools of New York during the 1930s and 1940s, group IQ tests were regularly given to students to help determine the appropriate academic tracks in which students were to be placed. Students who obtained IQ scores above 120 were assigned to special "rapid advancement" classes, and Thomas Sowell reports being assigned to such a class in the seventh grade. In addition, students at the end of junior high school regularly took entrance examinations to determine if they

(*continued*)

would be eligible to attend one of a handful of elite high schools in the city. On the basis of these test scores, Thomas was selected to attend Stuyvesant High School in 1945.

As a young child, Ben Carson remembers doing well in school up until the fifth grade, when the family moved from Boston to Detroit. Due to this abrupt change, Ben discovered that he was far behind the rest of his class. This was immediately noticed by his classmates, earning him the moniker of being the "dumbest kid in the fifth grade." Ben's mother, fed up with his poor grades, required Ben and his brother to watch only three television shows of their choosing each week, and to fill up their extra time by reading books from the local library and writing two book reports for her every week about what was read. Soon, Ben was at or near the top of his classes academically. Ben joined his high school's Reserve Officer's Training Corps (ROTC) in the tenth grade, and he quickly earned promotions through the ranks up to master sergeant. After posting the highest score in the city on the ROTC exam, Ben was promoted to the rank of lieutenant colonel by the end of his junior year in high school. By the time Ben graduated high school, he was the third highest student academically in his senior class. This ranking, in addition to high scores on the Scholastic Aptitude Test (SAT), resulted in his being accepted into Yale University for pre-med studies.

Ben did notice something remarkable about his cognitive strengths while he was in medical school at the University of Michigan. He noticed that he had an unusually strong facility for being able to see objects and think about them in three dimensions—or what psychologists would call a strong spatial visualization ability (i.e., the ability to retain, rotate, and understand the distance and positional relationships among objects and visual images in one's head). While he was a medical student, Ben carefully observed his professors and discovered a novel method for finding a hole at the base of a patient's skull without using invasive probes. This ability, coupled with his excellent eye-hand coordination, led Ben to pursue brain neurosurgery as a medical specialty.

Tom Sowell's life trajectory between high school and college was not as smooth. Due to debilitating family conflicts at home, Thomas Sowell left home and dropped out of high school at 16, subsisting on odd jobs and taking night classes to obtain his high school diploma before enlisting in the Marine Corps in 1951 during the Korean War.

Thomas Sowell's high scores on the College Board exams and recommendations by two professors helped him gain admission to Harvard University, where he graduated magna cum laude in 1958 with a Bachelor of Arts degree in economics. He received a Master of Arts from Columbia University the following year, and published his first article in the *American Economic Review* in 1960 while he was still a student at Columbia. He was accepted into the PhD program in economics at the University of Chicago, and he studied under George Stigler, who later received a Nobel Prize in Economics. Sowell received his PhD in Economics from the University of Chicago in 1968.

Thomas Sowell has taught Economics at Howard University, Rutgers University, Cornell University, Brandeis University, Amherst College, and UCLA. Since 1980, he has been a Senior Fellow in the Hoover Institution at Stanford University, where he holds a fellowship named after Rose and Milton Friedman, his mentor at the University of Chicago and a world-famous economist in his own right. He is the author of more than 30 books to date on a wide range of subjects, including the history of ethnic groups in America, the philosophical foundations of political movements, social policies on race in the United States and worldwide, the nature of education and decision making, classical and Marxist economics, the role of intellectuals in society, and the problems of late-talking children (see www.tsowell.com).

Over the course of his career, Dr. Sowell has received numerous awards, which have included the Francis Boyer Award, presented by the American Enterprise Institute, the Sydney Hook Award from the National Association of Scholars, the National Humanities Medal for prolific scholarship melding history, economics, and political science, and the Bradley Prize for intellectual achievement. For those national figures who have reviewed his books and followed his career, he has been called "the most important and original thinker of the late 20th century," "America's leading philosopher," and a "national resource . . . [who] fulfills the true calling of the intellectual."

After graduating from medical school, Ben Carson became the youngest Director of Pediatric Neurosurgery at Johns Hopkins Hospital (in Baltimore, MD) at age 33. He is known worldwide for conducting the first intrauterine procedure to relieve pressure on the brain of a hydrocephalic fetal twin, and for performing a successful hemispherectomy, in which a young girl suffering from uncontrollable seizures had one half of her brain removed. In 1987, Carson made medical history by being the first surgeon in the world to successfully separate Siamese twins who were conjoined at the back of the head. Operations to separate twins joined in this way had always failed, resulting in the death of one or both of the infants. Carson led a 70-member surgical team that worked for 22 hours on this history-making procedure. At the end, the twins were successfully separated and can now survive independently (see http://conversations.psu.edu/episodes/ben_carson).

Ben Carson has received numerous honors and many awards over the years, including 61 honorary doctorate degrees. He was also a member of the American Academy of Achievement, the Horatio Alger Association of Distinguished

(*continued*)

Americans, the Alpha Omega Alpha Honor Medical Society, the Yale Corporation (the governing body of Yale University), and many other prestigious organizations. On June 19, 2008, Dr. Carson received the Presidential Medal of Freedom from President George W. Bush.

On February 7, 2009, a television movie titled *Gifted Hands: The Ben Carson Story* was aired, starring Academy Award winner Cuba Gooding Jr. in the lead role.

These two remarkable life stories are notable for three things: First, neither person was born with a "silver spoon" in his mouth, and in fact their difficult and humble beginnings did not bode well for their futures. Second, both men attended integrated and segregated schools growing up. Third, both men easily excelled in school, and after leaving school their exceptional abilities resulted in staggering personal achievements.

Not only are the life stories of these remarkable men notable for what can be observed, *but their life stories are equally remarkable for what was not observed—at least in light of current fashions.* Nowhere in the life stories of these men have teachers and/or schools lowered academic standards for them—in the interests of so-called fairness. Equally absent from these stories is any complaining about not being able to perform well on "culturally biased" tests, or resentment over teachers' inability to understand their "cultural learning styles." Despite the unenlightened times in which they grew up, these men—like gifted children of all backgrounds—are easily identified through their personal drive, advanced intellectual capabilities, rapid progress through school, and exceptional achievements.

For more contemporary and in-depth narratives on gifted minority students growing up in difficult inner-city environments, readers are encouraged to consult *And Still We Rise: The Trials and Triumphs of Twelve Gifted Inner-City High School Students* by Miles Corwin, published in 2000 by William Morrow.

(Adapted from Carson, 2011; Lewis & Lewis, 2009; Sowell, 2000)

All intellectually superior children—despite their race, ethnicity, or language—can either have their talents recognized and nurtured, or they can be unrecognized and discouraged simply by virtue of supports or hindrances in their immediate social or school environments. Teachers who are sensitive to signs of unusually high intellectual abilities notice that some students grasp abstract concepts easier than others, are quicker to "catch on" to difficult academic material, tend to finish their school assignments more quickly than their classmates, and generally "ace" the material found on group-administered achievement tests. Good teachers know how to alert parents and other educators to this advanced potential, and facilitate opportunities for such students to be exposed to an accelerated curriculum, opportunities to pursue their interests outside of the school setting (particularly if sufficient school resources are not available), and opportunities to display their creativity and divergent thinking skills in complex tasks.

Although high-ability children are more likely to have better inner resources to overcome a poor education, many professional advocacy groups and scholars feel that these children are just as educationally vulnerable as slower children (The Council of State Directors of Programs for the Gifted & The National Association for Gifted Children, 2009; Murray, 2008).

In reality, however, many intellectually advanced minority students find that they struggle in school, either because the family/school environment is not conducive to intellectual development or pursuits, or negative social, personal, and attitudinal traits undermine the development of their natural abilities. Many such students find their motivational spark much later in life, sometimes through purely fortuitous circumstances. Once this spark turns into a flame, however, the superior intellectual capabilities and achievements of such children become undeniable (e.g., see Carson, 2011; Sowell, 2000; Sidebar 5.10).

Some minority students may not have the intellectual firepower of their more-advanced peers, but they do have the cognitive potential to achieve much more than their slower-learning classmates. When such students find themselves in failing urban schools with poor teaching, no academic role models, and a pervasive schoolwide anti-achievement ethic, their achievement potential is wasted. The only chance for many students trapped in failing schools is to obtain a brand-new chance to succeed in a totally transformed educational setting. Many educators, particularly those who support the goals of charter schools, find that new school environments can be created that are built on a bedrock of academic structure, clear and uncompromising disciplinary standards, and personal character development as necessary precursors to learning (see Chapter 7). The academic curriculum in such schools is carefully broken down into specific instructional objectives that are developed commensurate with the principles of explicit instruction and mastery learning (see Archer & Hughes, 2011; Jensen, 1993). Here, frequent assessments are tied to each instructional objective (see Chapter 6). Students who attend such schools find that a school culture and achievement-oriented climate is created that rewards academic excellence, and is infused with the idea that "being smart and achieving is cool." In such schools, failure is not an option, and students who chose not to learn or behave appropriately either drop out voluntarily or are simply not promoted to the next grade level. Once these conducive school environments are in place (and expectations consistently enforced), students begin to internalize the "achievement first" message, and effective learning can proceed for students who want to learn (see Chapter 7).

A key component of helping students succeed in school is to have realistic expectations. The "all children should go to college" mantra makes a good political speech, but not all children are cut out for college. Non-college-oriented students can succeed in life through different but equally as rewarding employment trajectories. Jensen (1998) effectively captures this principle in the following words:

> [B]y high-school age, ideally, real work apprenticeship programs would be available for students who wished to learn specific job skills that are best learned under supervision on the job. Many jobs, such as sailing a boat, cooking a dinner, or playing a musical instrument, require the automatization of many subskills and are not all that interesting or learnable without "hands on" experience and the informative feedback that comes only from trying to perform the task itself. Imagine trying to learn how to swim by listening to a lecture or reading a book on swimming! (p. 127)

Realistically, some minority students simply do not have the academic aptitude or the general cognitive proclivities to pursue an elite college educational experience. As seen in the Additional Resources section at the end of Chapter 7, the documentaries *The Pressure Cooker* and *Chops* vividly illustrate how rigorous high school–level apprenticeship programs (one involving the culinary arts and the other involving instrumental music performance) for minority students can inculcate the character traits and work habits that eventuate in outstanding skill performance—laying the foundation for lucrative and rewarding adult job careers.

In closing, a first step for the school psychologist, educational diagnostician, and classroom teacher in applying these cognitive principles is to properly assess where students are in their skills, and where they need to go in the course of instruction. Such diagnostics need to be both accurate and sensitive to signs of student progress. It is to this topic that we now turn.

ADDITIONAL RESOURCES

Supplemental Readings

Archer, A. L., & Hughes, C. A. (2011). *Explicit instruction: Effective and efficient teaching.* New York, NY: Guilford Press.

Ashlock, R. B. (2010). *Error patterns in computation: Using error patterns to help each student learn* (10th ed.). Boston, MA: Allyn & Bacon.

Carnine, D. W., Silbert, J., Kame'enui, E. J., & Tarver, S. G. (2009). *Direct instruction reading* (5th ed.). Upper Saddle River, NJ: Prentice Hall.

Carnine, D. W., Silbert, J., Kame'enui, E. J., Tarver, S. G., & Jungjohann, K. (2005). *Teaching struggling and at-risk readers: A Direct Instruction approach.* Upper Saddle River, NJ: Prentice Hall.

Cawelti, G. (Ed.). (2004). *Handbook of research on improving student achievement.* Arlington, VA: Educational Research Service.

Choate, J. S. (Ed.). (2004). *Successful inclusive teaching: Proven ways to detect and correct special needs* (4th ed.). Boston, MA: Pearson.

Engelmann, S. (2007). *Teaching needy kids in our backward system: 42 years of trying.* Eugene, OR: ADI Press.

Jensen, A. R. (1992). Psychometric g and achievement. In B. R. Gifford & M. C. O'Conner (Eds.), *Changing assessments: Alternative views of aptitude, achievement, and instruction.* Boston, MA: Kluwer Academic.

Marchand-Martella, N. E., Slocum, T. A., & Martella, R. C. (2004). *Introduction to Direct Instruction.* Boston, MA: Pearson.

Murray, C. (2008). *Real education: Four simple truths for bringing America's schools back to reality.* New York, NY: Random House.

Stein, M., Kinder, D., Silbert, J., & Carnine, D. W. (2005). *Designing effective mathematics instruction: A Direct Instruction approach* (4th ed.). Upper Saddle River, NJ: Prentice Hall.

Web Sites

Gifted Child Information/Resources: http://giftedkids.about.com
(See also websites in Sidebar 5.8, Direct Instruction)

CHAPTER

6

❖

Testing and Assessment

For better or worse, school psychologists are identified most closely with individualized assessment of students for determining special education eligibility. In many school contexts, appropriately trained school psychologists are expected to have knowledge and competencies, over and above the average educator, in a variety of classroom assessment methods, as well as in basic psychometric principles of applied measurement, test development, and score interpretation. This begs the question: How can knowledge of testing and assessment assist educators and school psychologists to adequately serve the psychoeducational needs of minority students in schools?

Traditionally, there have been two avenues for approaching this important issue. One approach is to be vigilant for ways in which the design, administration, and/or interpretation of tests and assessments may be inaccurate for racial/ethnic/language minority students. It is quite obvious that non-English speakers may require language modifications in tests. It comes as no surprise, however, that Quack Multiculturalism has marshaled an extraordinary amount of energy and resources to attack the validity and legitimacy of standardized cognitive and academic achievement testing for English-speaking, native-born cultural minority groups (e.g., Helms, 1997; Hilliard, 1982; Kohn, 2000; Phelps, 2009; Samuda, 1998; Williams, 1971, 1974). Such efforts are energized by a politicized interpretation of *The Equity Doctrine* (see Chapter 2), which holds that any test/assessment outcome showing differences in score distribution means constitutes *prima facie* (on its face) evidence of bias or unfairness (see discussion in Reynolds, 2000). This view advocates "alternative testing" for students who are not white or middle class.

This alternative testing movement adopts the view that traditional testing practices should be altered for English-speaking cultural minority groups in favor of one or more of the following proposals:

a. Traditional test administration and interpretation is so inappropriate that cultural minorities should be exempted outright from taking tests, and instead need qualitatively different types of tests and/or assessments.
b. If cultural minorities cannot be exempted from traditional tests, they should be held to different standards in the interpretation of test scores and/or the resulting decisions that are made from such scores.
c. Cultural minorities can take traditional tests, but these tests need to be altered in their administration procedures, in order to be fair.
d. If cultural minorities take traditional tests with standard administration procedures, the diagnostician needs additional assessment information in order to arrive at more accurate interpretations.

Alternative testing proposals, in order to build their case, rely on pointed criticisms of traditional standardized testing (Feuerstein, Rand, & Hoffmann, 1979; Lidz & Elliott, 2000; Reynolds & Lowe, 2009). These traditional testing criticisms can be distinguished by the extent to which they do or do not rely on empiricism to bolster their arguments. As discussed in Frisby (1999), one method of criticizing intelligence tests (for use with native-born, English-speaking culturally diverse groups) offers no data or concrete empirical evidence to support the credibility of anti-testing arguments (e.g., see Helms, 1992, 1997). Such criticisms

> must rely . . . on complex rationalizations. These rationalizations, with few differences, share a similar underlying logic. First, profound cultural differences between two or more racial, ethnic, or social class groups are argued from a psychological, philosophical, sociological, or historical point of view. Second, it is implied (either implicitly or explicitly) that "intelligence" or "intelligent behavior" is entirely relative and "culture specific." . . . [T]hese hypothesized links should cause practitioners to be insecure or cautious about how cognitive tests are interpreted with test takers from certain groups. (Frisby, 1999, p. 265)

Other test critics will spend a significant portion of their academic careers attempting to develop alternative instruments that presumably correct perceived shortcomings of traditional IQ testing. The following quote from the late 1970s, in support of the now-defunct System of Multicultural Pluralistic Assessment (SOMPA), typifies such advocacy:

> SOMPA is philosophically committed to a pluralistic view of American society. It sees American society as composed of a dominant Anglo core culture and many identifiable, unique cultural groups that vary in their degree of identification with Anglo values, language, life styles, habits, and social systems. The

more distinct and homogeneous the ethnic group, the greater the difference in the life experiences of the children and the greater the need to look at the child within the context of his or her experiences. SOMPA does this by providing assessment with norms appropriate to a child's sociocultural group. The procedure is not only equitable for youngsters, it also reflects cultural pluralism, or the belief that all cultures have equal worth and value, and that social strength comes from the continuance of diversity. (Figueroa, 1979, p. 30)

Fast-forward 30 years. When a typical beginning school psychology student is asked if they know what the SOMPA is or what these letters stand for, blank stares are the likely result. This typifies the utter failure of the alternative testing movement that was in vogue from the 1970s to the 1990s in school psychology, which left in its wake failed attempts to replace IQ testing with methods that were perceived to be more appropriate for English-speaking, native-born cultural minority groups. Some methods, like the SOMPA, have completely disappeared from the current scene. Other methods, such as the *Learning Potential Assessment Device* (Feuerstein, Rand, & Hoffmann, 1979; Feuerstein, Feuerstein, & Gross, 1997), were tried in progressive school districts such as the San Francisco Unified School District during the 1980s, but were eventually abandoned (Elliott, 1987). Other methods, like curriculum-based measurement, are still in use today, but they have not provided the "multicultural panacea" so hoped for by many. The various methods that have been suggested as replacements or supplements for traditional IQ and achievement testing (presumably to eliminate test bias), and their shortcomings, are listed in Table 6.1. Reasons for the failure of these attempts can be consolidated and summarized as follows:

1. Some alternative assessment proposals may be intuitively appealing, but they are not supported by a coherent body of data-based research that justifies their implementation in education settings for high-stakes decision making. Many alternative assessment proposals—for a variety of reasons—simply do not meet minimally acceptable standards of reliability or validity for educational decision making.

2. Some alternative assessment proposals (that are appropriate for native-born English speakers) advocate treating examinees differently (either in test administration or in the interpretation of test scores) based solely on their ethnic/racial group membership, which is ethically and morally questionable. At the time of this writing, California is the only state in the United States in which it is permissible to discriminate against African American students by denying them the opportunity to be evaluated for educational decision making in public schools with an intelligence test (Powers et al., 2004).

Table 6.1 Alternative Assessment Nostrums for Reducing or Eliminating Assumed Racial/ Ethnic/Language/Cultural Bias in Individual and Group-Administered Standardized Cognitive and Achievement Tests

Strategy	Underlying Assumptions/Rationale	Major Flaws
Banning cognitive test administration altogether for select groups (Bersoff, 1980)	Because individually administered IQ tests are assumed to be "culturally biased," banning use of such tests in schools will eradicate racial disproportionalities in selection outcomes (Bersoff, 1980; Elliott, 1987).	Such decisions stem from political, not empirical, reasons; in finding alternatives, schools that depend on testing are thrown into chaos; banning tests fails to reduce racial/ ethnic disproportionalities; test bans discriminate against groups that are disallowed from taking tests (Powers et al., 2004; Rauh, 2004).
Assessment of nonverbal intelligence (McCallum, 2003)	Because verbally loaded items require skills that are assumed to put some groups at a disadvantage, a purely nonverbal test should significantly reduce gaps in group mean scores (Bracken & McCallum, 1998; Noll, 1960).	Tests developed on exclusively nonverbal items and administered nonverbally do not completely erase subgroup differences in mean scores; important verbal abilities are not assessed, resulting in construct underrepresentation (Braden, 2000, 2003; Braden & Elliott, 2003).
Bio-cultural assessment (Armour-Thomas & Gopaul-McNicol, 1998)	Adding more instruments to a single IQ assessment permits a more comprehensive, and thus more fair and accurate, evaluation of intelligence.	Adding assessments is not time-efficient for busy professionals in schools; there is no evidence that this practice adds significantly to predictive validity.
Curriculum-based assessment/ measurement (CBA/CBM)	Evaluates students in specific academic skills that are directly taught and learned in classrooms, thus avoiding inferences about intelligence.	Despite its advantages for instructional decision-making, CBA/CBM is not designed to assess comprehensive intellectual functioning; racial/ ethnic group differences still persist (Hixson & McGlinchey, 2004; Kranzler, Miller, & Jordan, 1999; Mehrens & Clarizio, 1993).
Portfolio, performance, or authentic assessment	Evaluates students on specific work products from instruction, thus reducing reliance on skills that examinees have not had an opportunity to learn.	These methods do not yield smaller differences among racial/ethnic subgroups; they are subject to rater bias, higher costs, and poorer reliability (Braden, 1999).
Extended time limits (Elliott, 1987)	Assumed to be more fair to examinees who manifest a slower work/ thinking pace.	Standardized test administration procedures are altered significantly, thus invalidating test results (Elliott, 1987).

Table 6.1   (*Continued*)

Strategy	Underlying Assumptions/Rationale	Major Flaws
Learning potential/ dynamic assessment	Evaluating the change in test performance that results after examiner coaching is a more accurate picture of the examinee's potential for future learning.	Methods boil down to teaching the test; administration procedures are often unstandardized in some models; gain scores are less reliable; scores from "static" testing predict outcomes better than gain scores; dynamic measures are not validated for the purposes for which they are being used, i.e., determining special education eligibility (Elliott, 1987; Frisby & Braden, 1992; Glutting & McDermott, 1990; Reynolds, 1986).
System of Multicultural Pluralistic Assessment (SOMPA; Figueroa, 1979)	Uses "race norming" in selection score cutoffs, because environmental factors are assumed to put some groups at a disadvantage; persons who are the same in relative position on a test score distribution within their own racial/ethnic group are assumed to be essentially similar in underlying skills; traditional assessment is supplemented by health and physical history and adaptive behavior assessment in order to give a more complete picture of the child.	Standardization data is limited to only one state; conventional validity is poor or nonexistent; administration is not cost or time efficient (Goodman, 1979; Oakland, 1979).
Interviews/ examination of work samples	Provides a more comprehensive evaluation of personality traits and academic skills that are not measured by conventional testing.	Interviews or work samples have less demonstrated validity, thereby potentially increasing unfairness to groups or individuals (Hunter & Schmidt, 1976, p. 1065).
Redefining criteria for giftedness and eligibility standards for gifted program placement (Ford, 1996)	Minority children are seen as gifted according to culturally specific traits that are under-recognized or under-appreciated according to traditional test criteria.	No statistical evidence is provided to support these claims; presumed culturally specific intellectual traits are, in essence, noncognitive talents, personality, or behavioral traits (Gottfredson, 2004b).
Tests developed and normed in non-English language	Permits a more accurate assessment in the examinee's native language.	Large test companies do not have the resources and/or a large enough pool of subjects to justify test development on smaller language groups.

(*continued*)

Table 6.1   (Continued)

Strategy	Underlying Assumptions/Rationale	Major Flaws
Use of third-party language translators within English-language testing	Permits a more accurate assessment of non- or limited English speakers whenever non-English language standardized tests are not available.	There may be unintentional distortions in accuracy, or deletions of information, in relaying information from examiner to examinee or from examinee to examiner (Martines, 2008).
Test preparation programs	Allows examinees to practice test taking, thereby reducing their anxiety on future high-stakes testing.	Score improvements from test preparation programs are typically small/modest in size (Briggs, 2002).
Attempts to counteract the effects of stereotype threat	Minority examinees are intimidated by the possibility that negative stereotypes about their intellectual capabilities will be confirmed; hence examiners must behave in a manner that counteracts this possibility.	Stereotype threat theory cannot explain outcomes over and above what is predicted by generalized test anxiety theory (Jensen, 1998b); stereotype threat cannot fully account for performance differences among subgroups (Sackett, Hardison, & Cullen, 2004).

3. Some alternative assessment proposals may be adequate in providing information in one or more educationally relevant domains, but they are an inadequate substitute for gathering information that is useful for assessing general cognitive ability.

4. Some procedures were found to be awkward, clumsy, and/or too time consuming to justify usage in busy school settings where efficiency is prized.

This text takes the position that there is nothing to be gained from school psychologists pursuing alternative testing proposals that (a) contain higher degrees of measurement error compared to traditional testing; (b) cannot be used for purposes for which they have not been validated; or (c) promote claims that are *blatantly contradicted* by a solid foundation of empirical research (e.g., claims that usage will eliminate disproportional outcomes; or accusing traditional tests of bias when in fact research shows that tests are not biased—see Sidebar 5.2).

The cold, hard reality is that standardized tests are here to stay, and no American school-aged student is exempt from their consequences. As soon as an individual is born, that infant is evaluated at the hospital and given an APGAR score (which yields a score from 0 to 10 on **A**ppearance, **P**ulse, **G**rimace, **A**ctivity, and **R**espiration). Sometime around the fifth year of life, individuals are assessed as to their developmental readiness to begin attending school. As children matriculate through school, their daily existence involves completing seatwork and homework assignments, taking end-of-unit tests and quizzes, and taking yearly standardized academic achievement tests to assess their progress. In some communities, students must pass standardized tests in order to be admitted into the next higher grade level in exclusive public schools. If school professionals find that students are suspected of needing a qualitatively different educational experience (e.g., special or gifted education), then they are assessed by appropriately trained professionals who use the highest quality standardized tests. Once students reach high school age, they will have to achieve respectable scores on Advanced Placement (AP) tests, the Scholastic Aptitude Test (SAT), the American College Test (ACT), or the Graduate Record Exam (GRE) in order to be competitive for selective colleges. Citizens must take tests to obtain a driver's license, or to be hired for jobs as police officers, mail carriers, firefighters, and other civil service positions, and teachers must pass state certification tests in order to secure jobs in the public schools. In short, there is practically no area of life that is not impacted by tests.

To seriously argue that American minority groups should be exempted from taking tests, or to seriously entertain different test interpretation standards for different groups (particularly when no credible evidence exists that uncovers psychometrically defined test bias), is to invite total anarchy into American society. *This chapter is unapologetic in the conviction that nothing is to be gained by encouraging educators to explore alternative assessment schemes whose benefits are not supported by a reliable, high-quality program of data-based research.*

However, researchers' efforts to improve testing for English-language learners (ELLs) provides just such an occasion for optimism. The first section of this chapter provides an overview of the benefits of test accommodations for ELLs who take standardized state tests.

All students benefit whenever teachers, parents, and school support personnel prepare students adequately to display the best of their abilities on large-scale standardized tests. The second part of this chapter reviews strategies that teachers and psychologists can use to not only prepare students for testing, but also to help lessen test anxiety that can undermine students' best performance.

Finally, school psychologists are very familiar with Curriculum-Based Measurement procedures and materials, particularly as applied within the context of the Response-to-Intervention (RtI) identification model (see Glossary). Curriculum-Based Measurement is only one among many different models of Curriculum-Based Assessment (CBA) that can be used to help all children in schools. Unfortunately, other CBA models have been relatively overlooked in school psychology, hence the final section of this chapter discusses how these less-familiar models can be used in classrooms to benefit struggling students.

IMPROVING STANDARDIZED LARGE-SCALE TESTING FOR ENGLISH-LANGUAGE LEARNERS

According to 2007–2008 statistics by the National Center for Education Statistics (2009), approximately 11 percent of the nation's students attending traditional public schools—and 16 percent of the nation's students attending charter schools—are classified as Limited English Proficient (LEP). When the U.S. Congress passed Public Law 107-110, the No Child Left Behind (NCLB) Act of 2001, the term *limited English proficient* (LEP) was used in referring to students who are acquiring English during their educational years. These students are also known as ESL (English as a second language) students or bilingual students. In recent years, these students are more frequently being referred to as ELLs (English-language learners).

According to the federal government, an LEP or ELL is a student who (a) is 3 to 21 years of age; (b) is enrolled or preparing to enroll in an elementary or secondary school; (c) was not born in the United States or whose native language is a language other than English; who is a Native American or Alaska Native, or a native resident of the outlying areas; and who comes from an environment where a language other than English has had a significant impact on the individual's level of English-language proficiency; or who is migratory, whose native language is a language other than English, and who comes from an environment where a language other than English is dominant; and (d) whose difficulties in speaking, reading, writing, or understanding the English language may be sufficient to deny the individual the ability to meet the State's proficient level of achievement on State assessments, the ability to successfully achieve in classrooms where the language of instruction is English, or the opportunity to participate fully in society (P.L. 107-110, Title IX, Part A, Sec. 9101, [25]).

However, there is considerable inconsistency in ELL classification criteria both across and within states, which can directly affect the accuracy of Adequate Yearly Progress (AYP; see Glossary) reporting for these students (Abedi, 2004a). American school districts are held accountable by large-scale state-standardized assessments of academic skills, because federal funds are distributed proportionally based on the results of such assessment programs (Mihai, 2010). The passage of Goals 2000 stipulated that state standards and assessments must apply to all students, including ELLs (Abedi & Dietel, 2004), and that all students must make Adequate Yearly Progress (AYP). The No Child Left Behind Act has required that all students demonstrate a high level of proficiency in English Language Arts and Mathematics by 2014. Although some education observers feel that this deadline will likely be abandoned (e.g., see Mihai, 2010), the theme of accountability for academic progress—and tests being used as a very important component of this evaluation—continues to be the cornerstone of state assessments and changes in legislation. NCLB stipulates that every child be assessed in grades 3 through 8 and once in high school, the results of which are used to determine the yearly performance of the state and of each local educational agency and school in the state.

Numerous studies show that ELLs achieve significantly lower scores on state achievement tests compared to many comparison subgroups (Abedi & Dietel, 2004), and that this effect is particularly pronounced on Language Arts tests. It would be grossly naïve to conclude that, were it not for language challenges, there would be no significant test score gaps between ELLs and non-ELLs. Factors that are significantly correlated with test achievement gaps (e.g., parent education levels, socioeconomic status) interact in complex ways to explain such gaps (Abedi, 2004a). Further complicating matters is the fact that cultural/linguistic subgroups of ELLs show significant performance differences with each other. For example, ELL students with a Chinese-speaking background achieve significantly higher scores on state achievement tests compared to ELL students with a Spanish-speaking background (Abedi & Dietel, 2004).

When a content-specific achievement test is given to a non-ELL student, only knowledge and skills related to the test's measured content area are being assessed. For ELL students, achievement tests measure a combination of (a) content-specific knowledge and skills measured by the test, and (b) English language ability. Due to the confounding of test language comprehension with student demonstration of content knowledge, LEP students may show improvement in content knowledge (such as math) only when their level of academic English proficiency increases (Abedi & Lord, 2001). Researchers have suggested that ELL students are often assessed in content areas without proper time to develop sufficient English proficiency for valid testing. Some studies show that difficult English-language demands of tests can undermine an accurate measurement of an ELL student's knowledge and skills in the specific content measured by the test, which has led some to question the validity and reliability of large-scale state assessments for ELL students (Abella, Urritia, & Shneyderman, 2005).

Large-scale research studies have found that the gap in performance on content-based state assessments between ELL and non-ELL increases as the language load of the assessment tools increases. In addition, the internal consistency reliabilities of selected subtests were found to be lower in ELL groups compared to non-ELL groups, suggesting that construct-irrelevant variance caused by the language backgrounds of ELL students may be suspect as a source of measurement error (e.g., see Abedi & Leon, 1999; Abedi, Leon, & Mirocha, 2003). Because of these factors, all states have developed test accommodation policies for ELLs when they are taking state-standardized large-scale tests.

What Are Test Accommodations?

Test accommodations are practices and procedures that are intended to increase access to grade-level content for students who are potentially impacted by conditions that may interfere with their ability to demonstrate their knowledge on the test. Quite simply, test accommodations can be defined as changes to a test or testing situation that facilitate students' access to test content (Illinois State Board of Education, 2010). For ELLs, test accommodations help students to access the English content of the assessment, thereby enabling them to better demonstrate what they know academically (Mihai, 2010). Although test accommodations are intended to help students demonstrate their knowledge of test content, they must do so without altering the measured construct (i.e., what the test is intended to measure) and be comparable in interpretation to results from an un-accommodated test administration.

How Is ELL Eligibility for Test Accommodations Determined?

Students can be eligible to receive accommodations for several reasons. For example, some students have the need for accommodations written into their IEPs or 504 plans. Some testing access skills—usually taken for granted by test takers without disabilities—can present difficulties for students with disabilities in demonstrating their knowledge and skills on large-scale standardized tests (see Elliott, Kratochwill, & Gilbertson-Schulte, 1999; Elliott & Roach, 2006). These necessary skills are attending, listening, reading, remembering, writing, following directions, working alone, sitting quietly, turning pages, locating test items, locating answer spaces, erasing completely, seeing, processing information in a timely manner, working for a sustained period of time, and spelling. Some of these testing access skills may be problematic for English learners as well.

In the case of students who struggle with the English language, test accommodations ideally minimize the impact of language difficulties (and related stress) on the measurement of content area performance. Francis, Rivera, Lesaux, Kieffer, and Rivera (2006) categorize state accommodations eligibility criteria into four broad categories: (1) language competency, (2) academic criteria, (3) time criteria, and (4) professional/parental opinion.

Language Competency

Educators must first determine a student's language proficiency in order to make appropriate decisions for further psychoeducational assessments. The assessment of language competency includes the following components: (a) language proficiency in English, (b) language proficiency in the ELL student's native language, (c) the language of instruction that is used in a particular educational institution, and (d) program placement (Mihai, 2010). Martines (2008) defines the assessment of language proficiency as activities designed to "[provide] information that determines how efficiently individuals can converse in, read, write, and comprehend a language in comparison with their peers" (p. 404). Language dominance (i.e., the main language that a student uses) does not necessarily imply that a student is proficient in that language. A thorough language proficiency assessment involves language usage surveys, individually administered standardized tests, and clinical observations and interviews.

A thorough discussion of language proficiency assessment is beyond the scope of this chapter. For more detailed guidance on this important topic, readers are encouraged to consult the citations in the Additional Resources section at the end of this chapter.

Academic Criteria

The academic criteria that are used to assist in determining test accommodations for ELLs include (a) the academic background of ELLs in their native language (Mihai, 2010), and (b) the quality of the English-language instruction to which ELLs are exposed (Kopriva, 2008). Among the many education-related factors that influence an ELL student's native-language proficiency are the number of years these students have spent in schools within their native country (Kopriva, 2008). Further complicating matters is the quality of schooling experienced in a different country. In some circumstances, students do not experience continuous, steady exposure to education experiences—as these may be interrupted by personal or political turmoil.

Once in the United States, students classified as ELL within a given school district within a state are exposed to a wide range of qualitatively diverse instructional experiences with learning English (see Chapter 4). The quality of an ELL student's English-language instruction may vary as a function of differences in the aspects of English-language development emphasized, the social environment of the classroom, and the types of assessment activities that are used to determine language proficiency (see review in Kopriva, 2008).

Time Criteria

ELL eligibility for accommodations is also determined, in part, by (a) the length of time that an ELL student has been in the United States or in English-speaking schools, and (b) the length of time that an ELL student has been in a particular state's schools.

Professional/Parental Opinion

ELL eligibility for accommodations is also determined, in part, by (a) the parents' or guardians' opinions about whether an ELL student needs test accommodations, and (b) a teacher or other education professional's observations or recommendations. According to Mihai (2010), nearly half of all states specifically name the professionals whose opinions contribute to ELL test accommodation eligibility decisions: language acquisition professionals (e.g., ESL or bilingual teachers, interpreters); general education teachers (e.g., ELL classroom or content area teachers); parents, students, and community members; test coordinators or administrators (e.g., reading specialists, guidance counselors); and school administrators (e.g., principals, other school/district officials). Although school psychologists are not specifically mentioned by Mihai (2010), there is no reason why appropriately trained and skilled bilingual school psychologists cannot be included in one or more of these categories.

Many states have developed ELL-specific accommodation policies and guidelines, but these can differ considerably from state to state (see Mihai, 2010), as well as from district to district within states. Generally, test accommodations fall within four broad categories: presentation, response, setting, and timing/scheduling accommodations.

Presentation Accommodations

Translation

When ELL students continue to use their native languages frequently, some educators feel that translating test directions or actual test items from English to the students' native languages is appropriate. Unfortunately, problems may occur when the practice of translating items lowers the reliability and validity of test score interpretations, or unintentionally raises the item difficulty level (Abedi, 2002). In addition, test translation is time consuming (considering the need to translate items from multiple content areas across multiple grade levels; Cawthon, 2010).

Linguistically Modified Forms

When test forms are linguistically modified, it means that the language of test items are modified to plain or simplified English that retains the same meaning and content, but eliminates or reduces unnecessary complexity that causes the items to be more difficult for ELLs. Different methods for simplifying the English found on state-standardized tests are shown in Table 6.2.

Customized English Dictionaries and/or Glossaries

Whenever the test taker encounters potentially unfamiliar or difficult English words, definitions (or paraphrases) of such words can be printed in the margins of test booklets to aid in item comprehension. A variation on this accommodation is to provide built-in English glossaries in computerized tests, or for the program to include an item-appropriate synonym for difficult words that are unrelated to the academic or technical content of the item (Francis et al., 2006).

Bilingual Dictionaries and/or Glossaries

Test takers are given access to dictionaries and/or glossaries containing words written in both English and the test taker's native language. A variation of this accommodation is for computerized tests to include built-in bilingual glossaries.

Table 6.2   Item Linguistic Modifications on State-Standardized Tests for English Language Learners

Modification	Original Text	Modified Text
Shortening sentences (by eliminating nonessential noun phrases with complex modifiers)	This past year's class secretary counted the votes from Mrs. Brown's English class, and discovered a pattern in how girls voted.	The class secretary discovered a voting pattern.
	At a nearby mall in a small town, Debra played a noisy video game in which she received the highest score of two hundred sixty-six thousand, thirty-seven.	Debra played a video game and received a score of two hundred sixty-six thousand, thirty-seven.
Using simpler sentence structure (e.g., replacing conditional *if* clauses with separate sentences)	Because the package was a cube with six equal sides, Roy calculated the area by . . .	The package is a cube with six equal sides. Roy calculates the area of the cube by . . .
	If pencils cost $1.15 each, including tax, and Mary has $8.75, how many can she buy?	Pencils cost $1.15 each, including tax. Mary has $8.75. How many pencils can Mary buy?
Using more familiar and frequently used words (or omitting less frequently used words)	Bill is in charge of the raffle. Circle the clumps of pears in the illustration.	Bill is in charge of the bake sale. Find the groups of pears and draw circles around the pears.
	A certain culinary file contains approximately fifty recipes for making crepes.	A file contains fifty food recipes.
Sentences in active rather than passive voice	The test was failed by over one-third of the applicants to the school.	One-third of the school applicants failed the test.
	The girl was bitten by the cat.	The cat bit the girl.

(Adapted from Abedi, 2004b, 2006)

Side-by-Side Dual Language

Here, short and/or extended response items are presented both in English and in another language (e.g., Spanish). Depending on the print space required, both languages of side-by-side items may be organized vertically on a single page, or face each other on separate, opposite pages.

Reader Scripts

Reader scripts are special test booklets designed for the instructions, test items, and item choices to be read aloud by the test administrator. Partial read-alouds designate situations where portions are read aloud at the student's request. Here, test administrators still must read aloud from a reader script, not a standard test booklet. In addition, all students in the test session must be eligible for a reader script accommodation (e.g., see Illinois State Board of Education, 2010).

Audio Recordings

Audio recordings (in the form of cassettes or compact discs) include test directions, items, or item choices that can be listened to by individual examinees. Examinees can be provided with personal earphones/headphones that would allow them to independently repeat portions of the recording.

Test Directions

Sometimes the test directions can be modified to help examinees better understand how to approach test content. Scripted test directions can be written in an examinee's native language and read aloud. Or, test directions are in English but can be repeated in response to an examinee's request. Test directions may also be restated in simplified/modified English. In some instances, test directions can be repeated, but vocal emphasis is placed on key words in the directions. In some instances, the examiner can verify the student's understanding by having the student repeat the directions in English. Some states allow test directions to be locally translated into languages other than those provided by the state, but this must be done by a professional translator or educator who is familiar with state assessment policies, procedures, and practices—and who is under the line-of-sight supervision of an appropriately certified on-site educator (e.g., see Illinois Board of Education, 2010).

Word Clarification

In some state policies, ELL students can ask for decoding or meaning clarification on isolated words or phrases. Depending on specific state policies, the test proctor can provide limited assistance with student requests (see Sidebar 6.1).

⌦ Sidebar 6.1   Example of a Linguistic Accomodation on a Statewide Test

BACKGROUND

Minh is a Vietnamese third grader who has lived in America for two years. Mr. Taylor, her Language Arts and ESL teacher, will administer the statewide test to Minh. Because Mr. Taylor works with Minh each day, he knows the kind of English she can and cannot understand, and thus tailors the language he uses accordingly. A sample reading comprehension item on the test is shown as follows.

READING PASSAGE

Mr. and Mrs. Huntsman had a potbellied pig named Bonkers. The pig lived indoors like a pet dog or a cat. They all lived happily in their home in Texas. One summer Mr. and Mrs. Huntsman went camping and took Bonkers with them. Mr. Huntsman went fishing one morning. Mrs. Huntsman didn't feel well, so she and Bonkers stayed in the camper. Suddenly, Mrs. Huntsman fell to the floor. She needed a doctor. Bonkers pushed the camper door open and climbed out to locate* help. She went up to the road. Car after car passed by. Bonkers returned to the camper several times to check on Mrs. Huntsman. Finally Bonkers walked to the middle of the road. When a car came by, she lay down in front of it. When the driver got out, Bonkers led him back to the camper.

TEST ITEMS

1. The word <u>locate</u> means to:
   ___ try to find
   ___ leave alone
   ___ run around
   ___ make noise
2. Which of these would be the best title for a newspaper story about Bonkers?
   ___ Pig Fakes an Illness
   ___ Pig Saves Owner's Life
   ___ Pig Stops a Car
   ___ Pig Causes an Accident
3. What happened right after Bonkers lay down in the road?
   ___ A driver followed Bonkers back to the camper.
   ___ Bonkers pushed the camper door open.
   ___ Mrs. Huntsman needed a doctor.
   ___ The Huntsmans lived happily in Texas.

ACCOMMODATION REQUESTS/RESPONSES

<u>Question</u>: Minh asks for reading (decoding) assistance with the word *potbellied* in the passage.

<u>Responses</u>: Mr. Taylor will read the word aloud. If Minh asks what the word means, Mr. Taylor can provide clarification (e.g., "a potbellied pig is a kind of pet pig with a big stomach").

<u>Question</u>: Minh asks for help with the meaning of the word *camper*.

<u>Responses</u>: Because *camper* can have multiple meanings, Mr. Taylor explains the meaning of this word as it is used in the story (this may include drawing a picture to help explain the meaning if necessary).

(*continued*)

Question: Minh asks for help with the underlined word _locate_ in either the passage or the item.

Responses: Because this word is a tested vocabulary word, Mr. Taylor is only permitted to read the word aloud. If needed, he can read the entire item aloud. He is not permitted to provide any assistance with the meaning of the word.

Question: Minh requests help with the meaning of _right_ or _right after_, in the third item.

Responses: Mr. Taylor may clarify that "What happened right after" means to tell the next thing that happened. Mr. Taylor is also allowed to use words from the test question itself to clarify the meaning for Minh.

Question: Minh asks for clarification in the meaning of the response choices in Item 2.

Responses: Mr. Taylor may read aloud or explain the meaning of the words _fake, illness, owner's,_ or _accident._

*Tested vocabulary words are underlined.

(Adapted from Texas Education Agency, 2011a, 2011b)

Response Accommodations

Language of Responses

Under the proper allowances, examinees have a choice of responding in either English or their native language on short and/or extended response items.

Dictation

Test takers may dictate answers (English or non-English) from a short/extended response item to a live scribe (e.g., a school staff member who is under the line-of-sight supervision of a certified education professional) or to an audio recording device. The audio recording is then transcribed onto a regular answer document after testing is completed. Or, examinee responses must be scribed verbatim. Although the scribe may ask the test taker to pause, slow down, repeat, or speak more clearly, the test taker must not be prompted, reminded, or otherwise assisted in formulating his or her response during or after the dictation. Such requests must not be communicated in a manner suggesting that the student make a change or correction. Students who dictate to a live scribe may review and modify their response before the end of the testing session. No one may suggest corrections or improvements during this review, but they may clarify that the student can make any desired changes to the response. Students who dictate to only a recording device may review the recording before the end of the testing session and append material or re-record the response, but they may not later review the scribed response on their answer document.

A word dictated in a language other than English must be scribed in that language, if known. If such a word is not known, the scribe may insert, in its place, a note to the scorer in parentheses, such as "(Polish word)" or "(unknown word)." The student may correct native words or inserted notes during the post-dictation review mentioned previously, but the scribe may not make any special marks or provide other hints to the student suggesting changes (e.g., circled or underlined words, arrows, symbols, etc.; see Illinois State Board of Education, 2010).

Setting Accommodations

Setting accommodations consist of modifying the setting or environment in which testing takes place in order to assist the examinee in demonstrating skills and knowledge on the test. For example, the assessment may be administered in a space or location that is more free of distractions, or in a setting that is more familiar to the test taker. The test may be administered in a smaller group, or even on an individual basis as needed.

Timing/Scheduling Accommodations

Extended Time

In an impromptu manner, extra time can be allowed at the end of a standard time administration (e.g., 10 minutes) if test takers are still engaged when standard time has elapsed. However, extended time can be planned beforehand. For preplanned time allowances, there is no specified time limit for these sessions other than that they must begin and end in a single school day. Students receiving this provision are typically tested separately from students receiving standard time allowances.

More Frequent Breaks

ELLs may be provided with more frequent breaks that essentially divide the testing time into smaller segments. Regardless of the number or length of breaks provided, each individual test session must begin and end in the same day. Test security is a key issue when allowing more frequent breaks, because students must not have the opportunity to share or seek answers to test items. Students can be permitted to take breaks either in or out of their seats. For in-seat breaks, the testing session is simply stopped for a brief period, which can be easily implemented in group settings. For out-of-seat breaks, a student is instructed to stop working and close the test booklet after completing a specified portion of the session. Security is protected more easily for out-of-seat breaks when the student is being assessed individually.

A thorough review of accommodations research is beyond the scope of this chapter. Interested readers can consult Mihai (2010; Table 13). Little research has been available on how a state's accommodation policies are carried out in practice in local schools (for an exception, see Wolf, Griffin, Kao, Chang, & Rivera, 2009).

How Is Eligibility for ELL Test Accommodations Determined in a Local School?

Test accommodations are an important topic of decision making for ELL students with and without disabilities. As such, reliable and knowledgeable decision making at the school site is crucial for protecting the validity of standardized academic testing and the ability to use scores properly in comparing student performance across states and across school districts within states. When the assignment of individual testing accommodations to student needs is sloppy, there is a potential for test results to misrepresent student knowledge and abilities, and for classroom, school, and district comparisons to be misrepresented as well (Kopriva, 2008).

The policies for school sites in deciding who receives test accommodations (and what type) vary both among states and across districts within states. In nearly every state, the IEP team at the local school is given guidance by state assessment policies, which helps the team to determine the appropriate testing accommodations for individual students with disabilities. For ELL students without disabilities, other teams established by district policies make accommodations decisions. An illustrative description of these procedures is given in Sidebar 6.2.

Sidebar 6.2   Procedures for Accessing Standardized Test Accommodations for ELL Students

States require school districts to collect information from a brief Home Language Survey for every new student at enrollment. This information is used to identify the students whose families speak a language other than English at home, or if the student's first language is a language other than English (which helps identify students who are adopted, or who are children of email-ordered-brides whose American stepfathers do not allow the mother and child to use their first language). It also helps identify the students who need to be assessed for English-language proficiency. If the answers to one or more survey questions indicate that a non-English language is spoken, then students are eligible to be screened for ESL (English as a second language) services.

Educators in many states screen potential ELL students with the WIDA— ACCESS Placement Test (W-APT). WIDA (World-Class Instructional Design and Assessment) is a consortium of states dedicated to the design and implementation of high standards and equitable educational opportunities for English-language learners. As of August 2011, the WIDA consortium consists of 26 states and Washington, D.C. The W-APT is an individually administered instrument used by educators to measure the English-language proficiency of those students who have been identified as potential ELL students in a particular school district. It can help determine whether or not a child is in need of English-language development services. Any district employee who, at a minimum, meets the requirements of a paraprofessional under Title I (i.e., noncertified staff who work under the direct supervision of a certified teacher), and has received training, may administer and score the W-APT.

The W-APT Score Calculator (http://wida.us/assessment/w-apt/ScoreCalculator .aspx) is a tool that can be used to manually convert raw scores and calculate the composite proficiency level (CPL) scores. With the click of a button, it calculates Speaking, Reading, Writing, and Listening proficiency scores, along with the CPL score and a grade-adjusted CPL score. Using the calculator will also generate a basic printable score report. If a student, on the basis of his or her W-APT score, is found to be eligible for ELL services, then that student is entered into a state tracking system. Eligibility is based on their English proficiency level (EPL) score and state criteria for determining English proficiency.

Every year that a student is identified as limited English proficient (LEP), that student must be assessed annually to determine growth toward English proficiency. The ACCESS for ELLs is one of several different English proficiency assessments that can satisfy the NCLB requirement for the annual assessing of English proficiency development. All students identified as LEP are assessed annually, even if parents opt out of ESL services. ELL students in WIDA states are assessed with ACCESS (Assessing Comprehension and Communication in English State-to-State), which is a standards-based, criterion-referenced, English-language proficiency test designed to measure social and academic proficiency in English. It assesses social and instructional English used within the school context as well as the language associated with language arts, mathematics, science, and social studies across the four language domains (reading, writing, listening, and speaking). Within the grade-level clusters (i.e., 1–2, 3–5, 6–8, 9–12), ACCESS for ELLs consists of three test forms called *tiers*, which are written with test items reflecting second-language acquisition stages.

The nature of a school's test accommodations policies for ELLs varies as a function of whether a state is characterized as a district-controlled state (i.e., districts have freedom to develop their own policies as to which ELL students require

(*continued*)

accommodations) or whether districts must follow state-controlled guidelines (i.e., districts within a state must follow state-approved practices).

In some districts, a team consisting of ESL teachers, an ESL coordinator, an administrator, and non-ESL content area teachers meets typically at least twice per year to examine the instructional accommodations practices used in classrooms for ELL students, and to use this information to decide (a) if students are eligible to be included in state-mandated English grade-level assessments and end-of-course content assessments (administered to all students at the secondary level), and (b) if they are eligible, what test accommodations students may need.

IEP teams discuss needs for state test accommodations for ELL students receiving special education services. States vary in the number and types of test accommodations that are allowed in state-mandated assessments (see reviews in Mihai, 2010). All ELL students are required to take the state-mandated assessments. If students have been in the United States for less than one calendar year at the opening of the assessment window, they can be exempt from the communication/language arts assessment. That is the only place where an ELL student would not be included in the state-mandated assessment.

For a detailed study of the various factors and procedures used in urban districts for making accommodations decisions for ELL students on NAEP tests (see Glossary), readers are encouraged to consult Willner, Rivera, and Acosta (2007).

ELL students whose English skills are still poor and/or underdeveloped can be exempted from having to take state academic achievement tests. In some states, ELL students may be excused from state accountability testing in the subject areas of reading and writing. These decisions are based on the length of time that the students have attended school in the United States before having to take a state accountability test.

However, for those ELL students whose English skills exceed a minimum level of proficiency, test accommodations can help them demonstrate what they know in content areas without being hampered by underdeveloped English-language skills. Most ELL school professionals would agree with the adage that "test accommodations are only as good as the instructional accommodations in the classroom." This means that ELL students must have some familiarity with instructional efforts to accommodate underdeveloped English skills on English-language tasks, so that related test accommodations will not be unfamiliar to them. An innovative computerized program containing problem-solving algorithms for helping school officials to determine test accommodations for ELL students is described in Sidebar 6.3.

✍ Sidebar 6.3   STELLA System for Assisting Educators in Making Test Accommodation Decisions for ELL Students

Although teachers of English language learners (ELLs) appear to be competent at identifying and accommodating students' needs and challenges in the classroom, there is scant evidence that teachers can translate their knowledge into reliable recommendations for matching student characteristics to accommodations on large-scale academic tests (e.g., Douglas, 2004; Kopriva, 2008). Fortunately, emerging developments in standardizing decision-making algorithms for selecting test accommodations for ELL students show much promise in reversing this trend.

The Selection Taxonomy for English Language Learner Accommodations (STELLA) is a computerized decision-making system designed to provide a systematic mechanism for (a) defining and identifying different types of English-language learners in grades K through 12, and (b) matching these students to accommodation opportunities that are appropriate for each student on large-scale academic assessments.

The development of STELLA was supported through federal funding by the U.S. Department of Education and a collaboration among the University of Maryland, South Carolina Department of Education, North Carolina Department of Public Instruction, Maryland State Department of Education, District of Columbia Public Schools, Austin Independent School District, and the American Association for the Advancement of Science.

In the development of STELLA, three areas of student characteristics are deemed to be most relevant for making test accommodation decisions (see review in Kopriva, 2008): (1) language proficiency, (2) cultural proximity, and (3) quality of experiences in U.S. schooling.

The relationship between *language proficiency* in reading, writing, speaking, and listening in both a student's native language and English is complex (see discussions in Baker, 2011; Kopriva, 2008), and has a significant impact on the quality in which a test taker understands test information and performs on standardized tests. According to Kopriva (2008), *cultural proximity* refers to the extent to which an ELL student's home and previous school environments are or are not similar to school environments in which students are currently learning content in the United States. Certain variables can serve as proxy measures for these similarities and dissimilarities, which include the time, consistency, testing, and instructional experiences to which ELL students have been exposed in schools in their native country. Teachers of ELL students in American schools are in a key position to observe the strengths, weaknesses, and challenges of these students as they learn in

(continued)

classrooms. ELL students' *quality of experiences in U.S. schooling*, as observed by teachers, other educators, and parents, can be informative for deciding how the most appropriate test accommodations are selected.

Data is collected for entry into STELLA via three forms accessed as pull-down menus within the program. A *teacher form* requests information from teachers of ELL students related to their assessment of English and native-language proficiency, students' experience with a variety of standard test formats, and teacher judgments about conditions that help a particular student on classroom tests and evaluations. The *Parent Form* requests information from parents of ELL students related to the length and consistency of time the student has spent in U.S. schools, as well as the school atmosphere in the student's native country (e.g., how many hours per day and days per week were required to attend school, quality of school resources, types of tests and assessments taken in native country schools, and student's experience with various test formats). *Records Forms* allow the user to enter data related to English-language proficiency information, the language of instruction within an academic content area, and test information in the student's native language, among other information. At the time of this writing, a revision of the STELLA program is currently underway, which will reduce the student information input load to one form rather than three.

Pre-loaded information in STELLA includes four English-language proficiency tests, the output from which (and other tests selected by the user) are converted to a common scale with four levels: Beginner ELL, Low-Intermediate ELL, High-Intermediate ELL, and Grade-Level Competitive ELL (i.e., students deemed to be thriving in mainstream English classrooms).

Computer algorithms consolidate information from multiple questions in order to arrive at an appropriate evaluation. For example, a student can be rated in the low category for his or her time spent in a U.S. school if (a) the student has been in the United States less than one academic year, or (b) the student has been in the United States between one and two years AND has missed more than two months of school per year to date, or (c) the student has been in the United States between two to three years and has missed more than two months of school per year for at least two years.

Test Accommodation Decision-Making Rules are written into the STELLA program, where relevant student information is paired with relevant test accommodation factors that identify which particular set of test accommodations would be most appropriate for a particular student. According to STELLA developers, decision-making rules can be adapted to suit individual state agencies, because different states do not follow uniform rules for establishing which test accommodations to allow.

After all information is entered into STELLA, a computerized profile of each student includes a student profile (on language proficiency, cultural proximity, and quality of U.S. schooling), and then lists (a) recommended accommodation decisions for each student that are consistent with best practice for students with their profile, and (b) best-fit accommodation decisions consistent with accommodations currently allowed by individual state agencies for the purpose of participating in the statewide large-scale content testing program. Associated materials for STELLA include a Data Collection Forms Handbook, an Output Interpretation Handbook, and a Technical Manual.

The STELLA program has been field tested in a study by Kopriva, Emick, Hipolito-Delgado, and Cameron (2007). These researchers studied a sample of third- and fourth-grade ELLs in South Carolina (N = 272), who were randomly assigned to various types of test accommodations on a mathematics assessment. Results indicated that those students who received the appropriate test accommodations, as recommended by STELLA, had significantly higher test scores than ELLs who received no accommodations or those who received incomplete or no recommended accommodation packages. Additionally, students who were given no test accommodations scored no differently than those students who received accommodation packages that were incomplete or not recommended, given the students' particular needs and challenges.

A classroom version of STELLA is presently being considered, along with professional development plans for helping teachers adapt their own lessons consistent with addressing the individual needs of their ELL students. For more information about STELLA, visit the STELLA website at www.WIDA.us

(Adapted from Kopriva, n.d.)

Once the decision has been made to provide an ELL student with test accommodations, the test coordinator at the school site (in conjunction with site teachers who are responsible for proctoring the test) must indicate the accommodations given on test answer sheets (e.g., see Illinois State Board of Education test accommodations guide accessed at http://www.isbe.net/assessment/pdfs/ell_guidance.pdf). This documentation may differ by subject area.

TEST PREPARATION/TEST ANXIETY REDUCTION

The term *test preparation* is a generic concept that refers to all of the ways in which educators can help all students (of all backgrounds) perform to the best of their abilities on classroom and/or standardized tests. A wide variety of specific terms and concepts fall under this rubric. Strategies for developing effective test preparation skills range from generic good habits for being an effective student (see Sidebar 6.4) to very specific test-taking skills for handling particular item types on tests (see Sidebar 6.5).

Some educators may still experience some confusion related to a clear understanding of which test preparation activities are or are not ethical. At the time of this writing, some minority schools in large urban districts have gotten into serious ethical and legal troubles related to cheating on standardized tests (e.g., see Sidebar 4.6). Activities determined to be unethical and ethical according to most testing experts are listed in Sidebar 6.4. Readers may wish to consult Cizek (2003) for an excellent and comprehensive text on ways to detect and prevent cheating on tests in classrooms.

✍ Sidebar 6.4   Comparing the Legality, Appropriateness, and Ethics of Test Preparation Activities in Schools

Test Preparation Activities That Are Illegal, Inappropriate, or Unethical	Test Preparation Activities That Are Legal, Appropriate, or Ethical
• Giving students opportunities to practice on parallel versions of the test to be taken • Giving students opportunities to practice on items taken directly from the test • Altering or modifying test items at the school site before administering them to students • Changing students' answers on the test after it has been completed and submitted	• Encouraging students to get a good night's rest and to eat a healthy breakfast before testing • Familiarizing students with good test-taking behaviors (e.g., familiarizing students with the answer sheet format; encouraging students to read directions carefully; informing students whether they will be penalized for guessing) • Teaching general content from the domain that will be tested (e.g., if the test will test long division skill, teach skills in long division) • Giving students practice in using general test-taking strategies for solving problems presented in different item formats (e.g., multiple choice, short answer, completion) • Giving students opportunities to practice with state- and/or district-provided sample items that are similar, but not identical, to those on the test • Giving students opportunities to practice with commercial test preparation materials • Giving students opportunities to practice with older versions of the test to be taken

(Adapted from Perlman, 2004)

⚱ Sidebar 6.5   Strategies for Applying Test-Wiseness Skills to Different Test Item Types

True/False Items

- Generally, items that include "absolute" words (e.g., *all, always, everyone, never, none, no one*) are most often false, as exceptions can be found in most true statements.
- In longer statements, if one part is false, then the entire statement is false.
- A long statement composed of two true clauses can be false simply from a connector that makes the entire sentence false. For example, although both clauses in the statement "Abraham Lincoln is famous because he has black hair" are true, the connector *because* causes the entire statement to be false.

Matching Items

- When presented with two columns, read down each column carefully first to obtain a broad overview of all response options.
- As matches are made, cross the item off the list. This helps to limit subsequent choices as you move through the test and increases the chances of getting more answers correct.

Multiple-Choice Items

- If allowed, circle key words in the stem that may provide clues for the correct answer.
- Eliminate immediately response choices that you are sure are incorrect, which can give you greater chances for selecting the correct response.
- As with True/False items, response choices containing "absolute" words are usually not correct.
- If the response choices include "all of the above," and one of the other response choices is incorrect, then you know that "all of the above" is not the correct choice.

Fill-in-the-Blank Items (answer choices not provided)

- Look for context clues in words that may assist you to find the correct answer (e.g., matching the grammatical form of the stem with the grammatical form of the answer that goes in the blank).

Essay Items

- Understand key words that provide clues as to whether the essay requires recall, analysis, evaluation, or synthesis—in order to understand exactly what is being required.

(*continued*)

- Briefly outline the structure of the essay (e.g., introduction, body, conclusion) before beginning to write it.
- To assist with essay content, ask and answer the six W/H questions (who, what, when, where, why, and how).
- Learn to properly use linking/connection words that can assist in tying ideas together (e.g., *next, finally, in comparison, likewise, as a result, in summary*)

(Adapted from Rozakis, 2003)

STUDY SKILLS

Study skills are "processes individuals use to digest and learn information," which are seen as "critical for maximizing learning" (Crespi & Bieu, 2005, p. 539). Teaching effective study skills can certainly help students to prepare for tests, although study skills can be helpful for a wide variety of school activities and assignments. Interested readers are encouraged to investigate the study skills resources provided in the Additional Resources at the end of this chapter.

Test anxiety (TA) is a construct that is considered to be a special form of more generalized anxiety (Cizek & Burg, 2006). Zeidner (1998) defines TA as a constellation of cognitive, emotional, and behavioral responses associated with excessive concern over possible negative consequences of, or failure on, an exam or other similar evaluative situation. These responses are evoked when a person believes that his or her intellectual, motivational, and/or social capabilities are exceeded by the demands of the test situation.

Although all students feel anxious at some time or another about taking tests or from a possibly negative consequence stemming from poor test results, test-anxious students have an unusually low threshold for anxiety in evaluative situations. When confronted with an evaluative situation, these students show physical symptoms such as rapid and shallow breathing, increased sweating, or a racing heart rate (for additional symptoms, see Huberty, 2009). They may manifest specific behavioral symptoms such as fidgeting, looking frequently at their watch or a clock in the room, or cheating. These symptoms interact closely in a recursive and transactional manner (see Sidebar 6.6) that forms a continuous and negative cycle. For example, a student's nagging feeling that the test is threatening often increases TA symptoms that negatively impact the student's test performance. Poor test performance, in turn, confirms the student's perception of the threat posed by the evaluation. As the next evaluation/test nears, the student experiences stronger negative feelings and expectations of performing poorly.

✎ Sidebar 6.6   An Illustration of the Transactional Model of Test Anxiety in Two High School Students*

Roberto	Juan
Roberto is an average student who regularly attends classes, turns in his homework on time, and has made a reasonable attempt to study for his high school biology test.	Juan is an average student who regularly attends classes, turns in his homework on time, and has made a reasonable attempt to study for his high school biology test.
Roberto begins the test by carefully examining the first question, which is a multiple-choice item. He is immediately concerned about what he perceives to be the high level of difficulty in this question, and he experiences a strong sense that he is not prepared to answer it correctly. He tells himself that he is not going to answer the remaining test items satisfactorily either. The constant repetition of this thought begins to trigger sweating, and he feels his heart beginning to race.	Juan begins the test by remembering a test-taking skill that he practiced in class (to the point of overlearning) with his teacher in previous weeks. He begins by skimming over the test first, and then makes a conscious choice to respond to test question #6, because this item strikes him as the easiest question to answer—as the information is at "the tip of his tongue."
These responses, in turn, begin to cloud his thinking processes. In a panic, he finds that he is unable to remember the biology material he studied, and he finds it difficult to organize the material that he does remember.	Although he begins to feel some twinges of worry, these feelings are calmed somewhat by memories of the past week when his teacher drilled the class on the look, length, and format of the test, the topics that would be covered, and provided practice on how to pace oneself in working through a sample test. He also remembers how his teacher spent two full class periods giving students opportunities to write short essays in response to content-specific prompts, which helped him to practice extended writing skills that are helpful for short-answer test items.
He hastily marks an answer to this first question, but he knows that it is merely a "guesstimate." He is frustrated with the fact that he studied hard for this test, yet he feels that he bombed the very first question.	
As Roberto approaches the second question, his confidence has been drained, and he cannot shake the fear that he is going to receive a subpar grade on this test and be grounded by his parents. Furthermore, he worries that his chances for being competitive for a good college will be diminished as well.	Juan begins to feel that, although he perceives the test to be a challenge, this challenge is manageable. He then skims the test again to select the second item that he feels most confident in answering, and he periodically checks the clock to ensure that he does not spend an inordinate amount of time on any one question.

*Examples represent students who studied for the test, and not students who failed to study or prepare for the test.

(Adapted from Cizek & Burg, 2006)

TA is a complex phenomenon that manifests itself in a variety of ways among students. One type of student simply fails to prepare adequately for tests and understandably is quite anxious about not doing well. Another type of student may have prepared adequately for the test (as well as having good test-taking skills), but becomes easily distracted during the test and thereby performs poorly. Another type of student believes that they have adequate test preparation and test-taking skills, when in reality they do not. When these students are confronted with poor test performance, the conflicting information engenders confusion, worry, and apprehension about future performance (see Mealey & Host, 1992).

DO CULTURAL MINORITY STUDENTS EXPERIENCE HIGHER LEVELS OF TEST ANXIETY COMPARED TO OTHER STUDENTS?

This question is difficult to answer definitively, as numerous racial/ethnic groups are small in size, and the difficulty of gathering quality data on such groups is prohibitive (Cizek & Burg, 2006). Nevertheless, Hembree (1988) summarized more than 500 studies of test anxiety and found that across all studies (conducted in grades 4–12) comparing Hispanic and white students, Hispanic groups displayed a consistently higher level of TA compared to whites. Hembree's review identified a substantial effect size in TA levels between white and African American groups in the early elementary grades (African Americans show higher TA), but differences begin to narrow during middle school and disappear in high school (Cizek & Burg, 2006).

The perception of greater TA for minority students is energized by scholarly interest in *stereotype threat* theory (see Glossary). This theory holds that test takers belonging to lower-scoring racial/ethnic/gender groups suffer greater potential for anxiety stemming from fear that their performance on cognitive tests may conform to the stereotype of their group as less intellectually capable. Jordan and Lovett (2007) provide school psychologists with a range of conditions that presumably trigger stereotype threat within students in schools, as well as offer practical suggestions for school diagnosticians to consider in reducing this threat. The validity of stereotype threat theory (as an explanation for subgroup differences in cognitive test performance) is undermined by the theory's failure to provide a credible explanation for the fact that (a) racial differences in cognitive test performance appear as early as 2 years of age (e.g., see Rushton & Jensen, 2005), when young children do not possess the cognitive maturity or life experiences to grasp and internalize societal stereotypes about ability; (b) racial/ethnic differences in cognitive test performance are equally as pervasive in predominantly minority educational/social environments with little or no exposure to whites; and (c) the size of racial group differences in cognitive test performance have been reliably shown to vary as a function of the size of a test's *g* loadings (Jensen, 1998).

Finally, the effects of race/ethnicity and test anxiety are hopelessly intertwined, with effects on test anxiety stemming from variables other than race or ethnicity alone. For example, higher TA levels are associated with lower IQ scores, lower scores on other ability tests, lower grade point averages, and poorer study skills (Hembree, 1988).

What Can Teachers Do to Address the TA of Students?

Given the ambiguity in literature on the construct validity of stereotype threat theory—as well as the absence of any clear research on how stereotype threat theory leads to symptoms that are conceptually distinct from general test anxiety symptoms experienced by students from all groups—no interventions are deemed to be particularly effective *solely as a function of a student's racial/ethnic minority status*. Some practical suggestions that experienced teachers have used to address TA in all students are listed in Sidebar 6.7.

Sidebar 6.7   Strategies Used by Teachers for Helping Text-Anxious Students

General Tone Set in the Classroom

- Teacher expresses confidence in students' abilities
- Teacher rewards student effort, even if the outcome is less than stellar
- Teacher helps students to put tests and test results into a proper perspective (e.g., tests do not define who they are as persons, a bad grade is not the end of the world, etc.)

Specific Pretest Strategies

- Build student confidence through extra exposure to practice quizzes
- Encourage students to prepare for written tests (i.e., essay, short answer) by practicing actually writing responses as they study for the test
- Prepare for the test in class by discussing and practicing test-taking strategies
- Prepare for the test by reviewing the test format with students

Test-Session Strategies

- Allow for frequent breaks when needed
- "Brain flush" technique: Encourage students to use the first 5 minutes of a test to write down everything they remember about the topic, and use these notes on the test
- Break the test up into chunks and allow students extra time to complete the test if needed
- Encourage students to ask questions of the teacher when they do not fully understand what a test question is requiring

(continued)

- Encourage students to employ positive self-talk during testing
- Encourage students to move on if they are stumped by a question, but to return to it at the end of the test
- Ensure that students check their work before turning it in
- Permit individual testing where students can orally explain their thoughts first before writing down their answers
- Permit students to take tests at a different (less formal) time
- Permit students to take tests in smaller groups
- Permit students to underline key terms in test questions (as an aid to recall)
- Provide liberal access to water and snacks during the test (for relaxing the thoughts)
- Lead class in practicing deep-breathing exercises at strategic points during the test (which calms students and helps them to focus)

(Adapted from Morris, 2010)

INTERVENTIONS USING CURRICULUM-BASED ASSESSMENT

The term *curriculum-based assessment* (CBA) aggressively appeared in the school psychology literature during the 1980s, although its conceptual roots have been around (though not necessarily recognized in school psychology) in earlier decades. CBA can be defined as "any set of measurement procedures that use direct observation and recording of a student's performance in the local curriculum as a basis for gathering information to make instructional decisions" (Deno, 1987, p. 41). CBA is a broad umbrella term that represents a larger number of distinct assessment procedures that form the foundation for both assessing students' academic skills and providing information that is useful for intervention. Shinn, Rosenfield, and Knutson (1989) wrote a seminal article that described four models of CBA used in educational diagnostic and intervention work with vulnerable learners.

One of the models, called *curriculum-based measurement* (CBM), is the most well known within school psychology and currently forms the basis for special education identification procedures in a few school districts nationwide (e.g., see Bollman, Silberglitt, & Gibbons, 2007). CBM employs brief fluency measures in the basic and readiness skills reading, spelling, math, and written expression content areas. The essence of the CBM approach is to monitor student progress weekly, beginning at the start of the school year, in skills expected to be mastered by the *end* of a school year. Both administration and scoring directions are standardized, and the actual measures used are based on extensive programs of technical adequacy research (Fuchs & Fuchs, 2002; Hosp

& Hosp, 2003). Through the use of trend lines, the progress of target students is compared with the progress of a norm group, and the discrepancy in trend-line slopes or absolute levels of attainment are evaluated for special education decision making within a Response-to-Intervention (RTI; see also Glossary) framework (Case, Speece, & Molloy, 2003; Dexter & Hughes, 2011).

In addition to using CBM procedures, school psychologists can utilize their curriculum-based assessment skills from three other CBA models discussed by Shinn et al. to assist teachers in helping struggling learners (of any ethnicity, language, or racial group). These three CBA models are *Curriculum-Based Assessment for Instructional Design* (CBA-ID), *Criterion-Referenced Curriculum-Based Assessment* (CR-CBA), and *Curriculum-Based Evaluation* (CBE). Examples of how these three assessment models can be applied to intervention work is briefly described as follows.

Curriculum-Based Assessment for Instructional Design (CBA-ID)

In explaining how to understand academic failure within an Instructional Consultation model, Rosenfield (1987) discussed the concept of the "instructional mismatch" between vulnerable learners and a "muddled" design of classroom tasks. In a nutshell, vulnerable learners who interact with classroom tasks that are too difficult for them experience significant frustration and failure in schools. Conversely, vulnerable learners who interact with tasks that are consistently too easy for them (i.e., do not provide a sufficient degree of challenge) are likely to become bored and disengaged. Under the CBA-ID philosophy, the optimal condition is to have students interact as frequently as possible with tasks that provide the appropriate degree of challenge, but yet are sufficiently familiar in order to provide a high rate of success. Gickling and others developed a straightforward assessment paradigm that school psychologists and other educational diagnosticians can use to facilitate a better instructional match between struggling students and tasks, thereby providing the optimal degree of intellectual challenge (Gickling & Havertape, 1981; Gickling & Thompson, 1985; Gravois & Gickling, 2008).

A CBA-ID assessment intervention begins with an analysis of the classroom tasks on which a student is experiencing significant failure (which, in most instances, is first identified by teachers). The task on which the student experiences difficulty is broken down into its constituent units. For reading tasks, these units represent the individual words read. For math computation tasks, these units represent individual computation problems. For spelling tasks, the units represent individual words spelled. The interventionist assesses student performance on the difficult task by subdividing and categorizing task units into "knowns" versus "unknowns." *Knowns* represent units that the student has no difficulty performing correctly, accurately, and rapidly. For reading tasks, known units are words that are instantly pronounced correctly, with no hesitation. For math computation and spelling tasks, known units are problems computed or words spelled rapidly and accurately. *Unknowns* represent units on which the student cannot perform the correct answer, or units on which the student is significantly hesitant or slow in performing the correct answer. For example, if a student cannot correctly decode the word *neighbor*, or pauses for five or more seconds before saying this word correctly, then *neighbor* is an unknown unit in the reading decoding task.

According to Gickling and his associates, tasks can be subdivided into three categories that reflect the relative ease or difficulty with which students can perform on the task. Tasks that are at the *frustration level* are experienced by the student as being too difficult, where the proportion of unknown to known units is high. Tasks that are at the *independent level* represent maximum comfort and ease for students, because the proportion of unknown to known units is very low. Optimally, tasks that are at the *instructional level* are easy enough to maintain students' interest, yet are difficult enough so that they challenge the student. Students profit most from classroom tasks at the instructional level and least from tasks at the frustrational level. The goal of a CBA-ID intervention is to take tasks that are at the *frustrational level* for students and modify them to fall within the *instructional level* range for vulnerable students as they learn.

Gravois and Gickling (2008) review literature designed to determine optimal unknown-to-known ratios for *instructional level* tasks. They note that various *best-fit ratios* have been generated from this research, which have been found to vary slightly as a function of idiosyncratic study characteristics, the nature of the population under investigation, and the nature of the instructional tasks used. They conclude that an unknown units to total units ratio of 30 percent or more unknowns is at *frustration level* for most tasks; a ratio of 11 percent to 29 percent unknowns is at *instructional level* for most tasks; and a ratio of 10 percent or fewer unknowns will be at an *independent level* for most tasks. However, individual researchers have recommended smaller proportions of unknowns (e.g., 3 percent to 7 percent) for instructional tasks as a function of the nature of the task under consideration (e.g., see comprehension versus rehearsal/practice tasks discussed by Gravois & Gickling, 2008).

An Illustration of a CBA-ID Intervention With a Reading Task

The application of a CBA-ID assessment/intervention can be illustrated in the reading domain. Suppose a teacher requests consultation for reading problems she is having with a third-grade student. The teacher complains that Freddie struggles with reading tasks and experiences significant difficulty with word decoding in grade-level material. These struggles have led to auxiliary behavior problems in the classroom. The school psychologist decides to privately assess Freddie's word decoding skills on a brief passage in a basal reader that the class is currently using. The school psychologist makes a copy of the reading passage on which to follow as the child reads. The reading passage, entitled "One Day at the Park," is shown in Sidebar 6.8.

Sidebar 6.8   Curriculum-Based Assessment for Instructional Design: Transition Stories in Reading

TARGET STORY

One Day at the Park

Bill <u>wandered</u> away from his teacher and class <u>while</u> they were <u>visiting</u> the park. After an <u>hour</u> passed, Bill looked up and said to <u>himself</u>, "I am not in the park, I am in the <u>mountains</u>." Bill <u>yelled</u> <u>loudly</u>, but his teacher and class did not <u>answer</u>. Bill's teacher had told the class that bears live in the <u>mountains</u>. Bill was <u>afraid</u> that a bear <u>would</u> come out of the <u>mountains</u> and eat him up.

After a <u>while</u> Bill saw a <u>sign</u> that said "Big Pines <u>Ranger</u> <u>Station</u>." Bill's uncle Don works at Big Pines <u>Ranger</u> <u>Station</u>. Bill <u>became</u> very <u>excited</u> and <u>yelled</u> "Help!" very <u>loudly</u>. Soon, he <u>heard</u> the <u>voice</u> of his uncle Don. When Bill saw uncle Don, the teacher and class were with him. They <u>laughed</u> very hard at Bill when he came down from the <u>mountains</u>. Bill <u>smiled</u> and said, "I am so glad that you are not bears!"

- (A) Total words in story (including title): 159
- (B) Total occurrences of unknown words (underlined): 28
- Percentage story unknowns to knowns (B/A): 17 percent

Known Words (in addition to story words not underlined):

about	book	dog	good	into	make	no
add	boy(s)	dress	grass	it	man	not
again	bus	egg	green	jump	map	old
air	but	end	gun	just	mark	open
all	call	even	hand	keep	may	play
an	can	fat	has	kid	maybe	pool
any	car	feed	head	kill	me	ride
asked	cat	feet	her	last	mean	run
bag	clock	fish	hill	late	men	sad
ball	cook	flew	hit	leg	mom	so
be	cow	for	hole	let's	more	then
bed	cut	fun	home	like	my	too
bird	dad	get	hot	long	name	took
black	did	girl	how	look	near	who
boat	do	go	if	lot	neck	will

(continued)

TRANSITION STORY 1

One Day at the Park

Bill's uncle Don works at the park, so Bill was glad to go to the park. Bill's teacher and class were at the park. Bill looked up and saw a bird at the park. Bill <u>laughed</u> when he looked up and saw the bird. When Bill <u>laughed</u>, a bear <u>wandered</u> to the park. Bill looked up and said, "A bear!" The bear looked up and saw the bird, and said, "A bird!" The bird <u>laughed</u> at the bear, and the bear <u>laughed</u> at the bird. The bear <u>wandered</u> away from Bill and to the bird. Then the bird flew away. When Bill looked up and saw his teacher and class at the park, Bill said, "I saw a bird that <u>laughed</u> at a bear!" The class <u>laughed</u>, and the teacher <u>laughed</u>. The teacher said to the class, "Bill <u>wandered</u> away too long. Too, too long. Maybe Bill is a bird!"

   NOTE: Previously unknown words introduced: *laughed, wandered*

- (A) Total words in story (including title): 155
- (B) Total occurrences of unknown words (underlined): 10
- Percentage story unknowns to knowns (B/A): 6 percent

TRANSITION STORY 2

One Day at the Park

Bill was glad to go to the park to play with his teacher and the boys in his class. The boys said to Bill, "Uncle Don is in the <u>mountains</u>!" Bill asked, "When will he come down from the <u>mountains</u>?" The teacher <u>yelled</u> for Uncle Don. The class <u>yelled</u> for Uncle Don. Then Bill <u>yelled</u> for Uncle Don. Bill <u>yelled</u> again for Uncle Don. The teacher said, "Uncle Don will come down from the <u>mountains</u> when Bill <u>yelled</u>." Soon, the bird flew down from the <u>mountains</u>. The bird said, "Who <u>yelled</u>?" Soon, a bear came down from the <u>mountains</u>. Then, Uncle Don wandered down from the <u>mountains</u>. The bear said, "Who <u>yelled</u>?" The bird said, "Who <u>yelled</u>?" Uncle Don said, "Who <u>yelled</u>?" The teacher and the class looked at Bill. Bill looked down at his feet. Then Bill looked up and said, "I <u>yelled</u>!" The teacher, the class, and Uncle Don laughed and laughed. Bill laughed and said, "I had fun one day at the park!" The bear, the bird, the class, the teacher, and Uncle Don all had fun one day at the park.

   NOTE: *Laughed* and *wandered* are now knowns; previously unknown words introduced: *mountains, yelled*

- (A) Total words in story (including title): 190
- (B) Total occurrences of unknown words (underlined): 16
- Percentage story unknowns to knowns (B/A): 8 percent

As Freddie reads, the school psychologist underlines all words that are either not pronounced correctly, not pronounced at all, or are pronounced correctly only after a delay of five or more seconds. These underlined words represent the unknown units in the passage. In order to obtain a valid assessment, the school psychologist does not correct mispronunciations or provide corrections to Freddie as he reads. The percentage of unknown units, divided by the total number of units in the passage, is 17 percent, which is determined to be at an unacceptable frustration level for this student (given teacher comments about Freddie's reading performance in relation to classroom peers).

Next, the school psychologist gathers additional data necessary for developing transitional reading passages on which Freddie can perform at an instructional level. The school psychologist gathers word lists and basal reading passages appropriate for earlier grades and has Freddie read these so that the school psychologist can develop a pool of known words that can be used later in transitional stories.

In making transitional stories, the school psychologist limits the new words to be practiced to only a few words at a time, which is necessary for maximizing the proportion of known words and building Freddie's reading confidence. As shown in Sidebar 6.8, the percentage of unknown words in the first transitional passage has been reduced to 6 percent. In creating transition stories that maximize learning, the school psychologist uses frequent repetition of known word phrases and unknown words to be learned. Once the school psychologist is assured that Freddie can read the first transition story smoothly with no unknowns (after explicit teaching of the unknown words), the previously unknown words from the target story now have become known words. The stage is set for the school psychologist to develop a second transition story (see Sidebar 6.8), which again introduces a small number of additional unknown words from the original target story. This process continues for as many iterations as needed until the student has gradually transitioned into being able to smoothly read the original target reading passage. The speed at which the student catches up to his or her classroom peers (if at all) is a function of how focused the student is in interacting with and mastering transition tasks.

This intervention provides a useful template for interventionists to apply to any academic task that is susceptible to being broken down into measurable and observable units that can be categorized as knowns or unknowns. As with any academic intervention, there are challenges that require forethought and planning. The effective use of this intervention assumes that the interventionist has both the time and expertise to create effective transition tasks to use during the length of the intervention. If the school psychologist has limited time (particularly given a large intervention caseload), then it may be useful to train peer tutors, resource teachers, university practicum students, and/or parents in the fundamentals of this approach to use with academically vulnerable students.

Criterion-Referenced Curriculum-Based Assessment (CR-CBA)

Criterion-Referenced Curriculum-Based Assessment has been defined as "the practice of obtaining direct and frequent measures of a student's performance on a series of sequentially arranged objectives derived from the curriculum used in the classroom" (Blankenship, 1985, p. 244, quoted in Shinn et al., 1989, p. 301). The CR-CBA model begins with the recognition that the teacher's responsibility is to ensure that the class learns the skills necessary for mastering instructional objectives that are hierarchically arranged and temporally sequenced in a coherent manner. For example, in most commercial math curricula, addition is taught before subtraction; addition that does not involve regrouping is taught before addition that involves regrouping; place value concepts are taught before addition involving decimals. Any one of these singular objectives can be further broken down into sub-objectives that reflect sequenced learning in even smaller steps.

The CR-CBA model is based on the assumption that problems in mastering a particular objective most likely can be attributed to a failure to master earlier objectives in the instructional sequence. The essence of the CR-CBA assessment model is to first pinpoint the hierarchical sequence of earlier objectives that may be helpful in understanding why students are having difficulty mastering a later or more complex objective. By translating earlier objectives into "mini achievement tests" (via the creation of specific skill probes), students can be assessed in prerequisite skills that can more closely identify the area of student difficulty, and the resulting information can be used by teachers to tailor instruction to the students' unique needs. There are two major ways that tasks can be broken down into constituent parts so that a student's instructional needs can be assessed: through identification of skill hierarchies or by conducting a task analysis.

Identification of Skill Hierarchies

A skill hierarchy is a logical sequence of skills in an academic curriculum area, where simpler skills and/or concepts precede more advanced skills and/or concepts. For example, in order for a first-grade student to be proficient in elementary word recognition skills, he or she must first be able to discriminate likenesses/differences in shapes and letters, match the same letters written in different type fonts, or efficiently identify the same letter written in an upper-/lower-case format. In order for a second-grade student to be proficient in decoding four- or five-letter words, he or she must first be able to correctly identify three-letter consonant-vowel-consonant words, correctly apply the rule that activates a long vowel sound whenever an *e* is at the end of a word (e.g., in *make, dine, zone*).

Performing a Task Analysis

Some complex tasks cannot be broken down into skill hierarchies, because successful task completion involves mastering a set of procedures performed correctly and in the proper sequence. In this instance, a *task analysis* is the more appropriate analytical procedure to use in a CR-CBA. In a task analysis, the essential procedural components of a particular skill or task are isolated in order to pinpoint specific procedures that are weak or underdeveloped. As an example, the complex skill of driving an automobile can be subjected to a task analysis. Here, the essential component skills that are involved in driving a car can be sequenced as follows:

a. Adjust the driver's seat to a comfortable position upon entering the car
b. Attach the driver seatbelt
c. Place foot on the brake pedal (and keep it in place until ready for the car to move)
d. Turn on the engine with the ignition key
e. If driving at night, turn on the car lights
f. Adjust the left sideview mirror, the center car mirror, and right passenger mirror to positions that allow clear viewing of the road/cars toward the rear of the vehicle
g. Release the emergency brake
h. Look in all mirrors and the windshields to see if cars are approaching from either the rear or front of the vehicle
i. Shift the car into gear
j. Gently release foot from the brake pedal
k. Gently press the gas pedal (to enter traffic, back out of garage, etc.)

To the novice driver, these 11 steps represent a bewildering array of procedures that initially seem almost impossible to remember and sequence accurately. However, with sufficient practice and repetition, experienced drivers become so automatic with these steps that they are barely conscious of them when driving. If an instructor finds, for example, that a new driver has difficulty remembering Step h (i.e., checking mirrors before moving), then an intervention can be designed that makes this step salient in the driving algorithm. With sufficient practice and repetition in driving interventions that highlight the importance of Step h, the new driver can correctly perform the complex driving task.

An Illustration of CR-CBA Interventions With a Math Task

A CR-CBA intervention using a skill hierarchy and task analysis approach is shown in Sidebars 6.9 and 6.10, respectively.

As an illustration of a skill hierarchy analysis, suppose that a teacher requests consultation for a student who is currently struggling with double-digit times double-digit multiplication skills practiced in the classroom. The teacher shows the interventionist a worksheet showing multiple errors on these types of computation problems. The CR-CBA approach begins by identifying the prerequisite skills that must be sequentially mastered in order to be proficient at the current task on which the student is failing. If the interventionist does not already know how to construct a hierarchy of prerequisite skills that must be mastered before demonstrating proficiency in double-digit times double-digit multiplication, then he or she may wish to consult math teaching manuals, published math curriculum guides, or published criterion-referenced tests for identifying prerequisite skills.

In this hypothetical scenario, the interventionist can reasonably assume that double-digit times double-digit multiplication without regrouping is taught before regrouping skills, and double-digit times single-digit multiplication is taught before double-digit times double-digit multiplication. Fundamentally, all multidigit multiplication tasks assume proficiency with single-digit multiplication facts. Because a portion of the algorithm for successfully completing double-digit times double-digit multiplication problems involves proficiency with addition, then multidigit addition facts (with and without regrouping) are also a necessary prerequisite. The point is, only by administering prerequisite skill probes can the interventionist pinpoint the source of the difficulty with the original double-digit times double-digit multiplication task. Once this information is shared with teachers, it is more likely that the teacher can use this information to modify instruction for the struggling student. Examples of prerequisite skills that are taught before double-digit times double-digit multiplication are shown in Sidebar 6.9.

◿ Sidebar 6.9   Criterion-Referenced Curriculum-Based Assessment: Skill Hierarchy Analysis for Double-Digit Times Double-Digit Multiplication

Target Skill

- Double-Digit Times Double-Digit Multiplication With Regrouping
  (e.g., $45 \times 56 = \square$)

Prerequisite Skills (Latest to Earliest)

- Double-Digit Times Double-Digit Multiplication Without Regrouping
  (e.g., $23 \times 13 = \square$)
- Double-Digit Times Single-Digit Multiplication With Regrouping
  (e.g., $45 \times 6 = \square$)
- Double-Digit Times Single-Digit Multiplication Without Regrouping
  (e.g., $23 \times 3 = \square$)
- Single-Digit Times Single-Digit Multiplication Facts
  (e.g., $3 \times 7 = \square$)

- Three-Digit Plus Four-Digit Addition With Regrouping
  (e.g., $276 + 2259 = \square$)
- Three-Digit Plus Four-Digit Addition Without Regrouping
  (e.g., $270 + 2210 = \square$)
- Three-Digit Plus Three-Digit Addition With Regrouping
  (e.g., $648 + 378 = \square$)
- Three-Digit Plus Three-Digit Addition Without Regrouping
  (e.g., $648 + 211 = \square$)
- Double-Digit Plus Double-Digit Addition With Regrouping
  (e.g., $37 + 58 = \square$)
- Double-Digit Plus Double-Digit Addition Without Regrouping
  (e.g., $37 + 31 = \square$)
- Double-Digit Plus Single-Digit Addition With Regrouping
  (e.g., $37 + 8 = \square$)
- Double-Digit Plus Single-Digit Addition Without Regrouping
  (e.g., $37 + 2 = \square$)
- Single-Digit Plus Single-Digit Addition Facts
  (e.g., $3 + 5 = \square$)

A different kind of approach to conducting a CR-CBA is presented in Sidebar 6.10. Here, it is assumed that finding the solution to double-digit times double-digit math problems is taught by requiring students to follow a prescribed set of procedural steps, as is often the case as math becomes more difficult in the upper elementary grades. In the first example, it is assumed that the student makes procedural errors at the point in which he or she must use regrouping skills after multiplying the numbers in the ones column. The first intervention probe consists of simple problems asking students to indicate (by circling Y for YES or N for NO) whether or not a double-digit times double-digit multiplication problem requires regrouping. By giving students extensive practice in this rudimentary step, they will become sensitized to, and proficient in, this step in future problems. The second intervention probe requires the student to simply evaluate the first multiplication step (i.e., multiplying numbers in the ones column) and to write the ones column number in the product in the bottom box, then carry the tens column number of the product in the top box. By limiting the skill to be mastered to just this step, the student is exposed to frequent practice and error correction in this important step in the procedural algorithm.

Sidebar 6.10   Criterion-Referenced Curriculum-Based Assessment: Task Analysis Using Sequenced Probes for Double-Digit Times Double Digit Multiplication

Target Skill

- Double-Digit Times Double-Digit Multiplication With Regrouping (e.g., $45 \times 56 = \Box$)

<u>Probe 1</u>: When shown a series of _____ double-digit times double-digit multiplication problems, the student will indicate whether the problem requires regrouping (Y for YES) or does not require regrouping (N for NO) by circling the correct answer, getting _____ out of _____ problems correct.

24	58	97	84	14	23
× 35	× 18	× 45	× 50	× 21	× 22
Y / N	Y / N	Y / N	Y / N	Y / N	Y / N

<u>Probe 2</u>: When shown a series of _____ double-digit times double-digit multiplication problems, the student will write the correct number in the box under the ones column and the correct number (if needed) in the box above the tens column.

□	□	□	□
24	36	75	47
× 35	× 16	× 24	× 33
□	□	□	□

<u>Probe 3</u>: When shown a series of _____ double-digit times double-digit multiplication problems with zero included in the ones column in the products step, the student will write in the remaining correct numbers for _____ out of _____ problems.

58	43	52	67
× 18	× 39	× 48	× 93
_ _ _	_ _ _	_ _ _	_ _ _
_ _ 0	_ _ 0	_ _ 0	_ _ 0
_ _ _ _	_ _ _ _	_ _ _ _	_ _ _ _

Probe 4: When shown a two-digit number, the student will rewrite the number as a tens and ones number, making no errors.

	Number	Tens	Ones
(Sample)	68	60	8
	71	—	—
	50	—	—
	26	—	—

Probe 5: After being shown a correctly worked double-digit times double-digit multiplication problem based on the distributive property, the student will write the correct products in the spaces, making no more than one error (adapted from Ashlock, 2010).

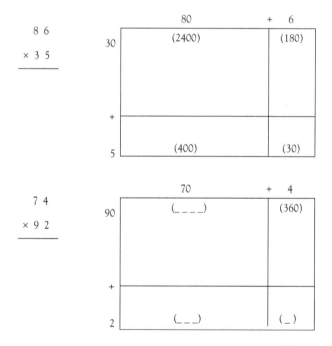

Probe 6: After being shown a correctly worked double-digit times double-digit multiplication problem based on the distributive property, the student will sum all products to arrive at the correct answer, making no more than one error (adapted from Ashlock, 2010).

(continued)

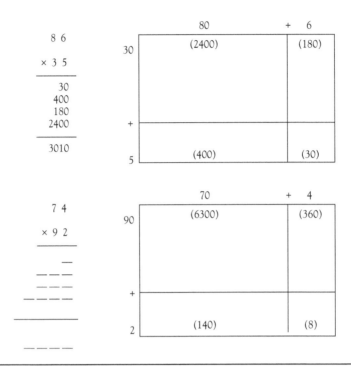

Suppose that a student is discovered to consistently show difficulty with the step that requires him or her to place a zero in the ones column in the second line of the summation of all products. A third probe can be designed that includes the zero in the appropriate step in all problems. Here, the student is required to provide the product numbers to all multiplication steps (except the zero) before adding them all. Regular and frequent practice in probes of this type reinforces inclusion of the zero in the appropriate step in the multiplication process. Subsequent probes can be used that gradually "fade out" the zero, where it is hoped that students will have learned to automatically include it in its proper position.

Suppose that the *distributive property* (see Glossary) of math equations are taught and emphasized in the classroom. A CR-CBA task analysis requires that the interventionist break down the task into procedural elements that are unique to this type of math instruction. Many assessment probes can be designed to provide students with practice at a variety of steps in the multiplication algorithm. In the fourth example, a simple probe can be designed that requires students only to separate a double-digit number into its tens and ones components. Once this is mastered, additional probes can carefully guide students through the proper steps (based on the distributive property) of solving multiplication problems. In the fifth example, students are first shown a correctly worked problem, then are required to fill in the proper products in the appropriate cells. In the sixth example, students are also shown a correctly worked problem, then are required to align the correct products in the math problem before providing the final sum.

Curriculum-Based Evaluation (CBE)

Curriculum-Based Evaluation (CBE) shares with Criterion-Referenced Curriculum-Based Assessment (CR-CBA) an emphasis on breaking down performance on complex tasks into skill hierarchies or task analyses (Shinn et al., 1989). The most salient feature of a CBE perspective, however, is to conduct a thorough *error analysis* of students' work in order to develop reasonable hypotheses as to why students are not performing as expected (Howell & Morehead, 1987). Once reasonable error hypotheses are generated, these hypotheses are tested with specific skill probes that are targeted specifically to the subskill responsible for poor performance in the original task.

An Illustration of a CBE Intervention With a Spelling Task

The results from a hypothetical spelling task administered to a fourth-grade student is shown in Sidebar 6.11. From analyzing the errors made for each word, coupled with knowledge of common phonetic rules for correct word spelling, the interventionist can arrive at a reasonably accurate hypothesis as to the source of the spelling error. Next, assessment probes requiring responses in several different modalities (e.g., "see/say," "hear/write") can be designed that target the specific error requiring correction. Examples of sample items within such error correction probes are shown in Sidebar 6.11.

Sidebar 6.11   Curriculum-Based Evaluation: Probe Templates Designed for Assessing and Remediating Spelling Errors

Objective: Discriminating the correct spelling application of the 'ie' versus 'ei' digraph words with the long ē sound

- **Probe (hear/write):** Oral dictation of *ie* and *ei* digraph words (*receive, retrieve, conceive, grieve, achieve, perceive, deceive, believe*); student writes words
- **Probe (see/write):** Fill in the blank with either an *ie* or *ei* digraph:
  - rec__ve, retr__ve, conc__ve, gr__ve, achi__ve, perc__ve, dec__ve, bel__ve

(continued)

Objective: *Discriminating soft vs. hard consonant sounds and their spellings*

- **Probe (hear/write):** Oral dictation of hard and soft words beginning with consonant *g* or *c* (*go, genie, civil, crown, cents, crash, gentle, great, giraffe, germ, group*); student writes words
- **Probe (see/write):** Circle the correct word (focus on correct identification of soft consonant words):
  - I paid Jim in dollars and (cents, sents).
  - I (urje, urge) you to vote for my candidate.
  - Bill tried to move the chair, but it would not (budge, budje).
  - The ballerina was a good (danser, dancer).

Objective: *Discriminating correct usage of 'oy' vs. 'oi' digraphs*

- **Probe (see/write):** Read sheet of sentences in which a word may be spelled incorrectly; student must cross out and correct misspelled words
  - The bois and girls all played outside.
  - It was quite a joi to see you today.
  - Mary did a good job playing with her tois.
  - Please joyn me in moving this couch.
- **Probe (see/write):** The following sentences presented to students on a worksheet; student must fill in missing letters
  - Please be quiet and stop making _oi_ _ (noise).
  - After coming through the front door, meet me in the _ oy_ _ (foyer).
  - The beauty queen showed grace and _ oi_ _ (poise).
  - The politician is very _ oy _ _ (loyal) to his party.

ADDITIONAL RESOURCES

Supplemental Readings

Language Proficiency Assessment

Gottlieb, M., & Hamayan, E. (2007). Assessing oral and written language proficiency: A guide for psychologists and teachers. In A. E. Brice (Ed.), *Multicultural handbook of school psychology: An interdisciplinary perspective* (pp. 245–264). New York, NY: Routledge.

Rhodes, R. L., Ochoa, S. H., & Ortiz, S. O. (2005). *Assessing culturally and linguistically diverse students: A practical guide.* New York, NY: Guilford Press.

Standardized Test Accommodations for ELL Students

Bolt, S. E., & Roach, A. T. (2009). *Inclusive assessment and accountability: A guide to accommodations for students with diverse needs.* New York, NY: Guilford Press.

Educational Testing Service. (2009). Guidelines for the assessment of English Language Learners. Accessed January 2012 from http://www.ets.org/Media/About_ETS/pdf/ELL_Guidelines.pdf

Kopriva, R. J. (2008). *Improving testing for English Language Learners.* New York, NY: Routledge.

Study Skills

Woodcock, S. K. (2009). *SOAR study skills: A simple and efficient system for earning better grades in less time.* Grand Blanc, MI: Grand Lighthouse Publishing.

Test-Taking Support

Cizek, G. J., & Burg, S. S. (2006). *Addressing test anxiety in a high stakes environment: Strategies for classrooms and schools.* Thousand Oaks, CA: Corwin Press.

Durham, G. (2007). *Teaching test-taking skills: Proven techniques to boost your students' scores.* Lanham, MD: Rowman & Littlefield.

Fuhrken, C. (2009). *What every elementary teacher needs to know about reading tests (from someone who has written them).* Portland, ME: Stenhouse Publishers.

Grossberg, B. (2009). *Test success: Test-taking and study strategies for all students including those with ADD and LD.* Plantation, FL: Specialty Press/ADD Warehouse.

Learning Express. (2007). *Test-taking power strategies.* New York, NY: Learning Express.

Rozakis, L. (2003). *Test taking strategies and study skills for the utterly confused.* New York, NY: McGraw-Hill.

Curriculum-Based Assessment

Hall, T., & Mengel, M. (2002). *Curriculum-based evaluations.* Wakefield, MA: National Center on Accessing the General Curriculum. Retrieved January 2012 from http://aim.cast.org/learn/historyarchive/backgroundpapers/curriculum-based_evaluations.

Websites

Study Skills: http://www.homeworkandstudyskills.com/studylinks.html

National Center on Student Progress Monitoring: Documents describing research on progress monitoring in school districts may be accessed here: http://www.studentprogress.org/library/articles.asp

CHAPTER

7

------◆-◆------

School Discipline and Behavior Management

MS 739 (a pseudonym) has been called New York City's worst-performing middle school by one newspaper article writer (Edelman, 2011). According to insideschools.org, the school's racial/ethnic makeup is 75 percent black and 24 percent Hispanic. The school also has the dubious distinction of making the state's notorious list of "persistently dangerous" schools. One teacher who worked at the school reported being pushed, shoved, scratched, thrown against the wall, spit on, and pickpocketed by students. This same teacher also reported finding a used condom that was anonymously placed in her purse at school. One male teacher is reported to have transferred out of the school after a student threatened to rape his wife. The overall atmosphere of the school can only be described as "hellish." According to Edelman (2011), students hoot and yell so loudly during class that the noise drowns out the teacher. Students have been known to literally throw books and supplies out of the windows. Class trash cans are overturned, and the classroom floors are littered with garbage during school hours. Mouse droppings have been found on class computers. Weaker students are routinely robbed by tougher kids at school, with little to no intervention by the school administration. Academics at MS 739 are equally abysmal, no doubt as a result of the general level of chaos and mayhem that characterizes school life. According to a description of the school's academic performance on insideschools.org (http://inside schools.org/?fs=1745), as of 2010, only 3 percent of students were on grade level in English language arts, and only 9 percent were on grade level in math. As of April 2011, insideschools.org reports that the school will be closed down after years of poor academic performance.

Contrast this scenario with another taken from McCloskey's (2008) account of a day in the life of Rice High, a Harlem Catholic high school serving essentially a similar pool of urban minority students:

> On the first day of class . . . Christopher M. Abbasse stands at the top of the flight of stairs that lead from Rice's front door up to the foyer. As Rice's current dean of students, Abbasse fulfills his duties with enough strictness to establish that he is firmly in charge of behavioral standards from the first minute of the school year. Every morning, Abbasse greets the students to "make sure they're dressed properly and to set a business-like tone for the day. . . . Otherwise they'll shuffle into cafeteria all disheveled, listening to their head-phones, and talking on their cell phones." . . .
>
> Ricky springs up the one front step to grab Rice's door. Hanging over his head on the glass bricks above the door is a sign with green letters on gold proclaiming: RICE MEN WELCOME TO SUCCESS! You are worthy! "Excuse me," a voice slams Ricky the moment his foot lands in the school vestibule. "Take off that hat before you come in the building." . . . [Ricky] swipes the black do-rag . . . from his head and stuffs it into his book bag. From now on, he'll do this automatically as soon as he crosses Rice's threshold.
>
> This simple gesture concretizes Rice's educational prerequisite: discipline based on respect and reinforced by constant adult supervision. . . . Rice is small enough to function as a family in which new teachers will soon know all the students by name. It's also a family in the traditional sense that the adults in charge impose consequences for missteps. Being late even by one second after the bell rings . . . earns an automatic detention. Five lates or absences warrant an in-school suspension.
>
> With such a focus on acting correctly, neither Rice nor any Catholic school in the country needs the metal detectors that have been installed at entrances to New York City's public junior high and high schools. Although the same proportion of Rice students would be eligible for the free or reduced lunch program—the standard measure of poverty—as their peers at zoned public high schools (where violence is as common as it is underreported), they wouldn't dare bring a weapon to class. . . . The Rice handbook states: "Any behavior, in or outside of school, that reflects unfavorably on Rice High School will bring immediate expulsion."
>
> One of Abbasse's major challenges over the first weeks of September will be to impress this behavioral ethos on the freshmen before anyone faces the con-sequence. . . . Once the students get past Abbasse's inspection, they walk along the side of the foyer past the school office, and then turn left under an archway

mounted with posters listing the 105 names on last year's honor roll. This is Rice's Arc de Triomphe, which [was] installed so students would have to pass beneath it every morning and at lunch. . . .

Success at Rice rests on [the] ability to keep street culture out of the school and create an attractive alternative. Urban Catholic schools stop gang activity and other street rivalries at the front door, as symbolized when Rice students take the do-rags off their heads as they step into the building. The ritual is almost sacramental. The young men instantly lose their street swagger and transform into students not much different than their peers at predominantly white Catholic schools. Securing the school's psychological perimeters via discipline and structure allows Orlando to offer his boys an option that is both a proven, traditional path to manhood and one that nurtures the young men's African American or Hispanic identity without developing a false sense of self-esteem. (pp. 43–48, 206)

Reprinted with permission from University of California Press.

DISCIPLINE AS A FUNDAMENTAL PRIORITY THAT SUPPORTS ACADEMICS

These examples show that without effective discipline and behavior management in schools and classrooms, there can be no effective learning. When students matriculate through schools year after year and are exposed to a lax school environment that is largely apathetic to the development of key behaviors that support learning and academic achievement, the deleterious effects can seem almost insurmountable.

Behavior modification is an equal opportunity scientific construct. That is to say, its fundamental principles are applicable to all human beings regardless of their race, ethnicity, or language. Stated bluntly, all human beings are more likely to engage in behaviors for which they are consistently rewarded, and similarly are more likely to refrain from behaviors for which they are punished or not rewarded. There is no credible research in behavioral modification, of which this author is aware, that has uncovered qualitatively distinct principles for modifying the behavior of individuals who belong to different racial, ethnic, or language groups. To be sure, a middle-schooler living in Pakistan may be motivated to clean up his room if he is promised to receive a Bal Mithai (small chocolate fudge-coated sugar balls), while a similar-aged New Yorker is motivated by an ice cream sundae. Despite this superficial cultural difference, both children are similar in being motivated to emit a desired behavior by the promise of their favorite dessert.

Yet even among individuals sharing the same ethnic group, applied behavior specialists in schools recognize that the effectiveness of different positive and negative contingencies varies widely as a function of *individual differences, not group stereotypes*. One child may be terrified at a threat from an angry teacher to call the student's parents at home, whereas another child may simply laugh it off.

The rank-and-file school psychologist has been socialized by his or her profession and training program to apply behavior modification principles typically within the context of individual teacher consultation activities or participation in school behavior support team meetings for individual problem students. Contemporary school psychologists may also learn about schoolwide programs such as Positive Behavioral Support (e.g., see Sugai, Horner, & McIntosh, 2008), and they may serve on school-based teams for helping to get such schoolwide programs off the ground and running smoothly.

Many excellent texts guide school psychologists in working with teachers and school teams to design behavioral interventions for individual students, classes, and schools (e.g., Bambara & Kern, 2005; Crone, Hawken, & Horner, 2010; Schloss & Smith, 1998). The principles elucidated in these texts are applicable to students from all ethnic and racial backgrounds (e.g., see Frank, Horner, & Anderson, 2011), provided that basic conditions are in place that support cooperation among the school administration, teaching staff, and students.

The PATHS Program

One brand-name program (see Glossary) for improving behavior in traditional schools is the Promoting Alternative Thinking Strategies (PATHS) program. The PATHS curriculum is a program for educators and counselors that is designed to facilitate the development of self-control, emotional awareness, social competence, and interpersonal problem-solving skills in elementary school-aged children. The program is based on the theory that young children's language functions can be trained to be a cognitive mediator for regulating emotions. This, in turn, will help children to (a) become less impulsive and more planful in their social interactions, and (b) use language to regulate their behavior and communicate more effectively with others.

The PATHS curriculum is organized into grade-specific classroom modules for Pre-K/Kindergarten, Grade 1, Grade 2, Grade 3, Grade 4, and Grades 5/6. The curriculum is taught two to three times per week for a minimum of 20 to 30 minutes per day. According to promotional materials, the PATHS curriculum provides teachers with systematic, developmentally based lessons, materials, and instructions to facilitate their students' emotional literacy, self-control, social competence, positive peer relations, and interpersonal problem-solving skills. In some venues, the PATHS curriculum is touted as a violence-prevention curriculum for elementary school-aged students. The PATHS curriculum is designed to be taught by regular classroom teachers and integrated into regular classroom lessons. The program emphasizes the development of students' generalization skills for applying competencies throughout the school day to new contexts.

The PATHS curriculum consists of an instruction manual, curriculum manuals, feelings pictures and photographs, and additional materials. A research book is also available.

The PATHS curriculum has been studied intensively in a series of randomized trials over the past 30 years. These include controlled trials with regular children (including sizeable numbers of ethnic/racial minority children), special education–classified children, and deaf/hearing-impaired children. Studies have been conducted in both urban and rural contexts. Particularly noteworthy are the results from a study that examined the effects of the PATHS curriculum in a group of inner-city public schools with very low academic performance and high rates of poverty (i.e., the majority of children receiving free and reduced lunch; Kam, Greenberg, & Walls, 2003). The researchers found that in classrooms where teachers implemented the program in a high-quality fashion, and where the school principal showed strong support, significant decreases in aggression were found within the first four months of program implementation (see also Bardon, Dona, & Symons, 2008).

The PATHS program developers recommend that interested educators participate in a two-day workshop followed by phone/e-mail consultation as the program is being implemented in schools (see contact information in the Additional Resources section at the end of this chapter).

The Rise of Paternalistic Schools

Unfortunately, many inner-city schools serving low-income minority students are plagued by a critical mass of low-functioning and academically unmotivated students, school violence, low teacher morale, minimal student expectations, and administrator/staff incompetence—such that basic disciplinary standards are poor to nonexistent.

Such poor-performing schools have not escaped the attention of popular culture—as depicted in movies and on television. Popular films such as *To Sir With Love*, *Freedom Writers*, *Stand and Deliver*, *Dangerous Minds*, *Sister Act*, and *Music of the Heart* dramatize the "dedicated charismatic teacher" as the obvious solution for difficult discipline and classroom management problems in inner-city schools. In such films, all that is needed to motivate students is to have a winsome and mercurial "tough love" teacher who "lays down the law," integrates street culture into school subjects, and shows that he or she cares by listening to the students' hopes, dreams, and fears. Although some elements of the charismatic teacher formula have some merit, this depiction drastically oversimplifies the problem. This is not to say that all inspirational school reform films miss the mark. Films like *Lean on Me* probably come closest to characterizing the schoolwide changes (and challenges) that are required to accomplish truly outstanding results for vulnerable minority students who are in most need of a quality educational experience.

Educators who must seriously grapple with the dismal academic and behavioral conditions of many minority schools have come to recognize that the key to school reform for vulnerable populations lies in the overhauling of broken *systemic and organizational variables*. Attempts to modify the discipline and behavioral problems of individual students in seriously failing schools/districts—without modifying broken organizational factors—are about as effective as a doctor treating a coal miner for black lung, then sending the patient back to work in the coal mines.

It therefore comes as no surprise that the most effective schools for accomplishing amazing behavioral and academic outcomes for low-income minority students are schools that, in Whitman's (2008) words, function "mostly outside the reach of the long arm of the education establishment" (p. xiv). Such schools are explicitly *paternalistic*, in that they are infused with a school culture that incorporates explicit instruction for students on how to behave, what academic and behavioral goals to aim for, and how to get there (see Sidebar 7.1 for a more detailed description).

Sidebar 7.1   The "New Paternalism" and Its Critics

The New Paternalism is a phrase, coined by Whitman (2008), that refers to a common characteristic of successful inner-city schools for low-income minority students. Such schools are characterized by inspiring, dedicated principals and teachers, high academic standards, motivated and respectful students, and what Whitman calls "a healthy, forceful, modern version of paternalism" (see Foreword in Whitman, 2008, p. x).

Paternalism, as applied to educational contexts—particularly those involving ethnic minority and immigrant students—dates back to the early 20th century. With the growing popularity of trendy progressive education movements of the 1940s through 1980s, educational paternalism fell out of fashion—only to be revived in the 1990s when it became increasingly clear to education observers that paternalistic methods were achieving results where previous other methods had consistently failed. As an abstraction divorced from educational contexts, the concept of *paternalism* connotes a fatherly care and concern, which closely manages the affairs of others and is to some degree restrictive of their freedom, but is nevertheless done "for their own good."

Case studies in some of the worst-performing inner-city schools show that when principals, teachers, and other school staff function like firm but loving parents, the students respond in ways that support learning. Paternalistic schools create policies that set clear expectations for behavior, then establish close supervision and monitoring procedures to ensure that students meet (or exceed) these expectations. Unlike schools in more economically advantaged communities, paternalistic schools follow the "broken window" philosophy of school management (i.e., if more serious misbehavior is to be avoided, focus like a laser beam on seemingly trivial misbehavior; see Glossary). In such schools, students are shown exactly and precisely how they are expected to behave in school (e.g., how to sit in a chair in class without slouching, how to track the teacher with their eyes, how to walk silently down the hall, how to greet visitors with a firm handshake and assertive verbal introduction, and how to keep track of daily assignments, among other behaviors).

Superficial impressions can easily lead to the misunderstanding that paternalism involves little more than "telling poor people how to live." In reality, the essence of paternalism is to honestly recognize and acknowledge destructive attitudes, behaviors, and habits that undermine success and perpetuate failure—and to correct these.

Not surprisingly, a chorus of criticism of the new paternalism comes from the "educational establishment" represented by teachers' unions, education school professors, multicultural activists, and bilingual educators. The success of paternalistic methods in low-income minority schools blatantly contradicts trendy progressive theories that dominate training curricula in colleges of education. The behaviors required by paternalistic schools are unapologetically middle class, which violate multicultural bromides that lecture audiences not to "impose their culture" on poor minority children. Equally embarrassing for these groups is the fact that many teachers in paternalistic schools have obtained alternate routes for certification that do not involve four or more years of exposure to a traditional teacher education program. The positive results experienced by such teachers are not supposed to happen apart from traditional teacher education training, which predictably causes criticism and resistance to paternalistic methods among the "education experts."

But results do not lie. Academic achievement at paternalistic schools far exceeds nearby schools with the same population of low-income minority students. While college attendance among affluent high school graduates approximates 75 percent, the three low-income but paternalistic high schools featured in Whitman's (2008) case studies send more than 85 percent of their graduates to college (whereas only 31 percent of low-income 18- to 24-year-olds nationwide ever enroll in college).

(Adapted from Whitman, 2008)

The clear and positive outcomes achieved by paternalistic schools make a mockery of the "conventional wisdom" of traditional teacher training programs, tired multicultural education canards, and the dire predictions of teachers' unions. Although some traditional district schools for predominantly minority populations can achieve dramatic results (although they are exceptions within their respective districts), most schools that do so are charter or parochial schools (see Chapter 4). What the majority of these schools share in common is the freedom to function outside of the confines of district "central office" bureaucratic rules and teacher union contracts.

HABITS OF HIGHLY EFFECTIVE PATERNALISTIC SCHOOLS

All public schools, even those institutions that are not considered to be paternalistic in the sense described by Whitman (2008), are paternalistic to some degree. That is, most schools mandate student attendance, prohibit violence and/or drug abuse, enforce rules for behavior, and attempt to teach values. Although these characteristics may be effective for students who come from more advantaged backgrounds, they are "too little, too late" for many vulnerable low-income inner-city students. The kinds of paternalistic institutions profiled by Whitman (2008) are qualitatively different from regular public schools, and this difference is immediately evident to observers who visit them. The characteristics of paternalistic schools are outlined in the following sections.

Inculcate a Strong Work Ethic

When predominantly minority public schools avoid (for whatever reason) the obligation to seriously develop basic work attitudes and study skills in students, any serious attempt at meaningful academic learning beyond high school is an uphill, if not impossible, battle. A stark illustration of this problem is described by one well-meaning black journalist in his efforts to teach basic journalism skills to seriously underprepared students at a historically black college (see Sidebar 7.2)

⌦ Sidebar 7.2   A Dying Dream

Tampa Bay Times (formerly the *St. Petersburg Times*) journalist Bill Maxwell wrote about his observations of students from his brief experience as a journalism professor at a small historically black college:

> Driving my 13-year-old, un-airconditioned Chevy Blazer past the guard house, I became apprehensive when I noticed about a dozen male students wearing baggy pants, oversized white T-shirts, expensive sneakers and assorted bling standing around shooting the breeze. At least two had "jailhouse tats" on their arms, crude tattoos suggesting that these young men had spent time behind bars. They carried no books or anything else to indicate they were on a college campus. . . . Behind them, several others sat on a low brick wall near the dorm entrance. They, too, were clad like extras in a gangsta rap video. It was a scene straight out of "the

hood"—young black men seemingly without direction or purpose, hanging out on the corner. In this case, they were hanging out on what is popularly known as "The Yard" on a college campus where they were supposed to be preparing for a more productive life. . . . When I began my first day . . . I would be a professor who would inspire and guide the lives of young black women and men who wanted to become successful journalists. As it turned out, I would last just two years before returning to the *Times*. I left the campus disheartened and disillusioned, and I regretted leaving behind a handful of dedicated students with real potential. . . .

At 8 on that first morning, I met my freshman English class. . . . The room was noisy. . . . I put my books on the table and raised an arm for silence. When only a few students paid attention I raised my arm again, and this time I yelled. "All right, knock it off! Take your seats and be quiet!"

I could not believe that I had to yell for college students to behave in a classroom. This is not going to be a good experience, I thought, unfolding the roster and preparing to call the roll. . . . After getting the room quiet, I instructed the students to "write an in-class essay of no more than 500 words describing at least three positive or negative things about your high school." I told them I would read the essays and return them the next time we met. "This is a diagnostic essay," I said. "I won't grade it. I simply want to see how well you write. If you plan to major in journalism, I want to see you after class. I will hand out the syllabus next time." . . .

During office hours and lunch, I read the essays. I wondered what I had gotten myself into when only one paper demonstrated college-level writing. During my 18 years of previous college teaching, I had never seen such poor writing—sentence fragments, run-on sentences, misspellings, wrong words and illogical word order. From one paper: "In my high school, prejudism were bad and people feel like nothing." From another essay: "Central High kids put there nose in other people concern." I was surprised and disappointed that the two prospective journalism majors had as many mistakes in their copy as their classmates. I shared the results with a colleague who had taught journalism and English . . . for three years. Her response was discouraging. The abysmal writing was par for the course, and I had better brace myself if I intended to keep my sanity.

That afternoon, I met my opinion writing and news writing/reporting classes. . . . Again, I called the roll and took writing samples. That night at home, I eagerly read the papers. . . . But after an hour of reading, I did not see how any of them would become reporters and editors without

(continued)

superhuman efforts on their part and mine. None had any sense of how a news article comes together. None knew how to write a compelling lead or how to use the active voice. Only one, a young woman in the opinion writing class, had written for a high school newspaper.

During the next class meetings, I returned the papers. I did not mark the work, but I explained the writing was disappointingly bad and that they would have to work overtime to learn to write at an acceptable level. All except the one student who had a decent essay were outraged. . . . I did tell them we would follow the syllabus, which required eight essays and four revisions. I also told them they would have to complete the grammar quizzes in the textbook. Everyone, except the competent writer, groaned.

"I ain't taking this class," one of the students who had been in front of King Hall said. He stood, nodded to his three friends and walked out of the room. One of them followed. The other two stared at me and scowled for the remainder of the period. . . .

After a week, I faced another problem that my seasoned colleagues knew well but failed to warn me about: Most . . . students refuse to buy their required textbooks. I discovered the problem on a Friday when I met my English class to discuss the assigned essay in the text. They were to write an essay in response to the reading. Only one student, the young man who wrote well, had read the essay. He had the text in front of him. The others had not purchased the text. I warned them that if they returned to class without their books, they would receive an F. But only five of 31 students brought their texts to the next class. Most students had book vouchers as part of their financial aid, so I told those without books to walk with me to the bookstore, a distance of about three football fields. Some did not follow me, and I tried to remember who they were.

At the store I watched students wander around, obviously trying to avoid buying the book. Only about eight wound up buying one. I became angry that I had to deal with such a self-destructive, juvenile problem. I saw the refusal to buy the text as a collective act of defiance. I knew that if I lost this battle, I would not have any control in this class and no respect. The next Monday, I went to class dreading a showdown. While calling the roll, I asked the students to show me their texts. Eighteen still did not have them. One said he had bought the book but left it in his dorm room "by mistake." I told him to go get it. He gathered his belongings and left. He never came to class again. . . .

As I settled into my routine . . . that first fall, I researched the backgrounds of the students in the English class. None had an SAT score above 1000. The average combined SAT score for the nation was 1026; the best possible score was 1600. None of them had taken advanced placement courses in school. Of the 33 students, 21 came from single-parent, low-income families who lived mostly in Alabama. Some came from the state's Black Belt, one of the poorest areas in the nation with some of the worst public schools. . . .

I tried my best to cultivate a love of language and reading. Two sayings were on my office door. One was a Chinese proverb: "It is only through daily reading that you refresh your mind sufficiently to speak wisely." The other came from me: "Being Smart is Acting Black." But the messages were lost on students who had read so little growing up and had never acquired basic academic skills. I was not surprised to learn that only two of my students had read more than three of the books most high school students have read, books such as *Moby Dick, The Sun Also Rises, The Color Purple* and *Invisible Man*. Those of us who were teaching the required general education courses—all of us from the nation's respected universities, such as the University of Chicago, Indiana University, the University of Florida and Princeton—had to face a harsh reality. We primarily were practicing remediation. Every day in my classes, I reviewed basic grammar and showed students how to use the dictionary effectively, lessons normally taught in elementary and middle school.

Homework was another major problem. Writing courses, especially journalism courses, are labor intensive for students and the professors. Reporting—going into the field, interviewing sources, finding official records and verifying information for accuracy—is essential. After most of my students continued to hand in articles that had only one interview, I began requiring at least four interviews, with the sources' telephone numbers, for each story. Most of the students balked and continued to hand in work with an insufficient number of interviews. Meeting deadlines, a must in journalism, was yet another problem. Few of my students regularly met the Monday deadline. I would deduct a letter grade for each day the copy was late. Some students received F's on all of their work. To avoid flunking them, I let them write in class. But that required them to show up, and I seldom had all students present. Attending class seemed to be an inconvenience. The college had an official attendance policy, but few professors followed it strictly because most of our students would have flunked out before mid-term. On most days, I did not call the roll. I simply tried to remember who was present. . . .

I hardly ever saw anyone take notes during lectures in the English class. Instead, I had to regularly chastise students for text messaging their

(continued)

friends and relatives and for going online to read messages and send messages. The college issued free laptops to all students who maintained a passing grade-point average. When I confronted students about text messaging, I was met with hostility. I even had a few students leave class to make calls or send text messages. Two male students threatened to physically attack . . . another female professor because [she] demanded that the students put away their laptops in class. Each time, I would leave the English class exhausted, angry and sad. I would go home on many evenings during my first month wanting to cry, and things didn't get much better as the year progressed. . . .

I became even more hopeful [when the college president] . . . agreed it was time to order new computers and other supplies to open a newsroom for the student newspaper and for editing and design classes. During those first few weeks of school, the new equipment began arriving and my hopes continued to rise. . . . I believed that with a real newsroom we were ready to make significant progress. . . . With a campus newsroom, we assumed that our students would begin to take the profession seriously and would love hanging out in their own space.

We soon learned that we had been naive. Nothing changed. Students rarely came to the newsroom except for classes. The majority preferred to socialize with their friends during their spare time, and others knew that one way to avoid an assignment for the newspaper was to avoid the newsroom where story leads and tips were posted on the bulletin board. My colleagues and I were witnessing the result of low admission standards. [W]e [were] expecting too much of young people who scored poorly on the SAT, who were rarely challenged to excel in high school, who were not motivated to take advantage of opportunities to learn. . . .

A white professor labored to get her students to critically read the assignments. She could not discuss the major themes and literary conventions when her students did not read. When she got nowhere with Zora Neale Hurston's novel *Their Eyes Were Watching God*, she asked me to speak to the class. Perhaps a black professor would have more success talking about one of the best-known black authors. A few minutes into my exchange with the class, I realized the white professor was not the problem. The students simply did not—or could not—read closely. My colleagues and I could not teach what we had been trained to teach. . . .

Many of my . . . colleagues regularly invited their students to their homes for dinner. The discussions often were about personal matters involving romantic relationships, family crises and money problems. Professors were the first confidants many students ever had. Indeed, they often became surrogate parents. . . . The bottom line was the same as it is at most [Historically Black Colleges and Universities]. Professors who had the best success connecting with students, especially below-average male students, emphasized friendly, personal and supportive involvement in their lives. . . . This style of teaching, which I grudgingly adopted, was unlike anything I had used during my previous 18 years of teaching on traditional campuses such as those of the University of Illinois at Chicago and Northern Illinois University. On those campuses, professors were respected for their achievements and position. Subject matter usually was taught without developing strong personal relationships between students and professors, and professors may not have cared if students liked them.

[Here], being professional but impersonal created frustration for the student and the professor. Students, especially males, liked and respected the flexible professor, and they learned when they respected the professor. The flexible professor encouraged lively exchanges of subject matter, ideas, beliefs and opinions during class discussions. The flexible professor often did not require written responses or exams. The flexible professor let students keep pace by retaking exams, completing take-home exams or giving classroom presentations. I had difficulty becoming flexible. The majority of my students in the English class failed to complete most of the assigned readings. Most of their essays were unacceptable, and attendance was low. I had a choice: Abandon my syllabus or flunk more than half of the class. I abandoned the syllabus. Instead, I lectured and made assignments based on the problems and errors in the students' writing. I went over the same material, such as writing the topic sentence, again and again because some students could not master it. "We're crippling these kids by mothering them," I told a colleague over a drink one evening. "We're loving them to death," he replied. . . .

During the fall semester, I would try to make eye contact with students and speak to them as we passed in the halls and on The Yard, the grassy campus gathering spot. Very few of them would return my greetings. Most were sullen. But I also saw something more disturbing in their faces: Many of these young people were sad and unhappy. Very few smiled. A colleague . . . confirmed my observations. "Our kids haven't had many good things in their lives," she said. "Many of them are angry and negative and rude. They've had hard lives. Some of them don't belong here." She was right.

(continued)

A number of students had criminal records, and others were awaiting trial on criminal charges. [This college] accepted them because they could not attend college anywhere else. . . . The college did not keep an accurate count, but we knew many young women on campus were mothers.

One of my students was a 20-year-old mother of two pressed for time and money. But she had good attendance and turned in passable home-work. I met several students who had legally adopted their siblings. For one reason or another, their parents were temporarily or permanently absent. Some of my colleagues and I empathized and gave these students breaks, such as giving them take-home quizzes and exams and sometimes excusing them from class if they had written excuses from their employers. . . . Instead of taking pride in being exemplary students, many were devotees of hip-hop culture. They were anti-intellectual, rude and profane. . . . Personal insult, crude language and threatening behavior were a way of life for many students. . . . I had no doubt that the influences of hip-hop contributed greatly to this ugly reality and other deleterious trends.

"Have you noticed that our students never have a sense of urgency?" a colleague asked one afternoon as we walked to a faculty meeting. "They don't seem to be going anywhere in particular. They just stand around or mosey along. Frivolity." He was right. Greek organization activities such as step shows—the rhythmical, patterned dance movements favored by fraternities and sororities—and any excuse to party and play music were the most important events on campus. When a professor brought a special lecturer to campus, the rest of us would require our students to attend the event. But more often than not only a handful would show up, a great source of embarrassment for the professors. I never invited any of my fellow journalists to campus. Besides the stinging embarrassment of low attendance, I resented the hassle of rounding up students for their own enlightenment. . . .

While disagreeable staff members and financial red tape were constant irritants, nothing was more appalling than the students' disregard for college property. During the spring semester, the . . . Fire Department put out trash can fires in King Hall. I was angry and embarrassed to see a team of white firefighters trying to save a dormitory named for the Rev. Martin Luther King Jr. that black students had trashed. . . . I went inside the dorm to see the damage. Students had stuffed trash cans with paper and fabric and set them on fire. The smoke damage was enormous. The walls were blackened, the windows were smudged and the pungent smell of smoke lingered and stuck to everything. Even without the fire damage, the place would have looked like a war zone. Holes had been kicked and punched in the walls. Windows were broken, floors were scarred and most of the furniture was damaged. The two dorms routinely underwent major repairs after each semester. . . .

By the end of the spring semester, I knew that I could not remain [at this college] another year. I had a few good students, but a few were not enough. One morning as I dressed for work, I accepted the reality that too much of my time was being wasted on students who did not care. I felt guilty about wanting to leave. But enough was enough. . . . In my office, I sat at my desk staring at a stack of papers to be graded. I'm wasting my time, I thought. I've wasted two years of my professional life. I don't belong here. I put the papers in a drawer. I did not read them. Why read them?

(Excerpted and adapted with permission from "I Had a Dream" and "A Dream Lay Dying," published May 13 and 20, 2007, by the *St. Petersburg Times*)

In a longitudinal study of approximately 300 white and black eighth graders in a northeast Philadelphia magnet school, Duckworth and Seligman (2005) concluded that the failure to exercise self-discipline is an overlooked but crucial variable for explaining school underachievement—even going so far as to suggest that students with lower IQs with high levels of self-discipline perform better in school in certain ways than higher-IQ students with low levels of self-discipline (Duckworth & Seligman, 2005). Awan (1997) articulates the matter in down-to-earth terms:

If a boy dreams of driving exotic and legendary sports cars, lunching at the Jockey Club in an Armani suit, and flying off to Paris for a night cap, he has a lot of work ahead of him. Fulfillment is likely to demand years and years of planning and right decisions, in addition to a great deal of education and achievement. Along the way, of course, priorities will likely rearrange themselves in his mind, and he may never enjoy such a "Hollywood day" as he dreamed about in his youth. Indeed, the man may decide to get a big, comfortable house in a quiet and friendly neighborhood where his daughter will grow up in safety. But no matter what career path he takes, he will need a powerful work ethic to help him achieve it. (p. 55)

Unfortunately, the lack of a powerful work ethic lies at the root of many students' difficulties with even minimal levels of achievement—both within and outside the classroom. Rothstein (2004) summarized results from nine large-scale surveys conducted by business groups, government agencies, and education policy groups on employers' perceptions of the deficiencies in employees who are recent high school and college graduates (pp. 151–152). According to survey findings, employers highly value communication skills, honesty and integrity, effective interpersonal skills, motivation and initiative, *a strong work ethic*, and teamwork skills. Although cognitive skills are also important, many employers opined that once potential job applicants generally met a "B" average in academic skills, their grade-point averages were relatively unimportant in comparison to the aforementioned noncognitive skills that are highly valued.

When employers were asked which characteristics were most significant in causing workers to be fired or not initially hired at all, they mentioned deficient timeliness (trouble being on time) and *a low work ethnic*, poor attitudes and reliability, insufficient perseverance in the face of obstacles, a lack of pride in one's work, a lack of enthusiasm for the job, an unwillingness to accept responsibility, poor problem-solving skills, poor communication skills, the lack of minimal ability to resolve interpersonal conflicts, a lack of respect for the rights of others, poor reading, writing, and/or math skills, and a poor appearance.

Paternalistic schools take on a piece of the parental role by unapologetically requiring students to live up to a highly specific and detailed code of conduct based on middle-class values and *a Protestant work ethic* nurtured within an explicit culture of achievement. These schools explicitly define the elements of good character necessary for achievement both inside and outside of the school setting. Students are taught specifically how they are to behave, similar to the guidance provided by a firm but loving father, which many of the students do not have in their own lives. Roth (1994) writes:

> Among the many functions of schools, one is certainly the grooming of individuals to take their place in the workforce. Punctuality, reliability, toleration of boredom, and acceptance of unearned authority are among the habits of mind terribly important for success in most jobs. Bravado, daring, respect for charismatic authority, and impatience with routine, while essential for participation in the "action" of the inner-city youth culture, are useless and counterproductive when it comes to getting and holding a job. In other words, schools, when successful, socialize young people to smoothly take their place in the workplace, and this socialization is every bit as important as the ability to read and write. (p. 247)

In the Cristo Rey Jesuit High School work experience program, students are held to high standards of work and behavioral accountability (Whitman, 2008). Here, students are treated as real employees who are personally responsible to their employer sponsors. For example, work experience students are regularly evaluated by their sponsors on 12 different measures of work performance (e.g., professional appearance, punctuality, work accuracy, and respect for authority). If students miss work for any reason, they are fined $100. If students accrue more than one absence from work that has not been made up, they receive an automatic "F" on their report cards. According to Whitman (2008), each year about a dozen of the school's students get fired from their jobs, and as a result are required to attend the school's re-employment program.

Surround Students With Structure, Structure, and More Structure

Paternalistic schools assume that economically disadvantaged students do best when "structure and expectations are crystal clear, rather than presuming that kids should learn to figure things out for themselves" (Whitman, 2008, p. 36). These schools "surround students with a total environment, a holistic set of habits and messages, and they dominate students' lives for many hours a day" (Whitman, 2008, p. 42). Specifically, paternalistic schools are characterized by a highly structured organizational scheme for how discipline standards are created, administered, and enforced; how curriculum is aligned to state standards and academic performance assessed; and how day-to-day classroom instruction is delivered.

Structured Discipline Standards/Enforcement

On day one, students in paternalistic schools are told exactly what behavioral standards they are expected to meet, and how these will be enforced, which effectively socializes them early on into the structured disciplinary culture of the school. For example, the material in Sidebar 7.3 describes KIPP (Knowledge Is Power Program) students' first exposure to the structured expectations of a KIPP school.

🖎 Sidebar 7.3   A KIPP (Knowledge Is Power Program) Student's First Day of Summer School Before Entering Fifth Grade

As fifth grade students arrive at their new school, teachers and returning students greet them and direct them to the gym. The students, predominantly African-American, sit silently on the floor and begin their "morning work." At 7:45 A.M., the staff welcomes the new students and immediately recognizes students who are in proper uniform. Throughout the morning, teachers call the parents of students who are not dressed appropriately, e.g., wearing the wrong color pants, a white shirt without a collar, or sneakers, or not wearing a belt. After the staff and returning students are introduced, students learn how to stand properly in line—silently and with a book in their hand. They are taught that lines should be SILENT, STRAIGHT, and SERIOUS. Students then learn how to walk in a straight line, silently.

(continued)

They repeat standing and walking in line a few times, until they get it right, before they walk to the cafeteria for breakfast.

At breakfast, students are given a few minutes to eat and then continue their morning work. During breakfast, they are taught how to write a KIPP header on a paper and the "Clap Praise" (a teacher counts 1-2-3 and everyone claps in unison). When students return to the gym, the principal singles out students who were late and reminds students the value of being on time. Students then learn silent hand signals for yes and no, the clap that teachers use to get students' attention, and are taught how to use the bathroom and keep it clean. Throughout the morning, students who are off-task or not in proper attire must apologize publicly to their teammates. Working hard, being nice, and following directions are constantly promoted as values that will get them to college.

The one academic lesson for the day is that students learn to "roll their nines" by repeating "9, 18, 27, 36, 45, . . ." over and over, and using their fingers to indicate the multiplier (1 times 9, 2 times 9, etc.). Before students leave for the day, they receive their first homework assignment. They are told that tomorrow, the second day of summer school, teachers will be checking to see that homework is complete and that "agendas" are signed by parents. Teachers will call the parents of students who do not complete their first homework assignments.

From David, J. L., Woodworth, K., Grant, E., Guha, R., Lopez-Torkos, A., & Young, V. M. (2006). *Bay Area KIPP schools: A study of early implementation (First Year Report 2004–05)*. Menlo Park, CA: SRI International. Reprinted with permission from SRI International.

Student behavior (and misbehavior) is more closely monitored in paternalistic schools than is typical in other schools. Paternalistic schools closely supervise students' lives in ways that even the strictest public schools cannot, as typified by what happens in SEED (Schools for Evolution and Educational Development) schools (see Glossary). Because SEED officials are responsible for students' behavior even while they live in the school-affiliated boarding dormitories, school administrators needed to create from scratch a detailed code of conduct for students. This code of conduct includes rules for how rooms are to be kept clean, how beds need to be made, how clothes are to be stored, and how personal items are to be arranged in rooms. Exemplary behavior is rewarded with "SEED dollars" that can be used for buying extra snacks at the school store, staying up a little later on weekdays, or earning the privilege of having additional time on the dormitory house phone.

The standard privileges and freedoms that young people take for granted in contemporary culture (e.g., watching TV, talking on cell phones, using pagers, listening to boom boxes, playing on video games and home entertainment systems) are prohibited while students are at SEED. Although SEED students report that they miss these privileges at first, they eventually come to adapt and view SEED as their second home (Whitman, 2008).

Many paternalistic schools require students to wear uniforms or at least to conform to strict dress codes. As examples, male students in the SEED program must wear ties to class every day, and there are even rules for the kinds of ties that are/are not allowed. In the SEED program, any adult in authority who has regular contact with the kids can feel free to comment on whether or not shoelaces are tied and shirts are tucked in properly.

A primary reason for the emphasis on structure in SEED schools is to ensure student safety and a sense of security. After an armed intruder hid in a SEED dormitory and was eventually captured, school officials erected an iron gate and fence around the campus to prevent unauthorized visitors from entering (Whitman, 2008).

Structured Assessment Programs

Because the paternalistic schools profiled by Whitman (2008) serve a predominantly minority population, administrators are sensitive to the yawning achievement gap between white and minority students, and they strive to narrow this gap on state assessments—or at least to work toward earning achievement test scores that surpass state averages for schools that serve a similar socioeconomic demographic. As discussed in Whitman (2008), paternalistic schools align a rigorous and structured curriculum with state standards, with benchmarks and performance outcomes explicitly specified for students.

Contrary to the "standardized-tests-are-bad-for-minority-students" rhetoric of test critics (e.g., see http://fairtest.org/; Kohn, 2001; Lomax, West, & Harmon, 1995), paternalistic schools for minority students regularly assess student progress—and use the test results to target academically struggling students, as well as to alter classroom instruction when needed (see also Carter, 2000). Whitman (2008) notes:

> [N]o-excuses schools bear little resemblance to the mechanistic, zombie-like institutions that critics deride. Rather, they show that secondary schools can prepare their pupils for [state] tests, assess them regularly, and still have a stimulating core curriculum. (p. 265)

Structured Academic Classroom Instruction

Although classrooms in paternalistic schools allow wide room for instructional variety, the routines in paternalistic classrooms share a similar structure. For example, when students enter class each day, teachers have already written a series of reflection questions on the board to which students must silently write answers when they sit down. Homework assignments, the ideas to be covered in class, as well as the discussion subjects, are often outlined on the board for all students to see. In most classes in paternalistic schools, students are required to write regularly in journals and read aloud in front of the class on a daily basis. Many of the paternalistic high schools reviewed by Whitman (2008) require students to correct and/or rewrite papers and homework assignments. These literacy-rich environments are intentionally provided daily in order to help low-income students compensate for growing up in homes that often have little to no literary and writing resources.

Whitman (2008) describes how SEED middle-school teachers document student conduct in writing as a routine part of each class period. Here, each student is required to carry a yellow School Note from class to class listing 12 target behaviors that can be evaluated under one of two columns titled Responsible Behaviors or Irresponsible Behaviors. At the end of each class, teachers assign letter grades in either column for each of the 12 behaviors for each student. At the close of the day, points are tabulated in order to determine how many SEED dollars the student earned for the day. For ninth- to 12th-grade students who demonstrate exemplary behaviors in leadership, character, academics, and school service, the requirement to carry School Notes from class to class is waived.

Structured Post-Graduation Monitoring

The structure provided by paternalistic schools even extends to students after they graduate. The Cristo Rey high school and KIPP middle school in the South Bronx profiled by Whitman (2008) have both developed counseling and support programs for students as they move into high school and then on to college. Since 2002, the KIPP school tracks all of its graduates and obtains copies of their grades throughout high school. In addition, the school provides a weekly after-school academic and character-building curriculum plus tutoring and counseling services. Once KIPP middle-schoolers reach high school, a "KIPP to College" staff becomes closely involved in monitoring students throughout the college applications process—helping alumni with writing college application essays and preparing for college admission interviews. These efforts are supplemented by KIPP alumni attendance at a two-day college-application preparation retreat at a nearby camp. In addition, the KIPP school oversees paid summer internships in closely monitored jobs for KIPP alumni (Whitman, 2008).

Build a School Culture of Achievement

To reiterate a point made earlier, the entire purpose of having rigorous discipline and behavior standards at paternalistic schools is to support the primary mission of building a school climate that is conducive to academic effort and achievement. When the

University Park Campus School (UPCS) in Worcester, Massachusetts, started in 1997, its founder vowed to create a neighborhood noncharter school for 7th to 12th graders that had a demanding culture of academic achievement—as well as enforced a paternalistic code of conduct that barred street talk, swear words, and various manifestations of disrespect toward authority. As described by Whitman (2008), the first class of 35 seventh graders included four students who could not read. The rest of the students read at or below the third-grade level, were special needs students, or spoke English as a second language (with parents who spoke little or no English at home). Half of the students were Hispanic, Vietnamese, or Cambodian.

To address these glaring deficiencies, the UPCS founder secured funding for a five-week August Academy for new students, to be held at Clark University. Each morning, prospective seventh graders took 90-minute block classes in math, reading, and writing that included intensive remedial instruction and diagnostic testing. Although these students were seventh graders, they had to be taught using picture books, and the teachers actually needed to read aloud to students as part of literacy instruction.

Fast-forward to 2003. As reported by Whitman (2008), UPCS was the only public school in Massachusetts where not a single student had failed the 10th-grade state Massachusetts Comprehensive Assessment System English and math tests, having achieved proficient or advanced skills in both subjects. In addition, 31 out of 35 students in the first UPCS class graduated, and all were accepted into a college. In 2005, a *Newsweek* article ranked the school as the fourth best high school in the country compared to schools where half or more of the students were low-income.

Amistad Academy, a charter school in New Haven, Connecticut, has no admissions standards and automatically enrolls all children who win spots in a lottery. According to Whitman (2008), roughly two-thirds of its students are African American and one-third are Hispanic. Nearly 85 percent qualify for free and reduced-price lunch programs, and nearly three-fourths of the students come from single-parent households. A typical entering fifth grader scores at the 27th and 25th percentile on standardized reading and math tests, respectively. However, Amistad students make dramatic academic gains on standardized tests once they have an opportunity to spend a few years in a system in which academic achievement is the number-one focus of the entire school. In 2006, Amistad's seventh graders had the largest single jump in academic performance of any of the 181 public middle schools in Connecticut (Whitman, 2008). In 2007, 93 percent of Amistad's eight graders were proficient in math, 76 percent were proficient in reading, and 99 percent scored "basic" or above on the writing section of the Connecticut Mastery Test.

The College Focus of Paternalistic Schools

As soon as a low-income minority student enters a SEED school, for example, the first thing noticed is that the hallways are lined with pennants from various colleges and universities around the country, and SEED school teachers and principals begin talking to students about college as soon as they arrive on campus. In SEED schools, students within each grade are divided into "houses" (dormitory units) that are named after colleges. Each house is staffed with a Life Skills Counselor, whose job it is to serve as a surrogate parent to the students while they are away from home. Among the many responsibilities of Life Skills Counselors is to ensure that students regularly attend evening study hall sessions on weekdays.

Consistent with their college-prep focus, SEED schools must focus like a laser beam on academics, because most students entering seventh grade have reading and math skills that are typical of a fifth grader (Whitman, 2008). As a result, SEED teachers work intensively on academic remediation and preparation for a college-prep high school curriculum. During these crucial years, students receive intensive after-school tutoring if they struggle in classes. In a similar fashion, Amistad Academy regularly assigns its best teachers to tutor students with the weakest academic skills.

SEED schools do not practice social promotion, where students are passed on to higher grades even if they have not demonstrated passable academic skills in previous grades. SEED schools are known for having a strict ninth-grade gate, which students are required to pass before they can be promoted to high school. If students do not demonstrate proficiency in even one of many academic strands, they must repeat the eighth grade or make up the work satisfactorily during the summer before entering the ninth grade.

Once SEED students pass the ninth-grade gate, they must take a rigorous college-prep curriculum consisting of four credits in English, three in social studies (World Studies and U.S. History), four in math (through Algebra 2), three credits of science (including at least two in biology, chemistry, or physics), and three credits in a modern language. As a result of these efforts, Whitman (2008) reports data showing that students in SEED schools perform considerably higher than students in comparable schools with the same socioeconomic characteristics, and has one of the highest college enrollment rates of any inner-city schools in the country.

Emphasis on Accountability

In traditional schools, students who miss class are simply marked as "tardy," with little accountability for attendance in schools serving highly truant populations. At the American Indian Public Charter School (see Sidebar 7.4), a missed school day has to be made up in a Saturday class, and a student is automatically held back a grade if five absences are accrued. Because of paternalistic schools' strict emphasis on consistent attendance, in contrast, teachers find that they do not have to constantly retrace instructional steps for students who miss class.

🏫 Sidebar 7.4   American Indian Public Charter School of Oakland, CA

When the American Indian Public Charter School (AIPCS) first opened in Oakland, California, in September 1996, it was a multicultural dream that would soon become an educational nightmare. . . . [T]he novel approach of the new middle school . . . inadvertently foreshadowed the disaster to come. . . . The school's distinctive curriculum . . . was designed chiefly to build student pride in being Native American: "The curriculum will integrate Indian culture in all subjects. Students will be involved in various ethnic-related projects from planting crops and learning traditional cooking to Native American storytelling and researching their individual tribes. . . . Other activities students will participate in include pottery, making musical instruments, basket weaving, and cultural art." . . .

Cut to the summer of 2000, by which time the American Indian Public Charter School had become a caricature of almost everything that can go wrong with a parent-driven, multicultural school. . . . Student achievement was pitiful. In 2001, AIPCS students scored a 436 out of 1000 on California's Academic Performance Index—one of the worst scores in a city already renowned for its dreadful public schools. Students roamed in and out of class at will. One school board member at the time said, "There were supposed to be sixty kids enrolled but you were lucky to find one kid in class" during school visits. . . . Finally, the Oakland School Board decided it had had enough: It was going to close AIPCS and revoke the school's charter. But then one member persuaded the district school board to give the school one last shot under the new leadership of Ben Chavis, a Lumbee Indian who had taught in the ethnic studies department at San Francisco State University. . . .

[W]hen Chavis arrived at AIPCS in July 2000, even he was outraged by the educational charade that school administrators had perpetrated on poor kids in the name of developing their Native American identity. "What the school and students had been doing was playing Indian," he recalls scornfully. The school day started . . . at 9:00 or 9:30 a.m. . . . "[t]he school believed in what it called 'Indian Time'—students were supposed to show up when they showed up because Indians can't get up early. . . . Then there was a culture class, where students would bang drums and were taught basket weaving and bead-making. . . . The school was filthy, and the walls were covered with graffiti and gang markings . . ."

(continued)

Within days of his appointment as principal, Chavis began to undo every decision of his predecessors. He fired all but one member of the staff and eliminated every curricular consultant. . . . He eliminated every multicultural offering, requiring instead that students have a minimum of three hours of English language arts and math each morning that followed state-adopted textbooks, step-for-step. Arriving one minute late to school would henceforth earn a student a guaranteed hour of silent detention after school; so would talking out of turn in class or uniform violations of the new school dress code. . . .

Today, seven years later, Chavis's reforms have produced one of the great educational turnaround stories in recent history. American Indian Public Charter School is currently the highest performing middle school in the Oakland area. After raising its Academic Performance Index (API) scores each year for seven years running, in 2006 AIPCS's 196 students even bested the Piedmont Middle School, the school for the "rich kids" in the hills above Oakland's gritty "flatlands" neighborhoods. AIPCS students on average scored 920 out of 1000 on California's API in 2006, far above the 800 point target that California has set as a statewide goal. . . . In October 2006, AIPCS became the first public school in Oakland to win a coveted Blue Ribbon award from the U.S. secretary of education. That same year, 35 students participated in the prestigious Johns Hopkins Center for Talented Youth summer programs at universities around the country. [AIPCS] has made such a name for itself that families from other ethnic backgrounds, including low-income Asian Americans and Latinos, have started seeking the school out. During a 2006 visit to AIPCS, California governor Arnold Schwarzenegger hailed it as "an educational miracle." . . .

The secret of [AIPCS]'s success lies not in its resources but rather in its paternalistic blend of instruction and discipline. . . . AIPCS . . . reflects the contrarian passions of its self-described "control freak" and "dictator," mad-dog principal Ben Chavis. . . . While students see Dr. Chavis as a no-nonsense disciplinarian, they also ultimately see him as "family"—a substitute father figure who cares about them, even as he wheedles, shames, and scolds. . . . AIPCS's authoritarian policies have often evolved directly out of Chavis's own experiences of childhood poverty. AIPCS, for instance, requires students to attend three weeks of summer school, lengthening the year from 180 days to 200 days. American Indian has increased instructional time during the school day, too, by cutting down on electives, shortening the lunch hour to 20 minutes, and reducing classroom rotation. It is an academically rigorous institution and one of only two middle schools in Oakland to require every eighth grader—including special ed students—to take Algebra I. . . . During detention, students must sit upright for an hour after school in absolute silence with nothing on their desks. By contrast, other schools allow students to do their homework, write notes of apologies, clean, or read during detentions. . . .

Chavis's first-hand exposure to poverty left him deeply skeptical of progressive rhetoric about multicultural education and parental involvement. He came to believe that "[t]he whole concept of parental involvement in schools for poor kids is b*******. . . . Focusing on parent involvement alone is the worst idea in the world in these schools, and I don't care whether you are talking about poor white parents in Kentucky or poor Mexicans in Oakland. My mom was a maid. She had six kids and couldn't read—how was she supposed to volunteer at school? It's fine for white, middle-class soccer moms to talk about the nuclear family and getting parents involved in school. But in schools for poor kids, "parental involvement" has become an excuse to blame somebody—Johnny can't read because his momma didn't work with him. I say, you get your kid to school dressed and on time. And we'll do our job to educate him."

Chavis was also disillusioned with multicultural education and bilingual instruction. In an August 2006 interview with National Public Radio, Chavis observed that progressive educators "have no standards for minorities. They're like, you know, let's give them freedom. Let's understand their learning style. Let's give them multiculturalism. And no discipline, no structure, no game plan. They've destroyed a whole generation." Once again, Chavis's strong convictions stemmed largely from lessons he learned the hard way.

Excerpt from Whitman, D. (2008). *Sweating the small stuff: Inner-city schools and the new paternalism* (pp. 68–77). Washington, DC: Thomas B. Fordham Institute. Reprinted with permission from Thomas B. Fordham Institute.

It is not unusual for students in paternalistic schools to feel that they constantly face peer pressure—that is, pressure to avoid being disruptive, to do their homework, and to not reflect poorly on their classmates or school. As reported by Whitman (2008, p. 267), one student attending University Park High School in Worcester, Massachusetts, commented that since "everybody at University Park is always doing their work, you feel awkward if you are not doing your work."

Tell Students Exactly How to Behave and Tolerate No Disorder

The fundamental problem crippling (particularly urban) schools for low-income minority students is behavioral disorder and its visible manifestations (e.g., graffiti on the walls; broken and/or vandalized furniture; fights, sexual activity, and drug use in bathrooms; rowdy behavior in hallways and stairwells; and dirty/noisy cafeteria environments). This creates an environment of indifference and unaccountability, which in turn breeds more disorder. Contrary to the chaos found in many inner-city schools for low-income minority students, paternalistic schools "sweat the small stuff"—meaning that there is zero tolerance for disruption and disorder in even the smallest details of school life (see *broken windows theory* in Glossary). Stated differently, a surly student in a paternalistic school will most likely never get to the point where he throws a classroom chair against the wall, if he is instead repeatedly monitored for how he walks up and down hallways or sits in his chair while in the classroom.

In paternalistic schools, one does not encounter the rowdiness, chaos, and disrespect commonly observed in traditional schools (regardless of the makeup of the student population). In paternalistic environments, students do not speak unless they have been called on, and there is no horseplay, giggling, and whispering in the back of the classroom. No student is slouching, slumping, or sleeping at his or her desk. Observers are struck by the serious atmosphere of the classroom, which is fostered in part by the students' attire. None of the males wear baggy pants, baseball caps turned backward, or shirts that are not neatly tucked in. None of the females wear heavy jewelry, make-up, or distracting and immodest clothing.

Students are taught exactly how to behave, and disorder is not tolerated. Such expectations are applied to the most minute details of school life—often encompassing behaviors that other schools overlook or take for granted. Summarizing behavioral expectations in paternalistic schools, Whitman (2008) writes:

> Pupils are typically taught not just to walk in the hallway—they learn how to walk from class to class: silently, with a book in hand. In class, teachers constantly monitor whether students are tracking them with their eyes, whether students nod their heads to show that they [are] listening, and if any students have slouched in their seats. Teachers repeatedly admonish students to sit up, listen, nod, and track the speaker with their eyes. Looking inattentive, or merely tapping a pen on the desk, can lead to students losing . . . special privileges at school. (p. 37–38)

Discipline is enforced with *certainty* in paternalistic schools, and does not represent, as is the case in so many high-poverty schools, empty threats with little follow through.

In SEED schools, for example, approximately 5 percent to 6 percent of its pupils are expelled each year for displaying behavior that represents a danger to themselves or others.

One ninth-grade girl in the SEED program was suspended for two weeks after she and her friends trashed a fellow student's dorm room. The girl was required to remain at home and regularly attend counseling sessions. After returning to school from her suspension, the girl had a Disciplinary Board hearing, and she was placed on probation for five months. She was required to write a note of apology to the girl whose room she helped trash, and to pay $50 in damages (Whitman, 2008).

Students who get a detention at the American Indian Public Charter School are required to serve their detentions after school for an hour by being required to sit silently with no books, pencils, or other materials at their desk. As reported in Whitman (2008, p. 81), one street-tough seventh grader earned an after-school detention every day for the first four months of school. Finally, at the start of the winter semester, the boy decided that he just "couldn't take it anymore," and he started to buckle down on his schoolwork and behavior.

Provide Character Education and Social Skills Training

The key theme that characterizes paternalistic schools is that "obligation trumps freedom." That is, students in paternalistic schools are inculcated early on with the idea that they are *obligated* to be boys and girls of good character, they are *obligated* to do their best in their academic work both inside and outside of school, and they are *obligated* to make something of themselves once they leave school. These obligations can only be realized in an environment in which exemplary character traits are explicitly taught, reinforced, and modeled by the school.

Paternalistic schools are characterized by an intensive form of focused character education, building and modeling that goes well beyond mouthing abstract platitudes such as "be kind to your neighbor" or "put forth your best effort." All public schools, by and large, promote these clichés to some degree, even though these words mean absolutely nothing to most students.

Character education and social skills training is just as much a part of the curriculum in paternalistic schools as academics. In many cases, character education and academics are viewed as inseparable. This is vitally necessary for paternalistic schools in which the majority of students grow up in fatherless homes without the strong guidance necessary for optimal development (see Chapter 3). Although mothers are just as important for providing character education and guidance to children, fathers are particularly important for providing moral/character guidance to growing boys who are "beginning to feel the testosterone." In two-parent families, fathers are particularly effective in providing close discipline that pre-empts misbehavior and disrespect toward authority. On the positive side, effective fathers make a point to celebrate their sons' accomplishments with well-earned praise. Fathers look for signs that their sons have internalized their teachings, and they can "ease up" on supervision when the son shows signs toward maturity. Sadly, a majority of minority (particularly black) children grow up in neighborhoods in which they rarely see a married couple or responsible males overseeing the activities of rambunctious boys (see Cosby & Poussaint, 2007).

To address this need, paternalistic schools drill into students the importance of traditional virtues such as hard work, politeness, diligence, respect for elders and authority, and good citizenship. As an example, the orchestra conductor at KIPP Academy required every student in the orchestra to stand quietly for two full minutes simply because one member of the orchestra looked at him disrespectfully (Whitman, 2008).

In one high school work-study SEED program, students are required to take etiquette classes that teach students how to properly meet potential employers for the first time by making appropriate eye contact, stating clearly their first and last names, and giving a firm handshake. Students also learn how to appropriately say "excuse me" before interrupting a conversation, as well as learn the finer points of how to distinguish between a dinner and salad fork when eating at a good restaurant. In several paternalistic schools, the students are responsible for the daily cleaning and maintenance of school grounds and bathrooms. In evaluating the criteria needed to determine SEED students' eligibility for promotion into high school, one administrator commented that "we couldn't promote a student who regularly refused to make his bed or clean up his room" (in the SEED dormitories; Whitman, 2008, p. 207). A quarterly SEED Academic Honors breakfast is held to recognize students who make the academic honor roll, but SEED students can also earn extra recognition through special awards given to students who exemplify SEED's core values through their daily attire.

The basic concept of *shame* is used as a powerful tool for developing character in paternalistic schools for poor children. When students at Amistad Academy middle school are suspended for fighting or from other equally serious forms of misbehavior, they are permitted to return to school only after they appear in front of the school and apologize for their actions. At the American Indian Public Charter School, a streetwise sixth grader pledged to the principal that if he was caught stealing at school, the principal could cut off all of the student's hair. When the child was caught stealing a short time later, the principal announced to the entire school that the haircut was going to happen.

As reported in Whitman (2008), some eighth graders attending a paternalistic school were overheard by the school janitor engaging in some mild teasing of an overweight peer. At traditional schools, such mild behavior (typical of students of middle-school age) does not raise eyebrows. At the paternalistic school, however, the students were immediately given in-house suspensions, and they were required to write essays explaining why they teased the boy and why they were not supposed to tease other students. When other teachers heard about this incident, they told one boy "we know you are a good kid, but you can't act like that and stay here" (Whitman, 2008, p. 232).

A Novel Vehicle for Character Education

As described by Whitman (2008), the KIPP middle school in the South Bronx boasts an 180-person string and rhythm orchestra. At this school, every KIPP student is required to take a music class, but no student is obligated to play in the school orchestra. However, because of its stellar tradition and reputation in the school, community, and even the nation, every student at KIPP signs up to be a part of the orchestra in some capacity. Managing that many rambunctious middle-schoolers is no easy task for any school. However, attempts to mold a cooperative ensemble of students from difficult backgrounds into musicians—most of whom have no prior training in classical music—is a daunting task. All of this practice results in an amazing scene—repeated at each practice—where the conductor walks into a room full of 180 noisy students, claps twice, and the entire room instantly falls dead silent. The methods used by the school's music teacher and orchestra conductor are illustrative of the no-nonsense disciplinary standards of paternalistic schools.

Training for the orchestra is carefully calibrated in incremental steps to help students manage more responsibilities as they gradually master basic musical and behavioral skills. Entering fifth graders wishing to become part of the KIPP orchestra are not allowed to play an instrument in the orchestra for the duration of their entire fifth-grade year. During the first two weeks of music class, however, fifth graders simply practice walking into the music room, taking their seats, and tracking the conductor with their eyes. Each time students walk into the music room, they must touch the glockenspiel by the door as a sign of respect. After students have learned to sit quietly and properly track the conductor with their eyes, they learn to clap out rhythms. From there, beginning students move on to learning elementary music theory and sight reading. By the end of the fifth grade, students are allowed to take a musical instrument home, take the instrument out of its case, and practice naming its parts (but not play it). They are also taught to call the instrument "my baby" in order to emphasize and personally internalize the instrument's value and need for care (Whitman, 2008).

When KIPP students reach the sixth grade, during the first month they simply learn how to open their instrument cases and lift their instruments from racks inside the cases. Then, they learn how to clean and maintain their instruments, *all before they learn how to play them*. By the end of the sixth grade, after being exposed to regular weekly music classes, after-school orchestra classes, and four-hour rehearsals every Saturday morning, students develop a relatively sophisticated knowledge of musical notation and music appreciation skills "that is alien to their peers in the South Bronx" (Whitman, p. 163). This rigorous music instruction continues into the seventh- and eighth-grade years.

By the time KIPP students finish the eighth grade, they have developed a deep love for the music of Brahams, Mozart, Mendelssohn, and other great historical and contemporary composers.

As detailed in Whitman (2008), if a student in the orchestra engages in mild horseplay or even looks bored and unengaged, the conductor abruptly stops the rehearsal and singles the student out for public rebuke before a hushed audience. The offending student is sometimes ordered to stand while being rebuked, or is sometimes required to leave the room. The rationale for these consequences are always framed in the context of "letting the team down," "being disrespectful to the conductor," or failing to "honor the KIPP tradition."

The emphasis on discipline and hard work pays off, to say the least. The KIPP orchestra has earned a national reputation for being one of the top middle-school orchestras in the country (in league with similar schools designed specifically for the performing arts). Within the span of a half-dozen years, the KIPP middle-school orchestra has performed at the Lincoln Center, Carnegie Hall, and the Apollo Theater. The orchestra has given concerts in a variety of cities around the country and has performed on the same stage with accomplished professional classical soloists.

The core lesson of this example is not to highlight the musical accomplishments of the KIPP orchestra. Rather, the lesson here is to highlight how student participation in an orchestra, and the discipline to which students must submit, is a *tool* for the greater goal of *character development as a foundation for academic learning*. Being a member of the KIPP orchestra is the one thing that every child in the school has in common. Once practically every student in the school is involved in a school activity, the fundamental focus is on creating a disciplined "achievement culture" around that activity. Although the orchestra is an elective, its value lies in its ability to develop the non-cognitive skills of patience, persistence, practice, thoroughness, teamwork, self-control, and striving for perfection that are just as important for nurturing academic skills. Most of the instruments that students learn to play are noted in the musical world as being the most challenging instruments to master in an orchestra. As quoted in Whitman (2008), the KIPP principal is noted for often repeating the phrase: "If you can play the violin, you can read *To Kill a Mockingbird*. If you can play the viola, you can do algebra" (p. 166).

Enjoy Freedom/Autonomy From Bureaucratic Regulations

Most schools described as paternalistic by Whitman (2008) are charter schools that are not bound by the same bureaucratic regulations by which public schools are bound. As a result, principals, teachers, and staff are freer to implement the changes needed to mold educational practices in order to accomplish performance objectives. The American Indian Public Charter School in Oakland, California, is a prime example of what freedom from bureaucratic regulations is able to accomplish (see Sidebar 7.4).

Principals in traditional schools usually have to accept whatever teachers are assigned to them by the district, and they have limited ability to set their own curriculum, to select textbooks, to mandate longer days or extended school years, to require longer workdays from teachers, or to free teachers from time-consuming and burdensome paperwork. In contrast, the charter school principals in the schools profiled by Whitman (2008) are not required to answer to the district's superintendent or school board. As a result, these schools can experiment "in ways that would be unimaginable in many neighborhood schools" (p. 271). To state the matter more bluntly, paternalistic school administrators have more freedom to design and run their schools as they see fit.

Freedom in Hiring Teaching Staff

Paternalistic schools have the freedom to handpick the instructors they want to teach in their schools (as opposed to having to accept often incompetent or oppositional teachers that are foisted on them by the district central office). In most instances, non-union teachers can be hired through unconventional means (e.g., through the Internet). This is a distinct advantage considering the fact that, by doing so, teachers can be required to work Saturdays (during the school year) and during the Summer. Teachers are also encouraged to carry cell phones so they can respond to students' needs during after-school hours. The hiring of non-union teachers is also an advantage when school administrators evaluate teacher performance. In paternalistic schools, teachers are evaluated by their principals directly on their ability to improve the students' academic performance. Teachers whose students continue to perform poorly in the assessment of their academic skills can be fired (which would not be possible with union teachers).

Many principals in paternalistic schools are free to hire prospective teachers who do not as yet have a teaching credential from the state, or who even have not matriculated through a college of education. There are many reasons why paternalistic (particularly charter) schools avoid hiring graduates from colleges of education. One major reason is that principals of paternalistic schools feel that traditional teachers are not socialized either educationally or attitudinally to have what it takes to be successful to teach a difficult population of needy students in schools that have a singular focus on raising academic achievement. That is to say, successful teachers in paternalistic schools are expected to have a "fire in their belly" for successfully teaching economically disadvantaged minority students. As a result, many paternalistic schools tend to recruit heavily from Teach for America graduates (see Sidebar 4.1), most of whom are bright, "book smart" students from top colleges who do not possess a teaching credential. Many principals hire new teachers who are guided by the conviction that "a teacher who did well in school is likely to be a better teacher than a mediocre student with a teaching credential" (Whitman, 2008, p. 87).

Most importantly, paternalistic schools (most of which are charter schools) are freed from the constraints of having to hire applicants who are members of teachers' unions. In order to hire teachers who are better suited to the goals of the American Indian Public Charter School, the principal used his own funds to pay higher salaries to non-union graduates from top-tier schools (Whitman, 2008). Because this particular principal already had personal wealth from real estate investments, he was able to pay teachers extra bonuses for going the "extra mile" with students by spending time with them in order to raise achievement test scores.

Freedom to Enact Curriculum Changes

The Oakland Charter Academy (OCA) was started in 1993 in Oakland, California, by Mexican American parents who were not happy with Oakland's programs for English-language learners. When it was first opened, OCA provided bilingual education in Spanish and heavily emphasized Mexican history. The school had no textbooks in English, and had no English language arts instruction. In order to move the OCA from a position where only seven students out of 170 were proficient in one subject area on state tests (year 2004) to achieving the most dramatic Academic Performance Index (API) gains of any school in Oakland (year 2006), its newly hired principal had to make drastic changes that could only be made without the bureaucractic constraints that are typical of traditional public schools (Whitman, 2008).

The new principal started by firing all of OCA's teachers and secretaries. No Spanish instructors were included in any of the new teachers who were hired. Instead, instructors lacking full teaching credentials, but who graduated from top-notch universities, were hired. In addition, the janitor was fired and replaced by a policy requiring students to be solely responsible for keeping the school clean. The principal then removed all computers and gave them away to the students. He replaced the entire curriculum with state-adopted textbooks that were aligned with state standards and emphasized English language arts, math, and reading. As a consequence for disciplinary infractions, a new policy was implemented whereby students were required to go to the principal's private residence and do yardwork.

Freedom to "Stay Small"

Of all of the paternalistic schools profiled by Whitman (2008), the smallest is a high school that enrolls no more than 530 students, which is approximately half the size of an average urban high school. The reason that highly effective schools have smaller enrollments comes as no surprise. Smaller schools enable principals and teachers to establish more intimate personal connections to students, to tailor academic assistance to the specific needs of struggling students, and to create a more cohesive sense of community among the students. In larger schools, "school spirit" is largely confined to cheering for the home team at athletic events. In smaller paternalistic schools, individual students come to feel that their success is closely tied to the success of their classmates. Thus, when classes of students take achievement tests, they spontaneously congratulate and spur each other on when their classmates do well. Such camaraderie is much more difficult to create in large, faceless schools enrolling thousands of students.

Reject "Street Culture," and Keep It Out of Schools

Quack Multiculturalism often attempts to romanticize (particularly black and Hispanic) street culture as an "authentic" manifestation of minority life that audiences are obligated to appreciate and respect if they are to be seen as "in step" with current fashions (e.g., see Hale-Benson, 1986; Kochman, 1981). To disapprove of, or to show an aversion to, street culture traits is viewed as middle-class naïveté or a lack of cultural sensitivity and enlightenment.

The paternalistic schools profiled by Whitman (2008) are founded on the observation that "minority parents want to do the right thing but often don't have the time or resources to keep their children from being dragged down by an unhealthy street culture" (p. 28). Many inner-city parents—many of whom are single mothers—actively choose to send their children to paternalistic schools because they feel that neighborhood schools are breeding grounds for gang membership, drugs, and early sexual activity. According to Whitman (2008), "[Inner-city parents] are often desperate for alternatives—and are particularly excited to find a no-nonsense public school committed to readying their children for college" (p. 40).

Paternalistic schools intentionally and assertively suppress all aspects of street culture, which includes, but is not limited to, street slang; the use of the "n-word" and other verbal cursing behavior; writing gang insignia on notebooks; or wearing gang-related clothing to school.

The concept of street culture refers not only to the outer, visible trappings of gang identification, but also to self-defeating attitudes that are celebrated on the streets but that undermine attitudes necessary for school success. McCloskey (2008) observes that working-class and underclass adolescents (of any ethnicity) often have difficulty making the transition to manhood, and often "act out" these difficulties within the context of school. These males tend to rebel against female authority figures in school, and they define their masculinity by skipping class, mouthing off to teachers, and getting into trouble by breaking school rules. In many instances, the "way of the street" is used to resolve conflicts in schools, and the results are often deadly.

In a typical scenario, two males accidentally bump into each other, or have a small, seemingly insignificant disagreement. Soon, this escalates into angry words that morph into personal insults. As described by McCloskey (2008):

> Soon the two young men stand squarely, chest to chest, exchanging threats. The problem is neither can back down without losing face, so it becomes difficult to defuse the confrontation, even if one or both want to. (p. 207)

Gang membership, fighting, and other forms of antisocial behavior give school-aged males (most of whom grow up with absent fathers) a tangible means to acquire power, status, and a sense of identity and belonging (McCloskey, 2008). Once out of school (i.e., by expulsion, dropping out, or graduation), many students gravitate toward membership in more dangerous gangs (see Chapter 8).

Educators with extensive school experience know all too well that no matter how hard a ghetto student works to get through school and avoid getting into trouble, he can lose everything in the blink of an eye if he loses his temper to the wrong person, or simply finds himself in the wrong place at the wrong time. Because of these omnipresent dangers, educators in paternalistic schools are constantly guiding (particularly male) students on ways to control their emotions, avoid dangerous situations, and/or de-escalate potentially deadly conflicts (McCloskey, 2008).

Embody Teacher/Administrator Devotion to Students

The core feature that describes the emotional bond between adults and students in paternalistic schools is reflected in the *in loco parentis* doctrine. Here, school leaders in paternalistic schools implicitly assume that school administrators and staff will need to periodically serve as surrogate parents to their students. Paternalistic schools serve a population in which most children are raised by single parents, most of whom are overburdened by raising more than one child, working at low-wage jobs (some working multiple jobs), and who speak little English and/or are high school dropouts.

As a condition for the privilege of having their children enrolled in a high-achieving paternalistic school, some schools initially required parents to volunteer 10 hours to the school each year. However, this requirement was abandoned once it became painfully evident that even this minimal requirement was too much for many parents to give (Whitman, 2008). Other paternalistic schools require parents to sign nonbinding contracts pledging to support their children by providing a quiet study space at home, getting their kids to school on time, and making sure that their children completed their homework. However, Whitman (2008) reports that these contracts are largely symbolic. Administrators in paternalistic schools know from experience that inner-city low-income parents, for whatever reasons, will not be involved in the schools to the extent that more affluent middle-class parents are. Although paternalistic schools certainly encourage parental involvement, they do not rely on parental involvement nor gravitate toward a "parent-driven school" concept for determining how the school is ultimately run.

In paternalistic schools, teachers have a relationship with students that allows them to oversee the character development of students in ways that are rare in regular schools. For example, teachers closely monitor students' use of street slang, attraction to adopting the symbolism and mannerisms of gang life, and students' general deportment while they are in school (Whitman, 2008).

In paternalistic schools, principals will go to extra lengths to enforce the school's academic rigor by making sure students do not miss school. As reported in Whitman (2008), the principal of one school would park her car outside of the homes of tardy students and honk on the horn until the students came out. At another school, the principal handed out alarm clocks to students with subpar attendance records, and actually sent taxis to pick them up at home if they did not show up at school on time. Another principal personally calls certain students at home each morning before school to wake them up because their parents work a night shift.

Strict discipline exists concurrently with support, genuine affection, and encouragement from adult administrators, teachers, and staff at paternalistic schools (for an illustration of this counter-intuitive relationship, see Sidebar 7.5). As one of many examples, the KIPP Academy employs full-time social workers on staff who assist students with personal problems (Whitman, 2008).

Sidebar 7.5   Do Tough Students Hate Tough Teachers?

Consider the following account of a Pakistani man's childhood memories growing up in a working-class, ethnically diverse West London public school:

> We'd often get a fresh-faced, idealistic teacher who had no doubt read Marx and Malcolm X and done an elective in post-colonial theory at polytechnic. We ate those suckers alive. Desperate to empathize with our persecution, they were knocked dead by our indifference and rampant misbehavior. At the first sniff of guilt-ridden middle-class weakness, the feral instincts of teenage boys were unleashed and the class descended into anarchy. They thought we'd been crazed by oppression, so didn't want to come down too hard on us. They wanted to "understand" instead. When it did get too much for them and they threatened to march one of us to the headmaster's office, our immediate protest would be: "You're a racist!" They'd cower behind their desks, mortified that we'd recognized some deeply suppressed prejudice

(continued)

within them, while we got back to hurling insults, beating the crap out of each other and rolling joints to smoke at lunchtime. . . . A stalwart gang of diehard traditionalists prevented us from leaving school illiterate. Chief among them was Mr. Garrett, my form tutor. He was an imposing behemoth of a man who couldn't have cared less about our ethnicity and historical subjugation. He had high expectations of how we should behave and apply ourselves, and flew into thunderous, terrifying rages whenever we failed to meet them. He was the kind of guy who'd never get a job in education today. For some kids he was the most solid male presence they had in their lives. Whenever I bump into former classmates in my old neighborhood, he's the teacher we remember most fondly, wondering how he's doing now. He didn't always have our affection, but he commanded our respect. He saw enough innate worth in us to set standards and be bitterly disappointed when we fell short. Things are very different today. I have a friend who teaches, and he says it's normal for teachers not to reprimand badly behaved black kids because "they suffer enough oppression as it is." The soft bigotry of wet liberals is as insidious as the racism of white supremacists. Lowering the bar for children because you consider them oppressed has the same effect as expecting little of them because you think them inferior. We could never pull our stunts on Mr. Garrett. He was hard on us all—black, white and brown—but rigorously fair. . . . It's 16 years since I left his care, and I'm now a writer who has just had his first novel published. If Mr. Garrett is reading this, I'd like to thank him for myself and on behalf of all the other boys whose lives he impacted so furiously, and so positively upon.

(© Nirpal Singh Dhaliwal, *Sunday Times*, April 9, 2006, retrieved from http://www .timesonline.co.uk. Reprinted with permission from Capel & Land Ltd.)

Critics who do not like the enhanced disciplinary structure of paternalistic schools disparage such schools as "harmful" to students, as illustrated by the Knowledge Is Power Program (KIPP) being mocked by some as the "Kids in Prison Program" schools (Whitman, 2008). The irony is that when students look back on their experiences in paternalistic schools, they speak fondly about them. As quoted in Whitman (2008), one student remarked:

They are extremely strict here but the teachers strive and strive for you to learn. . . . Being at KIPP is like being in your house without your parents—and that's why a lot of kids say KIPP is like a second home. (p. 162)

Adult Approval as a Natural Reinforcer

Professionals with years of experience applying behavioral modification principles in schools generally agree that using a balanced variety of positive reinforcements works best for students. In order to motivate students to develop and internalize desired behaviors in schools, educators use tangible rewards (e.g., stickers, crackers, certificates, pencils, etc.), activity rewards (e.g., in-class parties and games, field trips), status rewards (e.g., line leader or extra bathroom privileges, lunch with the teacher, name on a Most Improved Student wall plaque), and secondary rewards (e.g., tokens or school dollars that can be exchanged for tangible rewards at a school store; cards on which accrued stamps can be redeemed for a special class privilege).

However, educators know that they have reached students when they are motivated primarily by a teacher's approval, or the desire not to let them down. In paternalistic schools, the strict emphasis on good behavior and academic achievement—coupled with the close concern, support, and attention teachers shower on students in order to get them to succeed—fosters a motivation for students to emit desired behaviors simply because they want to please the school adults who they perceive as caring deeply for them (Whitman, 2008).

ADDITIONAL RESOURCES

Supplemental Reading

Mathews, J. (2009). *Work hard. Be nice: How two inspired teachers created the most promising schools in America.* Chapel Hill, NC: Algonquin Books.

McCloskey, P. J. (2008). *The street stops here: A year at a Catholic high school in Harlem.* Berkeley: University of California Press.

Tough, P. (2008). *Whatever it takes: Geoffrey Canada's quest to change Harlem and America.* New York, NY: Houghton Mifflin.

Whitman, D. (2008). *Sweating the small stuff: Inner-city schools and the new paternalism.* Washington, DC: Thomas D. Fordham Institute.

Films

Chops (2007). Filmed by Bruce Broder, follows a group of high school musicians from Jacksonville, Florida, as they pursue their goal to win the most prestigious jazz band competition in the country: the annual Essentially Ellington Festival in New York City. The film documents their journey, from the first day they played together as a band to overcoming their fears as they travel to New York to compete against the best of the best. The film centers on the collaborative process of building a top-notch ensemble, taking the audience through the rehearsal process and demonstrating how this dedicated bunch of student musicians learns to push against the edges of their talents.

Pressure Cooker (2008). This documentary, directed by Jennifer Grausman and Mark Becker, follows three African American students and their teacher in a culinary arts program at Philadelphia's Frankford high school. Wilma Stephenson teaches Culinary Arts at Frankford High to underprivileged kids whose only avenue for making it out of the ghetto lies in landing a scholarship to an institution of higher learning. She is a dedicated and devoted mentor to her students, and is a strict disciplinarian with 38 years of experience in the classroom. Consequently, her students dare not show up late or unprepared, or cut-up, step out of line, or fail to focus on the task at hand out of fear of incurring the wrath of this ever-vigilant taskmaster. Her dead serious approach to education comes out of love and wanting to maximize the potential of each and every one of her pupils. Since she knows that none of her students' parents can afford the cost of college tuition, she also gets personally involved in helping them understand the ins-and-outs of the scholarship application process. In fact, Wilma proudly points out that 11 members of last year's cooking class landed three-quarters of a million dollars in financial aid. Pressure Cooker is an uplifting bio-pic, which focuses narrowly on the fates of three aspiring chefs inspired to dare to dream big during their senior year despite hailing from humble origins.

The Street Stops Here (2010). This film chronicles one year in the life of legendary basketball coach Bob Hurley and his players on the St. Anthony high school boys' basketball team. St. Anthony's high school is a black parochial school in the ghetto of Jersey City, New Jersey. *The Street Stops Here* follows coach Hurley as he struggles to inspire and motivate those around him in order to keep St. Anthony's from closing due to financial shortfalls. The documentary also focuses on key players whose only ticket out of the ghetto is basketball and the hard wisdom of a fierce, demanding coach. In his tenure at the school, coach Hurley has had over 950 career wins and has sent over 150 players to college on scholarships. The team has garnered 23 state parochial championships, 10 Tournament of Champions titles, and 3 USA Today national championships. Seven of coach Hurley's players have received McDonald's All-American awards, 5 of his students became NBA first-round picks. Only two players in his 36 years of coaching have not gone on to attend college after graduation. Coach Hurley himself has received 3 national coach of the year awards. Despite St. Anthony's reputation, the school's athletic facilities reflect the poverty of the surrounding community. The school doesn't even have a gym, and the team must practice at a nearby building used as a bingo hall.

The school's outdoor trailers, the school auditorium, and school cafeteria must double as classrooms, locker rooms, and weight training rooms for the team.

Contact Information

Promoting Alternative Thinking Strategies (PATHS)
>For training information:
>PATHS Training LLC
>Carol A. Kusché, PhD
>PATHS Training LLC
>Phone and FAX: (206) 323-6688
>ckusche@comcast.net
>Dorothy Morelli
>dorothygm@hotmail.com
>(615) 364-6606

For curriculum information and materials:
>Prevention Science Customer Service Representative
>Channing Bete Company
>One Community Place
>South Deerfield, MA 01373-0200
>Toll free: 1-877-896-8532
>Fax: 1-800-499-6464
>Web site: www.preventionscience.com

8

Crime, Delinquency, and Gangs

Crime, juvenile delinquency, and violent gangs are problems that are of utmost concern to most Americans (Allen, Trzcinski, & Kubiak, 2012; Sourcebook of Criminal Justice Statistics, 2011a, 2011b), and young people appear to be disproportionately involved in these activities in American society (see Sidebar 8.1). Citizens expect students, teachers, and staff to be safe and secure in schools, which are a primary socialization agent of young people in society. Unfortunately, a disproportionately higher incidence of school crime is reported in public schools located in urban, inner-city areas. Many metropolitan inner-city schools are traditionally viewed as unsafe and dangerous places, where assaults, drugs, weapons, and gang-related warfare are fairly commonplace.

✎ Sidebar 8.1 Racial/Age Disproportionalities in American Crime Statistics for 2009

- 48 percent of all homicide victims were African American
- 9.8 percent of all homicide victims were under the age of 18
- 47 percent of all homicide victims under the age of 18 were African American
- 37 percent of all homicide offenders were African American
- 5.8 percent of all homicide offenders were under the age of 18
- 58 percent of all homicide offenders under the age of 18 were African American
- Out of all persons arrested for a variety of crimes, 69.1 percent were white, 28.3 percent were African American, 1.4 percent were Native American/ Alaskan Native, and 1.2 percent were Asian/Pacific Islander (data for Hispanics not provided).

(continued)

- Out of all persons arrested for a variety of crimes, 14.1 percent were under the age of 18.
- Out of all persons under age 18 arrested for crimes, the breakdown of arrests—from highest to lowest percentages—is as follows (only select crimes are shown):

Crime	Percentage of Arrests
Property crime[1]	24.4
Violent crime[2]	14.9
Disorderly conduct	8.8
Drug abuse violations	8.8
Curfew/loitering violations	5.9
Weapons possession	1.7

[1]Includes burglary, larceny/theft, motor vehicle theft, arson
[2]Includes murder, non-negligent manslaughter, forcible rape, robbery, and aggravated assault

Adapted from U.S. Department of Justice, Federal Bureau of Investigation (2010). *Crime in the United States 2009.* Clarksburg, WV: Criminal Justice Information Service Division.

Crime, juvenile delinquency, and gangs are inseparable from, and a function of, the conditions of the community that surrounds the school (Lawrence, 2007). However, this relationship is not always perfect. The spate of school shootings involving multiple deaths that were well publicized during the 1990s (e.g., Westside Middle School in Jonesboro, Arkansas; Columbine High School in Littleton, Colorado) focused the public's attention on the fact that school violence and crime are not limited only to inner-city schools.

School districts that are plagued by crime, juvenile delinquency, and gangs experience unusually high levels of violence, disorder, unruly behavior, and property damage, all of which make meaningful learning all but impossible. The role of the school psychologist, as with all other educational support personnel (e.g., guidance counselors, social workers), is typically conceived as helping at-risk students better adjust to school, cope with problems and stressors outside of school, or at a minimum, stay out of trouble. Secondarily, school psychologists seek to help teachers to better serve the needs of crime-prone students in regular or "alternative" classes. This is accomplished through the use of counseling and consultation skills in the context of meeting with individual students, student groups, families, and/or teachers.

Although these are perhaps the most typical roles for school psychologists (if they get to do these at all), common sense dictates that these roles are inadequate for meeting the needs of districts that serve large numbers of crime/gang-involved students. In such situations, a philosophical dilemma arises for the school psychologist. That is, should the school psychologist spend most of his or her time in attempts to help school officials *prevent* young children from being seduced by crime, delinquency, and gangs? Or, should the school psychologist spend most of his or her time working to ameliorate the personal problems of individual students who are already involved with gangs and crime? Or, would this time be better spent in efforts to *minimize the damage and disruption* that these students cause for other law-abiding students in the schools?

In an ideal world, it would be best if all of these professional objectives could be pursued with equal vigor. However, this is not reality. School psychologists working in difficult school districts must arrive at mutually beneficial agreements with their employers as to how they can best spend their time.

In an effort to be sensitive to this dilemma, the purpose of this chapter is to describe a wide variety of resources that are available to school psychologists (and other pupil personnel service professionals) who work in difficult school districts plagued by crime, juvenile delinquency, and gangs. By necessity, the chapter discusses the individual character traits of crime/gang-involved children and youth, which may be helpful in individual counseling contexts. As discussed in Chapter 7, some schools within districts can avoid many crime/gang problems altogether by starting charter schools that are explicitly designed to repel criminal chaos and mayhem. Unfortunately, many schools do not have this luxury. School psychologists can also assist districts as consultants if they are aware of local, state, and federal organizations and programs that exist primarily to provide helpful information and resources to troubled schools and school districts.

School psychologists can access many excellent texts devoted to broad-based scholarship on school violence, school bullying, juvenile justice, and delinquency (e.g., see Jimerson & Furlong, 2006; Jimerson, Swearer, & Espelage, 2009; Springer & Roberts, 2011). This chapter is narrower in scope, focusing on issues that impact primarily inner-city urban schools that traditionally educate high proportions of ethnic/racial minority students.

CONTEXTS FOR CRIME

The notion that multicultural problems in education can be fully understood while ignoring the vexing topics of crime, delinquency, and gangs in metropolitan schools is like a medical student training to be an oncologist without being exposed to the study of cancer. The proverbial elephant in the room is the inescapable fact that perpetrators of crime, as well as the victims of crime, are not evenly distributed across racial and ethnic subgroups in a given society (e.g., see Sidebar 8.1). In every country on the globe, such subgroup disproportionalities exist (e.g., Albrecht, 1997; Gabbidon, 2010; Gabor, 1994; Greene & Gabbidon, 2009; New Century Foundation, 2005; Tonry, 1997; U.S. Department of Justice, 2011). Within any country, disproportionalities in rates of crime and victimization typically are concentrated at higher levels in economically disadvantaged racial/ethnic minority communities and neighborhoods.

Neighborhood Characteristics Associated With Crime

What characteristics of neighborhoods are associated with high rates of crime? Sampson (2011) reviews research showing the significant correlation between geographic isolation of racial minority groups and higher rates of poverty, unemployment, family disruption and/or single-parent status, adolescent delinquency, teenage pregnancy, child mistreatment, dropping out of high school, crime, violence, and arrests—all of which are relatively stable over time. These are called areas of "concentrated disadvantage" in the sociological literature. These areas of concentrated disadvantage are also characterized by *social disorganization*, defined as "the inability of a community structure to realize the common interests of its residents in maintaining effective social controls" (Sampson, 2011).

More economically advantaged communities with higher rates of social organization tend to be characterized by a more dense concentration of both formal and/or informal interpersonal networks. When non-related adults have meaningful relationships that extend beyond the immediate household (i.e., through friendship, participation in common activities, or mutual membership in outside organizations), the adults are better able to observe children's actions and activities in different circumstances, talk to each other about children in the neighborhood, engage in informal surveillance of one another's homes, compare notes, establish norms, and reinforce each other's discipline of their children. In contrast, adults in socially disorganized neighborhoods are less likely to intervene in child/adolescent misbehavior if there is no mutual trust among residents, when rules governing appropriate behavior are unclear or nonexistent, or when residents fear one another (Sampson, 2011). In addition, Sampson (2011) reviews studies showing that neighborhoods characterized by high "moral cynicism" reflect higher levels of violence and crime. Moral cynicism is evident whenever respondents agree with statements such as "Laws were made to be broken," "It's okay to do anything you want as long as you don't hurt anyone," or "To make money, there are no right and wrong ways anymore, only easy ways and hard ways."

The crime and negative consequences from these processes, in turn, have a negative effect on further deteriorating community cohesion and structure. Neighborhoods and communities affected by higher crime rates result in (a) individuals physically or psychologically withdrawing from community life out of fear; (b) a decline of neighborhood property values; (c) a further weakening of the social control processes that inhibit crime; (d) a sharp decline in the ability of a community to mobilize and work together for common goals; and (e) deteriorating business opportunities and investments in the community (Skogan, 1990).

By extension, schools that serve socially disorganized communities experience higher rates of crime perpetration and victimization. Current data on the frequency and types of crimes committed in school systems can be gleaned from annual or biennial (once every two years) national surveys such as the *School Crime Supplement to the National Crime Victimization Survey* (U.S. Department of Justice), *Indicators of School Crime and Safety* (Bureau of Justice Statistics and National Center for Education Statistics), and the *School Survey on Crime and Safety* (National Center for Education Statistics)—to name a few (see Furlong & Sharkey, 2006; Lawrence, 2007, for additional sources).

School Crime

A crime can be generally defined as an action (or in some cases a lack of action) that breaches a rule or law, for which some governing authority can prosecute and prescribe a punishment (by law). Crimes that occur in the context of schools may or may not be punishable by state law, but all school crimes are susceptible to receiving some punishment or sanction by school authorities. School crimes are extremely heterogeneous, and can range from crimes having a clear victim (e.g., assaults, theft) to victimless crimes (e.g., possession of drugs); crimes directed toward property (e.g, vandalism) versus persons (e.g., armed robbery); nonviolent crimes (e.g., harassment, verbal threats) to violent crimes (e.g., rape, murder); and crimes in which the mere possession of a forbidden object or substance violates a rule or law (e.g., possession of a firearm, explosive device, or illegal drug).

At the time of this writing, a recently released study conducted by the U.S. Department of Education Office of Civil Rights reported results from 72,000 schools serving 85 percent of the nation's students. The data revealed stark racial disparities in discipline rates. According to advance reports of findings from newspaper articles, approximately 1 in 5 African American boys and 1 in 10 African American girls were suspended from school during the 2009–2010 school year. In addition, African American students in large school systems were arrested far more often than their white peers on campus (see http://ocrdata.ed.gov).

In March 2011, the *Philadelphia Inquirer* published a seven-part series of articles entitled "Assault on Learning" (http://www.philly.com/philly/news/special_packages/inquirer/school-violence/130788528.html), which detailed serious problems with daily school violence and crime in the Philadelphia public schools (enrolling approximately 63 percent black and 17 percent Hispanic students; see Sable, Plotts, Mitchell, & Chen, 2010). Reporters spent a full year conducting more than 300 interviews with teachers, administrators, students and their families, district officials, police officers, court officials, and school violence experts. The newspaper created a database to analyze more than 30,000 serious incidents—from assaults to robberies to rapes—that occurred during the five years prior to publication of the report. This information was supplemented by district and state data on suspensions, intervention, and 9-1-1 calls. Reporters also examined police reports, court records, transcripts, contracts, and school security videos.

In addition, the *Philadelphia Inquirer* also worked with researchers at Temple University to conduct an independent survey of the district's 13,000 teachers and aides. More than 750 teachers and aides responded to questions about violence and its impact on students' education.

The newspaper also obtained internal district documents detailing violent incidents during the past five years. On specific cases, reporters interviewed victims, perpetrators, police officers, attorneys, witnesses, and attended court hearings. One reporter had regular access over nearly six months to students, teachers, and administrators inside South Philadelphia High School, one of the city's most dangerous schools.

According to the series, in the 2010 school year, 690 teachers were assaulted—a number that totaled 4,000 in the years between 2005 to 2009. On an average day in Philadelphia's 268 schools, approximately 25 students, teachers, or other staff members were beaten, robbed, sexually assaulted, or victims of other violent crimes. These figures did not include lesser offenses of extortion, threats, or bullying incidents in a school year (for related information at the national level, see Figures 4.2, 4.3, and 4.4).

CRIME PREVENTION IN SCHOOL SETTINGS

Preventative School Design Features

With proper planning, the physical design of schools can incorporate safety and security elements that can deter crime on school grounds (Ohio School Facilities Commission, 2008). According to Schneider (2010), the designs of safe and secure schools are built on a tripartite model of natural surveillance, natural access control, and territoriality.

Natural Surveillance

Natural surveillance is quite simply the physical ability to see what is going on in and around the school. Impediments to natural surveillance include solid walls, tall shrubs, large signs, parked cars, and other large physical structures that may block a clear view of school grounds (Schneider, 2010). The presence of security cameras strategically placed near trouble spots around the school is one obvious method of implementing surveillance. School corridors can be designed so that they do not include hidden spaces or many outside entrances. In addition, corridors should allow for clear lines of sight between one end of the corridor to the other, so that potential problem situations (such as student bullying and fighting) can be recognized and addressed as quickly as possible. There are other ways to increase natural surveillance, which include (but certainly are not limited to) installing windows in solid walls or replacing solid walls with iron fencing, installing convex mirrors in order to provide visibility around corners, or installing lighting.

Natural Access Control

Natural access control is quite simply the ability to decide who gets in and out of the school. Impediments to natural access control include open breezeways, unlocked doors, and open windows. There are a variety of ways in which schools can be designed to give administrators more control over access to the school. Schools with fewer safety/security problems are designed such that all visitors must enter or leave the building through centralized entrances that are physically near administrative areas (e.g., central offices). Ideally, office staff should be able to observe approaching visitors before they reach school entrances. Two-way pagers provide quick and easy voice access from classrooms to administration areas and to all areas of the building, a feature that is essential for identifying and responding to health and/or behavioral emergencies. Other methods of controlling access include (but are not limited to) the reconfiguration of entry access doors to automatically lock when closed, covering windows with secure metal grates, and wiring the school so that a chief receptionist in the main office can implement a schoolwide lockdown during a crisis emergency with the touch of a button.

Territoriality and Maintenance

Territoriality refers to building indicators that reinforce a message of ownership over the school. Examples of territoriality include signs restricting access, the practice of directing visitors to the office, or posting campus closing times. Maintenance reinforces territoriality by making sure that no part of the school campus remains unkempt for extended periods. Unkempt sections of campus unintentionally communicates that no one is particularly concerned about, or possessive of, that particular part of the school. That appearance, in turn, can lead to the attitude that any part of the school is fair game for abuse and misbehavior. For a wealth of practical ideas for designing schools to enhance school safety, readers are encouraged to consult Schneider, Walker, and Sprague (2000). A partial list of security measures used by schools to reduce crime is provided in Sidebar 8.2.

Sidebar 8.2   Partial List of Security Measures Used by Schools in High-Crime Areas to Reduce Crime

Monitoring the Presence/Activities of Campus Outsiders

- Post guard(s) at main entry gate/door to campus
- Have greeters in strategic building locations
- Enforce uniforms/dress codes for all students, making outsiders easier to identify
- Require regular staff, students, and teachers to wear photo ID badges

(continued)

- Require visitors to prominently wear ID badges
- Require vehicle parking stickers for all cars

Swift Response to Fights on Campus

- Provide alarm whistles to all staff and teachers
- Strategically place cameras that can relay events quickly to central office

Vandalism Prevention

- Apply graffiti-resistant coatings to walls
- Add aesthetically pleasing wall murals that discourage graffiti
- Install glass-break sensors

Anti-Theft Measures

- Install interior intrusion and/or motion-detection sensors
- Install bars on windows
- Bolt down computers and TVs

Anti-Drug/Alcohol Measures

- Use drug-detection dogs
- Have random drug-detection searches
- Require clear/open mesh backpacks
- Require students to remain on-campus for lunch

Weapon Prevention/Detection

- Install walk-through metal detectors
- Use handheld metal detectors
- Implement "crime stopper" phone hotlines with rewards for useful information
- Have random locker, backpack, and vehicle searches
- Inspect book bags and purses with x-ray technology

Parking Lot Problems

- Use card identification systems for parking lot entry
- Have roving guards patrol lot areas
- Install parking lot cameras that feed images to the central office

False Fire Alarms/Bomb Threats

- Install sophisticated alarm systems that allow assessment of alarms first before they become audible
- Install caller ID phone system

- Record all incoming phone calls
- Route all incoming phone calls through a district office
- Remove pay phones from campus

Bus Problems

- Randomly test school bus drivers for drug/alcohol use
- Install and mount video cameras within buses
- Employ security aides on buses
- Provide cell phones to bus drivers

Teacher Safety

- Install video cameras in classrooms
- Provide "duress" alarms for teachers to use in emergencies
- Leave classroom doors open during class
- Install intercom systems in classrooms with direct access to the central school office
- Provide teachers with two-way radios to school-site security guards

(Adapted from Siegel & Welsh, 2009)

School Resource Officers (SROs)

The employment of School Resource Officers (SROs) is one way that schools attempt to prevent crime on school campuses (see also Chapter 9). SROs are police officers who are employed either part- or full-time during school hours by school administrators (Lawrence, 2007). The cost for employing SROs is generally shared with a local police department, and the specific duties and responsibilities are agreed upon by the police department and the school system. In some locations, SROs are assigned to a single school, whereas other SROs may split their time between two or more schools. Although SRO roles may vary slightly among districts and schools within districts, SRO officers function as law enforcement officers, counselors, and teachers (Burke, 2001). Some SROs conduct their work dressed in full police uniforms, whereas others work in schools as plain-clothes officers. According to the 2011 National Association of School Resource Officers webpage (http://www.nasro.org/mc/page.do?sitePageId=114180&orgId=naasro), there are currently more than 6,000 members of this school-based police organization.

Kupchik and Bracy (2010) conducted research in four public high schools in a southwestern and a mid-Atlantic state. The purpose of the research was to gain a deeper understanding of how SROs administer discipline and security on school sites. Within each state, one school comprised mostly of low-income students of color was included in the overall sample. The researchers observed the following practices by SROs at the sites studied (Kupchik & Bracy, 2010, pp. 24–28):

1. *Watching the halls.* SROs spend a substantial portion of their time in schools patrolling the hallways (particularly during high-traffic breaks between classes), supervising cafeterias during lunch times, and overseeing students as they board school buses at the end of the day. Depending on the particular school site, SROs can either perform these duties silently, or they can interact personally with the students while on duty. These behaviors accomplish the following goals: (a) the unavoidable presence of the SRO served as a reminder to students of their close presence, and (b) SROs could quickly respond to disruptions.

2. *Administrative police work.* When not involved in patrolling activities, SROs work in their school offices reviewing incident reports or completing arrest reports for students who have been arrested at school.

3. *Investigating minor incidents.* SROs spend a large part of their time investigating minor incidents such as suspected thefts, vandalism, fights between students, or drug/alcohol possession.

4. *Mentoring.* Some SROs have additional non-police duties in schools (e.g., assistant coaches for sports teams, teaching special classes) that bring them in close contact with students, thereby fostering mentoring relationships. Sometimes the close proximity of SROs encourages some students to approach SROs for counseling on minor personal issues. However, a close mentoring relationship may conflict at times with students' need to avoid divulging personal crime violations.

5. *Helping with school discipline.* Although school discipline issues that have little to no impact on overall school safety are not part of an SRO's negotiated job responsibilities, the researchers identified occasions in which SROs insert themselves (or are asked by administrators to insert themselves) into minor school discipline issues.

6. *Lending legitimacy to school safety initiatives.* Administrators can showcase the presence of SROs in their schools as public relations evidence for how seriously they handle security threats. SROs help administrators defend school policies to concerned parents, and they can help administrators target certain behaviors for harsher consequences. For example, if the administrator establishes a rule that suspended students can only be reinstated to school when accompanied by a parent, and the suspended student attempts to return to the school grounds without a parent, the SRO can arrest the student for trespassing.

7. *Benefits to police departments.* SROs, in the course of their service in schools, get to know students, their families, and their families' problems. Because SROs are still members of police precincts, they can easily share useful information with other police officers that can prevent and/or intervene quickly on problems. SROs can also gather useful information that helps detect and respond to crimes involving students outside of school.

8. *Helping students to feel safer.* According to Kupchik and Bracy's (2010) research, almost all students interviewed reported favorable feelings toward the presence of SROs in their schools. Some felt that SROs deterred crime and others looked to SROs to handle crisis situations. Although some students who were interviewed felt that the presence of SROs did relatively little to decrease crime, they reported feeling pleased that SROs regularly patrolled their schools.

The use of SROs in schools is not without its critics. Critics of the proliferation of police officers in schools claim that several abuses occur, because school-assigned police personnel are not directly subject to the supervisory authority of school administrators, and have not been adequately trained to work in educational settings. Such criticisms include the following (Mukherjee, 2007):

- Derogatory, abusive, and discriminatory comments and conduct
- Intrusive searches
- Unauthorized confiscation of students' personal items, including food, cameras, and essential school supplies
- Inappropriate sexual attention
- Physical abuse
- Arrest for minor non-criminal violations of school rules

Threat Assessment

In 2002, the U.S. Secret Service completed the Safe School Initiative, a study of school shootings and other school-based attacks that was conducted in collaboration with the U.S. Department of Education. The study examined school shootings in the United States as far back as 1974 and involved extensive review of police records, school records, and court documents, including interviews with 10 school shooters. The focus of the study was on developing information about school shooters' pre-attack behaviors and communications. The goal was to identify information about a school shooting that may be identifiable or noticeable before shootings occur, and to help inform efforts to prevent school-based attacks. The findings from the study suggest that some school attacks may be preventable, and that students can play an important role in prevention efforts.

Using the study findings, the Secret Service and Department of Education have modified the Secret Service threat assessment approach for use in schools—to give school and law enforcement professionals tools for investigating threats in school, managing situations of concern, and creating safe school climates (see also Jimerson & Furlong, 2006). At the completion of the Safe School Initiative, the Secret Service and Department of Education published two reports that detail the study findings and lay out a process for threat assessment in schools (e.g., Reddy et al., 2001; Vossekuil, Fein, Reddy, Borum, & Modzeleski, 2002).

Federal Initiatives to Help Schools

The Improving America's Schools Act of 1994, sometimes referred to as the Safe and Drug-Free Schools and Communities Act of 1994, was enacted to (a) prevent violence in and around schools; (b) strengthen programs that prevent the illegal use of alcohol, tobacco, and drugs; (c) involve parents; and (d) coordinate efforts and resources with related federal, state, and community agencies. In addition to providing grants to institutions of higher education, state community-based organizations, and nonprofit agencies, federal assistance is provided to states for grants to local educational agencies, educational service agencies, and consortia. These grants help agencies to establish, operate, and improve local programs of school drug and violence prevention, early intervention, rehabilitation referral, and education in elementary and secondary schools (including intermediate and junior high schools). Under the No Child Left Behind (NCLB) Act of 2001, school districts receiving federal funds must have a policy requiring that any student who brings a firearm or weapon to school will be referred to the criminal justice or juvenile delinquency system.

JUVENILE DELINQUENCY

The term *juvenile delinquency* refers to participation in illegal behavior by a minor who falls under a statutory age limit (usually 15 to 17 years of age, which varies by state; Springer & Roberts, 2011). However, juvenile delinquency encompasses much more than illegal behavior. Juvenile delinquency also includes *status offenses*, which may include consumption of alcohol, tobacco smoking, truancy, and running away from home. These acts may be illegal for persons under a certain age, while remaining legal for all others, which makes them status offenses. Juvenile status offenders are distinguished from juvenile delinquent offenders in that status offenders have not committed an act that would be considered a crime if it were committed by an adult, whereas delinquent youths have committed these acts.

In U.S. society, the illegal actions of adults are sanctioned by both criminal and civil laws. Youth delinquent behavior is sanctioned less heavily in the U.S. judicial system than adult criminality because the law considers juveniles as being less responsible for their behavior compared to adults (Siegel & Welsh, 2009). According to Siegel and Welsh (2009), adolescents are generally characterized as (a) having a stronger preference for risk and novelty, (b) not being as skilled in assessing the potentially negative consequences of risky conduct, (c) being more impulsive and more concerned with short-term rather than long-term consequences, (d) being less able to exercise self-control, and (e) being more susceptible to peer pressure.

Although youths share a lesser degree of legal responsibility than adults for their illegal deeds, they are still subject to being arrested and required to attend a trial, with a chance of incarceration. In addition, they are also granted legal protections that include the right to consult an attorney, to be free from self-incrimination, and to be protected from illegal searches and seizures (Siegel & Welsh, 2009). However, some youth are considered by the state to be so incorrigible that they are tried and convicted as adults.

Risk Factors

It is much too simplistic to characterize juvenile delinquency as being caused by a single issue, event, or set of circumstances. Rather, researchers and theorists frame discussions in terms of *factors* that may contribute to juvenile delinquency—fully recognizing that factors often interact in ways that increase the probability of juvenile delinquency. For example, it is quite normal for many adolescents to want to test their parents', schools', or society's limits on occasion. The propensity to test such limits may, in part, have its roots in constitutional factors (e.g., see Figure 8.1 on page 373). Although adolescents often test limits, this testing does not necessarily have to involve the regular commission of crimes. One factor that may contribute to the regular commission of crimes by juveniles is the negative dynamics of the family and neighborhood environment in which they are raised (e.g., single-parent households in neighborhoods high in social pathology; see Chapter 3). However, many individuals who grow up in dysfunctional situations *do not* fall into patterns of juvenile delinquency. For example, many adults in single-parent situations nevertheless apply strong, consistent parenting skills that help prevent certain law-breaking tendencies from taking root in their children.

Sometimes caregivers can have strong parenting skills, but constitutional factors deeply entrenched in children's personalities and temperaments lure such children to seek opportunities to regularly commit crimes. As examples, many juvenile delinquents diligently seek opportunities where parents are at work or preoccupied, in order to lessen the chances of scrutiny. Other youths are simply more susceptible to peer pressure than others, or are attracted to gangs and other criminal groups despite their parents' best efforts to shield them from these negative influences. Although the factors that influence juvenile delinquency are quite complex (see Springer & Roberts, 2011), there are statistically significant relationships between certain factors and the incidence of juvenile crime. These factors are listed briefly in Sidebar 8.3.

📖 Sidebar 8.3   Correlates of Youth Crime
_____

AGE

- Studies overwhelmingly show that delinquent and criminal behavior is most heavily concentrated in the period of time between ages 11 to 30.
- All of the available research suggests that a positive correlation exists between a diagnosis of conduct disorder as a child, adolescent, or young adult and later involvement in antisocial behavior, criminality, and/or delinquency.
- Childhood aggression is positively associated with delinquent and criminal behavior later in life. Longitudinal studies conclude that persistent childhood aggression is the single best childhood predictor of serious criminality (with the exception of illegal drug use).
- Regardless of the type of crime committed, early-onset offenders commit more crimes later in life than do late-onset offenders.

GENDER

- Although girls tend to physically mature more rapidly than boys, boys begin exhibiting criminal offenses earlier than girls.
- Studies conducted worldwide show, practically without exception, that males are more likely than females to be diagnosed with antisocial personality or antisocial disorder, engage in more violence-laden and sex offenses, and be identified by law enforcement as having committed homicide.
- In the general class of property crime offenses, females tend to be more involved in shoplifting compared to males.

RACE/ETHNICITY/IMMIGRANT STATUS

- In general, nonwhites are more criminally involved than whites in North America. Blacks commit more violent offenses (e.g., assaults, robberies) than do whites, and the extent of these differences usually exceed a ratio of 3 to 1. Violent crime rates are significantly higher in neighborhoods and/or cities with the highest proportions of black residents.
- Blacks are more likely than whites to be the victims of crime, especially involving violent offenses. Blacks have a probability of being murdered that has been found to be close to six times greater than that for whites. U.S. studies estimate that the homicide victimization rate of Native Americans is about twice the average for the country as a whole. Criminal offenders (regardless of race/ethnicity) are more likely to be crime victims than are persons in general.
- Whites surpass blacks in having higher rates of self-reported illegal drug offenses.

- Alcohol abuse is considerably higher among Native Americans than for any other racial/ethnic group in North America. Native Americans are over-represented in criminal offenses related to alcohol consumption (e.g., public drunkenness, disorderly conduct, interpersonal/domestic violence).
- Descendants of East Asia (i.e., Japanese, Chinese, and Koreans) exhibit significantly lower crime rates than do whites. Most studies conducted in the United States show that the crime rates for Pacific Rim Asian Americans is typically about half the rates exhibited by white Americans. In studies conducted in Hawaii, native Oceanic Islanders tend to exhibit substantially higher crime rates than do whites.
- Studies conducted in the United States that investigate the prevalence of immigrant crime reveal a mixed picture, which is complicated by more detailed comparisons of immigrants' countries of origin (i.e., immigrants from some countries show higher rates of crime compared to whites, and immigrants from other countries show lower rates of crime compared to whites).

SOCIAL STATUS

- Antisocial behavior and criminality tends to be more prevalent in the lower social strata than in the upper social strata. The majority of studies conclude that as an individual's years of education increase, or level of income/wealth increases, his or her probability of criminal behavior decreases.
- Regions with relatively high rates of divorced or separated individuals have higher rates of crime than do regions with low divorce or separation rates.
- Children who are born out-of-wedlock as opposed to those whose parents were married at the time of their birth are more likely than children in general to exhibit criminal/delinquent behavior. Most research indicates that offspring who have relatively young parents are more often involved in crime and delinquency than are the offspring of older parents.
- Studies are consistent in showing that persons who engage in delinquent and criminal behavior are significantly more likely to have one or both parents who have been criminally involved than is true for persons in general. Some researchers conclude that criminality in a parent is the strongest family-related variable for predicting a child's probability of serious delinquency or crime, which is elevated even more when both parents have a criminal record.
- Familial alcoholism (especially by the father) and illegal drug use are positively correlated with the offspring's antisocial behavior, illegal drug use, and/or other forms of criminality.

(continued)

- Mental illness is more common among family members of delinquents than among those of non-delinquents. In addition, children who are reared in families with the greatest degree of marital/family discord are significantly more likely to engage in delinquent, criminal, and/or antisocial behavior than are children reared in families with less conflict.
- Studies show that as parental supervision and monitoring increases, the probability that offspring would exhibit delinquent/criminal traits decreases. In addition, harsh and erratic parental discipline is positively associated with delinquent/criminal involvement in offspring, whereas firm and loving parental discipline is negatively related to offspring delinquent/criminal involvement.
- The association between gang membership and involvement in crime and delinquency is positive and statistically significant, and some delinquency usually occurs prior to participation in juvenile gangs. A few studies show that gang members are more likely to be antisocial or physically aggressive than their age-peers.

ECOLOGICAL FACTORS

- Crime rates are higher in urban compared to rural areas.
- Crime rates are generally higher in areas where taverns and liquor stores are most prevalent.
- As religious membership, level of education, and level of income in a geographic region increase, the region's crime rates tend to decrease.

SCHOOL FACTORS

- Nearly all available research shows that high school dropouts exhibit higher rates of criminal offending than do peers who stay in school. School truancy is positively correlated with delinquency/criminality.
- School discipline problems (such as misbehaving in class, smoking during school time, vandalism of school property) are positively associated with delinquent and criminal behavior.

PSYCHOLOGICAL/PERSONALITY CORRELATES

- Persons who engage in habitual criminal behavior are more likely to feel bored than are persons in general. Novelty seeking (i.e., the tendency to search for unusual experiences) is positively correlated with involvement in crime and delinquency. All available evidence points to the positive correlation between sensation seeking (i.e., the active desire for novel, varied, and extreme experiences, often to the point of taking physical and social risks to obtain such experiences) and various factors associated with criminality.

- Nearly all studies find a positive relationship between childhood bullying, callousness (i.e., a temperamental attitude of insensitivity, indifference, and lack of sympathy or concern for the suffering of others), and delinquent/criminal behavior.

- Studies show a consistent tendency for persons who quickly fly off the handle when irritated to be involved in crime to a greater degree than persons who are more reserved.

- According to studies across many countries, persons who are impulsive have a higher probability of committing crimes and exhibiting conduct disorders, psychopathy, and externalizing behavior. Risk taking and recklessness (i.e., willingness to sustain injury or even death in order to obtain a goal) is substantially correlated positively with criminality. The evidence suggests overwhelmingly that criminals and delinquents have lower levels of self-control than the general population. There is a consistent negative correlation between the ability to delay gratification and delinquent behavior. Nearly all relevant studies indicate that delinquents are less future oriented (which is the tendency to think generally about both the short- and long-term consequences of one's actions) than persons in general.

- Lying and deception are behavioral patterns found to be more common among persons involved in criminality as compared to persons who are more law abiding.

DRUG USE/CIGARETTE SMOKING

- Nearly all available research findings show a positive correlation between recreational use of depressants (drugs that slow down brain functioning), stimulants (drugs that speed up brain functioning), and hallucinogens (drugs that distort the brain's processing of perceptual information) and criminality.

- Antisocial behavior and other factors associated with criminality are positively associated with cigarette smoking.

SEXUAL BEHAVIOR

- All available evidence indicates a positive correlation between involvement in illegal drugs and sexual intercourse prior to marriage.

- Persons diagnosed as antisocial first experience sexual intercourse earlier on average than do persons without such diagnoses. Delinquents and criminals begin engaging in sexual intercourse earlier than do persons who are law abiding.

(continued)

COGNITIVE/ATTITUDINAL FACTORS

- Nearly all available studies find that a commitment to becoming educated, and/or a belief in the value of education, is negatively correlated with involvement in delinquent and criminal behavior. Children with conduct disorders express less favorable attitudes toward becoming well educated than do children generally.
- Delinquents have more hostile attitudes toward authority (i.e., government officials, parents, teachers, police) than their similar-aged peers.
- Criminal offenders have lower levels of moral reasoning than do their peers. Most studies indicate that, regardless of their chronological age, delinquents and criminals are similar to toddlers in their levels of moral reasoning.
- Most studies indicate that persons who can take the perspective of another person (particularly in the emotional aspects of role-taking) are less likely to become involved in crime and delinquency than those who find such role taking difficult.
- Most studies show a relationship between criminal offending and lower scores on intelligence tests. Children with conduct disorders have lower IQs than children without conduct disorders. Antisocial persons have lower emotional intelligence (the ability to empathize/sympathize with others) than those who are not antisocial.
- Studies overwhelmingly show a positive relationship between learning disabilities and antisocial behavior in childhood, adolescence, and adulthood. Several forms of slow development in reading ability are unusually common among delinquents and criminals.

MENTAL ILLNESS/DISORDERS

- Persons who engage in criminal or delinquent behavior are more prone to be moderately depressed than are people in general. Studies show a positive relationship between major clinical depression and antisocial behavior.
- Schizophrenics are more likely than non-schizophrenics to display antisocial behaviors during childhood, adolescence, and adulthood.
- Studies show a positive correlation between attention deficit hyperactivity disorder (ADHD) and antisocial behavior, alcoholism, and drug abuse. ADHD is predictive of persistent criminality. ADHD is one of the most robust correlates to criminal conduct and related behavior.
- Oppositional defiant disorder (ODD) is positively correlated with both antisocial behavior and physical aggression.

(Adapted from the *Handbook of Crime Correlates*; Ellis, Beaver, & Wright, 2009)

Race/ethnicity is one significant factor that influences the relative frequency of juvenile offenses that come to the attention of the court system. Although nonwhites are less than 30 percent of the American population, certain groups are overrepresented in various types of offenses reported by Juvenile Court Statistics (see Tables 8.1, 8.2, and 8.3).

According to Greenwood and Turner (2011), many have attributed the sharp rise in juvenile and young adult armed homicides of the latter 1980s to the introduction of crack cocaine in the mid-1980s. This was accompanied by disorganized street markets through which crack cocaine was sold, and the recruitment of young minority males to do most of the street-level selling. They argue that increased involvement in dangerous street-level drug markets led many of these youth to arm themselves, initially for protection. This, in turn, led many of their peers to also engage in defensive arming. The end result of this process, particularly in large cities, was much more gun carrying and use

Table 8.1   National Racial Profiles of Juvenile Delinquency Cases Within Offense: 2008

Race	Offense			
	Person	Property	Drugs	Public Order
White	56%	66%	73%	62%
Black	41%	31%	24%	36%
American Indian	1%	2%	2%	1%
Asian	1%	2%	1%	1%
(Total)	100%	100%	100%	100%

NOTE: Juveniles of Hispanic ethnicity can be of any race; however, most are included in the White racial category. The racial classification American Indian includes American Indian and Alaskan Native. The racial classification Asian includes Asian, Native Hawaiian, and Other Pacific Islander.
(Puzzanchera, Adams, & Sickmund, 2011)

Table 8.2   National Offense Profiles of Juvenile Delinquency Cases Within Race: 2008

Offense	Race			
	White	Black	American Indian	Asian
Person	22%	30%	22%	20%
Property	39%	34%	40%	45%
Drugs	13%	8%	12%	9%
Public Order	27%	29%	26%	26%
(Total)	100%	100%	100%	100%

NOTE: Juveniles of Hispanic ethnicity can be of any race; however, most are included in the White racial category. The racial classification American Indian includes American Indian and Alaskan Native. The racial classification Asian includes Asian, Native Hawaiian, and Other Pacific Islander.
(Puzzanchera, Adams, & Sickmund, 2011)

Table 8.3   National Offense Profiles of Serious Status Offense Cases Within Race: 2008

Offense	Race			
	White	Black	American Indian	Asian
Runaway	9%	21%	5%	21%
Truancy	32%	37%	25%	36%
Curfew	9%	13%	13%	13%
Ungovernability	11%	19%	3%	4%
Liquor Law	28%	5%	44%	16%
Miscellaneous	11%	5%	10%	10%
(Total)	*100%*	*100%*	*100%*	*100%*

NOTE: Juveniles of Hispanic ethnicity can be of any race; however, most are included in the White racial category. The racial classification American Indian includes American Indian and Alaskan Native. The racial classification Asian includes Asian, Native Hawaiian, and Other Pacific Islander.
(Puzzanchera, Adams, & Sickmund, 2011)

by a population "not noted for their dispute-resolution or decision-making skills" (p. 92). Although the initial motive for most of these youths in carrying guns was to defend themselves, the end result was a much higher rate of homicide and aggravated assault among this population that persists to present times.

A General Theory of Juvenile Crime

Social scientists have spent decades attempting to understand the origins and causes of juvenile crime, no matter where it occurs. All policies, rules, and crime-prevention efforts (both inside and outside of schools) are based on a coherent system of beliefs as to what causes juvenile crime. On the one hand, many argue in favor of get tough policies that assume implicitly that offenders act rationally and will be deterred by stringent rules and harsh punishment for offenses. On the other hand, those who favor rehabilitative and therapeutic interventions assume that juvenile crime originates in underlying psychological problems or alcohol/drug abuse that impairs the offender's judgment (Lawrence, 2007). Of course, these two categories are not mutually exclusive. According to Lawrence (2007), no single explanation can comprehensively account for the variety of criminal behaviors of youth, because the problem—and factors that contribute to the problem—are multifaceted.

In their seminal work *A General Theory of Crime*, Michael Gottfredson and Travis Hirschi (1990) integrated concepts from a variety of biological, social, and psychological theories to describe latent traits that, in combination, help explain why individuals engage in criminal behavior. Since publication of their theory, numerous research efforts using a variety of methodologies and subject groups have found empirical support for the basic components of their theory (see reviews in Siegel & Welsh, 2009). The components of Gottfredson and Hirschi's general theory of crime are depicted in Figure 8.1.

Impulsive Personality and Low Self-Control

The propensity to commit antisocial acts begins with an impulsive personality type. Impulsivity, by itself, is not viewed as inevitably leading to delinquency. Rather, impulsivity is a condition that inhibits people from appreciating the long-term consequences of their behavior. Impulsivity sets the stage for a predisposition to enjoy risky behaviors that provide immediate, short-term gratification (e.g., smoking, drinking, gambling, illicit sex). When there is inadequate monitoring of these personality types from home rearing and other contexts, a lack of self-control is a common feature of criminal behavior. In addition to having a predisposition toward impulsivity, persons with limited self-control tend to be self-centered and insensitive to other people's feelings; they prefer physical rather than mental stimulation; and they have a shortsighted here-and-now orientation that finds it difficult to work patiently on tasks and delay gratification for distant goals. Others would describe such persons as adventuresome and/ or reckless, and such persons enjoy behaviors that are exciting, thrilling, and dangerous. As they mature and begin adulthood, such persons tend to have unstable marriages, jobs, and friendships.

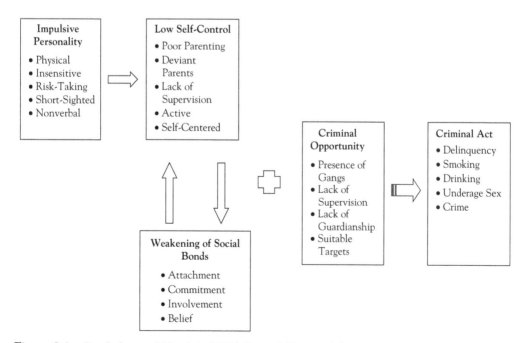

Figure 8.1   Gottfredson and Hirschi's (1990) General Theory of Crime

Impulsivity does not unavoidably lead to delinquent behavior, particularly if adequate and effective parental controls are present. Unfortunately, parents who are unable to properly monitor their child's behavior (due to absence of positive personal traits or the presence of deficient personal traits), unable to recognize deviant behavior when it occurs, or unable to appropriately punish misbehavior will exacerbate a lack of self-control in children who are constitutionally predisposed for impulsivity. Delinquent children are much more likely to be raised by parents who themselves are criminally deviant (Murray & Farrington, 2005; Shaw, 2003; Smith & Farrington, 2004). Social class is inextricably linked to these issues. In the words of Siegel and Welsh (2009), "parental competence is required if a youngster hopes to escape the carnage wrought by residence in a disorganized lower-class neighborhood" (p. 255).

Weakening of Social Bonds

Parents of delinquent youngsters tend to be less likely to show interest in their children and to display higher levels of hostile detachment (Siegel & Welsh, 2009). Juvenile delinquency tends to be lower if both or at least one parent can provide the type of structure that integrates children into their families, while giving them the opportunity to assert their individuality and regulate their own behavior (Simons & Conger, 2007). Adolescents whose parents maintain close, supportive relationships with them report less delinquent behavior and substance use regardless of the type of family structure (Wainright & Patterson, 2006).

Criminal Opportunity

Delinquents, like non-delinquents, have days filled with boring, conventional behaviors such as attending school, church, and concerts. However, when confronted with delinquent *opportunities* (e.g., unguarded homes containing valuable merchandise), crime-prone individuals will have a higher probability of violating the law.

The Developmental Trajectory of Criminality

Stability vs. Continuity of Criminal Behavior

Wright et al. (2008) opine that "the evidence on the stability of criminal behavior [across human development] is so strong that the relationship between past and future misbehavior constitutes one of the 'brute facts' of crime" (p. 17). Wright et al. (2008) review research pointing to the conclusion that young children who act impulsively are difficult to manage, tend to be hyperactive, and are more likely to commit delinquent acts as adolescents. These adolescents, in turn, are more likely to engage in repeated criminal behavior as adults. That is, virtually every study they reviewed that includes measures of early problem behavior (measured as early as age 4 or younger) significantly predicts individual differences in frequent and serious adult criminal behavior.

When researchers talk about the *stability* of criminal behavior over time, they mean that children who score high on measures of misbehavior at an earlier age also tend to score high on misbehaviors at a later age. In contrast (but often confused with stability), *continuity* is defined as the consistency of underlying personality traits or dispositions over time, some of which explain misbehaviors that may have a different form at different developmental stages. Wright et al. (2008) distinguish among three types of continuity.

Homotypic continuity refers to continuity over time in behaviors that are the same. Examples of homotypic continuity is reflected in an individual who displays aggressive physical behaviors (e.g., punching, pushing, kicking, etc.) towards peers at age 2 and also at age 13. *Heterotypic continuity* refers to behaviors that may take a different form over time, but are caused by the same underlying personality or temperamental characteristic. For example, a 4 year old may engage in chronic lying, cheating, and stealing (antisocial behaviors), but as a 16 year old s/he may engage in chronic drug abuse, credit card fraud, or reckless driving (also antisocial behaviors). *Cumulative continuity* occurs when anti-social behaviors lead to adverse consequences that, in turn, create and sustain other antisocial behaviors that, in turn, create additional adverse consequences, and so on. For example, aggressive and impulsive school behaviors may lead to failing grades and other academic sanctions from school officials. This leads to dropping out of school without a degree. The lack of education credentials may lead to later financial hardships, which in turn motivates criminal behavior designed to secure "quick cash". This, in turn, leads to incarceration, which may lead the individual to learn more criminal behaviors from the prison culture.

Adolescent-Limited versus Life-Course-Persistent Offenders

According to Moffitt (1993), two qualitatively different types of criminal offenders can be distinguished, which can be identified as the *adolescent-limited offender* and the *life-course-persistent offender*. The adolescent-limited offender (ALO) begins and engages in delinquent behavior only during adolescence. These adolescents engage in relatively minor delinquent acts, and then only for short periods. The developmental history of these adolescents is not riddled with patterns of chronic antisocial behaviors, and they cannot be characterized as committed to an antisocial lifestyle. ALOs typically do not continue antisocial behavior into adulthood, as they instead choose more appropriate adult roles to adopt. For this group, acts of delinquency are usually situation-specific (e.g., being egged on by a peer group to vandalize a neighbor's house or engage in occasional shoplifting).

In contrast, life-course-persistent offenders (LCPO) exhibit antisocial tendencies very early in life, commit criminal offenses across a variety of settings, and generally remain offenders throughout their adulthood. Generally, the types of crimes committed by LCPOs tend to be more serious than those committed by ALOs. In short, LCPOs are committed from an early age onward to an unabated criminal lifestyle. LCPOs generally lack the self-control and restraint necessary for life success. This, in turn, leads to school failure, ostracism by pro-social peers, and close associations with like-minded criminal peers. As they become adults, LCPOs are more likely to be divorced as adults; to drop out of school before acquiring their degree; and to experience prolonged periods of unemployment and incarceration (Wright, Tibbetts, & Daigle, 2008).

Criminal Thinking Patterns

Simplistic sociological theories, including those influenced by Quack Multiculturalism, are prone to offer glib, simplistic explanations for criminal behavior (e.g., it is "caused" by poverty, racism and discrimination, poor upbringing). The reality is that some children and youth never get into trouble regardless of growing up in adverse circumstances. Other individuals, in contrast, grow up to become "dangerous, predatory, and pathological" (Wright, Tibbetts, & Daigle, 2008, p. 13). To this latter group, social rebuke and risk of adverse consequences (e.g., incarceration) is of little concern to them. Comprehensive explanations of criminal behavior must explain why there is an unequal likelihood of engaging in criminal behavior despite growing up in nearly identical circumstances.

Stanton Samenow is a clinical psychologist who has spent the majority of his professional life (beginning in the late 1970s) interviewing, evaluating, and counseling literally hundreds of men, women, adolescents, and children who have committed crimes—"everything from a housewife apprehended for shoplifting to a man sentenced to death for lethally assaulting a total stranger with a baseball bat to rob him of a few dollars" (Samenow, 1998, p. xv). Dr. Samenow has worked with criminals in a variety of settings, which have included juvenile detention centers, psychiatric hospitals, county jails, penitentiaries, and in his private practice. Dr. Samenow has shared his findings with a variety of professionals nationwide who work with juvenile and adult offenders (e.g., judges, attorneys, police officers, school/drug/alcohol counselors, teachers, social workers, psychologists, psychiatrists, probation/parole officers, parents, and politicians).

Samenow argues that so-called career criminals (see previous discussion of LCPOs) display qualitatively different thinking patterns than non-criminals. These thinking patterns are summarized in Sidebar 8.4. The cornerstone of Dr. Samenow's work is that factors routinely assumed to cause crime actually *do not* cause crime. In his experience, criminals and their sympathizers use these assumed "causes" for crime as excuses to justify bad behavior. A summary of the common myths related to criminals and criminal behavior, contrasted with Samenow's counterarguments, are summarized in Sidebar 8.5.

🖎 Sidebar 8.4   Criminal Thinking Patterns

How Criminals View Themselves

- Despite the barbarity or heinous nature of their crimes, they believe that they are good people "deep inside"
- Expect circumstances to go their way, on their terms, whenever they want (when this doesn't happen, their egos are threatened)
- Do not see themselves as accountable for their own behavior
- See themselves as no different from anybody else, except that they have "made mistakes" and suffered from occasional "bad breaks"
- Pride themselves for having a highly developed ability to defraud others and "play the system"
- The slightest discrepancy between their expectations and reality is perceived as a personal affront to their self-esteem
- While committing a crime, feel that they have everything under control and will not get caught
- At the drop of a hat, can alternate between savage brutality and maudlin sentimentality

How Criminals View Other People

- Expect others to treat them according to their own inflated view of themselves
- Skilled at sizing up others in order to identify their vulnerabilities, which in turn can be preyed upon
- Employ a winsome, sincere personality in order to manipulate others for their own selfish purposes
- Tell therapists, psychologists, and counselors "what they want to hear" as a means of getting reduced consequences or easier treatment
- Use the psychotherapy/counseling process in a self-serving manner
- Attracted to the company of other criminals, because they find them appealing and exciting
- View non-criminals as "boring," "losers," "lame," "weak," "dopes," and "suckers"
- In intimate relationships, they maneuver to gain advantages over others; they are takers rather than givers
- When caught or arrested, others discover that they never "knew" the criminals, but knew only the carefully constructed image they had created of themselves

How Criminals View Their Environment

- Will seek out and exploit weaknesses in organizational rules/policies to commit crimes

(continued)

- Feel there is little reason to pay attention to, work hard at, or persist with tasks that are considered boring
- Often despise school and consider regular employment as being for "suckers"
- Life is exciting and has deep meaning only if one can engage in illicit and/or forbidden behavior
- Are continually angry, because the world never meets their expectations

How Criminals View Their Crimes

- Their crimes are always someone else's fault, and they are the perennial victims
- Feel that victims of their crimes "had it coming to them" or deserved their fate
- Feel that the negative consequences of their crimes (for other people and property) are exaggerated, and are less than they really are
- Are able to shut off their competing feelings (i.e., remorse, fear, guilt) in deference to the greater objective of successfully committing crimes
- Although some may profess to believe in God, they are a "law unto themselves" and can justify/rationalize any crime they commit

(Adapted from Samenow, 1989, 1998, 2004)

◪ Sidebar 8.5   Common Myths About Criminals vs. Observations From Samenow Case Studies/Interviews With Criminals

Common Myths About Criminals	Observations From Samenow Case Studies/Interviews
Criminals are forced into crime against their will because of adverse circumstances.	Criminals commit crimes because they want to commit crimes.
Criminals get into trouble because they are unable to learn from their experiences.	Criminals can learn from experience, but they don't care to learn what family, teachers, and others want them to learn. They are capable of learning how to be "better criminals."
Poverty propels citizens into a life of crime.	Most poor people are not criminals, and many economically affluent people are.
Disproportionately higher rates of minorities in the juvenile justice and prison systems "prove" endemic racial/ethnic discrimination that is unfair to these groups.	Criminals come from all types of racial, ethnic, and social class backgrounds. Lower rates of economically advantaged groups in the juvenile justice and prison systems can be partly attributed to access to resources that enable them to avoid punishment.

Common Myths About Criminals	Observations From Samenow Case Studies/Interviews
Low intelligence plays an important role in explaining criminal behavior.	Many criminals score high on conventional IQ tests. Some, although scoring low on conventional IQ tests, are nevertheless street-smart, savvy, and are capable of planning and carrying out elaborate schemes.
Criminals have no conscience, otherwise they could not do terrible things.	Criminals have a conscience that is *selective* and is applied only to certain areas but not other areas (particularly not those areas that involve their crimes).
Environment is the critical factor that creates criminals (i.e., they are "victims of their circumstances").	Environments can create greater or fewer opportunities for crime to occur, *but how people choose to deal with their environment* is the key to understanding criminal behavior.
Vocational training (e.g., computer skills) will enable criminals to turn their lives around for the better.	Vocational training will only create criminals with vocational skills (because their underlying thinking patterns have not been altered).
Environmental stress causes criminal behavior.	Individuals respond to stress differently in ways that align with their personality traits.
Lax (school) organizational rules that are not 100% airtight will cause criminal behavior.	Persons with a well-developed inner sense of personal responsibility will not commit crimes no matter how lax the (school) organizational rules are.
The high inner-city crime rate proves that the environment is a significant factor in creating criminals.	Most people who live in inner-city areas are not criminals. Criminals are disproportionately attracted to highly chaotic and unstable locations with low deterrence of criminal behavior.
Portrayals of violence and criminality in the entertainment media encourages criminal behavior.	The critical issue is not the content of entertainment media, but what is already in the mind of media consumers.
Youth join gangs in order to find a sense of acceptance and belonging that is missing at home.	Criminals can easily obtain a sense of acceptance through legitimate organizations (e.g., athletic teams, church groups), but they are not attracted to these groups. Youth join gangs because they are primarily attracted to the excitement of criminal activity and street life.
Individuals become criminals because of the absence of positive role models at home, or the influential presence of negative role models at home.	Many youth with positive role models in the home nevertheless become criminals, and many youth with negative role models in the home do not become criminals.

(*continued*)

Common Myths About Criminals	Observations From Samenow Case Studies/Interviews
One type of parenting style or one type of home environment produces more criminals compared to other types.	Criminal offenders come from all types of homes, raised by parents who use a variety of parenting styles.
Criminals suffer from low self-esteem.	Criminals have an inflated view of themselves as powerful, special, and unique people.
Children grow up to become criminals because they were physically abused at home.	Because of their criminal personalities, temperament, and behavior, criminals will often provoke abusive responses in otherwise nonabusive parents.
The cause for criminal behavior can usually be traced to the influence of a specific environmental stressor that negatively impacted otherwise normal children.	Parents of criminal children observe that these children are usually different from others in the family long before peer, school, and other outside influences have had a chance to have a significant influence.
If children have a genetic predisposition toward criminality, there is nothing that can be done to prevent a criminal lifestyle and eventual incarceration.	If detected early, and administered consistently, preventive measures can be taken to help crime-disposed children/youth to make responsible choices.

(Adapted from Samenow, 1989, 1998, 2004)

The more accurate approach is to understand how criminals view themselves, their circumstances, and other people. From this approach, methods can be developed to help some criminals correct their errors of thinking and take the appropriate steps needed to become responsible members of society (e.g., see Sidebar 8.6).

Sidebar 8.6   Counseling Strategies for Change in Individuals With Criminal Thinking Patterns

- Criminals, regardless of their backgrounds, have strikingly similar thinking patterns. Therefore, do not spend much time in rapport building, but rather take control of interviews by describing (for the counselees' benefit) their criminal thinking, behavior, and predilections.
- Treat counselees as responsible and accountable for their behavior.
- Do not search for "explanations" of the counselees' behavior. Communicate that the circumstances of the counselees' life, or "hard-luck" stories, are of no concern to the counselor.
- Communicate that no aspect of the counselees' life is off limits or sacred.

- Systematically expose and describe the counselees' criminal thought patterns without ridicule or condescension.
- Dissect every statement or question made by the counselees for signs of manipulation, where appropriate.
- The counselor seeks to *intensify*, rather than *alleviate*, the counselees' guilt over past criminal actions. That is, nothing is designed in the counselor–counselee interaction to help counselees feel good about themselves. In contrast, a sign of progress is for the counselees to feel "fed up" with themselves.
- Beware of counselees' attempts to erect a façade of respectability, contrition, and responsibility, as criminals use this to get away with more crimes.
- Be aware of attempts to mislead and confuse, by not accepting self-serving explanations, diversions, or excuses for criminal behavior.
- Reinforce the idea to counselees that commitment to a changed life *follows* (not precedes) correct knowledge, behaviors, and experiences.
- Counselees are required to keep a daily detailed journal documenting their thinking related to their work, leisure time, and important relationships.
- Since yesterday's thoughts contain the seeds of tomorrow's crimes, counselees are required to discuss these journaled thoughts (without embellishing, editing, or omitting them) with a counselor in weekly group/individual sessions.
- Eventually, counselees must learn to anticipate situations in which they will experience temptations to commit crimes, and think them through in advance in order to change behavior.

(Adapted from Samenow, 1989, 1998, 2004)

RESPONSES TO JUVENILE DELINQUENCY

The Juvenile Justice System

According to Greenwood and Turner (2011):

> No matter what the theory, no matter how hard we try, we come back to a few facts. The primary risk factors now known to be associated with criminal behavior, particularly serious criminal behavior, are all primarily in play during the years when the youth and his parents would fall under the jurisdiction of the juvenile or family court. (p. 88)

In current U.S. society, the philosophical underpinning of the juvenile justice system encourages the state to take control of "wayward children" who fall under the statutory age limit and provide care, custody, and treatment to remedy delinquent behavior. Crimes committed before the designated birthday (i.e., 17 to 19, which varies by state) fall within the jurisdiction of juvenile courts. Originally, four basic characteristics distinguish the juvenile court system from the criminal courts (Greenwood & Turner, 2011): (1) informality in procedures and decorum; (2) a separate detention center for juveniles; (3) contributory delinquency statutes that encourage the judge to punish adults, primarily parents, who actively contributed to the delinquency of juveniles; and (4) probation. For a student who enters the juvenile justice system, the specific steps that are followed as the student matriculates through the system are briefly discussed in Sidebar 8.7.

Sidebar 8.7   The Juvenile Justice Process

1. *Police investigation.* Most children and youth enter into the juvenile justice system as a result of a first contact with a police officer. Children and youth who commit less-serious offenses may be given a warning or referred to a social service agency/program. Those who commit more-serious offenses are arrested.

   When children/youth commit a crime, the police have the authority to investigate the incident and decide whether to release the children/youth or commit them to the juvenile court. The juvenile court has the discretion to exclude certain classes of offenders or offenses from the juvenile justice system (referring them instead to the adult court system) if they decide that there is little chance for rehabilitation under the juvenile system.

   If the police file a petition to refer the children/youth to juvenile court, then a decision is made as to whether the children/youth should remain in the community or be placed in a detention facility until their court appearance. In other cases, a detention hearing is held to determine whether to remand the children/youth to a shelter home (if appropriate). If the children/youth are not detained, then they will be released to a parent or guardian to await further court action.

2. *Pretrial procedures.* A pretrial hearing occurs where a juvenile court determines whether there is sufficient evidence to sustain the allegations against the youth in a petition. It is here that juveniles are informed of their right to a trial, that any plea or admission of guilt is voluntary, and whether they fully understand the charges and consequences of a plea. If the children/youth admit to the crime at this hearing, then the case will not be further adjudicated (i.e., taken to trial).

3. *Diversion.* One alternative to adjudication is diversion, where youths suspected of law violations are encouraged to participate in some specific program or activity in order to avoid further prosecution. Here, the youth are placed into a treatment-oriented program prior to a formal trial and disposition, in order to minimize their penetration into the justice system.

4. *Adjudication.* If the children/youth do not admit guilt at the initial hearing, do not agree to a diversion program, and are not transferred to an adult court, then the court hears evidence on the allegations in the delinquency petition. The children/youth are entitled here to the right to counsel, freedom from self-incrimination, the right to confront and cross-examine witnesses, and the right to a jury trial. At the end of this hearing, the court enters a judgment against the juveniles.

5. *Disposition.* If the children/youth are found to be delinquent at the adjudication stage, then the court makes a decision as to what is to be done for the children/youth. This decision is based on several factors, which include the seriousness of the offense, the youths' prior records, and their family background. A dispositional hearing is held where the judge prescribes a wide range of outcomes, the majority of which are described as follows:

   - *Informal consent decree.* In minor or first offenses, no formal trial or disposition hearing is held. Instead, the judge will ask the youth and their guardians to agree to a treatment program, such as counseling.
   - *Probation.* Youth are placed under the control of the county probation department and are required to obey a set of probation rules and participate in a treatment program.
   - *Home detention.* Children/youth are restricted to their home in lieu of a secure placement. Rules include regular school attendance, curfew observance, avoidance of alcohol or drugs, and notification of parents and the youth worker of the children's whereabouts.
   - *Court-ordered school attendance.* In cases where truancy is the problem, a judge may order mandatory school attendance. Some courts have established court-operated day schools and court-based tutorial programs staffed by community volunteers.
   - *Financial restitution.* A judge can order juvenile offenders to make financial restitution to the victims. In most jurisdictions, restitution is a part of probation, but in some states, restitution can be the sole judgment.
   - *Fines.* Some states allow fines to be levied against juveniles aged 16 and older.
   - *Community service.* Courts in many jurisdictions require juveniles to spend time in the community working off their debt to society. Community

(continued)

service orders are usually reserved for victimless crimes, such as drug possession or vandalism of school property. Community service orders are usually carried out in schools, hospitals, or nursing homes.

- *Outpatient therapy.* Youth who are diagnosed with psychological disorders may be required to undergo therapy at a local mental health clinic.
- *Drug and alcohol treatment.* Youth with drug/alcohol-related problems may be allowed to remain in the community if they agree to undergo drug or alcohol therapy.
- *Commitment to secure treatment.* In serious cases, a judge may order offenders to be admitted to a long-term treatment center, such as a training school, camp, ranch, or group home. These may be either state or privately run institutions, usually located in remote regions. Training schools provide educational, vocational, and rehabilitation programs in a secure environment.
- *Commitment to a residential community program.* Youth who commit less-serious crimes, but who still need to be removed from their homes, can be placed in community-based group homes or halfway houses. They attend school or work during the day and live in a controlled, therapeutic environment at night.
- *Foster home placement.* Foster homes are usually used for dependent or neglected children and status offenders. Judges place delinquents with insurmountable problems at home in state-licensed foster care homes.

(Adapted from Siegel & Welsh, 2009)

Brand-Name Intervention Programs

In the early 1990s, several researchers, usually with funding from the National Institute of Mental Health (NIMH) or the National Institutes of Health (NIH), began to develop and test treatment protocols that have proven to be far more cost-effective than the traditional programs offered by the juvenile system in the past. The reported outcomes from such programs have led many to call for the greater use of evidence-based programming in working with juveniles.

In recent years, several carefully designed and rigorously tested program models have proven their ability to produce strong, positive impacts on youth behavior in a variety of organizational settings and pay for themselves in cost savings. These brand-name programs (see Glossary and Greenwood & Turner, 2011, for details) have been developed by a single investigator or team over a number of years, are proven through careful replications, and are supported by millions of dollars in federal grants. These programs have already met the criteria established by various federal review groups for identifying proven programs.

Federal Review Groups

The Coalition for Evidence-Based Policy (CEBP) utilizes a review group of distinguished scientists to develop a list of effective programs whose evaluations meet the most rigorous standards. The Center for the Study and Prevention of Violence at the University of Colorado in Boulder, under the leadership of Professor Delbert Elliot, has developed a systematic process (called Blueprints) for describing and evaluating prevention programs that target youth violence and substance abuse. For Blueprints to certify a program as *proven*, the program must (a) demonstrate its effects on problem behaviors with a rigorous experimental design; (b) show that its effects persist after youth leave the program; and (c) be successfully replicated at another site. The current Blueprints website (http://www .colorado.educspvblueprints) lists 11 "model programs" and 20 "promising programs." Promising programs have positive, lasting results from one rigorous evaluation but not a second (Greenwood & Turner, 2011). Both the CEBP and Blueprints evaluation processes are very strict in requiring strong evaluations, whereas many other lists contain programs that sound interesting but for which there is no strong evaluation evidence.

The Washington State Institute for Public Policy (WSIPP) runs the best website (see http://www.wsipp.wa.gov) for checking out the estimated effectiveness of both brand-name and generic models. At the individual researcher level, Professor Mark Lipsey (currently Director of the Peabody Research Institute at Vanderbilt) began utilizing meta-analysis to identify correlates or predictors of success in delinquency prevention programs in the early 1990s. Since that time, he has published several articles identifying effective general (generic) intervention strategies and principles for applying them (see Greenwood & Turner, 2011).

In the material that follows, select brand-name programs that have been shown to reduce recidivism, substance use, and/or antisocial behavior in at least two trials, using strong research designs, are described.

BRAND-NAME INTERVENTION PROGRAMS FOR CRIME-INVOLVED YOUTH

Adolescent Diversion Project

The Michigan State University (MSU) Adolescent Diversion Project (ADP) is a local program (based in Lansing, MI) founded in 1976 through a collaborative agreement between the National Institute of Mental Health (NIMH) Center for Studies of Crime and Delinquency, the MSU Department of Psychology, and the Ingham County Juvenile Court. The impetus for the creation of the ADP came from the observation that juvenile crime was growing at alarming rates, and that most traditional attempts to reduce juvenile crime had been found to be ineffective. This issue represented a threat to community safety and local government expenditures.

As a result, three federal grants were written and funded to establish a model intervention program and to scientifically examine its efficacy. The ADP group developed an evidence-based practice approach to juvenile delinquency, which they believed would result in reductions of crime. The goal of the program is to provide court-referred young persons with a program of services tailored to their needs, and to help them avoid further involvement with the juvenile justice system. ADP volunteers are MSU undergraduates trained in specific intervention techniques to use with the court-involved youth and their families. ADP volunteers work six to eight hours per week for 18 weeks with the court-involved youth, but some time is spent with the parent(s) and significant others in the youth's life. ADP volunteers work on many different areas, depending on the youth's needs and interests. These areas typically involve: (a) teaching the youth and family how to negotiate and resolve problems in their relationships, the ultimate goal being to strengthen and improve these relationships; and (b) helping and teaching the youth and their families how to access the resources from the community in order to meet needs. These resources may include getting a job, working on school issues, or seeking activities for the youth's free time. The goal is to teach the youth and their families how to access these community resources themselves after the program is over. According to the ADP online program manual (accessed at https://www.msu.edu/course/psy/371/manual.pdf), roughly 50 percent of the court-involved youth are racial minorities.

The university contributed faculty and student time, theoretical and intervention information, and research and methodological acumen. The community provided a setting, organizational support, referrals of juvenile offenders from the local juvenile court as an alternative to court processing (diversion), experiential expertise, and access to records. The ADP has sought to generate scientifically credible information about intervention efficacy, provide unique and expanded educational experiences for graduate and undergraduate students, and expand its outreach/engagement mission to an underserved area (juvenile justice).

The ADP group is composed of faculty and graduate students from MSU, administrators and staff from the Ingham County Juvenile Court, and representatives of the Ingham County community. This group designed and validated an intervention model as the foundation of the diversion program. These models jointly engaged the university and the community, providing an effective alternative intervention for juvenile delinquency and a platform for long-term sustainability of the partnership.

According to its website, more than 4,000 youth have been diverted from the local juvenile court since 1976. Similarly, a comparable number of undergraduates have participated in a two-semester course where they received training in diversion work and carried out eight hours per week of structured mentoring. Through a series of longitudinal field experiments, the ADP has demonstrated that the recidivism rate for participating youth is half that of those youth who are randomly assigned to a control group. In addition, participating youth attended school at significantly higher rates.

Aggression Replacement Training

Aggression Replacement Training (ART) is a cognitive-behavioral intervention program designed to help children and adolescents improve their social skill competence and moral reasoning, better manage anger, and reduce aggressive behavior (Glick, 2006). The program was first developed for aggressive and violent adolescents aged 12 to 17 who were incarcerated in juvenile institutions. Over the years, ART has been adapted for chronically aggressive children in schools and mental health settings, as well as for adults. ART has been implemented in schools and juvenile delinquency programs across the United States and throughout the world.

The ART program is a multimodal intervention consisting of three components: social skills training (e.g., learning more appropriate methods of responding to threatening/stressful situations), anger control training (e.g., monitoring anger-producing situations and learning more appropriate was to express anger), and training in moral reasoning (e.g., learning how to be aware of others' points of view). Clients attend a one-hour session in each of these components each week for 10 weeks (a total of 30 sessions). Incremental learning, reinforcement techniques, and guided group discussions enhance skill acquisition and reinforce the lessons in the curriculum. ART has been taught to children and adolescents from all socioeconomic backgrounds in rural, urban, and suburban communities. In addition to being implemented in schools, ART has been used in juvenile delinquency programs and in mental health settings to reduce aggressive and antisocial behavior and to promote anger management and social competence.

Research has shown that students who develop skills in these areas are far less likely to engage in a wide range of aggressive and high-risk behaviors. A sampling of research studies on ART can be accessed at http://uscart.org/new/resources/research-articles

Life Skills Training (LST)

LifeSkills Training (LST) is a substance abuse prevention program developed by Dr. Gilbert J. Botwin, which aims to reduce the risks of alcohol, tobacco, drug abuse, and violence by targeting the major social and psychological factors that promote the initiation of substance use and other risky behaviors. The LST curriculum can be taught in school, community, faith-based, summer school, and after-school settings. According to its website, LST has been evaluated and shown to be effective with students from a wide variety of ethnic, racial, and social class backgrounds from elementary up to the high school grades (e.g., see http://www.lifeskillstraining.com/evaluation.php). The ultimate objective of the program is to provide young teens with the confidence and skills necessary to successfully handle challenging situations. Program efficacy has been documented by more than 30 scientific studies, and the program is recognized as a model program by an array of government agencies, including the U.S. Department of Education and the Center for Substance Abuse Prevention.

According to its online website, LST program activities go beyond merely transmitting information to students about the dangers of drugs. There are three major components of the program that cover the critical domains found to promote drug use. Program developers believe that students who develop skills in these three domains are far less likely to engage in a wide range of high-risk behaviors. The three components are:

1. *Drug resistance skills*—which include activities that enable students to recognize and challenge common misconceptions about tobacco, alcohol, and other drug use. Through coaching and practice, they learn resistance skills for dealing with peers and media pressure to engage in tobacco, alcohol, and other drug use.
2. *Personal self-management skills*—which include activities that help students learn how to examine their self-image and its effects on behavior, set goals and keep track of personal progress, identify everyday decisions and how they may be influenced by others, analyze problem situations and consider the consequences of each alternative solution before making decisions, reduce stress and anxiety, and look at personal challenges in a positive light.
3. *General social skills*—which include activities designed to help students develop the necessary skills to overcome shyness, communicate effectively and avoid misunderstandings, initiate and carry out conversations, handle social requests, utilize both verbal and nonverbal assertiveness skills to make or refuse requests, and recognize that they have choices other than aggression or passivity when faced with tough situations.

Customizable training services are available through National Health Promotion Associates, Inc., a health consulting, research, and development firm developed by Dr. Botvin, the developer of the Botvin LifeSkills Training program. LST workshops for training teachers can be delivered online, on school sites, or through open training workshops sponsored by National Health Promotion Associates, Inc.

Project Toward No Drug Abuse

Project Toward No Drug Abuse (PTNDA) is advertised as an effective, interactive classroom-based substance abuse prevention program based on more than two decades of research at the University of Southern California. The program is designed for high school youth (ages 14 to 19) and is implemented in both regular and alternative high schools with students from diverse ethnic and socioeconomic backgrounds.

The overall objectives of the PTNDA program are to help participants stop or reduce the use of cigarettes, alcohol, marijuana, and hard drugs; stop or reduce weapon carrying; be able to articulate accurate information about the various consequences of drug use and abuse; and demonstrate behavioral and cognitive coping skills that support reduced drug use.

Project PTNDA focuses on three factors that predict tobacco, alcohol, and other drug use, violence-related behaviors, and other problem behaviors among youth. These factors include (1) motivation factors (i.e., students' attitudes, beliefs, expectations, and desires regarding drug use), (2) skills (i.e., social, self-control, and coping skills), and (3) decision making (i.e., how to make decisions that lead to health-promoting behaviors).

The program is designed for school classroom implementation by a trained teacher or health education specialist using highly participatory and interactive lessons. Trainers will come to the school site to train interested school professionals. Scheduling and fees for training workshops are arranged by contacting the University of Southern California Institute for Prevention Research. The program includes twelve 40- to 50-minute classroom-based sessions delivered over a four-week period (i.e., three sessions per week) or twice a week over a six-week period.

According to the PTNDA website, the effectiveness of the program has been validated using randomized experimental designs with more than 3,000 ethnically diverse youth from 42 high schools in southern California. Links providing research summaries can be accessed at http://tnd.usc.edu/overview_research.php

Big Brothers/Big Sisters Mentoring

Big Brothers/Big Sisters of America (BBBS) is a nonprofit organization that represents the nation's largest donor-based volunteer network of mentors for youth. BBBS is a one-on-one mentoring program in which mentoring pairs set an individualized goal that typically falls into the following categories: improving parent-child and peer relationships, improving self-esteem, reducing antisocial behaviors, and promoting academic achievement. BBBS is an example of a community-based mentoring program where mentors and mentees make their own arrangements for activities, within guidelines distributed by the organization.

BBBS volunteers must first apply to one of approximately 500 BBBS affiliates throughout the country to be approved for service. To be accepted, potential volunteers must complete a formal written application, successfully pass background and reference checks, pass an in-person interview, and participate in an orientation and training process that outlines the individualized needs of the mentee child and provides information and resources on how to encourage that child's development. Adult mentors (called "bigs") come from business corporations, community agencies, or universities, and they are matched with elementary or middle school students to spend time together during the school day. Mostly during lunchtime, or another time period that works, mentors come to the school three to four times per month and spend time with their mentees (called "littles") for 45 to 60 minutes. Shared activities include, but certainly are not limited to, educational games, outdoor activities, eating lunch together, working on computers, or going to the library.

According to their national and affiliate websites, the majority of children needing mentoring are African American and Hispanic, whereas only a minority of volunteers come from these groups. Although no explicit ethnic matching is required to participate in the program, minority mentors are strongly encouraged to apply in order to provide ethnicity-matched mentors to children who need this the most.

In demonstrating support for BBBS, its developers point to a nationwide impact study conducted by Public/Private Ventures, an independent Philadelphia-based national research organization. The study, conducted in 1994–1995, looked at more than 950 boys and girls from eight BBBS agencies across the country. Approximately half of the children were randomly chosen to be matched with a Big Brother or Big Sister. The others were assigned to a waiting list. The matched children met with their Big Brothers or Big Sisters about three times per month for an average of one year. Researchers surveyed both the matched and unmatched children (and their parents) on two occasions: when they first applied for a Big Brother or Big Sister and again 18 months later. Researchers found that after 18 months of spending time with their mentors, the Little Brothers and Little Sisters—compared to those children not in the program—were less likely to begin using illegal drugs, less likely to begin using alcohol, less likely to skip school, less likely to skip a class, less likely to hit someone, more confident of their performance in schoolwork, and getting along better with their families (according to the BBBS national organization website). A report of the actual study can be accessed at http://www.ppv.org/ppv/publications/assets/111_publication.pdf

Olweus Bullying Prevention Program

The Olweus Bullying Prevention Program is advertised as a whole-school program aimed at preventing or reducing bullying primarily in elementary, middle, and junior high school settings. According to Dr. Dan Olweus, creator of the program, students are bullied when they are exposed, repeatedly and over time, to negative actions on the part of one or more other persons, and they have difficulty defending themselves (Olweus, 1993). As this definition is quite general, more specific manifestations of bullying can be identified, which include, but are not limited to, derogatory verbal comments, social exclusion, physical violence and intimidation, personal theft, racial and/or sexual intimidation, and cyber-bullying (e.g., bullying via computer or cell phone). According to its program materials, the goals of the program are to reduce bullying incidents and problems among students in school, prevent new bullying problems, and achieve better peer relations at school.

According to program materials, field research for the program began in the early 1970s in Norway, and its success has subsequently spread to implementation in U.S. schools beginning in the 1990s. With the assistance of Dr. Susan Limber of Clemson University in South Carolina and others, the Olweus Bullying Prevention Program has been systematically evaluated and has been found to result in significant reductions in adult observations of bullying and student reports of bullying in school settings (see Additional Resources for web links to program research).

A prescribed sequence of steps is required for persons interested in implementing the program in their schools and communities. The process begins with the formation of a Bullying Prevention Coordinating Committee (composed of school administrators, teachers, counselors, school psychologists, parents, custodial/cafeteria staff, and bus drivers), who attend a two-day training workshop conducted by a certified Olweus trainer. The committee then serves as the on-site resident experts for the program in the school setting. Following the initial two-day bullying prevention training, the certified Olweus trainer is available (for up to a year) to provide telephone consultations to the program coordinator (designated head) of the on-site coordinating committee. In instances where entire districts desire training in the program, it is more economically feasible to designate a district representative who can be trained to become a certified Olweus trainer, who in turn can then train multiple groups within the district.

After the Coordinating Committee is formed at the school site, the program provides anonymous student questionnaires that can be administered and interpreted to ascertain the nature, extent, and physical locations in individual schools where bullying incidents are most likely to occur. This can be followed by in-school meetings to discuss teacher, school staff, and student perceptions of bullying at the school site. Further activities may include, but are not limited to, developing (a) school/district-wide anti-bullying rules, (b) strategies to monitor bullying hot-spots in the schools, (c) a confidential bullying reporting system for students to use, (d) procedures for adults to use when handling observed bullying incidents, (e) procedures for counseling children who are victims of bullying, and (f) ways to involve parents in working with the school to resolve bullying issues.

The program provides a wealth of supportive resource material, which includes training workshops, instructional workbooks for teachers and students, video training materials, book resources, and assessment/evaluation materials. Program developers note that the program can (and has been) infused in nonschool and other community settings (e.g., juvenile justice residential facilities), but it has not yet been systematically evaluated for these applications.

GANGS

A major consequence of community/neighborhood social disorganization is a weakened or nonexistent ability to control the formation, development, and proliferation of adolescent gangs (Sampson, 2011). As discussed in the previous section, much delinquency occurs in groups. Gangs develop primarily through activities that are unsupervised by responsible adults, whether it is in the home or in the neighborhood. The lack of adults' ability to adequately supervise youth (or at least challenge kids who "seem to be up to no good"), for whatever reasons, is a key link between neighborhood/community characteristics and the heightened incidence of crime.

What Are Gangs?

Even social scientists who have devoted their professional lives to the study of gangs acknowledge that there is no commonly accepted definition as to exactly what a street gang is (for a variety of definitions, see Siegel & Welsh, 2009, p. 292). The difficulty is that once a characteristic is assigned to the definition, one can easily identify exemplars that do not fit the connotation of a street gang. According to the Office of Juvenile Justice and Delinquency Prevention National Gang Center website (http://www.nationalgangcenter.gov/About/FAQ#q1), the following criteria of youth gangs have the most consensus among gang researchers:

1. The group has three or more members, generally aged 12 to 24.
2. Members share an identity, typically linked to a name, and often other symbols.
3. Members view themselves as a gang, and they are recognized by others as a gang.
4. The group has some permanence and a degree of organization.
5. The group is involved in an elevated level of criminal activity.

In the "pecking order" of criminal organizations, youth street gangs are said to "occupy the lowest rung of the organized crime ladder" (Diaz, 2009, p. viii). Traditional criminal syndicates (such as La Cosa Nostra or Russian-American organized crime) are "businesslike" and are highly regimented/hierarchical in their delegation of internal power and authority. These sophisticated organizations specialize in money-producing schemes (e.g., drug sales and distribution, prostitution, gambling, money laundering, loansharking, embezzlement, robberies), and violence is primarily used within the ranks to enforce the efficient "business" of crime. For these criminal syndicates, gratuitous violence for its own sake, or the harming of innocent citizens, is viewed as attracting unwanted attention and "bad for business" (Diaz, 2009).

Like the more traditional criminal syndicates, youth street gangs are criminal networks. In contrast, however, youth street gangs have a less disciplined and more informal structure. Youth street gangs use violence to intimidate the general public and establish their identity. A youth's affiliation with street gangs is displayed openly through distinctive clothing (e.g., see Arciaga, Sakamoto, & Jones, 2010; Delaney, 2006), body tattoos, specialized hand signs (see Capozzoli & McVey, 2000), "tagging" neighborhoods using graffiti gang symbols, and ritualized hand sign greetings to fellow gang members.

Youth as young as 13 years of age are actively recruited to join gangs. Initiation rituals for joining gangs include forced sex or violent crimes (e.g., robbery, killing, maiming) committed against civilians. A more complete list of gang crimes written in state laws is provided in Sidebar 8.8.

✏ Sidebar 8.8   Synthesis of Exemplars of Gang Crime from State Law

Aggravated arson
Aggravated battery or second-degree battery
Aggravated kidnapping
Aggravated mayhem
Aggravated promotion of prostitution
Armed robbery
Arson
Assault and battery
Assault with a deadly weapon or by means of force likely to produce great
    bodily injury
Bringing armed men into the state
Burglary
Carjacking
Carrying a concealed weapon
Computer crime
Criminal damage to property
Criminal damage to or threat to criminally damage the property of a witness
Criminal mischief
Criminal solicitation
Discharging or permitting the discharge of a firearm from a motor vehicle
Evidence falsified or concealed and witnesses intimidated or bribed
False imprisonment
Felony extortion
Felony vandalism
First- or second-degree intentional homicide
Forgery and counterfeiting
Gambling
Grand theft
Grand theft of any firearm, vehicle, trailer, or vessel
Homicide
Illegal use of weapons or dangerous instrumentalities

(continued)

Intimidation of witnesses and victims

Kidnapping

Looting

Malicious harassment

Manslaughter

Manufacture, distribution, or delivery of a controlled substance or controlled substance analog

Mayhem

Money laundering

Possession of a deadly weapon by a prisoner

Possession of a destructive device

Possession of explosives

Possession of a pistol, revolver, or other firearm

Prostitution

Racketeering

Rape

Robbery

Sale, delivery, or transfer of a firearm

Sale, possession for sale, transportation, manufacture, offer for sale, or offer to manufacture controlled substances

Sexual assault of an adult or child

Sexual intercourse without consent

Shooting at an inhabited dwelling or occupied motor vehicle

Taking, driving, or operating a vehicle, or removing a part or component of a vehicle, without the owner's consent

Taking hostages

Tampering with witnesses and informants

Terrorism

Theft

Threats to commit crimes resulting in death or great bodily injury

Torture

Unlawful possession of a firearm by a convicted person

Unlawful taking or driving of a vehicle

Use of threat to coerce criminal street gang membership or use of violence to coerce criminal street gang membership

(for a complete state-by-state list, consult http://www.nationalgangcenter.gov/Content/Documents/Definitions.pdf)

Law enforcement agencies overwhelmingly report a greater percentage of male gang members versus female gang members. Some reports estimate the male-to-female ratio of gang members as approximately 2 to 1 (Snyder & Sickmund, 2006). However, more recent data has reported higher percentages of female gang involvement (see Howell, 2010).

Violence between gangs normally occurs within one ethnic group (e.g., one Latino gang vs. another Latino gang) as opposed to between ethnic groups (e.g., Latino gang vs. African-American gang). Rivalries tend to be based on neighborhood or location-based affiliation and turf issues.

How Many Youth Are Members of Gangs?

Estimates vary, as there exists no consistent, uniform, well-maintained system in place for recording data about gangs and gang members (Diaz, 2009). In the mid-1990s, estimates of the total number of persons belonging to American street gangs ranged from 660,000 to 1.5 million. More recent estimates have gang membership up to at least 1 million youth nationally (Johnson, 2009). A survey of nearly 6,000 eighth graders conducted in 11 cities with known gang problems found that 9 percent were currently gang members and 17 percent said they had belonged to a gang at some point in their lives (Esbensen, Peterson, Taylor, & Freng, 2010). This percentage varied from 4 to 15 percent depending on location (see Howell, 2010, p. 3).

Characteristics of Nonwhite Gangs

With rare exceptions, youth gangs tend to be ethnically/racially homogeneous. When analyzed proportionally in light of the total number of youth gang memberships in the United States, such membership is disproportionately nonwhite. According to recent law enforcement estimates, roughly 49 percent of gang members are Hispanic/Latino, 35 percent are African American/black, 9 percent are white, and 7 percent are other racial/ethnic categories (National Youth Gang Center, 2009). The racial/ethnic composition of gangs is an extension of the characteristics of the larger communities of which gangs are a part. For example, the overwhelming majority of gang members in Philadelphia and Detroit are African American. In New York and Los Angeles, Latino gangs predominate. A significant portion of gangs in Honolulu, Hawaii, are Filipino. Relevant information related to Hispanic, African American, Asian, and Native American youth gangs are described in the following sections.

Hispanic Youth Gangs

Hispanics are currently the largest minority group in the United States, and Hispanic/Latino youth constitute the majority of gang members nationwide. There are more than 500 Chicano gangs in Los Angeles County alone (Shelden, Tracy, & Brown, 2004), found predominantly in the San Fernando Valley, San Gabriel Valley, Long Beach community, and South Central Los Angeles. According to Shelden et al. (2004), the Chicano gangs in Southern California have arguably the longest history of any youth gangs in America. According to Regoli and Hewitt (2003), most Latino gangs are organized around age cohorts separated by two to three years. Hispanic gangs are motivated by the protection of territory, as loyalty to one's barrio lies at the root of intergang violence. With rare exceptions, Hispanic gangs do not identify with specific colors (as is more typical with African American youth gangs). For a more detailed description of case studies with Hispanic gangs in the Phoenix area, see Petersen (2004, Chapter 6).

African American Youth Gangs

A brief history of the development of African American gangs in Los Angeles and Chicago is given by Siegel and Welsh (2009, p. 305–306). Currently, the largest and most well-known African American youth gangs are the Bloods and the Crips, which are umbrella terms linking a large confederation of subset groups. Subset gangs are generally organized around neighborhoods and typically have anywhere from 20 to 30 members. Shelden et al. (2004) opine that the Crips and Bloods have so influenced African American street gangs in Los Angeles that the only distinction between the thousands of gang members is the blue (Crips) and the red (Bloods) colors. African American gangs are noted by slang words, secret hand signals, and ostentatious clothing, which borders on the outrageous in order to attract attention and to advertise gang identity (Shelden et al., 2004).

Asian Youth Gangs

There are several varieties of Asian gangs (e.g., Chinese, Japanese, Korean, Vietnamese, Cambodian, Pacific Islanders). Filipino youth gangs, like Hispanic youth gangs, operate primarily out of California. However, Filipino youth gang activity has also been reported in Alaska, Washington, and Nevada (Shelden et al., 2004). Vietnamese gangs have been found to operate in Southern California towns (e.g., Garden Grove, Westminster), as well as in other cities outside of California (e.g., Atlanta, Houston, New Orleans, to name a few). Chinese youth gangs operate from traditions that date back to the organized crime groups (called "tongs" or "triads") in China and Taiwan. Often low-skilled Chinese youth would learn the ropes from adult members of organized crime groups (e.g., running errands for gamblers or serving as couriers or lookouts). Thus, Chinese youth gang membership is viewed as the first rung on the journey toward involvement with Chinese organized crime. Chinese youth gangs are found in San Francisco, Los Angeles, Boston, Toronto, Vancouver, and New York City.

Although the behavioral characteristics between Asian and non-Asian youth gangs may overlap to some degree, researchers note many significant differences in Asian American youth gangs compared to African American and Hispanic gangs. Asian American youth gangs are the most difficult for law enforcement to penetrate, because of their heightened secrecy. In many close-knit communities, Chinese youth gangs in particular terrorize their own people, who are often too frightened and unskilled in utilizing the American legal system to report crimes to the police. It is estimated that between 80 percent to 90 percent of Chinese businesspeople pay Chinese youth gangs on either an occasional or regular basis for protection (Shelden et al., 2004).

Asian gangs differ from Hispanic or African American gangs in that they avoid detection by being deeply embedded in community organizations and legitimate businesses, and they avoid behaviors that would draw unwanted attention (e.g., particular modes of dress, hand signals, wearing highly visible tattoos). Some Asian gangs fight among themselves infrequently, whereas others are more similar to African American and Hispanic gangs in their intergang conflicts. An overall theme is the preference to concentrate most of their efforts in making money through robbery, theft, burglary, and extortion.

Native American Youth Gangs

Gangs have existed on Native American reservations since the 1970s (Delaney, 2006). The largest Native American reservation in the United States is the Navajo nation reservation in Window Rock, Arizona, which is also home to numerous gangs. The proliferation of such gangs are responsible for skyrocketing murder, assault, robbery, and drug trafficking rates within the 25,000 square miles that frame this reservation (Sahagun, 1997). As recently as 2009, as many as 39 gangs have been identified as operating in the South Dakota Pine Ridge reservation (Associated Press, July 31, 2009). According to Elsner (2003), gangs are so prevalent in local schools that it creates tremendous pressure on kids to drop out of school. The most well-known gangs and their ethnic/racial affiliation, at least at the time of this writing, are briefly summarized in Sidebar 8.9.

Where Do Gangs Proliferate?

Gang activity occurs in big cities, small cities, and rural areas throughout the United States, although serious gang activity is more prevalent in big-city locations. Howell, Egley, Tita, and Griffiths (2011) summarize regional trends in gang activity (of all ethnicities) as viewed by FBI and police agencies nationwide. This information is summarized as follows:

- *Northeast region.* In the early 1900s, New York City was considered to be the epicenter of serious street gang activity in the Northeast. Gradually, gang activity in this region expanded to include other East region and New England states, particularly Pennsylvania, New Jersey, and Connecticut. According to the FBI's

Sidebar 8.9   Partial List of Nonwhite American Street Gangs That Are National and/or Regional in Scope

Primary Name	Primary Ethnicity	Origins	National Scope	Primary Source of Income
18th Street	Illegal aliens from Mexico and Central America	Los Angeles	Membership estimated at 30,000–50,000 active in 44 cities in 20 states	Street-level distribution of cocaine, marijuana, heroin, methamphetamines
Latin Kings	Mexican and Puerto Rican	Chicago	Membership estimated at 20,000–35,000 active in 158 cities in 31 states	Street-level distribution of powder/crack cocaine, marijuana, heroin
Asian Boyz	Vietnamese and Cambodian	Southern California	Membership estimated at 1,300–2,000 active in 28 cities in 14 states	Producing, transporting, and distributing methamphetamines, marijuana
Black P. Stone Nation	African American	Chicago	Membership estimated at 6,000–8,000	Street-level distribution of cocaine, marijuana, heroin
Bloods	African American	Los Angeles	Membership estimated at 7,000–30,000 active in 123 cities in 33 states	Street-level distribution of cocaine, marijuana; transporting and distributing methamphetamines, heroin, and PCP
Crips	African American	Los Angeles	Membership estimated at 30,000–35,000 active in 221 cities in 41 states	Street-level distribution of powder/crack cocaine, marijuana, PCP
Florencia 13	Mexican	Los Angeles	Membership estimated at 3,000+ active in 5 states	Producing and distributing methamphetamines
Fresno Bulldogs	Mexican	Fresno, California	Membership estimated at 5,000–6,000 active in Central California	Street-level distribution of methamphetamines, marijuana, heroin

Gangster Disciples	African American	Chicago	Membership estimated at 25,000–50,000 active in 110 cities in 31 states	Street-level distribution of crack cocaine, marijuana, heroin
Latin Disciples	Puerto Rican	Chicago	Membership estimated at 1,500–2,000 active in Great Lakes and Southwest U.S.	Street-level distribution of powder cocaine, marijuana, heroin, PCP
Mara Salvatrucha (MS-13)	Central Americans	Los Angeles	Membership estimated at 30,000–50,000 worldwide; 8,000–10,000 active in five U.S. cities	Drug smuggling and distribution (powder cocaine, marijuana)
Sureños and Norteños	Mexican	Southern and Northern California	Membership estimated at 53,000+ members active in 20 states	Retail-level distribution of cocaine, heroin, marijuana, methamphetamines, PCP within prisons and in communities
Tiny Rascal Gangsters	Southeast Asian-American	California	Membership estimated at 5,000–10,000 members active in Southwestern, Pacific, and New England regions of the U.S.	Street-level distribution of powder cocaine, heroin, marijuana, methamphetamines
Vice Lord Nation	African American	Chicago	Membership estimated at 30,000–35,000 members active in 74 cities in 28 states	Street-level distribution of cocaine, heroin, marijuana

(Adapted from National Gang Threat Assessment 2009, National Gang Intelligence Center, available from http://www.fbi.gov/stats-services/publications/national-gang-threat-assessment-2009-pdf) intelligence reports, the most significant gangs operating in the East region are the Crips, Latin Kings, MS-13, Ñeta, and United Blood Nation. The most significant gangs operating in the New England region are Hell's Angels, Latin Kings, Outlaws, Tiny Rascal Gangster Crips, and United Blood Nation (UBN).

- *Central region.* In the Midwest region, traditional Chicago gangs still have the strongest presence. In 2008, the largest street gangs in Chicago included the Gangster Disciple Nation (GDN), Black Gangsters/New Breeds (BG), Latin Kings (LKs), Black P. Stone Nation, Vice Lords (VLs), Four Corner Hustlers, and Maniac Latin Disciples (MLDs). The most recent chapter in Chicago's gang history is the proliferation of gangs outside of the city. By 2006, 19 gang turfs were scattered around Chicago, throughout Cook County. Next, gangs began emerging in the larger region surrounding Chicago on the north, west, and south sides. Other cities in this region that have extensive gang activity include Cleveland, Detroit, Joliet, Kansas City, Minneapolis, Omaha, and St. Louis.

- *Southern region.* The most significant gangs operating in the Southeast region (Deep South states) are said to be the Crips, Gangster Disciples, Latin Kings, Sureños 13, and United Blood Nation. According to the FBI, the increased migration of Hispanic gangs into the region has contributed significantly to gang growth. In the Southwest region (Texas, Oklahoma, New Mexico, Colorado, Utah, and Arizona), the most significant gangs are Barrio Azteca, Latin Kings, Mexikanemi, Tango Blast, and Texas Syndicate. Among 25 major Houston gangs, the Tango Blast, Houston Tango Blast, and Latin Disciples are said to be the main regional gangs that are Houston-based.

- *Pacific region.* Street gangs in Los Angeles remain legendary. According to Diaz (2009), Los Angeles, California, is the "epicenter" of America's gang problem. One writer describes Los Angeles as the "world capital of gang life and culture" (Myers, 2000). As of 2007, the Los Angeles Police Department designated the 11 most notorious gangs in the city: 18th Street Westside (Southwest Area), 204th Street (Harbor Area), Avenues (Northeast Area), Black P-Stones (Southwest, Wilshire Areas), Canoga Park Alabama (West Valley Area), Grape Street Crips (Southeast Area), La Mirada Locos (Rampart, Northeast Areas), Mara Salvatrucha (Rampart, Hollywood, and Wilshire Areas), Rollin 40s (Southwest Area), Rollin 30s Harlem Crips (Southwest Area), and Rollin 60s (77th St. Area). California continues to have the most gangs and gang-related problems compared to any other state in the country, with more than 200 communities within the state that are seriously affected by gang-related problems. Many of the largest and most violent street gangs (such as Mara Salvatrucha, or MS-13, the Crips, and Bloods) began in Los Angeles and spread eastward to cities and towns all throughout the United States. One webpage (www.streetgangs.com/resources/programs) lists

45 gang intervention/violence prevention organizations just in the Los Angeles area alone, and a different website lists slightly more programs (http://www .illnevergiveup.com/files/Resource_List_for_Gang_Programs.pdf), while cautioning readers that even this list may not be comprehensive.

What Are Risk Factors for Joining Gangs?

At a certain point in life, a young person makes a conscious choice to join a gang, and multiple personal and environmental factors influence this choice. Obviously, many young children experience multiple risk factors, but they do not join gangs. The active presence of gang activity in communities and schools is a necessary, but not sufficient, condition that increases the probability of gang membership. Because schools in gang communities must provide security officers, metal detectors, and security cameras as deterrents for violence, an unfortunate by-product of such measures is heightened fear among teachers, staff, and students. This, in turn, increases the perceived power of gangs in schools, which in turn may lead some students to join gangs for protection (Thompkins, 2004).

Rather than immediately joining serious, violent gangs, some youth become involved in less delinquent groups, called *starter gangs* (Howell, 2010). Here, young children and adolescents are introduced to gang culture (i.e., distinctive attitudes, jargon, rituals, and symbols). In many locations, established gangs sometimes create cliques or sets composed of younger youth (with commensurate names such as "wannabes," "juniors," "pee-wees," and the like). While older members of established gangs are involved in serious and violent offenses, younger members of starter gangs engage in more minor delinquent behaviors. A brief summary of risk factors contributing to gang membership is listed in Table 8.4.

Once a young person joins a gang, he or she is part of a lifestyle that is largely unknown to persons who have little contact with gangs. Nevertheless, those who work closely with gang members have identified a common set of behaviors and attitudes that characterize gang life. These characteristics are listed briefly in Sidebar 8.10.

Sidebar 8.10   Behavioral and Attitudinal Characteristics of Persons Belonging to Delinquent Gangs

Excitement. Gang members seek "thrills" that come from taking risks in dangerous activities such as fighting, automobile racing, using firearms and explosives in ambushing enemy gangs, having frequent sex, and taking dangerous amounts of illegal drugs.

Fatalism. Many delinquent youth grow up in an environment of hopelessness and despair. Such an upbringing fosters the attitude that fate has worked against

(*continued*)

them. They believe that life is determined by forces outside of their control, and that they will never succeed in legitimate enterprises no matter how hard they work.

Group autonomy. Gang members/delinquents rarely respect, recognize, or obey conventional authority figures (e.g., parents, teachers, police) other than those figures in leadership positions within the gang.

Loyalty to the group. Gang members are socialized to put the gang above all other priorities in life. Many gangs have elaborate, specialized initiation rituals that new members must pass in order to join or establish loyalty to the gang. Members must faithfully wear the proper gang attire, display the correct hand signals and greetings, shun/denigrate all corresponding symbols belonging to rival gangs, and must not disobey gang rules. The physical turf owned by the gang (e.g., neighborhood, city block/section, or favorite hangout) must be protected at all times from enroachment by rival outside gang members. Gang members must come to the aid and defense of their fellow gang members at all times, and must avenge any violence perpetrated against their gangmates by outside rival gangs.

Maliciousness. Some crimes committed by gangs are an outgrowth of deep-seated spite, animosity, or bitterness directed at perceived enemies. Other acts, such as vandalism, are committed simply for the rush and/or thrill of inflicting injury, harm, or suffering on others.

Non-utilitarianism. Delinquent acts are committed for the sheer satisfaction of committing crimes, and not because such acts serve a specific or useful purpose.

Oppositional. Gangs take pride in turning middle-class norms and values of the surrounding society upside down.

Rationalization. When confronted by authority figures, law enforcement, or social service workers, delinquents will often rationalize their behavior by denying responsibility for wrongdoing, denying having any guilty feelings about injury to others, justifying violence against enemies (e.g., "they had it coming"), or deflecting blame by attacking others who disapprove of or criticize their behavior (e.g., "the police are more corrupt than we are").

Respect. Gang members are socialized to be hypersensitive to any sign of personal or group disrespect by those within or outside of the gang. Perceived disrespect, whether intentional or unintentional, is often met with violent consequences.

Short-term hedonism. Gang members live for the momentary pleasures (e.g., getting into fights, committing robberies, drinking, getting high, and sexual conquests) and have little regard for planning in relation to long-term goals for self-improvement.

Sloth. The gang life involves extended periods of "hanging out," "shooting the breeze," playing cards (or other games), listening to music, getting high, and in general doing nothing. Interspersed with these periods are short bursts of often intense, violent activity.

Street smarts. Gang members value the ability to outsmart, outfox, "con," or "run a game" on others who are perceived to be more socially naïve, in order to attain a desired goal.

Survivalist worldview. Gang life becomes an issue of predators trapping prey, nurtured by an environment of drug dealers preying on drug users, pimps preying on prostitutes, and robbers preying on their victims. Gang members view neighborhood derelicts and persons dependent on public assistance as weak failures, and they are determined not to fail like these people by surviving and fighting. They look around them and see the material things that more affluent people have, and they are determined to obtain these things through illegal methods. Youths learn that trust is not something to be automatically conferred or earned, but is rather something to be negotiated and "calculated" ultimately for personal gain. These traits are evident not so much because youth are in a gang, per se, but because these traits are nurtured by living in low-income communities.

Toughness. Being tough is a critical element in a male gang member's concept of what it means to be a man. Male delinquency/gangs value physical strength and prowess, being masculine (i.e., body building, tattoos), bravery in the face of danger, avoidance of appearing sentimental or soft, and an all-around "macho" attitude.

(Adapted from Delaney, 2006 Shelden, Tracy, & Brown, 2004)

Table 8.4   Risk Factors That Increase the Probability of Youth Gang Involvement

Individual Factors	
Attractions	Provides a family structure missing in the home; confers a well-defined social identity; enhances prestige/status; provides protection/safety from bullying; enhances sexual access to the opposite sex; lure of easy money from drug trafficking; popular media glamorizes gang life; close friends or boyfriends/girlfriends have already joined a gang
Personal Problems	Early involvement in delinquency; precocious sexual activity; attraction to aggression/violence as a means of solving problems; alcohol and/or drug use; conduct and other externalizing disorders; physical/sexual abuse from home
Peer Group Factors	
Peer Characteristics	Associations with aggressive peers, particularly those who engage in delinquency; higher levels of peer rejection

(continued)

Table 8.4   (*Continued*)

School Factors	
Cognitive/Academic	Generally perform poorly in school; learning disabilities more frequent
Student/School Relationships	Low degree of commitment to and involvement in school; weak attachment to teachers; hatred and rejection of anything that represents school order/authority
School Characteristics	Schools characterized by higher levels of student victimization by bullies, self-reported violence, discipline practices despised by students (suspensions, expulsions, referrals to juvenile courts); low levels of school's ability to protect students from physical harm/harassment
Community Factors	
Neighborhood Characteristics	Gang activity flourishes in high-crime, economically disadvantaged neighborhoods that promote widespread availability of firearms and drugs

(Adapted from Howell, 2010)

GANG IMPACT ON SCHOOLS

Many schools that are situated in communities with a long history of gang activity are well aware of the presence of gangs and gang influence on their campuses. In contrast, other schools and communities that have had no previous history of a significant gang presence are beginning to experience the influx of youth gangs from other locations. Many of these schools and communities have been described as being in denial over the presence of youth gangs. Even when schools eventually acknowledge a significant gang presence on their campuses, such schools are caught unprepared for how to deal with this troublesome issue. The next discussion highlights information for how to recognize a gang presence and associated activity in schools, followed by a discussion of effective schoolwide strategies culled from the field for dealing with gang influence.

Recognizing Gang Presence/Activity in Schools

Gangs and gang activity within the nation's schools are often linked to increased levels of school violence in areas in which gangs proliferate. Some gangs operate under the radar, thus teachers and administrators must gather information about their presence through indirect means. In other communities, gang presence is obvious to anyone who is knowledgeable about the overt signs of gang influence (e.g., graffiti, gang insignias, gang clothing, hand signals).

Indirect Means for Learning About Gang Presence in Schools

In many instances, adults in schools are unaware of the slow infiltration of gangs in schools, but students are not. Schools are known as an ideal place for gang members to recruit new members and conduct other gang business (e.g., selling drugs). Here, gang members consciously keep a low profile in order to maintain smooth and unfettered access to students. Important information about gang involvement in schools can be obtained simply by talking with students or administering confidential surveys to them.

As an example, the Healthy Youth Survey (HYS; Vogeler, 2009) is voluntarily administered every two years to school students in Washington State. Surveys such as this reveal data on how many students report being gang members. This data should be interpreted with caution, however, because the most criminally involved hard-core gang members have spotty attendance records resulting from frequent suspensions and/or expulsions.

Overt Signs of Gang Presence in Schools

Students are both psychologically and/or physically intimidated by gang activity at school. Many have reported that they sometimes fear they will be harmed at school, and some will avoid school or class out of fear (Vogeler, 2009). In 2007, the Washington state legislature directed the Office of Superintendent of Public Instruction to convene a task force to examine how gangs are affecting school safety. The task force was directed to recommend methods to prevent and eliminate gangs in schools, gather intelligence on gangs, and share information about gangs. The task force released a comprehensive report in December 2008 that included school administrators' observations about how the gang presence negatively affects schools over which they have responsibility (Vogeler, 2009). Anecdotal information in the Washington state school gang task force report revealed that students as young as kindergarten age were being sent to school (by older siblings or parents) dressed in gang-related attire.

Gang Presence in the Vicinity Surrounding Schools

Gangs are not only problematic for schools when they disrupt life within schools, but they can be just as problematic when they operate *in the vicinity of schools* (i.e., on the fringes of school property). A frequent complaint heard from school administrators in gang-infested communities is that

> nonstudent gang members congregate around schools where they intimidate staff and students, attempt to recruit students into the gang, stir up trouble with gang rivals, or engage in criminal activity. They may engage in trafficking of drugs and weapons, flash gang signs, tag school and private property with gang graffiti, or start fights with students. (Vogeler, 2009, p. 8)

School administrators express frustration that gang-involved students who are expelled or suspended from school are not allowed to trespass on school property, but no restrictions can prevent them from loitering around the surrounding vicinity of schools.

Expelled or suspended students who do this often return to seek retaliation for the incident that caused them to be removed from school in the first place. School administrators—and even school security officers—do not have the authority to order students to leave properties that are adjacent to schools, which is a weakness that is exploited by gang-involved students. In some instances, gang members live directly across the street from a school, which guarantees their continued presence and harassment of school students.

GANG INTERVENTION

According to Vogeler (2009), schools are a strategic location to establish gang prevention and intervention efforts for two primary reasons: (1) the majority of students who are vulnerable to gang joining and involvement can be easily accessed in one central location, and (2) intervention can focus on strengthening school attachment and academic success, which are viewed as protective factors that help counteract negative correlates of gang involvement.

However, it would be profoundly naïve for school psychologists to think about intervention in terms of stopping gangs from starting or even getting rid of gangs altogether. Youth gangs are so entrenched in numerous locations throughout America that one Mexican gang intervention worker opined (whether rightly or wrongly) that "the gang tradition is part of our culture" (Myers, 2000).

Nevertheless, positive steps designed to deal with gang problems in schools must first begin with an understanding of important distinctions between children and adolescents who are the intended targets for intervention efforts (adapted from Howell, 2010; Wyrick, 2006). These distinctions can be applied to the following four student subgroups:

Subgroup 1 (General Student Population)

The largest subgroup consists of all children and youth in a community where gangs are present. Members of this subgroup receive primary prevention services. *Primary prevention* refers to services and supports that reach the entire population in communities with large amounts of crime or gang activity. These efforts address needs or risk factors and are characteristic of all youth and families in a community. Government, local schools, community organizations, or faith-based organizations may deliver these services. Examples of primary prevention include public awareness campaigns, one-stop centers that improve access to public services, school-based life skills programs, community cleanup and lighting projects, and community organizing efforts.

The Gang Resistance Education And Training (G.R.E.A.T.) program is a school-based primary prevention program that has demonstrated effectiveness in helping dissuade youth from joining gangs (Esbensen, Osgood, Taylor, Peterson, & Freng, 2001). Law enforcement officers offer middle school students a 13-week curriculum that describes the dangers of gang involvement. The lesson content emphasizes cognitive-behavioral training, social skills development, refusal skills, and conflict resolution. The G.R.E.A.T. program also offers an elementary school curriculum, a summer program, and training for families (see weblink in the Additional Resources at the end of this chapter).

Subgroup 2 (At-Risk Non-Gang-Involved Youth)

This subgroup consists of high-risk youth who have already displayed early signs of delinquency and an elevated risk for gang membership but are not yet involved in gangs. Most of these youth may not have joined gangs yet, but they represent a pool of candidates for future gang membership. Members of this subgroup are candidates for secondary prevention services, which are less intensive than those provided to Subgroup 3 but are more intensive than those provided to youth in the community at large (see Brand-Name Interventions, previous section of this chapter).

In addition to several of the brand-name programs mentioned in the previous section on juvenile delinquency, other programs have shown promise. Some programs have demonstrated some ability to prevent delinquency and other juvenile problems, reduce risk factors, or enhance protective factors. However, compared to the superior brand-name programs discussed earlier, they employ limited research methods and often do not include a control group in their research design. The programs in this category appear promising, but their success must be strengthened using more rigorous scientific research designs.

These programs include Boys & Girls Clubs Gang Prevention Through Targeted Outreach, which is a program that substitutes the desire of at-risk youths (between ages 6 to 18) for gang membership with alternative social activities, a place to belong, and supportive adults who can reinforce more positive behaviors (Arbreton & McClanahan, 2002). In California, the Gang Resistance Is Paramount program provides a school-based anti-gang curriculum, recreational activities, gang awareness education for parents, and counseling for parents and youth (Solis, Schwartz, & Hinton, 2003).

The Preventive Treatment Program in Montreal, Canada, is an instructive example of an early intervention program that has reduced gang involvement, even though it was not developed primarily with this purpose in mind. It was designed to prevent antisocial behavior among boys ages 7 to 9 with a low socioeconomic status who had previously displayed disruptive behavior in kindergarten. The program improved school performance, reduced delinquency and substance use, and showed that a combination of parent training and childhood skill development can steer some children away from gangs before they reach mid-adolescence (Gatti, Tremblay, Vitaro, & McDuff, 2005; Tremblay, Masse, Pagani, & Vitaro, 1996).

Growing public concern in Mountlake Terrace, Washington, over juvenile crime and youth gang involvement led some frustrated and outspoken residents to demand a citywide curfew (Thurman & Mueller, 2003). In response, the police chief convened public meetings to discuss the problem. From these meetings, the formation of a Community Neutral Zone (at a centrally located elementary school gymnasium) was recommended as a safe place where at-risk youth could voluntarily congregate and engage in prosocial activities. In addition to participating in sports and other entertainment, youths receive various forms of counseling and other essential services. Each Friday and Saturday evening from 10:00 P.M. to 2:00 A.M., program staff and volunteers work with youth between the ages of 13 to 20 who are at high risk for gang involvement. Each evening's events include recreational activities (e.g., volleyball, basketball) and social service presentations such as Alcoholics Anonymous, Narcotics Anonymous, and AIDS awareness. Movies, music, and hot meals are also provided. A minimum number of rules for participation are imposed by adult supervisors in the interest of encouraging inclusion. Program materials such as sporting equipment, food, and, occasionally, door prizes typically are donated by local merchants.

A study of the program found that more than half of participating youths said they attended the program every weekend, that 84 percent said it exceeded their expectations, and that if the youth were not attending the Community Neutral Zone, it was likely they would be at considerably greater risk of committing delinquent and/or criminal acts. More than half of the interviewed youths cited improved interpersonal skills from their participation. Some evidence from an analysis of police arrest data suggested a possible reduction in juvenile crime that may have been linked to the program (Thurman & Mueller, 2003).

Subgroup 3 (Gang-Involved Youth)

This group consists of gang-involved youth and their associates, who make up a relatively smaller share of the general population compared to Subgroup 2. These youth are involved in significant levels of illegal gang activity but are not necessarily in the highest offending category. Members of this subgroup are candidates for intensive treatment, which may include, but certainly not be limited to, individual counseling, group therapy, family therapy, mentoring, and/or cognitive-behavioral therapy.

Many programs that seek to make a difference in school settings are community-based programs. Such programs initially seek funding outside of schools, but they apply services within schools to demonstrate positive gains. Once positive gains are demonstrated, funding from schools (or funding significantly facilitated by schools) is easier to secure. An example of an effective community-based program is the Violence-Free Zone Initiative developed by the National Center for Neighborhood Enterprise (see Sidebar 8.11).

🖎 Sidebar 8.11   The Milwaukee Violence-Free Zone Initiative

Milwaukee is the largest city in the state of Wisconsin and the 28th most populous city in the United States, according to the 2010 U.S. Census. Along with many cities, it has been listed as one of the 100 most dangerous cities in America (see http://www.neighborhoodscout.com/neighborhoods/crime-rates/top 100dangerous/). Part of this reputation comes from entrenched youth gang activity in the city (e.g., see Trevey, 2012).

Approximately 84 percent of students enrolled in the Milwaukee public schools are nonwhite, with the majority of this group comprised of African American (approximately 60 percent of the total) and Hispanic (approximately 20 percent of the total) students. At one point within the past 5 years, the Milwaukee public schools had the dubious distinction of having the highest school suspension rate in the nation.

In 1981, Robert Woodson Sr.—a community development activist and leader—founded the National Center for Neighborhood Enterprise (NCNE). NCNE was founded on the following core principles that guide the activities, governance, and overall direction of the group:

1. Individuals within communities that are suffering most from a problem *must* be involved in the creation and implementation of solutions for the problem.
2. Principles of the market economy should be applied to the solution of societal problems. When beginning new initiatives like the Violence-Free Zones (see below), for example, the NCNE initially relies on private funding. After positive qualitative and quantitative results (that show a positive impact with cost savings) are demonstrated, then public agencies are approached for funding.
3. Value-generating and faith-based programs and groups are uniquely qualified to address problems stemming from poverty in communities.
4. Effective community-based programs originate in suffering communities, and not necessarily from theories originating from the ivory tower (academia), civil rights organizations, or subject matter "experts", most of whom have little or no practical first-hand knowledge of, or experience in, suffering communities.

Robert Woodson's Violence-Free Zone (VFZ) is the name given to an NCNE program started in the late 1990s in response to gang violence in the local

(*continued*)

neighborhood surrounding Madison High School in Dallas, Texas. The NCNE enlisted the help of a former gang member named Omar Jahwar. With the help of a $100,000 grant facilitated by NCNE and the school district, Jahwar hired six youth advisors to help him establish and nurture relationships with a select number of youths, most of whom were responsible for much of the school violence at Madison High.

The intervention model is based on the observation that, in a high school of 1,000 students, approximately 10 percent (n = 100) are responsible for most of the disruptions occurring within the school. Of this group, 10 percent (n = 10) are typically leaders who orchestrate these disruptions and are the driving force behind school conflicts and mayhem. By working with and redirecting these leaders, significant reductions in gang-related violence in schools can occur. Because of a significant reduction in incidents of school violence as a result of the VFZ presence in the school, the VFZ's work expanded to 14 middle and high schools in the Dallas area.

Robert Woodson's long history of community work with the NCNE taught him that some of the most violent leaders of youth gangs have tremendous influence on other at-risk young people in crime-ridden neighborhoods. If these leaders could be turned around by the activities of the NCNE, they could be key players in helping to guide communities in a more positive direction. Here, former gang members can serve as coaches of neighborhood athletic teams, and motivate young children to complete their schoolwork and behave in school through their role as Youth Advisors for VFZ initiatives.

VFZ Youth Advisors are individuals typically between the ages of 19 to 30, who come from, as well as continue to live in, the same neighborhoods as at-risk students. In most cases, Youth Advisors have struggled with the same issues of gang-related crime and drug abuse as the young people they work with. Under the VFZ model, a day in the life of a Youth Advisor (YA) working in schools consists of the following activities:

- *Walking the streets.* YAs walk within about 1,000 feet around the school building, typically before the school day begins. This helps YAs to pick up any information on any gang conflicts that may be brewing, so that they can touch base quickly with police officers in the immediate vicinity.
- *Greeting the students.* YAs greet students as they come into school. By doing this, YAs can offer support to any students who may have issues at home or who may have other personal issues needing support.
- *Monitoring tardiness.* When students arrive late to school, YAs meet with those who are chronically late to find out why they have continuing difficulties being on time. Occasionally, YAs will call the homes of late or absent students to identify issues that may affect their tardiness.
- *Walking the halls.* Between classes, YAs walk up and down school hallways, redirecting students and maintaining a noticeable presence. YAs monitor

the presence of individual conflicts, neighborhood rivalries, or gang conflicts, as well as touch base with teachers to monitor any potentially explosive behavioral issues in the classroom.

- *Lunch with students.* Lunchtimes in school cafeterias are prime opportunities for YAs to build informal relationships, trust, and visibility with students.
- *Mediation.* YAs participate in teacher–student, parent–student, and student–student mediation to help resolve problematic issues causing disruption within the school and within classrooms.

In addition to these roles, each YA has a caseload of anywhere from 10 to 25 students, who are referred to them by principals, teachers, or counselors. These referrals are not all necessarily students who are experiencing problems; they can be model students who are academic and/or social leaders in the schools. This effectively counteracts any stigma for youth who form close relationships with YAs.

In order to elicit cooperation from different political groups in the Milwaukee community, the NCNE worked closely with the Latino Community Center, located on the south side of Milwaukee where most Hispanic residents live. The Latino Community Center was already involved in placing staff in the local high school to help with gang problems, hence they were natural allies in VFZ initiatives. The NCNE also established a working relationship with the Running Rebels Community Organization (RRCO), whose mission is to provide high-risk (predominantly African American) youth living on the north side of Milwaukee with athletic, academic, life skills, and career training services. The RRCO has a strong working relationship with the courts for youth in the community, but no strong presence in the local schools. By being a partner with the NCNE on the VFZ initiative, the RRCO gains further legitimacy and stature with Milwaukee's youth and schools.

The effectiveness of the VFZ initiatives in Milwaukee schools is assessed annually using the following outcome indicators: (a) number of both violent and nonviolent incidents that occur; (b) total number and rates of school suspensions; (c) positive increases in school climate survey results; and (d) the number of crime incidents (e.g., auto thefts) in the neighborhoods surrounding the school. The VFZ has shown vast improvements in all of these indicators in the sites in which it has been implemented, which makes it a highly sought-after program around the country. Online testimonials about the VFZ can be accessed at http://www.cneonline.org/files/RESULTS_WHAT_SAID_VFZ.pdf, and contact information is provided in the Additional Resources at the conclusion of this chapter.

(Adapted from Johnson & Wubbenhorst, 2010)

Once inside the gang world, the term *gang intervention* has been loosely defined as any activity designed primarily to help active gang members from visiting violence and mayhem on their communities, and secondarily to become somewhat functional members of the larger society (e.g., getting them back into school or an alternative educational institution, helping with pending court cases, providing job readiness skills and job placement). Los Angeles, in particular, has had extensive experience in recruiting Gang Intervention Workers (GIW) to assist them in gang intervention efforts. The activities of these workers is briefly described in Sidebar 8.12.

✑ Sidebar 8.12   The Role of Gang Intervention Workers

According to one estimate, Los Angeles is home to 400 youth gangs with approximately 39,000 members. In June 2010, a first-of-its-kind training academy for gang intervention workers graduated its inaugural class. Twenty-seven students received certificates from the Los Angeles Violence Intervention Training Academy after finishing a 140-hour course taught over 14 weeks at the UCLA Downtown Labor Center. The curriculum provides study and practical experience developing skills in mediation and conflict resolution, community crisis intervention, establishing gang truces and mutual understanding, and the "ethnic dynamics" about which one must be aware when working with a variety of ethnic and language groups. In a nutshell, the goal of this unique training academy is to professionalize the field of gang intervention work.

A gang intervention worker (GIW), as the name suggests, is a person who works closely with youth gang members to (a) broker peace between warring gang factions, (b) help prevent gang actions that would damage communities and schools, (c) forge personal mentoring relationships with gang members for the purpose of helping them navigate personal problems, and (d) help them take steps to pursue positive goals for the future (which may include leaving the gang altogether).

The theme that guides the work of GIWs is to replace antisocial values and behaviors of impressionable young gang members with prosocial values and behaviors. This work is much more difficult than it initially sounds, as the goal of intervention is to develop a total change in a gang member's thinking, values, and lifestyle. Once gang members decide to leave gang life, they are referred to case managers, who use case plans to follow through with clients to help eliminate barriers to leaving the gang life. Sometimes GIWs will work with newly exited gang members to encourage them to work with individuals who are still involved with gang life, in order to help them leave the life. Sometimes GIWs assist parents of recovering gang members by steering them to parenting classes, where they can learn how to provide an emotional support system to their children that effectively replaces the emotional support system that was provided by the gang.

Due to the nature of this work, the most effective GIWs are former gang leaders, since their own experiences with gang life gives them a natural insight into the thinking and actions of gang members. These former "gang bangers," some of whom have prison records, are the only persons with the credibility to earn the trust, respect, and support of active gang members, which is necessary for encouraging gang leaders and members to sit down at the "peace table" with rival gang leaders and members.

Negotiating gang truces is a full-time job, with peacekeeping required for the most innocuous circumstances. For example, if a gang wants to simply use parking spaces in territory occupied by a rival gang, or a gang member simply needs to attend school in a rival gang territory, truces must be negotiated. Although gang truces are celebrated when they happen, they do not always last.

Services that exiting gang members need include academic support, family support, mental health counseling, life skills training, and job readiness skill development (e.g., learning how to show up for work consistently and on time, dressing appropriately, how to interact with customers). Job readiness skills are particularly crucial, because many employers are reluctant to hire gang members. Tattoos, sagging clothes, and other physical elements of the gang lifestyle do not mix well in professional environments. Many youth need an appropriate environment to see the benefits of working and earning a living, which will in time prompt them to change their habits and presentation to more appropriate demeanors. Job placement programs recognize that entry-level options must also be accepting of the youths and the obstacles that they face, and provide some tolerance of them.

The long road toward the professionalization of GIWs has had its share of successes and setbacks. A recurring problem for GIWs is the perception that they lack the appropriate credentials to be effective in gang intervention work. Particularly in the Los Angeles area, some lucrative state grants have occasionally been terminated in part because ex-gang members with criminal records were hired as caseworkers. In some cases, such concerns have been justified, as some GIWs have been re-arrested for new crimes.

Another problem is that gang intervention efforts and programs are difficult to evaluate by funding agencies. According to one gang intervention program director, "You can count the number of times someone pulls the trigger . . . but you can't count the number of times they don't." According to one contracts and grants manager, "You don't know if a kid is not a gang member because of the program, or if the kid was just not going to join a gang."

According to one estimate, the top salary for gang intervention workers in Los Angeles is about $36,000 per year. Some GIWs work part-time for as little as

(*continued*)

$10 per hour. Because gang intervention programs sponsored by federal, state, and local governments come and go as different approaches to gang intervention come into vogue, consistent funding for such programs is never secure.

To combat these problems and perceptions, and to empower GIWs, the Association of Community-Based Gang Intervention was established in 1998 to give a unified voice to GIWs from 56 agencies in the Los Angeles area. The first youth and gang violence intervention specialist program in the nation was started in the year 2000 at Cal State University in Los Angeles (http://www.calstate.edu/newsline/Archive/00-01/001211-LA.shtml). The program was hailed as a groundbreaking effort to establish professional standards for gang intervention workers. The certificate program was designed to improve the quality of services provided by violence intervention and prevention workers by increasing their skills and expertise in gang intervention strategies.

The Center for Citizen Peacebuilding at the University of California, Irvine, has been working in conjunction with the Edmund G. "Pat" Brown Institute for Public Affairs at California State University, Los Angeles, and L.A. Bridges, a gang intervention program developed by the City of Los Angeles, to train community counselors in alternative dispute resolution techniques to help defuse conflict in urban environments, particularly between gangs and at-risk youth and other members of their communities. The training program is 15 weeks long and includes five separate courses in Youth and Adolescent Development, Gang Intervention Strategies, Mediation, Community Organizing, and Field Research. In 2007, the JAMS Foundation developed a training manual with accompanying DVDs of simulated mediations for dispute resolution facilitators working in informal settings in schools and communities with high levels of gang violence across the nation.

(Adapted from Adams, 2010; Myers, 2000; Uller & Martinez, n.d.; see also http://www .peacebuilding.uci.edu/pb_gangs)

Because Los Angeles is widely considered to be the epicenter of gang activity in America (Diaz, 2009), it comes as no surprise that the Los Angeles Police Department's (LAPD) police gang unit, initiated in the 1980s, is the most widely used model for local law enforcement's response to gang violence throughout the country.

Subgroup 4 (Hard-Core Gang-Involved Youth)

This subgroup consists of serious, chronic, and violent gang offenders. These offenders make up a relatively small portion of the population, but they commit a dispropor-tionately large share of the more serious illegal gang activity. Members of this group are candidates for targeted enforcement and prosecution because of their high level of involvement in crime and violent gangs and the small probability that other strategies will reduce their criminal behavior.

There are very few individuals who have both the professional credentials and the street credibility to successfully conduct gang intervention work with hard-core gang members. This chapter concludes with a brief profile of one such extraordinary individual, presented in Sidebar 8.13.

Sidebar 8.13   One Man's Experience on the Front Lines of Youth Gang Intervention

Dr. Stan Bosch is many things—a former college football player, a graduate of a PsyD program and skilled psychotherapist, and a Catholic priest. Last, but certainly not least, Stan (age 54) spends a large part of his time working intimately with youth who belong to the toughest street gangs of Compton, Watts, and East Los Angeles.

As a Caucasian man working closely with primarily African American and Latino youth, Stan's experiences represent a living, practical example of how the so-called "multicultural competencies debate" in counseling psychology is resolved and lived out in real life. For those needing a reminder, the multicultural competencies debate is the name given to a spirited disagreement among professionals within the counseling psychology literature over the construct validity, practical significance, and value of the multicultural counseling competencies endorsed by the Association for Multicultural Counseling and Development (AMCD) and other professional groups (Patterson, 2004; Sue, Arredondo, & McDavis, 1992; Sue & Sue, 2003; Thomas & Wubbolding, 2009). On one side of this debate are those who feel that effective counselors and psychotherapists must develop culturally specific counseling/ helping competencies in order to be effective with clients from groups that are racially/ethnically different from the counselor/therapist. On the other side of this debate are those who feel that developing culturally specific skills for every conceivable racial/ethnic group is impossible, and that a counselor/therapist's personal qualities are the key to effective helping for all groups.

Stan rejects the fundamental premise of this debate as an either/or proposition. That is, the life experiences and work ethic that guide his service represent a unique blend of views that are greater than the sum of their parts. Stan grew up in northern Virginia, the son of an Air Force father who served two tours of duty in Vietnam and a mother who was a devoted homemaker. Stan credits his early outlook on the world to his father, who ministered to Vietnamese orphans on weekends. The Bosch family then sponsored Vietnamese refugees who settled in the United States after the war. For Stan, life was not particularly easy growing up. Stan's brother was mentally handicapped, and his sister died unexpectedly as a

(continued)

result of a car accident. Despite these hardships, Stan recalls growing up in a home with a solid sense that he was affirmed and loved by his family. Stan recalls that he grew up with a sense of "transcendence," or the awareness that life has a higher purpose and meaning than just existing to get by from day to day.

When it came time to attend college, Stan attended Florida State University on a football scholarship from 1973 to 1976, years immediately following the turbulent times of massive civil unrest in the late 1960s. When in high school, he vividly remembers when Martin Luther King Jr. was assassinated, and how—being one of the few whites on his high school football team—he felt the tension between he and his African American buddies. Through this experience Stan learned to communicate to his friends that, although there is nothing he could possibly do to truly understand what life is like as an African American, he is willing to listen and learn.

Stan completed his undergraduate work in psychology and sociology at George Mason University, after which he earned an MS degree in Counseling Psychology while serving as a probation counselor at a boys' group home. He then taught psychology, sociology, and religion, in addition to coaching football and baseball, at Bishop James O'Connell High School in northern Virginia for four years.

At age 27, Stan studied for his master's degree in theology at the Washington Theological Union. In addition to working as a student chaplain at a District of Columbia jail, he found himself drawn to religious communities that minister to very poor areas in Latin America. He was not entirely ignorant of the Spanish language, as he was able to draw from the little bit of Spanish he learned in high school and college. Stan traveled to El Salvador and Guatemala, and he worked with children and youth whose parents had been killed in the extensive civil unrest there. He spent three and a half years in Mexico, and he was there during the devastating earthquake of 1985. Through these experiences, Stan became knowledgeable and conversant in Mexican culture.

These experiences made a profound impact on Stan, and when he returned to America in 1987, gang-infested Los Angeles was in many ways no different from the communities he had worked with overseas. After relocating to Los Angeles to begin work as a parish priest, he knew intuitively that the most effective way he could make an impact on actual lives was to return to the streets—and to go where others were reluctant to go.

Soon, Stan found himself to be on the ground floor of community-based youth gang intervention efforts in Los Angeles. Since the Los Angeles riots in 1992, former gang members—many of whom were ex-felons—began to work on their own to make a positive difference in the lives of increasingly younger gang members. At the same time, the LAPD was realizing that its style of policing youth gangs (i.e., by making endless arrests) was not working.

On October 29, 2007, the Mayor's Office of Gang Reduction and Youth Development released requests for proposals to conduct community needs assessment and resource mapping for 12 Gang Reduction and Youth Development (GRYD) zones. GRYD is an acronym used to refer to a collaborative and community-wide approach to reducing gang-related crime and violence, and promoting positive youth development via the application of best practices. The main objectives of the GRYD program are (a) prevention work with youth between the ages of 10 and 15 who display specific at-risk social behavior, and (b) intervention work with hard-core gang-involved youth and adults from 14 to 24 years of age who were in unhealthy relationships, displayed antisocial behavior, and were returning from incarceration.

The GRYD program focuses on a dozen gang-reduction zones throughout Los Angeles, which are neighborhoods where gang violence is at least four times the citywide average. Stan oversees four of those zones, supervising 24 intervention workers (called Gang Intervention Specialists, or GIS) and eight case managers. GIS are the primary persons who work to diffuse potentially volatile situations before they get out of control. This requires keeping on top of potentially dangerous rumors, preventing such rumors from spreading or being misinterpreted, and conducting "shuttle diplomacy"—where GIS workers go back and forth between rival gangs to broker truces and diffuse tensions.

Stan's gang intervention work also involves the monthly training of case managers to use psychodynamic clinical skills as one approach to understanding the roots of why youth are attracted to gang involvement. In his direct work with gang members, Stan's first order of business is to get to know the youth and earn their trust. This means spending time with them, listening to them, and modeling the attitude that he is there to both learn from them and help them to achieve positive goals in life. Once one gets past their tough exterior, gang members are real human beings who fundamentally want to be loved and listened to. Stan has discovered a basic truth in life, which is that genuine empathy and compassion can penetrate and make inroads into any human problem. Trust is crucial, but it can be very tricky to maintain in street-level gang intervention. For example, GIS can help prevent dangerous situations by alerting the police of gang retaliations before they occur. At the same time, they must be careful not to violate the confidentiality of information shared with youth and GIS mentors, even if it may involve the commission of a crime. Doing so would ruin the trust that they have worked so hard to earn with gang members.

Stan's work is supervised by the deputy mayor's office. Each of the 12 GRYD areas have a program manager, and all divisions meet together weekly or biweekly. Whenever there is a shooting, a report has to be filed, and the GRYD program

(continued)

manager must be notified. The work of each GRYD area is in turn monitored by Urban Institute and Harder+Company Community Research, which must receive monthly reports.

Stan is proud of the fact that the GRYD program is a model for other gang intervention programs around the country to follow. However, ongoing challenges remain. Programs struggle continually with the dilemma of how growth and improvement is measured. As one among many examples, it continues to be a challenge to measure the emotional growth or impulse regulation in young gang members. For now, program evaluation must rely on variables such as crime recidivism rates and attendance rates in schools. Data from these variables are a start, but much more work needs to be done to design evaluation models that capture the spirit of the positive changes that Stan sees happening every day in the streets.

ADDITIONAL RESOURCES

Supplemental Readings

School Safety Preparedness

Trump, K. (2011). *Proactive school security and emergency preparedness planning.* Thousand Oaks, CA: Corwin Press.

Working With Children of Incarcerated Parents

Eddy, M., & Poehlmann, J. (2010). *Children of incarcerated parents: A handbook for researchers and practitioners.* Washington, DC: Urban Institute Press.

Siegel, J. A. (2011). *Disrupted childhoods: Children of women in prison.* New Brunswick, NJ: Rutgers University Press.

Methods for Documenting Crime in Schools

Crime, Violence, and Discipline Task Force, National Forum on Education Statistics. (2002). *Safety in numbers: Collecting and using crime, violence and discipline incident data to make a difference in schools.* Washington, DC: U.S. Department of Education. (http://nces.ed.gov/pubs2002/2002312.pdf)

Resources/Clearinghouses for Scholarship on Gangs

Journal of Gang Research. The Journal of Gang Research is the official publication of the National Gang Crime Research Center (www.ngcrc.com). It is a peer-reviewed, quarterly interdisciplinary journal that is edited by well-known gang researchers and experts. The journal publishes original research, book reviews, and interviews dealing with gangs and gang problems. Articles published by the journal include a wide range of topical areas that address promising theories, scientifically grounded research, and useful policy analyses related to gangs and gang problems.

Websites

School Safety Design

- *National Clearinghouse for Educational Facilities (NCEF) Crime Prevention Through Environmental Design (CPTED) resource list* (http://www.ncef.org/rl/cpted.cfm). According to the section of its website pertaining to safe school facilities (http://www.ncef.org/safeschools/index.cfm), the NCEF provides information on the nation's best school facility assessment measures in one online source for assessing the safety and security of school buildings, school surroundings, school facilities, communications systems, building access control and surveillance, utility systems, mechanical systems, and emergency power. The site also provides access to numerous links on recent magazine and journal articles about safe school facilities, and continuously updated links, books, and journal articles on safe school facilities topics.
- School Security Technologies (http://www.ncef.org/pubs/security_technologies .pdf)
- Schneider, T., Walker, H., & Sprague, J. (2000). *Safe school design: A handbook for educational leaders.* Eugene, OR: ERIC Clearinghouse on Educational Management, University of Oregon. Accessed June 2011 at https://scholarsbank .uoregon.edu/xmlui/handle/1794/3258?show=full

Juvenile Justice School Curriculum

- The Texas Attorney General's office website provides an overview of, and materials for, the "Consequences Curriculum" (see https://www.oag.state.tx.us/consequences/index.php), which is designed to assist school students in understanding how the juvenile justice system operates and how criminal behavior impacts their lives. The Consequences Curriculum is divided into 10 units that each focus on a different offense (e.g., Texas juvenile justice system, school crime and discipline, truancy, property crime, theft offenses, alcohol/drugs/tobacco, assault crimes, hate crimes, gangs/violence, and making healthy choices). This comprehensive curriculum includes a lesson plan and teacher's guide for each unit, the latest changes in Texas law related to juvenile justice, and video segments that include interviews with students from the Texas Youth Commission (TYC), the state agency that incarcerates and rehabilitates juvenile offenders.

Information for Parents

- *Warning Signs* (www.warningsigns.info/index.html). This website is designed to serve as a resource for parents to help them in identifying the warning signs of their children's involvement in drugs, alcohol, smoking, pornography, school, violence, and gangs.

Gang Awareness (Gang Life/Activities) Resources

- *Gangs Or Us* (www.gangsorus.com). This site was created by Robert Walker, who uses his experience of more than 50 years in law enforcement to include the latest information on state gang laws, gang identifiers, major types of prison and street gangs, useful information for parents and teachers, and a variety of well-researched books on gang life and culture.
- *Office of Juvenile Justice and Delinquency Prevention (OJJDP), National Gang Center Gang-Related News Articles* (http://www.nationalgangcenter.gov/Gang-Related-News). This website provides a list of newspaper articles pertaining to gangs and gang-related activities from various U.S. and Canadian news sources. A link to the source of each article is provided. The list of articles can be accessed by date and a specific state or Canadian province/territory.
- *Street Gangs Resource Center* (http://www.streetgangs.com). This website is updated on a daily basis, providing users with the latest news articles, information, photos, gang intervention and prevention programs, latest books, and research dealing primarily with gangs and gang culture in the southern California region. According to website developers, the information on this site is frequented by actual gang members, but information contained on the site is also useful for parents, educators, law enforcement, and at-risk youth in understanding how the geography of gangs has had a major impact on residents of Los Angeles and the surrounding communities.
- *Gang Prevention Services* (http://www.gangpreventionservices.org/resources.asp). This Washington state–based website is maintained by Gabriel Morales, who, according to his webpage, has worked in the area of gang prevention and intervention in both adult and juvenile systems for approximately 30 years. The site provides a wealth of information on black, Asian, Hispanic, and white supremacist gangs and other security threat groups in America. The site provides a wealth of links and resources on Gang Investigator Associations, national gang

prevention and intervention groups, profiles of the most dangerous gangs in America, and links to anti-gang law enforcement groups.

Interprofessional Communication Forums About Gangs

○ GANGINFO (www.nationalgangcenter.gov/GANGINFO) is an Internet-based forum through which school practitioners, researchers, law enforcement officers, probation and parole officers, social workers, youth agency workers, and others with an interest in gangs can share information and exchange communication about (a) ways to identify gang activity and presence, (b) strategies for countering gang-related crime, (c) strategies and programs for gang prevention and intervention, and (d) the latest research on gangs. Access to GANGINFO is granted by subscription, which requires participants to complete an online application.

○ *National Alliance of Gang Investigators' Associations* (NAGIA; www.nagia.org). According to its website, the NAGIA is a cooperative organization representing 19 state and regional gang investigators associations. It provides for leadership in developing and recommending strategies to prevent and control gang crime, administer professional training, as well as assist criminal justice professionals and the public in identifying and tracking gangs, gang members, and gang crime around the world.

○ *The Coroner's Report* (www.gangwar.com). This website is created by Steve Nawojczyk (*Na-VOY-check*), who brings many decades of experience as a coroner in Little Rock, Arkansas, and advisor to the Arkansas Attorney General's Youth Gang Task Force to researching youth gangs and other forms of juvenile violence. In addition to a wealth of information on youth gangs, the site includes descriptions and guidelines for teachers and law enforcement training and seminars, school assembly programs, and public presentations.

Gang and Violence Intervention/Prevention and Community Partnership Efforts in School Districts

○ Bethel School District (Building Bridges Intervention Program), http://media.bethelsd.org/website/resources/pdf/diversity_gang.pdf

○ Miami Partnership for Action in Communities Task Force (MPACT), http://www.lisc.org/files/8306_file_csi_metlife_MPACT.pdf

○ Building the Bridges Organization (based in Tacoma, Washington), http://www.tiptopwebsite.com/websites/index2.php?username=magic32&page=1

○ Fort Worth Independent School District (ISD) Project Protect, http://www.fwisd.org/safe/Pages/ProjectProtect.aspx

o Gang Resistance Education And Training (G.R.E.A.T.) Program, www.great-online.org

Films

Crips and Bloods: Made in America (2008), directed by Stacy Peralta. Narrated by Academy Award–winning actor Forest Whitaker, this unflinching documentary chronicles one of the longest-running youth gang wars in the history of America. This documentary gives viewers an upfront and up-close look at the Crips and Bloods youth gangs, and examines the conditions that have lead to decades of devastating gang violence among young African Americans growing up in South Los Angeles. The documentary includes brief interviews with various community activists and gang interventionists.

"Will I Be Next?" (2009, August 4). In this YouTube video, Chicago youth discuss the effects of gun violence in their neighborhoods (accessed May, 2011, at http://www.wiretapmag.org/race/44392/).

Contact Information

Brand-Name Programs (Working With Crime-Involved Youth)

Adolescent Diversion Project
   Michigan State University
   58 Baker Hall
   East Lansing, MI 48823-5239
   Phone: 517-353-5015
   Website: http://universitydesign.asu.edu/db/adolescent-diversion-project-at-michigan-state-university
Aggression Replacement Training (http://uscart.org/new/)
   Contact ART by completing an online contact form at http://uscart.org/new/contact/
Life Skills Training (LST)
   National Health Promotion Associates
   711 Westchester Ave.
   White Plains, NY 10604
   Phone: 914-421-2525
   Toll-free: 800-293-4969
   Fax: 914-421-2007
   Email: lstinfo@nhpamail.com
Project Toward No Drug Abuse (http://tnd.usc.edu)
   USC Institute for Prevention Research

1000 S. Fremont Ave., Unit #8
Alhambra, CA 91803
Toll-free: 800-400-8461
Email: leahmedi@usc.edu
Olweus Bullying Prevention Program (www.olweus.org/public/index.page)
Training: Clemson University (nobully@clemson.edu)
Research: (http://www.clemson.edu/olweus/evidence.html)

Establishing Violence-Free Zones

Center for Neighborhood Enterprise Violence-Free Zones
1625 K St. NW, Ste. 1200
Washington, DC 20006
Phone: 202-518-6500
Toll-Free: 866-518-6500
Fax: 202-588-0314
Email: INFO@cneonline.org
Website: www.cneonline.org

Information About Gangs

National Gang Center Institute for Intergovernmental Research
P.O. Box 12729
Tallahassee, FL 32317
Phone: 850-385-0600
Fax: 850-386-5356
Email: information@nationalgangcenter.gov
Website: http://www.nationalgangcenter.gov

CHAPTER

9

━━━═>•<═━━━

School District Resources

Large, urban school districts across America face unique challenges that smaller, non-urban districts do not. Using ecological theory (Bronfenbrenner, 1989), Truscott and Truscott (2005) have organized these challenges as reflecting *macrosystem issues* (e.g., political and social influences on schooling; school funding equity issues; resegregation and hypersegregation issues), *mezosystem issues* (e.g., the relationship between poverty and school academic achievement; qualified teacher shortages; overly complex system bureaucracies), and *microsystem issues* (e.g., issues that arise from educators' efforts to work with families impacted by difficult social problems).

For the specific purposes of this chapter, school districts faced with the responsibility of serving the psychoeducational needs of large percentages of racial/ethnic/language minority children find that these needs stem from three basic sources: (1) challenges that can be attributable to disproportionately higher rates of social problems, (2) challenges that can be attributable to non-English language and/or immigration status, or (3) challenges that reflect a combination of these two sources.

GREATER SCHOOL PSYCHOLOGY ROLE DIFFERENTIATION IN LARGE DISTRICTS

A basic observation from the organizational psychology literature is that, as organizations succeed, grow, and expand, the greater the differentiation of roles within an organization will be (Schein, 1998). School psychologists working for small districts find that, in addition to traditional school psychologist responsibilities, they may also be called on to serve as researchers, mental health counselors, social workers, crisis interventionists, special education staffing and child study team leaders, and in-service workshop trainers and presenters. In contrast, school psychologists working for large (particularly urban) school districts find that their job responsibilities are narrowly prescribed to encompass very specific

425

role responsibilities that do not overlap with other colleagues' responsibilities. Although some school psychologists may actually prefer the expanded role functions afforded by small districts, an advantage of greater role differentiation in larger districts is that more in-depth services can be provided for very serious problems that disproportionately impact minority populations. Because a significant percentage of racial/ethnic/language minority children are served in large metropolitan school districts, the role differentiation that is characteristic of psychological services in such districts is deserving of further analysis. The psychological services department in the Memphis City School System is an excellent exemplar of this differentiation in school psychology job roles and functions.

Memphis City Schools Mental Health Center

Memphis is the biggest city—in terms of population—in the state of Tennessee, the third-largest city in the Southeastern United States, and lies somewhere between the 18th- and 20th-largest city in the United States. Within the state, its entire metropolitan area is second in size only to Nashville, Tennessee. Demographically, the city of Memphis is approximately 62 percent African American, 32 percent Caucasian, and 5 percent Hispanic/Latino. However, its city public schools are approximately 85 percent African American, 8 percent Caucasian, and 5 percent Hispanic. Close to 20 of its more than 180 schools are all-black in enrollment (Thomas, 2008).

The Memphis City Schools Mental Health Center (MCSMHC) is a state-licensed mental health center that provides outpatient mental health services and adolescent nonresidential alcohol and drug treatment/prevention services. Administratively, the MCSMHC is a component of the Memphis City Schools Division of Exceptional Children and Health Services. All services provided by MCSMHC are free of charge to Memphis City Schools students and their families.

According to its promotional materials (Schnell, 2011a), the MCSMHC employs more than 120 supervising psychologists, school psychologists, school social workers, and alcohol/drug counselors. These professionals provide a wide array of services, which include, but are not limited to, psychoeducational and functional behavioral assessment, individual/group counseling, crisis intervention and postvention, threat assessment, alcohol/drug counseling, parent training, academic/behavioral consultation, and case management services to pregnant and parenting students. An overview of the administrative structure of the MCSMHC is provided in Figure 9.1.

The MCSMHC Director reports to the Executive Director in the Memphis City Schools Department of Exceptional Children and Health Services, and oversees four regional teams and four specialty teams. Each regional team is headed by a doctoral-level supervising school psychologist, who in turn has responsibility for overseeing the activities of 90 to 95 school psychologists, school psychology interns, and school social workers in the Memphis City Schools. At the time of this writing, Memphis City school psychologists within the regional teams test children for special education and Section 504

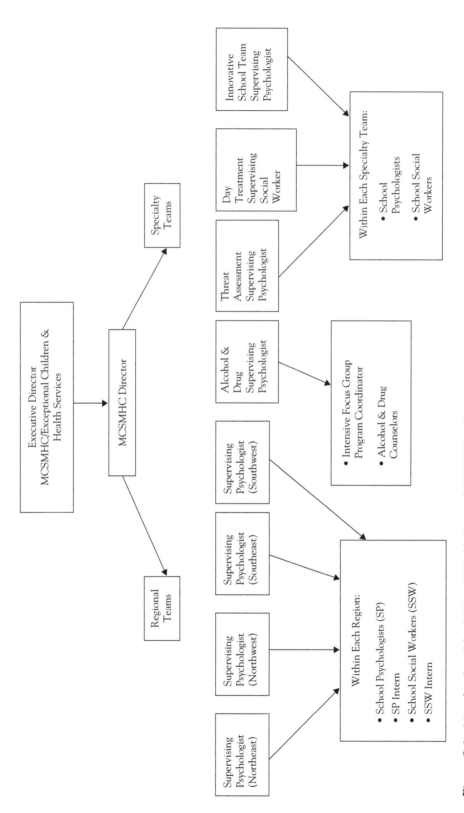

Figure 9.1 Memphis City Schools Mental Health Center (MCSMHC) Administrative Structure

eligibility, conduct functional behavioral assessments, participate in behavior intervention planning and teacher training/consultation, respond to school/family crises, and participate as members of Student Support and Individualized Education Program (IEP) teams.

Specialty teams, as the name implies, are smaller groups of school professionals (school psychologists, school social workers, school counselors) who are responsible for delivering services in a niche area of need. These specialty teams are described within different sections throughout this chapter.

MCSMHC Innovative School Team

The purpose of this team is to serve students who, for whatever reason, require a special learning environment (either enrichment or remedial) in which student/teacher ratios are low. These may include students who have been expelled or suspended, as well as students who are enrolled in college preparatory classes. The service received by "Innovative Schools" students are equivalent to services delivered by regular school psychologists/school social workers, with the exception that these services are more frequent and more collaborative with other service providers (e.g., school guidance, behavior specialists, nurses, physical/speech therapists, homecare agents, and other outside agencies). These services may include academic and social skills training.

Crisis Response Services

In the event of a crisis (e.g., a suicide threat, the unexpected death of a student, or a school shooting), school administrators call a crisis hotline at the MCSMHC. The Center then deploys a team of professionals (including social workers and school psychologists) to provide on-site assessment, specific counseling services (e.g., defusing and debriefing), and needed assistance to school administrators (e.g., follow-up with students, teachers, and parents). Details of the crisis and activities conducted by the response team are recorded and entered into a confidential database.

Prevention Services and Training

All MCSMHC clinicians provide ongoing prevention services to students throughout the school year in the areas of suicide, alcohol/drug, and violence prevention. These services are also provided to school faculties, school counselors, and parents.

Summer Programs

MCSMHC summer staff offer services in the context of specialized programs offered to students during the summer months (Schnell, 2011b). These students may be referred by their schools for a summer camp, or students may be seen as an adjunct to summer school programs. These summer programs support improved adaptive functioning in areas of social skills training, trauma recovery, and resilience. Play therapy techniques are frequently used in these summer intervention experiences (see Other Innovative Counseling/Therapy Services, this chapter).

General Prevention Services

In the Memphis City School District, school psychologists work closely with school counselors to train all elementary school faculties and some secondary school faculties on the Student Support Team process in each school. School psychologists also provide professional development services to teachers to assist them with enhancing instructional strategies with students showing traits of Attention Deficit Hyperactivity Disorder (Schnell, 2011a).

School psychologists and other mental health professionals who serve under the MCSMHC provide annual suicide prevention instruction to all ninth graders in the district. This service is coordinated with teachers and folded into the Family Life Curriculum unit on depression and suicide.

RESOURCES FOR ADDRESSING SOCIAL PROBLEMS IMPACTING LARGE SCHOOL DISTRICTS

Teenage Pregnancy

According to recent national statistics summarized by the Guttmacher Institute, 13 percent of the nation's teens have had sex by the age of 15, and seven out of ten teens have had sexual intercourse by their 19th birthday. When a teen pregnancy occurs, approximately 82 percent of these are unplanned (Guttmacher Institute, 2012). On average, black and Hispanic teens have the highest teen pregnancy rates relative to their representation in the national population (see Table 9.1). One majority black high school in Memphis Tennessee reported a stunning 90 students who were currently pregnant or had already had their baby in a given year (Madden, 2011).

School district programs that are designed to serve students in the general area of sexuality and health fall into two main categories: (1) sex education/prevention programs for teens who have not as yet had a pregnancy, and (2) education/childcare programs for teens who are pregnant or who have had their babies.

Sex Education/Prevention

Sex education/prevention programs for teens in schools are designed to demonstrate positive behavior changes in the following areas (Advocates for Youth, 2008): (a) postponement or delay of sexual initiation; (b) reduction in the frequency of sexual intercourse; (c) reduction in the number of sexual partners and a corresponding increase in monogamy; (d) increase in the use, or in the consistency of use, of effective methods of contraception; (e) reduction in the incidence of unprotected sex.

Table 9.1   State Number/Percentages of Births to Mothers Under Age 20: Breakdown by Race/Ethnicity for Year 2008

State	# Births to Mothers Under 20	Percentage White	Percentage Black	Percentage Hispanic	Percentage American Indian*	Percentage Asian or Pacific Islander*	Percentage Mothers Not Married	Percentage Repeat Births
U.S. Total	440,522	38.5	24.2	33.4	2.0	1.7	87	19
Alabama	8,719	48.0	43.0	8.2	0.4	0.2	78	19
Alaska	1,135	38.2	4.0	6.4	44.5	7.6	80	19
Arizona	12,215	24.7	4.9	59.6	9.9	0.9	88	22
Arkansas	6,016	59.7	28.9	9.5	0.8	0.4	82	20
California	52,355	13.7	8.7	72.6	1.1	3.6	86	18
Colorado	6,722	35.2	6.5	54.8	1.9	1.2	70	19
Connecticut	2,815	26.9	23.6	48.4	0.3	0.5	93	16
Delaware	1,260	36.7	40.7	21.6	—	0.6	94	19
D.C.	1,115	1.7	80.7	16.5	—	0.6	98	16
Florida	24,433	36.6	33.7	28.5	0.4	0.9	90	19
Georgia	17,531	33.6	45.3	17.4	0.1	0.9	87	20
Hawaii	1,640	16.6	2.1	23.9	—	72.8	86	17
Idaho	2,279	62.6	1.4	30.7	4.6	0.8	73	18
Illinois	17,664	31.0	36.8	31.2	0.2	0.5	91	19
Indiana	9,721	68.3	20.0	10.9	0.1	0.4	89	18
Iowa	3,629	73.6	10.0	14.4	1.4	1.0	90	17
Kansas	4,443	58.9	13.3	24.9	1.5	1.5	86	19
Kentucky	7,728	80.6	13.8	4.9	0.1	0.5	80	19
Louisiana	8,956	39.2	54.9	4.3	0.8	0.4	91	21
Maine	1,123	92.1	2.7	2.3	1.7	0.8	90	15
Maryland	6,658	29.7	53.3	15.7	0.1	0.9	94	18
Massachusetts	4,626	45.0	14.3	36.7	0.3	3.3	94	13
Michigan	12,129	49.1	38.4	10.5	0.9	0.7	92	18
Minnesota	4,951	51.7	17.3	16.0	7.1	8.7	92	18
Mississippi	7,325	39.3	56.1	3.4	0.7	0.2	88	23
Missouri	9,252	65.5	26.2	6.8	0.6	0.7	87	19
Montana	1,321	66.7	1.0	4.9	26.1	1.4	86	17
Nebraska	2,309	53.7	12.6	29.2	5.3	1.1	87	17
Nevada	4,329	28.0	13.6	51.0	1.8	3.4	84	21
New Hampshire	902	89.0	1.6	8.4	—	—	92	12
New Jersey	7,077	19.1	34.6	45.1	0.2	0.9	92	18
New Mexico	4,603	15.2	1.6	68.7	15.5	0.4	88	19

Table 9.1   (*Continued*)

State	# Births to Mothers Under 20	Percentage White	Percentage Black	Percentage Hispanic	Percentage American Indian*	Percentage Asian or Pacific Islander*	Percentage Mothers Not Married	Percentage Repeat Births
New York	17,533	29.7	26.7	39.8	0.6	1.6	90	14
North Carolina	15,370	41.0	37.6	17.8	2.3	1.0	86	19
North Dakota	666	57.0	2.2	7.3	36.0	—	90	16
Ohio	16,405	62.3	29.8	6.2	0.3	0.4	92	18
Oklahoma	7,583	53.9	13.0	15.6	17.0	0.8	82	21
Oregon	4,514	56.8	4.0	34.3	4.3	1.6	84	15
Pennsylvania	13,882	49.2	29.6	18.1	0.4	1.6	94	17
Rhode Island	1,144	33.6	12.5	39.5	2.5	3.5	94	17
South Carolina	8,437	42.1	47.4	8.9	0.6	0.7	89	20
South Dakota	1,130	51.0	1.3	7.6	40.2	0.8	90	18
Tennessee	11,307	57.6	32.3	9.3	0.4	0.7	85	20
Texas	55,127	21.8	14.1	63.1	0.3	0.6	83	22
Utah	3,781	53.9	1.7	38.0	3.0	2.5	75	18
Vermont	478	94.3	3.3	1.8	—	—	90	14
Virginia	8,906	45.0	39.0	14.6	0.1	1.0	86	18
Washington	7,468	50.7	6.1	34.4	5.3	4.5	83	16
West Virginia	2,798	93.7	4.7	1.0	—	—	81	17
Wisconsin	6,117	49.0	25.9	16.6	4.2	4.5	89	18
Wyoming	879	72.2	1.0	19.5	7.8	—	80	15

*Figures for American Indian and Asian/Pacific Islander teens include teens of Hispanic origin.
(Adapted from Ikramullah, Barry, Manlove, & Moore, 2011)

Effective school-based education/prevention programs that used experimental or quasi-experimental evaluation designs (using treatment and control comparison conditions) to demonstrate positive changes in these behaviors are described in more detail in the document *Sex Education and Other Programs That Work to Prevent Teen Pregnancy, HIV & Sexually Transmitted Infections* (Advocates for Youth, 2008).

Challenges Faced by Teen Mothers

Young pregnant teens face many significant challenges, as these impact their futures. Although each pregnant teen's life circumstances are unique, all pregnant teens share many challenges in common. For example, pregnant teens have a higher risk of dropping out of school in order to take care of their babies. If these teens manage to stay in school after they have had their babies, many find that they need to miss school more often than their peers in order to make doctor's appointments, and many who lack home supports struggle to find appropriate daycare services. Many pregnant teens, particularly those who are pregnant for the first time, understandably lack knowledge of child developmental expectations, or even what to expect in terms of needed life, financial, and social adjustments once a child is born.

Many teen mothers in low-income areas come from fragmented families themselves (many of whom represent single-parent situations), where the adults in their lives suffer from poverty, substance abuse, incarceration, or mental health issues. As a result, their own parents are not able to provide the knowledge or support for young teen mothers that would properly assist them in negotiating home and school responsibilities. Schools struggle with getting young mothers to internalize the message that in order to build a better life for their babies, it is necessary to finish school and concentrate on one's studies even though this seems like the last thing they would want to do. School districts have a variety of ways in which they serve teen mothers, some of which are described briefly in the following sections.

Short-Term Grants

The Memphis City Schools has received short-term grants to provide academic, social development, and mental health services to teen parents in the schools. Paraprofessionals working in the schools collaborate with outside agencies (and other Memphis City School resources) to ensure that pregnant and parenting students have the resources needed to complete their high school education. These services include, but are not limited to, providing personal and academic support and counseling, employment and career planning, and life/healthy living skills training. Examples of specific services involve helping students to learn the importance of reading to their babies, and in general helping young parents to understand how literacy impacts the lives of their children. These student advocacy services also assist teens in obtaining clothing items and diapers.

School Childcare Programs

The Living for the Young Family Through Education (LYFE) program, funded by the New York City Department of Education, provides a variety of supports for pregnant students and teenage parents who are enrolled in New York City public schools (see LYFE directory in Additional Resources). The LYFE program has 38 centers, most of which are located within a high school (while others are located in community centers). The program essentially provides free childcare while the teen parents are attending school, and serves infants and toddlers up to three years of age.

The California School-Age Families Education program (CAL-SAFE) provides school-based resources, which includes free childcare, to teen parents and their children throughout California. In the Los Angeles Unified School district alone, CAL-SAFE programs operate in five of its schools. The program's objectives are to help students to avoid repeat pregnancies, to graduate from high school, to pursue postsecondary educational opportunities, and to develop effective parenting skills (see CAL-SAFE directory in the Additional Resources).

The Round Rock Independent School District in central Texas has a Teen Parent program that provides pregnant and parenting teens with counseling, health services, home-bound learning for up to six weeks after the teen gives birth, parenting classes, and a childcare program. Childcare centers are located in two of the district's elementary schools. The program is free as long as the student is enrolled and working toward graduation. An optional bus service is available for both the teen parent and her child.

The Miami-Dade County Public School (M-DCPS) system offers childcare services to teen parents through its Teenage Parent Program. The program offers free childcare, transportation, social services, healthcare referrals, and parenting courses. Students who are enrolled in the program may be homeschooled or attend a special school for pregnant and parenting teens. For childcare, the school district contracts with Miami-Dade County's Child Development Services to provide free childcare services that are closest to the student's home.

The Fort Worth Independent School District serves 700 to 800 pregnant and parenting students each school year in grades 6 to 12 (Jackson, 2011). These students can apply to attend the Center for New Lives alternative school, which includes programs designed specifically for these students. Students also have a choice to remain enrolled in their regular middle or high schools. If pregnant and parenting students choose to remain in their regular schools, they can receive case management services from the district's Project Reach (see Sidebar 9.1).

Sidebar 9.1   Fort Worth Independent School District Project Reach

WHAT IS PROJECT REACH?

Project Reach (PR) is an in-school case management program that coordinates the medical/health, vocational, academic, support, and social services for pregnant and parenting Fort Worth Independent School District (FWISD) students enrolled in the program.

WHAT IS THE OVERARCHING GOAL OF PROJECT REACH?

The goal of PR is to assist pregnant and parenting students to remain in or return to school in order to graduate. Thus, all PR services interact to increase the school continuation and graduation rates of program participants.

(continued)

WHO IS ELIGIBLE FOR PROJECT REACH SERVICES?

PR services are voluntary and are open to any pregnant and parenting teen enrolled in the FWISD who is not enrolled in the district's alternative school (New Lives School, see chapter text). PR services are also provided to teen fathers who voluntarily admit to fathering a child and who consent to receiving PR services.

WHO SERVES ELIGIBLE STUDENTS?

PR staff consists of five full-time licensed social workers and one vocational counselor. Each social worker is assigned to three high schools and the feeder middle schools, while the vocational counselor has district-wide responsibilities. The Director of Adolescent Pregnancy Services supervises the program.

WHAT ON-CAMPUS SERVICES ARE PROVIDED BY PROJECT REACH?

- *Individual, peer, and group counseling.* These services are provided by PR case managers, Life Skills Program coordinators, PR vocational counselor, and school/community staff. A wide variety of topics, from academic concerns to healthcare, are discussed.
- *Parenting education.* In-school parenting classes are offered at all of the 13 regular high schools for 12 weeks in the Fall semester and 12 weeks in the Spring semester. Pregnant students voluntarily choose to attend these classes, which are taught during lunch periods or during class periods in some schools. Health educators from local community agencies and local colleges/ universities teach these classes. The March of Dimes Pregnancy Workshop curriculum is used as the foundation of the classes, with added sessions on breast-feeding and prevention of family violence. PR also collaborates with community agencies in sponsoring conferences for pregnant and parenting students. PR participants also receive early literacy education through the Read with Me Program. Here, teen parents receive children's books and attend a parenting group meeting on how to read to their children.
- *Childcare assistance.* PR staff counsel with teen parents about their childcare needs. Referrals are made to appropriate programs that assist with childcare. PR pays childcare costs for teen parents who are not eligible for federal assistance or who cannot pay all of the childcare costs. Two high school childcare centers exist in the FWISD.
- *Transportation assistance.* PR assists pregnant and parenting students to go to and from doctor appointments, social service appointments, and childcare centers. Upon request, students are issued monthly reduced-rate bus cards and cab vouchers. School bus transportation is also provided to specific events.

- *Academic interventions.* PR case managers regularly monitor the grades and attendance of project participants. The PR vocational counselor meets with the pregnant and parenting students to discuss their four-year plans and ensure that they are taking the needed courses and are on track for graduation. Students who are not making academic progress are counseled about various options, such as extended days, school attendance and credit recovery, night school, and summer school.

- *Case management and service coordination.* PR staff are knowledgeable of local agencies and the services they provide. Individual plans are developed for each student outlining their social service needs (e.g., food, clothing, shelter, prenatal care, well-child care). Referrals are made based on these plans and ongoing contact with the students.

- *Coordination of the academic tutoring program.* PR case managers ensure that pregnant students who are out of school because of complications and those who have delivered receive the required academic tutoring hours in order to earn attendance days. Tutoring is provided in the homes and hospitals for those who are on bed rest and at the schools for those who can come to the schools with medical approval. Tutoring services are provided by a certified teacher in the district, so that students will not get so far behind in their academic subjects that they choose to drop out of school.

- *Parenting education for special education students.* PR case managers ensure that eligible special education students receive the required number of hours each week of parenting instruction while they are out of school because of complications and delivery.

- *Advocacy.* PR staff advocates for participants in the schools and with community agencies. PR staff also educates the community and the schools on the needs of pregnant and parenting students.

WHAT ARE THE RESULTS OF AN EVALUATION OF PROJECT REACH?

A PR case manager completes a PR Student Information Form and intake forms for each student who enters the program. The FWISD Adolescent Pregnancy Services Department enters the information obtained into the PR database, which is updated regularly. According to Jackson (2011), while 30 percent to 40 percent of pregnant and parenting students nationally remain in school until graduation, PR sees approximately 80 percent to 90 percent of its seniors graduate in most years of the program. According to graduation data for the 2009–2010 school year, 88.2 percent of PR 12th graders graduated, which showed an increase from the previous year's rate of 76.7 percent.

(Adapted from Jackson, 2011)

Drug Abuse

Miami-Dade County Schools TRUST Program

At the time of this writing, Suzanne Berrios is the Director of Mental Health and Crisis Management Services for M-DCPS. Her job requires her to supervise a variety of programs, which include the District's Crisis Response Team, the Mental Health Consultation/ Response Team, the School Social Work Program, and the TRUST (To Reach Ultimate Success Together) program (S. Berrios, personal communication, November 2011).

The TRUST program is a comprehensive student assistance program designed to provide prevention, intervention, referral, and follow-up services to students and their families who may be experiencing problems in the area of substance abuse—among other self-defeating behaviors. The TRUST program was piloted during the 1987–1988 school year in all middle schools and three senior high schools, and is currently providing services in all middle and senior high schools, as well as six elementary schools. The program is funded from Safe and Drug-Free Schools and the M-DCPS.

All TRUST Specialists have Master's or higher-level degrees in a human services area and documented experience in alcohol/drug programs. According to Suzanne Berrios, school psychology in the M-DCPS system is largely an itinerant position where the school psychologist's responsibilities are spread around to as many as three different schools. In contrast, TRUST specialists are assigned to one school on a full-time basis.

According to the M-DCPS website (http://mhcms.dadeschools.net/trust/curriculum .asp), the TRUST program has both a prevention and intervention component. The prevention component of the TRUST Program provides curricula and activities to assist students in accepting themselves as capable and unique; developing and maintaining positive relationships; making responsible decisions; becoming aware of accurate drug information; and planning and participating in healthful alternatives to using alcohol, tobacco, and other drugs. The intervention component of the TRUST Program offers curricula and counseling activities that target at-risk students. Individual, group, and family counseling and referral services are offered to students and their families for problems related to alcohol, tobacco, and other drugs, stress, suicide, isolation, family violence, and general problem solving. Students and families receive help not only with the symptoms, but also with the causes of substance abuse.

Memphis County Schools Adolescent Alcohol/Drug Treatment Program

The Adolescent Outpatient Alcohol and Drug Treatment Program of the MCSMHC is funded in part by a grant from the Tennessee Department of Mental Health and Developmental Disabilities, Division of Alcohol and Drug Abuse Services. The program is designed to serve students (at no cost) who are experiencing problems with alcohol and other drugs, and who fit the profile of a DSM-IV diagnosis of substance abuse/dependence. Many of these students have been suspended from school for alcohol/drug offenses, or are returning from a period of residential or inpatient treatment. Services provided to students include comprehensive substance use assessment, individual/family/group counseling, relapse prevention counseling, family consultation, and referral services to students who are unable to benefit from outpatient therapy.

The Intensive Focus Group Program within the MCSMHC (see Figure 9.1) is a prevention/intervention program designed to identify substance use and prevent the personal deterioration that is associated with substance abuse. Services are provided to students when they first come to the attention of the school for alcohol or other drug-related offenses. Students are screened and assessed in order to determine whether they are in need of more intensive drug/alcohol treatment services.

Services are organized and delivered according to the students' age and developmental level and the extent of their substance abuse. Intervention services provided by the program include lectures and experiential/self-awareness activities designed to impart accurate health information. Health specialists with expertise in HIV/AIDS and other sexually transmitted diseases are called in to conduct group sessions. Members of the Memphis Police Department's Crime Prevention Unit conduct group sessions as well. Woven throughout these services is a commitment to assisting students in developing decision-making, impulse control, communication, and stress management skills.

Gangs and Violence

Memphis City Schools Threat Assessment Team

When students display behaviors that suggest threats of impending physical violence to others, the Memphis City Public Schools Threat Assessment Team (a) evaluates the students' mental health/emotional adjustment, (b) evaluates the students' intent and motivations for making threats, (c) makes recommendations intended to reduce the risk of impending violence and enhance school adjustment in the potential offender. This team (see Figure 9.1) consists of a licensed supervising school psychologist, three licensed school psychologists, and two licensed school social workers with advanced degrees in their respective areas of expertise.

District Police Forces

In order to properly handle the sheer volume of crime and gang violence that is endemic in communities served by some schools, many larger urban school districts find that they must employ their own police forces. The nature of police work in two large urban school districts is briefly described in Sidebar 9.2.

⚓ Sidebar 9.2   Districts' Use of Police and Security Services

For many school districts situated in large urban areas, the bottom line is that students cannot learn, teachers cannot teach, parents cannot feel completely comfortable sending their children to school, and administrators cannot properly enforce appropriate behavioral standards if there is widespread chaos and crime within schools. For this reason, many large districts find it necessary to create and employ their own school police and security services. The Dallas, Texas, and Miami, Florida, school districts are two prime examples of this necessity.

The Dallas Independent School District (Dallas ISD) is the largest employer in the city of Dallas, Texas, enrolling more than 157,000 students and employing more than 20,000 employees who serve 225 campuses. The racial/ethnic composition of the Dallas ISD is approximately 68 percent Hispanic, 26 percent black, 5 percent non-Hispanic white, 1 percent Asian, and 0.2 percent American Indian.

The Miami-Dade County Public School (M-DCPS) system has the distinction of being the fourth-largest school district in America. The M-DCPS system enrolls more than 380,000 students and employs more than 54,000 employees. The racial/ethnic composition of the M-DCPS is approximately 65 percent Hispanic, 25 percent Black, 9 percent non-Hispanic white, 1 percent Asian/Pacific Islander, and 0.1 percent American Indian or Native Alaskan.

ROLES AND FUNCTIONS FOR SCHOOL DISTRICT POLICE FORCES

The levels of responsibility shouldered by school district police forces are more complex that what typically meets the eye. The Dallas ISD police force has an administrative structure that encompasses six divisions (Blackburn, 2011). The *Schools Division* oversees police officers who staff patrol cars that are present at all secondary campuses in the district throughout the day. The *Patrol Division* is responsible for the active patrolling of the streets surrounding Dallas schools 24 hours a day, 7 days a week. Officers within this division are primarily responsible for rounding up and transporting school truants, as well as responding immediately to unforeseen needs that originate from the schools. Officers who work under the *Criminal Investigations Division* play an active role in fighting illegal drugs in Dallas schools. In addition to drug enforcement issues, these officers investigate criminal offenses that occur in the schools and refer cases to the Dallas County District Attorney's Office. Officers working in the *Security Division* are primarily responsible for supervising district facilities (and maintaining a strong presence at select secondary schools) 24 hours a day, 7 days a week. The *Communications Division* maintains radio and telephone contact with officers in the field 24 hours a day and

7 days a week, which includes screening and dispatching police response calls. The *Records and Administration Division* documents and records crime statistics and operational functions of the Dallas ISD police department.

As discussed in detail in Chapter 8, youth gang activity is an integral feature of many large, metropolitan urban minority communities, and Dallas is no different. The Dallas ISD police department oversees a Gang Unit, composed of a Director of Operations, three gang specialists, and a gang response team consisting of a police lieutenant, three police sergeants, two campus officers, and four patrol officers (Blackburn, 2011). In an average week, the DISD Gang Unit receives eight requests per week for intervention services, approximately 12 requests per week for visits to various campuses to obtain gang intelligence, and approximately four requests per week to conduct training or deliver presentations to staff, parents, and students (Blackburn, 2011). The Gang Unit meets with Dallas ISD police department sergeants to exchange gang intelligence information. Gang suppression efforts at various campuses are planned in the hope that potential criminal offenses can be thwarted.

Although these functions certainly reinforce an assurance of safety, vigilance, and protection in schools, readers must not lose sight of the fact that school police departments also play a crucial role in helping school mental health professionals. Criminal offenses and mental health problems are often intertwined in vulnerable groups, hence school police departments find that they need to work closely with school mental health professionals in helping students.

At the time of this writing, the Miami-Dade Schools Police Department (M-DSPD) is the fourth-largest police department in Dade County, Florida. Similar to the Dallas ISD, M-DSPD assigns a state-certified police officer to every high school in the county.

The job of a school police officer requires an entirely different set of assumptions to be effective in one's job, compared to what is typically required of municipal police officers. According to the M-DSPD, those desiring to be school police officers must be reprogrammed to understand the important role of individual differences among students with mental health issues. Toward this end, police officers who will eventually work in the Miami-Dade County schools are required to complete a 16-week field training program that helps them understand mental health issues in addition to school law enforcement issues.

In this context, the proper manner in which police–student altercations should be handled is not protocol-driven (where all problems are handled according to a standard procedure), but instead issues are handled according to the individualized dynamics inherent in specific situations. That is to say, properly trained school

(continued)

police officers are sensitive to mental health issues that may cause similar incidents to be handled differently. In order to know how to best handle a situation, school police officers need to examine a child's grades, school attendance, IEP goals, and family situation. Compared to older models of school policing, much progress has been made in the M-DSPD in integrating mental health knowledge and modern-day policing techniques.

(Adapted from Blackburn, 2011)

Other Innovative Counseling/Therapy Services

The MCSMHC summer staff participate in specialized summer programs designed to address the socioemotional development of students. These programs, sometimes taking the form of brief summer camps, are offered at a limited number of school locations. Here, students are referred by their schools for a summer camp, or students may be seen as an adjunct to summer school programs. The camps are designed to support improved adaptive functioning in social skills, emotional sensitivity, trauma recovery, and resilience. These skills are taught in an enjoyable environment, often utilizing play therapy techniques. Three of these camps (Camp Treetops, Camp Steady, and Camp WhyTry) are briefly[1] described as follows (from Schnell, 2011b).

Camp Treetops

Camp Treetops is a two-week therapeutic summer camp serving middle school students who are at risk for becoming aggressive and /or involved in violent behavior—as a result of having been exposed to violence in their homes or community. These students tend to display increased incidents of depression, posttraumatic stress disorder, aggression, and acting-out behaviors. Camp Treetops' therapeutic curriculum focuses on decreasing the probability that students will participate in destructive behaviors that frequently undermine their ability to achieve a positive and successful school experience. This is accomplished through the teaching and modeling of pragmatic prosocial skills to help students cope with an array of difficult emotions that are associated with perilous and violent communities, homes, and lifestyles.

Evaluation of the Camp Treetops program occurs through giving participating students a pretest and a posttest consisting of true/false, Likert, and open-ended survey items that assess their reactions to the program. Program developers built the evaluation model around the following three objectives, expected to be accomplished by the end of the summer experience: (1) 80 percent of students in the camp will identify at least one resource upon completion of the program; (2) 50 percent of students in the camp will identify at least one preferred nonviolent way of resolving conflict upon completion of the program; and (3) 80 percent of students in the camp will identify at least one individual strength upon completion of the program (Schnell, 2011b). Schnell (2011b) reports that in all four sites in which the program was implemented in the summer of 2011, students met all three objectives.

According to Schnell (2011b), sample student responses to the following open-ended questions at posttest were provided as follows: "What did you learn?" (sample responses: "How to deal with bullies and people that tease you"; "How to make better decisions"); "What did you like most?" (sample responses: "The teachers and how much fun we had"; "I like everything"); "What did you like least?" (sample responses: "There was nothing I disliked"; "What I liked least is all the writing"); "What was most helpful?" (sample responses: "The Life Laws"; "sitting in the circle talking"; "social workers"); and "What would you tell others about the program?" (sample responses: "Come on and you will never regret it"; "It was fun but you have to do work").

Camp Steady

A significant number of children have been identified as homeless within the Memphis area. The Memphis City Schools currently serves increasing numbers of these children, most of whom have difficulties with school attendance, academic deficits, health concerns, and social and behavioral problems. Camp Steady is a summer camp activity sponsored by Memphis City Schools in which students experiencing homelessness are provided with fun and relevant socioemotional learning activities in a safe, interesting, and caring environment. In addition to participating in academic and recreational activities, the children receive skills-based group training from MCSMHC clinicians.

When going through the Camp Steady experience, students attend skills-based training sessions twice per week for six weeks. Here, social workers and school psychologists conduct 12 group sessions on the topics of stress management, dealing with anger and aggression, and study skills—the purpose of which is to enhance participants' socioemotional and academic adjustment.

Camp WhyTry

The Camp WhyTry Program is a strength-based approach to help elementary-aged students with disabilities (and with a significant number of school suspensions/ expulsions) in the Memphis City Schools to overcome their school adjustment challenges and improve outcomes in the areas of truancy, behavior, and academics. Camp WhyTry services are delivered to students for three hours per day for two weeks in the summer (and held at two local high school sites). The design of Camp WhyTry is based on the principles that undergird solution-focused brief therapy, social and emotional intelligence, and multisensory learning. Here, social and emotional principles are taught to youth in a way that they can understand and remember. This is accomplished using a series of 10 pictorial metaphors. Each metaphor teaches a discrete principle, such as resisting peer pressure, obeying laws and rules, and that decisions have consequences. The visual components are then reinforced by music and physical activities. The major learning modalities (i.e., visual, auditory, and bodily-kinesthetic) are all used in teaching activities.

For each visual metaphor in the Camp WhyTry Program, two different hands-on group experiential activities are used. These activities are used as attention grabbers to introduce the visual metaphors and as object lessons to follow up and reinforce the principles taught in the visuals. According to Schnell (2011b), the experiential activities are particularly helpful in group environments for increasing participation and learning among those involved.

High School Graduation

According to recently published data on national high school dropout rates (between 1972–2009) compiled by the National Center for Education Statistics (Chapman, Laird, Ifill, & Kewal-Ramani, 2011), Hispanics consistently display the highest high school dropout rates compared to black non-Hispanics and white non-Hispanics. Although these rates have been steadily decreasing for all groups since 1972, 2009 data show high school dropout rates of 5.2 percent for white non-Hispanics, 9.3 percent for black non-Hispanics, and 17.6 percent for Hispanics. However, one Texas school district has institutionalized a comprehensive program for addressing this troubling issue.

Fort Worth ISD Project Prevail

Fort Worth is the fifth-largest city in the state of Texas and the 16th-largest city in the United States. The racial/ethnic breakdown of the city is approximately 63 percent Caucasian, 18 percent African American, and 34 percent Hispanic/Latino (of any race, which is why summing percentages exceeds 100). The racial/ethnic breakdown of the Fort Worth Independent School District (ISD) is listed on its website as 60 percent Hispanic/Latino, 25 percent African American, and 13 percent Caucasian.

The Fort Worth ISD is noted for Project Prevail (Diaz, 2011), which is a comprehensive plan for increasing the number of students graduating from Fort Worth high schools fully prepared for postsecondary education or gainful employment. The comprehensive nature of the plan is illustrated in the district's efforts to involve businesses, parents, colleges, churches, and social service agencies (in addition to student requirements) in this goal. A brief summary of the contributions of all of these stakeholders to Project Prevail goals are given in Sidebar 9.3.

☜ Sidebar 9.3   Fort Worth Independent School District Project Prevail: Stakeholder Practices and Responsibilities for Increasing High School Graduation Rates, College Attendance Rates, and Gainful Employment

Student Practices/Responsibilities

- Attend school every day, arriving on time and with homework completed
- Develop an Academic Learning Plan that includes learning goals
- Take college prep (if applicable) or other courses to prepare for postgraduation employment
- Sign up for PSAT and SAT testing and take an SAT preparation class
- Consult with knowledgeable adults/counselors for how to access and apply for scholarship money

Parent Practices/Responsibilities

- Closely monitor school attendance, homework, progress reports, report cards, and classroom grades
- Participate in parent classes offered at school
- Consult with school about how to access and apply for scholarship money
- Schedule at least one conference per year with your child's teachers
- Ensure that your child takes an SAT preparation class

School Practices/Responsibilities

- Redirect human and financial resources to support district-wide school completion initiatives
- Establish protocols for early identification, support for, and tracking of at-risk students
- Conduct annual transcript audits to monitor students for on-time graduation
- Expand prevention/intervention counseling and support services at all levels
- Evaluate programs and services for outcomes and impact

Higher Education Practices/Responsibilities

- Sponsor campus "VIP tours" to acquaint parents with college
- Provide freshman with transition camps and student support groups
- Send college/university representatives to district career fairs and career days/nights
- Sponsor/develop college student mentoring programs for high schoolers
- Waive tuition and fees for high schoolers who are taking dual-credit courses

(continued)

Business Practices/Responsibilities

- Make school attendance/enrollment a condition of employment for teens
- Provide incentives for school performance and attendance
- Limit employee student work schedules to 10 P.M. on school nights
- Allow adult parent employees to attend school/teacher conferences without penalty
- Establish internships and other school-to-work opportunities

Faith Community Practices/Responsibilities

- Provide homework help/tutorials during weeknights at places of worship
- Host school events and community forums to support educational initiatives
- Establish a scholarship fund for eligible youth
- Develop community service and/or work opportunities that provide financial support for college
- Celebrate youths' academic and school accomplishments at church events and in church newsletters

Social Services Practices/Responsibilities

- Establish/expand campus and Family Resource Center collaborations and services
- Establish/expand medical and health services through Family Resource Centers and campus-based clinics
- Sponsor back-to-school events that include provision of school clothing and supplies
- Provide on-site tutorial and homework support
- Include information about campus educational requirements and opportunities during service delivery

(Adapted from Diaz, 2011)

Interventions at the School Level

One strategy implemented by Project Prevail is to intervene in unproductive student behaviors that lead to students eventually dropping out of school. Guided by the moniker "Relevance, Rigor, and Relationships," middle and high schools have reduced class sizes for core subjects, and school curriculum has been revamped to support these 3 R's.

The AVID Program

Advancement Via Individual Determination (AVID) is a special academic program that is in every Fort Worth ISD middle and high school. AVID targets students in the middle of the achievement spectrum (i.e., students not at the top or bottom of their class academically) who express a desire to go to college after high school graduation.

Academic Teaming is a concept that gives secondary school teachers who share the same students (but teach in different subject areas) opportunities to share useful information about students. This gives teachers opportunities to plan and design lessons that may support the students' learning in other classes.

"Transition Camps" are held for sixth graders facing a transition time, which helps them to become acclimated to new schools and new classmates.

Local Media

In 2009, the Fort Worth ISD partnered with local broadcast media to air District-produced 10-, 15-, and 30-second public service announcements (PSAs) about the importance of students completing their education. In these PSAs, businesses, churches, and civic organizations are asked to work with schools to keep kids in class, engaged in learning, and college-bound.

District Attorney's Office

One of the school district's partners is the Tarrant County district attorney's office. The district attorney's office sends notices to families of students who are repeatedly absent or tardy for no excused reason. On any given Monday night of the school year, hundreds of parents and students are personally invited to come to the Billingsley Field House to review truancy laws and the legal consequences for breaking these laws. Students who repeatedly violate these laws eventually are required to go to on-campus truancy court hearings. When the same judge issues rulings from an on-campus location (instead of different judges making rulings from an off-campus municipal court), then rulings and associated punishments/sanctions are consistent among all students.

Higher Education

The district holds a "college night" at one of the local elementary schools. More than 200 colleges and universities across the country participate by answering questions students have about the college experience. Campus Go Centers are places where students can go to receive information and consultation about how to select and apply to college. These Go Centers are staffed by school staff, Project Prevail community partners, and actual college students.

The Fort Worth ISD partners with the Princeton Review, a top test-preparation company. Princeton Review consultants work with both Fort Worth ISD teachers and students to help them prepare for SAT and ACT exams.

Faith Community Partners

A local baptist church has agreed to devote one evening per week and church meeting space for Project Prevail staff to help local students with their homework and to prepare them for important high-stakes standardized tests.

Fort Worth Hispanic Chamber of Commerce

Through Project Prevail, Fort Worth Hispanic Chamber of Commerce representatives have visited schools to mentor students and give talks on local career opportunities. Many Fort Worth ISD students have part-time jobs while they attend school. It is important for these students to be successful in these jobs, but to not have these jobs interfere with their schoolwork. When local businesses support the broad objectives of Project Prevail, then the Chamber of Commerce in turn will actively support these local businesses. Businesses that are accepted into the Chamber of Commerce's teamworkers program provide student employees with flexible hours.

Student Engagement and School Completion Department

The Fort Worth ISD has its own department—called the Student Engagement and School Completion (SESC) Department—whose sole purpose is to coordinate all Project Prevail stakeholders in implementing a wide variety of programs and initiatives that help fulfill the objective of ensuring that students graduate from high school fully prepared for postsecondary education. A summary of the various programs administered by the SESC is provided in Table 9.2.

Table 9.2   Fort Worth Independent School District (FWISD) Student Engagement and School Completion (SESC) Department Projects

Mission: To engage all Project Prevail* stakeholders in implementing initiatives to ensure that students graduate from high school fully prepared for postsecondary education		
Project	Grade Level/ Stakeholders	Mission Description
College Foundations Program	High School	SESC staff, college volunteers, and university representatives help prepare FWISD 10th- to 12th-grade students for college admissions by guiding them through the college admissions process, helping them look for scholarship opportunities, and helping them complete college applications.
Community Action Team	Community	Community Action Teams (i.e., members of the business, faith, government/social service communities, parents, students, and educators) are responsible for helping to achieve the Project Prevail goals.

Table 9.2 (*Continued*)

Mission: To engage all Project Prevail* stakeholders in implementing initiatives to ensure that students graduate from high school fully prepared for postsecondary education

Project	Grade Level/ Stakeholders	Mission Description
Community Volunteer Corp	All Schools	High school and local college students participate in service projects in the FWISD community, which helps raise enthusiasm and awareness for community service.
Developmental Assets Training	Community	Developmental Assets are common-sense, positive experiences and qualities that help influence choices young people make to help them become caring, responsible adults and to avoid at-risk behaviors. Two train-the-trainer sessions are held to develop a cadre of 60 trainers who would share the Developmental Assets message with FWISD staff, students, parents, and members of the community.
Education & Immigration Summit	All Schools	Creates a college/career-bound culture for all families in the FWISD (including undocumented immigrant families) by providing a variety of informational workshops and resources (covering such topics as legal advice, current immigration laws, college access, and the college application process).
Elementary Student Leadership	Elementary School	A leadership development curriculum is used to teach students about a variety of leadership skills (collaborative problem solving, consensus building, and expressing opinions in a productive manner).
Helping Youth Pursue Excellence	Middle School	Eighth-grade students gain a positive self-image and develop communication skills by participating in art, comedy, dance, drama, or poetry classes taught by teachers, high school students, and college volunteers. A parent component involves Saturday workshops on preparing their children for high school and college.
iDream, iLearn, iWin	All Schools	Workshops are provided for K through 12th-grade students and their parents, the goals of which include creating a vision of achievement for students and parents, creating trust and knowledge of educational, community, and government systems, and creating an understanding of the value of education.
Leadership Academy	High School	Incoming freshmen and sophomores learn leadership skills while engaging in challenging mental and physical activities during a four-day, three-night stay at a local university.
Middle School Student Leadership	Middle School	A leadership development curriculum includes daily lessons and activities that teach middle schoolers about leadership skills through collaborative problem solving, consensus building, and expressing opinions in a productive manner.

(*continued*)

Table 9.2   (Continued)

Mission: To engage all Project Prevail* stakeholders in implementing initiatives to ensure that students graduate from high school fully prepared for postsecondary education

Project	Grade Level/ Stakeholders	Mission Description
MLS/LA Reunion	High School	Three follow-up meetings are conducted with students who participated in the Leadership Academy (LA) and the Multicultural Leadership Seminar (MLS). These meetings are held at institutions of higher learning and include parent participation.
Multicultural Leadership Seminar	High School	Incoming 11th- and 12th-grade students stay at a college campus for one week, at which time they tour the campus, visit surrounding universities, and attend workshops that discuss the college admissions process, how to apply for scholarships, and campus life for multicultural students.
Prevail to Graduation	High School	Volunteers participate in a Stay-in-School walk to personally contact students who were enrolled in Spring and did not return to school in the Fall. These volunteers encourage students to persist toward graduation.
Scholarships	High School	Texas Christian University (TCU) and Texas Wesleyan University (TWU) have partnered with the FWISD SESC to provide scholarships to students who have participated in SESC initiatives. Scholarships are awarded to students who have demonstrated academic excellence, leadership, and dedication to the community.
United High School Council (UHSC)	High School	Serves the FWISD and community through service learning and leadership training. Students in the UHSC are trained in student leadership processes and implement these processes on their campuses. In addition, UHSC members complete school year volunteer projects for the community. Students and their sponsors attend both state and local conferences for the National Association of Secondary School Principals and Texas Association of Student Councils.
Youth Engagement Opportunities	Middle School	Develops the leadership potential of middle school students through one-on-one mentoring with adult role models and through community volunteer projects.
Youth Forum	High School	Engages students in "listening sessions" through which their issues, concerns, and aspirations are identified and responsive actions are proposed. These events are youth-led and youth-facilitated.

*Project Prevail is a comprehensive and coordinated effort by the Fort Worth Independent School District that involves businesses, parents, students, colleges, middle/high schools, faith communities, and social services to increase the number of students graduating from district high schools fully prepared for postsecondary education or gainful employment (Diaz, 2011). (Adapted from Diaz, 2011)

School psychologists working in the FWISD are not directly involved in various SESC initiatives, as they are administratively hired and supervised under a completely different department within the district. As in most other districts, the work of school psychologists tends to focus on special education eligibility and the needs of special education students. However, this does not mean that there are not opportunities for psychological services personnel to contribute in meaningful ways to the district's Project Prevail initiatives. For example, the FWISD SESC has Community Action Teams (CATs), which are composed of members from postsecondary institutions of learning, the business, faith, and social service communities, and parents, students, and educators. The FWISD Director of Psychological Services serves on the CAT Social Services Committee, whose job it is to help CATs understand the social, emotional, and cognitive developmental expectations for those youth whom they serve who belong to various grade levels. As an example, children are often informally referred to as "immature." The Director of Psychological Services has conducted informative workshops to help CAT members understand what this means *specifically* in terms of skills young people should have acquired at various ages (M. Parker, personal communication, May 2012).

SCHOOL DISTRICT SERVICES FOR IMMIGRANT STUDENTS

Immigrants Are Not Monolithic, But Extremely Heterogeneous

An immigrant is generally defined as a person from a foreign country who enters a host country to establish permanent residence. Although there are some notable common-alities in all immigrant groups, immigrant status does not denote homogeneity in all respects. There are important differences among immigrants that are ultimately relevant to their educational experiences, which are briefly summarized in the following sections.

Foreign versus American Born

Many American immigrant students were first born in a foreign country but then came to the United States with their families in the middle of their formal schooling years. Other immigrant students were born in the United States after their families had settled in America. Although both groups have been called immigrants, the former group is generally referred to as first-generation immigrants, whereas the second group is generally referred to as second-generation immigrants. Third-generation immigrants would be those whose grandparents migrated to America, and their offspring were born in America (i.e., third-generation immigrants have parents who were born in America).

Age at Immigration

In studying schoolchildren and their families, some researchers have recently begun to make more fine-tuned distinctions among immigrant families by using the moniker *1.5 generation.* This moniker refers to children who were born abroad, but who moved to the United States before the age of 5. Researchers argue that the social, language, and psychological acculturation processes differ significantly for these students, as opposed to those who moved to the United States in their early/mid-teens (Coll & Marks, 2012).

Source Country of Immigration

Asian students who are more recent immigrants have been shown to have more positive academic attitudes, higher test scores, higher school grades, and higher graduation rates compared to immigrants from non-Asian countries, as well as in comparison to later-generation peers (Pong & Zeiser, 2012).

Education, Skill Level, and Social Status of Immigrants

Some immigrants are highly skilled workers who are also highly educated, being over-represented within the category of persons with doctorates and American Nobel prizes (Suárez-Orozco, 2001). Others are poorly schooled, semiskilled, or unskilled workers, many of whom are in the United States without proper documentation. According to Ruiz-de-Velasco, Fix, and Clewell (2000), large numbers of students from Mexico, Central America, and the Caribbean have significant gaps in formal schooling from their native countries before arriving in the United States. Further complicating matters is the fact that public schooling in many of these countries ends at the equivalent of sixth grade, and in some countries adolescents are only required to attend school part time.

Suárez-Orozco and her colleagues (2008) note that second-generation immigrants (i.e., those born in the United States) generally tend to display higher levels of academic achievement, better jobs, and higher income levels compared to first-generation immigrants. Paradoxically, however, there are certain health and well-being outcomes where first-generation immigrants fare better than second-generation immigrants (Coll & Marks, 2012; Hernández & Charney, 1998).

Language Spoken in the Home Environment

The linguistic home environments of immigrant families vary considerably in the extent to which English is spoken. According to Coll and Marks (2012), a small percentage of children (in the single digits) in immigrant families live with parents who speak no English at home, while more than twice this percentage have parents who speak only English. The largest percentage of immigrant children have parents who speak both English and another language. Parents of immigrant children differ not only in the languages spoken at home, but also in the extent of their English proficiency. Children whose parents have limited English proficiency are most likely to have limited English skills and to be classified by schools as English-language learners (ELLs). Children with English-fluent parents are least likely to be classified by schools as ELLs (Coll & Marks, 2012).

Legal versus Illegal Status

The term *undocumented immigrant* often serves as a polite euphemism for an immigrant who is in the country illegally. While all second-generation immigrant children are U.S. citizens, many first-generation children must contend with the realities of undocumented status (Suárez-Orozco, Suárez-Orozco, & Todorova, 2008; see also Tables 3.9 and 3.10).

Educational Strengths of Non-English Language and Immigrant Status

According to Suárez-Orozco (2001), schooling for immigrant children serves as the primary point of sustained and close contact with a crucial institution of the host society that their parents have chosen to join. In their longitudinal study of immigrant students' adaptation to American education (see Chapter 3 for more details), Suárez-Orozco et al. (2008) found that many immigrant children hold deeply ingrained cultural attitudes toward education that are sadly lacking in many American children. In a nutshell, the researchers concluded that immigrant children generally hold very positive attitudes toward school. For example, immigrant children are keenly aware of the sacrifices that their parents have made for them in coming to America. At home, they are constantly exposed by their parents to the idea that a person cannot have a reasonably good and successful life without a good education. For many immigrant families, it is hoped that the children will eventually become high-status professionals (e.g., businesspersons, lawyers, doctors) who will be a source of pride and bring recognition to the family name, specifically, and to their country, generally. In sentence completion surveys administered to immigrant students, when asked to complete the sentence "I know I cannot succeed unless . . . ," an overwhelming majority provided a response indicating the importance of studying hard (Suárez-Orozco et al., 2008). Many teachers commented that, in contrast to first-generation immigrant students, second- and third-generation immigrant students are observed to become more Americanized and more prone to lose their fierce desire to achieve.

When teachers and administrators were interviewed and asked to compare their experiences working with immigrant versus nonimmigrant students, their responses tended to reflect a perception of immigrant students as (paraphrased here) "being easier to develop a teacher/student bond with," "being more disciplined," "more prone to value education," "being nicer students," being "more respectful of authority figures," and "more motivated to make something of themselves after high school" (Suárez-Orozco et al., 2008).

Educational Challenges of Non-English Language and Immigrant Status
District Guidelines vis-à-vis Undocumented Status

The U.S. Department of Justice and U.S. Department of Education have issued important guidelines reminding school districts nationwide of their obligation under federal law to provide equal educational opportunities to all children residing in their districts, regardless of their race, color, national origin, citizenship or immigration status, or the immigration status of their parents and guardians. This guidance responded to discriminatory enrollment practices, documented in part by the American Civil Liberties Union, that unnecessarily and unlawfully inquire—directly or indirectly—into the immigration status of students and their families. These practices create fear among undocumented immigrants that the attempt to enroll their children in public school may bring both the students and their families to the attention of the immigration authorities. The guidance instructed school districts to cease all enrollment practices that may "chill," discourage, or exclude students from school based on immigration status. This guidance did not establish any new policy but simply reinforced existing law established by the Supreme Court's 1982 decision in *Plyler v. Doe* that a state may not deny access to a basic public education to any child residing in the state, regardless of immigration status.

The guidance made clear that a school district may not ask about a child's citizenship or immigration status to establish residency within the district, or deny a homeless child (including an undocumented homeless child) enrollment because she or he cannot provide the required documents to establish residency. The guidance further specified that a school district may not prevent a child from enrolling in school because a child has a foreign birth certificate; or a child or parent chooses not to provide the child's social security number; or a child or parent chooses not to provide the child's race or ethnicity.

The guidance also instructed school districts to assess their current policies to determine whether they discourage the enrollment of undocumented students and to eliminate any possible chilling effect on enrollment. This U.S. Department of Justice and Department of Education guidance can be accessed online at http://www.aclu.org/files/assets/DOJ-DOE_re_Plyler_May_2011.pdf Relevant legal issues faced by school districts related to the education of undocumented immigrant children are briefly discussed in Sidebar 9.4

◢ Sidebar 9.4   Legal Issues for School Districts Related to the Education of Undocumented Immigrant Children

The National Association of School Psychologists (NASP) has joined with at least 17 other professional organizations in endorsing the online document *Legal Issues for School Districts Related to the Education of Undocumented Children* (http://www.nsba.org/SchoolLaw/COSA/Search/AllCOSAdocuments/Undocumented-Children.pdf). The document is based on an analysis and broad interpretation of the 1982 U.S. Supreme Court case *Plyler v. Doe*, which held that undocumented immigrant students have a constitutional right to attend public elementary and secondary school for free. Although many questions that school officials have concerning the education of undocumented immigrant children have no definitive answers, the following 13 issues summarize the counsel of this document, which, according to the document writers, has been sent to every school district in the country.

1. The *Plyler* Court concluded that undocumented immigrant children are entitled to the same K–12 education that the state provides to children who are citizens or legal residents. The Court in *Plyler* concluded that for the state to deny undocumented children access to a free public education, the state must demonstrate that doing so serves a "substantial goal." Arguments that denying access to a free education for undocumented children (a) protects the state from an influx of illegal immigrants; (b) relieves the state of the added, unique costs of educating undocumented children; and (c) is rooted in the claim that undocumented children are "less likely than other children . . . to put their education to productive social or political use within the State" were rejected as compelling arguments.

2. Although not explicitly discussed in the *Plyler* ruling, the document implies that an undocumented child's right to an education *probably* includes secondary benefits of public education like participating in extracurricular activities.

3. Undocumented students are probably permitted or required to receive services that other students receive from school districts and other local government agencies. Services like free and reduced meals and educational assistance to manage a learning disability would be most likely protected by *Plyler* because they are central to a student's educational experience.

4. School districts probably cannot ask questions about immigration status to determine if a student is a resident of the district. Asking students questions about their immigration status when determining residency is argued to violate the *Plyler* decision, because it may discourage undocumented students from enrolling in school.

5. In some states, students must live with their parents/guardians in order to qualify as residents of the district—the purpose of which is to ensure that students do not move to a particular district solely to obtain an education. However, some undocumented children do not live with their parents and

(*continued*)

may not be able to establish an alternative legal guardian. School districts are *probably* required to educate an undocumented student who is not living with a parent or legal guardian. School districts should be cautious about denying enrollment to undocumented children living in the district who are unable to establish that their parents/guardians are residents of the school district if they otherwise meet residency requirements. Denying enrollment may violate *Plyler* and may be prohibited if the undocumented students are homeless.

6. No federal law requires school districts to report undocumented students to immigration authorities, and arguably school districts are prohibited from reporting them by the *Plyler* decision.

7. Even when asking to see visa documents is permissible under state law, school districts should be cautious about this issue, because doing so could "chill" undocumented student enrollment, arguably in violation of the *Plyler* decision.

8. Even when denying enrollment to B-2 visa* bearers is permissible under state law, school districts should be cautious because doing so could "chill" undocumented student enrollment, arguably in violation of the *Plyler* decision. In addition, a B-2 visa-bearing student who has been denied enrollment may claim *Plyler* has been violated because—despite the limitations of the visa—he or she intends to stay beyond the length of the visa as undocumented and he or she otherwise meets the district's residency requirements.

9. If a school district calls Immigrations and Customs Enforcement (ICE) to report a student who tries to attend school in violation of his or her visa, parents of undocumented students may become wary of continuing to send their children to school, thus "chilling" undocumented children's access to an education. Applicable state laws, regulations, or state agency policies should be considered before reporting a student who tries to attend school in violation of his or her B-2 visa.

10. The Family Educational Rights and Privacy Act (FERPA) generally prohibits school districts from providing third parties (such as ICE) with information about students contained in student records.

11. In some circumstances, a school district may have to allow ICE agents to interview students at school, but ICE's policy is to generally avoid enforcement actions on school grounds.

12. During an ICE enforcement action, school employees should not assist parents in remaining in the U.S. illegally, but may offer caregiving

assistance to undocumented students whose parents have been detained by ICE.

13. To avoid claims of negligent supervision, school districts should take adequate steps to ensure the safety of children whose parents are detained.

The authors of this document openly acknowledge that the document generally favors providing undocumented students an education in a very broad sense, based only on a few court cases. However, they argue that the spirit of the *Plyler* case supports an important principle that all children in the United States should be educated regardless of immigration status.

*The B-2 visa is a nonimmigrant visitor visa for persons desiring to enter the United States temporarily for pleasure, tourism, or medical treatment.

(Adapted from National School Boards Association & National Education Association, 2009)

School Challenges Posed by Immigrant Students/Families

Gershberg, Danenberg, and Sánchez (2004) interviewed elementary/middle school principals and district officials in five of the largest districts in the state of California (Fresno, Long Beach, Los Angeles, San Diego, and San Francisco) noted for hosting approximately 24 percent of recent immigrant students in the state. At least 20 percent of interview respondents mentioned the following challenges faced by recent immigrant students/families (in decreasing order of frequency):

- Communication/language issues
- Cultural assimilation issues
- Poverty
- Navigating the school system/understanding school system policies
- Low prior schooling of immigrant students
- Low educational levels of parents
- General health issues
- Housing concerns
- Parental participation and involvement in their child's school work
- Parental participation and involvement at school
- Immigrant children not living with their parents
- Need for childcare to assist immigrant parents

- Lure of, and problems caused by, gangs
- Legal issues and fear of Immigration and Naturalization Service (INS)
- Stigmatization by school system, school staff, or others
- Transportation to and from school and/or school events

According to the Center for Mental Health in Schools (2010), educators have expressed grave concerns over several problems involving immigrant students in schools, which include (a) the need for many immigrant students to leave school early in order to go to work; (b) early school termination for immigrant girls as young as 14, whose families have obligated them to arranged marriages; (c) the presence of illiterate refugee children who have never attended school in their native country; (d) the presence of families who speak many different languages when schools do not employ enough translators to facilitate communication; (e) the stigmatization of newcomer immigrant students by nonimmigrant students; (f) the negative impact on a school or district's ability to demonstrate Adequate Yearly Progress (AYP, see Glossary), due to high enrollment of immigrant students.

Most immigrant students in the Suárez-Orozco et al. (2008) study (see Chapter 3) attended highly segregated schools where the majority of their peers were nonwhite and came from poor families. Such settings are antithetical to a healthy climate of learning and/or physical safety. When Suárez-Orozco and her colleagues interviewed immigrant students about their perceptions of the schools they attended, "an alarming number of them spoke of crime, violence, feeling unsafe, gang activity, weapons, drug dealing, and racial conflicts" (p. 91). According to Suárez-Orozco and her colleagues, such students are "at a significant disadvantage as they strive to adapt to a new culture, master the necessary skills to pass high stakes tests, accrue graduation credits, get into college, and attain the skills needed to compete in workplaces shaped by the new global economy" (p. 96).

According to Ruiz-de-Velasco, Fix, and Clewell (2000), districts serving large numbers of immigrant students face four primary challenges: (1) the search for ways to address the literacy needs of students within secondary schools that are not designed to focus on basic literacy development, (2) the challenge of accelerating subject learning for students who are not ready for English instruction in mainstream classes, (3) the lack of appropriate assessment tools for evaluating the progress of LEP students in secondary schools, and (4) long-term shortages of new teachers who are specially trained to work with English-language learners.

According to Ruiz-de-Velasco et al. (2000), high school teachers report that the single strongest predictor of academic success for immigrant newcomers, outside of English language fluency, is how much prior schooling students have had in their native countries. This has a significant effect on their basic understanding of grammatical rules in their native language. For example, students who can identify the functions of an adjective, subject, or verb in a sentence are well positioned to make successful transitions to English language literacy, whereas students who are unable to do so are not.

Grammatically underprepared immigrants who enter U.S. secondary schools have a weak foundation for learning a second language, as well as having difficulty working at age-appropriate levels in required subjects even when taught in their native/primary languages. According to Ruiz-de-Velasco et al. (2000), teachers report that under-schooled immigrant teens also tend to lack basic study skills that promote classroom learning. Some new refugees of middle-school age did not even know how to use a pencil, and they were unaccustomed to sitting in a classroom for extended periods or raising their hands to be recognized.

According to Ruiz de Velasco et al. (2000), teachers would also complain about immigrant students from African and Carribean nations who were orally proficient in English but continued to experience serious difficulties in reading comprehension and writing. These students also tend to perform poorly in mainstream classes. Although the data on which their research is based is now over a decade old, investigators found that more than 42 percent of the district's secondary Limited English Proficient (LEP) students in one northern California school district were still classified LEP after six or more years in U.S. schools.

The dilemma for teachers working with these students is that they have typically already taken, and been promoted from, their schools' English language development (bilingual/ESL) programs and so have exhausted all available special language development services. Although still formally classified as LEP, they are now served almost exclusively in mainstream classes by regular subject-area teachers with no language development support. Many of these students speak only English and usually have no formal training in their parents' native languages. The education needs they face are no longer rooted in language per se, but rather in the more basic reading and writing skills usually acquired in primary grades.

According to Ruiz-de-Velasco et al. (2000), schools face institutional challenges in strengthening education programs for immigrant children. The first challenge is the limited capacity of school staff to instruct these learners. At one level, this capacity issue is caused by a simple shortage of teachers who are specially trained to teach LEP/immigrant students. At another level, it is the result of the limited number of content teachers (i.e., math, science, or social studies) who can communicate effectively with LEP/immigrant children. Schools with large numbers of immigrant children face significant challenges about how to simultaneously build both language and subject-matter learning among LEP/immigrant students. Both types of learning are necessary for immigrant teens to graduate from high school in the limited number of school years that are available to them.

A second challenge to teaching LEP/immigrant students derives from the ways in which secondary schools are organized. The division of secondary schools into departments (e.g., mathematics, sciences, social sciences), the isolation of language development teachers, and the division of the day into 50-minute periods militate against the kind of individualized instruction students with special learning needs may require (Ruiz-de-Velasco et al., 2000).

Without curriculum standards, individual teachers are left on their own to determine what instructional methods they would use and what content they would cover. As a result, teachers often focus only on the most basic oral English and reading comprehension skills. Because there was little standardization, the content of instruction at any given level often varied widely across schools in the same district and across classes in the same school. In the absence of a clearly articulated set of skills and knowledge to be mastered at each level of a language development program, it was also difficult for teachers of upper-level courses to make assumptions about what students could be expected to have mastered when they completed lower-level courses.

In the nation as a whole, only a small share of teachers, administrators, and guidance counselors are specially trained to work with English-language learners. These challenges mean that shortfalls in trained teachers could not be overcome by new hires alone, but would have to be met by veteran classroom teachers. They, in turn, would have to be trained and engaged more fully in meeting the needs of immigrant students.

Ruiz-de-Velasco et al. (2000) found that the task of preparing LEP/immigrants to participate effectively in mainstream classrooms is organizationally conceived by many schools as a special or add-on activity outside what school staff often consider to be the normal functions of the secondary school. Consequently, not only are key nonteaching staff frequently unprepared to work effectively with LEP/immigrants, but the departmentalized nature of most language development programs actually encourages administrators, counselors, and others to see the integration of LEP/immigrant youth as a duty assigned to special language development staff, and thus outside the scope of their own duties. As a result, language development teachers assume administrative, placement, and advising functions that for mainstream students would be routinely handled by principals, counselors, registrars, librarians, or other administrators.

In one demonstration school, for example, an ESOL teacher noted that she and other language development instructors were responsible for providing a full range of counseling, placement, and pre-college planning services to their ESOL students (Ruiz-de-Velasco et al., 2000). Language development teachers also noted that administrators' lack of training and foreign language skills often meant that language development teachers ended up mediating conflicts among parents, administrators, and regular classroom teachers, thereby assuming responsibility for disciplinary matters that were normally handled by assistant principals.

SCHOOL DISTRICT RESPONSES TO EDUCATIONAL CHALLENGES OF NON-ENGLISH LANGUAGE AND IMMIGRANT STATUS

Federal Support

Several federal education programs are available to support newly arrived students. In addition to Title III's emphasis on ensuring that LEP students master English, schools with high poverty rates can use Title I resources in addressing concerns related to newly arrived students and their families. In addition, 15 percent of IDEA funds may be used for Coordinated Early Intervening Services. Such services are for students who are not currently identified as requiring special education, but who need additional academic and behavioral support to succeed in a general education environment (U.S. Department of Education, 2009). The Refugee Children School Impact Grant Program in the Office of Refugee Resettlement also provides for some of the costs of educating refugee children (Morse, 2005).

Welcome Centers and Newcomer Programs

Many American school districts located in regions that are significantly impacted by immigration have a central location for the enrollment of "newcomer students" from other countries. Newcomer programs are short-term programs (usually 6 to 18 months) for recent immigrant students who have little or no English proficiency and who may have had limited formal education in their native countries. Newcomer programs are funded solely from, or as a combination of local district, state, and/or federal funds.

Newcomer students have needs that traditional English as a second language (ESL) and bilingual programs are usually not designed to address (Short & Boyson, 2003). The focus on newcomer programs is on orienting newcomers and assessing students' skill level in their native language in order to plan the best academic placement. In some cases, student support services are available to assess social and emotional needs and provide follow-up support to the students and family. The intent is to address limited English proficiency, low literacy, limited schooling, and to ease the transition to the American schooling culture. Other services for students may include healthcare, mental health, career counseling, and tutoring. Programs sometimes serve families as well, providing not only outreach specific to the school, but also adult ESL, orientation to the community, and help with accessing social services, healthcare, housing, and employment. Schools often partner with the community to serve parents and families.

National Surveys of Newcomer Programs

Under the auspices of the Center for Applied Linguistics in Washington, D.C., Boyson and Short (2003) first led a four-year research study designed to identify and document services provided by newcomer and welcome programs for new immigrant students in middle and high schools across the United States. During the 1999–2000 school year, 115 newcomer programs across 29 states and the District of Columbia were studied.

According to Short and Boyson (2012), 75 percent of the programs had opened in the 1990s, when the economy was stronger than the present day and No Child Left Behind (NCLB) had not yet been enacted. A new survey of newcomer programs was inaugurated in 2008, and many of the programs analyzed in the first survey no longer existed. Many separate-site programs, for example, were particularly hard hit, because programs that only served newcomers for one year or so could not make adequate yearly progress (AYP; see Glossary) because their students were always at the lowest levels of English proficiency. Some states, such as California, Arizona, and Massachusetts, have limited the duration that English-language learners can be in language support programs and, as a result, programs have closed. Budget constraints resulting from the economic downturn of 2008 were another reason for disbanding some programs. However, although some of the older newcomer programs closed in the past 10 years, many newer ones were established. A full 60 percent of the programs in Short and Boyson's (2012) 2011 database began operation in the 2000s.

Short and Boyson (2012) developed a second survey to identify promising middle and high school newcomer programs and gather information about the program design, policies, student population, instructional and assessment practices, staffing, materials, funding sources, and evidence of effectiveness. Through various venues (e.g., Web postings, electronic lists, conference presentations), newcomer programs across the United States were invited to complete a comprehensive survey from 2008 to 2009. Those programs that were interested in participating in the survey were able to send the data to the Washington, D.C., Center for Applied Linguistics via an online form, electronic Word file, hard copy, or phone interview. Follow-up phone calls and emails were made to clarify any information that was unclear. Their 2011 database contains 63 programs serving 10,899 secondary newcomer students in 24 states.

According to Short and Boyson (2012), 13 of the states with newcomer programs in 2000—Alaska, Connecticut, Florida, Georgia, Maryland, Missouri, Nevada, New Mexico, Pennsylvania, Utah, Washington, Wisconsin, and the District of Columbia—did not have any programs (or chose not to participate in the second Short and Boyson survey) in 2011. Seven states—Arkansas, Kentucky, North Dakota, Rhode Island, South Carolina, Tennessee, and Wyoming—did not report newcomer programs in 2000–2001 but had programs in 2011. Short and Boyson (2012) note that, with the exception of Rhode Island, these seven states represent what demographers currently refer to as "new destination" states: Immigrants might arrive in the United States at the traditional ports of entry, but they settle in nontraditional states.

Student Demographics

Newcomer students in Short and Boyson's (2012) database were reported as being from more than 90 countries and speaking more than 55 languages or dialects. The languages that were most common across the programs were Spanish (in 90 percent of the programs), Arabic (38 percent of the programs), Mandarin (19 percent of the programs), French (17 percent of the programs), and Korean and Vietnamese (both 14 percent of the programs). Some programs reported that they had refugee students, exclusively or in addition to immigrants. Around 96 percent of the newcomer programs served some students with interrupted formal education; nearly one-third of all the students enrolled across the programs had interrupted formal schooling. More than 90 percent of the students across programs qualified for the free/reduced lunch program.

Language of Instruction

According to Short and Boyson's (2012) database, English is primarily used for instruction in language and content courses offered by newcomer programs. Some courses are taught in the students' native languages when enough students in a program speak the same language and teachers who also speak the language are available to provide instruction. Spanish is the most common language used for the bilingual content courses. Other languages include Arabic, Vietnamese, French, Swahili, and Burmese. Support in languages other than English is provided through teachers and paraprofessional educators who speak the students' native languages. Some programs offer a foreign language course to students as well, usually Spanish and/or French. A few programs offer Spanish language arts and literacy.

Entry Criteria

In all school districts, entry into the newcomer program is entirely voluntary. In general, most newcomer programs serve students who are recent arrivals to the United States and have limited or no English language proficiency (as opposed to ESL and bilingual education students who have some English language proficiency). The criteria for "recent arrival" ranges from students who have been in the United States for one year or less to students who have been in the United States for four years or less.

Seventy-three percent of participating programs surveyed by Short and Boyson (2012) also rely on the results of the English-language proficiency assessment that students take at registration. At this juncture, a student who scores below a certain benchmark is given the option of entering the newcomer program. Thirteen percent of the programs only enroll students with limited English proficiency and interrupted formal schooling or academic performance that is at least two years below grade level. Programs also use referrals and recommendations by principals, teachers, or guidance counselors from the home school (i.e., the school that an English-language learner would otherwise attend were he or she not enrolled in a newcomer program) and parents to determine placement into newcomer programs.

Site Location

Each of the 63 programs studied by Short and Boyson (2012) were characterized by one of three site location models: (1) a program-within-a-school model (which constituted the majority of programs), (2) a separate-site (but not an entire school) model, or (3) a whole-school model.

In the program-within-a-school model, newcomer students are served in their home school or designated attendance area school. Here, they have opportunities to interact with mainstream students at least for part of the day (e.g., within classes such as physical education, music, art, or other extracurricular activities). When it comes time for newcomer students to exit programs that adhere to this model, most simply remain at the same school to continue their studies in the regular language-support program (i.e., ESL or bilingual services).

In the separate-site model, the district houses the program at a former school that previously closed, or in another separate space that may be leased or purchased. In some sites studied, students attend their home schools for a portion of the day and then are transported to the newcomer program location site for a half-day or less of specialized instruction. In other programs, students attend the newcomer program site of either a half-day or a full day, depending on their individual needs.

The least common newcomer program model is the whole-school model. Whole-school programs are designed especially for students who may have experienced interrupted schooling or who lack formal education in their native language. In this model, students enter the program, usually at the lowest grade of the school level, and remain at the site until promotion from middle to high school, or graduation. Students enrolled in these schools may remain in the program until they graduate, or they may transfer to a regular ESL, bilingual, or mainstream program at another high school.

Short and Boyson (2012) profile a national network of newcomer high schools called the Internationals Network. Of the 14 international high schools profiled, two exist in California and the remaining 12 are located throughout the boroughs of New York City. These four-year high schools provide students with a quality education and incorporate career and college planning opportunities, as well as all required courses for graduation. Most offer internships and the opportunity to take Advanced Placement or college-level courses through partnerships with colleges in the communities. Students may remain in most of these programs for five or six years to graduate if they are unable to complete the graduation requirements in four years.

Length of Daily Program/Overall Program Enrollment

Three programs surveyed by Short and Boyson (2012) offer services for less than one school year. Two programs are one-semester programs, and the third is a four-week summer program. One school year is the maximum stay for 36 percent of the programs in the Short and Boyson (2012) database, while one-year or more-than-one-year options account for 59 percent of the programs. Some of the longer programs were designed especially to accommodate the students who lack formal schooling in their native language and hence need more time to close achievement gaps. Other longer programs represent the whole-school model. The majority of the students (64 percent) are enrolled in more-than-one-year programs. According to Short and Boyson (2012), an additional 24 percent of the students are enrolled in programs that offer one-year or more-than-one-year options, depending on student needs, for a total of 88 percent of students who may remain in a newcomer program for more than one year.

Grade Level Served

Grade levels served in each newcomer program vary according to the program design and students' needs. According to Short and Boyson (2012), middle school programs generally assign students to grades 6, 7, or 8, but may offer curricula for one or more classes that draw from a combination of grades, such as Newcomer Science (which covers some life and physical science topics). Whole-school high school programs instruct students in Grades 9–12. Students are placed according to the number of credits they have. Although most newcomers have no credits upon entry, a few come with transcripts from their own countries and can receive credit for comparable courses. Some non-whole-school high school programs deliver a ninth-grade or pre-ninth-grade curricula to all the newcomers. In a number of programs, students are assigned to some content classes by grade level and to other classes by their language-proficiency levels.

Class Size

Small class size is an important feature for newcomer programs that serve preliterate students, or those with low literacy levels in their native language. According to Short and Boyson's (2012) findings, 45 percent of the programs reported that their average class size was fewer than 15 students. Forty percent have an average of 15 to 24 students. Only 9 percent of the programs had an average class size of 25 students or more. The largest average class size was 34 students, and this was in the largest four-year high school, which enrolls more than 900 students.

Instruction/Curriculum

Newcomer programs are generally designed to provide courses and instructional experiences that are distinct from what is provided in regular language-support programs.

All newcomer programs offer English-language development courses. A good portion of newcomer programs offer courses designed to develop the students' literacy skills in their native language. Nearly all newcomer programs provide some content instruction (e.g., math, language arts, social studies) through English or the native language of the students. Many of the students become literate for the first time in English rather than in their native language when resources for that language are not available in the district. Many programs supplement the classroom curricula with field trips, cultural activities, and special events designed to serve American acculturation goals.

According to Short and Boyson (2012), newcomer students may have more periods of ESL, for example, than students in the regular ESL program. Newcomer courses have a stronger focus on literacy development and provide more explicit instruction in the social uses of English. In some of these programs, the first ESL course that newcomers take is at a basic level, below what is covered in a traditional ESL class.

According to Short and Boyson (2012), the percentages of newcomer programs that offer certain types of instruction, listed in descending order, are as follows: English-language courses (100 percent); orientation to the United States (68%); content instruction via sheltered instruction (67%); reading intervention (56%); school study skills (54%); content instruction via both sheltered and native language instruction (27%); native-language literacy (25%); career/vocational content (14%); content instruction via native-language instruction (3%).

Literacy, Literacy, and More Literacy

All newcomer programs in Short and Boyson's (2012) survey acknowledged the need to develop students' academic literacy skills as soon as possible, although the approach taken depends on the native-language literacy levels of students. For example, all programs make sure the students know the Roman alphabet and phonemes of English, and they incorporate decoding and fluency instruction as part of their basic literacy curriculum. The most important component of literacy instruction for newcomer students is the building up of their vocabulary knowledge (i.e., classroom- and school-based words, general academic and subject-specific words, and word parts such as prefixes and suffixes). All newcomer programs employed vocabulary development instructional activities such as word studies, creating word walls in the classroom, practicing word attack skills, creating picture cards, and drafting personal dictionaries. For students who need to develop literacy skills for the first time in their lives, instruction first begins with the basics (i.e., introduction to the alphabet, vowel sounds, letter/sound correspondence, phonemic awareness, phonics, and syllables). Next, books are introduced early in emergent literacy instruction to demonstrate book orientation and voiceprint matching. Wordless picture books and picture walks are used to promote vocabulary, speaking, and writing. Depending on a student's native language, stage of literacy development, and the resources available, the initial literacy instruction may be provided one on one with the instructor for part of the day. Students coming into a program from different languages and backgrounds often need an individualized literacy plan. When possible, primary language literacy development and support is provided.

After students have acquired the basics, explicit comprehension strategy instruction and balanced literacy practices are implemented, most commonly by using guided reading groups and leveled readers. Other techniques are used as well, which include choral reading, interactive read-alouds, echo reading, partner reading, reciprocal reading, and shared reading techniques. All newcomer programs also promoted reading instruction across the curriculum. Students develop expository reading skills in their content courses and engage in literature-based instruction and novel analysis in their language classes. Newcomer teachers stress the importance of reading many books both inside and outside of school. Silent, independent reading is practiced frequently in newcomer classrooms, and students are encouraged to read books of personal interest. Some newcomer programs have students take books home for pleasure reading or content reinforcement. Program instructors teach students to use the school library, and, in some programs, teachers help students apply for library cards at their local public library so that they may check out books on their own. Most programs promote reading in the native language as well as in English both at home or after school in book clubs.

Teachers use both commercial products and teacher-made materials. Besides textbooks and leveled readers, teachers use flashcards, visuals (e.g., picture cards, photos), word walls, picture dictionaries (in English and the native language, where available), grammar and vocabulary practice books, and audio books. Teachers also incorporate authentic materials, such as environmental print and newspaper and magazine articles, in lessons. Technology is present in most classrooms, and students learn to use interactive computer software (e.g., Rosetta Stone) for language practice. Some teachers use technology tools (e.g., interactive whiteboards) to enhance their presentations in the classroom with visuals, graphics, audio files, and video clips.

Writing instruction in newcomer programs begins with the basics, such as tactile letter formation and handwriting in print and cursive. All students receive instruction for spelling and mechanics (e.g., capitalization), sentence construction, and paragraph construction. Process writing activities emphasize prewriting tasks, such as generating charts, graphs, and thinking maps, and introduce the basics of editing. Students participate in a variety of writing assignments across the curriculum, including journal writing, interactive writing, shared writing, language experience summaries, personal stories, script writing, emails, blogs, and recipes. Students are given opportunities to create their compositions in the school's computer lab. None of the programs teaches reading and writing in isolation, as teachers integrate reading, writing, speaking, and listening.

Assessments Used

The 63 programs reviewed by Short and Boyson (2012) reported a variety of reasons for using data from standardized assessments: placement in the newcomer program, monitoring progress, determining achievement, meeting federal or state accountability requirements, and determining readiness for program exit. The standardized assessments used by newcomer programs are listed in Sidebar 9.5

▨ Sidebar 9.5   Standardized Assessments Used by Newcomer Programs

Listed below are standardized assessments reported by the 63 newcomer programs for placement, progress monitoring, or exit from the program, in order of decreasing frequency:

- IDEA Oral Language Proficiency Tests (IPT; English and Spanish)
- Assessing Comprehension and Communication in English State-to-State (ACCESS) for English Language Learners
- World-Class Instructional Design and Assessment (WIDA)—ACCESS Placement Test (W-APT)
- Woodcock-Muñoz Language Survey (English and Spanish)
- Language Assessment Scales (LAS; English and Spanish)
- Texas English Language Proficiency Assessment of Skills (TELPAS)
- New York State English as a Second Language Achievement Test (NYSESLAT)
- Measures of Academic Progress (MAP)
- English Language Development Assessment (ELDA)
- New York State Regents Exams
- Language Assessment Battery—Revised (LAB-R; English and Spanish)
- Texas Assessment of Knowledge and Skills (TAKS)

(Adapted from Short and Boyson, 2012, p. 22)

Support Services

Newcomer program staffing most frequently consists of an administrator, teachers, and guidance counselors. The larger the student body, the greater the number of staff that are involved in meeting the students' diverse needs. In some smaller programs, teachers serve as program administrators, and the students are served by the guidance counselors at the home school (for separate-site programs) or the counselors in the main school (for programs within a school). Some programs employ paraprofessionals, especially when students in the program represent a wide range of native languages or have limited formal schooling. Staff sometimes include parent liaisons and social workers. In 98 percent of the programs surveyed by Short and Boyson (2012), at least one staff member in each program spoke one or more of the students' native languages. When available, bilingual staff who are familiar with the students' languages and cultures are the preferred hires.

Most of the newcomer programs rely on guidance counselors to help students adjust to school life. Guidance counselors assist with the students' schedules and help students make the transition from the newcomer program to other language support programs. Counselors in four-year newcomer high schools provide guidance in college and career planning for graduating students. About 25 percent of the newcomer programs in the Short and Boyson (2012) database have their own guidance counselors, but the majority of the programs rely on the regular school counselors to provide this service for the newcomer students (as for other students). Students in smaller, full-day, separate-site programs, however, have more difficulty accessing guidance services.

Short and Boyson (2012) found that close to one-half of the programs have access to a parent/family liaison position or social worker dedicated to serving the newcomer students and their families. Tasks that these staff perform may vary, but their main purpose is to facilitate communication among the schools, between schools and the families, and among social services providers available to newcomer families. Communication is accomplished by translating school correspondence into the parents' languages, by acting as interpreters, or by bringing trained interpreters into conversations with parents when needed, and by contacting families to share information (including home visits). Parent liaisons and social workers assess families' basic needs and refer parents to the appropriate social services in the community.

Throughout the year, the social worker or parent liaison plans meetings and/or workshops aimed at helping parents make the transition to U.S. culture. When families arrive, the social worker may introduce parents to teachers, give them a tour of the campus, and provide them with the school calendar. At the meetings held during the school year, topics of interest to parents of adolescent children are presented, sometimes with guest speakers. Transportation may be an issue in some locations, and the programs often help parents attend meetings by providing them with transportation or with complimentary passes for public transportation. Programs typically hold special events throughout the year or around holidays to highlight aspects of the students' cultures and to showcase student performances.

According to Short and Boyson (2012), many newcomer programs attempt to connect parents with educational opportunities. For example, they may provide on-site adult education classes that direct parents to classes in the district or community. Many programs also provide parents with orientation to U.S. culture (e.g., holidays, parenting expectations), as well as offer an orientation to U.S. schools (e.g., student schedules, handling absences, school lunch options). Many of these programs also provide native-language literacy and family literacy classes, adult ESL courses, adult basic education courses, or General Equivalency Degree (GED) courses.

Most programs surveyed offer social services to newcomer students and their families. Many do this through referrals to outside social agencies, including refugee resettlement agencies. Some newcomer programs have a social worker on staff who helps facilitate communication between the families and the social agencies, health, and counseling services. Some programs also offer health screening on site and assist parents with the paperwork for health insurance for children. To ensure that students are provided with basic necessities, programs connect families with food banks and clothing distribution centers and provide free and reduced-price school lunches and free school uniforms to qualifying students.

Other services that social service agencies provide to families are job referrals and job training, housing assistance and help for the homeless, assistance with utilities, family intervention and parenting classes, legal services, immigration services, preschool and daycare programs, transportation, and training in financial management, and training in technology with access to computers. Some agencies offer services to students outside of school, including youth academic services, recreational activities, youth dance and choir, summer programs, and college or postsecondary referrals (Short & Boyson, 2012).

Newcomer programs that offer social services to families have multiple ways of letting parents know about these services. Awareness is first activated at the intake/registration center: While their children are being assessed, parents are informed about local services. If a family has refugee or asylee status, the refugee resettlement agency is the first point of contact, and local community organizations or churches may be in touch with the family even before they register their children for school. At the program site, newcomer program staff (e.g., parent coordinators, teachers, nurses, social workers, and guidance counselors) tell students and their families about services available to them and make referrals. This is accomplished in a variety of ways, including holding orientation meetings, sharing information via parent-teacher conferences and classroom presentations, and showing informational videos to newcomer families (Short & Boyson, 2012). Parents learn of services by word of mouth and from bilingual parent networks that are active in some programs. Other methods of notification reported by the surveyed programs include mailing letters to parents in English and the parents' native languages, providing monthly calendars marked with specific events, distributing multicultural brochures and fliers, placing notices in local newspapers, calling homes directly using the district automated calling systems, and broadcasting information through websites and other multimedia, such as district cable television and radio programs, sometimes in the students' native languages (Short & Boyson, 2012).

Community organizations, such as libraries, local museums, county health departments, transit authorities, youth and family services, and sports clubs, are partners with newcomer programs. These groups range from large businesses to private foundations to nonprofit organizations. Readers are encouraged to consult Short and Boyson (2012) for specific examples of community/newcomer program partnerships in various states.

Exit Criteria

Newcomer programs use a variety of criteria to determine when students are ready to transition out of the program. Districts use test scores, portfolio assessment, teacher recommendations, or evaluations of student progress by program staff. In whole-school models, students merely fulfill district graduation requirements in order to successfully complete the program.

HOW CAN SCHOOL PSYCHOLOGISTS HELP SCHOOL DISTRICTS SERVE IMMIGRANT STUDENTS/FAMILIES?

At the time of this writing, save for rare exceptions (e.g., Pilon, 2007), few publications give the school psychology profession guidance and examples for how to best serve immigrant students in high-impact school systems. Until this knowledge base matures, the most that can be done is to describe the challenges that such districts face and how school psychologists can potentially be of service. This potential help has both direct and indirect service features.

Direct Services

Counseling

Obviously, a school psychologist cannot be effective working with non-English-speaking immigrant students if he or she is unable to communicate with them in their native language. Some school districts must take this into account when hiring school psychologists. As an example, the Division of Psychological Services within Miami-Dade County Public Schools employs more than 240 mostly bilingual school psychologists who are able to communicate in one or more languages, including Spanish, Haitian-Creole, French, Portuguese, Korean, Hebrew, Hindi, and American Sign Language.

Pilon (2007) provides an informative discussion of his role as a bilingual school psychologist serving the Los Angeles Unified School District's Newcomer Center housed within the Belmont High School. Each year, the Los Angeles Unified School District's Newcomer Center enrolls 450 newly arrived immigrant students, most of whom are Latino, into its one-year high school program. The program serves as a point-of-entry orientation experience, where students receive beginning ESL and primary language instruction, as well as a variety of specialized services in the areas of medical care, parent education, and individual and family counseling (Pilon, 2007).

From his years of experience, Pilon (2007) observes that the difficult psychological adjustment issues experienced by immigrant children can ultimately be traced to effects stemming from family disruption. For example, many immigrants have parents who left them in their native country to migrate to America, and in doing so left their children to be raised by relatives in the native country. Thus, relatives had the main responsibility for bonding with the children, administering discipline, and imparting values. Meanwhile, the parents living in America have moved on with their lives, which may include divorce, remarriage, and the added responsibility of raising new biological children or stepchildren in America. When the children of these parents eventually move to America to join their parents, a host of difficult readjustment issues come to the fore. The by-products of these difficult readjustment issues are negative feelings, moodiness, and poor concentration in American schools.

In Pilon's (2007) experience, counseling groups for these students provide a sense of relief, particularly when they see that they are not alone in coping with difficult home adjustment issues. The sharing in these sessions can be intense and quite emotional, and often results in crying. The psychological facilitator needs to display much support, encouragement, sensitivity, and compassion in order to be effective in working with this vulnerable population. A brief summary of the objectives and content of group counseling sessions for newcomer students, as discussed in Pilon (2007), is provided in Sidebar 9.6.

⌂ Sidebar 9.6   Content of Group Counseling Sessions for Newcomer Immigrant Students at Belmont High School Newcomer Center, Los Angeles Unified Schools

Counseling groups at the Newcomer Center (consisting of 8 to 12 students) meet for six sessions led by the bilingual school psychologist. The school psychologist guides participants through discussions involving the sharing of personal experiences and home and family issues, as well as their reactions and adjustment to American life and culture. According to Pilon (2007), the primary objective of group counseling for newcomers is to "reduce each student's sense of isolation and self-doubt stemming from the difficulties they have experienced in coming to [America], and replacing these feelings with pride and motivation to make their sacrifices pay off" (p. 10). In the course of the counseling sessions, students are encouraged to set academic goals and learn about vital information that would help them to advance their academic careers and aspirations. The essential content and related procedures involved in the six counseling sessions are briefly described below:

Session One

    I. *Explanation of rules for group functioning* (i.e., assuring students that they are free to discuss all aspects of their immigration experience; parameters for confidentiality; procedures for taking turns; prohibition of eating, earphones, rudeness, etc.)

    II. *General discussion of the immigrant experience* (i.e., what the word "immigration" means; history of U.S. immigration)

    III. *Ice-breaker exercise* (e.g., facilitator and students introduce themselves, state their country of origin; each student shares one special talent/quality they possess; facilitator uses a map to discuss each country represented in the group)

Sessions Two–Five

    I. *In-depth student interviews* (here, each student is given an opportunity to share with the group more in-depth information about his or her immigration-related experiences; other students use and develop interviewing skills with their peers)

    II. *Facilitator-led mini-lessons* (where appropriate, the facilitator educates students on the variety of personal reactions to immigration, family issues related to immigration, and facets of American culture)

    III. *Group processing of important feelings/concerns:*
        A. Culture shock
        B. Ambivalence about life in the United States
        C. "I want to go home!"
        D. Abandonment issues
        E. Conflicted feelings of disloyalty to, and worry about, relatives back home
        F. Resentment toward parents
        G. Doubts regarding ability to learn English and succeed academically
        H. American dating practices
        I. Fear of gangs
        J. Drug and alcohol use
        K. Getting along with half siblings and step-parents
        L. Legal issues related to domestic violence and child abuse

(*continued*)

Session Six

    I. *Group reflection/summarization* of content/issues discussed in previous lessons (e.g., stresses living in more dangerous neighborhoods; how to handle boredom; problems in getting along with parents; adjustment issues involved with undocumented immigration status)

    II. *Facilitator provides direct teaching* that helps students plan for their future (e.g., the importance of a high school degree; college entrance requirements; how to apply for college scholarships; career/salary opportunities)

    III. *Wrap-up exercise* (here, each student is given an opportunity to share the story or person in the group that made the most impact on them; students are given information about how to refer themselves for individual counseling both within and outside the school setting)

(Adapted from Pilon, 2007).

According to Pilon (2007), newcomer counseling groups are widely recognized by staff, parents, and students as quite effective for integrating immigrant students into American high schools. The emotional bonds that newcomers develop toward others who share their immigration experiences, combined with each student's goal of improving his or her life through education, makes these students highly receptive for receiving school orientation information. According to Pilon (2007), teachers often observe that—as a result of their participation in these newcomer counseling groups—students are calmer, more communicative, and their confidence increases as a result of this intervention. Parents of newcomers express relief and appreciation that their children have been given a safe forum in which to vent their feelings and experiences.

Indirect Services

School psychologists have opportunities to help school districts serve newcomers in more indirect ways. These methods for helping are not limited to the specific expertise of school psychologists only, and some indirect methods can be arguably judged to lie outside typical or traditional roles for school psychologists. Nevertheless, it is hoped that a simple awareness of school districts' needs and challenges in successfully serving newcomers can spur new opportunities for the practice of school psychology in vulnerable districts. Opportunities for service are briefly described as follows.

Improving Schools' Communication to Immigrants

Gershberg, Danenberg, and Sánchez (2004) interviewed elementary/middle school principals and district officials in five of the largest districts in the state of California

(Fresno, Long Beach, Los Angeles, San Diego, and San Francisco) noted for hosting approximately 24 percent of recent immigrant students in the state. According to Gershberg et al. (2004), immigrant families find that navigating the school system on behalf of their children can be overwhelming. The schools' inadequate translation of basic school documents and important school notices represents a major obstacle for immigrant families. Specifically, immigrant families require assistance understanding (a) school enrollment procedures, (b) choices available for both schools and language programs, (c) their basic rights to educational and other related services, and (d) the causes and potential consequences inherent in school disciplinary actions (Gershberg et al., 2004). Gershberg et al. (2004) also found that the training of front office nonteaching staff significantly determines the amount and quality of guidance that immigrant parents receive. Unfortunately, Gershberg et al. (2004) found few instances where any formal policies were in place for how nonteaching front office staff interact with immigrant families—nor were there opportunities for such staff to be properly trained.

School psychologists can work with teachers early in the school year to identify a parent or school aide who can assist the school in rapidly translating important school documents before they are sent to students' homes. If the school psychologist is ambitious, he or she can assist districts in compiling a database of employees in the district who speak various languages, which may include individuals from nearby universities and political advocacy groups in the state (Gershberg et al., 2004). Gershberg et al. (2004) opine that "[t]he impact of a newcomer who speaks an uncommon language on a small district could be overwhelming in the absence of such a database" (pp. 90–91). Even though districts may have elaborate translation databases in place, it could take several months before appropriate translation services are available. The site school psychologist can facilitate the securing of these services more quickly with a little advance planning and coordination.

Facilitating School/Home Face Time

Gershberg et al. (2004) found that most school personnel interviewed recognized that immigrant families' home workloads significantly undermined their participation in their children's education. As a result, schools that desire to reach out to immigrant parents must seriously consider making more frequent and regular home visits—or alternatively provide bus transportation for parents to visit the school.

Some states provide funding for school district staff to visit places where the parents of newcomer students are most likely to be found, which sometimes consists of agricultural fields or motels. In most cases, such state funding is the only incentive for school staff to visit homes after school hours and/or on weekends. There is a role for school psychologists to play in helping districts to access sources of funding, assisting in writing grant proposals to access needed funds, or possibly accompanying teachers on home visits.

Many districts have a parent coordinator, parent liaison, or home-school liaison whose job is to promote better communication between the schools and parents and increase parental involvement at a variety of levels. These individuals are sometimes certified teachers, while others are immigrants from countries with significant representation in the school district. Parent liaisons help with translating school notices for immigrant parents, brokering effective meetings between parents and school staff, and helping parents understand ways in which they can become involved in their children's schooling. It is imperative that school psychologists develop close relationships with parent liaisons, who are invaluable for facilitating school psychologists' direct and indirect services to newcomer and immigrant families.

Cultural Gaps in Expectations of Parenting and Parent/School Involvement

School officials interviewed noted a profound disconnect between American educators' expectations for parental participation in schools versus immigrant families' cultural attitudes toward this issue. That is, American educators typically value parental input on school parent/teacher councils, where parents feel free to give their input on school matters. In contrast, most immigrant parents come from cultural traditions that entrust the education of their children fully to professional teachers, and it is considered inappropriate to presume equal status with teachers' expertise in educational matters. As a result of these different expectations, schools find that they must be intentional and creative in designing supports for parents to feel empowered to participate comfortably in formal or informal parent/teacher collaborations.

To be blunt, many of the difficulties schools face in increasing parental involvement is a direct outgrowth of the undocumented status of many parents. Although schools are required to serve undocumented immigrants and not play any role in federal immigration investigations (see Sidebar 9.4), many parents are simply unaware that schools have no connection or obligation to the Immigration and Naturalization Service (INS). As a result, undocumented parents are terrified that someone from the school is going to discover their status and report them to the INS. Because undocumented families do not want to draw attention to themselves, they tend to drag their feet in accessing needed federal and/or state social services (Gershberg et al., 2004). As one of many examples of this fear, one principal interviewed by Gershberg et al. (2004) related the story of a child who was hurt on the playground and needed to go to the hospital, but the parents did not have MediCal because they feared what the application process would reveal.

There may be instances where there is a need for school personnel to serve as intermediaries between immigrant parents and state child protective services agencies in instances in which cultural differences play a key role in miscommunication and mis-understandings. For example, Gershberg et al. (2004) interviewed an elementary school principal who was concerned about the home disciplinary practices of Somali families, which tend to be more physical and punitive compared to American practices. The principal was concerned that these families were vulnerable to Child Protective Services intervention if no effort was made to at least expose these families to more effective home discipline practices. If these kinds of issues are salient in school districts, the school psychologist can be quite useful in helping to coordinate parenting classes that can provide an informal forum for discussion of a variety of useful methods for administering discipline and child management at home. To quote Gershberg et al. (2004), "[t]hese are turbulent waters that schools must navigate with care" (p. 90).

Ad Hoc Practices to Assist Immigrants in Schools and Classrooms Lacking Newcomer Programs

For whatever reason, many districts do not have separate newcomer programs and must rely on existing resources to help integrate new immigrants into schools. For example, many schools require immigrant newcomers to enroll in existing bilingual education or English immersion programs. Some schools employ instructional assistants, who give primary language support to all English-language learners (including newcomer immi-grants) for a specified number of hours per day. Other schools assign a "peer partner" to immigrant newcomers, whose job is to help newcomers understand classroom procedures and school culture. Sometimes these peer partners help translate new immigrants' class written assignments to English for the teacher. In turn, the teacher may award extra credit to these partners for the work they do in helping new immigrants (Gershberg et al., 2004).

Gershberg et al. (2004) found that partnering newcomer students with a more experienced classmate is a common practice within school districts. Teachers with experience with this practice attempt to select a student mentor who is mature, kind in temperament, patient, and who cares about the academic progress of their mentee. Unfortunately, some mentors use their translating duties as an excuse for not com-plying with other required assignments in the classroom. The authors state "[m]ore research is needed about the effects of [student mentoring/translation] practices" (p. 77). The school psychologist can assist teachers who may need help in selecting suitable student mentors for newcomer students, and can possibly provide direct sup-port and encouragement to these mentors as they work with newcomers. In addition, school psychology graduate students in nearby training programs can also assist site school psychologists in conducting research on the effects of student mentors on the adjustment of newcomers.

ADDITIONAL RESOURCES

Websites

Supports for Teen Mothers in Schools

CAL-SAFE Program Directory: http://www.cde.ca.gov/ls/cg/pp/calsafedirectory.asp

Fort Worth ISD Project Prevail: http://fortworthisd.granicus.com/MediaPlayer.php?view_id=2&clip_id=35 (promotional video)

Living for the Young Family Through Education (LYFE) Program Directory: http://schools.nyc.gov/Documents/MISC/FINAL%20LYFE%20directory%2009.02.09.pdf

Miami-Dade Teen Parent Program: http://www.miamidade.gov/socialservices/teenage-parent.asp

Round Rock Independent School District Teen Parent Program: http://schools.roundrockisd.org/teenparentprogram/index.html

Support for Immigrants in Schools

CELLA Document links, including CELLA testing site: http://bilingual.dadeschools.net/BEWL/cella.asp

Comprehensive English Language Learning Assessment (CELLA): http://www.awschooltest.com/photos/CELLA_Brochure_v2.pdf

Miami-Dade County Public Schools *New Beginning Program*: http://bilingual.dadeschools.net/BEWL/pdfs/NB_registration_10-11.pdf (registration packet)

Steinhardt School of Culture, Education, and Human Development Immigration Studies: http://www.academicwebpages.com/preview/pathways/towardsyouth/index.html

CHAPTER

10

❧

Where Do We Go From Here?

Perhaps the most disturbing aspect of contemporary education is the extent to which the very process of testing ideas and procedures by their actual results has been superseded by a process of testing them by their consonance with existing preconceptions about education and society.

(Sowell, 1986, p. 36)[1]

This quote captures, in a succinct nutshell, the central discovery of the research and practices discussed in this book. As observed in the real world, some minority children do well in school, and some do not. Knowing the ethnic/racial status of a student, by itself, provides absolutely no useful information about the factors responsible for these differences. That is, the conditions responsible for disproportionate psychoeducational difficulties experienced by individuals within certain ethnic subgroups—as well as the interventions applied by teachers, schools, and school districts to effectively address these problems—have precious little to do with prescriptions originating from Quack Multiculturalism (as it has been traditionally sold to school psychology audiences). Never before has an ideology been promoted so endlessly in school psychology, yet has contributed so little to helping real "flesh and blood" minority children in real-world educational settings.

In fact, effective practices for minority children *have much more in common with basic common sense than they have with abstract multicultural theories.* Most (but certainly not all)

---

[1]Originally published in Sowell, T. (1976). "Patterns of black excellence," *The Public Interest, 43,* 57. Reproduced with permission from National Affairs.

school districts know this intuitively. However, those in academia who are farthest removed from real-world practice, for a variety of reasons, continue to be enamored with theories that sound good—yet have no empirical support or basis in reality. In order to propose a credible direction for how training in school psychology (and related professions) can better prepare future practitioners for serving the psychoeducational needs of minority children, it is first necessary to understand where the profession currently stands—and what needs to happen—in order to make significant progress.

THE CURRENT STATE OF AFFAIRS VIS-À-VIS MULTICULTURAL ISSUES

Over three decades, this author has been exposed to colleagues, students, and professionals in many different states, either in the capacity of a graduate student, a school-based practitioner, a national/state conference attendee or speaker, or a member of a university's faculty. The tone, climate, and "flavor" of multiculturalism ideology—as it is manifested in national/state professional organizations, school psychology training programs, students' attitudes, and working conditions in schools—is influenced by a host of interlocking variables, as depicted in Figure 10.1.

In the material that follows, the manner in which multiculturalism ideology is promoted at all levels of school psychology—beginning with professional organizations, down to training programs, to graduate students in training programs, concluding with practice within individual school districts—is briefly described. Although this material is geared specifically to the profession of school psychology, the multicultural dynamics discussed are also common to a wide variety of applied education and psychology professions.

National/State Professional Organizations

The primary objectives of professional organizations are to serve as a central clearing-house for new developments in the field, promote the legislative interests of their constituencies, and develop/monitor professional standards for training programs and public practice. However, they are also political organizations. As political entities, national/state professional organizations must be attuned to the current political winds in order to ensure that any official positions that are adopted come down on the politically correct side of current trends. This enables them to maintain smooth, mutually beneficial working relationships with outside organizations, as well as reduce tensions and promote harmony among subgroups within the organization.

Viewed in this light, it takes no extraordinary degree of courage to endorse and publish position statements with which most other professional organizations can easily agree (e.g., condemning racism, child abuse, or school bullying). In the same vein, it comes as no surprise that the current trend in contemporary professional organizations

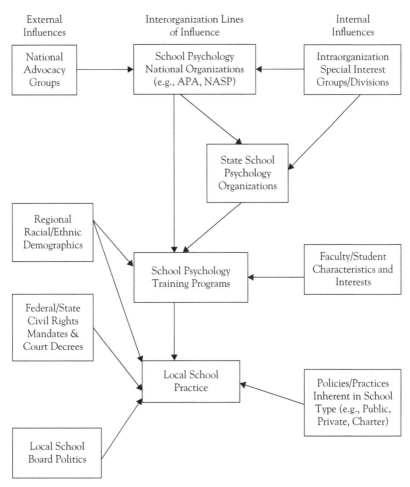

Figure 10.1   Variables Influencing the "Multicultural Tone" of School Psychology Organizations, Training, and Practice

representing teachers, psychologists, school counselors, and school administrators is to promote multiculturalism as their unofficial/official ideology.

As described in Chapter 2, the rationale for multiculturalism advocacy in NASP and APA stems from the belief (whether real or imagined) that minority groups are under-served by professional psychologists, or are culturally "misunderstood" by non-minority professionals (which presumably leads to lower-quality services). The hope is that once a professional organization can officially mandate multicultural advocacy as a condition for approval and accreditation of training programs, then this will magically translate into increased and/or better services to, and positive outcomes for, underserved groups.

An organization's position statements and policy proposals are internally debated over long periods of time, particularly within organizations comprising a dizzying array of special interest subgroups (e.g., APA divisions and committees). Proposals for multicultural service guidelines must survive a veritable gauntlet of internal political maneuvering, endless debates, discussions, and revisions. The end result of this process are vague generalities that appease, and avoid giving offense to, the political sensibilities of influential multicultural advocacy groups within the organization. In short, multicultural guidelines are most often determined by a *political process*, and are not necessarily a natural outgrowth of findings from empirical research and/or case studies. *The intent of some multicultural guidelines for practitioners is to support practices or viewpoints that are consistent with multiculturalism ideology, not necessarily to promote practices that have actually been demonstrated to help minority children.* Training programs are then left to their own devices for operationalizing multicultural guidelines the best way they can, absent clear and specific guidance from their professional organizations.

As an example, Rogers et al. (1999) discuss efforts to update the APA *Guidelines for Providers of Psychological Services to Ethnic, Cultural, and Linguistically Diverse Populations* (American Psychological Association, 1993) to address school psychology practice issues in schools. These guidelines cover six domains, one of which addresses legal and ethical issues. Within this domain, one recommendation for practice states:

> Psychologists working in the schools are cognizant of major legislation and litigation regarding bilingual education and English as a second language (ESL) programs, are familiar with the ways that bilingual education and ESL programs are implemented in the schools, and are aware of the effectiveness of different models of bilingual education and ESL programs. (Rogers et al., 1999, p. 246)

One cannot help but wonder, however, how school psychologists are supposed to apply this guideline to the "politically incorrect" observation that some non-English speakers actually begin to *thrive* when they are required to speak and learn in English only (see Sidebar 10.1). Because multiculturalism ideology is the silent inspiration behind such professional guidelines, school psychologists are highly unlikely to be exposed to articles like the one depicted in Sidebar 10.1.

Sidebar 10.1   The Bilingual Ban That Worked

The following passages are excerpted in part from Heather MacDonald, "The Bilingual Ban That Worked," *City Journal*, 19(4). Reprinted with permission from *City Journal*.

Before Proposition 227 got rid of them, bilingual classes were taught mostly in Spanish. In 1998, Californians voted to pass Proposition 227, the "English for the Children Act," and dismantle the state's bilingual-education industry. The results, according to California's education establishment, were not supposed to look like this: button-cute Hispanic pupils at a Santa Ana elementary school boasting about their English skills to a visitor. Those same pupils cheerfully calling out to their principal on their way to lunch: "Hi, Miss Champion!" A statewide increase in English proficiency among all Hispanic students.

Instead, warned legions of educrats, eliminating bilingual education in California would demoralize Hispanic students and widen the achievement gap. Unless Hispanic children were taught in Spanish, the bilingual advocates moaned, they would be unable to learn English or to succeed in other academic subjects.

California's electorate has been proved right: Hispanic test scores on a range of subjects have risen since Prop. 227 became law. But while the curtailment of California's bilingual-education industry has removed a significant barrier to Hispanic assimilation, the persistence of a Hispanic academic underclass suggests the need for further reform.

The counterintuitive linguistic claims behind bilingual education were always a fig leaf covering a political agenda. The 1960s Chicano rights movement ("Chicano" refers to Mexican-Americans) asserted that the American tradition of assimilation was destroying not just Mexican-American identity but also Mexican-American students' capacity to learn. Teaching these students in English rather than in Spanish hurt their self-esteem and pride in their culture, Chicano activists alleged: hence the high drop-out rates, poor academic performance, and gang involvement that characterized so many Mexican-American students in the Southwest. . . . The role of American schools, according to this nascent ideology, became the preservation of the Spanish language and Mexican culture for Mexican-origin U.S. residents.

Novel linguistic theories arose to buttress this political platform. Children could not learn a second language well unless they were already fully literate in their native tongue, the newly minted bilingual-ed proponents argued. To teach English to a five-year-old who spoke Spanish at home, you had to instruct him in Spanish for several more years, until he had mastered Spanish grammar and spelling. . . . Such ad hoc justifications rested on shaky scientific ground. Psycholinguistics research supports what generations of immigrants experienced firsthand: the younger you are when you tackle a second language, the greater your chances of achieving full proficiency. Children who learn a second language early in life may even process it in the same parts of the brain that process their first language, an advantage lost as they age.

(continued)

Only one justification for bilingual education made possible sense. The bilingual theorists maintained that children should be taught academic content—physics, say, or history—in their home language, lest they fall behind their peers in their knowledge of subject matter. But this argument applied most forcefully where bilingual education has always been the rarest: in high school, where, one would hope, teachers use relatively sophisticated concepts. In the earliest grades, however, where bilingual education has always been concentrated, academic content is predominantly learning a language—how to read and write B-A-T, for example. Moreover, most Hispanic children who show up in American elementary school have subpar Spanish skills to begin with, so teaching them in Spanish does not provide a large advantage over English in conveying knowledge about language—or anything else. . . .

In 1965, just as the [bilingual education] movement was getting under way in the United States, the Canadian province of Quebec decided that not enough Quebecois children were learning French. It instituted the most efficient method for overcoming that deficit: immersion. Young English-speaking students started spending their school days in all-French classes, emerging into English teaching only after having absorbed French. By all accounts, the immersion schools have been successful. And no wonder: the simple insight of immersion is that the more one practices a new language, the better one learns it. . . .

McGill professor Genesee—who opposed Prop. 227 in 1998, [argues that] . . . if you start American Hispanics off in English . . . "they won't want to speak Spanish" because it is a "stigmatized, low-prestige language." Genesee's argument exposes the enduring influence of Chicano political activism on academic bilingual theory. Hispanic students do risk losing their home tongue when taught in the majority language. Such linguistic oblivion has beset second- and third-generation immigrants throughout American history—not because of the relative status of their home languages but simply because of the power of language immersion and the magnetic force of the public culture. . . .

Bilingual education was the activists' primary weapon in fighting assimilation because, as they rightly understood, English-language teaching is a powerful tool for encouraging assimilation. In a country as diverse as the United States, fluency in the common tongue is an essential bond among citizens, and the experience of learning it alongside classmates of different ethnic origins reinforces the message that Americans share a common culture. Bilingual-ed proponents often accuse immersion advocates of opposing multilingualism or wanting to stamp out Spanish. This is nonsense. But it is true that maintaining students' home language for the sake of strengthened ethnic identity is not part of a school's mandate. Its primary language duty, rather, is to ensure that citizens can understand one another and participate in democracy.

Despite its conceptual contradictions, bilingual education spread inexorably through the federal and state education bureaucracies. . . . In 1968, Congress passed the Bilingual Education Act, which provided federal funds for bilingual teaching. When not enough school districts applied for the funds, advocacy groups sued, claiming that the districts were violating Hispanic children's civil rights. The federal Department of Education agreed, issuing rules in 1975 that penalized schools for not establishing bilingual programs for their non-English-speaking students. Though the Reagan administration cut back on several bilingual-education mandates from the Ford and Carter years, the federal bilingual bureaucracy remained firmly entrenched for decades.

In California, which contains the vast majority of the country's so-called English learners—students from homes where a language other than English is regularly spoken—the rise of the bilingual machine was swift and decisive. The 1976 Chacon-Moscone Bilingual-Bicultural Education Act declared that bilingual education was the right of every English learner. Elementary schools had to provide native-language instruction if they enrolled a certain number of English learners; bilingual education in the lower grades became the default mode for anyone with a Hispanic surname. . . . Even after Governor George Deukmejian refused to reauthorize the Chacon-Moscone bill in 1987, the bilingual establishment in Sacramento continued to enforce the law's mandates. The state's department of education sponsored numerous conferences and reports alleging that bilingual education was necessary for Hispanic success and showered an additional $5,000 a year on bilingual teachers. Administrators and teachers in heavily Hispanic areas often saw themselves as part of the Chicano empowerment movement. "You weren't worthwhile if you didn't speak Spanish," recalls a Santa Ana teacher. "The attitude was: 'No one should teach our kids but native language speakers.'" . . .

Many low-skilled native Spanish speakers were lured into the education profession by the generous stipends available to bilingual teachers, but they didn't speak English well enough to make the transition into English teaching. English instruction, when it happened at all, was

(continued)

haphazard and unsystematic, recalls Jane Barboza, director of Student Support Services for the Green Dot Charter Schools. "It was left to the end of the day or to the playground. You'd sing 'Old MacDonald,' accompanied by a guitar," she says. Jose Hernandez, the elementary education coordinator for District Six in the Los Angeles Unified School District, admits: "We never implemented bilingual education with the idea of moving kids into English; we weren't great at delivering the dual-language aspect of it."

Such problems were not lost on parents. In 1996, a group of them in the Ninth Street Elementary School in downtown L.A. tried to remove their children from all-Spanish classes and place them in English immersion. When their letters and petitions produced no response, 63 families, organized by poverty advocate Alice Callahan, pulled their children out of classes in protest. The school was jeopardizing their children's futures by not teaching them English, these poor Central American garment workers maintained. Case in point: after six years in Ninth Street's "bilingual" program, reported Jill Stewart in *New Times LA*, a fifth-grader wrote the following passage for his English class: "I my parens per mi in dis shool en I so feol essayrin too old in the shool my border o reri can grier das mony putni gire and I sisairin aliro sceer." . . .

The Ninth Street boycott caught the attention of Silicon Valley software entrepreneur Ron Unz. Stunned to learn that schools were imprisoning children in Spanish classes against their parents' will, Unz, along with Santa Ana teacher Gloria Mata Tuchman, drafted a ballot initiative that mandated that all children be taught "overwhelmingly" in English and integrated into mainstream classes, following one year of specialized English instruction. Waivers for bilingual education would be granted only on an individual basis, following a parental request and a school certification that the child had "special . . . needs" that made a bilingual setting more appropriate. Unz could not refrain from an ironic jab at bilingual theory: "All children in California public schools shall be taught English by being taught in English," announced the English for the Children Act.

The national bilingual-education establishment reacted with fury. Unz was a nativist who wanted to eradicate Spanish and drive out immigrants, it charged. Dismantling bilingual education would put "generations at risk," as the title of a 1998 educrat conference convened by the University of California at Riverside proclaimed. . . .

The establishment pointed to studies that showed that bilingual education produced better results than English immersion—and it still points to them whenever challenged. But according to Russell Gersten, an expert in educational-research design, most evaluations in the bilingual-ed field are "poorly constructed and utterly unpersuasive, consisting of makeshift, descriptive research open to multiple interpretations." Manhattan Institute senior fellow Jay Greene conducted a meta-analysis of the extant studies in 1998. After winnowing out the vast majority on quality grounds, he found a slight edge to bilingual education in conveying academic content. But the programs he reviewed were irrelevant to California's version of bilingual education, Greene says: "Most were highly resource-intensive pilot programs from the 1960s that resembled French écoles or Jewish day schools. They attracted high-quality teachers and were accountable for results." Furthermore, most comparisons of bilingual and immersion methods have an inherent bias, since bilingual regimes exempt the lowest-performing English learners from taking tests in English until the teacher deems them ready, whereas immersion regimes test a far greater percentage of English learners.

The establishment marshaled President Bill Clinton and California's political elite from both parties against Prop. 227. Unions lined up in opposition. The California Teachers Association contributed $2.1 million to defeat the initiative; the American Federation of Labor also pitched in. . . .

The vote wasn't even close. The initiative passed, 61 to 39 percent. Though pre-election polls showed 60 percent of Latinos supporting Prop. 227, only 37 percent voted for it in the end. Many may have been moved at the last minute by claims that the measure was anti-immigrant.

Lawsuits to invalidate or water down 227 began the day after the vote and have continued ever since. Outside the courthouse, efforts to torpedo the initiative were hardly more subtle. The Los Angeles County Office of Education ruled that teaching "overwhelmingly in English" meant teaching in English for 51 percent of the school day; the Riverside and Vista school districts made that 60 percent. Soliciting waivers from parents to put their children back into bilingual classes became so successful a crusade in some districts that the bilingual teaching load barely budged.

The bureaucratic resistance wasn't able to suppress the good news, however. In Los Angeles, young Hispanic pupils placed in immersion were absorbing spoken English far more quickly than expected and were starting to read and write in English as well, their teachers told the *Los Angeles Times*. The Oceanside school district, on the Pacific coast north of San Diego, became the emblem for the new English immersion. Superintendent Kenneth Noonan, a former bilingual teacher himself and cofounder

(continued)

of the California Association of Bilingual Education, had opposed Prop. 227, but once it passed, he determined that Oceanside would follow the law to the letter. He applied the criteria for granting bilingual waivers strictly and ended up creating no Spanish-taught classes. He then sat back with considerable trepidation and waited. "Trained bilingual teachers started calling me," he says. " 'You've got to see what's happening down here,' they said. I thought: 'I guess it's true, the sky has fallen.' " But when Noonan visited their classrooms, he found that these new converts to immersion were "glowing with a sense of success."

The first four months were difficult, Noonan recalls, but then the students took off. Second-grade test scores in reading rose nearly 100 percent in two years—with the average student moving from California's 13th percentile to its 24th—after staying flat for years. These accomplishments didn't stop protesters from holding candlelight vigils outside the Oceanside school board's offices and from filing federal and state civil rights complaints challenging the district's strict waiver policies. Those complaints were eventually rejected.

Oceanside and its inland neighbor, the Vista Unified School District, formed a natural experiment of sorts. Advocates in Vista actively solicited waivers, and Vista officials granted them to everyone who asked, so that half the eligible students remained in bilingual education. Oceanside's test-score increases from 1998 to 2000 were at least double those of Vista in nearly every grade, reported the *New York Times*, despite the districts' similar English-learner populations—low-income, largely agricultural Spanish speakers. Critics dismissed Oceanside's test-score gains as nothing remarkable. But today, the Vista Unified School District has shrunk its bilingual program to minimal proportions, and its coordinator of English-language development—Matt Doyle, another former bilingual teacher—speaks like an immersion true believer: "Almost all our students come at such an early age that it's the perfect opportunity to develop English."

Two broad observations about the aftermath of Prop. 227 are incontestable. First: despite desperate efforts at stonewalling by bilingual diehards within school bureaucracies, the incidence of bilingual education in California has dropped precipitously—from enrolling 30 percent of the state's English learners to enrolling 4 percent. . . .

Second: California's English learners have made steady progress on a range of tests since 1998. That progress is all the more impressive since school districts can no longer keep their lowest-performing English learners out of the testing process. In 1998, 29 percent of school districts submitted under half of their English learners to the statewide reading and writing test; today, close to 100 percent of the state's English learners participate. Despite this, the performance of English learners has improved significantly, from 10 percent scoring "proficient" or "advanced" (the top two categories) in 2003 to 20 percent in 2009. Similarly, on the English proficiency test given to nonnative speakers, the fraction of English learners scoring as "early advanced" or "advanced" (the top two categories) has increased from 25 percent in 2001, when the test was first administered, to 39 percent this year. If the critics of Prop. 227 have the burden of proof to substantiate their warnings of catastrophe, they clearly haven't met it. . . .

The schools that have abandoned bilingual education have not regretted it. Every school that has done so in Los Angeles's District 6 has improved its rating on California's 800-point Academic Performance Index at least 150 points, says district elementary coordinator Hernandez.

The bilingual industry also argues that Prop. 227 has failed in its mission because the gap between English learners and native English speakers on statewide reading and math tests hasn't closed. . . .

[This] "persistent test-score gap" argument has a more fundamental flaw. California defines English learners as students who are less than fluent in English *and* who occupy the bottom rungs of reading and math achievement. To be reclassified out of English-learner status, a student must score well not just on the test of English proficiency but also on statewide reading and math tests. As soon as a student becomes more capable academically, he leaves the English-learner pool and enters a new category: Reclassified Fluent English Proficient, or RFEP. By fiat, then, the English-learner pool contains only the weakest students, whereas the native-speaker pool contains the entire range of students, from the highest achievers to the lowest. Eliminating the gap between English learners and native speakers (known as "English only" students) is logically impossible. A fairer test of how English learners are performing in relation to English-only speakers would combine English learners and RFEP students into one category and compare them with the English-only students. Yet this the state does not do.

The test-score gap between English learners and English-only students is so large that even narrowing it significantly would take Herculean efforts. In 2003, recall, 10 percent of English learners scored "proficient" or above in a statewide reading and writing test. By 2009, 20 percent of them did, a 100 percent improvement. During the same time, English-only students improved their performance on the same test only 32 percent,

(continued)

from 44 percent proficient or above to 58. The gap between the two groups nevertheless grew from 34 to 38 percentage points, because gains in the English-only category started from such a higher base level than those of the English learners.

Notwithstanding the complexities and inadequacies of the data and the persistence of the achievement gap, the steady advance of English learners on both English proficiency and academic tests vindicates Prop. 227. . . .

Prop. 227 changed the debate in California; widespread bilingual education is no longer on the agenda. To be sure, some die-hard districts are quietly trying to increase Spanish-language classes without attracting attention, but they are in the minority. In public, the bilingual industry finds itself reduced to fighting rearguard actions, such as demanding NCLB tests in Spanish or separate textbooks (in English) for English learners. . . .

And the transformation in the classroom has to be seen to be believed. It is extraordinary, for example, to observe elementary school teachers in Santa Ana, once a bastion of bilingual education, talking to their young Hispanic students exclusively in English about the Great Wall of China. It is just as extraordinary to see those students eagerly raising their hands to read English workbooks aloud in class. The main sign that the students are not native English speakers is an occasional reminder about past-tense formation or the pronunciation of word endings, but plenty of English-only speakers in the state need such assistance, too. Schools are not universally following the time frame set out in Prop. 227: a year of separate instruction in English followed by integration with English-only students. In some schools, English learners remain cloistered for a longer period. But regardless of classroom composition, English learners *are* being taught "overwhelmingly in English," which is the most important goal of 227.

Self-esteem seems fine. "I didn't know how to speak English in first grade," says a husky fourth-grade boy at Adams Elementary School in Santa Ana. "I just figured out at the end of the year and talked all English." The boy's classmates, who are sitting next to him at a picnic table under a pepper tree for lunch, jostle to get in on the interview. They are fluent in schoolyard insults. "He's a special ed!" one boy says of another. "I am not a special ed, you liar!" retorts the target. The fifth-grade girls at a table nearby complain that the boys are lazy. A slender girl has recently arrived from Mexico. Her translator for that day, a tiny blue-eyed girl named Lily, drapes her arm lovingly around the new immigrant and will sit next to her in all their classes, explaining what the teacher is saying. The pair and their fellow pupils amble back into the school after lunch, any signs of psychological distress well concealed. No one reports unhappiness at speaking English in class; on the contrary, they brag that it's easy.

Such students are clearly better off liberated from California's inept version of bilingual education. But though test scores have risen, the educational situation for Hispanics remains troubling. Bilingual ed has come and gone, but the conditions that provided the pretext for it— Hispanics' low academic achievement, high drop-out rates, and gang involvement—live on.

Some multicultural advocates candidly admit that there is absolutely no data that gives training programs any guidance whatsoever for how to translate multicultural guidelines from professional organizations to practice in the field (e.g., Robinson-Zanartu, Butler-Byrd, Cook-Morales, Dauphinais, & Charley, 2011). To its credit, NASP has recognized this problem and has attempted to address it by producing and marketing an instructional video entitled *Portraits of the Children: Culturally Competent Assessment*. According to the NASP webpage (http://www.nasponline.org/resources/culturalcompetence/B%20&%20W%20flyer%201-29-04.pdf) that advertises this product, the video

> provides schools with the tools to look at each child individually and carefully examine what are the real issues that impact their ability to learn. It encourages educators to develop a system that allows them to work effectively in a diverse, cross-cultural setting. This multi-media professional development resource package is specifically designed to provide viewers with the background information and effective practice techniques necessary in order to provide culturally competent assessment for special education eligibility.

The video includes vignettes of four children, each representing various degrees of cultural differences, interspersed with interviews with educators involved in all phases of determining these children's eligibility for special education. This author contacted a school psychologist acquaintance who bought this tape for her district. The psychologist stated that, after one viewing, the tape has been relegated to collecting dust on a shelf— as it was found to be of little use to school psychologists in the district.

In all fairness to NASP, this represents only one isolated anecdote, as a larger sample of persons who have bought this tape have not been scientifically surveyed as to their reactions. Nevertheless, this anecdote perfectly illustrates a crucial point made in Chapter 1. That is, *minority students are not kitchen appliances that come equipped with a multicultural instruction manual.* Abstract multicultural theory does not often translate smoothly to the real world. Practitioners who want to be educated about multicultural issues must first learn about a variety of factors that affect school outcomes. As many have no doubt discovered, a professional organization can only issue guidelines that deal in the broadest of generalities. It is up to individual training programs to decide which specific resources and strategies are most useful for preparing students to serve vulnerable minority populations in schools. Even after they leave their training programs, it takes time for new professionals to develop the skills, experience, and clinical acumen to flexibly apply their knowledge and modify their services to the unique *individual characteristics and needs* of clients in specific settings.

School Psychology Training Programs

According to NASP, approximately 200 school psychology training programs exist in the United States (http://www.nasponline.org/certification/becoming.aspx). There is considerable diversity in where these programs are housed (i.e., departments of education versus departments of psychology), as well as their training emphases. Some programs are informally referred to as "practitioner programs"—meaning that less emphasis is placed on preparing researchers and more emphasis is placed on learning concrete skill sets that can be applied to school settings. Other programs emphasize training graduates to be effective consumers and producers of research. Programs also differ considerably in how they approach and incorporate multiculturalism ideology. These factors are briefly described in the following sections.

Program Geographic Location

The program's geographic location within the United States, and the demographic makeup of surrounding communities, has a significant degree of influence on the content of multicultural information to which students are exposed. For example, a program located near vibrant Native American communities will, by necessity, include a greater awareness of, and intentional emphasis on, Native Americans. Similarly, a program located in close physical proximity to urban black communities will understandably include practicum experiences in which students are more regularly exposed to these groups.

General Approach/Attitudes Toward Multiculturalism

Nearly all training programs have to engage in at least a minimum degree of Bean-Counting Multiculturalism (see Chapter 2) in order to remain in good graces with national program approval and accreditation bodies. Nevertheless, programs differ considerably in their general approach and attitudes toward multiculturalism ideology. Some programs readily acknowledge that almost nothing in their program model addresses multicultural issues, and they include only the bare minimum requirements necessary to please national accreditation bodies to which they are accountable. Other programs make a concerted effort to include multicultural content and experiences in their training, but the depth of analysis goes no deeper than Kumbayah or Light-and-Fluffy Multiculturalism (see Chapter 2). Other programs consider themselves to be "multicultural-friendly" programs, only because they admit a larger than usual number of racial/ethnic minority students, or because they make a concerted effort to saturate their training with multiculturally themed publications and topics. A few programs gain reputations for being "multicultural specialty" programs. These programs serve geographic areas that naturally attract higher numbers of racial/ethnic minority students, or such programs receive special training grants to train bilingual school psychologists in serving primarily Hispanic children and families (e.g., www.nasponline.org/publications/cq/mocq344multiculturalspot.aspx).

Faculty Interests

On one end of the continuum, there are program faculty who have little to no interest in multicultural issues, and do no research and writing on multicultural topics. At the opposite end of the spectrum are faculty who devote most of their professional careers to research and writing about multicultural issues. Complicating matters is the fact that faculty research interests may or may not translate directly to what students are taught within the program. Even though a faculty member may conduct extensive research on multicultural issues, students in the program may have only a cursory exposure to this research.

Program Climate for Dealing With Controversial Issues

An intangible, but no less real, quality of training programs concerns the freedom with which controversial multicultural topics are aired, discussed, and researched. Due to a variety of contributing factors, some programs are characterized by a free, open, and unfettered exchange of a full range of ideas, without fear of disapproval, criticism, or reprisal. Other programs consider some multicultural topics to be too "radioactive," and hence they are terrified of openly discussing such topics seriously for fear of giving offense. On the opposite end of the continuum, some training programs are little more than indoctrination centers for Quack Multiculturalism. Here, activist program faculty view their position as a platform from which they can indoctrinate students in advocacy for their pet sociopolitical agendas. In these programs, both students and faculty understand implicitly that certain opinions/attitudes toward controversial multicultural topics are off-limits, while other opinions/attitudes are rewarded. In these programs, opinions/attitudes that deviate substantially from those that are expected will be negatively sanctioned in some regard.

Playing the "Fair and Balanced Game"

There are wide individual differences with which program faculty are or are not comfortable in dealing with "radioactive" multicultural issues in their respective areas of expertise. Some faculty simply ignore or avoid discussing topics with which they are not comfortable. Other faculty have no problem openly discussing these topics or publicly endorsing an empirically supported position that may not be politically popular with students or colleagues.

A third group of faculty attempt to straddle the fence when faced with a situation where they privately endorse a controversial position that is substantially supported by empirical research, yet fear negative reactions from publicly supporting the position in front of students. When faced with this situation, many faculty play the *fair and balanced game*. Here, faculty will include articles supporting the controversial topic in their syllabi (i.e., the position with which they privately agree), but they will also include articles taking an opposing but more politically palatable position (i.e., the position with which they privately disagree). This is presented to students as a "fair and balanced exposure to all sides of the issue." Students read and discuss the articles representing both sides, and then are encouraged to decide for themselves which side they personally prefer. This fair and balanced game allows the faculty member to expose students to the unpopular idea (even though it has more substantial empirical support), yet provide an psychological "escape hatch" that allows some students to reject the idea if it is too emotionally painful to accept. Through this process, the faculty member avoids potentially upsetting students, and gains a reputation as being fair and balanced.

Students

Students come in all personality types, temperaments, and backgrounds. Yet professional organizations are under the naïve impression that requiring training programs to infuse multiculturalism ideology into course content will mold students into ways of thinking and feeling that conform to how professional organizations imagine that they should think and feel. This is not the case, for the simple reason that any material to which students are exposed in training is first filtered through their own private experiences, personal backgrounds, and unique psychological characteristics. *Stated simply, not all students process multiculturalism ideology in the same way.* In this author's experience, student attitudes toward multiculturalism ideology cluster into six categories. Although some students may not fit neatly into some of these categories, the full range of student responses to multiculturalism ideology is reflected in the following six archetypes:

- *The Apathetic/Indifferent.* Students who fall into this category couldn't care less about multiculturalism ideology or developing "cultural competence," and they find it difficult to muster any enthusiasm for multicultural initiatives originating from national organizations and promoted through professional training programs. This apathy is not ideology-driven, but can be explained from the fact that multicultural issues/concerns are simply not salient in their background experiences, current lives, and/or future professional goals. In their view, the primary reason for attending a training program is to secure a comfortable job, with comfortable working conditions in a "nice" district, located in a "nice" community, and that pays a comfortable salary. Thus, their enrollment in a professional training program is quite simply a means to secure a comfortable employment lifestyle after graduation. When confronted with multiculturalism or any other sociopolitical ideology in their training program, such students simply "go along to get along"—at least superficially agreeing with whatever they are told and doing whatever is needed to graduate from their programs as quickly and as efficiently as possible.

- *The Guild Loyalists.* Guild loyalists believe that the ultimate and final authority for all matters relating to what they should believe, how they should think, and what attitudes they should adopt, ultimately emanates from the national organizations that oversee their profession (e.g., the American Psychological Association and National Association for School Psychologists). Due partly to youth, naïveté, and the fact that they are in the beginning stages of learning in a new profession, these students hold their professional organizations in awe. That is to say, professional organizations are thought to be always right, never biased, and all-knowing as to what is best for practitioners. From a critical thinking perspective (e.g., see Ruggiero, 2001), Guild Loyalists reason from an *appeal to authority*, which means that policy positions adopted by professional organizations should never be negatively evaluated or challenged. Guild Loyalists would be horrified at the prospect of ignoring—let alone disagreeing with—any multicultural training guidelines that emanate from their professional organizations. Guild Loyalists truly believe that taking "multicultural" classes, being exposed to multicultural content in their training program, or adopting the political attitudes of multicultural special interest groups within these organizations effectively prepares them for achieving "cultural competence." For all practical purposes, these students are relatively unconcerned with questions of whether policy/training initiatives that emanate from professional organizations have any solid research support, or even whether such initiatives make any significant difference in the real world.

- *The Open-Minded.* Some students, because of prior life experiences and/or from personal proclivities, appear to have a natural affinity for, and heartfelt interest in, serving children and families from racial/ethnic/cultural groups that are different from their own. The trait that characterizes these students most accurately is that they are *unafraid*. That is, they are comfortable interacting closely with cultural minority children and families, and they do not fear working in an environment in which they may be a minority. These students are willing to do whatever it takes to gain the trust and cooperation of the clients with whom they work and serve. They do not fear letting their practice be guided by "politically incorrect" research, because, unlike the *True Believers* (see below), they are not fundamentally motivated by a sociopolitical agenda. Although they may work successfully in multicultural environments, they cannot be characterized as multiculturalism ideologues.

- *The Skeptics.* Students characterized as skeptics are those who, for whatever reasons, are not personally persuaded by—and in some cases may actively resist— multiculturalism indoctrination within their training programs. These students often complain, in private to like-minded peers, that multiculturalism is being "crammed down their throats." There are a variety of reasons that may explain this skepticism to multiculturalism. Some students resist multiculturalism on purely empirical grounds, in that they feel that much of what they are taught about multiculturalism in their training programs has flimsy or nonexistent research support. Other students may feel that their personal experiences are not congruent with a so-called "multicultural worldview," and they resent being told that they cannot be good school psychologists if they hold opinions that deviate from the politically correct party line (e.g., see Sidebar 2.1). Some students have a politically conservative (see Glossary) or religious worldview, and they object to the pressure to adopt multicultural doctrines that violate deeply held personal convictions. The extent to which skeptics come to the attention of their training programs is often a function of how effectively they can hide their real views. For example, some skeptics immediately come to the attention of faculty as perceived "problem students," particularly if they are extremely vocal in their opinions and do not fear academic repercussions from peers or faculty. Others will simply keep their contrarian opinions to themselves while in their training programs as a means of "going along to get along."

- *The Tribalists.* Tribalists are primarily racial/ethnic/language minority students who enter school psychology training programs highly sensitized to the educational problems of school children belonging to their own "tribe," or cultural group. Many tribalists enter school psychology training programs believing that, by the time they graduate from their program, they will have developed a special repertoire of skills necessary for helping children and families from their own racial/ethnic subgroup. Hence, they have little to no interest in studying multi-cultural issues affecting groups other than their own. Said another way, their interests are in "my-culturalism," instead of multi-culturalism.

- *The True Believers.* True Believers identify so deeply with multiculturalism ideology, that it is central to their personal and professional identities. To these students, multicultural advocacy is a noble force for "social justice"—akin to the Rebel Alliance's battle against the Evil Empire in the original *Star Wars* movie trilogy. To the True Believers, a multicultural worldview is the only morally acceptable position for their profession to endorse, and any persons holding beliefs or attitudes that deviate from or contradict this view are suspected of having deep-seated character flaws requiring exposure, rebuke, and rehabilitation. True Believers see political activism, rather than patient scholarship, as the more emotionally satisfying route to change. Thus, research that contradicts multiculturalism ideology is simply ignored, and considered secondary to the superior moral good inherent in aggressive multiculturalism advocacy. Although the views of True Believers overlap in some ways with those of the Tribalists, the views of True Believers typically emanate from a broad-based left/progressive worldview, of which multiculturalism ideology is an integral component.

Local School-Based Practice

As discussed in Chapter 4, school settings differ in a wide variety of important ways that impact the education of minority children. For purposes of this specific discussion, school settings differ considerably in the extent to which multiculturalism ideology impacts school psychology roles and functions. For example, integrated school districts are often held hostage by worries over disproportionality statistics, where racial/ethnic imbalances in special education enrollment, graduation rates, suspension/expulsion rates, and gifted program enrollment can earn unwanted attention and/or sanctions from the U.S. Department of Education Office of Civil Rights (e.g., see Pollock, 2008). The underlying reasoning on which disproportionality concerns are based is succinctly summarized by Oswald (2006), who writes:

> The fact that disproportionality is widely viewed as a problem reflects a general belief that the proportion of children who have a disability should be about the same across all race/ethnicity groups. This belief leads to the conclusion that if the proportion for one race/ethnicity group is substantially different from the proportion for another group, then the system for identifying children with disabilities is not working the same way across groups. Further, if identification confers some benefit, or imposes some stigma, then the system is not only

working differently, but it is discriminatory. . . . Most statements about the causes of disproportionality fall under one of these two positions: (a) disproportionality is the result of a system that works in a biased, discriminatory fashion, or (b) disproportionality is the result of social factors that lead to higher rates of disability in some groups. It is common for scholars to maintain that the disproportionality that exists in the U.S. special education system is the result of some combination of these two factors. (p. 1, 6)

Even when readers substitute the terms "are gifted" or "are suspended" for "have a disability," this basic reasoning is the same. Knowledgeable audiences who are undeceived about these matters can readily recognize the 800-pound gorilla that this reasoning takes great pains to ignore—namely, that disproportionality statistics *are, more often than not, the result of real differences*, and not discrimination. Stated bluntly, if black males get suspended at greater rates than Asian females, it is simply because black males display higher rates of school misbehavior than Asian females. Even pious references to "social factors" cannot resolve this problem. If an angry student picks up a chair in the middle of an algebra class and hurls the chair through a window, the terrified teacher couldn't care less what social factors may be responsible for this misbehavior. If school rules stipulate that this behavior warrants instant suspension, then the student is fully deserving of this consequence—regardless of his or her race/ethnicity.

Too often, school psychologists who hold little power/influence in their school districts are under pressure to second-guess their assessment and eligibility decision-making practices in order to bring their judgments more in line with district mandates to equalize outcomes between racial/ethnic groups. In some instances, these directives can correct sloppy practices and improve school psychologists' clinical acumen. In other instances, however, school psychologists are encouraged to violate what they know to be best practice and are forced to resign themselves to adopting racial/ethnic double standards in their work.

FUTURE DIRECTIONS

A four-pronged approach is required in order to make significant progress toward preparing school psychologists and other school pupil service personnel to better serve minority children. This four-pronged approach requires that (1) school psychologists become more discriminating consumers of multicultural content in coursework; (2) students are exposed to more accurate and higher-quality information in training; (3) high-quality research is advertised more efficiently to school psychologists and schools serving minority children; and (4) school psychology audiences are exposed to real-world examples of effective schools for minority children.

School Psychologists Can Become More Discriminating Consumers of Multicultural Content in Coursework

Naïve students, particularly at the beginning of their training programs, are prone to accept uncritically any ideas that they see in print or that are told to them by authority figures. School psychology (and related disciplines) can continue to be hypnotized by multicultural lullabies, or it can smell the coffee and wake up to reality.

Reality has no higher authority to which it is obligated to conform. It is beholden neither to the decrees and opinions of professional organizations, nor to the dictates of politically correct orthodoxy. Reality is not impressed by fancy degrees or professional titles, pretentious-sounding theories, the earnestness and resolve of professional task forces, or millions of dollars poured into the latest social engineering agendas. Reality cares nothing about the prickly sensitivities of special interest groups, the pet agendas of political pressure groups, or the hardened ideological beliefs of political parties. Although clever thinkers throughout history have exerted much effort in convincing themselves (and others) that reality is optional, reality always ends up making a complete mockery of academics' most brilliant theories. *As such, reality will not be denied.* Reality waits quietly and patiently behind the scenes, and inevitably exposes itself at the most inopportune times—often causing embarrassment, pain, denial, and much frustration for those who try desperately (and in vain) to erase it from existence. Whereas social fads come and go with predictable regularity, reality remains constant, intractable, firm, and inescapable.

Quack Multiculturalism: The Road to Nowhere

As long as school psychology (or any other profession) continues to treat multicultural issues *ideologically*, instead of *scientifically and with an awareness of the real world*, the field will continue to wallow in total irrelevancy on these issues. As discussed in Chapter 2, multiculturalism ideology is sold to audiences using three primary philosophical approaches: the *Moral Model*, the *Culture Model*, and the *Social Engineering Model*. Each of these training models is supported by implicit (i.e., unspoken) assumptions, standard templates for how to effect change in individuals, specific ways in which strategies are manifested in education/school psychology, and predictable shortcomings of these change strategies (see Table 10.1). These ideas and practices are endlessly promoted in the applied social science fields, and have been tried but have largely failed to yield tangible, long-term results (see Chapter 2). Yet the assumptions on which these ideas and practices are based are never seriously questioned in a manner befitting rigorous scholarly inquiry. Simple progress can occur if school psychology openly revisits and re-examines four dead-ends that continue to plague the field:

Table 10.1 Three Philosophical Approaches to Training Rooted in Multiculturalism Ideology

Training Model	Underlying Assumptions	Strategies for Change	How Strategies for Change Are Manifested in Education and School Psychology	Shortcomings of Change Strategies
Moral Model	1. Faith in human goodness 2. People can be divided into a "good guy/bad guy" dichotomy. 3. Change comes through moral conversion, or "seeing the light." 4. Successful change depends on changing/modifying attitudes of "bad guys" to become more like the attitudes of the "good guys." 5. Once everyone is on board with the righteous cause, a better world can be realized.	1. Exercises that encourage audiences to feel guilty for their group's past sins and feel sorry for minority groups 2. Audiences are encouraged to do something noble or symbolic so that they can feel good about themselves. 3. "Bad guys" must be shamed into moral conversion through exhortation, ridicule, guilt, and/or intimidation.	1. Civil rights moralizing and anti-racism education in public schools 2. Promoting social justice ideology in school psychology training programs 3. Persons are encouraged to introspect and identify how their latent "Eurocentrism," white privilege, or racism makes them insensitive to the suffering/plight of minority groups.	1. Emotional intensity of moral crusades distorts priorities. 2. Ideological rigidity creates moral blind spots in "True Believers." 3. Moral crusades ebb and flow with changing fashions and emotional fatigue. 4. Those with different, but legitimate, viewpoints are caricatured as evil. 5. Cultural minorities are viewed as "mascots" who are useful for manipulating white guilt. 6. Majority groups are intimidated into avoiding making judgments of the bad behavior of minority groups.
Culture Model	1. Assumes that "culture" and "cultural differences" are the penultimate variables that explain all problems and conflicts. 2. People can be divided into the culturally ignorant vs. the culturally enlightened. 3. Assumes that the majority group is experientially and constitutionally ignorant of minority group culture.	1. Personal testimonials by victimized minorities presumably generate empathy, eliminate ignorance, and foster enlightenment. 2. Perfecting human beings by eliminating their cultural skill deficits (e.g., developing "cultural competence").	1. School psychologists are told that they must re-examine and reinterpret what they know about psychology, interventions, and assessment principles in conformity to "cultural differences."	1. Culture writing, used to influence professional practice, is rarely (if at all) based on accurate, sound science. 2. Since acknowledging individual differences requires too much effort, educating others about cultural differences must rely on lazy, crude stereotypes. 3. Actual practices observed to improve outcomes for minority children blatantly

Model	Assumptions	Description / Examples	Criticisms
			...contradict the practices supported by multiculturalists. 4. The politicized quality of re-education efforts alienates many people.
	4. Assumes that the majority group's ignorance of minority group culture lies at the root of minority problems, and that ignorant majority group members cannot properly serve minority groups. 5. Once the ignorant are properly re-educated and enlightened, they will do the right thing. 6. Better knowledge is the antidote to intergroup conflicts.		
Social Engineering Model	1. The world is comparable to a giant chess board that can be manipulated and controlled by judges, lawmakers, social scientists, and professional organizations. 2. Assumes that the "problem" is sufficiently understood (people know what is wrong and hence what needs to be fixed). 3. Assumes that the right solution to the problem can be found. 4. Assumes that an acceptable solution can readily be implemented. 5. If activists are clever, persistent, and have enough funds, any desired change is possible.	1. Requires enforceable power, centralized decision making, and strategies for coercion (e.g., using the force of law) in the service of social goals 1. The use of court-ordered desegregation efforts (e.g., forced busing) or testing bans (e.g., Larry P. case) 2. Civil rights enforcement agencies requiring organizations to correct disparate impact outcomes, under threat of lawsuits 3. NCATE, TEAC, APA, and NASP requiring commitment to diversity goals as a condition for program approval or accreditation.	1. Social engineering schemes are too simplistic (e.g., see Bean-Counting Multiculturalism, Chapter 2) when compared to the complexity of real-life settings. 2. No perfect solutions exist in real-world settings, only trade-offs. 3. Social engineering schemes frequently backfire and cannot account for negative unintended consequences.

(Adapted from Fein, 2001)

499

1. School psychology endlessly expresses alarm over the fact that the racial/ethnic demographics of America's schoolchildren do not match the racial/ethnic demographics of school psychology (Lineman & Miller, 2012). Efforts to increase minority representation in the field gives the superficial impression that the field is involved in a noble enterprise for the betterment of children—yet no one ever seems to ask what this will accomplish in any meaningful sense. This writer is certainly sensitized to the need for the racial/ethnic demographics of a school districts' psychological services staff to "look good" to outside observers. However, school psychology is not about "looking good", but is about the discovery of documented practices that yield tangible *results*. The field offers no explanation for why racially/ethnically homogeneous schools (where teachers, administrators, counselors, school psychologists all represent the same race/ethnicity) often demonstrate *worse* outcomes compared to more racially/ethnically heterogeneous schools.

2. School psychology (and other applied education and psychology fields) engages in endless hand-wringing over racial/ethnic disproportionalities in special and regular education. Yet constant failure has shown that the field has done nothing to meaningfully correct such disproportionalities—without resorting to blatant double standards or ethically questionable practices designed to artificially manipulate outcomes (see Sidebars 4.6, 6.1).

3. "Cultural competence" is an endless topic of concern in the field, yet to date there is no compelling research that has demonstrated its construct validity (Frisby, 2009). With the sole exception of the obvious need for bilingual school psychologists to serve non-English-speaking populations, the field has not provided any tangible evidence of the relationship between cultural competence (whatever this may be) and positive outcomes for children in schools.

4. A dwindling band of die-hard multiculturalists continue to accuse traditional standardized cognitive testing of "cultural bias." However—with the exception of non-English-language assessments and standardized instruments—the field has not established any viable alternative multicultural assessment approaches that have demonstrated a sufficient degree of psychometric integrity to be used universally by schools.

Despite many researchers' best efforts, why do these movements continue to thrive in spite of their consistent lack of evidence? One compelling explanation is that these movements demonstrate *the triumph of symbolism over substance*. As the chapters in this text have shown, school outcomes for minority children are mediated by a host of complex home, school context, individual ability, and district factors. To take these variables seriously does not afford the opportunity for professional organizations and training programs to engage in the kinds of single-issue chest-thumping that galvanizes sociopolitical movements. Engaging in lazy group stereotyping and shouting politicized slogans is easy, but having one's cherished assumptions challenged—in light of reality— is painful.

When a painter needs to apply a fresh coat of paint to a house, the standard practice is to first strip the house of old paint, splinters, and dead bugs so that the fresh coat can be applied cleanly and smoothly. In much the same way, school psychologists need to first value, develop, and then master basic thinking skills that would enable them to be more discerning consumers of multiculturalism ideology before they can see clearly what truly has been found to be effective with minority children. This involves not only confronting outdated knowledge and attitudes, but also being exposed to information of which they are not aware.

The Application of Minimum Standards of Critical Thinking

As indicated in the opening quote of Chapter 2, the intent of ideologically driven advocacy movements is to persuade audiences to believe something, *not to give audiences tools to think for themselves*. Training audiences to think for themselves runs the risk of exposing the fatal flaws in the arguments of popular social ideologies, which may cause audiences to be wary of accepting an advocacy position just because it sounds good or is popular (e.g., see Table 2.2).

For decades, the fundamental hallmark of an educated citizenry was to develop the skills necessary for thinking critically (Willingham, 2007). Although critical thinking has been given a variety of definitions by researchers and educators (Moon, 2008), a brief sampling of its basic components are the ability to (a) identify multiple perspectives on an issue, (b) be open to new evidence that may disconfirm deeply held ideas, (c) avoid appeals to emotion and/or authority when reasoning, (d) demand that claims be backed by evidence, (e) deduce and infer conclusions logically from available facts, and (f) solve complex multistep problems. The fundamental goal for critical thinking education is to teach students *how* to think, rather than *what* to think. As such, critical thinking is the fundamental enemy of Quack Multiculturalism.

Lilienfeld, Ammirati, and David (2012) recently published an outstanding article in the *Journal of School Psychology* that outlines basic principles for scientific thinking, how to avoid cognitive errors in one's reasoning processes, and how to identify and avoid erroneous pseudoscience among popular beliefs in school psychology. If just one-tenth of these principles were applied to multiculturalism ideology, an entire book would need to be written in order to cover all relevant examples of how multiculturalism advocacy—no matter how well-intentioned—violates basic rules of critical thinking.

Sample passages excerpted from various multiculturism-friendly sources are displayed in Sidebar 10.2. For each passage, 50 others of similar sentiment could have been easily culled from the academic literature. Basic critical thinking skills are then defined, each of which can be easily applied to the ideas promulgated in these passages. A brief sampling of common emotional and perceptual barriers to critical thinking, as manifested in multiculturalism, are displayed in Table 10.2. When critical thinking skills are consistently practiced and applied, much of what passes for so-called "multicultural insights" falls apart like a house of cards in a windstorm.

Sidebar 10.2   Applying Critical Thinking Skills (Browne & Keeley, 2004) to Multiculturalism Ideology

Consider the following passages:

> **Passage 1:** "[I]f one's students are largely Filipino, a generic curriculum that barely mentions Filipinos teaches the unplanned lesson that Filipinos do not matter and have no significant history or culture. Why should Filipino-American students value education in which they are never reflected? Evidence suggests that students learn more when they can see themselves and their communities mirrored in their curriculum." (Grant & Sleeter, 2007, p. 170)

> **Passage 2:** "Sometimes behaviors that are totally appropriate for the child's native culture may seem inappropriate at school. For example, a male who has been taught that 'macho' means 'stand up for yourself' cannot be criticized for initiating a fist fight with a bully who called him a 'wimp.' . . . Knowledge about unique features of the child's culture may help prevent a misdiagnosis." (Openshaw, 2008, p. 74)

> **Passage 3:** "There are five essential elements that contribute to a system's ability to become more culturally competent. The system should (1) value diversity, (2) have the capacity for cultural self-assessment, (3) be conscious of the 'dynamics' inherent when cultures interact, (4) institutionalize cultural knowledge, and (5) develop adaptations to service delivery reflecting an understanding of diversity between and within cultures. Further, these five elements must be manifested in every level of the service delivery system. They should be reflected in attitudes, structures, policies, and services." (King, Sims, & Osher, 2001)

> **Passage 4:** "Being competent in cross-cultural functioning means learning new patterns of behavior and effectively applying them in the appropriate settings. For example, a teacher with a class of African-American children may find that a certain look sufficiently quiets most of the class. Often African-American adults use eye contact and facial expression to discipline their children. However, this is not effective with

all African-Americans. Intra-group differences, such as geographic location or socioeconomic background, require practitioners to avoid over-generalizing. With other students, one might have to use loud demanding tones, quiet non-threatening language, or whatever is appropriate for those students. The unknowing teacher might offend some students and upset others by using the wrong words, tone, or body language. Being culturally competent means having the capacity to function effectively in other cultural contexts." (King, Sims, & Osher, 2001)

Passage 5: "[T]he majority of the children referred for learning problems come from culturally/ethnically and linguistically diverse backgrounds which are dissimilar to many of the standardized samples used for the available tests. Such differences render these tests invalid . . . , thus the emphasis on informal/alternative assessment methods for CLD children and youth. The dubious reliability and validity of intelligence tests for CLD populations have triggered ethical and political reforms." (Martines, 2008, p. 46)

Passage 6: "[R]ap music or hip-hop music has a strong poetic or Ebonic influence that psychologically engages urban, suburban, or rural youth in today's changing society. Consequently, labeling students who use Ebonics as having a linguistic deficiency can lead to academic disengagement and behavior problems. In the long run, when these behavior problems are inappropriately addressed, students drop out of school and begin displaying antisocial behaviors and practicing criminal activities (e.g., drug dealing) that eventually land them in jail. Put another way, language and cultural valuing enhance academic engagement, student retention and graduation, and [a] productive life." (Obiakor, 2007, p. 10)

THE APPLICATION OF CRITICAL THINKING SKILLS

1. Where's the Data?

Definition: If authors make a claim or affirmation, ask them to provide empirical data that supports it.

Application: Where is the data showing that . . .

. . . students who have less exposure to their ethnic group in the school curriculum reliably achieve less than students who have more exposure? (Passage 1)
. . . the majority of children referred for learning problems who come from culturally/ethnically and linguistically diverse backgrounds outnumber those who do not? (Passage 5)

(continued)

. . . tests are invalid for test takers whose ethnic group is not represented in the standardization sample? (Passage 5)

. . . behavior problems of black students are caused by educators labeling Ebonics as deficient? (Passage 6)

2. Carefully Define Terms

<u>Definition</u>: Key words/terms that are not defined precisely are subject to shifting meanings, which muddies communication between the speaker and the audience, and impairs the audience's ability to evaluate the soundness of the argument.

<u>Application</u>: What is meant by . . .

. . . "native culture"? (Passage 2) If a child is born and raised in the United States (even though he or she is nonwhite), isn't his or her native culture American? Or, is his or her native culture limited to his/her race/ethnicity only?

. . . "culturally competent"? (Passage 3) Competent to do what? Does this mean to hold attitudes that are approved by a sociopolitical ideology? Does this mean to have insights into something about which one was previously unaware? Does this mean to learn some particular skill? Is a person culturally incompetent if he or she disagrees with the content of "politically correct" or "multiculturally approved" knowledge, insights, or attitudes?

. . . vague terms and phrases such as "value," "be conscious of," "institutionalize," or "develop adaptations to"? (Passage 3)

. . . "Ebonics"? (Passage 6). Does this mean the use of incorrect grammar? Talking in street slang? Can a person who is not black, but who uses the same speech patterns, be described as speaking Ebonics?

3. Examine Hidden Assumptions

<u>Definition</u>: The argument relies on beliefs that are unstated, but must be implicitly accepted in order for the argument to make sense. If the unstated assumption is found not to be true, or is not accepted, then the argument is considerably weakened.

<u>Application</u>: This argument assumes that . . .

. . . similarities in outward appearances or ethnic traits is the only—or most important—characteristic that students identify with in the curriculum. (Passage 1)

. . . specific behaviors can be attached to, or "owned" exclusively by, a particular cultural group. Many non-minority parents teach their children to defend themselves, and many non-minority parents do not. (Passage 2)

. . . it is wrong to teach or enforce adherence to behaviors in school that are not manifested in the home setting. (Passage 2)

. . . a system is a monolithic entity, which it is not. Individuals within a system have a variety of conflicting beliefs and preferences. (Passage 3)

. . . teacher behaviors for maintaining order and discipline are "culture specific." If a certain teacher behavior is effective for all students, or inconsistently works when applied to the cultural group for whom it is intended, then how can such teacher's behaviors be called "cultural" in the first place? (Passage 4)

4. Identify Faulty Reasoning

Definition: Reasoning is faulty when it does not use logic in order to justify acceptance of a conclusion; the conclusion does not follow from premises; or distracting material is made to seem relevant to the conclusion when it is not.

Application: Faulty reasoning is identified . . .

. . . in the assumption that students will be "empowered" if they see their group represented in the curriculum, versus being "demoralized" if they do not see their group represented in the curriculum. This creates an *artificial "forced-choice" dilemma*. There could be many reasons, having nothing to do with ethnic representation, that are responsible for positive or negative reactions to the curriculum. (Passage 1)

. . . in the fanciful notion that a teacher has the superhuman ability to know all of the geographic/social class backgrounds of each of his or her students, connect each background with their unique discipline preferences, and apply these differences to a classroom full of students without simultaneously offending some students. This is wishful thinking. (Passage 4)

. . . when a premise (teachers devalue Ebonics) and a conclusion (black students selling drugs) are juxtaposed next to one another, creating the false impression that the premise caused the conclusion. (Passage 6)

An expert in cognitive psychology reminds audiences that critical thinking skills cannot be effectively taught absent from a working knowledge of subject matter content (Willingham, 2007). This means that audiences must be given accurate information from which to make informed decisions, and not information that is purposely slanted to support predetermined conclusions.

This can be illustrated with a simple example involving racial/ethnic disproportionality statistics, which are often used to induce alarm and hand-wringing among school psychologists. As discussed in Chapter 2, disproportionality statistics are often used to justify pet multicultural agendas, such as those that are an outgrowth of standardized testing criticisms (e.g., see Green, Mcintosh, Cook-Morales, & Robinson-Zanartu, 2005). A simple exercise can illustrate how the reporting of simple statistics can be politicized to manipulate emotions. In Sidebar 10.3, the same hypothetical disproportionality data is interpreted using six different possible story "headlines." All of these headlines are factually true, but they are worded differently depending on how the source data is analyzed. These are arranged such that the wording of the beginning statements hardly raise an eyebrow, but the concluding statements are worded in a way that creates increased alarm (even though all statements refer to the same data). The point here is that data can be presented in a manner that manipulates attitudes and emotions to support whatever pet agenda needs sympathy.

Table 10.2   Emotional and Perceptual Barriers to Critical Thinking: Applications to Multiculturalism Ideology

Emotional/Perceptual Barriers to Critical Thinking	Definition	Sample Applications to Multiculturalism Ideology
Ad Hominem Attacks	To attack or insult a person by engaging in name-calling, rather than logically addressing the person's arguments	"Only far-right wingers would require minority children to say the pledge of allegiance."
Appeal to (Legitimate) Authority	The positions of a legitimate authority are blindly accepted, without making the effort to independently evaluate the empirical support for the positions.	"Practitioners cannot adequately serve minority children without training in cultural competence, because my professional organization says so."
Appeal to (Questionable) Authority	Supporting a conclusion by citing superficial or nonexistent criteria for expertise on the issue at hand	"This minority politician believes that smaller class sizes is the key to school reform for Hispanics, hence it is probably true."
Appeal to Popularity	Attempting to justify a claim by assuming that anything favored by a large group is inherently right, true, or desirable	"Since most people believe that ghetto violence is caused by living in poverty, this must be true."
Begging the Question	Attempting to justify a conclusion by merely restating it in different words	"A diverse gifted education program is to be pursued because diversity is highly desirable."

Table 10.2   (*Continued*)

Emotional/Perceptual Barriers to Critical Thinking	Definition	Sample Applications to Multiculturalism Ideology
Black/White "Either/Or" Thinking	Gratuitous assumption that only two alternatives exist, when it is possible that more than two alternatives exist	"Either you are a passionate advocate for multiculturalism, or you are a racist."
Egocentrism	The assumption that my beliefs are true even though I have never critically examined or questioned the basis for these beliefs	"I don't care what anyone says—the concept of 'white privilege' is true."
Explaining by Naming	False assumption that because you have provided a name for a state of affairs, you have also adequately explained the state of affairs	"Schools fail minority children because of their Eurocentrism."
Labeling	Using general labels that lump disparate elements into homogeneous categories, as a substitute for more nuanced, precise discriminators for categories	"We must treat Susie differently because she is a CLD child."
Limited Frame of Reference	When one's experience or perspective is limited, this also limits perception, the ability to recognize the variety of factors that influence problems, and the full range of acceptable solutions for problems	"In my experience growing up, all of the Hispanic parents I knew wanted bilingual education for their children, hence this is best for all Hispanic children."
Moral Judgments	Making a hasty moral judgment that supports our acquired moral value systems, but ignores or dismisses what doesn't, thus sacrificing insight and understanding in order to maintain a feeling of security	"Ability tracking in schools is evil because it leads to over-representation of minorities in lower tracks."
Red Herrings	When an irrelevant topic is raised in order to divert attention from the original issue or topic	"We can't properly understand minority underachievement on standardized tests without first understanding the problem of discrimination in society."

(*continued*)

Table 10.2 (*Continued*)

Emotional/Perceptual Barriers to Critical Thinking	Definition	Sample Applications to Multiculturalism Ideology
Searching for "Perfect Solutions"	Falsely assuming that because part of a problem would remain after a solution is tried, the solution should not be adopted	"Charter schools don't work for minority children, because the majority/minority achievement gap still remains."
Self-Interest	Holding fast to beliefs that justify getting more power, approval, or personal advantage, even though these beliefs are not grounded in sound reasoning or evidence	"I will be accepted by my academic peers if I publicly adhere to an Afrocentric worldview."
Self-Validation	Having a strong desire to maintain long-held beliefs, even without seriously considering the extent to which those beliefs are justified, given the evidence	"America is a racist society because I have always believed this."
Slippery Slope	The assumption that an action or belief will set off an uncontrollable chain of catastrophic negative or undesirable events	"If we acknowledge that cognitive tests are not culturally biased, then this will cause people to believe that lower scoring minority groups are genetically inferior."
Sociocentrism	The assumption that the dominant beliefs of fellow group members are true, even without ever questioning the basis for many of these beliefs	"Cognitive tests are culturally biased because The National Center for Fair and Open Testing, of which I am a member, believes that they are."
Straw Man Argument	Distorting an opponent's point of view so that it is easy to attack, thereby attacking a point of view that in reality does not exist	"Criticizing the behavior of poor minority parents is cruel, because it blames the victim and sides with the oppressor."
Virtue Words	The use of hackneyed, vague, and emotionally appealing words that distract from a close examination of an argument	"To overlook bad behavior of minority groups is to be tolerant, inclusive, and culturally sensitive."
Wish Fulfillment	The faulty assumption that because we wish a position were true or false, then it must indeed be true or false	"We know that all groups contain equal proportions of gifted individuals, hence we are morally obligated to eradicate any barriers to disproportionalities in gifted programs."

(Adapted from Browne & Keeley, 2004; Paul & Elder, 2003; Rudinow & Barry, 2008)

✍ Sidebar 10.3   Different Ways to Report Special Education Disproportionality Statistics

Mayview Unified School District (MUSD) has 5,000 students, 10 percent of whom are racial/ethnic minorities (n = 500). In MUSD, 300 students are enrolled in full-day special education classes, 60 of whom are racial/ethnic minorities. Which of the following headlines is most likely to generate the most hysteria?

- "A special ed student in MUSD is 4 times more likely to be a non-minority"
- "60 minority students in MUSD are in special ed"
- "1 percent of the students in MUSD are minority students in special ed"
- "Minority students are 10 percent of MUSD students, but 20 percent of students enrolled in special ed"
- "Minority students in MUSD are roughly 2 times more likely to be placed in special ed compared to non-minority students"
- "In MUSD, minority students are overrepresented by 100 percent in special ed"

Applied psychologists (i.e., clinical, school, counseling, industrial/organizational) have high levels of specific expertise in many areas, but they are not experts in important fields that have a direct bearing on the accurate understanding of many multicultural issues in education (e.g., cultural anthropology, economics, sociology, education organization and administration, to name a few). Applied psychologists are interested in "culture" only to the extent that it provides facile explanations that can explain away embarrassing facts (e.g., poor test performance is caused by "cultural bias"). If school psychologists are to learn accurate (i.e., non-ideological) information about cultural issues, then they must begin to be exposed to the best research on these issues that originate from fields outside of school psychology.

Sensitive, Inclusive, Equitable, . . . and Wrong

In the hermetically sealed world of Quack Multiculturalism, one's sociopolitical perspective (rather than the results of empirical research) is paramount in what is believed to be true or false. Pick up any advocacy article promoting multiculturalism and it will be liberally peppered with the terms *cultural fairness, diversity, equity, tolerance, sensitivity, social justice,* or a closely related variant of these words. The implicit message is that once the focus shifts to a discussion of what is best for minority children and families, then one is obligated to *think ideologically rather than scientifically.* Sometimes these terms are evoked in order to prevent audiences from thinking at all. As soon as these magic words are uttered, one can literally throw away one's Statistics, Measurement, Child Development, and Instructional Design textbooks. In the unspoken rules of Quack Multiculturalism, scientific concepts that would normally apply to non-minority children suddenly have no relevance whatsoever to psychoeducational issues involving minority children.

Ironically, intellectuals in academia are particularly susceptible to this thinking. Sowell (1986) writes:

> Academic intellectuals are especially subject to emotional enthusiasm and especially insulated from the chilling effects of objective reality. . . . Academics are protected not only by tenure but also by their own ability to rationalize, complicate, and mystify. They do not like objective processes whose results cannot be talked away. In short, the very people whose work is based on the relationship between ideas and reality are exempted from having to demonstrate such a relationship. . . . For academics, the only test is whether what they say sounds plausible to enough people, or to the right people. Tenure, "academic freedom," and other insulations . . . end up freeing the intellectual from a need to respect the intellectual process, or to recognize any objective reality beyond his fancies or the fashions of his fellow academicians. . . . Academics will research anything—except the effectiveness of their own schemes growing out of previous research. (Sowell, 1986, pp. 128–129)

If audiences are to take multicultural issues seriously, then it is unavoidable that situations will eventually arise where ideologically driven beliefs will conflict with what the research says. If multiculturalism ideology claims that intelligence tests are culturally biased, but the science says that they are not, which message should school psychologists believe? If "sensitivity" demands that educators overlook clear violations of school discipline rules in order to avoid subgroup disproportionalities in school suspension rates, but research shows that such disproportionalities are unavoidable, then how should school psychologists consult with educators? If school psychologists meticulously follow best practices in their use of the most reliable and valid instruments for gifted identification, yet political pressures within the district compel them to artificially lower gifted program admission standards for underrepresented groups, how should the school psychologists proceed? Are school psychologists truly supposed to be data-oriented problem solvers, or are they little more than mere pawns beholden to fashionable sociopolitical agendas?

Students Are Exposed to More Accurate and Higher-Quality Information in Training

Needed: A Climate for Professional Debate

The hallmark of scholarship that supports and guides good practice is the necessity for ideas to survive the gauntlet of peer review. Books and journal articles must be routinely reviewed by knowledgeable experts in a field before ever seeing the light of day. This improves the quality of research to which audiences are exposed, as well as focuses attention on those practical proposals that have the best research support.

As mentioned briefly in Chapter 1, the field of counseling psychology is notorious for being dominated by high-profile viewpoints that promote racialized (see under *racialism* in Glossary) multicultural counseling competencies as a professional mandate for counseling psychologists. To its credit, however, the counseling psychology field has provided opportunities for audiences to hear lively debates involving counseling psychology scholars who dissent from this view (e.g., see *Journal of Mental Health Counseling*, 2004, Vol. 26, No. 1).

With rare exceptions, no such climate of debate exists in school psychology on any critical issues related to multiculturalism. If multicultural school psychology could be likened to a political system, it can be characterized as a one-party system. For all practical purposes, multiculturalism is portrayed as a movement that is so noble, virtuous, and self-evident that it is exempt from any objective analysis or critical scrutiny from scholars within or outside of the field. Multicultural guidelines are promoted by professional organizations, and they are expected to be obediently followed absent any professional discussion of whether such guidelines even make sense—let alone whether they are even capable of being implemented in the real world.

In order for the field to benefit from the best knowledge and practices as to how minority children are helped in schools, state and national school psychology professional organizations should, at the very least, systematically provide open forums (through journal publications and/or professional conferences) for researchers, trainers, and practitioners to debate and discuss the construct and social validity of multicultural training guidelines.

A Rising Tide Lifts All Boats

A dejected student once came into this author's university office complaining that he could not find any literature in the campus library on school interventions that work effectively for Hispanic children. Assuming for a moment that his search was thorough, this illustrates how this student's thinking (as well as the thinking of countless other students) has been thoroughly hypnotized by Quack Multiculturalism.

If a severe thunderstorm showers rain on an area during an outside baseball game, all persons attending the game will get wet *regardless of their ethnicity*. If a state legislature votes to raise taxes, all persons within the affected jurisdiction will pay *regardless of their cultural background*. If a man ingests a large volume of strychnine, he will inevitably die, *regardless of his skin color*.

The obvious point here is that certain external events have the same predictable effects on all people regardless of their personal characteristics. In the same way, all students benefit when teachers, administrators, counselors, and psychologists provide the highest-quality services to children and youth under their professional care. Conversely, all students suffer when teachers, administrators, counselors, and psychologists fail to provide high-quality services to children and youth for whom they are responsible.

The problem is not that there is an insufficient corpus of research that can inform school psychologists on how to assist Hispanic children having problems in schools. *The real problem revolves around the manner in which such relevant research is identified*, as illustrated by this student's frustration. This issue is brought into sharper focus using the illustration in Sidebar 10.4.

Sidebar 10.4   Which of the Following Fictitious Articles Is Most Informative for Helping Hispanic Students in Schools?

ARTICLE #1

Title: The Effects of a Social Skills Training Program on Turn-Taking Skills for Behaviorally At-Risk Mexican American Third Graders

Abstract: The Patton Social Skills Training Program (PSSTP) is a classroom-based intervention for teaching pro-social skills to students in Grades 2–4. The PSSTP consists of a series of training modules designed to teach 15 distinct pro-social skills, which can be adapted to the individual needs of teachers. For the purposes of this study, a 12-week intervention was used, which consisted of a series of eight teacher-led 45-minute modules and four 20-minute role-play video vignettes. Participants consisted of three third-grade classrooms in a predominantly Mexican American school in Los Angeles, California. All participants (n = 89) were Mexican American third-grade students (mean age 8 years 5 months), who spoke English at least somewhat fluently and displayed levels of academic achievement (as measured by group-administered standardized achievement tests) within the average range. Three third-grade classrooms in the same elementary school participated in the program. Classroom 1 received 12 weeks of PSSTP training specifically on turn-taking skills. Classroom 2 received 12 weeks of PSSTP training specifically on how to talk with authority figures in the school. Classroom 3 (control classroom) received no intervention. All participants were given pre- and posttests on turn-taking skills. Results showed that students in Classroom 1 showed significantly higher increases in pro-social turn-taking skills compared to students in Classrooms 2 and 3.

ARTICLE #2

Title: The Effects of a Program to Teach Double-Digit Plus Double-Digit Borrowing Skills in a Sample of Low-Achieving Third Graders

Abstract: Hargrave and Olso (2003) illustrate a method for teaching double-digit plus double-digit borrowing skills to elementary school-aged students. The method uses multicolored print in addition problems that helps signal students as to which kinds of addition problems require borrowing skills, and how they are demonstrated. The method can be taught to students over five 30-minute classroom periods. Participants consisted of three third-grade classrooms in a suburban community in central Texas. The teacher-reported racial/ethnic breakdown of all participants (n = 89) was 55 percent Caucasian, 30 percent Mexican American, and 15 percent African American. The mean age of all participants was 8 years 5 months, and all participants came from working and middle-class backgrounds. All students spoke English fluently and displayed levels of academic achievement (as measured by group-administered standardized achievement tests) within the average range. Three third-grade classrooms in the same elementary school participated in the program. Classroom 1 received five training sessions involving the Hargrave and Olso (2003) method spread across two weeks. Classroom 2 received five training sessions spread across two weeks on general addition skills. Classroom 3 (control classroom) received no intervention. All participants were given pre- and posttests on double-digit plus double-digit borrowing skills. Results showed that students in Classroom 1 showed significantly higher increases in double-digit plus double-digit borrowing skills compared to students in Classrooms 2 and 3.

ARTICLE #3

Title: The Effects of a Note-Taking Intervention on End-of-Unit Classroom Test Scores for Rural Eighth-Grade Students

Abstract: The Novosinski method (see Peterson, 2006) for teaching secondary school students to take high-quality in-class notes is currently being promoted by the National Council for the Social Studies (NCSS). The method can be taught to students in six teacher-led training sessions. In these sessions, students first receive didactic instruction in the mechanics of the method, then listen to sample lectures, and finally have their notes evaluated and scored by expert scorers. An eighth-grade classroom (Classroom 1) in a rural central Montana district was taught the Novosinski method during the Fall 2004 academic semester. In Spring 2004, Classroom 1 and two additional eighth-grade classrooms (Classrooms 2 and 3) in the same junior high school were exposed to a series of three identical lectures on American government (obtained from NCSS). Students in Classroom 2 were taught general listening skills in Fall 2004, but not the Novosinski note-taking skills method. Classroom 3 (control group) did not receive any training. The demographic makeup of the district is reported in school records as 96 percent Caucasian. The majority of students in all three classrooms display average levels of academic achievement. All participants were given pre- and posttests evaluations on their note-taking skills. Results showed that students in Classroom 1 showed significantly higher scores on note-taking skills compared to students in Classrooms 2 and 3.

Three fictitious journal article titles and abstracts are shown in Sidebar 10.4, each of which describe a school intervention demonstrated to be effective for a particular problem. Article 1 mentions Hispanics explicitly in the title, and the sample on which the study was conducted is predominantly Hispanic. This represents the kind of article that this student was looking for, and which can be touted by multiculturalists as "an intervention that research shows is effective with Hispanics." At least superficially, Articles 2 and 3 do not seem to fit this description. *But to what extent is this true?*

Articles 2 and 3 deserve a closer look. There is no explicit reference to minority groups in the title to Article 2. Yet, 30 percent of the sample is described in the abstract as Hispanic (Mexican-American). If the intervention was effective with the entire sample as a whole, then obviously this means that it was also effective for Hispanic children in the sample. *Yet, because this article does not explicitly advertise race/ethnic information, or is not conducted in a predominantly Hispanic setting, it is likely to be overlooked as providing useful information for Hispanic children.* Article 3 not only has no race/ethnicity identifying information in the title, but the sample on which the study was conducted is predominantly Caucasian. Quack Multiculturalism would be quick to conclude that this article provides no useful information relevant to Hispanics. However, the *burden of proof* is on multiculturalists to demonstrate (either with strong conceptual arguments or with data) why the note-taking intervention described in Article 3 *cannot* be effective with Hispanic children. The most conservative interpretation is simply to remain agnostic about this question until further research can be conducted. Unfortunately, potentially valuable information in this article is completely missed if one's search is limited only to articles that explicitly identify racial/ethnic information.

Does the Field Need More Research on Multiculturalism?

Nearly all graduate students, faced with writing a discussion section of a master's thesis or doctoral dissertation, feel obligated to conclude their studies with the well-worn phrase "more research is needed." Multiculturalism is no exception. Books and articles that are sympathetic to multiculturalism often imply that progress toward helping minority children to succeed educationally or psychologically is contingent on some as-yet-undiscovered (multicultural) research that urgently needs to be conducted. In order to evaluate the question of whether school psychology needs more research on multiculturalism, some crucial distinctions need to be made.

Primary versus Secondary Research Questions

First, a crucial distinction must be made between primary versus secondary research questions applied to multicultural issues (see Sidebar 10.5). Data collected on primary research questions are designed to evaluate directly the central doctrines of multiculturalism ideology (e.g., see discussion of *Group Identity*, *Difference*, *Equity*, *Sensitivity*,

Inclusion, and *Sovereignty Doctrines* in Chapter 2 and in the Glossary). For example, ideologues often claim that standardized tests are culturally biased, even though primary research on this topic has established such claims to be baseless (see Sidebar 5.2). Some primary research questions have already been answered, *yet for ideological reasons*, multiculturalism ideology attempts to portray these research questions as inconclusive (e.g., see Gottfredson, 2005). Other primary research questions have no substantial support at all, for the simple reason that no research has been sufficiently designed or conducted to answer the research question. For example, a professional organization can claim in its membership publications that "interventions should be culturally appropriate." Not only is this phrase insufficiently defined, but to date no substantial body of primary research has established concrete, reliable, and effective interventions (or modifications on interventions) that have been shown to work specifically for a certain cultural group better than they do for a different cultural group.

Sidebar 10.5   Examples of Primary versus Secondary Research Questions Related to Multicultural Topics

Primary Research Questions

- What is the central tendency, range, and/or variance in a measured or observed construct within a group? Are these measurements statistically different from the same information collected on a different group?
- Does an intervention that is shown to be effective with a group in one setting generalize in effectiveness to the same group in significantly different settings? If not, is there a "setting times treatment interaction" in the application of interventions across two or more settings?
- Using appropriate statistical procedures, does a test measure the same psychological construct within two or more different English-speaking native-born groups? If not, what is the source of bias?
- Using appropriate statistical procedures, does a test predict a criterion similarly within two or more different English-speaking native-born groups? If not, what is the source of bias?
- Within the same setting, and controlling for extraneous variables, is there a "culture times treatment interaction" in outcomes when applying interventions to students' psychological, behavioral, and/or academic problems?

Secondary Research Questions

- What is the relationship between the racial/ethnic/language demographics of a school and teacher/staff satisfaction and student conflicts in a particular setting?

(continued)

- How is multicultural training incorporated within school psychology training programs?
- How are bilingual education and/or immigrant newcomer programs implemented in particular school districts?
- Does a standardized test translated into a different non-English language have the same psychometric properties as the English version of the test?
- What are the effects of standardized test accommodations on scores for limited-English-proficient students?

Data collected from secondary research questions do not fundamentally test basic assumptions of multiculturalism ideology but address topics that are applicable to typically setting- or situation-specific concerns. Examples of secondary research include survey research that collects information on how different settings implement multiculturalism in training, or the effects of different demographic configurations in a setting on important outcomes.

It's All About the Ideology

It comes as little surprise that multiculturalism's answer to the question of whether more research on multiculturalism is needed is *ideologically slanted*, rather than scientifically based. In a 1993 article, for example, Richardson (1993) stated that "only a modest amount of research has been conducted to investigate the pedagogy which will best meet the educational needs of black learners" (p. 566). Huckleberry (2009) argues that "the basis of most research lies in Eurocentric approaches" (p. 221), and criticizes current research paradigms for their "acceptance and utilization of culturally inappropriate research methodology" (p. 222). She opines that "the marginalization and quantitative exclusion of the culturally and linguistically diverse permeate most research" (p. 216). In her view, this exclusion "extends from the earliest participation in focus and survey groups, through selection and recruitment of research subjects and participation, to finalization of standardization pools" (p. 218–219). Bringing these criticisms to a crescendo, Mio and Awakuni (2000) state that "to oppose multiculturalism is to oppose scholarship itself" (p. xiv).

Discerning readers will recognize in these comments the two standard talking points that have become all too predictable in Quack Multiculturalism—namely, the minorities-as-victims and minorities-as-exotic messages (see Chapter 2). Here, minorities are thought to be so discriminated against in academia that they are "excluded" from participating in standard research activities. In addition, minority groups are viewed as so culturally exotic that traditional investigators have yet to discover the proper research methodology that will unlock the "cultural insights" necessary for providing appropriate solutions to psychoeducational problems.

Particularly noteworthy is the fact that these two criticisms cancel each other out when combined. If research is deemed to be too "Eurocentric," and therefore harmful to minorities, then what would be the point of complaining that minorities are not sufficiently included in research samples? In this twisted logic, conducting more "traditional" research on minorities turns out to be something that potential scholars need to avoid, if they are to protect minorities from harm. The utter absurdity of this conclusion is patently obvious. When we leave the world of ideology and return to the world of reality, a quite different picture emerges.

For starters, the claim that knowledge about minorities suffers because they are "excluded" from research fails to appreciate certain nuanced realities. African Americans are the most frequently researched minority group in the American social sciences (e.g., Hampton, Gullotta, & Crowel, 2011; Higginbotham, Litwack, Hine, & Burkett, 2001; Neville, Tynes, & Utsey, 2009), which includes research on educational issues and problems (Engelmann, 2007; Thernstrom & Thernstrom, 2003; Tillman, 2009). The reason why there may not be a comparable volume of research on other minority groups, at least in education, has nothing to do with intentional efforts to "exclude" them. Some groups generally do not present the same degree of educational problems as other groups, and they succeed at higher rates than other groups (e.g., Jews, Chinese). Thus, there is little urgency to conduct massive amounts of research on these groups unless it is to find out what they do right (in order to distill these findings in the service of helping other groups). Some groups are simply not as numerous in a state's population compared to other groups (e.g., Native Americans), hence the numbers necessary to create robust samples are difficult to generate in some geographic locations.

Perhaps the fundamental reason why multiculturalism complains about a perceived lack of research boils down to the simple observation that *the results of existing research do not tell multiculturalism ideology what it wants to hear.* Therefore, the only research conditions that are ideologically acceptable to multiculturalists are those that conclude that tests are culturally biased, minority children are disciplined unfairly in schools, or that learning problems experienced by minority children are caused by the fact that they do not see themselves represented in textbooks—to name a few.

The issue is not that educators and schools have no research to inform them of what to do to assist minority children. Voluminous research over the decades has clearly identified promising practices for vulnerable minority children—and is clearly and openly available to all. The *real problem* is that, for whatever reasons, *many schools are either unwilling or simply unable to put into practice what is already known.* It is here where audiences need to be made conscious of the corrupting influence of racial/ethnic politics in educational discussions.

Corrosive Politics

Unfortunately, *contentious politics* are a staple feature of contemporary debates on what educational practices are most effective for minority children. As examples, the teacher education establishment has vehemently resisted the Teach for America (TFA) program that prepares bright and motivated college graduates to teach in America's toughest inner-city schools (see Sidebar 4.1). This resistance is based on the claim, in part, that TFA graduates shortchange students by not matriculating through a traditional teacher education program. Hispanic activists and scholars denounce English-only school programs as "racist" (Zarate & Conchas, 2010), even in the face of clear evidence that such programs help some children to succeed (see Sidebar 10.1).

Even though Direct Instruction (see Sidebar 5.8) has demonstrated a clear superiority compared to other Head Start curricula for improving the academic skills of low-income minority children, its developers found that local school politics and the preference for more trendy curricula often thwarted its implementation in needy schools (Engelmann, 2007). Minority parents will go through tremendous personal sacrifices to give their children a chance to attend high-performing charter schools, even in opposition to politicized teacher unions and civil rights groups, who actively resist the right of such schools to compete for customers (see video documentaries in Additional Resources, Chapter 4). Researchers will painstakingly collect field data in actual schools on issues related to minority students, only to have this data completely ignored by the educational establishment when the research conclusions do not fit politically correct beliefs (e.g., see National Urban League, 2002; Ogbu, 2003; Sowell, 1986).

School psychologists, who are professionally socialized to value data-based methods for helping at-risk children (e.g., curriculum-based assessment for academic skills, progress monitoring), find that many teachers and school support services practitioners prefer to use less data-based methods that align with more trendy educational theories (see Grossen, 1997; http://www.illinoisloop.org/dap.html, click on Theories link; Jacobson, Foxx, & Mulick, 2009).

The glib juxtaposition of the word *multiculturalism* with *research* represents a fundamental oxymoron. As extensively discussed in Chapter 2, *multiculturalism is a sociopolitical ideology, not a science.* As an ideology, the fundamental goal of multiculturalism is quite simply *to advance multiculturalism.* In contrast, the aspirational goal of empiricism is to *discover objective truth.* Multiculturalism, essentially being a sociopolitical ideology, balks at the notion of an objective truth, often using the claim that cultural groups determine their own versions of reality (Huckleberry, 2009; Monteiro, 1996).

The essential (and incompatible) differences between sociopolitical ideologies (such as multiculturalism) and objective empiricism are depicted in Table 10.3. When high-quality, world-class research is typically applied to primary research questions involving

Table 10.3   Distinguishing Features of Sociopolitical Ideologies versus Objective Empiricism

Sociopolitical Ideologies	Objective Empiricism
Primary avenue of influence is through manipulating perceptions, emotions, and attitudes.	Primary avenue of influence is through application of the scientific method, critical thinking, analysis, reason, and reflection.
Central goal is to promote sociopolitical objectives, primarily, and to spread and defend the ideology at all costs, secondarily.	Central goal is to discover truth, primarily, and to find the best evidence-based solutions for solving practical problems, secondarily.
In order to most effectively manipulate perceptions, emotions, and attitudes, complex issues are reduced to simplistic morality plays.	In order to maximize persuasion, the design and execution of research is steadily improved.
In order to protect the ideology, large bodies of relevant research (that are damaging to the ideology) must be kept offstage and ignored.	Contradictory findings from exhaustive reviews of research are openly acknowledged; firm conclusions are established cautiously.
Audiences are told what to think and the "correct" attitudes and feelings they should have—through endless repetition of buzzwords, slogans, bromides, platitudes, and homilies.	Audiences are permitted the freedom to use their analytical skills and make up their own minds from the presentation of reliable, objectively determined facts.
Conformity of thought is enforced, in order to discourage debate and portray dissenters as having character flaws.	Independent thought is promoted in order to sharpen critical thinking skills.
Debate is discouraged, from fear that deficiencies in the ideology will be exposed.	Debate is encouraged, in the hope that more accurate knowledge will be discovered.
Some knowledge claims central to the ideology are considered to be so sacred as to be considered off-limits from debate and/or challenges.	There are no "sacred cows." All knowledge claims are open to evaluation, scrutiny, and debate.
Research consists of cherry-picking only those studies that appear to support or cast the ideology in a positive light.	Standards for evaluating the quality of research are independent from any particular ideological viewpoint; popular beliefs are readily abandoned if they are not supported or are contradicted by results from high-quality research.

some aspect of multiculturalism, the conclusions, more often than not, *contradict* multiculturalism's fundamental talking points. When this happens, the forces of multiculturalism orthodoxy reflexively mobilize to loudly denigrate and condemn such research. Simply witness the multicultural community's reaction to Arthur Jensen's *How Much Can We Boost IQ and Scholastic Achievement?*, Richard Herrnstein and Charles Murray's *The Bell Curve*, Daniel Patrick Moynihan's *The Negro Family: The Case for National Action*, James Coleman's *The Coleman Report*, Christopher Jencks's *Inequality: A Reassessment of the Effect of Family and Schooling in America*, Dinesh D'Souza's *The End of Racism*, or Robert Putnam's *E Pluribus Unum: Diversity and Community in the Twenty-first*

Century. Given these predictable reactions, multiculturalism's claim to "need more research" makes about as much sense as termites wanting homeowners to use a stronger brand of pesticide.

The Case for a Cross-Cutting Knowledge Base

As an ideology, multiculturalism often degenerates into *racialism* (see Chapters 2, Glossary). Here, audiences are marinated in the idea that human beings can be neatly partitioned into a smaller number of major racial/ethnic groups, and the goal of school psychology training is to learn the unique "psychologies" of each group, so that children from each group can be served "correctly." The problems that inevitably flow from this approach to training are described as follows.

Limitations of "Culture-Specific" Training

The sheer amount of racial, ethnic, and language diversity in America is nothing short of staggering (see Sidebar 2.11). According to the *Harvard Encyclopedia of American Ethnic Groups* (Thernstrom, 1980), America is host to more than 100 distinct cultural/ethnic groups. As examples, the broad term *Asian American* refers to Americans who have cultural ties, in varying degrees, to East Asian countries (e.g., China, Japan, Korea, Taiwan), Southeast Asian countries (e.g., Cambodia, Laos, Burma, Thailand, Vietnam), and South Asian countries (e.g., India, Pakistan)—all of whom have very different cultural traditions. There are more than 500 different Native American tribal groups in the United States, many of whom speak a distinctive language and dialect. Within American Hispanics, language proficiency levels range from persons who cannot speak a word of English to persons who do not speak Spanish fluently. Within any one cultural/ethnic group, socioeconomic conditions range from families living below the so-called poverty line, to multi-millionaires. American living conditions span the full range of persons residing in congested urban areas to persons living in sparsely populated rural areas, small towns/villages, and everywhere in between. *There is no professional preparation program, of which this author is aware, that makes even the most rudimentary efforts to acknowledge this diversity in its training model.*

The Lack of Standardization in Multicultural Training

Furthermore, the nature of school psychology multicultural training is often determined exclusively by parochial conditions that are unique to particular professional preparation programs. Training programs in school psychology have no common or standardized template for establishing the nature of multicultural training to which all school psychologists should be exposed. If a training program is located in an urban area within a large city, then multicultural training tends to focus exclusively on issues related to urban

African Americans. If a training program is situated in the Southwest, then multicultural training tends to focus on Hispanics, second-language assessment, and bilingual education issues. If a training program is situated in geographic locations where there is a significant presence of Native American tribal groups, then multicultural training will understandably focus on Native American issues in education.

If a professional preparation program is not located in racially or ethnically diverse areas, then there will most likely be no serious effort to acknowledge or even incorporate significant degrees of multicultural content in training. If a person graduates from a training program in State X that immersed students in culturally specific multicultural training content, then what will happen when this person selects a job hundreds of miles away in State Y? If the ethnic/racial demographics of State Y are significantly different from the demographics of State X, it will be as if the person has had no multicultural training to be effective in State Y.

Even if it were remotely possible to require pre-service school psychologists and teachers to spend 10 years of their training programs learning about the cultures of every conceivable American ethnic group, this would have absolutely no effect on helping them to develop skills in serving such children in schools—any more than reading a catalog of the many different varieties of surfboards can teach a person how to surf. Stated differently, how can generic multicultural training equip a school psychologist to help *this particular child*, who has *these particular personality/temperament characteristics*, who was raised in *this particular family configuration*, attending *this particular school*, who is in *this particular grade*, who has been taught by *this particular teacher*, and who is having *these particular psychoeducational problems*?

Study the Dollar Bill

A more defensible approach to answering these difficult questions can be gleaned from an understanding of how the U.S. Department of the Treasury trains its agents to identify counterfeit money. One method, which seems intuitive on its face, is for instructors to gather numerous examples of counterfeit bills that have been circulated within the economy in the past, and have agents diligently study these fakes. In the same way, this is how most professional organizations and training programs think about the best way to prepare students for so-called cultural competence. That is, students are typically trained by exposing them to articles, books, and/or speakers on culturally specific issues related to a small handful of cultural groups. Although this method may seem intuitively appealing, it leaves unanswered the issue of how the training program will find the time to discuss issues related to the other 95 cultural/ethnic groups living in America.

A second method of training U.S. Treasury agents to detect phony money is *counterintuitive* at first glance, yet it is the correct and most effective method of training used today. Here, Treasury agents study one and only one thing: *real United States currency*.

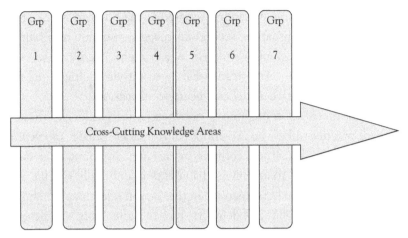

Figure 10.2   Cross-Cutting Knowledge Areas (Applicable to Seven Groups)
Grp = Racial/ethnic/language cultural groups

That is, agents will take a real dollar bill and devote months of intense study to the weight and quality of the paper, the type of printing ink used, the manner in which colors are combined to form images, the exact printing of the letters, the spatial positioning of the pictures, and the proper manner used to detect security watermarks on the bills when it is held up to the light. As a result of months devoted to the intense study of real currency, they are able to detect a counterfeit bill *within mere seconds* after looking at it, even though Treasury agents may have never seen this particular counterfeit bill before.

In the same manner, the only way that pre- and in-service school psychologists (or any other school-service professionals) attending geographically diverse programs can be exposed to a standardized model of high-quality multicultural training is to devote intense study to real dollar bills—or what can be called *cross-cutting knowledge areas.* Cross-cutting knowledge areas represent a smaller number of empirically supported constructs representing sources of variability within all groups, regardless of race, ethnicity, or language (see Figure 10.2).

These smaller numbers of cross-cutting knowledge areas have been shown by research to have a significant relationship with the quality of schooling experienced by all children—*regardless of race/ethnicity.* Cross-cutting training begins with the acknowledgement and study of human universals (see Sidebar 10.6). Next, by devoting intense study to a smaller number of cross-cutting knowledge areas, school psychologists in training are exposed to research that directly addresses psychoeducational problems of a wide variety of cultural minority students, *even though this material is not overtly identified as race or ethnicity specific.*

⚚ Sidebar 10.6   Partial List of Human Universals

Behavior

- Adjusting to the environment
- Conflict between individuals and groups, and means of dealing with conflict through consultation and/or mediation
- Cooking food
- Customs related to childbirth
- Distinction between behaviors that are or are not under self-control
- Distinction between normal versus abnormal behavior
- Gossiping
- Hygiene (standards for)
- Mood- and/or consciousness-altering techniques and/or substances
- Music (presence of)
- Practice believed to improve skill(s)
- Relationship of music to dance
- Rituals related to death
- Self-control
- Use of tools
- Wariness/fear of snakes

Beliefs

- Beliefs in the supernatural
- Religious beliefs
- Sickness seen as related to death

Cognition

- Abstract thought
- Ability to classify (e.g., colors, emotions, tools, weather conditions)
- Concept of past, present, and future (time)
- Distinction between what is true and what is false
- Dreams (presence of, and ability to)
- Making comparisons
- Measurement concepts
- Memory functions
- Numeracy
- Ordering elements along a continuum
- Planning for the future

(continued)

Development

- Belief in critical periods for learning
- Childhood fear of strangers
- Play in childhood (including use of toys)
- Pretend play
- Right-handedness is a population norm
- Status differences between adults and children
- Thumb-sucking
- Toilet training necessary for child socialization

Emotion

- Affection
- Distinction between likes and dislikes
- Empathy
- Envy
- Facial expressions of emotion (anger, disgust, sadness, surprise, fear)
- Fear
- Joking and jokes
- Mourning
- Preference for sweets
- Pride
- Sexuality (attraction, jealousy, modesty)
- Shame

Gender

- Females more involved in childcare
- Male domination in politics
- Males more aggressive/prone to lethal violence
- Sex differences in spatial cognition
- Status differences between male and female

Kinship

- Clear distinctions between close versus distant kin
- Husband older than wife (on average)
- Preference for own children (as opposed to others' children)
- Social organization among kinship groups

Language

- Black (word for)
- Distinctions in phonemes, morphemes, syntax within language

- Face (word for)
- Logical forms embedded in language
- One word can have several meanings
- Poetry (presence of)
- Proficient use of language associated with higher prestige
- Semantic categories
- Symbolic speech
- Use in manipulating others
- Use in misleading others
- White (word for)

Morality

- Concept of fairness
- Distinction between good and bad
- Distinction between right and wrong
- Prohibitions/taboos against incest, murder, rape

Social

- Awareness of, and concern for, what others think
- Collective decision making
- Division of labor within groups (and within age and sex groups)
- Economic inequalities within groups
- Etiquette
- Ethnocentrism
- Gift giving
- Government (need for)
- Greetings (customs for)
- Healers of the sick
- Hospitality
- In-groups clearly distinguished from out-groups
- Inheritance (rules for)
- Law (rules for rights and obligations)
- Leaders
- Marriage
- Prestige gradations/inequalities
- Property rights
- Sanction for crimes against the collective
- Taboos (speech, foods)

(Adapted from Brown, 1991, 2000; Pinker, 2002)

The Integration and Application of Cross-Cutting Knowledge

As observed in the Thernstrom and Thernstrom (2003, p. 66) quote from Chapter 2, children first develop values, attitudes, and skills as a result of their experience in the families that raised them. As discussed in Chapter 3, these differences are highly correlated with differences in families' social class status. Some children are born into two-parent families in which each parent holds advanced degrees, live financially comfortable lifestyles, and reside in neighborhoods that are relatively free of crime and associated mayhem. Children growing up in such homes are nurtured by adults who expose them to rich conversation, focused care and concern for their optimal development, and reliable, structured oversight of their school-related and social activities. Other children do not have such advantages early in life. These children grow up in homes run by parents who have limited cognitive abilities, minimal education attainment, and largely negative experiences with schools. These parents, many of whom were never married, must raise their children alone. Many (but certainly not all) of these parents struggle with personal and financial problems, chemical addictions, or a chaotic social life. As discussed in Chapter 3, most of these parents more than adequately provide for their children, but they do not have the time or skills to provide the focused oversight necessary for their children's optimal educational development. This child-rearing task is further complicated by the fact of living in communities in which biological fathers are largely absent from children's lives in a majority of homes, the lure of youth gangs is an ever-present temptation, and young girls dream of getting pregnant in order to gain a degree of status in the eyes of their peers.

Children continue to have variable experiences as they enter school, partly because of huge differences in schooling environments to which they are exposed for 12-plus years (see Chapter 4). Because of the presence of juvenile delinquency and street gangs in many communities, many students have to attend schools that are characterized by metal detectors, drug-sniffing police dogs, and uniformed officers patrolling the hallways (see Chapter 8). Due to a lack of options, many students emigrating from other countries attend such schools. In such schools, best practices are rarely encountered, partly because of a critical mass of students who care little about learning and are half-heartedly supervised by demoralized staff. Teacher incompetence and the control of powerful teachers' unions sap employee initiative, creativity, and drive. In contrast, other students attend schools run by energetic, driven principals who are freed from the bureaucratic constraints that afflict countless other public schools. These principals can establish academic achievement and character education as the number-one priority of the school, hire teachers and staff who share this vision, and establish expectations that teachers will go "far beyond the call of duty" to serve students, unencumbered by restrictive teacher unions (see Chapter 7).

Cognitively bright students eventually come to the attention of teachers for their rapid learning and exceptional test performance (see Chapter 5). If such pupils find themselves surrounded by a majority of peers who are much less academically inclined than they are, then a pervasive peer culture of anti-intellectualism and indifferent educators who fail to properly nurture their capabilities, the school psychologist (or another knowledgeable professional) can lead efforts to link students and families to needed resources and opportunities that can develop these students' talents and abilities. A classroom populated by a preponderance of students with IQs in the 80s to low 90s will have significant implications for the pace of classroom instruction and how lessons are taught for maximum retention and generalization (see Chapter 5). School psychologists can help teachers and student teams understand, in everyday language, these implications.

School districts that serve urban populations with a high incidence of crime, poverty, and single-parent families develop many more district-wide "specialty" intervention programs for combating drug abuse, teen pregnancies, and high school dropout rates (Chapter 9). School psychologists with unique training in these areas can be valuable assets to these programs by applying their knowledge of behavioral assessment, counseling, and program evaluation skills.

First-generation immigrant students who are new arrivals in the United States face significant challenges adjusting to a new American culture (Chapter 9). They and their parents are largely unfamiliar with American schooling, and they need considerable guidance in accessing services and adjusting to the stresses and demands of contemporary public schools. In turn, schools need assistance in how to inculcate English literacy skills, how to access and use standardized test accommodations (Chapter 6), and how to support these students when they experience emotional stresses associated with their newcomer status (Chapter 9).

Several specific cross-cutting knowledge areas are mentioned in the preceding paragraphs, a few of which are listed here:

- The correlation between socioeconomic status, home environment, and school/social outcomes
- The relationship between general cognitive ability and effective classroom instruction
- Understanding the essential features and distinctions between public, charter, and private schools, and how these differences relate to school-wide discipline and behavioral management policies and procedures
- Theory and methods of standardized test accommodations for English-language learners

- Understanding how specific social problems (e.g., teen pregnancy, drug addiction) impact school adjustment and performance
- Variables that influence a school's ability to address the adjustment challenges of immigrant students

Readers will notice that there is nothing race/ethnicity-specific in these cross-cutting knowledge areas. There is no special teaching pedagogy for blacks, no special counseling methods that supposedly are uniquely effective for Native Americans, and no EZ cookie-cutter recipes for "how to work with Hispanic families." Stated differently, one can gain invaluable information and skills from an in-depth study of these cross-cutting research areas without ever being required to accept racialized (see Glossary) psychology theories that are so popular (but ineffective) in Quack Multiculturalism. If specific racial/ethnic groups are observed to experience a disproportionately greater degree of problems or difficulties in any of these areas, the reasons for these difficulties, as well as proposals for their solution, can be easily explained by the universal principles inherent in these cross-cutting knowledge areas.

High-Quality Research Is Advertised More Efficiently to School Psychologists and Schools Serving Minority Children

School psychology can get the message out in several ways with respect to promising practices that help vulnerable minority children in schools.

Professional Organizations

The American Psychological Association (APA) includes 54 separate divisions representing specific sub-disciplines, each with their own officers, website, publications, email list, awards, convention activities, and meetings. The most well-known of these divisions is Division 45 (the Society for the Psychological Study of Ethnic Minority Issues).

The Education Directorate within the APA was established to advance the science and practice of psychology through educational institutions broadly defined, which include public primary and secondary education. One of its program offices is the Center for Psychology in (K–12) Schools and Education (http://www.apa.org/ed/schools/cpse/index.aspx), which conducts research, makes research-based policy recommendations related to education, and serves as a liaison between APA and national educational societies.

There are several separate free-standing ethnic minority psychology associations (e.g., Association of Black Psychologists, National Latino/a Psychological Association, Society of Indian Psychologists, Asian American Psychological Association) whose interests focus on the psychological and mental health of specific racial/ethnic minority populations. The National Association of School Psychologists Multicultural Affairs

Committee drives most of the organization's initiatives involving racial, ethnic, and language minority groups. This committee also oversees several specialty subgroups, who take responsibility for certain tasks and projects (e.g., see Sullivan, 2010).

NASP also has special interest groups that provide a forum for interested members to collaborate and communicate, become better informed, and share information in a particular area of common interest to smaller subgroups of organization members. Communication and sharing among special-interest group members occurs at conventions, and by having one's contact information listed on directories that can be disseminated through email listservs. Examples of school psychology special-interest groups are those devoted to autism, preschool issues, positive psychology, and behavioral psychology.

At least as far back as the 1980s, NASP has sponsored a special interest group called Urban School Psychology. The purpose of this group, as it was originally conceived, is to provide opportunities for school psychologists working in urban settings to share their experiences and learn about psychological service initiatives oriented toward the unique challenges of working in these settings. However, it remains unknown whether this group has maintained a consistent and vibrant presence within NASP in the past 30 years.

The Unfortunate Reality of Racial/Ethnic Politics

It would be quite easy to conclude that these organizations would be most likely to spearhead efforts to raise awareness of effective practices for minority students in schools. Unfortunately, reality is more complicated than this. First, not all of these organizations are focused exclusively on the psychoeducational challenges of children in schools. Second, many of these organizations are *ground zero* for an overtly politicized and racialized advocacy stance toward multicultural issues. According to one well-known black academic, for many race/ethnicity-specific professional organizations, "[t]he goal here is not to weigh evidence carefully in order to unearth the truth, but to construct interpretations of evidence that bolster a pre-conceived 'truth'" (McWhorter, 2000, p. 54). As an example, he offers the following observations on Afrocentric scholarship:

> All too often, black scholarship is devoted not to general scholarly inquiry about black people, but a subset of this: chronicling black victimhood past and present. . . . Because black people are no more perfect than anyone else and life past and present is complex, this abridged conception of academic inquiry inherently conflicts with the commitment of mainstream academia to striving for assessment as unbiased as possible. In this conflict between Victimology and truth, Victimology is naturally allowed the upper hand. . . . The result is a sovereign entity where the outward forms of academia—articles, books,

conferences, symposia—are harnessed to a local set of rules: a Separatist conception of academia. In "black" academia, as often as not, . . . sociopolitical intent is weighted more heavily than the empirical soundness of one's conclusions. . . . The fundamental commitment of much black academic work is not assessment of facts and testing of theories, but chronicling victimhood and reinforcing community self-esteem. (pp. 54–55)

Some topics and/or research conclusions are simply too threatening for civil discourse, which undermines the extent to which some organizations can evaluate data objectively. For the committed ideologue, to disagree with a cherished belief in multiculturalism ideology is akin to smashing one's fist through mom's freshly baked apple pie cooling on the windowsill. A brief sampling of conditions that upset and threaten militant multiculturalism is listed in Sidebar 10.7. Many race/ethnicity-specific organizations revel in group identity politics, for the simple reason that this style of interacting with the broader psychological and educational community confers the highest degree of political power and influence. A less-politicized emphasis on cross-cutting knowledge areas is likely to be resisted by these organizations, because this would effectively strip these entities of their most effective weapon—group identity politics based on victimology and real or imagined grievances.

✍ Sidebar 10.7   Conditions and Beliefs That Are Most Threatening to Militant Multiculturalism

- Psychologists and educators who do not subscribe to multiculturalism ideology as the penultimate value that trumps all other values
- Acknowledging individual differences within racial/ethnic/language minority groups, and rejecting simplistic generalizations and stereotypes
- The belief that some customs, achievements, and contributions to society from Western or European cultures are superior to those from non-Western or non-European cultures
- Racial/ethnic minorities who are socially, politically, or culturally conservative and/or who reject "progressive" politics
- Rejection of the belief that racism, prejudice, and discrimination are the fundamental societal problems responsible for stifling minority achievement
- Being comfortable with social or educational outcomes that are not sufficiently "diverse"

- Belief that observed differences are real across racial, ethnic, and socio-economic groups in the mean and variance of distributions in cognitive abilities, school misbehavior, and crime/delinquency rates
- Persons who are not susceptible to being manipulated by "white guilt" (see Glossary), or who reject the charge of "white privilege" as a moral problem from which they must repent
- Educators and psychologists who refuse to be bullied or intimidated from criticizing the negative or counterproductive behavior of cultural minorities
- Rejecting the notion that minority students must be marinated in their "culture" in order to succeed academically, behaviorally, or emotionally in schools
- Valuing the accoutrements of middle-class values, behaviors, and attitudes as worthy aspirations for students from poor and/or minority backgrounds

Nevertheless, there may be room for optimism. Making progress simply means replacing the emotional satisfaction a professional organization or training program gets from promoting largely *symbolic* initiatives (that have no effect on children in schools) with the satisfaction that comes from devoting time, effort, and resources to promoting *substantive* initiatives that actually do help children in schools.

Leadership from NASP Urban School Psychology Special Interest Group

The NASP Urban School Psychology group is uniquely positioned to raise awareness and educate the field on school setting and context variables that play a huge role in helping (particularly minority) children succeed. An excellent first step is for this organization to read and digest David Whitman's *Sweating the Small Stuff: Inner-City Schools and the New Paternalism* (see Chapter 7). This book is easy to read, and includes detailed case study information on inner-city public and charter schools that have substantially improved the school pride, personal adjustment, and academic performance of at-risk minority children and youth in urban settings. The book is written from a journalist's point of view and includes interview information from a wide variety of administrators, teachers, and students in each school. Although school psychologists do not figure prominently in the variables responsible for these schools' success, the book includes concrete principles that transcend specific disciplines.

The NASP Urban Special Interest Group can encourage colleagues to contribute position papers, workshops, or journal articles that expand on each of the principles identified by Whitman on creating effective schools for minority children—making these maximally relevant for school psychologists working in similar settings.

Expanding Practicum Sites

Needy schools for minority children often do not have qualified personnel or the internal infrastructure to support data-based monitoring and problem solving for academically at-risk students. These schools often struggle with finding high-quality teachers and other support staff. This author is familiar with one state in which a high official in the state department of education—who fortunately was quite sympathetic to school psychology—offered stipends to districts to hire school interns to help with Response-to-Intervention (RtI, see Glossary) implementation. This funding was short-lived, however, after only a few districts applied for the funding (C. Smith, personal communication, June 2012).

In states with school districts enrolling large numbers of high-needs minority children, state school psychology organizations and university faculty can work with interested state departments to fund well-trained school psychology interns for fledgling charter schools or promising public schools that are trying to implement best practices in data-based academic progress monitoring. One of the best ways to accomplish this is to help districts support instructional consultation teams (Rosenfield & Gravois, 1996). However, state departments are not going to give away money without having a good reason to believe that they will get something out of it. Therefore, state school psychology organizations and universities need to show carefully how money spent on interns is cost effective to districts and to the state (C. Smith, personal communication, June 2012). Rosenfield and Gravois (1996) articulate fundamental principles for what instructional consultation teams are, what they do, and the variables that facilitate their effectiveness in school districts. A detailed description of the processes involved in getting instructional consultation teams started in a district is described on the ICAT Resources website (http://icatresources.com/icteams/developing.cfm). According to their website, ICAT Resources consults with State Departments of Education and districts in nine states involving more than 400 schools.

Building on the Groundwork Laid by Brand-Name Intervention Programs

School psychologists may understandably be overwhelmed at the serious and long-standing problems that they see in the public schools in which they work. They realize intuitively that one person cannot single-handedly inaugurate or sustain the fundamental systems changes needed to support vulnerable children with difficult emotional, behavioral, and academic issues and problems.

However, if a critical mass of teachers, administrators, and support personnel are motivated to investigate interventions that can be introduced into the existing system, yet do not require them to re-invent the wheel, there are numerous examples of programs that have already laid the necessary groundwork for providing training, resources, and practical experience for supporting children in difficult educational settings. The fundamental issue here is whether schools/districts want to spend the money necessary to inaugurate needed changes. If schools/districts decide that such financial resources are available and money would be well spent, then there is no reason why school psychologists (or other key support personnel) cannot be the catalysts for spearheading these change efforts.

In these circumstances, schools and school districts may be open to taking a closer look at the evidence-based interventions that are key features of the brand-name programs (see Glossary) profiled in this text (see Chapters 3, 7, and 8). In addition to their empirically demonstrated outcomes, a common theme running through these programs is their explication of the steps needed to encourage and spread school/district-wide buy-in to the goals of the program.

These efforts usually begin with the formation of a small steering committee composed of key stakeholders (e.g., administrators, teachers, parents, and support staff representatives), whose purpose is to identify a program that appears to best fit the unique needs of the school/district. Next, key individuals are selected to receive training in the program methods (i.e., train-the-trainers model), with the understanding that they will serve as on-site trainers of other school personnel as the program is integrated into the educational setting. As program implementation progresses, key school representatives are taught how to document program outcomes, as well as how to access phone or on-site consultation with program developers to ensure that the program is being implemented with fidelity.

School Psychology Audiences Are Exposed to Real-World Examples of Effective Schools for Minority Children

There is simply no substitute for experience. Although reading a book, attending an interesting lecture, or watching an engaging documentary may indeed inspire, it cannot provide the kind of firsthand experience that is foundational for meaningful learning.

Outstanding schools for minority children exist, being based on principles that have little to do with abstract multicultural theory. Principals who have dramatically turned around academic and behavioral outcomes of previously poor-performing minority schools are noted for being "a walking testament to political incorrectness" (Whitman, 2008, p. 73) and their disdain for politically correct multiculturalism. In fact, a recruiting advertisement for a high-performing school catering to Native American children openly mocks potential applicants who are marinated in politically correct theory on how to teach minorities (see Joyce, 2009; http://www.aimschools.org/aipcs_job_posting.shtml).

High-performing minority schools with reputations of overcoming tremendous odds have been profiled in recent books (and one website) geared to the education community. These high-performing schools, and the source texts in which they are profiled, are listed in Sidebar 10.8. Many of these schools are still models of exemplary educational practices to this day. Unfortunately, many researchers observe that some schools experience a decline in academic and/or behavioral norms as a function of changing principals or funding cutbacks. After many years of neglect, some of these schools become empty shells that barely reflect the glory of former years. Sometimes high-performing schools for minority students close down for internal political reasons that have nothing to do with how well they educate students (e.g., see Tucker, 2012).

⌨ Sidebar 10.8   Public, Charter, or Private Schools Profiled for Demonstrating Effective Practices in Serving Minority Children and Youth[*]

Alabama

    West Jasper Elementary School$_1$ (PreK–5), West Jasper

Arkansas

    Oakland Heights Elementary School$_1$ (K–4), Russellville
    Portland Elementary$_4$ (PreK–6), Portland

California

    American Indian Public Charter School$_5$ (6–8), Oakland
    Bennett-Kew Elementary$_4$ (K–5), Inglewood
    Hobart Boulevard Elementary$_4$ (K–5), Los Angeles
    Imperial High School$_2$ (9–12), Imperial
    Marcus Garvey School$_4$ (PreK–8), Los Angeles
    Oakland Charter Academy$_5$ (6–8), Oakland

Connecticut

    Amistad Academy Elementary$_6$ (K–4), New Haven
    Amistad Academy Middle$_6$ (5–8), New Haven
    Bridgeport Academy Elementary$_6$ (K–4), Bridgeport
    Bridgeport Academy Middle$_6$ (5–8), Bridgeport
    Elm City College Preparatory Elementary$_6$ (K–4), New Haven
    Elm City College Preparatory Middle$_6$ (5–8), New Haven

Hartford Academy Elementary[6] (K–4), Hartford
Hartford Academy Middle[6] (5–8), Hartford

Delaware

East Millsboro Elementary School[1] (PreK–5), East Millsboro
Frankford Elementary School[1] (PreK–5), Frankford

District of Columbia

KIPP DC: KEY Academy[4] (4–8), Washington, DC
The SEED School[5] (6–12), Washington, DC

Georgia

Capitol View Elementary School[1] (K–5), Atlanta
Cascade Elementary School[4] (K–5), Atlanta
Centennial Place Elementary School[1] (PreK–5), Atlanta

Idaho

Lapwai Elementary School[1] (PreK–5), Lapwai

Illinois

Cristo Rey Jesuit High School[5] (9–12), Chicago
Earhart Elementary[4] (K–8), Chicago
George Washington Elementary[4] (PreK–8), Chicago
Marva Collins Preparatory School[4] (K–8), Chicago

Kansas

Ware Elementary School[2] (K–5), Fort Riley

Massachusettes

Charlestown High School[3] (9–12), Boston
Edward Everett Elementary School[3] (PreK–5), Dorchester
Edward W. Brooke Charter School[4] (K–12), Roslindale
Mather Elementary School[3] (K–5), Dorchester
Morse Elementary School[4] (K–8), Cambridge
Roxbury Preparatory Charter School[2] (6–8), Roxbury
South Boston Harbor Academy[4] (5–11), South Boston
University Park Campus School[1,5] (7–12), Worcester

(continued)

Michigan

    Cornerstone Schools Association[4] (PreK–8), Detroit

Minnesota

    Dayton's Bluff Achievement Plus[1] (K–6), St. Paul

New Jersey

    Chad School[4] (PreK–8), Newark
    Fourteenth Avenue School[4] (K–4), Newark
    North Star Academy[4] (Multiple campuses; K–12), Newark

New York

    Allen Christian School[4] (PreK–8), Queens
    Apollo Elementary[6] (K–2), Brooklyn
    Brooklyn High School[6] (9–12), Brooklyn
    Brownsville Elementary[6] (K–4), Brooklyn
    Bushwick Elementary[6] (K–4), Brooklyn
    Bushwick Middle[6] (5–8), Brooklyn
    Crown Heights Elementary[6] (K–4), Brooklyn
    Crown Heights Middle[6] (5–8), Brooklyn
    East New York Elementary[6] (K–4), Brooklyn
    East New York Middle[6] (5–7), Brooklyn
    Elmont Memorial Junior-Senior High School[1] (7–12), Elmont
    Endeavor Elementary[6] (K–1), Brooklyn
    Endeavor Middle[6] (5–8), Brooklyn
    Frederick Douglass Academy[4] (6–12), Manhattan
    KIPP Academy[4,5] (5–8), South Bronx
    Lincoln Elementary School[1] (K–6), Mount Vernon
    Mamie Fay School (P.S. 122)[4] (PreK–8), Long Island City
    Osmond A. Church School[2] (PreK–8), Queens
    Port Chester Middle School[1] (6–8), Port Chester

North Carolina

    Healthy Start Academy[4] (K–8), Durham

Ohio

    Wells Elementary School[2] (K–5), Steubenville

Pennsylvania

M. Hall Stanton Elementary School$_1$ (K–7), Philadelphia
Girard Academic Music Program (GAMP)$_4$ (K–12), Philadelphia

Tennessee

The Benwood Initiative$_1$ (16 Elementary Schools; K–5), Hamilton County
Rozelle Elementary$_4$ (K–5), Memphis

Texas

KIPP Houston High School$_4$ (9–12), Houston
Lockhart Junior High School$_2$ (6–8), Lockhart
Mabel B. Wesley Elementary$_4$ (PreK–5), Houston

Virginia

Graham Road Elementary School$_2$ (PreK–6), Falls Church

Washington State

Granger High School$_1$ (9–12), Granger

Source Publications

1. Chenoweth, K. (2008). *It's being done: Academic success in unexpected schools.* Cambridge, MA: Harvard Education Press.
2. Chenoweth, K. (2009). *How it's being done: Urgent lessons from unexpected schools.* Cambridge, MA: Harvard Education Press.
3. Leader, G. C. (2008). *Real leaders, real schools: Stories of success against enormous odds.* Cambridge, MA: Harvard Education Press.
4. Thernstrom, A., & Thernstrom, S. (2003). *No excuses: Closing the racial gap in learning.* New York, NY: Simon & Schuster.
5. Whitman, D. (2008). *Sweating the small stuff: Inner-city schools and the new paternalism.* Washington, DC: Thomas B. Fordham Institute.

Source Website

6. Achievement First (http://www.achievementfirst.org)

*Each school is followed by a subscript number corresponding to the source publication/website above in which it is described.

These schools offer ripe opportunities for school psychology faculty and graduate students in nearby universities to observe, study, and document what goes on in these and similar schools—either currently or from archival records that document past successes (e.g., see Sowell, 1986). The broader school psychology community can finally wean itself from an over-reliance on abstract multicultural theory to observing real-world examples of quality educational environments for at-risk minority children. At the very least, school psychologists (and other school professionals) can play a crucial role in facilitating linkages between administrators in these high-performing schools and struggling schools seeking to find ways to improve how minority children and youth are served.

Glossary

Academic Engaged Time. Previously called Academic Learning Time (ALT; Gettinger & Seibert, 2002). Academic engaged time refers to "the time during which students are engaged in relevant academic tasks while performing the tasks at a relatively high rate of success" (p. 1046). According to Gettinger and Ball (2008), the term *academic learning time* has been replaced with the broader term of *academic engaged time* to reflect the inclusion of cognitive and affective learner-centered variables such as initiative, self-motivation, and self-regulatory strategies (p. 1044).

Acculturation. Acculturation has generally been understood as "all the changes that arise following contact between individuals and groups of different cultural backgrounds" (Sam, 2006, p. 11). According to Sam (2006), *acculturation* should not be confused with *assimilation*, as these terms have their origins in separate social science disciplines and may be considered by some theorists to be subsets of each other conceptually. Acculturation should also not be confused with *enculturation*, which Vedder and Horenczyk (2006) define as "the process of becoming skillful in using tools, learning behaviors, knowledge and values that are part of the culture of one's own group" (p. 420). For complex issues related to the measurement of acculturation, readers are encouraged to consult Arends-Toth and van de Vijver (2006), and Ryan-Arredondo and Sandoval (2005).

Achievement Tests. Achievement tests are designed to measure a student's acquired learning from past schooling experiences. Achievement tests may assess knowledge or skill attained in one or more specific subject matter areas or content domains (e.g., reading, math, science, social studies, language arts). Achievement tests can be informally constructed, as in teacher-made tests given at the end of a unit of study, or they can be constructed and standardized using the considerable financial and technical resources of large testing companies. Achievement tests can be group or individually administered.

Advanced Placement (AP) Classes. The name given to college-level courses that can be taken in high school. AP classes are typically taken by honors program students who have completed all of the high school courses available in the subject. High school students can receive college credit for taking AP courses, although not all colleges grant college credit for AP courses.

African American. African American is a relatively recent term used to designate contemporary black Americans who descended from Africans brought against their will to America during the trans-Atlantic slave trade between the 16th and 19th centuries (see evolution of this term as discussed in Worrell, 2005), as well as blacks who did not. This term is somewhat imprecise, as (a) many contemporary black Americans have no cultural or psychological connections to the African continent; (b) contemporary black immigrants to America from Africa, the Caribbean, or South America often prefer to be designated by their specific country of origin (e.g., Kenyans, Sudanese); and (c) whites living in America who were born and raised in Africa are rarely (if at all) referred to as African Americans.

539

In published survey reports, Sigelman, Tuch, and Martin (2005) surveyed 2,300 black Americans in the 1998–2000 time frame, and found an even split in preference for the term "African American" (49%) vs. "Black" (48%). In more recent surveys (circa 2007), where respondents were given a choice of "Doesn't matter," a majority of blacks in America did not have a preference for the use of either term when they were given the explicit opportunity to say so (Newport, 2007).

According to 2008 Census figures (see BlackDemographics.com), African Americans constitute 13.5 percent of the U.S. population. Slightly more than half of all African Americans live in the South. The District of Columbia and the southern states of Georgia, Mississippi, and Louisiana have the largest proportion of African Americans. According to 2007 census figures, the cities with the highest percentage of African Americans (from highest to lowest) are Jackson, Mississippi; Memphis, Tennessee; Columbia, South Carolina; Augusta, Georgia; Baton Rouge, Louisiana; Atlanta, Georgia; Baltimore, Maryland; Mobile, Alabama; Washington, D.C.; and Detroit, Michigan.

According to various estimates, anywhere from 25 to 50 percent of African Americans belong to the "middle class" (Attewell, Lavin, Domina, & Levey, 2004). However, chronic poverty, broken families, out-of-wedlock births, disproportionate health problems, low educational attainment, and high crime rates continue to be significant problems in African American communities.

Afrocentrism.   Also known as Afrocentricity or Africentrism (Asante, 1988). As an ideology, Afrocentrism manifests itself in relatively mild to more radical forms. In its milder forms, Afrocentrism emphasizes the scholarly investigation of the heritage and influence of African cultures, which involves no additional sociopolitical agendas. The more radicalized versions of Afrocentrism ideology are rooted in the belief that Africans were responsible for many of the significant discoveries in ancient philosophy, science, and technology, but they are not recognized as such, because Europeans stole African discoveries and claimed credit (Bernal, 1987, 1991, 2006; James, 1954). Calls for Afrocentric education and/or schools are based on the theory that the relatively poorer academic and test performance of African American students must be caused by the fact that they are being unfairly evaluated using white or "Eurocentric" cultural standards (see Eurocentrism, this chapter). Afrocentrists believe that African American students can achieve academically at a level comparable to white students, as well as develop healthy self-images, only when the school curriculum is infused with Afrocentric values, standards, and concepts—and students "center" their identity, culture, and history in Africa (Webster, 1997).

AIMSWeb.   AIMSweb is the name of a web-based benchmarking, progress monitoring, data management, and data analysis system that is based on direct, frequent, and continuous student assessment of oral reading fluency (both English and Spanish), maze reading comprehension skills, early literacy skills (both English and Spanish), mathematics skills (e.g., number sense, measurement concepts, computation operations, geometry), early numeracy skills, as well as classroom behavior and social skills. The system is designed to help teachers, parents, school psychologists, and resource specialists implement a data-based Response-to-Intervention (RTI) problem-solving approach (see Response to Intervention, this chapter) in their districts. AIMSweb can be accessed online at http://www.aimsweb.com

Asian American.   The label "Asian American" is a broad label that refers to Americans who have immigrated or descended from East Asian countries (e.g., China, Japan, North and South Korea, Taiwan, and Mongolia; Yoon & Cheng, 2005), Southeast Asian countries (e.g., Cambodia, Laos, Burma, Thailand, Singapore, Vietnam; see Thao, 2005), and South Asian countries (e.g., Bangladesh, Bhutan, India, Maldives, Nepal, and Pakistan; see Thao, 2005).

As of 2009, the 10 states with the largest percentage of Asian American populations (in decreasing order) are California, New York, Texas, New Jersey, Illinois, Hawaii, Washington, Florida, Virginia, and Massachusetts (U.S. Census Bureau, 2011). According to 2000 Census data, the following American cities (having a population more than 100,000) recorded a majority of residents who are Asian or Asian American (in descending order): Honolulu, Hawaii; Daly City, California; Fremont, California; Sunnyvale, California; Irvine, California; Garden Grove, California; Santa Clara, California; Torrance, California; and San Jose, California (U.S. Census Bureau, 2002).

As late as 2009, Asian American households had the highest median income of all racial groups, a finding that has remained consistent since the mid-1980s (DeNavas-Walt, Proctor, & Smith, 2010). Some have suggested that this is a result of Asian families having more members in the workforce at higher levels of education (Rong & Preissle, 2009).

Assessment.   Assessment refers to a broad array of evaluative procedures that yield useful information about a person, which encompasses a much broader scope of activities than simply "testing." In school settings, assessment may include (but not be limited to) direct observation and clinical interviews, as well as the administration of rating scales and behavior checklists. Assessment can also involve the administration of personality tests, cognitive ability tests, and both formal and informal academic achievement tests.

Attention Deficit Hyperactivity Disorder (ADHD).   According to the *Diagnostic and Statistical Manual of Mental Disorders*—Fourth Edition (DSM-IV; American Psychiatric Association, 1994), ADHD is the clinical label given to individuals who display a persistent pattern of inattention (e.g., marked failure to give close attention to details; the manifestation of significant careless mistakes in schoolwork or other tasks) and/or hyperactivity/impulsivity (fidgetiness and difficulty in remaining seated when expected to do so; impatience with, or difficulty in, delaying responses and awaiting one's turn) that is more frequent and severe than is typically observed in individuals at a comparable level of development.

"Authentic" Minorities.   The term "authentic" minorities refers to members of racial/ethnic minority groups who possess characteristics that validate multiculturalism ideology. Members of cultural/ethnic minority groups who see themselves as perpetual victims of racism, have cultural characteristics that are most discrepant from the mainstream, are politically liberal or progressive, or who are in strong agreement with the implicit beliefs of ideological multiculturalism, are considered to be "real" or "authentic" minorities. In contrast, members of minority groups who work/study hard in school, have no difficulties speaking or pursuing the learning of standard English, perform well on standardized intelligence and achievement tests, have close friendships with members of different racial/ethnic groups, are politically conservative, or who do not see racism, prejudice, or discrimination as a significant hindrance to their personal goals, are a threat to multiculturalism ideology—and hence are viewed as "inauthentic." Multiculturalism ideology must downplay or denigrate the existence of "inauthentic" minorities, while promoting "authentic" minorities as the only valid characterization of minority groups (see also Clifton, 2004; McWhorter, 2001; Ogbu, 2008; Prager, 1995).

AYP (Adequate Yearly Progress).   *Adequate Yearly Progress* is a term applied to the minimum level of performance on standardized assessments that school districts and schools must achieve each year as determined under the federal No Child Left Behind (NCLB) Act. NCLB requires that each state establish a timeline for adequate yearly progress. These timelines are developed by state education agencies working under guidance from the federal government. All K–12 schools are required to demonstrate AYP in the areas of reading/language arts, mathematics, and either graduation rates (for high schools and districts) or attendance rates for elementary and middle/junior high schools. Every state education agency is required to determine which schools do not meet AYP every year. Schools that do not meet AYP for two years in a row are identified as "schools in need of improvement" and are subject to immediate interventions by the State Education Agency in their state.

Back Translation.   In back translation, a test is translated from the original language (e.g., English) into a second language (e.g., Spanish) by a translator who is proficient in both languages. However, this does not guarantee that the second-language translation communicates the same meaning as the test in the original language. In order to ensure accurate translation, an additional step is needed. Here, the translated test is then translated back into the original language by an independent, bilingually proficient translator, and the two original-language versions of the test (i.e., the original test and the back-translated test) are compared for equivalence in item meaning. If the two original-language versions are shown to be nonequivalent in item meaning, the process is repeated with an eye toward correcting areas of disagreement.

Barrio.   *Barrio* is a Spanish word meaning "district" or "neighborhood." In popular usage, barrios are lower-social-class ghetto neighborhoods with predominantly Hispanic residents. The two largest and most well-known barrios in the United States are the predominantly Mexican East L.A. section of Los Angeles, California, and the predominantly Puerto Rican El Barrio in the East Harlem section of New York City.

Behavioral Consultation.   A model of consultation developed by John Bergan (1977), in which a consultant and a consultee work together to modify a client's (child's) behavior in settings where the behavior takes place (e.g., classroom). Through the consultant's judicious use of verbal behavior, the consultee is helped to move through problem-solving stages in defining concerns in behavioral terms, helped in formulating and implementing behavior plans for changing client behavior, and helped in evaluating the attainment of consultation goals and the effectiveness of plans implemented to achieve goals (Bergan & Kratochwill, 1990). *Conjoint Behavioral Consultation* is based on the same theoretical principles as the Behavioral Consultation model, but differs in the fact that two parties involved with the client (e.g., parents and teachers) join together with the consultant to address the client's problem (Sheridan, Kratochwill, & Bergan, 1996).

Bell Curve, The.   *The Bell Curve* is a best-selling book published in 1994 by the late Harvard psychologist Richard J. Herrnstein and American Enterprise Institute political scientist Charles Murray. The book's title is named after the continuous probability distribution that is bell-shaped, with a peak at the mean and continuous decreasing probability as each point on the distribution deviates farther from the mean. The book's main thesis is that cognitive ability (operationalized as measured IQ) is normally distributed among human populations in the shape of a bell curve. Measured intelligence is a significant predictor of school achievement, highest educational and occupational attainments, income, and job performance—as well as negative social factors such as crime, unemployment, poverty rates, out-of-wedlock births, and welfare dependency.

The book includes 22 chapters and numerous tables, figures, and appendices, and is written in a style that is easily readable for both scientists and the lay public. The authors analyzed data from the National Longitudinal Study of Youth, sponsored by the U.S. Department of Labor's Bureau of Labor Statistics, in tracking more than 12,500 youths between the ages of 14 to 22 (beginning in year 1979) through college and beyond. In a little more than 800 pages, *The Bell Curve* is organized into four main sections. Part I (entitled "The Emergence of a Cognitive Elite") documents increasing American social stratification since the beginning of the 20th century on the basis of measured intelligence. Part II (entitled "Cognitive Classes and Social Behavior") documents the superiority of measured intelligence (compared to parents' socioeconomic status) in showing significant correlations with a variety of social and economic outcomes later in life. In Part III (entitled "The National Context"), the authors examine the role that IQ plays in racial/ethnic group differences in social and economic outcomes in the United States. Part IV (entitled "Living Together") examines social policy implications and limitations that arise from the reality of cognitive stratification in the United States.

The publication of *The Bell Curve* ignited immediate widespread attention, controversy, and commentary matched only by the publication in 1969 of Arthur Jensen's *Harvard Educational Review* article (Jensen, 1969). Most of the media and popular attention focused on Chapters 13 and 14, which discussed ethnic differences in cognitive ability and their social consequences. After showing in previous chapters that cognitive ability is significantly associated with both positive and negative social/economic outcomes in an exclusively white sample, Chapters 13 and 14 argue that much of the social and economic racial inequalities in American life are rooted (at least to a significant degree) by measured average racial differences in cognitive ability.

In addition to a slate of edited books offering responses from academics, responses to publication of *The Bell Curve* (both pro and con) appeared in popular periodicals such as *Newsweek*, *Forbes*, *National Review*, *Commentary Magazine*, the *New Criterion*, the *Weekly Standard*, the *Washington Post*, the *Wall Street Journal*, and the *New York Times*. Fifty-two professors, most of whom are research psychologists in intelligence and related fields, signed an opinion statement entitled "Mainstream Science on Intelligence." This statement supported the fundamental conclusions on intelligence as presented in *The Bell Curve*. The statement was written by Professor Linda Gottfredson, published in the *Wall Street Journal*, and reprinted in the journal *Intelligence* (Gottfredson, 1997). The American Psychological Association's Board of Scientific Affairs established a special task force to publish an investigative report on the research presented in *The Bell Curve*. The final report, entitled *Intelligence: Knowns and Unknowns*, was published in the *American Psychologist* in 1996 (see Neisser et al., 1996).

Brand-Name Programs.   This term, coined by Greenwood and Turner (2011), refers to home and/or school intervention programs known for the following characteristics: (1) the program was originally developed by a single investigator or a team of investigators, such that the program is closely associated with a single name or group of names; (2) the program has been developed, refined, and replicated in numerous sites both in America and in many international locations; (3) the program incorporates systematic, empirical evaluations of its effectiveness with a wide variety of target groups, and with independent investigators in different sites; (4) the program is typically supported by millions of dollars in federal grants; (5) the program has met and exceeded rigorous evaluation criteria established by formal review groups, whose purpose is to identify proven programs; (6) the program has established sites where groups of interested parties can receive formal training in the methods for implementing the program in a school or nonschool setting; (7) on-site consultation is usually provided for trained individuals/groups to maintain the treatment integrity of program methods; (8) there is a cost associated with initial, ongoing training and program materials; and (9) the program has a website where interested parties can access information about the program, contact information for training, and evaluation studies.

Broken Windows Theory.   The *Broken Windows Theory* was first coined by Wilson and Kelling (1982) in the context of neighborhood policing policy. The theory holds that a broken window in a neighborhood that is left unfixed is a sign that nobody cares, which in turn leads to more damage. Similarly, disorderly conditions and behaviors that are left unattended in neighborhoods are indicators of apathy, which in turn leads to more serious crimes, rapid urban decay, and the abandonment of entire neighborhoods to criminals.

As discussed in Wilson and Kelling (1982), a Stanford psychologist tested the Broken Windows Theory by leaving an automobile without license plates parked with its hood up on a street in the Bronx (a lower socioeconomic [SES] environment) and a comparable (but unaltered) automobile on a street in Palo Alto, California (a higher SES environment). The car in the Bronx was attacked by vandals within 10 minutes of its abandonment. The first to arrive were a family—father, mother, and young son—who removed the radiator and battery. Within 24 hours, virtually everything of value had been removed. Then random destruction began: Windows were smashed, parts were torn off, and upholstery was ripped. Children began to use the car as a playground. Most of the adult vandals were well-dressed, apparently clean-cut whites. The car in Palo Alto sat untouched for more than a week. The researcher then smashed part of it with a sledgehammer. Soon, passersby were joining in. Within a few hours, the car had been turned upside down and utterly destroyed. Again, the vandals appeared to be primarily respectable whites. The researchers concluded that vandalism can occur anywhere once communal barriers (i.e., the sense of mutual regard and the obligations of civility) are lowered by actions that seem to signal that no one cares.

Following these principles, the ethos discovered to be effective within paternalistic schools for low-income minority populations (see Sidebar 7.1) is to pay close attention to strict codes of behavior and dress (seemingly minor infractions similar to broken windows). When this is done consistently and regularly and is institutionalized as routine, then more serious discipline problems are virtually eliminated.

Bromide. A trite expression or phrase that has lost its originality through being overused.

Bureau of Indian Education (BIE). The Bureau of Indian Education (BIE) is one of two Bureaus (the other being the Bureau of Indian Affairs) that operate under the U.S. Department of the Interior to form policies/procedures, supervise program activities, and approve the expenditure of funds appropriated for the education of Native American tribal and Alaska Native children. The passage of the Indian Self-Determination and Education Assistance Act of 1975 (P.L. 93-638) gave authority to federally recognized tribes to contract with the Bureau of Indian Affairs for the operation of Bureau-funded schools, and to determine education programs suitable for Native children. Subsequent federal amendments provided funds directly to tribally operated schools, empowered Indian school boards, and permitted local hiring of teachers and staff. As of school year 2007–2008, the BIE funded 183 schools located on 64 reservations in 23 states. The BIE also funds or operates off-reservation boarding schools and dormitories near reservations for students attending public schools. The BIE directly operates two postsecondary institutions: the Haskell Indian Nations University in Lawrence, Kansas, and the Southwest Indian Polytechnic Institute in Albuquerque, New Mexico (accessed September 2010 from http://www.bia.gov/WhatWeDo/ServiceOverview/IndianEducation/index.htm).

Busing. In the wake of the 1954 *Brown v. Board of Education* Supreme Court decision outlawing state-sponsored racial segregation, many public schools throughout America continued to be de facto segregated due to long-standing segregated housing patterns in local neighborhoods. In the wake of the *Swann v. Charlotte-Mecklenburg Board of Education* ruling of 1971, the U.S. Supreme Court held that busing was an appropriate remedy for rectifying racial imbalances within and among public schools, even when such imbalances resulted from student selection based on geographic proximity to schools (e.g., as in neighborhood schools). *Busing* (sometimes called "forced busing") became a term used to describe the practice of assigning and transporting students by schoolbuses to schools over long distances (under court orders) for the purpose of overcoming the effects of residential segregation on a school's racial demographics.

Under federal supervision, numerous school districts throughout the United States implemented mandatory busing plans within their districts in the 1970s and 1980s. Although a few plans are still in effect today, busing to achieve school integration has experienced a sharp decline because of changes in residential housing patterns, the use of alternate plans for racial integration (e.g., magnet schools), and a host of unintended negative consequences (see discussion in Chapters 3 and 4). (See also Desegregation, Integration, and White Flight, this chapter.)

Charter Schools.   Broadly defined, *charter schools* are "publicly funded schools that are granted significant autonomy in curriculum and governance in return for greater accountability" (Buckley & Schneider, 2007, p. 1). Although the concept behind charter schools was first proposed in the 1970s, it was not until the early 1990s that Minnesota and California became the first states to pass charter school laws. As of 2005, more than 3,400 charter schools had been created in the United States, serving more than 1 million students (Vanourek, 2005). Charter schools are created when a local agency applies to the state to operate as a school at public expense. Thus, a governmental relationship is established between the charter school and the state agency that is responsible for granting charters, which allows the school to operate independently from state educational bureaucracies and local school boards. This allows the charter school to experiment with different methods of instruction and school organization (Spring, 2010).

In theory, charter schools are designed to be more responsive to the needs of parents, students, and the surrounding community, thereby improving the match between what the school offers and what parents, students, and the community prefer. By federal law, any time a charter school has more applications than seats available, it must conduct a lottery to fill the seats (see Shane, 2010, for an example of charter schools' popularity with parents). By some estimates, the parental waiting lists for admission to charter schools are equivalent in number to approximately 9 percent of the number of students currently enrolled in charter schools (Walberg, 2007). The Charter Schools division of the U.S. Department of Education provides web links to state laws governing charter schools, which can be accessed at http://www.uscharterschools.org

Chicano.   The terms *Chicano* and *Chicana* are used in reference to U.S. citizens of Mexican descent. The term began to be widely used beginning in the 1960s and early 1970s. For some people, the term connotes positive aspects of ethnic pride, identity, and political awareness. For others, the term may have pejorative connotations and is not universally accepted by all Mexican Americans.

Civil Rights Moralism.   "Civil rights moralism" (a phrase coined by Lynch, 1997) refers to a template, rooted in the history of the civil rights movement in America, that is used as a lens through which the dynamics of contemporary racial/ethnic conflicts and/or problems are interpreted. In this template, all racial/ethnic conflicts can be reduced to a simplistic morality play between innocent victim groups versus evil oppressor groups.

In this morality play, any statistical disparities among racial/ethnic groups in income, occupations, or education achievements are assumed to be the result of prejudice and discrimination of some form in society (Sowell, 1984). Therefore, the antidote to such perceived wrongdoing takes the form of political activism and/or intervention from the legal/court system. In the realm of public education, for example, civil rights moralism is played out when the federal Office of Civil Rights and state divisions of special education pressure school districts to remedy "disproportionate representation" of minority groups in certain special education categories. Similarly, when racial minority students are underrepresented in classes for the gifted, the application of civil rights moralism would interpret this situation as minorities being "denied access" to a higher-quality curriculum (analogous to blacks being denied service at commercial lunch counters in the segregated South during the Civil Rights era).

When commenting on observed group differences in IQ test scores, Williams (1974) states that "IQ and achievement tests are nothing but updated versions of the old signs down South that read 'For Whites Only'" (p. 32), which is designed to evoke vivid imagery rooted in civil rights moralism. As a result, educators and psychologists who advocate for lowering or abandoning admissions standards for gifted eligibility, or the abolishment of IQ testing in schools (in order to manipulate racial representation in special education), can feel virtuous in the sense that these positions are seen as analogous to the noble goals of the civil rights movement of the 1950s and 1960s.

Cognitive Styles.   (see Learning Styles).

Coleman Report.   The *Coleman Report* (Coleman, 1966) is the moniker given to a controversial (for its time) research report published in 1966, under the title *Equality of Educational Opportunity*. The Coleman Report is widely considered to be a landmark in policy research, being one of the first social scientific studies specifically commissioned by Congress in order to inform government policy related to schools. The report was named after its principal author, sociologist James S. Coleman, and was based on an extensive survey of approximately 650,000 students and teachers in more than 3,000 schools nationwide.

The design of the study provided answers to the question of how much, and in what ways, schools were able to overcome the inequalities (notably those associated with race) with which children came to school. The results of the report showed that variations in school quality (as indexed by such measures as expenditure per pupil, size of school library) showed little association with levels of educational attainment, when students of comparable social backgrounds were compared across schools. By comparison, differences in students' family backgrounds showed a substantial association with school achievement. Second, students' educational attainment was also related (although less strongly) to the backgrounds of the other students in the school.

The study was considered controversial because it challenged a major orthodoxy of the times, which was that increased spending on education could rectify social deficits. However, Coleman's findings on the effects of peer backgrounds were interpreted by policy makers to provide support for the notion that disadvantaged black children learn better in well-integrated classrooms. This conclusion is viewed as helping to set in motion the mass busing of students to achieve racial balance in public schools in the 1960s and 1970s, a practice that Coleman later evaluated as resulting in failure (due to white flight from many integrated schools).

Coleman's subsequent work was designed to identify those characteristics of schools that showed significant relationships to achievement outcomes. As examples, his later research (Coleman, Hoffer, & Kilgore, 1982) suggested that, after controlling for family background and other effects, pupils in private Catholic schools did better than others not attending such schools, because of the higher academic demands and disciplinary standards present in these schools (as well as the kinds of families and communities to which the children belonged). See Clark (1996) for an excellent summary and appraisal of the Coleman Report, subsequent research that was inspired by the report, and Coleman's contributions to education.

Conduct Disorder.   According to the *Diagnostic and Statistical Manual of Mental Disorders— Fourth Edition* (DSM-IV; American Psychiatric Association, 1994), a *conduct disorder* represents a repetitive and persistent pattern of behavior—usually present in the home, school, and community—in which the basic rights of others or major age-appropriate societal norms or rules are violated. Children and adolescents with this disorder often initiate aggressive behavior and react aggressively to others; initiate deliberate destruction of others' property; and engage in frequent deceit, lying, and/or breaking promises to others.

Conservative.   In a broad sense, conservatism represents an ideology that values the preservation of traditional principles, institutions, and practices that evolve slowly over time. In the United States, a conservative is a person who holds social, cultural, and political beliefs that are viewed as fundamentally different from those self-identified as liberal (see Liberal, this chapter). In reality, however, social, cultural, and political beliefs are multidimensional, and beliefs on a range of issues fall within a graded continuum rather than locked categories. A conservative tends to favor personal responsibility, limited government, the value of free markets, individual liberty, traditional American values, and a strong national defense. Many subcategories of American conservatism have been identified, which include (but are not limited to) social conservatism, fiscal conservatism, religious conservatism, and libertarian conservatism.

On social issues related to minority groups and schools, conservatives tend to favor preserving the definition of traditional marriage, and the use of school vouchers as a means of improving school performance. Conservatives tend to oppose illegal immigration, the use of race/ethnicity as a preferential factor in selection processes, and the removal of Christian (and other religious) symbols from public and government spaces.

Construct Bias (testing).   Construct bias is thought to occur when evidence shows that a mental test may not be measuring the same construct in one group compared to what is thought to be measured in another group. Evidence for construct bias is suggested whenever there are significant differences between groups in internal consistency, reliability estimates, temporal stability estimates, the correlation of raw scores with chronological age, the statistical interaction of test items by group membership, the rank order of item difficulties, item intercorrelations, the factor structure of tests and/or items and the magnitudes of factor loadings, differences between groups in item characteristic curves, and differences in the frequencies of distractors chosen in multiple-choice test items (see Jensen, 1980, Chapter 9).

Construct-Irrelevant Variance.   The variance in a set of test scores should, in theory, result from variance among examinees in whatever construct the test is designed to measure. *Construct-irrelevant variance* refers to the "extent to which test scores are influenced by factors that are irrelevant to the construct that the test is intended to measure" (AERA, APA, NCME, 1999, p. 173–174). Sources extraneous to the intended construct, which may cause a test to be more difficult for some individuals or groups, include—but are not limited to—language, cultural, emotional, or other disability-related factors. Sources extraneous to the intended construct, which may cause an examinee to respond correctly in ways that are irrelevant to the construct being assessed include—but are not limited to—"test-wiseness" (Messick, 1989). Thus, the presence of construct-irrelevant variance necessarily undermines the accurate interpretation of test scores (see Test Bias, this chapter).

Cooperative Learning.   *Cooperative learning* is the name given to an approach to organizing classroom academic and social learning experiences that uses small groups for enabling students to work together in helping their own and each other's learning (Johnson & Johnson, 2005). Three types of cooperative learning models have been identified in the literature. In *formal cooperative learning*, groups of students work together for anywhere from one class period to several weeks to achieve shared learning goals or to complete specific tasks/assignments. *Informal cooperative learning* involves students working together for anywhere from a few minutes to one class period in short, focused class discussions (e.g., 2–5 minutes). *Cooperative base groups* are long-term groups with stable memberships, the purpose of which is to provide mutual support and encouragement for making academic progress.

Some multicultural educators argue that cultural-minority children achieve better when cooperative learning strategies are used (e.g., see Lee & Slaughter-Defoe, 2004), while others argue that cooperative learning strategies have a positive effect on intercultural friendships and interactions (Cohen & Lotan, 2004).

Cultural Competence.   *Cultural competence* is a concept frequently found in healthcare, education, and applied psychology training. Although many definitions for this term have been advanced, the term generally implies a consolidation of knowledge, attitudes, and skills required to work effectively with persons or clients from different cultural backgrounds in reducing conflict, improving services, and facilitating positive outcomes in work settings (see additional definitions in Frisby, 2009, Table 40.1). Although this term has become ubiquitous in school psychology professional training since the 1990s, it is characterized by an amalgamation of scholars' professional (though subjective) opinions as to the ideal knowledge, attitudinal, and behavioral skill sets that should be circumscribed by the concept—as opposed to the objective measurement of actual behaviors, knowledge, or skills in work settings (for further discussion, see Frisby, 2009).

Cultural Equivalence (testing).   *Cultural equivalence* refers to a general standard used by psychometricians, test developers, and test users to evaluate the extent to which the same tests developed and used with different cultural groups (however defined) have the same psychometric properties and subsequent interpretation of test results (with or without appropriate translation procedures). As found in the social science and testing literature, however, this term has both a politicized (i.e., subjective) meaning and a nonpoliticized (i.e., empirical) meaning. In the former perspective, some critics use subjective rationalizations to accuse tests of not demonstrating cultural equivalence, primarily on the grounds that different racial/ethnic groups achieve different mean scores on tests (e.g., see Helms, 1992), which has been shown to be inadequate as a justification for test bias (see Test Bias, this chapter). From an empirical perspective (e.g., see Hambleton & Li, 2005; Hambleton, Merenda, & Speilberger, 2005; van de Vijver & Leung, 2001; van de Vijver & Tanzer, 2004), *cultural equivalence* serves as an umbrella term that subsumes the empirical evaluation of *linguistic equivalence* (where both spoken and written language translated for use in a different group nevertheless has the same meaning), *construct equivalence* (the same construct is measured by a translated or untranslated test across all cultural groups studied; sometimes labeled *structural equivalence* or *functional equivalence*), and *measurement unit equivalence* (score differences among examinees within each group have the same interpretation).

Cultural Immersion Schools.   Cultural immersion schools are schools in which subjects are taught from the perspective of a particular religious, cultural, ethnic, or language group. Many cultural immersion schools are private; however, some educators propose the creation of cultural immersion schools within the public school system as a means for combating low student academic achievement or educational failure within a specified subset of students (e.g., see Scott, 2009). Other educators create voluntary cultural immersion curricula within schools as a means of developing advanced proficiency in a culture or language (e.g., see Bellevue School District's Spanish immersion program, accessed from https://www.bsd405.org/puestadelsol/about/school-at-a-glance/what-is-spanish-immersion.aspx).

The Islamic Schools League of America operates approximately 30 schools across America designed to provide children of Muslim parents with an Islamic-centered K–12 education (accessed at http://www.theisla.org/staticpages/index.php/AboutUs). According to its website (http://muslimamericansociety.org/main/content/council-islamic-schools), the Muslim American Society Council on Islamic Schools "offers several technical and support services as well as professional training programs for teachers and administrators of full-time and part-time Islamic schools." According to its website (http://www.torah-umesorah.com), membership in the National Society of Hebrew Day Schools consists of more than 675 day schools with a total student enrollment of more than 190,000 students.

Culture.   *Culture* is a considerably complex social and psychological concept evoked to explain and describe patterns of human cognition and behavior. In order to understand the concept, different cultural groups have been closely observed and studied all over the world by scholars, dating back from ancient Greek history and up to present times (see Kitayama & Cohen, 2007). *Cultural anthropology* is the scholarly discipline that is best known for the serious study of the culture concept, with Franz Boas, Edward Sapir, Ruth Benedict, Margaret Mead, Abram Kardiner, and A. Irving Hallowell being the early scholars most notable for their scientific contributions to its study (LeVine, 2007). Due to the sheer complexity inherent in the culture concept, coupled with sociopolitical influences and pressures, contemporary applied psychology has oversimplified the culture concept as referring to a collection of traits that define particular groups or collections of people—typically (but not always) defined by race, geographic boundaries, or language. In this oversimplified view, culture is characterized as a monolithic entity that discrete, internally homogeneous groups "have"—and other groups "don't have." This leads to the popular (but oversimplified) notion that culture refers to a group's collective personality or character (Markus & Hamedani, 2007). Readers are encouraged to consult Chapter 2 for a critique of oversimplified characterizations of culture and how such characterizations have been used to serve sociopolitical objectives.

Literally hundreds of definitions for *culture* have been advanced in the social and behavioral sciences literature (e.g., see Borowsky, Barth, Shweder, Rodseth, & Stolzenberg, 2001; Kroeber & Kluckhohn, 1952; Sapir & Irvine, 2002), hence no single "definitive" definition will be offered here. Triandis (2007) opines that, on balance, most serious culture researchers share the following observations: (a) *Culture emerges in adaptive interactions between humans and environments.* The idea here is that culture is both constrained and shaped by a group's environment, leading to the development of language, writing, tools, skills, ways of organizing information, patterns of behavior, intellectual/moral/aesthetic standards, marriage/kinship behavioral patterns, systems of government and/or ways of controlling behavior, and social norms. (b) *Culture consists of shared elements.* Here, persons who share a common language, time period (e.g., living in the 19th versus 21st centuries), and geographic region are more likely to interact, and thus are more likely to share a common culture than those who do not. (c) *Culture is transmitted across time periods and generations.* Here, cultural transmission can occur *vertically* (as in transmission from parents to offspring), *horizontally* (as in transmission among colleagues in a work environment), and *obliquely* (as in transmission from social institutions such as schools, churches, and popular media to persons within a society).

Culture-Bound Fallacy.   This fallacy is committed whenever mental test items are judged, on their face, to be "culturally biased," and hence unfair to examinees from a particular group (see Jensen, 1980, p. 371–372). Such judgments are typically made on the basis of a non-empirical evaluation of the items' content and/or face validity, leading to the gratuitous conclusion that the cultural background experiences of examinees from a particular cultural group would place such individuals at an unfair disadvantage in responding correctly to certain test item(s). Research has demonstrated the failure of this method to reliably identify mental test items that have been empirically established to be relatively more or less difficult for members of particular cultural minority groups (e.g., see Jensen & McGurk, 1987; Sandoval & Mille, 1980).

Culture Broker.   A *culture broker* is an individual who functions as a bridge, link, or mediator between persons or groups who differ in cultural, social class, ethnic, racial, or language backgrounds—for the purpose of reducing conflict or facilitating cooperation and/or meaningful communication. In the school setting, for example, a culture broker can be a person who speaks both English and a non-English language. Such an individual can assist in helping non-English-speaking parents and English-speaking teachers to communicate in the context of school meetings. Sometimes schools employ *home/school communicators*, whose job is to serve as a go-between for interpreting community/neighborhood needs and concerns to school personnel, and at the same time encouraging community residents to cooperate with school initiatives.

Culture × Treatment Interaction.   *Culture × Treatment Interaction* is a name applied to the gratuitous assumption that the effectiveness of a school intervention for a given individual should necessarily differ as a direct function of differences between individuals in their racial/ethnic group membership (euphemistically designated as "culture"). If a suggested school intervention (e.g., promoted in professional training texts) makes no mention of racial/ethnic group membership, the belief in a culture × treatment interaction leads to the expectation that the intervention, in order to be effective, must be modified to some unspecified degree to accommodate that individual's cultural background (e.g., see discussions of "culturally sensitive interventions" in Bernal & Sáez-Santiago, 2006; Kemple et al., 2006; Quinn & Jacob, 1999).

Curriculum-Based Assessment.   *Curriculum-Based Assessment* (CBA) has been defined as any set of measurement procedures that use direct observation and recording of a student's performance in the local curriculum as a basis for gathering information to make instructional decisions (Deno, 1987). CBA is an umbrella term that encompasses at least four different models, each of which may differ according to each model's technical adequacy, item construction procedures, scoring procedures, and the school decisions for which the model is most appropriately used (Shinn, Rosenfield, & Knutson, 1989). Four of the most well-known models of CBA are *Criterion-Referenced* CBA (CR-CBA), *Curriculum-Based Assessment for Instructional Design* (CBA-ID), *Curriculum-Based Measurement* (CBM), and *Curriculum-Based Evaluation* (CBE; see discussion by Shinn, Rosenfield, & Knutson, 1989).

Curriculum-Based Measurement.   *Curriculum-Based Measurement* (CBM) is one among many models of Curriculum-Based Assessment (CBA). CBM has been defined as "a set of standardized and short duration tests (i.e., 1–5 minutes) used by educators to evaluate the effects of their instructional interventions in the basic skills of reading, mathematics, spelling, and written expression" (Shinn, 2008, p. 243). CBM is the most technically and psychometrically sophisticated assessment model among the various CBA models (see Shinn, Rosenfield, & Knutson, 1989). CBM procedures have been used, in varying degrees, by school districts to determine special education eligibility, instructional education plan (IEP) goal setting, and general progress monitoring (Shinn, 2008).

Desegregation.   This term refers to the act or process of removing segregation (i.e., social policies that keep groups apart) by allowing access to opportunities/activities by people of all race, ethnicity, or language groups. As applied to the *Brown v. Board of Education* Supreme court decision of 1954, desegregation is fundamentally a restriction on government power, where the state may not use race as the basis for school assignments. As such, racial groups may still remain separated as long as it is not compelled by government (D'Souza, 1995). Unfortunately, desegregation is often erroneously confused with "forced integration" (see Integration, this chapter). According to the Civil Rights Act of 1964, "desegregation means the assignment of students to public schools and within such schools without regard to their race, color, religion or national origin, but desegregation shall not mean the assignment of students to public schools in order to overcome racial imbalance" (quoted in D'Souza, 1995, p. 622).

DIBELS *(Dynamic Indicators of Basic Early Literacy Skills)*. DIBELS is a downward extension of Curriculum-Based Measurement (CBM) methodology for assessing early literacy skills in kindergarten and at-risk first-grade students (Kaminski & Good, 1998), and reading skills up to the sixth grade. DIBELS focuses primarily on early identification of reading problems through progress monitoring of early reading skill acquisition. Examples of skills measured by DIBELS tasks include, but are not limited to, initial sound fluency, phoneme segmentation fluency, nonsense word fluency, and letter naming fluency. Current materials, resources, research, and information related to the application of DIBELS measurement to school systems are available from the Center on Teaching and Learning at the University of Oregon (accessed at https://dibels.uoregon.edu).

DIF *(Differential Item Functioning)*. In psychometrics, DIF refers to a class of statistical procedures designed to evaluate the difference in item performance between two groups of examinees that are matched on the construct measured by a test, questionnaire, or scale (Dorans & Holland, 1993). Here, an item is said to display DIF if persons from different groups who possess the *same* latent ability or skill have a *different* probability of giving a certain response (e.g., item parameters estimated by Item Response Theory). For a readable treatment of DIF methods, see Embretson and Reise (2000).

Difference Doctrine. The *Difference Doctrine* is one among six implicit doctrines that comprise multiculturalism ideology (Frisby, 2005a). This doctrine assumes that racial/ethnic/language differences among groups or individuals must *necessarily* imply mutually exclusive and reliable historical, cultural, psychological, and/or behavioral differences. In order to preserve the integrity of multiculturalism ideology, the Difference Doctrine must exaggerate differences *between* racial/ethnic/language groups, while simultaneously downplay or ignore significant individual differences *within* groups. A related outgrowth of this doctrine is the assumption that the ways in which groups differ is much more important for pre- and inservice professionals to understand compared to ways in which groups are similar (see also Culture × Treatment Interaction, this chapter).

Digraph. In phonics, a digraph is a pair of letters that represent a single speech sound (e.g., the *ea* in *meat* or the *th* in *they*).

Discrimination. This term connotes slightly differing meanings depending on the contexts within which it is used. In cognitive psychology, discrimination refers to cognitive or sensory processes involved in perceiving differences between objects, concepts, or stimuli. In the social sciences, discrimination refers to (positive or negative) prejudicial treatment of an individual based on his or her membership in an identifiable group or category. In psychometrics, discrimination means "to show a reliable or statistically significant difference between individuals or groups on some measurement, index, or descriptive statistic" (Jensen, 1980, p. 375; see also Nondiscriminatory Assessment, this chapter).

Disparate Impact. *Disparate impact* is a legal phrase, found primarily in discussions of employment law, that attempts to prove "intentional discrimination by inference" (Ford, 2008). Disparate impact cases arise from situations where a neutral practice or policy (on its face) has an adverse disproportionate impact on members of a specified protected class. For example, if an employment policy states that workers must drive their own cars to work, but a disproportionate number of workers from a particular racial/ethnic minority group do not own their own cars, then one can say that this requirement (though not created from a deliberate intention to discriminate) has a "disparate impact" on said protected group. In disparate impact cases, defendants must show that the employment policy or requirement is job-related and consistent with a business necessity. However, the plaintiff may win disparate impact cases if it can be shown that the employer can adopt an alternative practice (which satisfies a business necessity) that avoids having a disparate impact on a protected class. In the employment arena, disparate impact is the legal strategy used to litigate situations where standardized test results (with a set cut score) allow one ethnic/racial group to be hired or promoted at greater rates than another group.

Distributive Property (math).   There are four properties that help make multiplication problems easier to solve. They are the commutative, associative, multiplicative identity, and distributive properties. According to the distributive property: *The sum of two numbers times a third number is equal to the sum of each addend times the third number.* For example, $6 \times (3 + 4) = 6 \times 3 + 6 \times 4$.

Diversity.   In a politically neutral sense, the word *diversity* simply means the state or quality of being dissimilar, varied, or different. Over decades, this term has morphed into a ubiquitous buzzword representing a sociopolitical ideology that has been infused throughout all aspects of America's social, civic, business, and educational life. In contemporary lexicon, the word *diversity* is the rallying cry for a movement that pursues racial, ethnic, and language group representation in outcomes as a pre-eminent social ideal. According to Wood (2003), diversity ideology is energized by the hope that "once individuals of diverse backgrounds are brought together, a transformation will take place in people's attitudes—primarily within the members of the formerly exclusive group, who will discover the richness of the newcomers' cultural backgrounds. Diversity will [presumably] breed tolerance and respect, and . . . will enhance the effectiveness of work groups . . . , contribute to economic prosperity . . . , [and] create good will and social betterment in every direction . . . The pursuit of diversity is held to be both practically good and personally redemptive" (p. 5, 6, 8, 9). As a practical application, diversity ideology is justified on the grounds that racial, ethnic, and language groups have a prescriptive right to special privileges and representation in valued outcomes "in proportion to how much their purported ancestors were victimized in the past" (Wood, 2003, p. 10). As a sociopolitical movement, diversity spawns the creation of "diversiphiles" ("professional multiculturalists" who appear to be obsessed with the aggressive promotion and dissemination of diversity ideology) and "diversicrats" (administrators in business, government, and/or academia hired specifically to regulate and enforce diversity quotas, goals, and timetables; Woods, 2003). (See also the Inclusion Doctrine, this chapter.)

Egalitarian Fallacy.   In the context of the test bias literature, this term refers to "the gratuitous assumption that all human populations are essentially identical or equal in whatever trait or ability [a] test purports to measure" (Jensen, 1980, p. 370). Therefore, any difference among population subgroups in the mean or standard deviation of obtained scores from a test is assumed to constitute evidence that a test is "biased"—and conversely, a test that does not reflect these differences is assumed, gratuitously, to be free of bias (see Test Bias, this chapter).

Egalitarianism.   Egalitarianism is an ideology or social philosophy that believes one or more of the following tenets: (a) all human subgroups are inherently equal in worth, dignity, and value; (b) all human subgroups should reflect equal social, educational, political, and economic outcomes in a society; (c) all human subgroups are assumed to have an equal distribution of abilities, talents, and developed skills. If an outcome reflects inequalities in outcomes among subgroups, then a person driven by egalitarianism ideology believes in the moral imperative to promote and advocate for equality in outcomes.

Emic vs. Etic Perspective.   Refers to terms originating in linguistics, which were then appropriated by cultural anthropologists in referring to two different ways of understanding data from the observation of human behavior. An *emic* perspective reflects the viewpoint of members within a culture (i.e., insiders) concerning their own interpretation of their group's customs and beliefs. An *etic* perspective reflects the viewpoint of observers who are outside of a culture (i.e., outsiders). These terms have been used in the field of counseling psychology when understanding clients in culturally specific terms (i.e., an "emic" perspective) as opposed to understanding clients in the context of human universals (i.e., an "etic" perspective; Sue & Sue, 2003).

Emotional Disturbance.   In federal special education eligibility law, *emotional disturbance* is defined as a condition exhibiting one or more of the following characteristics over a long period of time—and to a marked degree—that adversely affects a student's educational performance: (a) an inability to learn that cannot be explained by intellectual, sensory, or health factors; (b) an inability to build or maintain satisfactory interpersonal relationships with peers and teachers; (c) inappropriate types of behavior or feelings under normal circumstances; (d) a general pervasive mood of unhappiness or depression; (e) a tendency to develop physical symptoms or fears associated with personal or school problems. The term includes schizophrenia, and does not apply to students who are socially maladjusted, unless it is determined that they have an emotional disturbance (quoted from Pierangelo & Giuliani, 2007).

Environment.   This term encompasses every cause of both individual and group differences in a measured trait that is not genetic (see Heritability, this chapter). As outlined by Miele (2002), environmental causes include biological factors (e.g., exposure to toxic chemicals, mother's age and health during pregnancy, problems during childbirth), socioeconomic factors (e.g., family income), and qualitative sociocultural factors (quality of the neighborhood and family in which an individual is raised).

Ethnicity.   An ethnic group is a group of people whose members identify psychologically with one another on the basis of one or more commonalities in race, language, culture, country of origin, geographical residence, migration history, religion, folk traditions, or sociopolitical characteristics. However, ethnicity is not synonymous with any of these terms. That is, many distinct ethnic groups can exist *within* any one racial, cultural, or language group. Members of ethnic groups share an ethnic identity that is acutely aware of their group's distinctiveness from members of outgroups. According to the *Harvard Encyclopedia of Ethnic Groups* (Thernstrom, 1980), at least 100 distinct ethnic groups exist in America, and at least 500 distinct ethnic groups are distributed around the globe (see http://en.wikipedia.org/wiki/Lists_of_ethnic_groups).

Equity Doctrine.   The Equity Doctrine is one among six implicit doctrines that constitute multiculturalism ideology (Frisby, 2005a). There are both noncontroversial and controversial versions of this doctrine. In the noncontroversial version of the Equity Doctrine, nearly all education professionals agree that all students should be treated fairly and equally in the process of assisting them in achieving a successful educational experience. In the controversial version of this doctrine, equity is assumed to be achieved only when all subgroups of students achieve the same level of educational outcomes.

ESL (English as a Second Language) Programs.   According to Ochoa (2005), the major characteristic of ESL programs is that they do not provide native-language instruction to second-language learners, which differs from other types of bilingual education programs. In ESL programs, all instruction is provided in English. Here, students spend most of their school day in regular mainstream classrooms but attend daily ESL classes. In other models, students are pulled out from their mainstream classes to take ESL lessons with a special teacher, or ESL teachers may assist mainstream teachers in their classrooms with students who are not proficient in English. Some models segregate non-English speakers for concentrated high-intensity English learning for the entire day, which may last over a summer, semester, or full year before students are integrated into a school with native English speakers (see Brisk, 2006).

Eurocentrism.   As an abstraction, *Eurocentrism* can be defined as a belief, attitude, or mindset that values Europe, European culture, or European interests above all others. In contemporary application, however, the term *Eurocentrism* is frequently used by American multiculturalists to characterize methods, values, and beliefs that presumably originate with white people. Eurocentrism serves as a foil against which to contrast viewpoints and theories that are presumed by multiculturalists to more accurately reflect the psychology of "people of color" (e.g., Afrocentrism; see Helms, 1989). Multiculturalists view Eurocentrism as the main roadblock that impedes a correct understanding of minority psychology, and they take great pains to warn audiences against the dangers of Eurocentric epistemology, Eurocentric worldviews, or Eurocentric research paradigms (Padilla, 2004; Sleeter & Bernal, 2004).

European American.   A European American is a resident of the United States who is descended from the original peoples of the European continent or non-European countries who have a large European diaspora (for a more detailed discussion, see LoConto & Francis, 2005). Within the context of the vernacular of multiculturalism ideology, the term is used as a counterpart to the term *African American*, and as such is used as a more formal way for labeling white people.

Extinction.   A component of a behavior modification program in which the likelihood of a specific behavior is decreased following the removal of a rewarding condition from the environment. In a classroom setting, an example of extinction would be to require students in a class not to pay attention to, or laugh at, another student who misbehaves in class.

Factor Analysis.   *Factor analysis* refers to a class of mathematical techniques, aided by a computer, for reducing data from a large number of variables (collected from the same group) to a smaller number of underlying sources of variance in the data (called factors or principal components). In psychometrics and the social sciences, a factor analysis is applied to a matrix of intercorrelations (or covariances) among a number of variables (e.g., measurements, test scores). This results in a factor loading matrix, which displays the correlation between each variable and each of a number of hypothetical underlying factors (see Kline, 1994, for a more detailed explanation).

g Factor.   *g* stands for *general intelligence factor*, which was discovered and developed into a theory by Charles Spearman in the first two decades of the 20th century (see discussion in Jensen, 1998b). *g* refers to a highly heritable construct, identified through factor analysis, which represents the most fundamental source of variability in individual differences shared (in varying degrees) by all mental tests. Subsequent research has demonstrated the substantial correlation of the *g* factor with physical and biological variables (e.g., body stature, head size, brain size, frequency of alpha brain waves, latency and amplitude of evoked brain potentials, rate of brain glucose metabolism, peripheral and brain nerve conduction velocity, general health), educational variables (e.g., scholastic achievement, learning ability), and life variables (e.g., job training success, job performance, occupational level). The size of the average black/white differences in performance on a wide variety of mental tests is best explained by differences in the tests' *g* loading (Jensen, 1998b).

Genotype.   Genotype refers to the specific combination and location of the genes on the chromosomes, which reflect the inherited codes carried by the cells within all living organisms. This stored information is used as a blueprint or set of instructions for building and maintaining a living creature—and is passed from one generation to the next. A person's genotype cannot be observed, but it carries the instructions that are used and interpreted by the cells to produce the outward, physical manifestation, or phenotype, of the organism (see Phenotype).

Gifted. Within the context of public education, the term *gifted* describes students "who demonstrate extraordinary performance or have the potential to demonstrate outstanding performance in the areas of general intellectual ability, specific academic areas, the fine and performing arts, creativity, and leadership" (Callahan, 2005, p. 225). Such students require services beyond, or qualitatively different from, what is offered in the regular school program and curriculum.

Group Identity Doctrine. *The Group Identity Doctrine* is one among six implicit doctrines that constitute multiculturalism ideology (Frisby, 2005a). This doctrine holds that individuals are little more than representatives of their racial/ethnic/language/social class groups. The Group Identity doctrine assumes that efforts to understand and/or study a group *necessarily* lead to greater insight and understanding into the behavior and psychology of individuals from that group. In addition, individuals are seen as inextricably linked behaviorally and psychologically to the groups of which they are members.

Head Start. Head Start is the name given to an early intervention program started in the spring of 1965 as part of the Johnson administration's "War on Poverty." Currently, the stated purpose of Head Start is to promote school readiness and sociocognitive development in children from high-poverty backgrounds through the provision of educational, health, nutritional, social, and other services to children and their families. Historically, however, the program initially began with expectations that it would raise the IQs of poor children and put them on an equal cognitive and academic footing with their more economically advantaged classmates as they entered school (Ravitch, 1983). The program began as an eight-week summer experience that served approximately 561,000 children nationwide before they entered kindergarten. Head Start was subsequently expanded to a yearlong prekindergarten program in 1966.

In order to establish Head Start services in communities, public and private agencies (e.g., school system, private preschool provider, city governments) submit grants to the appropriate federal agencies. Head Start is administered through the Department of Health and Human Services through the Head Start Bureau within the Administration on Children, Youth and Families, and the Administration for Children and Families (Greenfield, 2005). Children in families who meet poverty income guidelines based on family size are eligible for Head Start services, as are children with disabilities, children from families receiving public assistance, and children living in foster care regardless of their family's income (Greenfield, 2005). According to Greenfield (2005), as late as the 2002–2003 school year, approximately 19,200 Head Start Centers were in operation nationally, which contained 47,000 classrooms serving 909,608 children. When these statistics are broken down by race/ethnicity, approximately 32 percent of children served are African American, 27 percent are white, 30 percent are Hispanic, 3 percent are Native American, 2 percent are Asian, and 1 percent are Hawaiian/ Pacific Islanders. To date, more than 22 million children have been served through Head Start since its inception, at a cumulative cost of more than $120 billion.

On December 12, 2007, the Improving Head Start for School Readiness Act of 2007 became law, representing the first reauthorization and major revision of the Head Start Act since 1998. The 2007 Act retains and slightly rewords many provisions from the prior version of the law, and contains significant changes that affect grantee recompetition, program governance, eligibility and enrollment, monitoring and corrective actions, staff credentials, salary limits, and political activities (Tipton, 2008). The most significant of these changes is the provision to begin serving homeless children under Head Start.

Heritability. *Heritability* refers to the proportion of the total variance in a measured trait (e.g., height, weight, IQ scores) that is caused by genes, not the environment. This estimate is represented by the symbol h^2. For example, if the heritability of blood pressure in a group of people is $h^2 = 0.8$, it means that 80 percent of the variation in blood pressure measurements for that group is due to differences in genes among individuals in the group. The methods of quantitative genetics (see Plomin, 1994) are used to determine the proportion of variation in any measurable trait (within a given population at a given point in time) that is caused by heredity and the proportion that is caused by environment (see Environment, this chapter).

High-Stakes Testing.   High-stakes testing is the moniker given to standardized educational testing, the results from which have important consequences for both students and educators. For students, as an example, the results from high-stakes tests may determine promotion between grades or graduation from high school. For teachers and school administrators, results from student testing can be used to measure schoolwide achievement performance, which may possibly lead to salary increases. For charter schools, test results may be used, in whole or in part, to determine whether the school will continue to exist. Low-stakes testing, in contrast, means that no significant consequences result from student test performance.

Hispanic.   Derived from the Latin word for Spain, *Hispania*, this term generally describes all Spanish-speaking peoples in both the Northern and Southern global hemispheres. Hispanics constitute approximately 14 percent of the total U.S. population (roughly 38 million persons; Ramirez & Cruz, 2003). Although this term emphasizes the common denominator of Spanish language among groups, the term refers to subgroups that are heterogeneous in country of origin and racial background. For example, those who identify as Hispanic may also identify as Brazilian, Cuban, Mexican, Portuguese, Puerto Rican, South or Central American, or Spaniard. However, there remains some disagreement as to which groups should or should not be included under the broad Hispanic label (see Lopez, Lopez, Suarez-Morales, & Castro, 2005). For certain segments of Spanish speakers, the term *Latino* is preferred to Hispanic (particularly for those living in Western American states; see Latino/a, this chapter). Not all persons who may self-identify as Hispanic speak Spanish or even have a Spanish surname. Likewise, persons with Spanish surnames may not necessarily identify with an exclusively Spanish heritage (e.g., Louisiana Creole persons).

Homeschooling.   Homeschooling refers to the worldwide practice of educating children at home for a variable period of time before the college years (usually by parents, neighbors, or professional tutors), rather than enrolling children in public or private schools. Estimates of the total number of American children who are homeschooled as of 2010 range from 1.3 to 2 million. There are a variety of reasons why parents choose to homeschool their children. These include, but are certainly not limited to, one or more of the following reasons: (a) the conviction that public schools teach moral/social values that are in opposition to parental values; (b) the conviction that religious values forbid public schooling; (c) dissatisfaction with the quality of education in public schools; or (d) idiosyncratic personal and/or family reasons that require homeschooling (e.g., child illness).

The question of the advantages/disadvantages of homeschooling is a matter of debate, and research supporting opposing sides of the pro- versus anti-homeschooling debate may be tainted by a lack of objectivity. Nevertheless, opponents of homeschooling marshal the following arguments against this practice: (a) Homeschooling undermines the healthy socialization of children with age peers; (b) parents do not possess the quality of training that is comparable to professionally credentialed teachers; (c) or the potential for children to be socialized in the political, religious, or antisocial extremism that falls outside the mainstream of acceptable societal norms. Supporters of homeschooling marshal the following arguments in favor of this practice: (a) Homeschooling affords more flexibility in tailoring teaching methods to individual child needs; (b) vulnerable children are not "corrupted" by values that are offensive to parents; and (c) homeschooled students often outperform their matched peers on standardized tests. For links to homeschooling networks nationwide, as well as updates to changes in state laws, readers may wish to consult the Home School Legal Defense Association website (www.hslda.org).

Homily.   A solemn, moralizing lecture that is intended to be inspirational, but instead comes off as banal, uninspired, and tedious.

Homonym.   Homonyms are sets of two or more words that sound the same but have a different spelling. Examples are *meat/meet, write/right, pair/pear, seas/sees/seize.*

Ideologue.   An ideologue is a person who is prone to blindly and uncritically follow a particular ideology, and who is rigid and doctrinaire in his or her support of the ideology. Conformity to the ideology is the primary litmus test in the ideologue's thinking as to what ideas are deemed to be worthy. Militant ideologues are genuinely bewildered and indignant when others share a different or opposing viewpoint, hence the remedy for nonconformity to the favored ideology is to browbeat and propagandize the opposition into conformity.

Ideology.   An ideology is a philosophical value or belief system that consists of a set of propositions about why the world is the way it is and how things got this way. Ideologies are accepted as facts and truth by a group, which provides "true believers" with a picture of what is "wrong" with the world and how such wrongs can be corrected to produce a world "as it should be" (e.g., see O'Neill, 1981).

Inclusion Doctrine.   *The Inclusion Doctrine* is one among six implicit doctrines that constitute multiculturalism ideology (Frisby, 2005a). According to the Inclusion Doctrine, the highest standards of moral virtue are reflected in "aggressive efforts . . . to ensure that the presence, perspectives, contributions, needs, or opinions of racial/ethnic minority group members are fully represented in all endeavors related to one's professional functioning" (p. 59). The corollary is that less-than-enthusiastic attempts to promote inclusion are indicative of a covert or overt intent to "exclude." As an ideological movement, the Inclusion Doctrine has spawned the related professional buzzwords *diversity* and *tolerance. Diversity* is a ubiquitous term which holds that outcomes reflecting the broad representation of individuals from a variety of racial/ethnic/language groups are to be preferred philosophically over outcomes that reflect an over-representation of any one group (Clare, 2009). *Tolerance* movements communicate the idea that educational and psychological professionals are morally obligated to strive to understand, revere, appreciate, or respect cultural groups or practices that are unusual or different from one's own cultural experiences and background (Daugherty & Stanhope, 1998).

Individuals with Disabilities Educational Improvement Act (IDEIA).   IDEIA was first enacted as the Education for All Handicapped Children Act of 1975 (Public Law 94-142), renamed the Individuals with Disabilities Education Improvement Act (IDEIA) in 1990 (Public Law 101-476), amended (Public Law 102-119) in 1991, and again in 2004. On December 3, 2004, President George W. Bush signed the revised IDEIA legislation. IDEIA is a revised law that provides access for children with disabilities to a free, appropriate public education and improves the educational experience of such children. The latest revision is an attempt to update and improve the criteria for identifying a specific learning disability by relaxing the requirement that students must exhibit a severe discrepancy between ability and achievement in order to be found eligible for services under IDEIA (see Response to Intervention, this chapter).

Instructional Consultation.   *Instructional consultation* (IC) is a form of consultee-centered consultation that is broadly designed to enhance the academic achievement of students in schools. The cornerstone of IC is the "instructional triangle" (Rosenfield, 1987), which conceptualizes academic problems as a mismatch between a vulnerable learner, inadequate instruction, and a muddled conception of the task to be learned. Instructional consultants work with consultees (i.e., teachers, parents, and school staff) to facilitate a more effective match between these components of the instructional triangle. The original IC model has been expanded through research to include the idea of IC teams (Rosenfield & Gravois, 1996; Rosenfield, Silvia, & Gravois, 2008), which are multidisciplinary teams that focus on "improving and enhancing school staff competence as a route to both systems improvement and positive individual student outcomes" (Rosenfield, 2008, p. 1645).

Integration.   In the field of education, *integration* typically refers to the combining, or bringing together, of students from different racial, ethnic, or language groups in schools. Integration is not to be confused with *desegregation* (see Desegregation, this chapter). Court-ordered integration is a state- or government-mandated result, where personal or parental choice is overridden in order to ensure that different racial, ethnic, or language groups obtain the same educational experiences together. Whereas desegregation establishes and protects personal choice, forced integration seeks to compel a particular result (D'Souza, 1995).

Intelligence   (see *g* Factor).

Islam.   The word *Islam* means "submission to God." The term also describes a religion founded on the teachings of the Qur'an and the life example of the prophet Muhammad. An adherent of Islam is called a Muslim. The Qur'an is considered by Muslims as being the verbatim word of God (or Allah, in Arabic). Muhammad is considered by Muslims to be the last legitimate prophet of God, who has primacy over Abraham, Moses, and Jesus.

There are approximately 1.5 billion Muslims worldwide, which constitutes about 21 to 23 percent of the world's population. The largest majority-Muslim country in the world is Indonesia (88 percent of Indonesia's population). According to recent estimates, roughly 13 percent of the world's Muslims live in Indonesia, followed by 25 percent in South Asia, 20 percent in the Middle East, 15 percent in sub-Saharan Africa, 4 percent in Southeast Asia, and 2 percent in Central Asia (Pew Forum on Religion and Public Life, 2009). According to 2009 estimates, more than 300 million Muslims, or one-fifth of the world's Muslim population, live in countries where Islam is not the majority religion (Pew Forum on Religion and Public Life, 2009). Approximately 2.4 million Muslims live in the United States.

During the first half of the 20th century, a small number of African Americans have chosen to establish and follow a brand of Islamic teaching as interpreted through the Nation of Islam (NOI). Founded in the 1930s by Wallace Fard Muhammad, the NOI promoted black supremacy and separation from white Americans. In 1934, Elijah Muhammad became the leader of the NOI. One of the most well-known spokespersons for the NOI was Malcolm X, and to a lesser extent, the celebrated boxer Muhammad Ali. Currently, the American political figure Louis Farrakhan broke away from the NOI, led by Elijah Muhammad's son, and reestablished the NOI as an organization that has some degree of influence in contemporary African American communities (at the time of this writing).

In the wake of the attack on the World Trade Center and Pentagon on September 11, 2001, a "culture war" is being fought over how to appropriately regard the Muslim presence in America. On one side are those who feel that law-abiding Muslims are being unfairly targeted for stereotyping, prejudice, and discrimination. On the other side are those who feel that America has gone too far in appeasing Islamic advocacy, and they fault moderate Muslims for not speaking out more forcefully against radical Islamic elements within their communities.

Kinship Studies.   Within the discipline of quantitative genetics, kinship studies are indispensable for understanding the contribution of genetics, environment, and gene–environment interactions to variability in a phenotypic trait (see Phenotype, this chapter). In such studies, researchers observe the strength of the correlations between pairs of individuals representing differing degrees of kinship (e.g., parents with their adopted children; adopted siblings reared together; natural parents with their biological children adopted and raised in a different home; biological parents with their biological offspring raised in the same home; full siblings reared apart; full siblings reared together; fraternal twins reared together; identical twins reared apart; identical twins reared together).

KIPP (Knowledge Is Power Program) Schools.   KIPP schools are a national network of free, open-enrollment, college preparatory public schools designed to prepare students in under-served communities for success in college. The core principles of a KIPP education are academic achievement, character education, and college attendance. According to its website as of January 2012 (www.kipp.org/about-kipp), there are currently 109 KIPP schools in 20 states and the District of Columbia, which combined serve more than 32,000 students. Nationwide, there are approximately 30 KIPP elementary schools (Grades K–4), 61 KIPP middle schools (Grades 5–8), and 18 KIPP high schools (Grades 9–12). More than 85 percent of KIPP students are from low-income families who are eligible for the federal free or reduced-price meals program—and 95 percent are African American or Latino. KIPP schools boast that approximately 95 percent of their middle school students graduate from high school, and more than 85 percent of KIPP alumni eventually enroll in college.

Latino/Latina.   A term officially adopted in 1997 by the U.S. government, in referring to a self-designated alternative to the term *Hispanic*. The terms *Latino* (generic label for both sexes) and *Latina* (label specifically for females) designate persons of Latin American origin or heritage. Latin America encompasses Mexico, most of Central and South America, Cuba, the Dominican Republic, and Puerto Rico. The term *Hispanic* is more commonly used in the eastern portion of the United States, whereas *Latino/Latina* is more commonly used in the western portion of the United States (see Hispanic, this chapter).

Learning Disability.   The definition of *learning disability* can vary as a function of differences in how professional organizations define this term, or whether the perspective for understanding this term is medical, social, or educational. According to the federal educational definition under IDEIA, the term means a disorder in one or more of the basic psychological processes involved in understanding or in using language, spoken or written, that may manifest itself in an imperfect ability to listen, think, speak, read, write, spell, or to do mathematical calculations, including conditions such as perceptual disabilities, brain injury, minimal brain dysfunction, dyslexia, and developmental aphasia. This term does not include learning problems that are primarily the result of visual, hearing, or motor disabilities, of mental retardation, or emotional disturbance, or of environmental, cultural, or economic disadvantage (34 C.F.R. 300.7(c)(10). (See also Pierangelo & Giuliani, 2007, p. 53.)

Learning Potential Assessment.   *Learning potential assessment* (Van Der Aalsvoort, Ruijssenaars, & Resing, 2002) is an umbrella term that designates a family of assessment methods and techniques (e.g., see Budoff, 1987; Campione, 1989; Feuerstein, Rand, & Hoffmann, 1979) that can also be referred to as *interactive assessment* (Haywood & Tzuriel, 1992) or *dynamic assessment* (Haywood & Lidz, 2007). The theoretical underpinnings of this model are rooted in Vygotsky's (1986) notion of a *zone of proximal development*, which describes cognitive tasks that a child is able to perform only with the help of a more knowledgeable and experienced collaborator (or, in learning potential theory, a "mediator").

Learning potential assessment describes an assessment methodology where the student performs (usually nonverbal) cognitive tasks without help (called traditional, or "static," assessment), is then exposed to teaching on how to successfully solve similar tasks, then is retested on related tasks (but different from the original task) to determine the degree of improvement. Persons who improve their performance substantially from the first static assessment are said to have demonstrated high learning potential.

The attraction of learning potential assessment to multiculturalism ideology is rooted in the idea that learning potential assessment promises to unlock untapped learning potential in economically and culturally disadvantaged populations, who typically obtain lower scores, on average, within the context of traditional cognitive testing. Current international interest in the work of Professor Reuven Feuerstein, an originator of learning potential theory and methods, can be accessed at the International Center for the Enhancement of Learning Potential (see www.amanforpeace.net).

Learning Styles.   Readers must be careful to distinguish among similar terms such as *cognitive style*, *learning strategies*, and *thinking styles* (see Frisby, 2005c). A *learning style* is considered by many to be a habitual pattern that reflects how a student learns or prefers to learn (Frisby, 2005c). Related to this belief is the associated idea that student learning styles can be reliably assessed, and that teachers are obligated to adapt their classroom instructional methods to best fit each student's identified learning style (in order to promote the best learning outcomes). Multiculturalists then promote the idea that distinct learning styles are associated with race and/or ethnicity (e.g., see Dunn & Griggs, 1995; Hale-Benson, 1986), and that disproportionate rates of school failure for specific groups can plausibly be attributed to the mismatching of instruction with a students' race/ethnicity. According to Pashler, McDaniel, Rohrer, and Bjork (2008):

> The learning-styles view has acquired great influence within the education field, and is frequently encountered at levels ranging from kindergarten to graduate school. There is a thriving industry devoted to publishing learning-styles tests and guidebooks for teachers, and many organizations offer professional development workshops for teachers and educators built around the concept of learning styles. (p. 105)

Scientifically credible research on these concepts requires careful experimental designs that match homogeneous groups of subjects (representing different learning styles) with distinct instructional treatments in order to identify reliable learning style × instructional treatment interactions (Pashler et al., 2008). Despite the enormous published literature on learning styles, Pashler et al. found that very few studies incorporate correct experimental designs, and those that do often report findings that flatly contradict the validity of learning style × instructional treatment interactions. Literature reviews of multicultural applications of learning style theory highlight its weaknesses and lack of empirical support (see Frisby, 1993; Kane & Boan, 2005).

LEP (Limited English Proficient).   The term *limited English proficient* (LEP) has been defined in Title IX of the No Child Left Behind Act of 2001 (under General Provisions Part A, Section 9101) as an individual aged 3 through 21 who is enrolled or preparing to enroll in an elementary school or secondary school; was not born in the United States or whose native language is a language other than English; who is a Native American or Alaska Native, or a native resident of the outlying areas; who comes from an environment where a language other than English has had a significant impact on the individual's level of English language proficiency; or who is migratory (whose native language is a language other than English) and who comes from an environment where a language other than English is dominant; and whose difficulties in speaking, reading, writing, or understanding the English language may be sufficient to deny the individual the ability to meet the State's proficient level of achievement on State assessments, the ability to successfully achieve in classrooms where the language of instruction is English, or the opportunity to participate fully in society.

Liberal.   In a broad sense, liberalism represents an ideology that values the preservation of "progressive" social change, liberty, and human/equal rights. In the United States, a *liberal* is a person who holds social, cultural, and political beliefs that are viewed as fundamentally different from those self-identified as *conservative* (see Conservative, this chapter). In reality, however, social, cultural, and political beliefs are multidimensional, and beliefs on a range of issues fall within a graded continuum rather than locked categories. A liberal tends to favor government action to achieve equal opportunity and equality, and believes in a strong government role in alleviating social ills and solving social problems (e.g., poverty and discrimination). Many subcategories of American liberalism have been identified, which include (but are not limited to) classical liberalism, sociocultural liberalism, and libertarianism.

   On social issues related to minority groups and schools, liberals tend to favor marriage rights for same-sex couples; the financial support of public schools (e.g., through raising teacher salaries and reducing class size); race/ethnicity-based affirmative action for rectifying past discrimination; legal rights, government services, and pathways to amnesty for illegal immigrants; and a strict separation of church and state.

Liberal Racism.   *Liberal Racism* refers to a condescending and patronizing set of assumptions about nonwhite minority groups held by those who identify closely with a politically liberal worldview. Liberal racism assumes that racial differences are so profound, and the social disadvantages and historical grievances associated with these differences to be so inevitable, that nonwhite groups cannot be expected to adhere to basic standards of morality and behavior assumed to be fundamental to a shared civic culture (see critique in Sleeper, 1997). In this view, nonwhite minorities are helpless and are incapable of succeeding without the benefit of government set-asides, affirmative action, quotas, and/or lowered standards. Ironically, persons whose views are characterized by liberal racism consider themselves to be sympathetic toward minority groups and free from conventional, overt racism.

Libertarian.   *Libertarianism* is a political philosophy that places a high value on individual liberty and freedom, and opposes governmental conditions perceived as limiting this freedom. Libertarians believe individuals should be free to make choices for themselves and to accept responsibility for the consequences of the choices they make. However, a libertarian's support of an individual's right to make life choices does not necessarily translate into approval or disapproval of those choices. Libertarians generally do not identify themselves as belonging to the political left or political right, and many advocate third or alternative political parties. Readers interested in understanding nuanced subdivisions of libertarian philosophy can consult Bevir (2010).

Lower Class (socioeconomic status).   *Lower class* is an imprecise designation for persons/families at the lower end of the socioeconomic scale as measured by occupation, educational attainment, and yearly income levels (see Chapter 3). There are a variety of models for making subdivisions among classes within the socioeconomic status continuum. Hence, the lower class can describe individuals who are also designated as working class, working poor, the poor, or the underclass (Gilbert, 2011).

Marxism (and its relationship to multiculturalism).   *Marxism* is a political/economic philosophy named after the 19th-century German philosopher Karl Marx. With co-author Friedrich Engels, Marx wrote *The Communist Manifesto* in 1848. Marxism, and its close cousin Communism, were political systems that have been tried (and have subsequently failed) in such diverse countries as Afghanistan, Albania, Angola, Benin, Bulgaria, Chile, China, Republic of Congo, Cuba, Czechoslovakia, East Germany, Ethiopia, Grenada, Hungary, Laos, Moldova, Mongolia, Mozambique, Nepal, Nicaragua, North Korea, Poland, Romania, Russia, the USSR and its republics, South Yemen, Yugoslavia, Venezuela, and Vietnam.

Many academics in archaeology, anthropology, media studies, political science, theater, history, sociological theory, art history and theory, cultural studies, education, economics, geography, literary criticism, aesthetics, critical psychology, and philosophy have allowed Marxist thought to influence their writings in these areas. Marxist thought and ideas have also heavily influenced multiculturalism ideology, which is currently popular in school and counseling psychology journals, books, and professional newsletters. Several parallels between Marxism and multiculturalism can be readily identified (Ellis, 2010):

(a) The core tenet of Marxism views life as a political class struggle between those who own the means of production (capitalists, landlords, and the bourgeoisie) and those who work the means of production (the proletariat, workers, and peasants). Multiculturalism views life through the lens of racial/ethnic (i.e., whites vs. nonwhites), economic (i.e., affluent vs. low-income groups), language (i.e., English speakers vs. non-English speakers), citizenship (e.g., immigrants vs. natives), and lifestyle (i.e., mainstream vs. non-mainstream groups) conflicts. Both ideologies couch these conflicts in terms of a morality play, pitting victims against their victimizers and/or the oppressed against their oppressors.

(b) According to Marxism, the oppressed classes must develop their own "class consciousness," in order to help them focus on stark differences between them and the ruling classes—and to be sensitized to the various subtle and not-so-subtle ways that the ruling classes oppress them. The proletariat must also become aware that television, literature, art, music, education, and other forms of culture tend to reflect the ideology of the class to which the artist belongs. Thus, Marxism holds that these areas merely reflect the ideology of the capitalist system. According to multiculturalism, cultural/racial minority groups (and their sympathizers) must develop a sharpened consciousness of racism and Eurocentrism in psychology, psychometrics, and education—and learn how these views undermine the education and mental health of their group (e.g., see Banks & Banks, 2004; Helms, 1992, 1997; Naidoo, 1996).

(c) In Marxist thought, there is no such thing as an objective truth that is discovered through rational inquiry or communicated using the rules of logic and evidence. Here, truth simply varies as a function of a speaker's class perspective. Multiculturalism ideology teaches that it is wrong to compare racial/ethnic groups on any universal standard, because each group is thought to have its own "psychology" and unique truth system that cannot be questioned by those outside of the group.

(d) Marxist thought is perpetuated through political control of education, psychiatry, ethics, and social behavior—accomplished by ensuring that these areas conform to Marxist orthodoxy. Multiculturalism ideology is perpetuated by "political correctness"—that is, making sure that audiences "think correctly," "feel correctly," and develop the "correct attitudes" that can be approved by the basic tenets of multiculturalism orthodoxy (e.g., see Clare, 2009).

(e) In Marxist regimes, those who dissent from Marxist ideology were viewed as mentally ill, and sometimes were incarcerated. Under multiculturalism ideology, dissenters are viewed as "racist," "dangerous," "confused," "unprofessional," "unenlightened," "offensive," "radical right-wing conservatives," "intolerant," and "Eurocentric," among other names. Dissenters from multiculturalist thought are subjected to related sanctions (e.g., lawsuits, name-calling, denial of program accreditation, denial of academic tenure, lack of opportunities to publish, lack of grant funding, social censure; see Gottfredson, 1994, 2007, 2010).

(f) According to Marxism, the ultimate goal of a just society is when the worker class, through revolution, overthrows the capitalist class. This, in turn, will presumably lead to a "just" society where there will be no more classes and all property and means of production are owned by all. Under multiculturalism, Eurocentrism must be overthrown (see Asante, 2005) as one of many necessary steps toward "social justice" (Darling-Hammond, French, & Garcia-Lopez, 2002). Once this occurs throughout all levels of the educational system, there will presumably be no more educational inequities among racial/cultural groups in achievment outcomes.

Mastery Learning.   *Mastery Learning* (ML) is the name given to an integrated instructional, learning, and teaching philosophy that was first introduced into American education as far back as the 1920s (Block, 1971) and that has experienced periodic resurgences in popularity since then (see review by Davis & Sorrell, 1995). Philosophically, the mastery learning model is rooted in the conviction that all children can learn, provided they are exposed to the appropriate and optimal learning conditions. ML is built on the following tenets: (1) The teacher breaks down the content to be learned into smaller, sequentially and hierarchically organized learning objectives; (2) learning objectives have a clearly specified condition [conditions that set the stage for demonstrating the skill], behavior [the learned skill clearly specified in observable, measurable terms], and criterion [observable and measurable standard that represents mastery] ; (3) learners are not advanced to the next learning objective until they have demonstrated proficiency with the previous learning objective; (4) diagnostic formative tests are given after instruction for each objective, for the purpose of giving corrective feedback and quickly identifying/correcting mistakes learners may make in their skill repertoire as they learn; (5) formative assessments are criterion-referenced rather than norm-referenced in design; (6) individual differences in student outcomes are conceptualized according to the time needed to learn specified objectives. That is, traditional instructional methods set a uniform period of time in which all students are expected to learn the curricular material, which by design results in individual differences in the amount learned. In contrast, mastery learning recognizes that all students can learn the material, but learners require different amounts of time to do so (assuming uniform learning conditions). Readers are encouraged to consult Guskey and Gates (1986), Guskey and Pigott (1988), and Kulik, Kulik, and Bangert-Downs (1990) for empirical reviews of mastery learning programs.

Mental Health Consultation.   *Mental Health Consultation* is a model of consultation developed by Gerald Caplan (Caplan & Caplan, 1999), in which a consultant and a consultee work together to assist the consultee with a current professional problem (usually with a client), which facilitates the development of skills that would allow the consultee to deal effectively with similar problems in the future (Caplan & Caplan, 1999). Caplan developed four types of mental health consultation models, which differ according to whether the content focus is a client or administrative concern, or whether the primary objective is to provide information drawn from the consultant's expertise or to improve the problem-solving capabilities of the consultee (Erchul, 2005). In the context of the consultee-centered mental health consultation model, an important goal of the consultant is to determine if the likely cause of consultee difficulty is a lack of knowledge, lack of skill, lack of confidence, or a lack of objectivity.

Mental Retardation.   *Mental retardation* is a term that describes a condition, manifested during the developmental period, which reflects significantly subaverage intellectual functioning manifested by a score of 70 or lower on an individually administered IQ test. A diagnosis of mental retardation is accompanied by concurrent deficits or impairments in adaptive functioning in at least two areas involving communication, self-care, home living, social/interpersonal skills, use of community resources, self-direction, functional academic skills, work, leisure, health, and safety (American Psychiatric Association, 1994).

Mental retardation is further subdivided into four categories of clinical/educational severity. Approximately 85 percent of the mentally retarded population is in the *mild mental retardation* category. This category describes individuals with an IQ level of approximately 50/55 to 70. Developmentally, persons in this range attain a mental age in adulthood of approximately 8 to 10.5 years of age. Educationally, persons in this range achieve academically up to a sixth-grade level. Although mild mental retardation can be caused by biological/environmental factors or genetic anomalies, cognitive functioning in this range also represents normal variation at the lower end of the intelligence distribution in human populations. Persons with mild mental retardation can become fairly self-sufficient and are able to live independently with appropriate community and social support.

Approximately 10 percent of the mentally retarded population is considered to have *moderate mental retardation*. Persons in this range have IQ levels between 35/40 to 50/55 and can develop intellectually in adulthood up to a mental age of 5.5 to 8 years of age. Educationally, persons with moderate mental retardation can achieve academic skills up to the third/fourth-grade level if provided with adequate special education. Such persons can complete simple work and self-care tasks with moderate supervision, but can function successfully in highly structured and supervised environments, such as group homes.

Approximately 3 to 4 percent of the mentally retarded population is classified as having *severe mental retardation*. Persons in this category have IQ scores of 20/25 to 35/40. Educationally, persons with severe mental retardation can achieve academic skills in adulthood up to a mental age of 3 to 5.5 years of age. Such persons can master only basic self-care skills and some communication skills, and require supervision in group homes.

Approximately 1 to 2 percent of the mentally retarded population is classified as having *profound mental retardation*. Persons in this category have IQ scores below 20/25 and develop a maximum mental age in adulthood of 2 to 3 years of age. Persons with profound mental retardation also have serious physical handicapping conditions, and many are non-ambulatory. Persons within this category need complete, supervised care for all physical and self-help needs.

Mestizo.   *Mestizo* is a term traditionally used to refer to people of mixed European and Native American heritage or descent.

Middle Class.   The label *middle class* refers to a diverse group of individuals that constitute anywhere from 45 to 50 percent of American families (Gilbert, 2011). A college education is one of the main indicators of middle-class status. Individual yearly incomes earned by persons in the middle class can range from near median yearly income estimates to well over $100,000 per year (according to Thompson & Hickey, 2005). The middle class can be subdivided into the upper middle and lower middle classes. Upper-middle-class occupations include many professionals with postgraduate degrees, such as medical doctors, engineers, dentists, lawyers, bankers, corporate executives, head teachers, university professors, scientists, pharmacists, airline pilots, ship captains, actuaries, high-level civil servants, politicians, military officers, and architects. Lower-middle-class occupations include lower-paid white-collar workers with Associate's or Bachelor's degrees, but who are not manual laborers. Lower-middle-class occupations include police officers, firefighters, primary and high school teachers, accountants, nurses, municipal office workers, low to midlevel civil servants, sales representatives, non-management office workers, clergy, technicians, and small business owners.

Morpheme.   A part of a word that represents a meaningful linguistic unit that cannot be divided into smaller meaningful parts. Thus, *ed* is a morpheme that, when placed after *walk*, meaningfully changes its interpretation (i.e., to past tense). Other examples of morphemes are *re* (e.g., *reimagine, relearn*) and *ing* (e.g., *playing, singing, working*).

Multiculturalism.   *Multiculturalism* is a sociopolitical ideology that describes a coherent (and at times incoherent) system of clearly identifiable assumptions, beliefs, attitudes, and practices associated with relations between racial, ethnic, and language subgroups within a society (Frisby, 2005a). Multiculturalism is the ideology that fuels multicultural education, social justice, anti-racist education, diversity, tolerance, and cultural competence movements and objectives in education and applied psychology. Multiculturalism ideology serves as a template for shaping how audiences view racial/ethnic/language groups, how the dynamics of problems involving these groups are interpreted, and the attitudes/perceptions that are viewed as socially acceptable in educating and working with individuals from these groups. The components of multiculturalism ideology are represented by six implicit doctrines (see *Difference, Equity, Group Identity, Inclusion, Sensitivity, and Sovereignty Doctrines,* this chapter) that shape the content of the ideology (see also Marxism, this chapter).

Muslim.   (see Islam).

Naïve Environmentalism.   *Naïve environmentalism* (labeled *egalitarian environmentalism* in Jensen, 1973) is a term coined by Sandra Scarr (Scarr & McCartney, 1983), which refers to the conviction that genetic factors play no part (or at least a very minimal role) in individual or group differences in behavioral traits, which are assumed to result entirely from environmental inequalities imposed by the capitalist economic system and its attendant social injustices (Jensen, 2000).

National Assessment of Educational Progress (NAEP).   The NAEP is the largest nationally representative and continuing assessment of what America's students know and can do in the subject areas of mathematics, reading, science, writing, the arts, civics, economics, geography, and U.S. history. NAEP assessments are conducted by the National Center for Education Statistics (NCES) and are released as *The Nation's Report Card.* As such, results are not reported at the individual student or school level, but are aggregated across age and grade groupings (which can also include aggregation by racial/ethnic/sex groupings). NAEP assessment is conducted on representative samples of public and nonpublic school students at grades 4, 8, and 12 for the main assessment, and additionally on samples of students at ages 9, 13, and 17 for long-term trend assessments. With the reauthorization of the Elementary and Secondary Education Act in 2001 (i.e., No Child Left Behind legislation), states that receive Title I funding are required to participate in state NAEP reading and mathematics assessments in grades 4 and 8 every two years.

NAEP assessments are administered uniformly to all participating students, who use the same test booklets and identical test administration procedures. NAEP results categorize results according to one of four achievement levels. A "Proficient" designation represents solid academic performance at the grade level assessed. Here students have demonstrated competency over challenging subject matter knowledge, the application of such knowledge to real-world situations, and the analytical skills appropriate to the subject matter. A "Basic" designation represents partial mastery of prerequisite knowledge and skills that are fundamental for proficient work in the grade level assessed. A "Below Basic" designation represents low scores that fail to equal or exceed the Basic cut score. An "Advanced" designation denotes superior performance at the grade level assessed. (Additional information on the NAEP can be obtained from the National Center for Education Statistics website at http://nces.ed.gov/nationsreportcard/about/) NAEP results for reading, mathematics, writing, and science can be reported at the state level. (The most current NAEP results broken down by states can be accessed at http://nces.ed.gov/nationsreportcard/states/) The NAEP also provides limited results separately for several large urban school districts (e.g., see www.nationsreportcard.gov/tuda.asp).

National Center for Educational Statistics (NCES). The NCES is the part of the U.S. Department of Education's Institute of Education Sciences (IES), which collects, analyzes, and publishes statistics on education and public school district finance information in the United States. It also conducts international comparisons of education statistics and provides leadership in developing and promoting the use of standardized terminology and definitions for the collection of those statistics. The NCES website can be accessed at http://nces.ed.gov.

National Congress of American Indians (NCAI). The NCAI is the oldest, largest, and most representative American Indian and Alaska Native organization in the United States. The NCAI was organized in 1944 in response to federal policies that were perceived as threatening the existence of Native American tribes. The NCAI advocates on behalf of more than 250 member tribal governments representing thousands of individual members. NCAI acts as a central hub to bring American tribes together and to develop unified consensus positions on issues of mutual concern. The organization also oversees U.S. commitments to Indian tribes and works to promote better understanding of American Indian and Alaskan Native governments, rights, and customs (National Congress of American Indians, n.d.).

Native Americans. The term *Native Americans* refers to the indigenous peoples of the continental United States, parts of Alaska, and the island state of Hawaii. Native Americans are extremely heterogeneous, as this term encompasses numerous distinct tribal and ethnic/language groups. Alternative or more precise subgroup names that may be used (that may or may not be synonymous with Native American) include Alaska Natives, Aleuts, American Indians, Arctic Indians, First Nations people, indigenous peoples, Inuit, or People of the Sovereign Nations and Tribes.

Approximately 0.8 to 1 percent of American citizens identify as Native Americans, who live in all geographic areas of the United States. According to the U.S. Census Bureau's American Community Survey Dataset for 2005–2009, the states with the highest percentages (within the total population of each state) of people who identify as American Indian and Alaska Native are as follows: Alaska (13.5%), New Mexico (9.3%), South Dakota (8.4%), Oklahoma (6.6%), Montana (6.2%), North Dakota (5.3%), and Arizona (4.5%).

In addition to living in cities, towns, and rural areas, many Native Americans settle on reservations, which are areas of land managed by a Native American tribe under the U.S. Department of the Interior's Bureau of Indian Affairs. Tribal councils, rather than the local or federal government, have jurisdiction over reservations. Since Native American tribes possess tribal sovereignty, tribal laws permit the establishment of legal gaming casinos, which attract tourists and generate revenue for reservations. Unfortunately, the quality of life on some reservations is so poor (e.g., infant mortality, life expectancy, nutrition, poverty, alcohol and drug abuse) that these areas are comparable to impoverished third world communities in other less-developed countries.

According to estimates from the year 2000, for example, the Pine Ridge Indian reservation in South Dakota has an unemployment rate between 80 to 85 percent, and 49 percent of residents were estimated to live below the federal poverty level (U.S. Census Bureau, 2000). Adolescent suicide was estimated to be four times the national average, and many of the reservation families have no electricity, telephone, running water, or sewage systems. Many families use wood stoves to heat their homes. The population on Pine Ridge has among the shortest life expectancies of any group in the Western Hemisphere (approximately 47 years for males and 52 years for females), with the infant mortality rate being five times the U.S. national average (for a *TIME* magazine photo essay showing life on the Pine Ridge reservation, see http://www.time.com/time/photogallery/0,29307,2048598_2235608,00.html). There are approximately 310 Native American reservations located in the United States, the majority of which are located west of the Mississippi River. Collectively, Native

American reservations total 55.7 million acres, representing approximately 2 percent of the area of the United States.

There are approximately 562 distinct, federally recognized Native American tribal/nation groups living in the United States (although the total number of tribes that have lived north of Mexico and have existed from the early 20th century to the present has been estimated at 2,500). According to the 2000 U.S. Census data, the 10 most populous tribes, in descending order, are Cherokee, Navajo, Latin American Indian, Choctaw, Sioux, Chippewa, Apache, Blackfeet, Iroquois, and Pueblo tribal groups.

Native American students continue to manifest troubling statistics compared to other American ethnic/racial groups. As examples, in 2006 some 14 percent of American Indian/Alaska Native children were served by the Individuals with Disabilities Education Act (IDEA), which was a higher percentage than the percentage of children in all racial/ethnic groups. In comparison, 9 percent of the general population was served under IDEA. In 2007, a larger percentage (66 percent) of American Indian/Alaska Native eighth-grade students reported absences from school in the preceding month than did eighth-grade students of any other race/ethnicity (36 to 57 percent). Also in 2007, 78 percent of American Indian/Alaska Native eighth-graders in public schools reported using a computer at home, which was lower than the percentage for eighth-graders of any other racial/ethnic group (82 to 96 percent). In 2007, fourth- and eighth-grade students in high-density schools—in which American Indian/Alaskan Natives made up at least one-fourth of the school enrollment—had school administrators who reported serious problems with student absenteeism, student tardiness, lack of family involvement, and low expectations. In 2006, some 21 percent of American Indian/Alaska Native children between the ages of 12 and 17 reported the use of alcohol in the past month, compared to 11 percent of black and 8 percent of Asian children who did so. In 2007, approximately 36 percent of American Indians/Alaska Natives had completed high school without continuing on to a postsecondary institution, and 20 percent had not even finished high school (National Center for Education Statistics, 2008). For a brief, readable overview of Native American life, see Martins, Widoe, Porter, and McNeil (2006). (See also Bureau of Indian Education, this chapter).

Negative Reinforcement.   A component of a behavior modification program in which the likelihood of a specific behavior is either maintained or increased following the removal of an aversive condition from the environment. An example of *negative reinforcement* in a classroom setting would be for the teacher to cancel a difficult homework assignment if students sit in their seats quietly.

No Child Left Behind (NCLB) Act.   NCLB refers to legislation that was proposed by President George W. Bush on January 23, 2001, and signed into law on January 8, 2002. The No Child Left Behind Act of 2001 (NCLB) is an Act of Congress that reauthorizes the Elementary and Secondary Education Act. This Act includes Title I, the government's flagship aid program for disadvantaged students. NCLB supports standards-based education reform, which is based on the premise that setting high standards and establishing measurable goals can improve individual outcomes in education. NCLB requires states to develop assessments in basic skills, and to give these assessments to all students at select grade levels in order to receive federal school funding. NCLB expanded the federal role in public education through annual testing, annual academic progress, report cards, teacher qualifications, and funding changes.

Nondiscriminatory Assessment.   In the 1970 case of *Diana et al. v. State Board of Education* in California, a class action suit was filed on behalf of all bilingual Mexican American children in California schools, challenging their placement in classes for children with mental retardation on the basis of scores obtained from IQ tests given in English. The court ruled that students cannot be placed in special education on the basis of culturally biased tests or tests given in other than the child's native language. This ruling resulted in requirements for schools to implement *nondiscriminatory assessment* methods, including testing referred students in their native language. This set the stage for Public Law 94-142 (The Education for All Handicapped Children Act of 1975; now called the Individuals with Disabilities Education Improvement Act), which requires schools to use nonbiased, nondiscriminatory assessment procedures for special education eligibility decision making. According to Ortiz (2008), "nondiscriminatory assessment is not a search for an unbiased test but rather a process that ensures every individual, not just those who are different in some way, is evaluated in the least discriminatory manner possible" (p. 662). Ortiz then summarizes 10 components for a comprehensive framework for nondiscriminatory assessment (see Ortiz, 2008, Table 1, p. 668).

This history underscores the need for practitioners to avoid use of assessment procedures that would introduce construct-irrelevant variance (see Construct Irrelevant Variance, this chapter) into assessment results, which erodes the correct interpretation of such information for culturally and linguistically different examinees.

Nonequivalent Exemplars Fallacy.   *Nonequivalent exemplars fallacy* is the name given to the gratuitous assumption that the magnitude of the cultural difference between two or more groups is a reliable basis for assuming that the same degree of cultural difference *must necessarily* exist between two or more different arbitrarily defined groups (see Frisby, 1999, for an extended discussion).

Nonverbal Intelligence (assessment of).   The assessment of nonverbal intelligence refers to the assessment of nonverbal cognitive processes involved in cognitive/intellectual functioning. Well-known examples are tasks that involve putting puzzles together while viewing a completed picture, pointing to a subgroup of pictures within a pictorial array that go together conceptually, or pointing to the correct missing part (from among an array of distractors) that would complete an incomplete pictorial/figural matrix. The *assessment of nonverbal intelligence* should not be confused with the *nonverbal assessment of intelligence* (see Braden, 2000). The former term implies that only a subset of all of the ways in which intelligent functioning can be displayed is being measured. Here, examiners may use, and examinees must understand, directions given verbally. In contrast, the latter term implies that the full range of intelligent functioning is being measured, but in a manner that reduces reliance on spoken language from the examiner and examinee (e.g., testing of deaf individuals using sign language; for additional details, see Braden & Athanasiou, 2005; McCallum, 2003).

Nostrum.   A nostrum is a popular remedy for social, political, or educational problems, the effectiveness of which remains unproven or ineffective (see also Quackery, this chapter).

Parochial Schools.   A subcategory of private schools (see Private Schools) that are affiliated with a religious denomination. Parochial schools teach religious lessons together with lessons from secular academic subjects. Although religious schools can be affiliated with Christian Protestant, Muslim, and Jewish faiths, the term *parochial* is most closely associated with Catholic Christian schools. Parochial schools have the freedom to refuse to teach any subject matter that is incompatable with the religious doctrines of the affiliated denomination. Many parents elect to send their children to parochial schools because they may object to certain elements of the curriculum taught in public schools; however, parents who do not necessarily subscribe to the religious doctrines of the affiliated denomination may elect to send their children to parochial schools for other reasons (e.g., greater discipline, better instruction, more academically rigorous curriculum).

Paternalistic Schools.   "Paternalism" is a term discussed at length by Whitman (2008) in referring to the instructional and child guidance philosophy of (primarily) charter schools that have demonstrated positive academic and behavioral outcomes with poor minority children. *Paternalistic schools* operate under the assumption that "the poor lack the family and community support, cultural capital, and personal follow-through to live according to the middle class values that they, too, espouse" (Whitman, 2008, p. 35). Paternalistic schools seek to change the school-related lifestyles of poor and minority children and families by (a) continually and unapologetically telling students what is good for them, (b) using "carrots and sticks" to compel good behavior and punish undesirable behavior, and (c) closely supervising students in the small details of school life, with a view toward changing behavior and creating new habits and attitudes.

Phenotype.   A phenotype is the observable manifestation of the interaction between a person's genotype (see Genotype, this chapter) and his or her environment, which can be observed and/or measured.

Platitudes.   A platitude is a frequently repeated saying that is intended to communicate a meaningful message, but instead has become hackneyed, trite, and meaningless through sheer overuse.

Political Correctness.   *Political correctness* is a term used to describe the social pressure to self-censor or monitor one's language in favor of only "socially approved" language, the thinking of only "socially approved" thoughts, the public endorsement of certain "socially approved" viewpoints, or taking great pains not to acknowledge certain truths or observations that have the potential of giving offense to politically organized advocacy groups (based on gender, race, ethnicity, language, sexual orientation, disability, etc.) or their designated or self-appointed spokespersons.

Positive Behavior Support (PBS).   *Positive behavior support* is a generic name given to a system of practices and procedures conceived and applied at the school (McKevitt & Braaksma, 2008), district (Johns, Patrick, & Rutherford, 2008), state (Knoff, 2008), and/or national levels (Sugai, Horner, & McIntosh, 2008) to promote and support appropriate student behavior in school settings. The key features of a schoolwide implementation of a PBS program involve (a) defining schoolwide expectations that are stated in a positive manner, (b) providing direct and explicit instruction of positive behaviors in the locations in which they are expected to occur, (c) developing effective methods for school staff to reinforce appropriate student behaviors, (d) developing clear and consistent responses to inappropriate behaviors, and (e) using data to monitor the effectiveness of, and areas needing improvement in, the system (McKevitt & Braaksma, 2008).

Positive Reinforcement.   *Positive reinforcement* refers to a component of a behavior modification program in which the likelihood of a specific behavior is either maintained or increased following application of a rewarding condition from the environment. In a classroom setting, positive reinforcement can be applied through tangible reinforcers (e.g., pencils, candy), intangible or secondary reinforcers (e.g., checkmarks on a behavior chart, redeemable tokens), activity rewards (e.g., pizza party, extra recess time), status rewards (e.g., line leader, special water fountain privileges), or social rewards (e.g., a smile, hug, thumbs-up sign).

Predictive Bias (testing).   Statistically speaking, "a test is a biased predictor if there is a statistically significant difference between [groups, however defined] in the slopes . . . , or in the intercepts . . . , or in the standard error of estimates . . . of the regression lines of the [groups under consideration], when these regression parameters are derived from the estimated true scores of persons within each group" (Jensen, 1980, p. 381–382). "Conversely, an unbiased test . . . is one for which the [groups under consideration] do not differ significantly in [slopes, intercepts, or standard error of estimates]" (Jensen, 1980, p. 379).

Prejudice.   As defined literally, *prejudice* is simply a prejudgment (i.e., making a judgment before having a complete set of facts about a person, group, situation, or event). In popular usage, prejudice connotes a negative attitude or emotional response to a group of people or to an individual from that group (Schneider, 2004). In the context of multiculturalism and "anti-racist" education movements, there is an implicit assumption that stereotypes, prejudice, and discrimination form a "neatly wrapped package" (Schneider, 2004, p. 266) that demands eradication from civilized society. Here, prejudice is viewed as a serious problem that primarily afflicts cultural majority groups and that in turn harms cultural minority groups (as assumed from unequal societal outcomes). This, in turn, leads to conscious efforts by professional groups and organizations to create counseling models and/or educational curricula for "reducing prejudice" in schools (e.g., see Sandhu & Aspy, 1997).

From a scientific perspective, however, prejudice is in reality a much more complex and nuanced construct. For example, no person is, can be, or ever will be completely free of prejudice. Prejudice involves not only negative feelings, but can involve positive feelings, as well as feelings of pity or envy (Schneider, 2004). Prejudicial feelings do not necessarily remain constant over long periods of time, but change concurrently with changes in mood, personal experiences, and personal goals (Schneider, 2004). Further complicating matters is the fact that individuals belong to multiple social categories and groups. Hence, multiple prejudices can often clash when directed at the same individual (e.g., a person who has negative prejudices about lawyers, but positive prejudices about Asians, will experience cognitive/attitude dissonance when confronted with an Asian lawyer).

Private Schools.   Private schools (sometimes referred to as independent schools) are schools not administered by local, state, or national governments. Private schools have the freedom to select their student body and are funded in whole or in part by charging their students tuition rather than funding their schooling with public (state) funds. Private schools range from preschool to post–high school institutions. Annual tuitions at K–12 private schools range from tuition-free schools to annual tuition rates of more than $40,000 at exclusive boarding, military, and/or preparatory ("prep") schools. Higher tuition costs at private schools are typically needed to pay higher salaries for the best teachers, to achieve lower student-to-teacher ratios and smaller class sizes, and to fund resources such as libraries, science laboratories, and computers. Trade or vocational schools are usually private schools where students can learn skills in a future occupation or trade, such as cosmetology or the performing arts (see also Parochial Schools, this chapter).

Progressivism (political).   *Progressivism* is the name given to a political movement first identified in the late 19th century, which has undergone several different waves in popularity over the ensuing decades, and which has been associated with notable figures such as Susan B. Anthony (who advocated alcohol prohibition), John Dewey (who advocated universal and comprehensive education), and former president Theodore Roosevelt (who instituted the largest government-funded, conservation-related projects in history at that time). In current times, progressivism is associated with social activism movements such as gay rights, women's rights, immigrants' rights, and environmental rights.

Public Schools.   Public schools in the United States are both mandated for, and made available to, all children by federal (U.S. Department of Education), state (state education agencies), and local (local education agencies) governments, and paid for in whole or in part by state taxes. Student attendance is compulsory for public schools, with ages for compulsory education beginning between 5 to 8 years old and ending between 14 to 18 years old (actual age ranges vary by state). Teachers and curricula must be state certified, and testing standards are set by both federal and state governments. A state superintendent of schools and state board of education oversee state education policies, which are in turn disseminated to school districts or their equivalents. Whereas private, parochial, and homeschooling groups are not required to abide by local school board policies, public schools must do so because of their taxpayer-funded status. According to current U.S. Census data, approximately 85 percent of American children are enrolled in primary and secondary public schools in more than 14,000 school districts.

Punishment.   *Punishment* is a term that refers to a component of a behavior modification program in which the likelihood of a specific behavior is decreased following application of an aversive condition from the environment. In a classroom setting, an example of punishment would be to require a student to spend recess time scraping gum from the bottom of desks as a consequence for breaking a "no gum chewing" rule in class.

Quackery.   *Quackery* is a pejorative term originally applied to the ostentatious promotion (by "swindlers," "hucksters," or "snake oil salesmen") of health products or services, for financial gain, that in reality have no supporting scientific research or demonstrated effectiveness. Such promotions are easily persuasive because of the consumer's deep-seated emotional need for quick fixes (e.g., promoting sugar water as a health tonic). In its more general application to education and psychology, quackery refers to an aggressively hyped or marketed fad (e.g., intervention, treatment procedure, or education philosophy) that promises dramatic results if implemented or adopted, but in the final analysis is not supported by quality research and/or ultimately fails to deliver on its promises (see also Nostrum, this chapter).

Race.   Traditional anthropology has subdivided human populations into three major racial groups (Caucasoid, Negroid, and Mongoloid), while more recent scholarship has expanded this taxonomy up to eight major subdivisions (e.g., see Cavalli-Sforza, Menozzi, & Piazza, 1994). Nonspecialists tend to categorize persons into racial categories based on observable characteristics related to skin color, hair texture, eye color/shape, and related geographic/climatic zone boundaries throughout the world that are associated with these physical characteristics. However, contemporary scholars disagree on the validity of mutually exclusive racial classification taxonomies for the human population.

For purposes of this discussion, those who believe in the validity of clearly defined racial groups are called *race-acknowledgers* (RA). Those who do not believe in the validity of clearly defined racial groups are called *race-deniers* (RD). RA groups believe that theirs is the traditional view among anthropologists (see Gill, 2000). They believe that racial groups are biological realities, particularly among anthropologists who specialize in certain branches of physical anthropology. RD groups among anthropologists (particularly those who specialize in blood analysis) largely believe that mutually exclusive racial classifications are arbitrary, meaningless, and ought to be abandoned in light of alternative methods for understanding human variation (Brace, 2000). For example, RD groups who study blood groupings hold that many traits show more gradual gradients of change (called *clines*) that cut across traditional racial boundaries. RD groups argue that race is a social construct, and RD groups among social scientists may argue that belief in the biological reality of racial classifications is socially dangerous—and will inevitably promote racism (see Racism, this chapter). RA groups acknowledge that, although social methods of classifying persons are indeed imprecise, and blood analysis shows much clinal variation, other anthropological and biological criteria can be used to assign persons in racial categories with reasonable accuracy (Gill, 2000).

Racialism.   (Not to be confused with *Racism*, see next entry). In a general sense, *racialism* refers to a mindset that injects race and racial differences as the central feature in the analysis and interpretation of social problems. In applied psychology, racialism manifests itself in the belief that race and racial differences are fundamental to understanding differences in cognition, personality, and behavior. Racialism believes that all members within racial subdivisions share certain heritable traits and characteristics that are unique to that race and are not characteristic of members belonging to a different race. Any innocuous event, despite the absence of any inherent discriminatory intent, can be instantly "racialized" by injecting racial grievances as the central feature of its analysis. Thus, for example, one writer racialized the natural disaster caused from Hurricane Katrina by citing it and its aftermath (on predominantly black sections of New Orleans) as an example of "environmental racism" (Wright, 2005).

In applied psychology, issues involving race and racial differences are rarely discussed overtly, but they are discussed covertly by framing discussions as issues of "culture" and "cultural differences." Multiculturalism ideology and rhetoric often serves as a sanitized cover for practices and beliefs that are essentially rooted in racialism. Ironically, racialist beliefs exist independently of the relative absence or presence of racial prejudice. Thus, an open-minded person with racially tolerant beliefs and an intolerant bigot can *both* hold racialist beliefs, because of the primacy that is placed on racial differences in explaining human behavior. (See also Civil Rights Moralism, this chapter.)

Racism.   *Racism* is originally defined as the belief or ideology that (a) race is a fundamental determinant of human traits and capacities, (b) all members of each racial group possess characteristics or abilities that are specific to that race, and (c) racial differences produce an inherent superiority or inferiority in worth of a particular racial group relative to another. Racism is then manifested in racially discriminatory actions among members within a society, whereby certain racially identifiable groups are denied rights or benefits, while others receive preferential treatment on the basis of racial group membership.

Ironically, as discriminatory laws have been abolished, and antidiscrimination laws are aggressively infused into every fabric of American economic, social and civic life, and as the overt expression of racism has receded into the outer margins of society, definitions of racism have been *considerably broadened* by social scientists as a means of explaining the origins of inequalities in outcomes between groups. Some claim that racism is present in seemingly innocuous interpersonal behaviors in everyday social life that, upon closer inspection, presumably signal racially motivated "microaggressions" (e.g., see Sue et al., 2007). Whenever overt acts of racism cannot be found, some claim that racism is unconscious (Jones, 2003). Others claim to uncover racism (in the form of unconscious bias) in persons' slower response reaction times (measured in milliseconds) to a computerized presentation of faces and words (Greenwald & Krieger, 2006). Others claim that certain manifestations of conservative religious or political beliefs represent "symbolic racism" (Kinder & Sears, 1981; Sears, 1988). According to some, simply conducting research on differences between racial groups is a form of "academic" or "scientific" racism (Erickson & Murphy, 2008; Ferris State University, 2010). If any political or policy decision is shown to have a disparate impact on racial groups, it is labeled by some as racist, despite the absence of any intentional prejudicial or discriminatory intent (see Ford, 2008, pp. 213–231, for an extended discussion). Finally, many have argued that entire institutions (simply on the basis of differences in group performance outcomes that result from an institutions' policies) can be guilty of "institutional racism" (e.g., see Better, 2002).

In the corrosive atmosphere of contemporary racial politics, irresponsible and reckless accusations of racism (or labeling as "racist" a person with whom one disagrees) has become a potent weapon useful for wielding power, attacking or intimidating opponents, and forcing schools and other organizations to make decisions that are favorable to various political constituencies (D'Souza, 1995; Ford, 2008).

Reaction Time (assessment of).   The phrase *reaction time* was first coined in 1873 by the Austrian physiologist Sigmund Exner, and extensively developed within the context of mental chronometry (i.e., measuring the speed of mental processes) by the Dutch physiologist Frans C. Donders in the 1800s (see Jensen, 2006). In contemporary usage, reaction time tasks are typically measured in milliseconds aided by computer technology. Reaction time refers to the time that elapses between the presentation of a stimulus on a computer screen and a physical response (e.g., pressing or releasing a key or button). Reaction time research has proven useful in the study of individual differences in general intelligence and learning disabilities (for an extended treatment, see Jensen, 2006).

Reading Recovery.   *Reading Recovery* (RR) is a 12- to 20-week accelerated program designed to move struggling first-grade readers in a short time from the bottom of their class to the average (Lyons, 1998). At the end of the RR program, children develop a self-extending system that uses a variety of strategies to read increasingly difficult text and to independently write their own messages (Clay, 1991). The RR program provides one-to-one tutoring, five days per week, 30 minutes per day, by a specially trained teacher. RR uses supportive conversations between teacher and child as the primary basis of instruction. More in-depth information about RR can be accessed at www.readingrecovery.org.

Recidivism.   The term *recidivism* refers to the chronic tendency to repeat, or fall back into, criminal or antisocial behavior patterns.

Red Herring.   *Red herring* is a term used in informal logic texts to refer to a rhetorical tactic of diverting attention away from an important or significant issue in an argument. For example, in murder mysteries in which the killer has yet to be revealed, the writer will divert suspicion to a minor character (who is not the killer) or a series of irrelevant clues as a means of surprising readers at the end with the identity of the real killer.

Response to Intervention.   Criticisms of, and dissatisfaction with, the IQ/achievement discrepancy model for identifying learning disabilities has been extensively documented (Aaron, 1997; Francis et al., 2005; Gresham, 2002; Restori, Katz, & Lee, 2009). *Response to intervention* (RtI) is the name given to an alternative model designed to (a) provide early instructional assistance to children who are experiencing learning difficulties, generally, and (b) provide one component of a data-based process for the accurate identification of learning disabilities. In the 2004 reauthorization of the Individuals with Disabilities Education Act (IDEA), a local educational agency is not required to take into consideration whether a child has a severe discrepancy between achievement and intellectual ability, but has the option of using a process that determines if the child responds to scientific, research-based intervention as a part of the evaluation procedures.

The key components of RtI involve three tiers of services, which are necessary to ensure the academic growth and achievement of all students. In the first tier, all students receive core classroom instruction that is differentiated and utilizes strategies and materials that are scientifically research-based. Any necessary interventions at this level are within the framework of the general education classroom and can be in the form of differentiated instruction, small group review, or one-on-one remediation of a concept. Progress monitoring (see Curriculum-Based Measurement, this chapter) displays individual student growth over time, to determine whether the student is progressing as expected. In the second tier, supplemental interventions (for students who do not make adequate progress with first-tier services) may occur within or outside of the general education classroom. Core instruction is still delivered by the classroom teacher. Small groups of similar instructional levels may work together under the teacher's instruction and guidance. This targeted instruction may occur in the general education setting or outside in a smaller group setting with a specialized teacher for struggling readers.

The main purpose of progress monitoring is to determine whether the intervention is successful in helping the student learn at an appropriate rate. Decision rules need to be created to determine when a student might no longer require Tier 2 and beyond services and can be returned to the general classroom (Tier 1), when the intervention needs to be changed, or when a student might be identified for special education. In one version of the RtI model, students who have failed to make expected progress with Tier 1 (classroom) and Tier 2 (standard protocol or problem solving methods, see Bender & Shores, 2007) interventions would be referred to special education to determine eligibility for Tier 3 services (McDougal, Graney, Wright, & Ardoin, 2010). Tier 3 is for students who require more intense, explicit, and individualized instruction. The instruction in Tier 3 is typically delivered outside of the general education classroom. If Tier 3 is not successful, a child is considered for the first time as potentially disabled.

SEED (Schools for Evolution and Educational Development) Schools.   SEED schools are high-performing, college-preparatory public boarding schools that serve primarily racial/ethnic minority students from traditionally underserved communities. SEED schools serve students in the 6th through 12th grades, but all new applicants are admitted in their 6th-grade year. SEED schools are funded by private donors, foundations, and corporations. According to the organization's website, a majority of SEED students come from families in which no member has attended college. Eighty percent of students live with a single parent or neither parent, and approximately 12 percent of SEED graduates are reported to have special education needs. The SEED model includes academic, residential, mental health, physical health, social, and enrichment programs delivered in the context of life skills training. SEED students arrive at school on Sunday evenings and go home for the weekend on Friday afternoons (as well as for summer vacation and holidays). Approximately 96 percent of SEED high school graduates have been accepted to a four-year college or university. The SEED Foundation operates one public charter school in Washington, D.C., and a public school in Maryland.

Self-Concept.   The self-concept is a multidimensional construct that "refers to an individual's own perceptions, both positive and negative, of his or her attributes, traits, and abilities" (Luhr, 2005, p. 490). Persons develop their sense of self concept from their unique life experiences, others' reactions, feedback, and evaluations of them, and their unique inner psychological and attitudinal tendencies. The self-concept is thought to become more differentiated over time, and can include global and specific areas of self-concept (Bracken, Bunch, Keith, & Keith, 2000). Self-concept can be assessed by open interviews, self-report measures, rating scales, Q sort methods, and sentence completion methods (Luhr, 2005).

Self-Esteem.   While the self-concept (see previous entry) refers to a person's more or less objective self-description (without necessarily implying affective connotations of self-worth; see Roth, 2005), *self-esteem* reflects a person's overall evaluation or appraisal of his or her own worth (which includes both subjective beliefs and emotions). According to the seminal work of William James (1890/1950), self-esteem is multidimensional (i.e., many different sources of information potentially influence its quality), idiosyncratic (i.e., each individual's sense of self-worth is determined subjectively from a different set of factors that are viewed as important), and hierarchical (i.e., broader and more global aspects of self-esteem are derived from narrower and more specific aspects of self-esteem).

Sensitivity Doctrine.   *The Sensitivity Doctrine* is one among six implicit doctrines that constitute multiculturalism ideology (Frisby, 2005a). This doctrine holds that members of racial/ethnic/language majority groups (however defined) are morally obligated to avoid giving offense (in words, ideas, viewpoints, actions, or deeds) to members of minority groups (or to those who style themselves as their "spokespersons"). A related belief is that members of minority groups (however defined) have a prescriptive right to be protected from any words, ideas, viewpoints, actions, or deeds that have the potential to be unflattering to their group or diminish their sense of group-esteem (Frisby, 2005b). The Sensitivity Doctrine has both proactive and avoidant aspects. In the proactive sense, for example, test developers will solicit the cooperation of minority group scholars in evaluating potential cognitive or achievement test items before publication for their possible offensiveness to minority groups (called *sensitivity reviews*). In the avoidant sense, scholars will avoid conducting or writing about any research whose conclusions may invite charges of racism or insensitivity (e.g., research on average group differences in cognitive ability; see Gottfredson, 1994; Jensen, 1981b).

Shibboleth.   The origin of this word can be found in the Biblical Old Testament book of Judges, chapter 12 (verses 1–6). In this chapter, the inhabitants of Gilead inflicted a military defeat upon the tribe of Ephraim. When the surviving Ephraimites tried to cross the Jordan River in order to return to their home territory, the Gileadites commandeered the river's fords to stop them. In order to accurately identify Ephraimite refugees in order to kill them, the men of Gilead would ask each river traveler to say the word *Shibboleth*. If the person said "Sibboleth" instead of "Shibboleth" (due to difficulty in pronouncing the word), they would be identified as an Ephraimite and be promptly killed.

Thus, the modern application of this term refers to a word, idea, symbol, phrase, attitude, or practice used to distinguish members of an in-group from outsiders. In the context of the dominance of multiculturalism ideology in psychology and education, a shibboleth is an informal litmus test that identifies the person as a "culturally sensitive" individual or a "culturally competent" psychologist/educator. When a person, group, or institution fails or refuses to pass the designated litmus test, they are identified as "outsiders" and are vulnerable to sanction, ostracism, or punishment.

Various examples in psychology and education are symbolic of multiculturalism shibboleths. Examples include a "celebrate diversity" logo that is required on all newsletters published by a professional organization; a publishing company refusing to print pictures of groups of schoolchildren in their educational textbook unless they are sufficiently "diverse"; requiring college applicants, as a condition for possible acceptance, to write an essay showing how they "value diversity"; a conference speaker feeling an obligation to praise social justice, tolerance, and inclusion in a keynote address in order to impress the listening audience; a job applicant who is automatically disqualified from employment consideration because of failure to use the latest up-to-date terminology in referring to a particular minority group (for further discussion, see Bernstein, 1994; Sowell, 2006, pp. 238–240).

Situational Bias (testing).   *Situational bias* is the name given to a source of test bias resulting from "factors in the external testing situation that interact with individual or group differences to produce systematic bias in the test scores of individuals or groups" (Jensen, 1980, p. 589). Sources of situational bias may include, but not be limited to, the quality of the interpersonal relationship between the examiner and examinee (e.g., examiner dialect, clarity of test instructions, motivational techniques), the effects of the testing environment (e.g., room temperature or lighting), the effects of timed versus untimed testing, or the examinee's attitudinal or behavioral reactions to different aspects of subtests' format or task demands (see also Test Bias, this chapter).

Social Justice.   *Social justice* is the moniker given to an advocacy movement currently in vogue in school psychology (e.g., see *School Psychology Review*, Vol. 37, No. 4) and multicultural education (e.g., see Darling-Hammond, French, & Garcia-Lopez, 2002). Sowell (1986) traces the origins of social justice advocacy to a 1793 treatise by philosopher William Godwin entitled *Enquiry Concerning Political Justice and Its Influence on Modern Morals and Manners* (reprinted in Godwin, 2009). Social justice advocacy is the natural outgrowth of one of two opposing social visions that underlie political, economic, cultural, and social conflicts that occur throughout history in every corner of the globe (Sowell, 1986). One of these two visions, called the "unconstrained vision" (Sowell, 1986), believes that social problems in the world (e.g., poverty, social inequalities) are fundamentally caused by foolish and/or immoral practices of individuals. According to this vision, such problems can be solved by the combination (either all or in part) of human brainpower, the superior ideas of a select group of enlightened persons, the moral conversion of "unenlightened" persons, large outlays of money to fund advocacy movements, social policies that impel the desired (i.e.,

socially correct) behavior, and/or from discoveries culled from the research of socially conscious "experts." The ultimate goal is to continuously improve fallible human nature and
discover the solution to intractable social problems.

The term *social justice* has no clear or universally agreed-upon definition in school psychology, but its characteristics can be inferred from recent survey research that summarizes
professionals' opinions about the meaning of this term (e.g., see Shriberg et al., 2008).
According to some "cultural diversity experts" in school psychology (Shriberg et al., 2008,
p. 456), social justice includes (but is not limited to) specific recommendations (e.g., ensuring
equal and appropriate service to all students irrespective of their cultural backgrounds,
overcoming barriers to hinder access to health and mental health services, advocacy for
sexual minority children and youth) to vague platitudes (e.g., "addressing inequality and
marginalization in research and practice," "facilitating the equal distribution of power in
schools," "making sure that students receive culturally competent services").

Social Maladjustment.   The term *social maladjustment* is most commonly known among special
educators as an exclusionary term for students who cause significant problems for schools, but
who are not eligible for classification as "emotionally disturbed" under the Individuals with
Disabilities Education Improvement Act (see Pierangelo & Guiliani, 2007)—unless they can
also be identified as suffering from emotional disturbance. According to Reither (2003), the
socially maladjusted student experiences difficulties in learning because of his or her conscious rejection of school values and norms (i.e., is often tardy, truant, rebellious, and
unmotivated), but a willingness to learn in areas relevant to a particular subculture (e.g., a
neighborhood youth gang). Such students may be excessively aggressive (i.e., engages in
violence or thievery) or passive (i.e., engages in work refusal or substance abuse). The
socially maladjusted student may be "street smart" and capable of good peer relationships
with his or her subculture, but is often manipulative, resistant to authority figures, and hurtful
to others as a means of personal gain.

Socioeconomic Status (SES).   *Socioeconomic status* (SES) refers to a designation of a person or
family's place or rank within society, based on a variety of social and economic factors. SES is
a multidimensional construct that is most typically determined by a combination of educational achievement, occupational status, and financial income variables (APA Task Force
on Socioeconomic Status, 2007; Bornstein, Hahn, Suwalsky, & Haynes, 2003). Higher levels
of education are associated with better economic outcomes, more social and psychological
resources, and fewer health risk behaviors. Income has a moderate, but not perfect, correlation with education. For example, persons can be highly educated but have lower-income-
producing jobs (e.g., college students on assistantships). Similarly, persons with less education can have jobs earning large incomes (e.g., sports or entertainment figures). A person's
occupational status is associated with the cognitive complexity and challenge required for
the job, autonomy and supervision, physical hazards, safety present in the work setting; the
degree of skill required; financial compensation schedules and amount; and social prestige.
(See also *Upper Class, Middle Class, Lower Class,* and *Underclass,* this chapter.)

Sociologist's Fallacy.   The *sociologist's fallacy* is the name given to the tendency for social scientists to interpret a correlation between a social variable and a phenotype (see Phenotype,
this chapter) as causal, without considering the role that genetics could play in mediating the
relationship. For example, suppose that Groups A and B differ with respect to the average
socioeconomic status of group members (e.g., level of education, income level, and occupation), in addition to the average IQ scores of group members (i.e., where Group A is higher
on both). The social scientist discovers that the difference in average IQ scores between the
two groups is considerably reduced as a result of equating groups on their socioeconomic

status (e.g., where high socioeconomic status Group A members are compared to only high socioeconomic status Group B members). The social scientist erroneously concludes that socioeconomic status differences between groups is the key variable that is most responsible for the initial group differences in IQ scores between the groups. The fallacy is that the social scientist failed to consider the fact that genetic factors could also play a key role in the initial socioeconomic differences between groups. Therefore, the social scientist has inadvertently equated the groups on genetic as well as environmental factors (see also Jensen, 1998a, p. 491).

Sovereignty Doctrine. *The Sovereignty Doctrine* is one among six implicit doctrines that constitute multiculturalism ideology (Frisby, 2005a). A person or entity that is sovereign is autonomous and not bound by any higher authority outside of itself. In the context of multiculturalism ideology, the Sovereignty Doctrine is evoked when racial/ethnic/language groups argue that they have a prescriptive right to establish their own truth, group psychology, and/or standards of behavior independently of outgroups. Membership in an ethnic/racial/language group is assumed to confer automatic sovereignty (i.e., credibility, knowledge, intuitive understanding, or expertise) in cultural matters related to the group of which they are members (e.g., only teachers from group X are thought to be most competent in teaching students from group X; only psychologists from group Y can best understand the psychology of individuals from group Y; only researchers belonging to group Z can interpret research on persons from group Z).

Standardization Fallacy. The *standardization fallacy* is an inadequate concept of test bias, which claims that, because a test has been standardized on a given subpopulation, it is by this fact biased or unfair when used with any other subpopulation (Jensen, 1980, p. 372). See research by Fan (1996) as an example of an empirical test of the standardization fallacy.

Star Trek Fallacy. The *Star Trek fallacy* is an informal name given to an empirically validated concept from social psychology called *outgroup homogeneity bias* (Schneider, 2004). Outgroup homogeneity bias occurs when an observer perceives outgroup members as more similar to one another than members of his or her in-group (however defined). In the *Star Trek* television series of the 1960s (and its subsequent reincarnations), the in-group (members of the starship *Enterprise*) is portrayed as wonderfully diverse—representing different races, ethnicities, personalities, and temperaments. However, whenever the *Enterprise* crew encountered aliens from other planets, they were usually portrayed as physically and tempermentally all alike. Quack Multiculturalism (see Chapter 2) often commits the Star Trek fallacy whenever attempting to describe the cultural traits of ethnic, racial, or language minority groups (e.g., see Sidebars 2.4, 2.5, 2.6, and 2.7).

Stereotype Threat. *Stereotype threat* refers to the threat felt in particular situations in which stereotypes relevant to one's group identity exist, and the mere knowledge of the stereotypes can be distracting enough to negatively affect one's performance in a domain related to the stereotype. Claude Steele first coined this term (Steele, 1997; Steele & Aronson, 1995) and developed laboratory studies to examine the impact of stereotype threat on the test performance of college-aged African American students. In these experiments, high-achieving majority and minority group college students were asked to take a test under two conditions. One group were told that the test was a problem-solving task (the nonthreat condition), and another group was told that the task was a test of intelligence (the threat condition). In reality, all participants received the same test. A larger majority/minority group difference in mean test scores was obtained in the threat condition compared to the nonthreat condition—a finding that was interpreted by the authors as confirming the existence of stereotype threat. Since these studies, stereotype threat is proposed by some as a partial explanation, at minimum, for majority/minority differences in mean scores on intellectual and academic achievement tests (see discussion in Sackett, Hardison, & Cullen, 2004). For arguments in opposition to this interpretation, see Jensen (1998a) and Sackett et al. (2004). For a comprehensive resource on issues and controversies within the field of stereotype threat research, readers are encouraged to consult http://reducingstereotypethreat.org.

Stereotypes.   As culled from the research literature, several classic definitions for a stereotype have been proposed (e.g., see review by Schneider, 2004). A brief sampling of definitions are as follows (see Schneider, 2004, for citations to each definition): "Whether favorable or unfavorable, a stereotype is an exaggerated belief associated with a category that justifies or rationalizes conduct in relation to that category"; "A belief that is simple, inadequately grounded, or at least partially inaccurate, and held with considerable assurance by many people"; "A collection of associations that link a target group to a set of descriptive characteristics." Disagreements among definitions appear to crystallize around three issues: (1) The extent to which stereotypes are or are not inaccurate; (2) the extent to which stereotypes are "bad" in the internal reasoning that gives birth to the stereotype, or in the real-world consequences for accepting stereotypes; and (3) questions of whether stereotypes are shared among groups, or whether stereotypes originate within an individual and hence are not shared by others (see Schneider, 2004, for an extended discussion of these issues).

System of Multicultural Pluralistic Assessment (SOMPA).   The SOMPA is a multifaceted battery of assessments, authored by Dr. Jane Mercer and June Lewis, that was originally designed to be responsive to the nondiscriminatory assessment mandates of Public Law 94-142 (see also Nondiscriminatory Assessment, this chapter). Development of the SOMPA was grounded in the ideological presupposition that "the average potential for learning is equivalent across ethnic groups and that observed between-group differences in average test scores reflect differing levels of cultural exposure to the materials in the test" (Mercer, 1979, p. 109). The full SOMPA battery comprises three models of assessment. The *Medical Model* employs six measures: Physical Dexterity tasks (sensory motor coordination), the Bender Visual Motor Gestalt Test (perceptual and neurological factors), the Health History Inventories, Weight by Height norms (for screening possible nutritional or developmental problems), Vision assessment (Snellen Test), and an Auditory Acuity assessment. The *Social System Model* includes the Adaptive Behavior Inventory for Children and the Wechsler Intelligence Scale for Children—Revised (WISC-R). The *Pluralistic Model* yields an index of the child's intellectual functioning via an Estimated Learning Potential score, which corrects the WISC-R score based on a comparison of how well the child performs in comparison to children from a similar sociocultural background. Separate norms are provided for black, white, and Hispanic children. The SOMPA was standardized on a sample of 2,100 California children ranging in age from 5 to 11 years old. After its publication, the SOMPA was extensively reviewed (see Humphreys, 1985; Nuttal, 1979; Reynolds, 1985; Sandoval, 1985) and was found to be psychometrically unacceptable for resolving major conceptual and technical problems/issues.

Teach for America (TFA).   *Teach for America* is an American nonprofit organization whose mission is to build a movement to address educational inequities by recruiting recent college graduates and professionals to teach for two years in low-income communities throughout the United States (see www.teachforamerica.org). TFA members do not have to be certified teachers, although certified teachers may apply. Uncertified TFA members receive alternative certification through coursework taken while completing the program. TFA members attend an intensive five-week summer institute to prepare for their commitment. TFA teachers are placed in schools in urban areas such as New York City and Houston, as well as in rural places such as eastern North Carolina and the Mississippi Delta. They then serve for two years and are usually placed in schools with other TFA members. For a first-person account of the professional life of a TFA graduate teaching in inner-city high minority schools, see Foote (2008).

Test Bias.   In the context of testing, *test bias* (sometimes called cultural bias in testing) has been defined conceptually as the effects of *construct-irrelevant variance* on examinees' performance/responses on all or parts of tests (American Educational Research Association, American Psychological Association, & National Council on Measurement in Education, 1999). Construct-irrelevant variance refers to something that is measured by a test that is irrelevant to the construct that the test was designed to measure, thereby creating a contaminating source of individual differences in scores. If select subgroups differ significantly in a construct that is irrelevant to what the test purports to measure, then there could be "systematic errors in the predictive validity or the construct validity of test scores of individuals that are associated with the individual's group membership" (Jensen, 1980, p. 375).

The scientific investigation of test bias is a "purely objective, empirical, statistical, and quantitative matter entirely independent of subjective value judgments and ethical issues concerning fairness or unfairness of tests and the uses to which they are put" (Jensen, 1980, p. 375). Psychometricians and researchers use empirical methods (some more sophisticated than others) to investigate bias in tests that are tailored to the particular research question under investigation. For a more detailed treatment of test bias concepts and procedures, see Jensen (1980), Reynolds and Carson (2005), and Reynolds and Lowe (2009).

Test Session Behavior.   In the context of school psychology assessment research and practice, *test session behavior* (TSB) can be broadly defined as examinee behaviors (observed by the examiner during individually administered cognitive or academic achievement testing) that are peripheral to scorable test responses (Oakland, Glutting, & Watkins, 2005). Examples of examinee behaviors of interest during testing include observable behaviors reflective of task persistence and/or interest, degree of attentiveness and ability to follow directions, and the degree of attitudinal or behavioral cooperation with examiner directions. The assessment of TSB differs markedly with respect to psychometric development and sophistication. That is, TSB assessment can take the form of informal nonstandardized behavior rating checklists printed on test protocols (e.g., see Frisby & Osterlind, 2007), to stand-alone standardized TSB scales co-normed with individually administered intelligence or achievement scales (Glutting & Oakland, 1993).

Tracking.   *Tracking* refers to the educational practice of separating students by academic ability into more homogeneous groupings for instruction in all or part of the school academic curriculum. Supporters of tracking argue that this practice permits teachers to design more effective lessons geared to pupils who are academically similar, as well as to reduce learner frustration that may result when students are forced to keep up with more advanced peers (Ansalone, 2003). Critics of tracking object to the racial stratification that is a by-product of this practice, the wide disparities in experience and skills among teachers across tracks, and differences in the quality of the curriculum across tracks (Oakes, 2005).

Tribalism.   Refers to the tendency of people to identify strongly with their kinship, cultural, racial, ethnic, or language group. Here, loyalty to and advocacy for their own group's interests becomes the primary driving force of one's personal and/or professional life. Many opine that the influence of multiculturalism ideology in academia, public education, and civic life feeds tribalist instincts, which inevitably leads to a splintering of the national common culture, heightened sensitivity to differences rather than similarities, and intensified group conflicts (e.g., Bernstein, 1994; Taylor, 2011). Roger Sandall coined the phrase *designer tribalism* to refer to the tendency of multiculturalism ideology to romanticize primitive nonwhite cultures as inherently more spiritual, free from corruption, and "in harmony with nature" (e.g., see movies *Dances With Wolves, Pocahontas, Avatar*) as compared to the denigration of Western science, culture, civilization, and technology (Sandall, 2001).

Underclass.   Within the context of socioeconomic class taxonomies, the *underclass* refers to persons/families who are at the bottom of the economic scale in their disenfranchisement and lack of access to scarce societal resources (Gilbert, 2011). Although members of the underclass and persons from other socioeconomic classes may both be poor, the underclass differs significantly from the "working poor" in major ways. For example, members of the underclass have been described as having a strong "present-time" orientation, with little ability to delay gratification and plan for the future. A vast majority of the underclass have not graduated from high school, are not active participants in the nation's labor force, have incomes that are far below the national poverty line, and are by and large isolated from mainstream society. They manifest many maladaptive ways of handling life's difficulties, which include passivity (e.g., long-term welfare recipients who refuse to look for work or actively improve their life circumstances), criminality (e.g., earning money through prostitution, drug dealing, and other street crimes), hustling (e.g., gambling or questionable "get rich quick" scams), and traumatization (e.g., becoming alcoholics, drug addicts, mental patients, or homeless). For more detailed research, scholarship, and commentary on the underclass, see Auletta (1999), Wilson (1987), and Wilson (1993).

Universal Test Design (UTD).   *Universal test design* (UTD) is a concept that is rooted in the notion of universal design in the field of architecture. In this context, architects began to appreciate the need for buildings to be designed, from the beginning, to accommodate the largest range of users. Thus, instead of adding ramps and elevators to an existing building in order to increase accessibility for persons with disabilities, the concept of universal design considers the needs of all possible building users at the very beginning stages of the building's design.

In the same way, UTD means that large-scale standardized assessments are designed from the beginning to be accessible to, and valid for, the widest range of students (including ELL students and students with disabilities). When a test is in the conceptual phase, for example, the developers will consider all students regardless of their level of language proficiency. In the test construction phase, test items are developed to maximize the testing of academic content while simultaneously minimizing the testing of language ability or the effects of a disabling condition. After a pilot test is administered to different populations, items are analyzed and revised so that items that perform differentially for different groups can be eliminated (Dolan & Hall, 2001; Mihai, 2010). Readers are encouraged to consult Thompson, Johnstone, and Thurlow (2002) for necessary elements of universally designed assessments.

Upper Class.   In the context of socioeconomic status taxonomies, the *upper class* is a broad designation that encompasses individuals/families who are also referred to as "the rich" or the capitalist class. Because of their wealth (according to some estimates, those with incomes in the top 1 percent), education, and/or the prestige of their social/occupational positions, persons within this class have disproportionate power and influence over public opinion and American political, social, educational, and economic institutions. Persons within this class include, but are certainly not limited to, high-level politicians, top business executives, highly paid sports/entertainment figures, high-level capitalists/investors, and heirs to major fortunes.

Vouchers (School).   Education vouchers are "grants [awarded] to parents to cover some or all of the costs associated with private school tuition" (Walberg, 2007, p. 35). When private schools are funded by the state, such grants are typically referred to as vouchers or public vouchers. When such grants are funded by private businesses, foundations, or philan-thropists, they may be referred to as scholarships or private vouchers (Walberg, 2007). Education voucher programs may vary according to the number and type of students allowed to participate, the size of the voucher, and/or the regulations that are imposed on partici-pating schools (Walberg, 2007). Voucher programs can be open to all children (as in the case in some foreign countries), or limited to children from low-income families, students who attend failing public schools, students with special education needs, prekindergarten chil-dren, or students who live in towns that do not operate public schools at their grade levels (see Walberg, 2007, for a detailed discussion).

White Flight.   *White flight* is a term (coined by sociologists and demographers) that describes a phenomenon, beginning in the 1950s, where whites rapidly leave urban residential areas (in favor of neighboring suburban areas) as the (generally poorer) nonwhite population increases. White flight is triggered, all or in part, by court-ordered school desegregation and its correlates (e.g., busing), the decline of manufacturing industries in inner cities, or urban rioting/crime. As a result of white flight, most major inner cities (and their associated school systems) experience greater racial/ethnic resegregation; accelerated social, civic, and eco-nomic deterioration; and the explosive growth of private schooling in outlying suburban areas (e.g., see Wolters, 1984, 2008).

White Guilt.   In the context of contemporary American race relations, *white guilt* refers to whites' individual or collective sense that they are obligated (on the basis of past historical injustices to nonwhite groups) to capitulate to the grievances of nonwhites (or those who style them-selves as minority spokespersons) as a way of showcasing their innocence to charges of racism (Steele, 2006; Will, 2006). White guilt can manifest itself in several beliefs and behaviors, which include, but are not limited to, giving a respectful hearing and/or exposure to bizarre ideas/theories that would ordinarily be laughed out of serious scholarly debate; administratively lowering merit standards in order to meet real or imagined diversity goals; feeling obligated to capitulate to minority demands, no matter how unreasonable; willingness to accept blame for specious charges of racism with little or no rebuttal; believing that whites bear sole respon-sibility for the negative social conditions of nonwhites—and conversely that negative social conditions for nonwhites cannot improve absent the benevolent actions of whites.

White Privilege.   *White privilege* is a concept which asserts that "whiteness" as a racial category confers real or perceived advantages in a society (e.g., access to better economic opportu-nities or civic resources; freedom from discrimination; more potent political power) to which "people of color" are denied access (McIntosh, 1988; Neville, Worthington, & Spanierman, 2001). According to Neville et. al (2001), "to combat and eliminate White privilege, the unacknowledged culturally laden symbols and protocols that reflect and maintain the racial hierarchy need to be clearly identified and expunged" (p. 269).

Youth Gangs.   Youth gangs are self-identified, organized groups of adolescents (who can range in age from a low of 12 years to a high of 24 years), banded together under common interests in activities that typically are regarded as illegal or menacing to society. Youth gang activities involve, but are not limited to, general delinquency, protection of a geographic area (e.g., neighborhood turf), burglary/armed robbery, drinking/drug use, drug trafficking, gun own-ership and use, and violent retaliation against rival gangs. Most youth gangs arise among poor urban, slum, ghetto, barrio, or changing working-class communities, and tend to be bound by a common race/ethnicity, social class, or other determinant. According to 2001 statistics, American youth gang activity is an overwhelmingly nonwhite phenomenon, where black, Hispanic, and Asian youth are 15, 19, and 9 times more likely (respectively) than whites to be gang members (New Century Foundation, 2005).

Gangs often employ distinctive symbols, including the style and color of clothing, distinctive hand signs, tattoos, and graffiti symbols. Youth gangs enforce a system of internal rules, rituals, and codes of behavior—signified by the "three Rs" of reputation, respect, and retaliation. Although many youth join gangs because of a palpable need for protection from other gangs, many are attracted to gang life because it provides a family structure they are missing in the home, it confers a well-defined social identity, it enhances one's prestige/status, it enhances access to the opposite sex, or it offers the lure of easy money from drug trafficking. According to the Office of Juvenile Justice and Delinquency Prevention (OJJDP) National Gang Center estimates (Egley, Howell, & Moore, 2010), 32.4 percent of all cities, suburban areas, towns, and rural counties (more than 3,330 jurisdictions served by city and county law enforcement agencies) experienced gang problems as late as 2008. Approximately 774,000 gang members and 27,900 gangs are estimated to have been active in the United States as late as 2008.

References

Aaroe, L., & Nelson, J. (2000). A comparative analysis of teachers', Caucasian parents', and Hispanic parents' views of problematic school survival behaviors. *Education and Treatment of Children, 23*(3), 314–324.

Aaron, P. G. (1997). The impending demise of the discrepancy formula. *Review of Educational Research, 67*(4), 461–502.

Abedi, J. (2002). Standardized achievement tests and English language learners: Psychometric issues. *Educational Assessment, 8*(3), 231–257.

Abedi, J. (2004a). The No Child Left Behind Act and English Language Learners: Assessment and accountability issues. *Educational Researcher, 33*(1), 4–14.

Abedi, J. (2004b). Will you explain the question? *Principal Leadership Vol. 4*(7), 27–31.

Abedi, J. (2006). Language issues in item development. In S. M. Downing & T. M. Haladyna (Eds.), *Handbook of test development* (pp. 377–398). Mahwah, NJ: Erlbaum.

Abedi, J., & Dietel, R. (2004). *Policy Brief 7: Challenges in the No Child Left Behind Act for English Language Learners.* National Center for Research on Evaluation, Standards, and Student Testing (CRESST/UCLA). Accessed January 2012 from http://www.cse.ucla.edu/products/policy/cresst_policy7.pdf

Abedi, J., & Leon, S. (1999). *Impact of students' language background on content-based performance: Analyses of extant data* (Final Deliverable to OERI, Contract No. R305B960002). Los Angeles: University of California, National Center for Research on Evaluation, Standards, and Student Testing (CRESST).

Abedi, J., Leon, S., & Mirocha, J. (2003). *Impact of students' language background on content-based assessment: Analysis of extant data* (CSE Tech. Rep. No. 603). Los Angeles: University of California, National Center for Research on Evaluation, Standards, and Student Testing (CRESST).

Abedi, J., & Lord, C. (2001). The language factor in mathematics tests. *Applied Measurement in Education, 14*(3), 219–234.

Abella, R., Urrutia, J., & Shneyderman, A. (2005). An examination of the validity of English-language achievement test scores in an English language learner population. *Bilingual Research Journal, 29*(1), 127–144.

ABT Associates. (1977). *Education as experimentation: A planned variation model.* Cambridge, MA: Author.

Adams, G. L., & Engelmann, S. (1996). *Research on Direct Instruction: 25 years beyond DISTAR.* Seattle, WA: Educational Achievement Systems.

Adams, J. (2010, June 12). A special graduation recognizes gang intervention. Accessed May 2011 from City News Service, NBC Los Angeles, http://www.nbclosangeles.com/news/local/A-Special-Graduation-Could-Make-Big-Difference-in-Gang-Intervention-96222174.htm

Advocates for Youth. (2008). *Sex education and other programs that work to prevent teen pregnancy, HIV & sexually transmitted infections.* Washington, DC. Accessed May 2012 from http://www.advocatesforyouth.org/storage/advfy/documents/sciencesuccess.pdf

Ahlert, A. (2008). *A racial chip on one's shoulder.* Accessed November 2010 from Political Mavens.com, http://politicalmavens.com/index.php/2008/02/23/a-racial-chip-on-ones-shoulder

Albrecht, H. (1997). Ethnic minorities, crime and criminal justice in Germany. *Ethnicity, Crime and Immigration: Comparative and Cross-National Perspectives, 21,* 31–99.

Allen, B. A., & Boykin, A. W. (1992). African-American children and the educational process: Alleviating cultural discontinuity through prescriptive pedagogy. *School Psychology Review, 21*(4), 586–596.

Allen, T. T., Trzcinski, E., & Kubiak, S. P. (2012). Public attitudes toward juveniles who commit crimes: The relationship between assessments of adolescent development and attitudes toward severity of punishment. *Crime & Delinquency, 58*(1), 78–102.

American Association on Mental Retardation. (2002). *Mental retardation: Definition, classification, and systems of supports.* Washington, DC: Author.

American Educational Research Association (AERA), American Psychological Association (APA), National Council on Measurement in Education (NCME). (1999). *Standards for educational and psychological testing.* Washington, DC: Author.

American Psychological Association (APA). (1993). *Guidelines for providers of psychological services to ethnic, linguistic, and culturally diverse populations.* Washington, DC: Author.

APA Task Force on Socioeconomic Status. (2007). *Report of the APA Task Force on Socioeconomic Status.* Washington, DC: Author.

American Psychiatric Association. (1994). *Diagnostic and statistical manual of mental disorders* (4th ed.). Washington, DC: Author.

Anonymous. (1993, August 28). The cash street kids. *The Economist, 328* (7826), 23–25.

Ansalone, G. (2003). Poverty, tracking, and the social construction of failure: International perspectives on tracking. *Journal of Children and Poverty, 9*(1), 3–20.

Arbreton, A., & McClanahan, W. (2002). *Targeted outreach: Boys and Girls Clubs of America's approach to gang prevention and intervention.* Philadelphia, PA: Public/Private Ventures. Accessed March 2012 from http://www.ppv.org/ppv/publications/assets/148_publication.pdf

Arciaga, M., Sakamoto, W., & Jones, E. F. (2010, November). *Responding to gangs in the school setting. National Gang Center Bulletin, No. 5.* Office of Juvenile Justice and Delinquency Prevention. Accessed May 2011 from http://www.nationalgangcenter.gov/Content/Documents/Bulletin-5.pdf

Archer, A. L., & Hughes, C. A. (2011). *Explicit instruction: Effective and efficient teaching.* New York, NY: Guilford Press.

Arends-Tóth, J. V., & Van de Vijver, F. J. R. (2006). Assessment of psycho-logical acculturation: Choices in designing an instrument. In D. L. Sam & J. W. Berry (Eds.), *The Cambridge Handbook of acculturation psychology* (pp. 142–160). Cambridge, UK: Cambridge University Press.

Armour-Thomas, E., & Gopaul-McNicol, S. (1998). *Assessing intelligence: Applying a bio-cultural model.* Thousand Oaks, CA: Sage.

Asante, M. K. (1988). *Afrocentricity.* Trenton, NJ: Africa World Press.

Asante, M. K. (2005). *The painful demise of Eurocentrism: An Afrocentric response to critics.* Trenton, NJ: Africa World Press.

Ashlock, R.B. (2010). Error patterns in computation: Using error patterns to help each student learn (10th Edition). Boston, MA: Allyn & Bacon.

Associated Press. (2009, March 1). *Race becomes more central to TV advertising.* Accessed September 2010 from http://www.msnbc.msn.com/id/29453960/from/toolbar

Associated Press. (2009, July 31). *Tribal leaders seek help with Indian gang activity.* Accessed May 2011 from http://www.kxnet.com/getArticle.asp?setCity=bis&ArticleId=413511

Associated Press. (2010, November 11). *Father sues district over reading about slavery: Dad says daughter racially harassed by reading.* Accessed December 2, 2010 from http://www.the denverchannel.com/education/25752532/detail.html

Associated Press. (2011, May 17). White teachers sue Philadelphia school, charge race bias. CBS Philly.com. Accessed July, 2011 from http://philadelphia.cbslocal.com/2011/05/17/white-teachers-sue-philadelphia-school-charge-race-bias/

Attewell, P., Lavin, D., Domina, T., & Levey, T. (2004). The black middle class: Progress, prospects, and puzzles. *Journal of African American Studies, 8*(1), 6–19.

August, D., & Shanahan, T. (2006). *Developing literacy in second-language learners: Report of the National Literacy Panel on language minority children and youth.* Mahwah, NJ: Erlbaum.

Auletta, K. (1999). *The underclass.* Woodstock, NY: Overlook Press.

Austin, A. (2011). *Reducing poverty and increasing marriage rates among Latinos and African Americans (Issue Brief #313).* Washington, DC: Economic Policy Institute.

Awan, M. (1997). Educational development in the black community. In S. Faryna, B. Stetson, & J. G. Conti (Eds.), *Black and right: The bold new voice of black conservatives in America.* Westport, CT: Praeger.

Baker, C. (2011). *Foundations of bilingual education and bilingualism* (5th ed.). Bristol, UK: Multilingual Matters.

Baker, S. K., & Good, R. (1995). Curriculum-based measurement of English reading with bilingual Hispanic students: A validation. *School Psychology Review, 24*(4), 561–578.

Baker, S. K., Plasencia-Peinado, J., & Lezcano-Lytle, V. (1998). The use of curriculum-based measurement with language-minority students. In M. Shinn (Ed.), *Advanced applications of curriculum-based measurement* (pp. 175–213). New York, NY: Guilford Press.

Bambara, L. M., & Kern, L. (Eds.). (2005). *Individualized supports for students with problem behaviors: Designing positive behavior plans.* New York, NY: Guilford Press.

Banaszak, N. (2011). *NAACP president attacks Huntsville school system, threatens legal action.* WHNT News 19. Accessed February 2011 from http://www.whnt.com/news/whnt-huntsville-schools-naacp-alice-sams-desegregation-white-black,0,27752.story

Banks, J. A., & Banks, C. M. (2004). *Handbook of research on multicultural education* (2nd ed.). San Francisco, CA: Jossey-Bass.

Banks, S. (2011, October 18). Once again, a focus on disparities in L.A. Unified. Accessed November 2011 from LATimes.com, http://www.latimes.com/news/local/la-me-banks-20111018,0,6348669.column?page=1

Bankston, C. L., & Caldas, S. J. (2002). *A troubled dream: The promise and failure of school desegregation in Louisiana.* Nashville, TN: Vanderbilt University Press.

Bardon, L. A., Dona, D. P., & Symons, F. J. (2008). Extending classwide social skills interventions to at-risk minority students: A preliminary application of randomization tests combined with single-subject design methodology. *Behavioral Disorders, 33*(3), 141–152.

Bebko, J. M., & Luhaorg, H. (1998). The development of strategy use and metacognitive processing in mental retardation: Some sources of difficulty. In J. A. Burack, R. M. Hodapp, & E. Zigler (Eds.), *Handbook of mental retardation and development* (pp. 382–395). New York, NY: Cambridge University Press.

Beeghley, L. (2004). *The structure of social stratification in the United States.* Boston, MA: Pearson/ Allyn & Bacon.

Bender, W. N., & Shores, C. (2007). *Response to intervention: A practical guide for every teacher.* Thousand Oaks, CA: Corwin Press.

Bennett, C. I. (2004). Research on racial issues in American higher education. In J. A. Banks & C. M. Banks (Eds.), *Handbook of research on multicultural education* (2nd ed., pp. 847–868). San Francisco, CA: Jossey-Bass.

Bereiter, C. (1987). Jensen and educational differences. In S. Modgil & C. Modgil (Eds.), *Arthur Jensen: Consensus and controversy* (pp. 329–337). New York, NY: Falmer Press.

Bergan, J. (1977). *Behavioral consultation.* Columbus, OH: Charles Merrill.

Bergan, J. R., & Kratochwill, T. R. (1990). *Behavioral consultation and therapy.* New York, NY: Plenum.

Bernal, G., & Sáez-Santiago, E. (2006). Culturally centered psychosocial interventions. *Journal of Community Psychology, 34*(2), 121–132.

Bernal, G., Trimble, J. E., Burlew, A. K., & Leong, F. (Eds.). (2003). *Handbook of racial and ethnic minority psychology.* Thousand Oaks, CA: Sage.

Bernal, M. (1987). *Black Athena: The Afroasiatic roots of classical civilization.* Piscataway, NJ: Rutgers University Press.

Bernal, M. (1991). *Black Athena: The Afroasiatic roots of classical civilization, Vol. 2.* Piscataway, NJ: Rutgers University Press.

Bernal, M. (2006). *Black Athena: The Afroasiatic roots of classical civilization, Vol. 3.* Piscataway, NJ: Rutgers University Press.

Bernstein, R. (1994). *Dictatorship of virtue: Multiculturalism and the battle for America's future*. New York, NY: Knopf.

Berry, K. A., Grossman, Z., & Pawiki, L. H. (2007). Native Americans. In I. M. Miyares & C. A. Airriess (Eds.), *Contemporary ethnic geographies in America* (pp. 51–70). Lanham, MD: Rowman & Littlefield.

Bersoff, D. N. (1980). *P. v. Riles*: Legal perspective. *School Psychology Review*, 9(2), 112–122.

Better, S. (2002). *Institutional racism: A primer on theory and strategies for social change*. Lanham, MD: Rowman & Littlefield.

Bevir, M. (2010). *Encyclopedia of political theory*. Thousand Oaks, CA: Sage.

Blackburn, J. (2011). *Dallas ISD police and security services: Safety is job one*. Unpublished manuscript. Dallas, TX: Dallas Independent School District.

Blair, C. (2001). The early identification of risk for grade retention among African American children at risk for school difficulty. *Applied Development Science*, 5(1), 37–50.

Blanchett, W. (2010). Telling it like it is: The role of race, class, and culture in the perpetuation of learning disability as a privileged category for the white middle class. *Disability Studies Quarterly*, 30(2). Accessed January 2011 from http://www.dsq-sds.org/article/view/1233/1280

Blankenship, C.S. (1985). Using curriculum-based assessment data to make instructional decisions. *Exceptional Children*, 52, 233–238.

Block, J. (1971). *Mastery learning: Theory and practice*. New York, NY: Holt, Rinehart, & Winston.

Blume, H. (2011, October 11). LAUSD agrees to revise how English learners, blacks are taught. Accessed November 2011 from LATimes.com, http://www.latimes.com/news/local/la-me-1012-lausd-feds-20111011,0,4458591.story?page=1

Bollman, K. A., Silberglitt, B., & Gibbons, K. A. (2007). The St. Croix River education district model: Incorporating systems-level organization and a multi-tiered problemsolving process for intervention delivery. In S. R. Jimerson, M. K. Burns, & A. M. VanDerHeyden (Eds.), *Handbook of response to intervention: The science and practice of assessment and intervention* (pp. 319–330). New York, NY: Springer.

Booker, K. (2009). Multicultural considerations in school consultation. In J. M. Jones (Ed.), *The psychology of multiculturalism in the schools: A primer for practice, training, and research* (pp. 173–190). Bethesda, MD: National Association of School Psychologists.

Bornstein, M. H. (Ed.). (2002a). *Handbook of parenting, Vol. 2: Biology and ecology of parenting*. Mahwah, NJ: Erlbaum.

Bornstein, M. H. (Ed.). (2002b). *Handbook of parenting, Vol. 4: Social conditions and applied parenting*. Mahwah, NJ: Erlbaum.

Bornstein, M. H., & Bradley, R. H. (Eds.). (2003). *Socioeconomic status, parenting, and child development*. Mahwah, NJ: Erlbaum.

Bornstein, M. H., Hahn, C., Suwalsky, J., & Haynes, O. (2003). Socioeconomic status, parenting, and child development: The Hollingshead Four Factor Index of Social Status and the Socioeconomic Index of Occupations. In M. H. Bornstein & R. H. Bradley (Eds.), *Socioeconomic status, parenting, and child development* (pp. 29–82). Mahwah, NJ: Erlbaum.

Borowsky, R., Barth, F., Shweder, R. A., Rodseth, L., & Stolzenberg, N. M. (2001). When: A conversation about culture. *American Anthropologist, 103*, 432–446.

Bouffard, K. (2008, February 25). Detroit schools graduation rate: 32%. Accessed February 2011 from *The Detroit News*, http://www.bridges4kids.org/articles/3-08/DetroitNews2-25-08 .html

Bowlby, J. (1982). *Attachment and loss, Vol. I: Attachment* (2nd ed.). New York, NY: Basic Books.

Boykin, A. W. (1986). The triple quandary and the schooling of Afro-American children. In U. Neisser (Ed.), *The school achievement of minority children: New perspectives* (pp. 57–92). Hillsdale, NJ: Erlbaum.

Brace, C. L. (2000). *Does race exist? An antagonist's perspective.* Accessed May 2011 from NOVA Online, http://www.pbs.org/wgbh/nova/first/brace.html

Bracken, B. A., Bunch, S., Keith, T. Z., & Keith, P. B. (2000). Childhood and adolescent multidimensional self-concept: A five-instrument factor analysis. *Psychology in the Schools, 37*, 483–493.

Bracken, B. A., & McCallum, R. S. (1998). *Universal Nonverbal Intelligence Test (UNIT) Manual.* Chicago, IL: Riverside.

Braden, J. P. (1990, February). People of color. *NASP Communiqué, 18*(5), 2.

Braden, J. P. (1999). Performance assessment and diversity. *School Psychology Quarterly, 14*(3), 304–326.

Braden, J. P. (2000). Editor's introduction: Perspectives on the nonverbal assessment of intelligence. *Journal of Psychoeducational Assessment, 18*, 204–210.

Braden, J. P. (2003). Accommodating clients with disabilities on the WAIS-III/WMS. In D. Saklofske & D. Tulsky (Eds.), *Use of the WAIS-III/WMS in clinical practice* (pp. 451–486). Boston, MA: Houghton Mifflin.

Braden, J. P., & Athanasiou, M. S. (2005). A comparative review of nonverbal measures of intelligence. In D. P. Flanagan & P. L. Harrison (Eds.), *Contemporary intellectual assessment* (pp. 557–578). New York, NY: Guilford Press.

Braden, J. P., & Elliott, S. N. (2003). Accommodations on the Stanford-Binet Intelligence Scales. In G. Roid (Ed.), *Interpretive manual for the Stanford-Binet Intelligence Scales* (5th ed., pp. 135–143). Itasca, IL: Riverside.

Bramlett, R. K., Murphy, J. J., Johnson, J., Wallingsford, L., & Hall, J. D. (2002). Contemporary practices in school psychology: A national survey of roles and referral problems. *Psychology in the Schools, 39*(3), 327–335.

Briggs, A. (2009, June). Social justice in school psychology: Moving forward. *NASP Communiqué, 37*(8), 8–9.

Briggs, D. C. (2002). Test preparation programs: Impact. In J. Guthrie (Ed.), *Encyclopedia of education* (pp. 2542–2545). New York, NY: MacMillan.

Brisk, M. (2006). *Bilingual education: From compensatory to quality schooling* (2nd ed.). Mahwah, NJ: Erlbaum.

Bronfenbrenner, U. (1989). Ecological systems theory. In R. Vasta (Ed.), *Annals of child development: A research annual* 6 (pp. 187–249). New York, NY: Taylor & Francis.

Brooks-Gunn, J., & Markman, L. B. (2005). The contribution of parenting to ethnic and racial gaps in school readiness. *The Future of Children, 15*(1), 139–168.

Broughman, S. P., Swaim, N. L., & Hryczaniuk, C. A. (2011). *Characteristics of private schools in the United States: Results from the 2009–10 Private School Universe Survey* (NCES 2011-339). Washington, DC: National Center for Education Statistics, Institute of Education Sciences, U.S. Department of Education.

Brown, D. (1991). *Human universals.* Philadelphia, PA: Temple University Press.

Brown, D. (2000). Human universals and their implications. In N. Roughley (Ed.), *Being humans: Anthropological universality and particularity in transdisciplinary perspectives* (pp. 156–174). Berlin, Germany: Walter de Gruyter.

Brown, K. (1993). Do African Americans need immersion schools? The paradoxes created by the conceptualization by law of race and public education. *Iowa Law Review, 78*, 813–881.

Brown, K. (2000). Afrocentric schools. Accessed November 2011 from http://www.jiffynotes .com/a_study_guides/book_notes/eamc_01/eamc_01_00060.html

Brown, M. B., Holcombe, D. C., Bolen, L. M., & Thomson, S. (2006). Role function and job satisfaction of school psychologists practicing in an expanded role model. *Psychological Reports, 98*(2), 486–496.

Browne, M. N., & Keeley, S. M. (2004). *Asking the right questions: A guide to critical thinking.* Upper Saddle River, NJ: Pearson.

Buck, S. (2010). Acting white: The ironic legacy of desegregation. New Haven, CT: Yale University Press.

Buckley, J., & Schneider, M. (2007). *Charter schools: Hope or hype?* Princeton, NJ: Princeton University Press.

Budoff, M. (1987). Measures for assessing learning. In C. S. Lidz (Ed.), *Dynamic assessment: An interactional approach to evaluation of learning potential* (pp. 173–195). New York, NY: Guilford Press.

Burke, S. (2001). The advantages of a school resource officer. *Law and Order, 49*, 73–75.

Caldas, S. J., & Bankston, C. L. (2005). *Forced to fail: The paradox of school desegregation.* Westport, CT: Praeger.

Calkins, A., Guenther, W., Belfiore, G., & Lash, D. (2007). *The turnaround challenge: Supplement to the main report.* Boston, MA: Mass Insight Education and Research Institute. Accessed July 2011 from http://www.massinsight.org/publications/turnaround/52/file/1/pubs/2010/04/ 15/TheTurnaroundChallenge_SupplementalReport.pdf

Callahan, C. M. (2005). Gifted students. In S. W. Lee (Ed.), *Encyclopedia of school psychology* (pp. 225–227). Thousand Oaks, CA: Sage.

Campeau, J. (2010, January 31). Illegal immigrant endures tough life to send money home. *Berks Community Television (BCTV.org)*. Accessed April 2012 from http://www.bctv.org/special_reports/community/article_3a2fc452-0e95-11df-9ac7-001cc4c03286.html

Campione, J. C. (1989). Assisted assessment: A taxonomy. *Journal of Learning Disabilities, 22*, 151–165.

Caplan, G., & Caplan, R. B. (1999). *Mental health consultation and collaboration*. Prospect Heights, IL: Waveland.

Capozzoli, T., & McVey, S. (2000). *Kids killing kids: Managing violence and gangs in schools*. Boca Raton, FL: St. Lucie Press.

Carnine, D. W., Silbert, J., Kame'enui, E. J., & Tarver, S. G. (2009). *Direct Instruction reading* (5th ed.). Upper Saddle River, NJ: Prentice Hall.

Carroll, D. (2009). Toward multiculturalism competence: A practical model for implementation in the schools. In J. M. Jones (Ed.), *The psychology of multiculturalism in the schools: A primer for practice, training, and research* (pp. 1–16). Bethesda, MD: National Association of School Psychologists.

Carroll, J. B. (1963). A model of school learning. *Teachers College Record, 64*, 723–733.

Carroll, J. B. (1989). The Carroll model: A 25-year retrospective and prospective view. *Educational Researcher, 18*(1), 26–31.

Carroll, J. B. (1993). *Human cognitive abilities: A survey of factor-analytic studies*. Cambridge, UK: Cambridge University Press.

Carson, B. (2011). *Gifted hands, 20th anniversary edition: The Ben Carson story*. Grand Rapids, MI: Zondervan Books.

Carter, S. (2000). *No excuses: Lessons from 21 high-performing, high-poverty schools*. Washington, DC: Heritage Foundation.

Case, L. P., Speece, D. L., & Molloy, D. E. (2003). The validity of a response-to-instruction paradigm to identify reading disabilities: A longitudinal analysis of individual differences and contextual factors. *School Psychology Review, 32*, 557–582.

Casimir, L. (2004, July 18). Cotillions make a comeback: Courtly tradition updated by African Americans. *NYDailyNews.com*. Accessed August 2011 from http://articles.nydailynews.com/2004-07-18/news/18269703_1_cotillion-whites-black-elite

Cavalli-Sforza, L. L., Menozzi, P., & Piazza, A. (1994). *The history and geography of human genes*. Princeton, NJ: Princeton University Press.

Cawthon, S. W. (2010). Assessment accommodations for English Language Learners: The case of former-LEPs. *Practical Assessment, Research and Evaluation, 15*(13), 1–9.

Ceballo, R., Dahl, T. A., Aretakis, M. T., & Ramirez, C. (2001). Inner-city children's exposure to community violence: How much do parents know? *Journal of Marriage and Family, 63*(4), 927–940.

Center for Mental Health in Schools. (2010). *Immigrant children and youth: Enabling their success at school*. Los Angeles, CA: School Mental Health Project, Department of Psychology, UCLA.

Chan, S. (1986). Parents of exceptional Asian children. In M. K. Kitano & P. C. Chinn (Eds.), *Exceptional Asian children and youth* (Exceptional Children Education Report, pp. 36–53). Reston, VA: Council for Exceptional Children.

Chan-sew, S. (1980). *Issues and concerns in the provision of services to Asians with developmental disabilities*. Paper presented at the First Annual Conference of the Committee on Asians with Developmental Disabilities, Berkeley, CA.

Chapman, C., Laird, J., Ifill, N., & Kewal-Ramani, A. (2011). *Trends in high school dropout and completion rates in the United States: 1972–2009*. Washington, DC: National Center for Education Statistics.

Christensen, B. (2004, October). *Time for a new 'Moynihan Report'? Confronting the national family crisis*. The Family in America (Online Edition). Howard Center for Family, Religion, and Society. Accessed June 2011 from http://www.profam.org/pub/fia/fia_1810.htm

Ciotti, P. (1998a, March 16). Money and school performance: Lessons from the Kansas City desegregation experiment. *Policy Analysis, No. 298*. Accessed January 8, 2011, from The Cato Institute, http://www.cato.org/pubs/pas/pa-298.pdf

Ciotti, P. (1998b, April 29). America's most costly educational failure. Accessed January 8, 2011, from The Cato Institute, http://www.cato.org/pub_display.php?pub_id=5552

Cizek, G. J. (2003). *Detecting and preventing classroom cheating: Promoting integrity in assessment.* Thousand Oaks, CA: Corwin Press.

Cizek, G. J., & Burg, S. S. (2006). *Addressing test anxiety in a high-stakes environment: Strategies for classrooms and schools.* Thousand Oaks, CA: Corwin Press.

Clare, M. (2009). Thinking diversity: A habit of mind for school psychology. In T. B. Gutkin & C. R. Reynolds (Eds.), *The handbook of school psychology* (4th ed., pp. 840–854). Hoboken, NJ: Wiley.

Clark, J. (Ed.). (1996). *James S. Coleman.* New York, NY: Taylor & Francis.

Clark, K. B., & Clark, M. K. (1939). The development of consciousness of self and the emergence of racial identification in Negro preschool children. *Journal of Social Psychology, S.P.S.S.I. Bulletin, 10*, 591–599.

Clauss-Ehlers, C. S. (Ed.). (2010). *Encyclopedia of cross-cultural school psychology.* New York, NY: Springer.

Clay, M. (1991). *Becoming literate: The construction of inner control.* Auckland, New Zealand: Heinemann Education.

Clifton, J. A. (Ed.). (2004). *The invented Indian.* New Brunswick, NJ: Transaction.

Cohen, E. G., & Lotan, R. A. (2004). Equity in heterogeneous classrooms. In J. A. Banks & C. A. Banks (Eds.), *Handbook of research on multicultural education* (2nd ed., pp. 736–750). San Francisco, CA: Jossey-Bass.

Coleman, H., & Hau, J. M. (2003). Multicultural counseling competency and portfolios. In D. B. Pope-Davis, H. Coleman, W. Liu, & R. Toporek (Eds.), *Handbook of multicultural competencies in counseling and psychology* (pp. 168–182). Thousand Oaks, CA: Sage.

Coleman, J. (1966). *Equality of educational opportunity*. Washington, DC: Government Printing Office.

Coleman, J., Hoffer, T., & Kilgore, S. (1982). *High school achievement: Public, Catholic, and private schools compared*. New York, NY: Basic Books.

Coll, C. G., & Marks, A. K. (Eds.). (2012). *The immigrant paradox in children and adolescents: Is becoming American a developmental risk?* Washington, DC: American Psychological Association.

Colson, C. (2010, December 8). Playing the hate card: One way to shut down debate. Breakpoint. Accessed November 2012 from http://www.breakpoint.org/bpcommentaries/entry/13/16011.

Conti, J. G., & Stetson, B. (1997). Are you really a racist? A common sense quiz. In S. Faryna, B. Stetson, & J. G. Conti (Eds.), *Black and right: The bold new voice of black conservatives in America* (pp. 65–76). Westport, CT: Praeger.

Cook, P. J., & Ludwig, J. (1997). Weighing the "burden of acting white": Are there race differences in attitudes toward education? *Journal of Policy Analysis and Management, 16*(2), 256–278.

Cosby, B., & Poissaint, A. F. (2007). *Come on people: On the path from victims to victors*. Nashville, TN: Thomas Nelson.

Cotton, K. (2003). *Principals and student achievement: What the research says*. Alexandria, VA: Association for Supervision & Curriculum Development.

Coulson, A. J. (2010, January 28). Head Start: A tragic waste of money. Accessed March 2011 from the *New York Post*, http://www.nypost.com/p/news/opinion/opedcolumnists/head_start_tragic_waste_of_money_L7V5dJC333RDC8QT8UEWaO

Council of State Directors of Programs for the Gifted & National Association of Gifted Children. (2009). *State of the states in gifted education: National policy and practice data*. Washington, DC: National Association for Gifted Children.

Coutinho, M. J., Oswald, D. P., & Best, A. M. (2002). The influence of sociodemographics and gender on the disproportionate identification of minority students as having learning disabilities. *Remedial and Special Education, 23*(1), 49–59.

Crespi, T., & Bieu, R.P. (2005). Study skills. In S.W. Lee (Ed.), *Encyclopedia of school psychology* (pp. 539–543). Thousand Oaks, CA: Sage.

Crockett, D., & Brown, J. (2009). Multicultural practices and response to intervention. In J. Jones (Ed.), *The psychology of multiculturalism in the schools: A primer for practice, training, and research* (pp. 117–138). Bethesda, MD: National Association of School Psychologists.

Crone, D. A., Hawken, L. S., & Horner, R. H. (2010). *Responding to problem behavior in schools* (2nd ed.). New York, NY: Guilford Press.

Cross, T., Bazron, B., Dennis, K., & Isaacs, M. (1989). *Towards a culturally competent system of care, Vol. I*. Washington, DC: Georgetown University Child Development Center, CASSP Technical Assistance Center.

Crouch, E. (2010, August 30). Big incentive for school attendance: Cash. Accessed February 2011 from the *St. Louis Dispatch*, http://www.stltoday.com/news/local/education/article_69e59029-9c22-52e7-99f4-162d02d2d814.html

Crouch, E. (2011, August 21). New city school blends learning with African cultural flavor. Accessed November 2011 from *Stltoday.com*, http://www.stltoday.com/news/local/education/article_c8feb096-d071-5f22-94c3-78cc351cc92d.html

Cummings, N. (2008, August 14). *Destructive trends in mental health: A 2008 progress report*. Paper presented at the 2008 American Psychological Association Convention, Boston, Massachusetts. Accessed April 2011 from http://www.narth.com/docs/DestructiveTrends.pdf

Cummins, J. (1991). Language development and academic learning. In L. M. Malavé and G. Duquette (Eds.), *Language, culture, and cognition* (pp. 161–175). Clevedon, England: Multilingual Matters.

Currie, J., & Thomas, D. (1995). Does Head Start make a difference? *American Economic Review*, 85, 341–364.

Daily Mail Reporter. (2011, January 27). School defends experiment to separate black students in a bid to boost their academic results. Accessed February 2011 from *Mail Online News*, http://www.dailymail.co.uk/news/article-1350864/School-defends-separation-black-students-boost-academic-results.html

Dalrymple, T. (2001). *Life at the bottom: The worldview that makes the underclass*. Chicago, IL: Ivan R. Dee.

D'Andrea, M., & Daniels, J. (2001). Expanding our thinking about white racism: Facing the challenge of multicultural counseling in the 21st century. In J. G. Ponterotto, J. M. Casas, L. A. Suzuki, & C. M. Alexander (Eds.), *Handbook of multicultural counseling* (2nd ed., pp. 289–310). Thousand Oaks, CA: Sage.

D'Andrea, M., & Daniels, J. (2003, February). White supremacy, racism and multicultural competence. *Counseling Today*, 45(7), 26–28.

Darling-Hammond, L. (1994). Who will speak for the children? How "Teach for America" hurts urban schools and students. *The Phi Delta Kappan*, 76, 21–34.

Darling-Hammond, L., French, J., & Garcia-Lopez, S. (Eds.). (2002). *Learning to teach for social justice*. New York, NY: Teachers College Press.

Daugherty, D., & Stanhope, V. (Eds.). (1998). *Pathways to tolerance: Student diversity*. Bethesda, MD: National Association of School Psychologists.

Davis, D., & Sorrell, J. (1995, December). Mastery learning in public schools. *Educational Psychology Interactive*. Valdosta, GA: Valdosta State University. Accessed May 2011 from http://teach.valdosta.edu/whuitt/files/mastlear.html

Dawsey, C. (2011, February 10). *Illegal grade-fixing allegations swirl at DPS*. Accessed February 2011 from *Detroit Free Press*, http://www.freep.com/article/20110210/NEWS05/102100562/Illegal-grade-fixing-allegations-swirl-DPS?odyssey=tab | topnews | text | FRONTPAGE

Decter, M. (1991). E. pluribus nihil. *Commentary*, 92(3), 25–29.

Delaney, T. (2006). *American street gangs*. Upper Saddle River, NJ: Pearson.

Delgado, R. (Ed.). (1995). *Critical race theory: The cutting edge*. Philadelphia, PA: Temple University Press.

DeNavas-Walt, C., Proctor, B., & Smith, J. (2010). *Income, poverty, and health insurance coverage in the United States: 2009.* U.S. Census Bureau, Current Population Reports, P60-238. Washington, DC: U.S. Government Printing Office.

Deno, S. (1987). Curriculum-based measurement. *Teaching Exceptional Children, 20,* 41.

Dent, D. J. (1996, August 4). *African-Americans turning to Christian academies.* Accessed June 2011 from New York Times.com, http://www.nytimes.com/1996/08/04/education/african-americans-turning-to-christian-academies.html?src=pm

de Ramirez, R. D., & Shapiro, E. S. (2006). Curriculum-based measurement and the evaluation of reading skills of Spanish-speaking English language learners in bilingual education classrooms. *School Psychology Review, 35*(3), 356–369.

Dexter, D., & Hughes, C. (2011). Progress monitoring within a Response-to-Intervention model. Accessed September 2011 from http://www.rtinetwork.org/learn/research/progress-monitoring-within-a-rti-model

Diaz, D. (2011). *Project Prevail: Guide for students, families and community.* Unpublished manuscript. Fort Worth, TX: Fort Worth Independent School District.

Diaz, T. (2009). *No boundaries: Transnational Latino gangs and American law enforcement.* Ann Arbor: University of Michigan Press.

Dolan, R. P., & Hall, T. E. (2001). Universal design for learning: Implications for large-scale assessment. *IDA Perspectives, 27*(4), 22–25.

Dorans, N., & Holland, P. W. (1993). DIF detection and description: Mantel-Haenszel and standardization. In P. W. Holland & H. Wainer (Eds.), *Differential item functioning* (pp. 35–66). Hillsdale, NJ: Erlbaum.

Dougherty, M. (2005, October 6). A day in the life of an illegal immigrant. Accessed April 2012 from *World Internet News,* http://soc.hfac.uh.edu/artman/publish/article_270.shtml

Douglas, K. (2004). *Teacher ideas on teaching and testing English language learners: Summary of focus group discussions* (C-SAVE Rep. No. 223). Madison, WI: University of Wisconsin, Center for the Study of Assessment Validity and Evaluation.

Dreher, M., & MacNaughton, N. (2002). Cultural competence in nursing: Foundation or fallacy? *Nursing Outlook, 50,* 181–186.

D'Souza, D. (1995). *The end of racism.* New York, NY: Free Press.

Duckworth, A. L., & Seligman, M. E. P. (2005). Self-discipline outdoes IQ in predicting academic performance of adolescents. *Psychological Science, 16*(12), 939–944.

Dunn, R., & Griggs, S. A. (1995). *Multiculturalism and learning style: Teaching and counseling adolescents.* Westport, CT: Praeger.

Eddy, J. M., & Poehlmann, J. (Eds.). (2010). *Children of incarcerated parents: A handbook for researchers and practitioners.* Washington, DC: Urban Institute Press.

Edelman, S. (2011, June 26). The school from hell. Accessed July 2011 from *New York Post,* http://www.nypost.com/p/news/local/manhattan/the_school_from_hell_nVSOubg9F7uzULCHOrNh2H

Edin, K., & Kefalas, M. (2005). *Promises I can keep: Why poor women put motherhood before marriage*. Berkeley, CA: University of California Press.

Egley, A., Howell, J. C., & Moore, J. P. (2010, March). *Highlights of the 2008 National Youth Gang Survey*. Washington, DC: U.S. Department of Justice, Office of Juvenile Justice and Delinquency Prevention.

Einzig, H. (1996). Parenting education and support. In R. Bayne and I. Horton (Eds.), *New directions in counseling* (pp. 220–234). London, England: Routledge.

Elliott, R. (1987). *Litigating intelligence: IQ tests, special education, and social science*. Dover, MA: Auburn House.

Elliott, S. N., Kratochwill, T. R., & Gilbertson-Schulte, A. (1999). *Assessment accommodations guide*. Monteray, CA: CTB McGraw-Hill.

Elliott, S. N., & Roach, A. T. (2006). The influence of access to the general education curriculum on the alternate assessment performance of students with significant cognitive disabilities. *Education Evaluation and Policy Analysis, 20*(2), 181–194.

Ellis, F. (2010). Multiculturalism and Marxism. Accessed August 2011 from *OrthodoxyToday.org*, http://www.orthodoxytoday.org/articles-2009/Ellis-Multiculturalism-And-Marxism.php

Ellis, L., Beaver, K., & Wright, J. (2009). *Handbook of crime correlates*. San Diego, CA: Academic Press.

Elshinnawi, M. (2010, July 12). Islamic schools in US raise hopes, fears. Accessed November 2011 from *Voanews.com*, http://www.voanews.com/english/news/usa/Islamic-Schools-in-US-Raises-Hopes-and-Fears-98247319.html

Elsner, A. (2003, December 13). *Pine Ridge: Youth Gangs flourish on Indian reservations*. Accessed June, 2012 from http://story.news.yahoo.com/news?tmpl=story&cid=572&ncid=572&e=11&u=/nm/20031211\/lf_nm/life_gangs_dc_1

Embretson, S. E., & Reise, S. P. (2000). *Item response theory for psychologists*. Mahwah, NJ: Erlbaum.

Englemann, S. (2007). *Teaching needy kids in our backward system: 42 years of trying*. Eugene, OR: ADI Press.

Ennis, S. R., Ríos-Vargas, M., & Albert, N. G. (2011). *The Hispanic Population: 2010*. Washington, DC: U.S. Census Bureau.

Erchul, W. P. (2005). Consultation: Mental health. In S. W. Lee (Ed.), *Encyclopedia of school psychology* (pp. 115–117). Thousand Oaks, CA: Sage.

Erickson, P. A., & Murphy, L. D. (2008). *A history of anthropological theory* (3rd ed.). Peterborough, Ontario, Canada: Broadview Press.

Erler, E. J., West, T. G., & Marini, J. A. (2007). *The founders on citizenship and immigration: Principles and challenges in America*. Lanham, MD: Rowman & Littlefield.

Esbensen, F., Osgood, D., Taylor, T., Peterson, D., & Freng, A. (2001). How great is G.R.E.A.T.? Results from a longitudinal quasi-experimental design. *Criminology and Public Policy, 1*, 87–118.

Esbensen, F., Peterson, D., Taylor, T. J., & Freng, A. (2010). *Youth violence: Sex and race differences in offending, victimization, and gang membership*. Philadelphia, PA: Temple University Press.

Espenshade, T. J., & Radford, A. W. (2009). *No longer separate, not yet equal: Race and class in elite college admission and campus life*. Princeton, NJ: Princeton University Press.

Esquivel, G. B., Lopez, E. C., & Nahari, S. (2007). *Handbook of multicultural school psychology: An interdisciplinary perspective*. Mahwah, NJ: Erlbaum.

Estes, W. (1992). Ability testing: Postscript on ability tests, testing, and public policy. *Psychological Science, 3*, 278.

Evans, M. (1995, December). Catastrophe in Kansas City: The latest colossal failure in forced equality. *American Renaissance, 6*(12). Accessed January 2011 from http://www.amren.com/ar/1995/12/index.html.

Fagan, T. (1990). Book review: *Testers and testing: The sociology of school psychology*. *Journal of Psychoeducational Assessment, 8*(4), 550–555.

Fagan, T., & Wise, P. S. (2007). *School psychology: Past, present, and future* (3rd ed.). Bethesda, MD: National Association of School Psychologists.

Fan, X. (1996). Ethnic group representation in test construction samples and test bias: The standardization fallacy revisited. *Educational and Psychological Measurement, 56*(3), 365–382.

Fein, M. L. (2001). *Race and morality: How good intentions undermine social justice and perpetuate inequality*. New York, NY: Kluwer.

Ferguson, A. (2000). *Bad boys: Public schools in the making of black masculinity*. Ann Arbor, MI: University of Michigan Press.

Ferris State University. (2010). *Institute for the study of academic racism*. Accessed July 2010 at http://www.ferris.edu/ISAR/homepage.htm

Feuerstein, R., Feuerstein, R. S., & Falik, L. H. (2010). *Mediated learning and the brain's capacity for change*. New York, NY: Teachers College Press.

Feuerstein, R., Feuerstein, R., & Gross, S. (1997). The learning potential assessment device. In D. P. Flanagan, J. L. Genshaft, & P. L. Harrison (Eds.), *Contemporary intellectual assessment: Theories, tests, and issues* (pp. 297–313). New York, NY: Guilford Press.

Feuerstein, R., Rand, Y., & Hoffmann, M. (1979). *Dynamic assessment of retarded performers*. Baltimore, MD: University Park Press.

Figueroa, R. A. (1979). The system of multicultural pluralistic assessment. *The School Psychology Digest, 8*(1), 28–36.

Figueroa, R. A. (1999). Special education for Latino students in the United States: A metaphor for what is wrong. In T. V. Fletcher & C. S. Bos (Eds.), *Helping individuals with disabilities and their families: Mexican and U.S. perspectives* (pp. 147–159). Tempe, AZ: Bilingual Review/Press.

Figueroa, R. A., & Hernandez, S. (2000). *Testing Hispanic students in the United States: Technical and policy issues*. Washington, DC: President's Advisory Commission on Educational Excellence for Hispanic Americans.

Fish, S. (1997). Boutique multiculturalism, or why liberals are incapable of thinking about hate speech. *Critical Inquiry, 23*(2), 378–389.

Fong, M. L., & Lease, S. H. (1997). Cross-cultural supervision: Issues for the white supervisor. In D. Pope-Davis & H. Coleman (Eds.), *Multicultural counseling competencies: Assessment, education and training, and supervision* (pp. 387–405). Thousand Oaks, CA: Sage.

Foote, D. (2008). *Relentless pursuit: A year in the trenches with Teach for America*. New York, NY: Knopf.

Ford, D. Y. (1996). *Reversing underachievement among gifted black students: Promising practices and programs*. New York, NY: Teachers College Press.

Ford, D. Y. (2008). Intelligence testing and cultural diversity: The need for alternative instruments, policies, and procedures. In J. VanTassel-Baska (Ed.), *Alternative assessments with gifted and talented students* (pp. 107–128). Waco, TX: Prufrock Press.

Ford, D. Y., & Grantham, T. C. (2003). Providing access for culturally diverse gifted students: From deficit to dynamic thinking. *Theory Into Practice, 42*(3), 217–225.

Ford, D. Y., Grantham, T. C., & Milner, H. R. (2004). Under-achievement among gifted African American students: Cultural, social and psychological considerations. In D. Boothe & J. C. Stanley (Eds.), *In the eyes of the beholder: Critical issues for diversity in gifted education*. Waco, TX: Prufrock Press.

Ford, D. Y., Grantham, T. C., & Whiting, G. W. (2008). Culturally and linguistically diverse students in gifted education: Recruitment and retention issues. *Exceptional Children, 74*(3), 289–306.

Ford, R. T. (2008). *The race card: How bluffing about bias makes race relations worse*. New York, NY: Farrar, Straus & Giroux.

Fordham, S., & Ogbu, J. U. (1986). Black students' school success: Coping with the "burden of 'acting white.'" *The Urban Review, 18*(3), 176–206.

France-Presse, A. (2011, February 10). *Multiculturalism "clearly" a failure: Sarkozy*. Accessed March 2011 from Nationalpost.com, http://www.nationalpost.com/news/Multiculturalism+clearly +failure+Sarkozy/4261825/story.html

Francis, D. J., Fletcher, J. M., Stuebing, K. K., Lyon, G. R., Shaywitz, B. A., & Shaywitz, S. E. (2005). Psychometric approaches to the identification of LD: IQ and achievement scores are not sufficient. *Journal of Learning Disabilities, 38*, 98–108.

Francis, D., Rivera, M., Lesaux, N., Kieffer, M., & Rivera, H. (2006). *Research-based recommendations for the use of accommodations in large-scale assessments*. Houston, TX: Center on Instruction. Retrieved September 2011 from http://www.centeroninstruction.org/files/ELL3-Assessments.pdf

Frank, J. L., Horner, R. H., & Anderson, C. M. (2011). Influence of school level socioeconomic status and racial diversity on Schoolwide Positive Behavior Support implementation. *PBIS Newsletter, 5*(4). Accessed February 2012 from http://www.pbis.org/pbis_newsletter/volume_5/volume5_issue4.aspx

Freedman, S. G. (2004, May 19). *Increasingly, African-Americans take flight to private schools*. Accessed June 2011 from NYTimes.com, http://www.nytimes.com/2004/05/19/nyregion/on-education-increasingly-african-americans-take-flight-to-private-schools.html

Frisby, C. L. (1993). One giant step backward: Myths of black cultural learning styles. *School Psychology Review, 22*, 535–558.

Frisby, C. L. (1996). The use of multidimensional scaling in the cognitive mapping of cultural difference judgments. *School Psychology Review, 25*(1), 77–93.

Frisby, C. L. (1999). Culture and test session behavior, Part I. *School Psychology Quarterly, 14*(3), 263–280.

Frisby, C. L. (2005a). The politics of multiculturalism in school psychology, Part I. In C. L. Frisby & C. R. Reynolds (Eds.), *Comprehensive handbook of multicultural school psychology* (pp. 45–80). Hoboken, NJ: Wiley.

Frisby, C. L. (2005b). The politics of multiculturalism in school psychology, Part II. In C. L. Frisby & C. R. Reynolds (Eds.), *Comprehensive handbook of multicultural school psychology* (pp. 81–136). Hoboken, NJ: Wiley.

Frisby, C. L. (2005c). *Learning styles*. In S.W. Lee (Ed.), *Encyclopedia of school psychology*. Thousand Oaks, CA: Sage.

Frisby, C. L. (2009). Cultural competence in school psychology: Established or elusive construct? *The handbook of school psychology* (4th ed., pp. 855–885). Hoboken, NJ: Wiley.

Frisby, C. L., & Lorenzo-Luaces, L. M. (2000). The structure of cultural difference judgments in a Cuban American sample. *Hispanic Journal of Behavioral Sciences, 22*(2), 194–222.

Frisby, C. L., & Osterlind, S. (2007). Hispanic test-session behavior on the Woodcock Johnson Psychoeducational Battery, Third Edition. *Journal of Psychoeducational Assessment, 25*(5), 257–270.

Frisby, C. L., & Reynolds, C. R. (Eds.). (2005). *Comprehensive handbook of multicultural school psychology*. Hoboken, NJ: Wiley.

Fry, R. (2009). *The rapid growth and changing complexion of suburban public schools*. Washington, DC: Pew Research Center.

Frycr, R. (2006). Acting white: The social price paid by the best and brightest minority students. Accessed July 2011 from *Education Next.org*, http://www.economics.harvard.edu/faculty/ fryer/files/aw_ednext.pdf

Fuchs, L. S., & Fuchs, D. (2002). Curriculum-based measurement: Describing competence, enhancing outcomes, evaluating treatment effects, and identifying treatment nonresponders. *Peabody Journal of Education, 77*, 64–84.

Funiciello, T. (1993). *Tyranny of kindness: Dismantling the welfare system to end poverty in America*. New York, NY: Atlantic Monthly Press.

Furlong, M., & Sharkey, J. (2006). A review of methods to assess student self-report of weapons on school campuses. In S. R. Jimerson & M. J. Furlong (Eds.), *The handbook of school violence and school safety* (pp. 235–256). Mahwah, NJ: Erlbaum.

Gabbidon, S. L. (2010). *Race, ethnicity, crime, and justice: An international dilemma*. Thousand Oaks, CA: Sage.

Gabor, T. (1994). The suppression of crime statistics on race and ethnicity: The price of political correctness. *Canadian Journal of Criminology, 36*, 153–163.

Garces, E., Thomas, D., & Currie, J. (2002). Longer-term effects of Head Start. *American Economic Review, 92*(4), 999–1012.

Gass, S. M., & Selinker, L. (2001). *Second language acquisition: An introductory text* (2nd ed.). Mahwah, NJ: Erlbaum.

Gatti, U., Tremblay, R., Vitaro, F., & McDuff, P. (2005). Youth gangs, delinquency and drug use: A test of selection, facilitation, and enhancement hypotheses. *Journal of Child Psychology and Psychiatry, 46*, 1178–1190.

Gay, G. (1973). Racism in America: Imperatives for teaching ethnic studies. In J. A. Banks (Ed.), *Teaching ethnic studies: Concepts and strategies* (pp. 27–49). Washington, DC: National Council for the Social Studies.

Gay, G. (2000). *Culturally responsive teaching: Theory, research, and practice.* New York, NY: Teachers College Press.

Gay, G. (2004). Curriculum theory and multicultural education. In J. A. Banks & C. A. Banks (Eds.), *Handbook of research on multicultural education* (2nd ed., pp. 30–49). San Francisco, CA: Jossey-Bass.

Gemma, P.B. (2010). The Southern Poverty Law Center: An introduction. *The Social Contract*, Vol. 20 (3), 150–151.

Genesee, F. (1976). The role of intelligence in second language learning. *Language Learning, 26* (2), 267–280.

Georgas, J., Weiss, L. G., Van de Vijver, F., & Saklofske, D. H. (Eds.). (2003). *Culture and children's intelligence: Cross cultural analysis of the WISC-III.* San Diego, CA: Academic Press.

Gershberg, A.I., Danenberg, A., & Sánchez, P. (2004). *Beyond "bilingual" education: New immigrants and public school policies in California.* Washington, DC: Urban Institute Press.

Gettinger, M., & Ball, C. (2008). Best practices in increasing academic engaged time. In A. Thomas & J. Grimes (Eds.), *Best practices in school psychology V* (pp. 1043–1058). Bethesda, MD: National Association of School Psychologists.

Gettinger, M., & Seibert, J. K. (2002). Best practices in increasing academic learning time. In A. Thomas & J. Grimes (Eds.), *Best practices in school psychology IV* (pp. 773–787). Bethesda, MD: National Association of School Psychologists.

Gibson, D. (2011, April 28). Angry 'Raza studies' mob shuts down Tucson school board meeting. Accessed August 2011 from Examiner.com, http://www.examiner.com/immigration-reform-in-national/angry-raza-studies-mob-shuts-down-tucson-school-board-meeting-w-video

Gickling, E. E., & Havertape, J. R. (1981). Curriculum-based assessment. In J. A. Tucker (Ed.), *Non-test-based assessment.* Minneapolis, MN: National School Psychology Inservice Training Network, University of Minnesota.

Gickling, E. E., & Thompson, V. P. (1985). A personal view of curriculum-based assessment. *Exceptional Children, 52*, 205–218.

Gilbert, D. (2011). *American class structure in an age of inequality.* Thousand Oaks, CA: Pine Forge Press.

Gill, G. W. (2000). *Does race exist? A proponent's perspective.* Accessed May 2011 from NOVA Online, http://www.pbs.org/wgbh/nova/first/gill.html

Giunca, M. (2011, March 24). Office of Civil Rights to examine discipline of black students. Accessed November 2011 from *Winston-Salem Journal*, http://www2.journalnow.com/news/2011/mar/24/wsmain01-office-of-civil-rights-to-examine-discipl-ar-886967/

Glaze, L. E., & Maruschak, L. M. (2008). *Parents in prison and their minor children.* NCJ 222984. Washington, DC: U.S. Department of Justice, Bureau of Justice Statistics.

Gleason, P., Clark, M., Tuttle, C., Dwoyer, E., & Silverberg, M. (2010). *The evaluation of charter school impacts: Final report.* Washington, DC: U.S. Department of Education. Accessed November 2011 from http://ies.ed.gov/ncee/pubs/20104029/pdf/20104029.pdf

Glick, B. (2006). ART: A comprehensive intervention for aggressive youth. In B. Glick, *Cognitive behavioral interventions for at-risk youth.* Kingston, NJ: Civic Research Institute.

Glutting, J. J., & McDermott, P. A. (1990). Principles and problems in learning potential. In C. R. Reynolds & R. W. Kamphaus (Eds.), *Handbook of psychological and educational assessment of children: Intelligence and achievement* (Vol. 1, pp. 296–347). New York, NY: Guilford Press.

Glutting, J. J., & Oakland, T. (1993). *GATSB: Guide to the Assessment of Test Session Behavior for the WISC-III and the WIAT (Manual).* San Antonio, TX: Psychological Corporation.

Godwin, W. (2009). *Enquiry concerning political justice and its influence on modern morals and manners.* Gloucester, UK: Dodo Press.

Goldsmith, S. (1999, June 17). The wizard of Pasadena. *NewTimesLA.com.* (see http://www.eoht.info/page/Christopher+Hirata)

Goodman, J. F. (1979). Is tissue the issue? A critique of SOMPA's models and tests. *School Psychology Digest, 8*(1), 47–62.

Goodyear, S. (2011, August 4). Student sues high school over "Wigger Day." Accessed August 2011 from *Cnews*, http://cnews.canoe.ca/CNEWS/WeirdNews/2011/08/04/18509901.html

Gottfredson, G. D., & Gottfredson, D. C. (2001). *Gang problems and gang programs in a national sample of schools: Summary.* Ellicott City, MD: Gottfredson Associates.

Gottfredson, L. S. (1994). Egalitarian fiction and collective fraud. *Society, 31*(3), 53–59.

Gottfredson, L. S. (1997). Mainstream science on intelligence: An editorial with 52 signatories, history, and bibliography. *Intelligence, 24*(1), 13–23.

Gottfredson, L. S. (2003a). g, jobs, and life. In H. Nyborg (Ed.), *The scientific study of general intelligence: Tribute to Arthur R. Jensen* (pp. 293–342). Oxford, UK: Elsevier.

Gottfredson, L. S. (2003b). The science and politics of intelligence in gifted education. In N. Colangelo & G. A. Davis (Eds.), *Handbook of gifted education* (3rd ed., pp. 24–40). Boston, MA: Allyn & Bacon.

Gottfredson, L. S. (2004a). Schools and the g factor. *Wilson Quarterly*, Summer, pp. 35–42.

Gottfredson, L. S. (2004b). Realities in desegregating gifted education. In D. Booth & J. C. Stanley (Eds.), *In the eyes of the beholder: Critical issues for diversity in gifted education* (pp. 139–155). Waco, TX: Prufrock Press.

Gottfredson, L. S. (2005). Implications of cognitive differences for schooling within diverse societies. In C. L. Frisby & C. R. Reynolds (Eds.), *Comprehensive handbook of multicultural school psychology* (pp. 517–554). Hoboken, NJ: Wiley.

Gottfredson, L. S. (2006). Social consequences of group differences in cognitive ability (*Consequencias sociais das diferencas de grupo em habilidade cognitiva*). In C. E. Flores-Mendoza & R. Colom (Eds.), *Introducau a psicologia das diferencas individuais* (pp. 433–456). Porto Allegre, Brazil: ArtMed Publishers. (English version accessed August 2011 from http://www.udel.edu/educ/gottfredson/reprints/2004socialconsequences.pdf)

Gottfredson, L. S. (2007). Applying double standards to "divisive" ideas. *Perspectives on Psychological Science, 2*(2), 216–220.

Gottfredson, L. S. (2009). Logical fallacies used to dismiss the evidence on intelligence testing. In R. P. Phelps (Ed.), *Correcting fallacies about educational and psychological testing* (pp. 11–65). Washington, DC: American Psychological Association.

Gottfredson, L. S. (2010). Lessons in academic freedom as lived experience. *Personality and Individual Differences, 49,* 272–280.

Gottfredson, M., & Hirschi, T. (1990). *A general theory of crime.* Stanford, CA: Stanford University Press.

Gould, S. J. (1981). *The mismeasure of man.* New York, NY: Norton.

Graham, L. O. (1999). *Our kind of people: Inside America's black upper class.* New York, NY: HarperCollins.

Grant, C. A., & Sleeter, C. E. (2007). *Doing multicultural education for achievement and equity.* New York, NY: Routledge.

Gravois, T., & Gickling, E. (2008). Best practices in instructional assessment. In A. Thomas & J. Grimes (Eds.), *Best Practices in School Psychology—Volume Five* (pp. 503–518). Washington, DC: National Association of School Psychologists.

Green, T. (2004, May). Journey to thinking multiculturally: New series of articles from school psychology students in multicultural counseling. *NASP Communiqué, 32*(7). Accessed March 2011 from http://www.nasponline.org/publications/cq/cq327journey.aspx

Green, T., Cook-Morales, V., Robinson-Zañartu, C., & Ingraham, C. L. (2009). Pathways on a journey of *Getting It*: Multicultural competence training and continuing professional development. In J. Jones (Ed.), *The psychology of multiculturalism in the schools* (pp. 83–116). Bethesda, MD: National Association of School Psychologists.

Green, T., & Ingraham, C. L. (2005). Multicultural education. In S. W. Lee (Ed.), *Encyclopedia of school psychology* (pp. 338–342). Thousand Oaks, CA: Sage.

Green, T., Mcintosh, A., Cook-Morales, V., & Robinson-Zanartu, C. (2005). From old schools to tomorrow's schools: Psychoeducational assessment of African American students. *Remedial and Special Education, 26*(2), 82–92.

Greene, H. T., & Gabbidon, S. L. (2009). *Encyclopedia of race and crime.* Thousand Oaks, CA: Sage.

Greene, J. P. (2005). *Education myths: What special interest groups want you to believe about our schools—and why it isn't so.* Lanham, MD: Rowman & Littlefield.

Greenfield, D. B. (2005). Head Start. In S. W. Lee (Ed.), *Encyclopedia of school psychology* (pp. 237–240). Thousand Oaks, CA: Sage.

Greenhut, S. (2003, September 7). Stop the racial bean-counting. Accessed September 2010 from *Orange County Register*, http://www.lewrockwell.com/ocregister/bean-counting.html

Greenwald, A. G., & Krieger, L. H. (2006). Implicit bias: Scientific foundations. *California Law Review, 94,* 945–967.

Greenwood, P. W., & Turner, S. (2011). Juvenile crime and juvenile justice. In J. Q. Wilson & J. Petersilia (Eds.), *Crime and public policy* (pp. 88–129). New York, NY: Oxford University Press.

Gresham, F. M. (1982). *Handbook for behavioral consultation.* ERIC Document Reproduction Service No. ED223953.

Gresham, F. M. (2002). Responsiveness to intervention: An alternative approach to the identification of learning disabilities. In R. Bradley, L. Donaldson, & D. Hallahan (Eds.), *Identification of learning disabilities: Research to practice* (pp. 467–519). Mahwah, NJ: Erlbaum.

Grieco, E. M., & Trevelyan, E. N. (2010). *Place of birth of the foreign-born population: 2009 (American Community Survey Briefs).* Washington, DC: U.S. Census Bureau.

Grisso, T. (2008). Adolescent offenders with mental disorders. *The Future of Children, 18*(2), 143–164.

Gross, J. (1992, March 29). Collapse of inner-city families creates orphans. *New York Times,* p. 1.

Grossen, B. (1997). *What does it mean to be a research-based profession?* Accessed June 2012 from http://personalweb.donet.com/~eprice/resprf.htm

Guskey, T., & Gates, S. (1986). Synthesis of research on the effects of mastery learning in elementary and secondary classrooms. *Educational Leadership, 43*(8), 73–80.

Guskey, T., & Pigott, T. (1988). Research on group-based mastery learning programs: A meta-analysis. *Journal of Educational Research, 81*(4), 197–216.

Gutman, H. G. (1976). *The black family in slavery and freedom, 1750–1925.* New York, NY: Pantheon Books.

Guttmacher Institute. (2012, February). Facts on American teens' sexual and reproductive health. Accessed May 2012 from http://www.guttmacher.org/pubs/FB-ATSRH.html

Hacker, H. K., & Hobbs, T. D. (2010, June). "Black flight" changing the makeup of Dallas schools. Accessed March 2011 from Dallasnews.com, http://www.dallasnews.com/news/education/headlines/20100609-black-flight_changing-the-makeup-of-dallas-schools.ece

Hale, J. (1993). Rejoinder to ". . . Myths of black cultural learning styles": In defense of Afrocentric scholarship. *School Psychology Review, 22*(3), 558–561.

Hale, J. (1994). *Unbank the fire: Visions for the education of African American children.* Baltimore, MD: Johns Hopkins University Press.

Hale-Benson, J. (1986). *Black children: Their roots, culture, and learning styles* (rev. ed.). Baltimore, MD: Johns Hopkins University Press.

Halpern, C. T., Joyner, K., Udry, J. R., & Suchindran, C. (2000). Smart teens don't have sex (or kiss much either). *Journal of Adolescent Health, 26*(3), 213–225.

Hambleton, R. K., & Li, S. (2005). Translation and adaptation issues and methods for educational and psychological tests. In C. L. Frisby & C. R. Reynolds (Eds.), *Comprehensive handbook of multicultural school psychology* (pp. 881–903). Hoboken, NJ: Wiley.

Hambleton, R. K., Merenda, P. F., & Speilberger, C. D. (Eds.). (2005). *Adapting educational and psychological tests for cross-cultural assessment.* Mahwah, NJ: Erlbaum.

Hampton, R. L., Gullotta, T.P., & Crowel, R. L. (Eds.). (2011). *Handbook of African American health.* New York, NY: Guilford Press.

Haney, W. (1977). *The Follow Through Planned Variation experiment, Vol. 5: A technical history of the National Follow Through Evaluation.* Cambridge, MA: Huron Institute.

Hanushek, E. A. (1997). Assessing the effects of school resources on student performance: An update. *Educational Evaluation and Policy Analysis, 19*(2), 141–164.

Harris, A. M. (1991). Response to *Testers and testing: The sociology of school psychology* by Carl Milofsky. *School Psychology Quarterly, 6*(4), 310–314.

Harris, P. (2009, March). Native Americans find their voice. Accessed November 2011 from *The Observer,* http://www.guardian.co.uk/world/2009/mar/22/native-americans-preserve-language-america

Harris, T. W. (2010). *Chasing the Joneses. Love isn't enough: On raising a family in a colorstruck world.* Accessed June 2011 from http://loveisntenough.com/2010/06/23/chasing-the-joneses/

Harry, B. (2006). *Why are so many minority students in special education?* New York, NY: Teachers College Press.

Hart, B., & Risley, T. R. (1995). *Meaningful differences in the everyday experience of young American children.* Baltimore, MD: Brookes.

Harvard Project on American Indian Economic Development. (2008). *The state of the Native Nations: Conditions under U.S. policies of self-determination.* New York, NY: Oxford University Press.

Haywood, H. C., & Lidz, C. (2007). *Dynamic assessment in practice: Clinical and educational applications.* New York, NY: Cambridge University Press.

Haywood, H. C., & Tzuriel, D. (Eds.). (1992). *Interactive assessment.* New York, NY: Springer-Verlag.

Healey, J. F. (2010). *Diversity and society: Race, ethnicity, and gender.* Thousand Oaks, CA: Pine Forge Press.

Hedgecock, R. (2010, January). "Too white" Berkeley science labs may be cut. Accessed November 2011 from *HumanEvents.com,* http://www.humanevents.com/article.php?id=35380

Helms, A., & Frazier, E. (2010, November 11). CMS vote highlights deep divide—District leaders face calls to build trust and dialogue, particularly with minorities. *The Charlotte Observer,* p. 1A.

Helms, J. E. (1989). Eurocentrism strikes in strange ways and in unusual places. *The Counseling Psychologist, 17*(4), 643–647.

Helms, J. E. (1992). Why is there no study of cultural equivalence in standardized cognitive ability testing? *American Psychologist, 47*(9), 1083–1101.

Helms, J. E. (1997). The triple quandary of race, culture, and social class in standardized cognitive ability testing. In D. P. Flanagan, J. L. Genshaft, & P. L. Harrison (Eds.), *Contemporary intellectual assessment: Theories, tests, and issues* (pp. 517–532). New York, NY: Guilford Press.

Hembree, R. (1988). Correlates, causes, effects, and treatment of test anxiety. *Review of Educational Research, 58*, 47–77.

Henggeler, S. W., Schoenwald, S. K., Borduin, C. M., Rowland, M. D., & Cunningham, P. B. (2009). *Multisystemic therapy for antisocial behavior in children and adolescents* (2nd ed.). New York, NY: Guilford Press.

Heritage Foundation. (2005). *The Heritage guide to the Constitution.* Washington, DC: Author.

Hernández, D., & Charney, E. (1998). *From generation to generation: The health and well-being of children of immigrant families.* Washington, DC: National Academy Press.

Herring, R. D. (1997). *Multicultural counseling in schools: A synergetic approach.* Alexandria, VA: American Counseling Association.

Herrnstein, R. J., & Murray, C. (1994). *The bell curve: Intelligence and class structure in American life.* New York, NY: Free Press.

Higginbotham, E. B., Litwack, L. F., Hine, D. C., & Burkett, R. K. (Eds.). (2001). *The Harvard guide to African-American history.* Cambridge, MA: Harvard University Press.

Hilliard, A. (1982). The Learning Potential Assessment Device and Instrumental Enrichment as a paradigm shift. *The Negro Educational Review, 38*, 2–3.

Hines, M.T. (2011). The skin they're in: An in-depth analysis of African American students from Irving Independent School District. Irving, TX: Irving Unified School District. Accessed June 2012 from http://www.scribd.com/doc/35725982/The-Skin-They-re-In

Hixson, M. D., & McGlinchey, M. T. (2004). The relationship between race, income, and oral reading fluency and performance on two reading comprehension measures. *Journal of Psychoeducational Assessment, 22*, 351–364.

Hoefer, M., Rytina, N., & Baker, B. (2012). *Estimates of the Unauthorized Immigrant Population Residing in the United States: January 2011.* Washington, DC: Department of Homeland Security. Accessed October 2012 from http://www.dhs.gov/xlibrary/assets/statistics/publications/ois_ill_pe_2011.pdf

Hoeffel, E. M., Rastogi, S., Kim, M. O., & Shahid, H. (2012). *The Asian population: 2010.* Washington, DC: U.S. Census Bureau.

Hoff, E., Laursen, B., & Tardif, T. (2002). Socioeconomic status and parenting. In M. H. Bornstein (Ed.), *Handbook of parenting* (2nd ed.), *Vol. 2: Biology and ecology of parenting* (pp. 231–252). Mahwah, NJ: Erlbaum.

Holcomb-McCoy, C. (2003). Multicultural competence in school settings. In D. B. Pope-Davis, H. Coleman, W. Liu, & R. Toporek (Eds.), *Handbook of multicultural competencies in counseling and psychology* (pp. 406–419). Thousand Oaks, CA: Sage.

Hood, J. (2011, November 14). CPS fails to close performance gap. Accessed November 2011 from *Chicago Tribune*, http://www.chicagotribune.com/news/education/ct-met-cps-racial-gap-1114-20111114,0,7622731.story

Hosp, M. K., & Hosp, J. (2003). Curriculum-based measurement for reading, math, and spelling: How to do it and why. *Preventing School Failure, 48*(1), 10–17.

Howe, S. (1998). *Afrocentrism: Mythical pasts and imagined homes.* New York, NY: Verso.

Howell, J. C. (2010). *Gang prevention: An overview of research and programs.* Washington, DC: U.S. Department of Justice, Office of Juvenile Justice and Delinquency Prevention.

Howell, J. C., Egley, A., Tita, G. E., & Griffiths, E. (2011). *U.S. gang problem trends and seriousness, 1996–2009 (National Gang Center Bulletin, No. 6).* Tallahasee, FL: Institute for Intergovernmental Research. Accessed March 2012 from http://www.nationalgangcenter.gov/Content/Documents/Bulletin-6.pdf

Howell, K. W., & Morehead, M. K. (1987). *Curriculum-based evaluation for special and remedial education.* Columbus, OH: Charles Merrill.

Huber, T., & Pewewardy, C. (1990). *Maximizing learning for all students: A review of literature on learning modalities, cognitive styles and approaches to meeting the needs of diverse learners* (ERIC Document Reproduction Service No. 324289).

Huberty, T. J. (2009, September). Test and performance anxiety. *Principal Leadership,* 12–16.

Huckleberry, T. M. (2009). Multicultural issues in research: Practical implications for school psychologists. In J. M. Jones (Ed.), *The psychology of multiculturalism in the schools: A primer for practice, training, and research* (pp. 215–226). Bethesda, MD: National Association of School Psychologists.

Humes, K. R., Jones, N. A., & Ramirez, R. R. (2011). *Overview of race and Hispanic origin: 2010.* Washington, DC: U.S. Census Bureau.

Humphreys, L. G. (1985). Review of system of multicultural pluralistic assessment. In J. V. Mitchell (Ed.), *Ninth mental measurements yearbook.* Lincoln, NE: Buros Institute.

Hunter, J. E., & Schmidt, F. L. (1976). A critical analysis of the statistical and ethical implications of various definitions of "test bias." *Psychological Bulletin, 83,* 1053–1071.

Hymowitz, K. S. (2005, Summer). The black family: 40 years of lies. Accessed June 2011 from *City Journal*, http://www.city-journal.org/html/15_3_black_family.html

Hymowitz, K. S. (2006). *Marriage and caste in America: Separate and unequal families in a post-marital age.* Chicago, IL: Ivan R. Dee.

Iarocci, G., & Burack, J. A. (1998). Understanding the development of attention in persons with mental retardation: Challenging the myths. In J. A. Burack, R. M. Hodapp, & E. Zigler (Eds.), *Handbook of mental retardation and development* (pp. 349–381). New York, NY: Cambridge University Press.

Ikramullah, E., Barry, M., Manlove, J., & Moore, K. A. (2011). Facts at a glance: A fact sheet reporting national, state, and city trends in teen childbearing. Accessed May 2012 from http://ww1.prweb.com/prfiles/2011/05/03/8373096/Child_Trends-2011_04_14_FG_2011.pdf

Illinois State Board of Education. (2010). *Assessment accommodations for English Language Learners guidance for 2011–2012.* Springfield, IL: Illinois State Board of Education.

Jackson, N. (2011). *Project Reach campus-based services.* Unpublished manuscript. Fort Worth, TX: Fort Worth Independent School District.

Jackson, Y. (Ed.). (2006). *Encyclopedia of multicultural psychology.* Thousand Oaks, CA: Sage.

Jacob, S., & Hartshorne, T. (2007). *Ethics and law for school psychologists* (5th ed.). Hoboken, NJ: Wiley.

Jacobson, J. W., Foxx, R. M., & Mulick, J. A. (Eds.). (2009). *Controversial therapies for developmental disabilities.* Mahwah, NJ: Erlbaum.

Jacoby, R., & Glauberman, N. (Eds.). (1995). *The Bell Curve debate.* New York, NY: Three Rivers Press.

Jalali, R., & Lipset, S. M. (1992). Racial and ethnic conflicts: A global perspective. *Political Science Quarterly, 107*(4), 585–606.

James, G. (1954). *Stolen legacy.* New York, NY: Philosophical Library.

James, W. (1950). *The principles of psychology* (Vol. 1). New York, NY: Dover. (Original work published in 1890).

Jencks, C. (1972). *Inequality: A reassessment of the effect of family and schooling in America.* New York, NY: Basic Books.

Jensen, A. R. (1969). How much can we boost IQ and scholastic achievement? *Harvard Educational Review, 39,* 1–123.

Jensen, A. R. (1973). *Educability and group differences.* London, UK: T&A Constable, Ltd.

Jensen, A. R. (1980). *Bias in mental testing.* New York, NY: Free Press.

Jensen, A. R. (1981a). Obstacles, problems, and pitfalls in differential psychology. In S. Scarr (Ed.), *Race, social class, and individual differences in IQ* (pp. 483–514). Hillsdale, NJ: Erlbaum.

Jensen, A. R. (1981b). *Straight talk about mental tests.* New York, NY: Free Press.

Jensen, A. R. (1982). The debunking of scientific fossils and straw persons. [Review of *The mismeasure of man.*] *Contemporary Education Review, 1,* 121–135.

Jensen, A. R. (1984). Test validity: *g* versus the specificity doctrine. *Journal of Social and Biological Structures, 7,* 93–118.

Jensen, A. R. (1989). The relationship between learning and intelligence. *Learning and Individual Differences, 1*(1), 37–62.

Jensen, A. R. (1993). Psychometric *g* and achievement. In B. R. Gifford (Ed.), *Policy perspectives on educational testing* (pp. 117–227). Boston, MA: Kluwer Academic.

Jensen, A. R. (1996). Giftedness and genius: Crucial differences. In C. P. Benbow & D. J. Lubinski (Eds.), *Intellectual talent: Psychometric and social issues* (pp. 393–411). Baltimore, MD: Johns Hopkins University.

Jensen, A. R. (1998a). The *g* factor and the design of education. In R. J. Sternberg & W. M. Williams (Eds.), *Intelligence, instruction, and assessment: Theory into practice.* Mahwah, NJ: Erlbaum.

Jensen, A. R. (1998b). *The g factor: The science of mental ability.* Westport, CT: Praeger.

Jensen, A. R. (2000). "Biological Determinism" as an ideological buzz-word. *Psycoloquy, 11*(021). Accessed May 2011 from http://kiwi.uni-psych.gwdg.de/home/ertel/erteldir/mysciencelinks/6psychometry/01a62c92ec0bc3c02.html

Jensen, A. R. (2003, August 23). *Individual differences and population differences in Spearman's g.* Acceptance speech at Kistler Prize Ceremony, Foundation for the Future, Seattle, WA.

Jensen, A. R. (2006). *Clocking the mind: Mental chronometry and individual differences.* Oxford, UK: Elsevier.

Jensen, A. R., & McGurk, F. (1987). Black-white bias in "cultural" and "noncultural" test items. *Personality and Individual Differences, 8*(3), 295–301.

Jimerson, S. R., & Furlong, M. J. (Eds.). (2006). *The handbook of school violence and school safety: From research to practice.* Mahwah, NJ: Erlbaum.

Jimerson, S. R., Swearer, S. M., & Espelage, D. L. (Eds.). (2009). *Handbook of bullying in schools: An international perspective.* Oxford, UK: Taylor & Francis.

Johns, S. K., Patrick, J. A., & Rutherford, K. J. (2008). Best practices in district-wide positive behavior support implementation. In A. Thomas & J. Grimes (Eds.), *Best practices in school psychology V* (Vol. 3, pp. 721–733). Bethesda, MD: National Association of School Psychologists.

Johnsen, S. (2011). *Identifying gifted students: A practical guide* (2nd ed.). Waco, TX: Prufrock Press.

Johnson, B. R., & Wubbenhorst, W. (2010). *Tracking the Milwaukee violence-free zone initiative.* Waco, TX: Baylor Institute for Studies of Religion, Baylor University.

Johnson, D. W., & Johnson, R. T. (2005). Cooperative learning. In S. W. Lee (Ed.), *Encyclopedia of school psychology* (pp. 117–120). Thousand Oaks, CA: Sage.

Johnson, K. (2009, January 29). FBI: Burgeoning gangs behind up to 80% of U.S. crime. Accessed March 2012 from *USA Today.com,* http://www.usatoday.com/news/nation/2009-01-29-ms13_N.htm

Johnson, S. (2000). *Taking the anxiety out of taking tests: A step-by-step guide.* Lyndhurst, NJ: Barnes & Noble Books.

Johnstone, C. J., Altman, J., Thurlow, M. L., & Thompson, S. J. (2006). *A summary of research on the effects of test accommodations: 2002 through 2004* (Technical Report 45). Minneapolis: University of Minnesota, National Center on Educational Outcomes. Accessed June 2011 from http://education.umn.edu/NCEO/OnlinePubs/Tech45/

Jones, B. D. (2007). The unintended outcomes of high-stakes testing. *Journal of Applied School Psychology, 23*(2), 65–86.

Jones, J. (2006, March 26). "Marriage is for white people." Accessed October 2011 from *Washingtonpost.com,* http://www.washingtonpost.com/wp-dyn/content/article/2006/03/25/AR2006032500029.html

Jones, J. M. (2003). Constructing race and deconstructing racism: A cultural psychology approach. In G. Bernal, J. E. Trimble, A. K. Burlew, & F. Leong (Eds.), *Handbook of racial and ethnic minority psychology* (pp. 276–290). Thousand Oaks, CA: Sage.

Jones, J. M. (Ed.). (2009). *The psychology of multiculturalism in schools: A primer for practice, training, and research*. Bethesda, MD: National Association of School Psychologists.

Jordan, A. H., & Lovett, B. J. (2007). Stereotype threat and test performance: A primer for school psychologists. *Journal of School Psychology, 45*, 45–59.

Jordan, M. (1992, April 11). Kansas City's costly integration strategy; Results mixed in $1.2 billion school plan. *Washington Post*, p. A1.

Joseph, L. M. (2006). *Understanding, assessing, and intervening on reading problems*. Bethesda, MD: National Association of School Psychologists.

Joyce, G. (2009, May 31). Oppression liberators need not apply. Accessed June 2012 from *American Thinker*, http://www.americanthinker.com/blog/2009/05/oppression_liberators_need _not.html

Kam, C., Greenberg, M. T., & Walls, C. (2003). Examining the role of implementation quality in school-based prevention using the PATHS curriculum. *Prevention Science, 4*(1), 55–63.

Kame'enui, E. J., & Simmons, D. C. (1990). *Designing instructional strategies: The prevention of academic learning problems*. Columbus, OH: Merrill.

Kame'enui, E. J., & Simmons, D. C. (1999). *Toward successful inclusion of students with disabilities: The architecture of instruction*. Reston, VA: Council for Exceptional Children.

Kaminski, R. A., & Good, R. H., III. (1998). Assessing early literacy skills in a Problem-Solving model: Dynamic indicators of basic early literacy skills. In M. R. Shinn (Ed.), *Advanced applications of Curriculum-Based Measurement* (pp. 113–142). New York, NY: Guilford Press.

Kane, E. (2010, November 21). African-centered education has a strong backer. Accessed December 2, 2010, from *Milwaukee Journal Sentinel* Online, http://www.jsonline.com/news/ milwaukee/109566374.html

Kane, H. & Boan, C.H. (2005). A review and critique of multicultural learning styles. In C.L. Frisby and C.R. Reynolds (Eds.), *Comprehensive handbook of multicultural school psychology*, pp. 425–456. Hoboken, NJ: Wiley.

Kaulback, B. (1995). Styles of learning among Native children: A review of the research. In B. Shade (Ed.), *Culture, style and the educative process* (pp. 92–104). Springfield, IL: Charles C. Thomas.

Kay, J. (2011, September 23). The brown dog. Accessed October 2011 from *American-Renaissance.com*, http://www.amren.com/mtnews/archives/2011/09/the_brown_dog.php

Kelling, G. L., & Coles, C. M. (1996). *Fixing broken windows: Restoring order and reducing crime in our communities*. New York, NY: Touchstone.

Kemple, A. E., Heath, M. A., Hansen, K., Annandale, N. O., Fischer, L., Young, E. L., & Ryan, K. (2006). Cultural sensitivity in school-based crisis intervention. *NASP Communiqué, 34*(7), 34–37.

Kersten, K. (2011, April 9). Always room in the budget for white guilt. Accessed April 2011 from *StarTribune*, http://www.startribune.com/opinion/otherviews/119508364.html

Kesselman, J., & Peterson, F. (1981). *Test-taking strategies*. Madison, WI: University of Wisconsin Press.

Kinder, D., & Sears, D. (1981). Prejudice and politics: Symbolic racism versus threats to the good life. *Journal of Personality and Social Psychology, 40*(3), 414–431.

King, M. A., Sims, A., & Osher, D. (2001). How is cultural competence integrated in education? Accessed May 2012 from http://cecp.air.org/cultural/Q_integrated.htm

Kitayama, S., & Cohen, D. (Eds.). (2007). *Handbook of cultural psychology*. New York, NY: Guilford Press.

Kline, P. (1994). *An easy guide to factor analysis*. New York, NY: Routledge.

Knoff, H. (2008). Best practices in implementing statewide positive behavioral support systems. In A. Thomas & J. Grimes (Eds.), *Best practices in school psychology V* (Vol. 3, pp. 749–764). Bethesda, MD: National Association of School Psychologists.

Kochman, T. (1981). *Black and white styles in conflict*. Chicago, IL: University of Chicago Press.

Koenen, K. C., Caspi, A., Moffitt, T. E., Rijskijk, F., & Taylor, A. (2006). Genetic influences on the overlap between low IQ and antisocial behavior in young children. *Journal of Abnormal Psychology, 115*(4), 787–797.

Kohn, A. (2000). *The case against standardized testing: Raising the scores, ruining the schools*. Portsmouth, NH: Heinemann.

Kohn, A. (2001). Fighting the tests: A practical guide to rescuing our schools. *Phi Delta Kappan, 82*(5), 349–357.

Koolhof, R., Loeber, R., Wei, E. H., & Pardini, D. (2007). Inhibition deficits of serious delinquent boys of low intelligence. *Criminal Behavior & Mental Health, 17*(5), 274–292.

Kopp, W. (2009, April 25). Teach for (some of) America. Accessed July 2011 from the *Wall Street Journal*, http://online.wsj.com/article/SB124061253951954349.html

Kopriva, R. J. (n.d.). What might disability practitioners learn from STELLA, a computerized system for selecting accommodations for ELLs? Accessed February 2012 from http://www.ets.org/Media/Research/conf_accomm2006_kopriva.ppt#2

Kopriva, R. J. (2008). *Improving testing for English language learners*. New York, NY: Routledge.

Kopriva, R. J., Emick, J. E., Hipolito-Delgado, C. P., & Cameron, C. A. (2007). Do proper accommodation assignments make a difference? Examining the impact of improved decision making on scores for English Language Learners. *Educational Measurement: Issues and Practice, 26*(3), 11–20.

Kozloff, M. (2002). *Three requirements of effective instruction: Providing sufficient scaffolding, helping students organize and activate knowledge, and sustaining high engaged time*. Wilmington, NC: University of North Carolina at Wilmington, Watson School of Education. Accessed August 2011 from http://people.uncw.edu/kozloffm/scaffolding.pdf

Kozol, J. (2005). *The shame of the nation: The restoration of apartheid schooling in America*. New York, NY: Crown.

Kramer, R. (2000). *Ed school follies: The mis-education of America's teachers*. Lincoln, NE: iUniverse.com.

Kranzler, J., Miller, D., & Jordan, L. (1999). An examination of racial/ethnic bias on curriculum-based measurement of reading. *School Psychology Quarterly, 14*(3), 327–342.

Kratochwill, T. R., Sheridan, S. M., Bergan, J. R., & Elliot, S. N. (1998). After all is said and done, more has been done than said. *School Psychology Quarterly, 13*(1), 63–80.

Kroeber, A. L., & Kluckhohn, C. K. M. (1952). *Culture: A critical review of concepts and definitions* (Papers of the Peabody Museum, Vol. 47, No. 1). Cambridge, MA: Harvard University.

KSBW.com. (2010, November 12). School forces boy to take flag off bike. Accessed December 2, 2010, from KSBW.com, http://www.ksbw.com/news/25763175/detail.html

KTVU.com. (2010, May). Racial tension mounts at South Bay high school. Accessed March 2011 from KTVU.com, http://www.ktvu.com/news/23470391/detail.html

Kulik, C. C., Kulik, J. A., & Bangert-Downs, R. L. (1990). Effectiveness of mastery learning programs: A meta-analysis. *Review of Educational Research, 60*, 265–299.

Kunjufu, J. (2002). *Black students. Middle class teachers.* Chicago, IL: African American Images.

Kunjufu, J. (2005). *Keeping black boys out of special education.* Chicago, IL: African American Images.

Kunjufu, J. (2011). *Understanding black male learning styles.* Chicago, IL: African American Images.

Kupchik, A., & Bracy, N.L. (2010). To protect, serve, and mentor? Police officers in public schools. In T. Monahan & R. D. Torres (Eds.), *Schools under surveillance: Cultures of control in public education* (pp. 21–37). New Brunswick, NJ: Rutgers University Press.

Ladson-Billings, G. (2004). New directions in multicultural education: Complexities, boundaries, and critical race theory. In J. A. Banks & C. M. Banks (Eds.), *Handbook of research on multicultural education* (2nd ed., pp. 50–65). San Francisco, CA: Jossey-Bass.

Lang, K. (2007). *Poverty and discrimination.* Princeton, NJ: Princeton University Press.

Lareau, A. (2011). *Unequal childhoods: Class, race, and family life* (2nd ed.). Berkeley, CA: University of California Press.

Laub, J. H., & Lauritsen, J. L. (1998). The interdependence of school violence with neighborhood and family conditions. In D. S. Elliot, B. A. Hamburg, & K. R. Williams (Eds.), *Violence in American schools: A new perspective* (pp. 127–158). New York, NY: Cambridge University Press.

Lawrence, R. (2007). *School crime and juvenile justice* (2nd ed.). New York, NY: Oxford University Press.

Le, C. N. (2011). Asian small businesses. *Asian-Nation: The Landscape of Asian America.* Accessed October 2011 from http://www.asian-nation.org/smallbusiness.shtml

Leahy, R. (1983). *The child's construction of social inequality.* New York, NY: Academic Books.

Lee, C. D., & Slaughter-Defoe, D. (2004). Historical and sociocultural influences on African American education. In J. A. Banks & C. A. Banks (Eds.), *Handbook of research on multicultural education* (2nd ed., pp. 462–490). San-Francisco, CA: Jossey-Bass.

Lefkowitz, M. R. (1996). *Not out of Africa: How "Afrocentrism" became an excuse to teach myth as history.* New York, NY: Basic Books.

Lehr, C. A. (2005). School climate. In S. W. Lee (Ed.), *Encyclopedia of school psychology* (pp. 471–472). Thousand Oaks, CA: Sage.

Levin, M. (1997). *Why race matters: Race differences and what they mean.* Westport, CT: Praeger.

LeVine, R. A. (2007). Anthropological foundations of cultural psychology. In S. Kitayama & D. Cohen (Eds.), *Handbook of cultural psychology* (pp. 40–58). New York, NY: Guilford Press.

Lewis, G., & Lewis, D.S. (2009). *Gifted hands: The Ben Carson story.* Grand Rapids, MI. Zondervan.

Lidz, C. S., & Elliott, J. G. (Eds.). (2000). *Dynamic assessment: Prevailing models and applications.* New York, NY: Elsevier.

Lieberman, M. (1997). *The teachers' unions: How the NEA and AFT sabotage reform and hold students, parents, teachers, and taxpayers hostage to bureaucracy.* New York, NY: Free Press.

Light, S. A., & Rand, K. R. (2005). *Indian gaming and tribal sovereignty: The casino compromise.* Lawrence, KS: University Press of Kansas.

Lilienfeld, S. O., Ammirati, R., & David, M. (2012). Distinguishing science from pseudoscience in school psychology: Science and scientific thinking as safeguards against human error. *Journal of School Psychology, 50*, 7–36.

Lineman, J. M., & Miller, G. E. (2012). Strengthening competence in working with culturally and linguistically diverse students. *NASP Communiqué, 40*(8), 20–21.

Littlewood, W. T. (1984). *Foreign and second language learning.* Cambridge, UK: Cambridge University Press.

Liu, W., & Pope-Davis, D. (2003). Moving from diversity to multiculturalism: Exploring power and its implications for multicultural competence. In D. B. Pope-Davis, H. Coleman, W. Liu, & R. Toporek (Eds.), *Handbook of multicultural competencies in counseling and psychology* (pp. 90–102). Thousand Oaks, CA: Sage.

Lobo, I., & Shaw, K. (2008). Phenotypic range of gene expression: Environmental influence. *Nature Education, 1*(1). Accessed February 2011 from http://www.nature.com/scitable/topicpage/phenotypic-range-of-gene-expression-environmental-influence-581

LoConto, D. G., & Francis, A. D. (2005). Cultural variation within European American families. In C. L. Frisby & C. R. Reynolds (Eds.), *Comprehensive handbook of multicultural school psychology* (pp. 205–233). Hoboken, NJ: Wiley.

Lomawaima, K. T. (2004). Educating Native Americans. In J. A. Banks & C. M. Banks (Eds.), *Handbook of research on multicultural education* (2nd ed., pp. 441–490). San Francisco, CA: Jossey-Bass.

Lomax, R. G., West, M. M., & Harmon, M. C. (1995). The impact of mandated standardized testing on minority students. *Journal of Negro Education, 64*, 171–185.

Long, S. (2010, October 16). NAACP's eye cast on W-Barea. Accessed December 2, 2010, from *The Times Leader*, http://www.timesleader.com/news/NAACPs-eye-cast-on-W-BArea.html

Lopez, C., & Bhat, C. S. (2007). Supporting students with incarcerated parents in schools: A group intervention. *Journal for Specialists in Group Work, 32*, 139–153.

Lopez, C., Lopez, V., Suarez-Morales, L., & Castro, F. (2005). Cultural variation within Hispanic American families. In C. L. Frisby & C. R. Reynolds (Eds.), *Comprehensive handbook of multicultural school psychology* (pp. 234–264). Hoboken, NJ: Wiley.

Lopez, E. C. (1997). The cognitive assessment of limited English proficient and bilingual children. In D. P. Flanagan, J. L. Genshaft, & P. L. Harrison (Eds.), *Contemporary intellectual assessment: Theories, tests, and issues* (pp. 503–516). New York, NY: Guilford Press.

Losen, D. J., & Orfield, G. E. (2002). *Inequality in special education.* Cambridge, MA: Harvard Education Publishing Group.

Losen, D.J. & Skiba, R.J. (2012). *Suspended education: Urban middle schools in crisis.* Montgomery, AL: Southern Poverty Law Center.

Louie, J. (2003). Media in the lives of immigrant youth. In C. Suárez-Orozco & I. Todorova (Eds.), *Understanding the social worlds of immigrant youth: New directions for youth development, Vol. 100.* San Francisco, CA: Jossey-Bass.

Luhr, M. (2005). Self concept and efficacy. In S. W. Lee (Ed.), *Encyclopedia of school psychology* (pp. 490–491). Thousand Oaks, CA: Sage.

Lynam, D., Moffitt, T., & Stouthamer-Loeber, M. (1993). Explaining the relation between IQ and delinquency: Class, race, test motivation, school failure, or self-control? *Journal of Abnormal Psychology, 102*(2), 187–196.

Lynch, F. R. (1997). *The diversity machine: The drive to change the "white male workplace."* New York, NY: Free Press.

Lyons, C. A. (1998). Reading Recovery in the United States: More than a decade of data. *Literacy Teaching and Learning: An International Journal of Early Reading and Writing, 3*(1), 77–92.

MacCluskie, K. (2010). *Acquiring counseling skills: Integrating theory, multiculturalism, and self awareness.* Columbus, OH: Merrill.

MacDonald, H. (2004, Summer). The immigrant gang plague. *City Journal, 14*(3). Accessed February 2011 from http://www.city-journal.org/html/14_3_immigrant_gang.html

MacDonald, M. (2010, September). Afrocentric school shines. Accessed November 2011 from *Toronto Sun,* http://www.torontosun.com/comment/columnists/moira_macdonald/2010/09/24/15469271.html

MacMillan, D. L., Gresham, F. M., Bocian, K. M., & Lambros, K. (1998). Current plight of borderline students: Where do they belong? *Education and Training in Mental Retardation and Developmental Disabilities, 33,* 83–94.

MacMillan, D. L., Gresham, F. M., Siperstein, G. N., & Bocian, K. M. (1996). The labyrinth of IDEA: School decisions on referred students with subaverage general intelligence. *American Journal on Mental Retardation, 101,* 161–174.

Madden, U. (2011, January 12). Teen pregnancy epidemic hits Memphis high school. Accessed May 2012 from *Wmctv.com,* http://www.wmctv.com/Global/story.asp?S=13824956

Madrid, A. (1986). Foreword. In M. S. Olivas (Ed.), *Latino college students* (pp. ix–xvii). New York, NY: Teachers College Press.

Maeroff, G. (1988). Withered hopes, stillborn dreams: The dismal panorama of urban schools. *Phi Delta Kappan, 69*(9), 632–638.

Manno, B. V. (2001). The case against charter schools. *School Administrator, 58*(5), 28–34.

Maranto, R., Redding, R. E., & Hess, F. M. (Eds.). (2009). *The politically correct university: Problems, scope, and reforms.* Washington, DC: American Enterprise Institute.

Marchand-Martella, N. E., Slocum, T. A., & Martella, R. C. (2004). *Introduction to Direct Instruction.* Boston, MA: Pearson.

Markus, H. R., & Hamedani, M. G. (2007). Sociocultural psychology: The dynamic interdependence among self systems and social systems. In S. Kitayama & D. Cohen (Eds.), *Handbook of cultural psychology* (pp. 3–39). New York, NY: Guilford Press.

Martines, D. (2008). *Multicultural school psychology competencies: A practical guide.* Thousand Oaks, CA: Sage.

Martines, D., & Rodriguez-Srednicki, O. (2007). Academic assessment. In G. B. Esquivel, E. C. Lopez, & S. Nahara (Eds.), *Handbook of multicultural school psychology: An interdisciplinary perspective* (pp. 381–405). Mahwah, NJ: Erlbaum.

Martins, R. K., Widoe, R. K., Porter, C. A., & McNeil, D. W. (2006). Native Americans. In Y. Jackson (Ed.), *Encyclopedia of multicultural psychology* (pp. 331–339). Thousand Oaks, CA: Sage.

Marzano, R. J., Waters, T., & McNulty, B. A. (2005). *School leadership that works: From research to results.* Alexandria, VA: Association for Supervision and Curriculum Development; Aurora, CO: Mid-continent Research for Education and Learning.

Masi, G., Marcheschi, M., & Pfanner, P. (1998). Adolescents with borderline intellectual functioning: Psychopathological risk. *Adolescence, 33*, 415–424.

Massey, D. S., & Sampson, R. J. (2009). Moynihan redux: Legacies and lessons. In D. S. Massey & R. J. Sampson (Eds.), *The Moynihan Report revisited: Lessons and reflections after four decades* (pp. 6–27). Thousand Oaks, CA: Sage.

Matteucci, M. (2010, March 3). Civil rights complaint file against DeKalb schools. Accessed November 2011 from *DeKalb County News,* http://www.ajc.com/news/dekalb/civil-rights-complaint-filed-345054.html

Maylor, U. (2009). "They do not relate to Black people like us": Black teachers as role models for black pupils. *Journal of Education Policy, 24*(1), 1–21.

McCallum, R. S. (Ed.). (2003). *Handbook of nonverbal assessment.* New York, NY: Kluwer Academic.

McCloskey, S. G. (2008). *The street stops here: A year at a Catholic high school in Harlem.* Berkeley, CA: University of California Press.

McDougal, J. L., Graney, S. B., Wright, J. A., & Ardoin, S. P. (2010). *RTI in practice: A practical guide to implementing effective evidence-based interventions in your school.* Hoboken, NJ: Wiley.

McIntosh, P. (1988). *White privilege and male privilege: A personal account of coming to see correspondences through work in women's studies* (Working Papers Series No. 189). Wellesley, MA: Wellesley College, Center for Research on Women.

McKeough, A., Lupart, J. L., & Marini, A. (Eds.). (1995). *Teaching for transfer: Fostering generalization in learning.* New York, NY: Routledge.

McKevitt, B., & Braaksma, A. (2008). Best practices in developing a positive behavior support system at the school level. In A. Thomas & J. Grimes (Eds.), *Best practices in school psychology* V (Vol. 3, pp. 735–747). Bethesda, MD: National Association of School Psychologists.

McNamara, E. (2011, July 8). Yale researcher wants to fix achievement gap. Accessed July 2011 from BethwoodPatch.com, http://bethwood.patch.com/articles/yale-researcher-wants-to-fix-achievement-gap

McNeil, H. (2011, June). Expert cites African-centered campus as way to reverse low achievement. Accessed November 2011 from BuffaloNews.com, http://www.buffalonews.com/city/article454207.ece

McWhorter, J. (2000). *Losing the race: Self-sabotage in black America.* New York, NY: Free Press.

McWhorter, J. H. (2001, Winter). What's holding blacks back? Accessed June 2010 from *City Journal*, http://www.city-journal.org/html/11_1_whats_holding_blacks.html

Mealey, D. L., & Host, T. R. (1992). Coping with test anxiety. *College Teaching*, 40(4), 147–150.

Medrano, L. (2010, December 31). *Ethnic studies classes illegal in Arizona public schools as of Jan. 1.* Accessed March 2011 from *Christian Science Monitor*, http://www.csmonitor.com/USA/Education/2010/1231/Ethnic-studies-classes-illegal in-Arizona-public-schools-as-of-Jan.-1

Mehrens, W.A. & Clarizio, H.F. (1993). Curriculum-Based Measurement: Conceptual and Psychometric Considerations. *Psychology in the Schools*, Vol. 30, Issue 3, 241–254.

Menzies, S. (2010). Cooking the books on "hate": A closer look at SPLC's famous list. *The Social Contract*, 20(3), 156–161.

Mercer, J. (1979). In defense of racially and culturally non-discriminatory assessment. *School Psychology Digest*, 8(1), 89–115.

Merluzzi, T. V., & Hegde, K. (2003). Implications of social and cultural influences for multicultural competencies in health psychology. In D. B. Pope-Davis, H. Coleman, W. Liu, & R. Toporek (Eds.), *Handbook of multicultural competencies in counseling and psychology* (pp. 420–438). Thousand Oaks, CA: Sage.

Merrell, K. W., Ervin, R. A., & Peacock, G. G. (2012). *School psychology for the 21st century: Foundations and practices.* New York, NY: Guilford Press.

Merton, R.K. (1973). *The sociology of science.* Chicago, IL: University of Chicago Press.

Messick, S. (1989). Validity. In R. Linn (Ed.), *Educational measurement* (3rd ed., pp. 13–103). New York, NY: American Council on Education and Macmillan.

Michaelis, B. (1997). Diversity of American Indians. *Children and Families*, 16(4), 35–39.

Miele, F. (2002). *Intelligence, race, and genetics: Conversations with Arthur Jensen.* Cambridge, MA: Westview Press.

Mihai, F. M. (2010). *Assessing English Language Learners in the content areas: A research-into-practice guide for educators.* Ann Arbor, MI: University of Michigan Press.

Milofsky, C. (1989). *Testers and testing: The sociology of school psychology.* Piscataway, NJ: Rutgers University Press.

Mio, J. S., & Awakuni, G. I. (2000). *Resistance to multiculturalism: Issues and interventions.* Philadelphia, PA: Brunner/Mazel.

Moe, T. (2011). *Special interest: Teachers unions and America's public schools.* Washington, DC: Brookings Institution Press.

Moffitt, T. E. (1993). Adolescence-limited and life-course-persistent antisocial behavior: A developmental taxonomy. *Psychological Review, 100,* 674–701.

Moffitt, T. E., Caspi, A., Silva, P. A., & Stouthamer-Loeber, M. (1995). Individual differences in personality and intelligence are linked to crime: Cross-context evidence from nations, neighborhoods, genders, races, and age-cohorts. In J. Hagan (Ed.), *Current perspectives on aging and the life cycle, Vol. 4: Delinquency and disrepute in the life course: Contextual and dynamic analyses* (pp. 1–34). Greenwich, CT: JAI Press.

Mohr, H. (2010, August 27). School's race rule prompts mom to pull kids out. Accessed December 2, 2010, from *Associated Press,* http://www.boston.com/news/education/k_12/articles/2010/08/27/schools_race_rule_prompts_mom_to_pull_kids_out/

Monahan, T., & Torres, R. D. (2010). Introduction. In T. Monahan & R. D. Torres (Eds.), *Schools under surveillance: Cultures of control in public education.* New Brunswick, NJ: Rutgers University Press.

Monk, D. H. (2007). Recruiting and retaining high-quality teachers in rural areas. *Future of Children, 17*(1), 155–174.

Monteiro, K. P. (Ed.). (1996). *Ethnicity and psychology.* Dubuque, IA: Kendall/Hunt.

Moon, J. A. (2008). *Critical thinking: An exploration of theory and practice.* New York, NY: Routledge.

Morris, A. (2010, November). *Strategies teachers use to help students with test anxiety in limited resource environments.* Master's research project. Accessed February 2012 from http://www.cehs.ohio.edu/gfx/media/pdf/morris.pdf

Morrow, R. D. (1989, June). Differences between Americans and Southeast Asians. *NASP Communiqué, 18*(1), 22.

Morse, A. (2005). *A look at immigrant youth: prospects and promising practices.* Washington, DC: National Conference of State Legislatures. Accessed at http://www.ncsl.org/default.aspx?tabid=18113

Mukherjee, E. (2007). *Criminalizing the classroom: The over-policing of New York City schools.* New York, NY: New York Civil Liberties Union. Accessed June 2011 from http://www.nyclu.org/pdfs/criminalizing_the_classroom_report.pdf

Murray, C. (1994). *Losing ground: American social policy, 1950–1980.* New York, NY: Basic Books.

Murray, C. (1999). *The underclass revisited.* Washington, DC: American Enterprise Institute.

Murray, C. (2008). *Real education: Four simple truths for bringing America's schools back to reality.* New York, NY: Crown Forum.

Murray, J., & Farrington, D. (2005). Parental imprisonment: Effects on boys' antisocial behaviour and delinquency through the life-course. *Journal of Child Psychology and Psychiatry, 46,* 1269–1278.

Myers, J. (2000). Is there a youth gang epidemic? *Youth Today*, 1, 34–39.

Myers, J. (2000, November 1). Retired gangsters gang up on youth. Accessed May 2011 from *Youth Today*, http://sparkaction.org/node/32166

Naglieri, J. A. (2003). Fair assessment of gifted minority children using the NNAT. *Gifted Education Press Quarterly*, *17*, 2–7.

Naidoo, A. V. (1996). Challenging the hegemony of Eurocentric psychology. *Journal of Community and Health Sciences*, *2*(2), 9–16.

National Association of School Psychologists. (2011). *What is a school psychologist?* Accessed March 2011 from http://www.nasponline.org/about_sp/whatis.aspx

National Center for Education Statistics. (2008, September). *Status and trends in the education of American Indians and Alaska Natives: 2008*. Washington, DC: U.S. Department of Education.

National Center for Education Statistics. (2009, June). *Characteristics of public, private, and Bureau of Indian Education elementary and secondary schools in the United States: Results from the 2007-08 schools and staffing survey*. Washington, DC: U.S. Department of Education.

National Center for Education Statistics. (2010). *Homeschooling in the United States: Parent and Family Involvement in Education Survey (2007) of the National Household Education Surveys Program*. Washington, DC: U.S. Department of Education.

National Center for Education Statistics. (2012). *Indicators of school crime and safety: 2011*. Washington, DC: U.S. Department of Education.

National Congress of American Indians. (n.d.). *An introduction to Indian nations in the United States*. Accessed August 2011 from http://www.ncai.org/fileadmin/initiatives/NCAI_Indian_Nations_In_The_US.pdf

The National School Boards Association & National Education Association. (2009). Legal issues for school districts related to the education of undocumented children. National School Boards Association. Accessed May 2012 from http://www.nsba.org/SchoolLaw/COSA/Search/AllCOSAdocuments/Undocumented-Children.pdf

National Urban League. (2002, December 4). *Statement by the National Urban League regarding "Black American students in an affluent suburb: A study of academic disengagement."* Press release accessed March 5, 2004, from http://www.nul.org/news/2002/ogbu_statement.html

National Youth Gang Center. (2009). *National Youth Gang Survey Analysis*. Accessed May 2011 from http://www.nationalgangcenter.gov/Survey-Analysis

Neisser, U., Boodoo, G., Bouchard, T. J., Boykin, A. W., Brody, N., Ceci, S. J., . . . Urbina, S. (1996). Intelligence: Knowns and unknowns. *American Psychologist*, *51*, 77–101.

Neville, H. A., Worthington, R. L., & Spanierman, L. B. (2001). Race, power, and multicultural counseling psychology: Understanding white privilege and color-blind racial attitudes. In J. G. Ponterotto, J. M. Casas, L. A. Suzuki, & C. M. Alexander (Eds.), *Handbook of multicultural counseling* (2nd ed., pp. 257–288). Thousand Oaks, CA: Sage.

New Century Foundation. (2005). *The color of crime* (2nd expanded ed.). Oakton, VA: Author.

Newell, M. L., Nastasi, B. K., Hatzichristou, C., Jones, J. M., Schanding, G. T., & Yetter, G. (2010). Evidence on multicultural training in school psychology: Recommendations for future directions. *School Psychology Quarterly*, *25*(4), 249–278.

Newport, F. (2007, September 28). Black or African American? Accessed October 2010 from *Gallup News Service*, http://www.gallup.com/poll/28816/black-african-american.aspx

Neville, H. A., Tynes, B. M., & Utsey, S. O. (Eds.). (2009). *Handbook of African American psychology*. Thousand Oaks, CA: Sage.

Nieto, S. (2000). *Affirming diversity: The sociopolitical context of multicultural education* (3rd ed.). New York, NY: Longman.

Noell, G. H., & Witt, J. C. (1996). A critical re-evaluation of five fundamental assumptions underlying behavioral consultation. *School Psychology Quarterly, 11*, 189–203.

Noll, V. H. (1960). Relation of scores on Davis-Eells Games to socio-economic status, intelligence test results, and school achievement. *Educational and Psychological Measurement, 20*(1), 119–129.

Nuttall, E. V. (1979). Review of System of Multicultural Pluralistic Assessment. *Journal of Educational Measurement, 16*, 285–290.

Oakes, J. (2005). *Keeping track: How schools structure inequality* (2nd ed.). New Haven, CT: Yale University Press.

Oakland, T. (1979). Research on the adaptive behavior inventory for children and the estimated learning potential. *School Psychology Digest, 8*(1), 63–70.

Oakland, T., Glutting, J. J., & Watkins, M. W. (2005). Assessment of test behaviors with the WISC-IV. In A. Prifitera, D. H. Saklofske, & L. G. Weiss (Eds.), *WISC-IV clinical use and interpretation* (pp. 435–463). Burlington, MA: Elsevier Academic Press.

Obiakor, F. E. (2007). *Multicultural special education: Culturally responsive teaching*. Upper Saddle River, NJ: Pearson.

Ochoa, S. H. (2005). The effectiveness of bilingual education programs in the United States: A review of the empirical literature. In C. L. Frisby & C. R. Reynolds (Eds.), *Comprehensive handbook of multicultural school psychology* (pp. 329–356). Hoboken, NJ: Wiley.

O'Connor, C. (2010, August). South High in Denver embraces diversity. Accessed March 2011 from *The Denver Post*, http://www.denverpost.com/news/ci_15834496

Office of Program Consultation and Accreditation. (2010). *Commission on Accreditation 2011 self-study instructions: Doctoral graduate programs*. Washington, DC: American Psychological Association.

Ogbu, J. (2003). *Black American students in an affluent suburb: A study of academic disengagement*. Mahwah, NJ: Erlbaum.

Ogbu, J. (Ed.). (2008). *Minority status, oppositional culture, and schooling*. New York, NY: Taylor & Francis.

Ohio School Facilities Commission. (2008). Building in safety. Accessed June 2011 from http://www.osfc.ohio.gov/LinkClick.aspx?fileticket=haxpQFwr%2fRQ%3d&tabid=79

Olweus, D. (1993). *Bullying at school: What we know and what we can do*. Malden, MA: Blackwell.

O'Neill, W. F. (1981). *Educational ideologies: Contemporary expressions of educational philosophy*. Santa Monica, CA: Goodyear.

Openshaw, L. (2008). *Social work in schools: Principles and practice.* New York, NY: Guilford Press.

Orange County (Florida) Public Schools, OCPS Curriculum and Student Services. (2008, June). *Strategies for improving instruction for Black and Hispanic male students.* Accessed September 2011 from https://www.ocps.net/cs/services/initiatives/Documents/Strategies %20Document.pdf

Orr, E. (1997). *Twice as less: Black English and the performance of black students in mathematics and science.* New York, NY: W.W. Norton.

Ortiz, S.O. (2008). Best practices in nondiscriminatory assessment. In A. Thomas & J. Grimes (Eds.), *Best practices in school psychology V* (pp. 661–678). Bethesda, MD: National Association of School Psychologists.

Osher, D., Cartledge, G., Oswald, D., Sutherland, K. S., Artiles, A. J., & Coutinho, M. (2004). Cultural and linguistic competency and disproportionate representation. In R. B. Rutherford, M. M. Quinn, & S. R. Mathur (Eds.), *Handbook of research in emotional and behavioral disorders* (pp. 54–77). New York, NY: Guilford Press.

Oswald, D. (2006). Why it matters: What is disproportionate representation? *The Special EDge,* 20(1), 1, 6–7. Accessed May 2012 from http://www.calstat.org/publications/pdfs/06fallE.pdf

Padilla, A. M. (2004). Quantitative methods in multicultural education research. In J. A. Banks & C. M. Banks (Eds.), *Handbook of research on multicultural education* (2nd ed., pp. 127–145). San Francisco, CA: Jossey-Bass.

Paige, R. (2007). *The war against hope: How teachers' unions hurt children, hinder teachers, and endanger public education.* Nashville, TN: Thomas Nelson.

Parham, T. A. (2002, October). Cultural competency is best for counseling. *Counseling Today, 45* (4), 31, 36–37, 41.

Parker, S. (2003). *Uncle Sam's plantation: How big government enslaves America's poor and what we can do about it.* Nashville, TN: WND Books.

Pashler, H., McDaniel, M., Rohrer, D., & Bjork, R. (2008). Learning styles: Concepts and evidence. *Psychological Science in the Public Interest,* 9(3), 106–119.

Passel, J. S. (2005). *Background briefing prepared for task force on immigration and America's future.* Washington, DC: Pew Hispanic Center.

Patterson, C. H. (2004). Do we need multicultural counseling competencies? *Journal of Mental Health Counseling,* 26(1), 67–73.

Patterson, G. R., DeBaryshe, B. D., & Ramsey, E. (1989). A developmental perspective on antisocial behavior. *American Psychologist,* 44(2), 329–335.

Paul, R., & Elder, L. (2003). *The miniature guide to critical thinking concepts and tools.* Tomales, CA: Foundation for Critical Thinking.

Paulson, A. (2011, September 20). How one school district won prestigious prize for narrowing achievement gap. Accessed November 2011 from CSMonitor.com, http://www.csmonitor .com/USA/Education/2011/0920/How-one-school-district-won-prestigious-prize-for-narrowing-achievement-gap

Pedersen, P. (Ed.). (1999). *Multiculturalism as a fourth force*. Philadelphia, PA: Brunner/Mazel.

Pennock-Roman, M., & Rivera, C. (2007). The differential effects of time on accommodated vs. unaccommodated content assessments for English language learners. *Center for Assessment Reidy Interactive Lecture Series*. Available from http://www.nciea.org

Perazzo, J. (1999). *The myths that divide us: How lies have poisoned American race relations*. Briarcliff Manor, NY: World Studies Books.

Perlman, C. L. (2004). Practice tests and study guides: Do they help? Are they ethical? What is ethical test preparation practice? In Wall, J. E., & Walz, G. R. (Eds.). *Measuring Up: Assessment Issues for Teachers, Counselors, and Administrators*, (Chapter 27, pp. 387–396). Greensboro, NC: CAPS Press.

Petersen, R. D. (2004). *Understanding contemporary gangs in America: An interdisciplinary approach*. Upper Saddle River, NJ: Prentice-Hall.

Petrill, S. A., Plomin, R., DeFries, J. C., & Hewitt, J. K. (Eds.). (2003). *Nature, nurture, and the transition to early adolescence*. New York, NY: Oxford University Press.

Pew Forum on Religion and Public Life. (2009, October). *Mapping the global Muslim population: A report on the size and distribution of the world's Muslim population*. Washington, DC: Pew Research Center. Accessed May 2011 from http://pewforum.org/uploadedfiles/Topics/Demographics/Muslimpopulation.pdf

Pew Hispanic Center. (2011a). *Census 2010*. Washington, DC: Pew Research Center.

Pew Hispanic Center. (2011b). *Statistical portrait of the foreign-born population in the United States, 2008*. Washington, DC: Pew Research Center.

Pew Hispanic Center. (2011c). *Unauthorized immigrant population: National and state trends, 2010*. Washington, DC: Pew Research Center.

Phelps, R. P. (2007). *Standardized testing primer*. New York, NY: Peter Lang.

Phelps, R. P. (Ed.). (2009). *Correcting fallacies about educational and psychological testing*. (pp. 247–256). Washington, DC: American Psychological Association.

Phelps, R. P., & Gottfredson, L. (2009). Summary and discussion. In R. P. Phelps (Ed.), *Correcting fallacies about educational and psychological testing* (pp. 247–256). Washington, DC: American Psychological Association.

Pierangelo, R., & Giuliani, G. (2007). *Special education eligibility: A step-by-step guide for educators*. Thousand Oaks, CA: Corwin Press.

Pilon, B. (2007). Counseling groups for Latino immigrant teens at the LAUSD newcomer center. *The Observer*, 23(1), 10–15. Accessed April 2012 from http://www.utahschoolpsychology.org/UASPObserverNovember07.pdf

Pinderhughes, E.E., Nix, R.F., Foster, E.M., & Jones, D. (2001). Parenting in context: Impact of neighborhood poverty, residential stability, public services, social networks, and danger on parental behaviors. *Journal of Marriage and Family*, 63(4), 941–953.

Pinker, S. (2002). *The blank slate*. New York, NY: Penguin Putnam.

Piquero, A. R. (2008). Disproportionate minority contact. *The Future of Children*, 18(2), 59–79.

Plomin, R. (1994). *Genetics and experience: The interplay between nature and nurture*. Thousand Oaks, CA: Sage.

Plomin, R., DeFries, J. C., McClearn, G. E., & McGuffin, P. (2008). *Behavioral genetics* (5th ed.). London, UK: Worth.

Pollock, M. (2008). *Because of race: How Americans debate harm and opportunity in our schools*. Princeton, NJ: Princeton University Press.

Pong, S., & Zeiser, K. L. (2012). Student engagement, school climate, and academic achievement of immigrants' children. In C. G. Coll & A. K. Marks (Eds.), *The immigrant paradox in children and adolescents* (pp. 209–232). Washington, DC: American Psychological Association.

Pope-Davis, D., Coleman, H., Liu, W., & Toporek, R. (Eds.). (2003). *Handbook of multicultural competencies in counseling and psychology*. Thousand Oaks, CA: Sage.

Powers, K. M., Hagans-Murillo, K. S., & Restori, A. F. (2004). Twenty-five years after *Larry P.*: The California response to overrepresentation of African Americans in special education. *The California School Psychologist, 9*, 145–158.

Prager, D. (1995). *Think a second time*. New York, NY: HarperCollins.

Putnam, R. (2007). E Pluribus Unum: Diversity and community in the twenty-first century: The 2006 Johan Skytte Prize lecture. *Scandinavian Political Studies, 30*(2), 137–174.

Puzzanchera, C., Adams, B., & Sickmund, M. (2011). *Juvenile court statistics: 2008*. Pittsburgh, PA: National Center for Juvenile Justice. Accessed March 2012 from http://www.ojjdp.gov/ojstatbb/njcda/pdf/jcs2008.pdf

Quinn, M. T., & Jacob, E. (1999). Adding culture to the tools of school psychologists. *NASP Communiqué, 28*(1), 34, 38–39.

Rado, D. (2010, November 24). School may end honors class—Proposal by Evanston Township High School to increase diversity in advanced course leads to charged debate. *Chicago Tribune*, p. 4.

Rainwater, L., & Yancey, W. (Eds.). (1967). *The Moynihan Report and the politics of controversy*. Cambridge, MA: Massachusetts Institute of Technology Press.

Ramirez, J. D. (1992). Executive summary. *Bilingual Research Journal, 16*, 1–62.

Ramirez, R. R., & de la Cruz, G. P. (2003). *The Hispanic population in the United States: March 2002*. Accessed June 2010 at http://www.census.gov/prod/2003pubs/p20-545.pdf

Rankin, B., Vogell, H., & Judd, A. (2010, November 30). Atlanta public schools cheating: Some teachers admit guilt. Accessed February 2011 from *Atlanta Journal-Constitution*, http://www.ajc.com/news/atlanta/atlanta-public-schools-cheating-758757.html?cxntlid=cmg_cntnt_rss

Rastogi, S., Johnson, T. D., Hoeffel, E. M., & Drewery, M. P. (2011). *The black population: 2010*. Washington, DC: U.S. Census Bureau. Accessed October 2011 from http://www.census.gov/prod/cen2010/briefs/c2010br-06.pdf

Rauh, G. (2004, June 23). Mother calls IQ test ban for black children racist; 1979 ruling sought to address high numbers of African-american students put in special education. *The Oakland Tribune*.

Ravitch, D. (1983). *The troubled crusade: American education, 1945–1980.* New York, NY: Basic Books.

Ravitch, S. (2007). *Multiculturalism and diversity: School counselors as mediators of culture.* Alexandria, VA: American School Counselor Association.

Ray, B. D. (1997). *Strengths of their own—home schoolers across America: Family characteristics, student achievement, and longitudinal traits.* Salem, OR: National Home Education Research Institute.

Ray, B. D., & Weller, N. (2003). Homeschooling: An overview and financial implications for public schools. *School Business Affairs, 69,* 22–26.

Rector, R., & Sheffield, R. (2011). *Air conditioning, cable TV, and an Xbox: What is poverty in the United States today?* Washington, DC: Heritage Foundation.

Reddy, M., Borum, R., Berglund, J., Vossekuil, B., Fein, R., & Modzeleski, W. (2001). Evaluating risk for targeted violence in schools: Comparing risk assessment, threat assessment, and other approaches. *Psychology in the Schools, 38*(2), 157–172.

Ree, M. J., Carretta, T. R., & Green, M. T. (2003). The ubiquitous role of *g* in training. In H. Nyborg (Ed.), *The scientific study of general intelligence: Tribute to Arthur R. Jensen* (pp. 261–274). Oxford, UK: Elsevier.

Regoli, R. M., & Hewitt, J. D. (2003). *Delinquency in society* (5th ed.). Boston, MA: McGraw-Hill.

Reich, R. (2002). The civic perils of homeschooling. *Educational Leadership, 59*(7), 56–59.

Reither, E. (2003). *The issues surrounding the seriously emotionally disturbed: Emotional handicapped or managing chaos?* Accessed February 2011 from http://www.reither.com/SED/SED%20Paperc.pdf

Renzulli, J. S., Reis, S. M., Gavin, M. K., Siegle, D., & Sytsma, R. (2003). *Four new scales for rating the behavioral characteristics of superior students.* Storrs, CT: Neag Center for Gifted Education and Talent Development. Accessed August 2011 from http://www.gifted.uconn.edu/siegle/Conferences/SRBCSSNAGC2003Handout.pdf

Reschly, D. (2000). The present and future status of school psychology in the United States. *School Psychology Review, 29*(4), 507–522.

Restori, A. F., Katz, G. S., & Lee, H. B. (2009). A critique of the IQ/Achievement discrepancy model for identifying specific learning disabilities. *Europe's Journal of Psychology, 4,* 128–145.

Reynolds, C. R. (1985). Review of System of Multicultural Pluralistic Assessment. In J. V. Mitchell (Ed.), *Ninth mental measurements yearbook.* Lincoln, NE: Buros Institute.

Reynolds, C. R. (1986). Transactional models of intellectual development, yes. Deficit models of process remediation, no. *School Psychology Review, 15,* 256–260.

Reynolds, C. R. (2000). Why is psychometric research on bias in mental testing so often ignored? *Psychology, Public Policy, and Law, 6*(1), 144–150.

Reynolds, C. R., & Carson, A. D. (2005). Methods for assessing cultural bias in tests. In C. L. Frisby & C. R. Reynolds (Eds.), *Comprehensive handbook of multicultural school psychology* (pp. 795–823). Hoboken, NJ: Wiley.

Reynolds, C. R., & Lowe, P. A. (2009). The problem of bias in psychological assessment. In T. B. Gutkin & C. R. Reynolds (Eds.), *The handbook of school psychology* (4th ed., pp. 332–374). Hoboken, NJ: Wiley.

Richardson, T. (1993). Black cultural learning styles: Is it really a myth? *School Psychology Review*, 22(3), 562–567.

Ridley, C. R. (1995). *Overcoming unintentional racism in counseling and therapy: A practitioner's guide to intentional intervention.* Thousand Oaks, CA: Sage.

Ridley, C. R., Espelage, D. L., & Rubinstein, K. J. (1997). Course development in multicultural counseling. In D. Pope-Davis & H. Coleman (Eds.), *Multicultural counseling competencies: Assessment, education and training, and Supervision* (pp. 131–158). Thousand Oaks, CA: Sage.

Rivera, C. (2006, July). An extended family for black students. Accessed July 2011 from *Los Angeles Times*, http://articles.latimes.com/2006/jul/06/local/me-village6

Riverside County Special Education Local Plan Area. (2010). *Guidelines for assessing African-American students.* Riverside, CA: Author. Accessed November 2011 from http://www.rcselpa .org/docs/policies/Section%20III%20EvaluationsIII.h%20Guidelines%20for%20Assessing %20African-American%20Students.pdf

Robers, S., Zhang, J., and Truman, J. (2010). *Indicators of school crime and safety: 2010* (NCES 2011-002/NCJ 230812). Washington, DC: National Center for Education Statistics, U.S. Department of Education, and Bureau of Justice Statistics, Office of Justice Programs, U.S. Department of Justice.

Robinson-Zanartu, C., Butler-Byrd, N., Cook-Morales, V., Dauphinais, P., & Charley, E. (2011). School psychologists working with Native American youth: Training, competence, and needs. *Contemporary School Psychology, 15*, 103–115.

Rogers, M. R., Ingraham, C. L., Bursztyn, A., Cajigas-Segredo, N., Esquivel, G., Hess, R., Nahari, S., & Lopez, E. (1999). Providing psychological services to racially, ethnically, culturally, and linguistically diverse individuals in the schools. *School Psychology International, 20*(3), 243–264.

Rogers, M. R., & Lopez, E. C. (2002). Identifying critical cross-cultural school psychology competencies. *Journal of School Psychology, 40*(2), 115–141.

Rolland, M. (2010, October 1). Oklahoma City district pushes pause on hip-hop curriculum. Accessed December 2, 2010, from *NewsOK.com*, http://newsok.com/oklahoma-city-district-pushes-pause-on-hip-hop curriculum/article3500154?custom_click=lead_story_title

Rong, X., & Preissle, J. (2009). *Educating immigrant students in the 21st century.* Thousand Oaks, CA: Corwin Press.

Root, M. (2003). Racial and ethnic origins of harassment in the workplace: Evaluation issues and symptomatology. In D. B. Pope-Davis, H. Coleman, W. Liu, & R. Toporek (Eds.), *Handbook of multicultural competencies in counseling and psychology* (pp. 478–492). Thousand Oaks, CA: Sage.

Rosenfield, S. (1987). *Instructional consultation.* New York, NY: Erlbaum.

Rosenfield, S. (2008). Best practice in Instructional Consultation and Instructional Consultation teams. In A. Thomas & J. Grimes (Eds.), *Best practices in school psychology V* (pp. 1645–1660). Bethesda, MD: National Association of School Psychologists.

Rosenfield, S., & Gravois, T.A. (1996). *Instructional consultation teams: Collaborating for change.* New York, NY: Guilford Press.

Rosenfield, S., Silvia, A., & Gravois, T. (2008). Bringing instructional consultation to scale: Research and development of IC and IC teams. In W. Erchul & S. Sheridan (Eds.), *Handbook of research in school consultation: Empirical foundations for the field* (pp. 203–223). New York, NY: Erlbaum.

Rosenshine, B. (1987). Explicit teaching and teacher training. *Journal of Teacher Education, 38* (3), 34–36.

Ross, B. (2011). Public school desegregation and the white flight: A case study of the Kansas City, Missouri school district. Accessed January 2011 from http://www.benross.net/Public%20School%20Desegregation%20and%20the%20 White%20Flight.htm

Rossell, C., & Baker, K. (1996). The educational effectiveness of bilingual education. *Research in the Teaching of English, 30,* 7–74.

Roth, B. (1994). *Prescription for failure: Race relations in the age of social science.* New Brunswick, NJ: Transaction.

Roth, B. (2005). Self-esteem, ethnicity, and academic performance among American children. In C. L. Frisby & C. R. Reynolds (Eds.), *Comprehensive handbook of multicultural school psychology* (pp. 577–610). Hoboken, NJ: Wiley.

Roth, P. L., Bevier, C. A., Bobko, P., Switzer, F. S., & Tyler, P. (2001). Ethnic group differences in cognitive ability in employment and educational settings: A meta-analysis. *Personnel Psychology, 54,* 297–330.

Rothstein, R. (2004). *Class and schools: Using social, economic, and educational reform to close the black-white achievement gap.* Washington, DC: Economic Policy Institute.

Rozakis, L. (2003). *Test-taking strategies and study skills for the utterly confused.* New York, NY: McGraw-Hill

Rudinow, J., & Barry, V. E. (2008). *Invitation to critical thinking* (6th ed.). Belmont, CA: Thomson Wadsworth.

Ruggiero, V. R. (2001). *Beyond feelings: A guide to critical thinking* (6th ed.). Mountain View, CA: Mayfield.

Ruiz-de-Velasco, J., Fix, M., & Clewell, B. (2000). *Overlooked and underserved: Immigrant students in U.S. secondary schools.* Washington, DC: Urban Institute.

Rushton, J. P. (2003). Race differences in g and the "Jensen Effect." In H. Nyborg (Ed.), *The scientific study of general intelligence: Tribute to Arthur Jensen* (pp. 147–186). Oxford, UK: Elsevier.

Rushton, J. P., & Jensen, A. R. (2005). Thirty years of research on race differences in cognitive ability. *Psychology, Public Policy, and Law, 11*(2), 235–294.

Rutter, M. (2006). *Genes and behavior: Nature-nurture interplay explained.* Malden, MA: Blackwell.

Ryan, W. (1971). *Blaming the victim.* New York, NY: Vintage Books.

Ryan-Arrendondo, K., & Sandoval, J. (2005). Psychometric issues in the measurement of acculturation. In C. L. Frisby & C. R. Reynolds (Eds.), *Comprehensive handbook of multicultural school psychology* (pp. 861–880). Hoboken, NJ: Wiley.

Sable, J., Plotts, C., Mitchell, L., & Chen, C. (2010). *Characteristics of the 100 largest public elementary and secondary school districts in the United States: 2008–09 (NCES 2011-301)*. U.S. Department of Education, National Center for Education Statistics. Washington, DC: U.S. Government Printing Office.

Sackett, P. R., Hardison, C. M., & Cullen, M. J. (2004). On interpreting stereotype threat as accounting for African American-white differences on cognitive tests. *American Psychologist, 59*(1), 7–13.

Sahagun, L. (1997, November 9). Tribes struggle with violent crime wave. *Los Angeles Times,* p. A18.

Sam, D. L. (2006). Acculturation: Conceptual background and core components. In D. L. Sam & J. W. Berry (Eds.), *The Cambridge handbook of acculturation psychology* (pp. 11–26). Cambridge, UK: Cambridge University Press.

Sam, D. L., & Berry, J. W. (Eds.). (2006). *The Cambridge handbook of acculturation psychology.* Cambridge, UK: Cambridge University Press.

Samenow, S. E. (1989). *Before it's too late: Why some kids get into trouble and what parents can do about it.* New York, NY: Times Books.

Samenow, S. E. (1998). *Straight talk about criminals: Understanding and treating antisocial individuals.* Northvale, NJ: Jason Aronson.

Samenow, S. E. (2004). *Inside the criminal mind* (revised and updated). New York, NY: Crown.

Sampson, R. J. (2011). The community. In J. Q. Wilson & J. Petersilia (Eds.), *Crime and public policy* (pp. 210–236). New York, NY: Oxford University Press.

Samuda, R. (1998). *Psychological testing of American minorities: Issues and consequences.* Thousand Oaks, CA: Sage.

Sandall, R. (2001). *The culture cult: Designer tribalism and other essays.* Boulder, CO: Westview Press.

Sandhu, D. S., & Aspy, C. B. (1997). *Counseling for prejudice prevention and reduction.* Alexandria, VA: American Counseling Association.

Sandoval, J. (1985). Review of System of Multicultural Pluralistic Assessment. In J. V. Mitchell (Ed.), *Ninth mental measurements yearbook.* Lincoln, NE: Buros Institute.

Sandoval, J., & Mille, M. (1980). Accuracy of judgments of WISC-R item difficulty for minority groups. *Journal of Consulting and Clinical Psychology, 48*(2), 249–253.

San Miguel Montes, L. E., Allen, D. N., Puente, A. E., & Neblina, C. (2010). Validity of the WISC-IV Spanish for a clinically referred sample of Hispanic children. *Psychological Assessment, 22*(2), 465–469.

Sapir, E., & Irvine, J. (1993). *The psychology of culture: A course of lectures.* New York, NY: Mouton.

Sapp, M. (1999). *Test anxiety: Applied research, assessment, and treatment interventions* (2nd ed.). Lanham, MD: University Press of America.

Sattler, J. M. (2008). *Assessment of children: Cognitive foundations* (5th ed.). San Diego, CA: Author.

Saunders, P. (2005, August 8). Defining poverty. Accessed October 2011 from *On Line Opinion*, http://www.onlineopinion.com.au/view.asp?article=3737

Scarr, S., & McCartney, K. (1983). How people make their own environments: A theory of genotype/environment effects. *Child Development, 54,* 424–435.

Schein, E. (1998). *Process consultation revisited: Building the helping relationship.* Boston, MA: Addison Wesley Longman.

Schloss, P. J., & Smith, M. A. (1998). *Applied behavior analysis in the classroom.* Boston, MA: Allyn & Bacon.

Schneider, D. J. (2004). *The psychology of stereotyping.* New York, NY: Guilford Press.

Schneider, T. (2010). *CPTED 101: Crime prevention through environmental design: The fundamentals for schools.* Washington, DC: National Clearinghouse for Educational Facilities at the National Institute of Building Sciences.

Schneider, T., Walker, H., & Sprague, J. (2000). *Safe school design: A handbook for educational leaders.* Eugene, OR: ERIC Clearinghouse on Educational Management, University of Oregon. Accessed June 2011 from https://scholarsbank.uoregon.edu/xmlui/handle/1794/3258?show=full

Schnell, R. (2011a). *Memphis City Schools Mental Health Center programs and services.* Unpublished manuscript. Memphis, TN: Memphis City Schools Mental Health Center.

Schnell, R. (2011b). *Summer programs.* Unpublished manuscript. Memphis, TN: Memphis City Schools Mental Health Center.

Schofield, J. W. (1982). *Black and white in school: Trust, tension, or tolerance?* Santa Barbara, CA: Praeger.

Schofield, J. W. (2004). Fostering positive intergroup relations in schools. In J. A. Banks & C. M. Banks (Eds.), *Handbook of research on multicultural education* (2nd ed., pp. 799–812). San Francisco, CA: Jossey-Bass.

Schrank, F. A., & Woodcock, R. W. (2001). WJ III Compuscore and Profiles Program [Computer software]. *Woodcock-Johnson III.* Itasca, IL: Riverside.

Scott, E. S., & Steinberg, L. (2008). Adolescent development and the regulation of youth crime. *The Future of Children, 18*(2), 15–33.

Scott, M. (2011, March 9). Grand Rapids schools hit with sanctions for suspending blacks, students with disabilities at higher rates. Accessed November 2011 from *Grand Rapids Press*, http://www.mlive.com/news/grand-rapids/index.ssf/2011/03/state_says_grand_rapids_school.html

Scott, S. (2009, May 6). African American students are thriving in Afro-centric schools. Accessed May 2011 from the *Florida Times-Union Jacksonville.com*, http://jacksonville.com/interact/blog/stanley_scott/2009-05-06/african_american_students_are_thriving_in_afro-centric_school

Sears, D. O. (1988). Symbolic racism. In P. Katz & D. Taylor (Eds.), *Eliminating racism: Profiles in controversy* (pp. 53–84). New York, NY: Plenum Press.

Sexton, T. L. (2011). *Functional Family Therapy in clinical practice: An evidence-based treatment model for working with troubled adolescents*. New York, NY: Routledge.

Shade, B. (Ed.). (1995). *Culture, style and the educative process*. Springfield, IL: Charles C. Thomas.

Shane, L.A. (2010, April 2). *Parents pin hopes on charter school lottery*. Mackinac Center for Public Policy. Accessed May 2012 from http://www.mackinac.org/12455

Shaw, D. (2003). Advancing our understanding of intergenerational continuity in antisocial behavior. *Journal of Abnormal Child Psychology, 31*, 193–199.

Shaw, S. R. (2001, April). *Slow learners: Condemned to failure or failed by schools?* Paper presented to the convention of the National Association of School Psychologists, Washington, DC.

Shaw, S. (2008). An educational programming framework for a subset of students with diverse learning needs: Borderline intellectual functioning. *Intervention in School and Clinic, 43*(5), 291–299.

Shaw, S. (2010, February). Rescuing students from the slow learner trap. *Principal Leadership*, 12–16.

Shaw, S., Grimes, D., & Bulman, J. (2005). Educating slow learners: Are charter schools the last, best hope for their educational success? *The Charter Schools Resource Journal, 1*(1), 10–19.

Shelden, R. G., Tracy, S. K., & Brown, W. B. (2004). *Youth gangs in American society* (3rd ed.). Belmont, CA: Wadsworth.

Shelvin, K. (2008). School-based interventions to reduce stereotype threat activation. *NASP Communiqué, 36*(7), 21–22.

Sheridan, S. M., Kratochwill, T. R., & Bergan, J. R. (1996). *Conjoint behavioral consultation: A procedural manual*. New York, NY: Plenum.

Sherman, L. W., & Strang, H. (2007). *Restorative justice: The evidence*. London, UK: The Smith Institute.

Sherman, L. W., Strang, H., Angel, C., Woods, D., Barnes, G. C., Bennett, S., & Inkpen, N. (2005). Effects of face-to-face restorative justice on victims of crime in four randomized, controlled trials. *Journal of Experimental Criminology, 1*, 367–395.

Shinn, M. R. (Ed.). (1998). *Advanced applications of curriculum-based measurement*. New York, NY: Guilford Press.

Shinn, M. R. (2008). Best practices in using curriculum-based measurement in a problem-solving model. In A. Thomas & J. Grimes (Eds.), *Best practices in school psychology V* (Vol. 2, pp. 243–261). Bethesda, MD: National Association of School Psychologists.

Shinn, M. R., Rosenfield, S., & Knutson, N. (1989). Curriculum-based assessment: A comparison of models. *School Psychology Review, 18*, 299–316.

Shipler, D. K. (2005). *The working poor: Invisible in America*. New York, NY: Vintage Books.

Shokraii-Rees, N. H. (2007). The self-esteem fraud: Why feel-good education does not lead to academic success. Accessed November 2011 from *Center for Equal Opportunity*, http://www .ceousa.org/content/view/162/92

Short, D. J., & Boyson, B. A. (2003). *Establishing an effective newcomer program*. Washington, DC: Center for Applied Linguistics.

Short, D. J., & Boyson, B. A. (2012). *Helping newcomer students succeed in secondary schools and beyond*. Washington, DC: Center for Applied Linguistics.

Shriberg, D. (2009). Social justice and school mental health: Evolution and implications for practice. In J. Jones (Ed.), *The psychology of multiculturalism in the schools* (pp. 49–66). Bethesda, MD: National Association of School Psychologists.

Shriberg, D., Bonner, M., Sarr, B., Walker, A., Hyland, M., & Chester, C. (2008). Social justice through a school psychology lens: Definitions and applications. *School Psychology Review, 37,* 453–468.

Sieff, K. (2011, November 6). Washington-area schools confront the "gifted gap." Accessed November 2011 from *WashingtonPost.com*, http://www.washingtonpost.com/local/education/2011/11/06/gIQAeYImtM_story.html

Siegel, L. J., & Welsh, B. C. (2009). *Juvenile delinquency: Theory, practice, and law* (10th ed.). Belmont, CA: Wadsworth.

Sigelman, L., Tuch, S. A., & Martin, J. K. (2005). What's in a name? Preference for "Black" versus "African-American" among Americans of African descent. *Public Opinion Quarterly, 69*(3), 429–438.

Simmons, R. G., & Rosenberg, M. (1971). Functions of children's perceptions of the stratification system. *American Sociological Review, 36,* 235–249.

Simons, L. G., & Conger, R. (2007). Linking mother-father differences in parenting to a typology of family parenting styles and adolescent outcomes. *Journal of Family Issues, 28,* 212–241.

Sireci, S. G., Li, S., & Scarpati, S. (2003). *The effects of test accommodation on test performance: A review of the literature.* (Research Report No. 485). Amherst, MA: Center for Education Assessment.

Sisk, D. A. (1977). What if your child is gifted? *American Education, 13*(8), 23–26.

Skehan, P. (1998). *A cognitive approach to language learning.* Oxford, UK: Oxford University Press.

Skogan, W. (1990). *Disorder and decline: Crime and the spiral decay in American cities.* Berkeley, CA: University of California Press.

Sleeper, J. (1997). *Liberal racism.* New York, NY: Penguin Books.

Sleeter, C. E., & Bernal, D. D. (2004). Critical pedagogy, critical race theory, and antiracist education: Implications for multicultural education. In J. A. Banks & C. M. Banks (Eds.), *Handbook of research on multicultural education* (2nd ed., pp. 240–258). San Francisco, CA: Jossey-Bass.

Smith, C., & Farrington, D. (2004). Continuities in antisocial behavior and parenting across three generations. *Journal of Child Psychology and Psychiatry, 45,* 230–247.

Smith, C., Perou, R., & Lesesne, C. (2002). Parent education. In M. H. Bornstein (Ed.), *Handbook of parenting, Vol. 4: Social conditions and applied parenting* (pp. 389–410). Mahway, NJ: Erlbaum.

Smith, D. L., & Smith, B. J. (2006). Perceptions of violence: The views of teachers who left urban schools. *The High School Journal, 89*(3), 34–42.

Smith, J. R. (2011, January 5). Big stimulus money for Detroit Public Schools. Accessed February 2011 from *American Thinker*, http://www.americanthinker.com/blog/2011/01/big_stimulus_money_for_detroit.html

Smith, M., & Shade, B. J. (1995). Social and cultural effects on Indian learning style: Classroom implications. In B. Shade (Ed.), *Culture, style and the educative process* (pp. 178–186). Springfield, IL: Charles C. Thomas.

Smydo, J. (2007, August 6). College Board cool to AP course in African-American History. *Pittsburgh Post-Gazette*, p. B-1.

Snyder, H. N., & Sickmund, M. (2006). *Juvenile Offenders and Victims: 2006 National Report*. Washington, DC: U.S. Department of Justice, Office of Justice Programs, Office of Juvenile Justice and Delinquency Prevention.

Sodowsky, G., Kuo-Jackson, P., & Loya, G. (1997). Outcome of training in the philosophy of assessment: Multicultural counseling competencies. In D. Pope-Davis & H. Coleman (Eds.), *Multicultural counseling competencies: Assessment, education and training, and Supervision* (pp. 3–42). Thousand Oaks, CA: Sage.

Sokal, A., & Bricmont, J. (1998). *Fashionable nonsense: Postmodern intellectuals' abuse of science*. London, UK: Profile Books.

Solis, A., Schwartz, W., & Hinton, T. (2003). *Gang Resistance Is Paramount (GRIP) program evaluation: Final report*. Los Angeles: University of Southern California, Center for Economic Development.

Sorokin, E. (2002). NEA blames America for 9/11; Critics say National Education Association lesson plans on Sept. 11 are anti-American and anti-Western civilization. Accessed November 2011 from *News World Communications*, http://findarticles.com/p/articles/mi_m1571/is_35_18/ai_92352724/

Sourcebook of Criminal Justice Statistics. (2011a). *Public attitudes toward crime and criminal justice-related topics*. Washington, DC: Bureau of Justice Statistics. Accessed March 2012 from http://www.albany.edu/sourcebook/pdf/t2362011.pdf

Sourcebook of Criminal Justice Statistics. (2011b). Attitudes toward the biggest problems facing public schools. Washington, DC: Bureau of Justice Statistics. Accessed March 2012 from http://www.albany.edu/sourcebook/pdf/t242011.pdf

Southern Poverty Law Center. (2012). Southern Poverty Law Center. Accessed December 2012 from http://www.splcenter.org/who-we-are

Sowell, T. (1984). *Civil rights: Rhetoric or reality?* New York, NY: William Morrow.

Sowell, T. (1986). *Education: Assumptions versus history*. Stanford, CA: Hoover Institution Press.

Sowell, T. (1993). *Inside American education: The decline, the deception, the dogmas*. New York, NY: Free Press.

Sowell, T. (1996, January 17). Teachers refuse to admit colleagues' poor quality. Accessed August 2011 from the *Seattle Times*, http://community.seattletimes.nwsource.com/archive/?date=19960117&slug=2309238

Sowell, T. (2000). *A personal odyssey*. New York, NY: Free Press.

Sowell, T. (2002, July 11). A scary report. Accessed August 2011 from *Jewish World Review*, http://www.jewishworldreview.com/cols/sowell071102.asp

Sowell, T. (2004). *Affirmative action around the world: An empirical study*. New Haven, CT: Yale University Press.

Sowell, T. (2006). *Ever wonder why?: And other controversial essays*. Stanford, CA: Hoover Institution Press.

Sowell, T. (2009). *Intellectuals and society*. New York, NY: Basic Books.

Sowell, T. (2010, September 8). The money of fools. Accessed September 2010 from *Jewish World Review*, http://www.jewishworldreview.com/cols/sowell091410.php3

Sowell, T. (2010, September 15). The money of fools: Part II. Accessed September 2010 from *Jewish World Review*, http://jewishworldreview.com/cols/sowell091510.php3

Sowell, T. (2010). *Dismantling America*. New York, NY: Basic Books.

Spearman, C. (1904). General intelligence, objectively determined and measured. *American Journal of Psychology, 15*, 201–293.

Spitz, H. H. (1986). *The raising of intelligence: A selected history of attempts to raise retarded intelligence*. Hillsdale, NJ: Erlbaum.

Spring, J. (2010). *American education*. New York, NY: McGraw-Hill.

Springer, D. W., & Roberts, A. R. (2011). *Juvenile justice and delinquency*. Sudbury, MA: Jones & Bartlett.

Steele, C. M. (1997). A threat in the air: How stereotypes shape intellectual identity and performance. *American Psychologist, 52*, 613–629.

Steele, C. M., & Aronson, J. (1995). Stereotype threat and the intellectual test performance of African Americans. *Journal of Personality and Social Psychology, 69*, 797–811.

Steele, S. (2006). *White guilt: How blacks and whites together destroyed the promise of the civil rights era*. New York, NY: HarperCollins.

Steinberg, L. D., Brown, B. B., & Dornbusch, S. M. (1996). *Beyond the classroom: Why school reform has failed and what parents need to do*. New York, NY: Simon & Schuster.

Steinberg, M. P., Allensworth, E., & Johnson, D. W. (2011). *Student and teacher safety in Chicago public Schools: The roles of community context and school social organization*. Chicago, IL: University of Chicago Consortium on Chicago School Research.

Steinberg, S. R. (2009). *Diversity and multiculturalism*. New York, NY: Peter Lang.

Stendler, C. (1949). *Children of Brasstown: Their awareness of the symbols of social class*. Urbana, IL: University of Illinois Press.

Stern, G. (2009, June 27). "Kumbaya, My Lord:" Why we sing it; why we hate it. Accessed September 2010 from the *Journal News*, http://www.lohud.com/apps/pbcs.dll/article?AID=/200906270230/COLUMNIST/906270343

Stern, S. (1997). How teachers' unions handcuff schools. Accessed November 2011 from *City Journal*, http://www.city-journal.org/html/7_2_how_teachers.html

Strang, H., & Sherman, L. W. (2006). Restorative Justice to reduce victimization. In B. C. Welsh & D. P. Farrington (Eds.), *Preventing crime: What works for children, offenders, victims, and places*. New York, NY: Springer.

Stronge, J. H., & Grant, L. W. (2009). *Student achievement goal setting: Using data to improve teaching and leaning*. Larchmont, NY: Eye on Education, Inc.

Suárez-Orozco, C., Suárez-Orozco, M., & Todorova, I. (2008). *Learning a new land: Immigrant students in American society*. Cambridge, MA: Harvard University Press.

Suárez-Orozco, M. (2001). Globalization, immigration, and education: The research agenda. *Harvard Educational Review, 71*(3), 345–365.

Sue, D. W. (2003). Hate crimes are illegal but racial microaggressions are not! In *Communiqué Special Section: Psychology and Racism Ten Years After the Miniconvention* (pp. 5–9). Bethesda, MD: National Association of School Psychologists.

Sue, D. W., Arredondo, P., & McDavis, R. J. (1992). Multicultural counseling competencies and standards: A call to the profession. *Journal of Counseling and Development, 70*, 477–486.

Sue, D. W., Capodilupo, C. M., Nadal, K. L., & Torino, G. C. (2008). Racial microaggressions and the power to define reality. *American Psychologist, 63*(4), 277–279.

Sue, D. W., Capodilupo, C. M., Torino, G. C., Bucceri, J. M., Holder, M. B., Nadal, K. L., & Esquilin, M. (2007). Racial microaggression in everyday life: Implications for clinical practice. *American Psychologist, 62*(4), 27.

Sue, D. W., & Sue D. (2003). *Counseling the culturally diverse: Theory and practice* (4th ed.). Hoboken, NJ: Wiley.

Sugai, G., Horner, R., & McIntosh, K. (2008). Best practices in developing a broad-scale system of school-wide positive behavior support. In A. Thomas & J. Grimes (Eds.), *Best practices in school psychology V* (Vol. 3, pp. 765–779). Bethesda, MD: National Association of School Psychologists.

Sullivan, A. L. (2010). Preventing disproportionality: A framework for culturally responsive assessment. *NASP Communiqué, 39*(3).

Sundaram, A. (2011, July 16). Freedom from fear awards: Fighting school violence, Asian immigrants find their voice. Accessed July 2011 from *New America Media*, http://new americamedia.org/2011/07/fighting-school-violence-asian-immigrants-discover-communal-voice.php

Suzuki, L. A., & Ponterotto, J. G. (Eds.). (2008). *Handbook of multicultural assessment: Clinical, psychological, and educational applications*. Hoboken, NJ: Wiley.

Shweder, Minow, & Markus (Eds.) (2002). *Engaging cultural differences: The multicultural challenge in liberal democracies*. New York: Sage.

Swisher, K. G. (1998). Why Indian people should be the ones to write about Indian education. In D. A. Mihesuah (Ed.), *Natives and academics: Researching and writing about American Indians* (pp. 190–200). Lincoln, NE: University of Nebraska Press.

Swisher, R. R., & Waller, M. R. (2008). Confining fatherhood: Incarceration and paternal involvement among unmarried white, African American, and Latino fathers. *Journal of Family Issues, 29*(8), 1067–1088.

Taylor, G. M., & Quintana, S. M. (2003). Teachers' multicultural competencies (K–12). In D. B. Pope-Davis, H. Coleman, W. Liu, & R. Toporek (Eds.), *Handbook of multicultural competencies in counseling and psychology* (pp. 511–527). Thousand Oaks, CA: Sage.

Taylor, J. (2004). *Paved with good intentions: The failure of race relations in contemporary America.* Oakton, VA: New Century Books.

Taylor, J. (2011). *White identity: Racial consciousness in the 21st century.* Oakton, VA: New Century Books.

Teitelbaum, P. (2011, February 6). Arizona law outlaws ethnic studies programs: Activists, community prepare to fight back. Accessed August 2011 from *Workers World,* http://www .workers.org/2011/us/arizona_0210/

Texas Education Agency. (2011a). *Grades 3–8 and 10 linguistically accommodated testing (LAT) test administrator manual 2011: Mathematics, Reading/ELA, Science.* Accessed September 2011 from http://www.tea.state.tx.us/student.assessment/ell/lat/

Texas Education Agency. (2011b). *Training test administrators on providing linguistic accommodations for LAT administrations of TAKS-Spring 2011.* Accessed September 2011 from http:// www.tea.state.tx.us/student.assessment/ell/lat/

Thao, P. (2005). Cultural variation within southeast Asian American families. In C. L. Frisby & C. R. Reynolds (Eds.), *Comprehensive handbook of multicultural school psychology* (pp. 173–204). Hoboken, NJ: Wiley.

Thernstrom, A., & Thernstrom, S. (2003). *No excuses: Closing the racial gap in learning.* New York, NY: Simon & Schuster.

Thernstrom, S. (Ed.). (1980). *Harvard encyclopedia of American ethnic groups.* Cambridge, MA: Harvard University Press.

Thernstrom, S., & Thernstrom, A. (1997). *America in black and white: One nation, indivisible.* New York, NY: Simon & Schuster.

Thomas, K. (2008). Macrononsense in multiculturalism. *American Psychologist, 63*(4), 274–275.

Thomas, K. R., & Wubbolding, R. E. (2009). Social justice, multicultural counseling, and counseling psychology research: A politically incorrect perspective. In A. M. Columbus (Ed.), *Advances in Psychology Research, 59,* 279–287.

Thomas, L. (2010, November 17). A brave new world controversy. Accessed December 2, 2010, from the *News Chick,* http://www.mynorthwest.com/category/news_chick_blog/20101117/ A-Brave-New-World-controversy

Thomas, W. P., & Collier, V. P. (2002). *A national study of school effectiveness for language minority students' long-term academic achievement.* Santa Cruz, CA: Center for Research on Education, Diversity and Excellence.

Thompkins, D. E. (2004). School violence: Gangs and a culture of fear. In R. D. Petersen (Ed.), *Understanding contemporary gangs in America: An interdisciplinary approach.* Upper Saddle River, NJ: Prentice Hall.

Thompson, S. J., Johnstone, C. J., & Thurlow, M. L. (2002). *Universal design applied to large scale assessments (Synthesis Report 44)*. Minneapolis, MN: University of Minnesota, National Center on Educational Outcomes. Accessed February 2012 from www.cehd.umn.edu/NCEO/onlinepubs/Synthesis44.html

Thompson, W., & Hickey, J. (2005). *Society in focus*. Boston, MA: Pearson.

Thurman, Q., & Mueller, D. (2003). Beyond curfews and crackdowns: An overview of the Mountlake Terrace Neutral Zone-AmeriCorps program. In S. H. Decker (Ed.), *Policing gangs and youth violence* (pp. 167–187). Belmont, CA: Wadsworth/Thompson Learning.

Tileston, D. W., & Darling, S. K. (2008). *Why culture counts: Teaching children of poverty*. Bloomington, IN: Solution Tree Press.

Tillman, L. C. (Ed.). (2009). *The SAGE handbook of African American education*. Thousand Oaks, CA: Sage.

Tipton, R. B. (2008). *Head Start update 2008: Overview of Head Start reauthorization*. Accessed March 2011 from http://www.caplaw.org/documents/Tipton-OverviewofHeadStartReauthorization .pdf

Tonry, M. (Ed.). (1997). *Ethnicity, crime, and immigration: Comparative and cross-national perspectives*. Chicago, IL: University of Chicago Press.

Torres, K. (2010, June 18). 100 Atlanta school employees implicated in test cheating scandal. Accessed February 2011 from *Atlanta Journal-Constitution*, http://www.ajc.com/news/atlanta/ 100-atlanta-school-employees-552164.html

Trainers of School Psychologists (2009). *Special edition: Social justice*. Washington, DC: American Psychological Association, Division 16.

Tremblay, R., Masse, L., Pagani, L., & Vitaro, F. (1996). From childhood physical aggression to adolescent maladjustment: The Montreal Prevention Experiment. In R. D. Peters & R. J. McMahon (Eds.), *Preventing childhood disorders, substance abuse, and delinquency* (pp. 268–298). Thousand Oaks, CA: Sage.

Trevey, M. (2012). The gangs of Milwaukee. Accessed March 2012 from *Today's TMJ4*, http:// www.todaystmj4.com/features/specialassignment/45608612.html

Triandis, H. C. (2007). Culture and psychology: A history of the study of their relationship. In S. Kitayama & D. Cohen (Eds.), *Handbook of cultural psychology* (pp. 59–76). New York, NY: Guilford Press.

Truscott, S. D., & Truscott, D. M. (2005). Challenges in urban and rural education. In C. L. Frisby & C. R. Reynolds (Eds.), *Comprehensive handbook of multicultural school psychology* (pp. 357–393). Hoboken, NJ: Wiley.

Tucker, C. M., & Herman, K. C. (2002). Using culturally sensitive theories and research to meet the academic needs of low-income African American children. *American Psychologist, 57* (10), 762–773.

Tucker, J. (2010, November 27). *Albany schools try to balance parent-funded extras*. Accessed December 1, 2010, from http://articles.sfgate.com/2010-11-27/news/24948346_1_public-schools-foreign-language-programs-public-education

Tucker, J. (2012, April 3). Oakland charter school accused of fraud may close. Accessed June 2012 from *SFGate.com*, www.sfgate.com/cgibin/article.cgi?f=/c/a/2012/04/02/MNSB1NTO21.DTL

Turner, A. (1986). *The behavior and style of black students* (ERIC Document Reproduction Service No. 282965).

Tutor, J. (1991). The development of class awareness in children. *Social Forces, 49,* 470–476.

Tyler, K. M., Uqdah, A. L., Dillihunt, M. L., Beatty-Hazelbaker, R., Conner, T., Gadson, N., . . . Stevens, R. (2008). Cultural discontinuity: Toward a quantitative investigation of a major hypothesis in education. *Educational Researcher, 37*(5), 280–297.

Tyrell, B. (2011, February 17). Multiculturalism has failed. Accessed March 2011 from *Jewish World Review,* http://www.jewishworldreview.com/cols/tyrrell021711.php3

Tyson, K., Darity, W., & Castellino, D. R. (2005). It's not "a black thing": Understanding the burden of acting white and other dilemmas of high achievement. *American Sociological Review, 70,* 582–605.

Uller, H., & Martinez, B. (n.d.). *Gang prevention and intervention cluster.* Accessed May 2011 from http://councilcommittee.lacity.org/youthdev/AP.Final.Appendix.05.pdf

U.S. Census Bureau. (2000). *DP-3 Profile of selected economic characteristics: Pine Ridge CDP, South Dakota.* Washington, DC: Author.

U.S. Census Bureau. (2002). *The Asian population: 2000.* Washington, DC: U.S. Department of Commerce.

U.S. Census Bureau. (2009a). *American Community Survey 2005–2009, M0201: Percent of the total population who are white alone.* Washington, DC: Author.

U.S. Census Bureau. (2009b). *American Community Survey 2005–2009, M0202: Percent of the total population who are black or African American alone.* Washington, DC: Author.

U.S. Census Bureau. (2009c). *American Community Survey, C16005: Nativity by language spoken at home by ability to speak English for the population 5 years and over.* Accessed October 2011 from http://www.census.gov/compendia/statab/2012/tables/12s0054.pdf

U.S. Census Bureau. (2009d). *American Community Survey, B16001: Language spoken at home by ability to speak English for the population 5 years and over.* Accessed October 2011 from http://www.census.gov/compendia/statab/2012/tables/12s0053.pdf

U.S. Census Bureau. (2010a). *Census redistricting data summary file, Table P1.* Accessed October 2011 from http://www.census.gov/compendia/statab/2012/tables/12s0019.pdf

U.S. Census Bureau. (2010b). *Income, poverty and health insurance coverage in the United States: 2009, Current Population Reports, P60-238.* Accessed October 2011 from http://www.census.gov/compendia/statab/2012/tables/12s0695.pdf

U.S. Census Bureau. (2011). *America's families and living arrangements: 2011.* Washington, DC: Author.

U.S. Center for Education Statistics. (2008). *School and staffing survey (SASS), Public School Questionnaire 2007–08 and Public Teacher Questionnaire.* Accessed November 2011 from http://www.census.gov/compendia/statab/2012/tables/12s0239.pdf

U.S. Center for Education Statistics. (2009, June). *Condition of education, 2009, NCES 2009-081.* Washington, DC: U.S. Census Bureau.

U.S. Commission on Civil Rights. (2009, April). *Minorities in special education.* Washington, DC: Author. Accessed January 2011 from http://www.usccr.gov/pubs/MinoritiesinSpecial Education.pdf

U. S. Department of Education. (2009). *Implementing RTI Using Title I, Title III, and CEIS Funds.* Accessed at http://www2.ed.gov/programs/titleiparta/rtifiles/rti.pdf

U.S. Department of Health and Human Services. (2010). *Head Start impact study.* Washington, DC: DHHS, Administration for Children and Families. Accessed July 2011 from http://www.acf.hhs.gov/programs/opre/hs/impact_study/reports/impact_study/executive_summary _final.pdf

U.S. Department of Justice. (2011, May). *Criminal victimization in the United States, 2008 statistical tables.* Washington, DC: Bureau of Justice Statistics. Accessed March 2012 from http://www .bjs.gov/content/pub/pdf/cvus0801.pdf

Valdés, G., Capitelli, S., & Alvarez, L. (2011). *Latino children learning English.* New York, NY: Teachers College Press.

Van Der Aalsvoort, G. M., Ruijssenaars, A. J., & Resing, W. C. (2002). *Learning potential assessment and cognitive training: Actual research and perspectives in theory building and methodology.* New York, NY: JAI Press.

van de Vijver, F., & Leung, K. (2001). Personality in cultural context: Methodological issues. *Journal of Personality, 69*(6), 1007–1031.

van de Vijver, F., & Tanzer, N. K. (2004). Bias and equivalence in cross-cultural assessment: An overview. *Revue européenne de psychologie appliquée, 54,* 119–135.

Vanourek, G. (2005). *State of the charter movement 2005: Trends and issues.* Washington, DC: National Alliance for Public Charter Schools (formerly Charter School Leadership Council).

Vasquez, J. A. (1998). Distinctive traits of Hispanic students. *The Prevention Researcher, 5*(1), 1–4.

Vedder, P. H., & Horenczyk, G. (2006). Acculturation and the school. In D. L. Sam & J. W. Berry (Eds.), *The Cambridge handbook of acculturation psychology* (pp. 419–438). Cambridge, UK: Cambridge University Press.

Vitaro, F., Brendgen, M., & Tremblay, R. E. (1999). Prevention of school dropout through the reduction of disruptive behaviours and school failure in elementary school. *Journal of School Psychology, 37,* 205–226.

Vogeler, T. J. (2009). *Gangs in schools task force: 2009 report to the legislature.* Olympia, WA: Washington State School Safety Center.

Vossekuil, B., Fein, R. A., Reddy, M., Borum, R., & Modzeleski, W. (2002). *The final report and findings of the safe school initiative: Implications for the prevention of school attacks in the United States.* Washington, DC: U.S. Secret Service and U.S. Department of Education.

Vygotsky, L. (1986). *Thought and language.* Cambridge, MA: MIT Press.

Wainright, J., & Patterson, C. (2006). Delinquency, victimization, and substance use among adolescents with female same-sex parents. *Journal of Family Psychology, 20,* 526–530.

Walberg, H. J. (2007). *School choice: The findings.* Washington, DC: Cato Institute.

Wallace, B., & Eriksson, G. (Eds.). (2006). *Diversity in gifted education: International perspectives on global issues.* New York, NY: Routledge.

Walker, C. (2001). *We can't go home again: An argument about Afrocentrism.* New York, NY: Oxford University Press.

Webster, Y. O. (1997). *Against the multicultural agenda: A critical thinking alternative.* Westport, CT: Praeger.

Webster-Stratton, C. (2000). *How to promote social and academic competence in young children.* London, UK: Sage.

Webster-Stratton, C. (2006). *The incredible years: A trouble-shooting guide for parents of children ages 3–8 years.* Seattle, WA: Incredible Years Press.

Webster-Stratton, C., & Herman, K. C. (2010). Disseminating Incredible Years series early-intervention programs: Integrating and sustaining services between school and home. *Psychology in the Schools, 47*(1), 36–54.

Weiner, L. (2006). *Urban teaching: The essentials.* New York, NY: Teachers College Press.

Weiss, J. (2006, November 12). How did 'Kumbaya' become a mocking metaphor? Accessed September 2010 from *Dallas Morning News,* http://www.dallasnews.com/sharedcontent/dws/dn/religion/stories/DN-kumbaya_11rel.ART0.State.Edition1.3e6da2d.html

Weissberg, R. (2010). *Bad students, not bad schools.* New Brunswick, NJ: Transaction.

Wellman, D. T. (1993). *Portraits of white racism* (2nd ed.). New York, NY: Cambridge University Press.

Western, B., & Wildeman, C. (2009). The black family and mass incarceration. *Annals of the American Academy of Political and Social Science, 621,* 221–242.

Westinghouse Learning Corporation and Ohio University. (1969). *The impact of Head Start: An evaluation of the effects of Head Start on children's cognitive and affective development* (Vols. 1 and 2, Report to the Office of Economic Opportunity). Athens, GA: Author.

Whitaker, J. D. (2005). Homeschooling. In S. W. Lee (Ed.), *Encyclopedia of school psychology* (pp. 245–247). Thousand Oaks, CA: Sage.

White, J. (1984). *The psychology of blacks.* Englewood Cliffs, NJ: Prentice-Hall.

Whitman, D. (2008). *Sweating the small stuff: Inner-city schools and the new paternalism.* Washington, DC: Thomas B. Fordham Institute Press.

Will, G. (2006, January 5). White guilt deciphered. *Newsweek,* p. 68.

Williams, D. A., & Wade-Golden, K. C. (2006). What is a Chief Diversity Officer? Accessed June 2011 from *Inside Higher Ed.Com,* http://www.insidehighered.com/workplace/2006/04/18/williams

Williams, R. L. (1971). Abuses and misuses in testing black children. *Counseling Psychologist, 2,* 62–77.

Williams, R. L. (1974, May). Scientific racism and IQ: The silent mugging of the black community. *Psychology Today*, 32–41.

Williams, W. E. (1990). Myth making and reality testing. *Society, 27*(4), 4–7.

Willingham, D. T. (2007, Summer). Critical thinking: Why is it so hard to teach? *American Educator*, 8–19.

Willner, L. S., Rivera, C., & Acosta, B. D. (2007). *Decision-making practices of urban districts for including and accommodating English Language Learners in NAEP: School-based perspectives.* Arlington, VA: George Washington University Center for Equity and Excellence in Education.

Wilson, E. (2001, November 14). Beating a new kind of drum. Accessed January 2011 from *East Bay Express*, http://www.emilywilsonreports.com/pdfs/ebexpress%20beating%20a%20different%20drum.pdf

Wilson, J. Q. (2002). Why we don't marry. Accessed October 2011 from *City Journal*, http://www.city-journal.org/html/12_1_why_we.html

Wilson, J. Q., & Kelling, G. L. (1982, March). Broken windows: The police and neighborhood safety. *Atlantic Monthly, 249*(3), 29–38.

Wilson, W. J. (1987). *The truly disadvantaged: The inner city, the underclass, and public policy.* Chicago, IL: University of Chicago Press.

Wilson, W. J. (1993). *The ghetto underclass: Social science perspectives.* Newbury Park, CA: Sage.

Winner, E. (1996). *Gifted children: Myths and realities.* New York, NY: Basic Books.

Wise, A., & Velayutham, S. (Eds.). (2009). *Everyday multiculturalism.* Hampshire, UK: Palgrave MacMillan.

Wolf, M. K., Griffin, N., Kao, J. C., Chang, S. M., & Rivera, N. M. (2009). *Connecting policy to practice: Accommodations in states' large-scale math assessments for English language learners* (CRESST Report 765). Los Angeles, CA: University of California, National Center for Research on Evaluation, Standards, and Student Testing (CRESST).

Wolfram, G. (2011, January 7). Is a lack of computers really the problem with Detroit schools? Accessed February 2011 from the *Michigan View*, http://detnews.com/article/20110107/MIVIEW/101070359/Is-a-lack-of-computers-really-the-problem-with-Detroit-schools

Wolters, R. (1984). *The burden of Brown: Thirty years of school desegregation.* Knoxville, TN: University of Tennessee Press.

Wolters, R. (2008). *Race and education, 1954–2007.* Columbia, MO: University of Missouri Press.

Wood, P. (2003). *Diversity: The invention of a concept.* San Francisco, CA: Encounter Books.

Woodcock, R. W., McGrew, K. S., & Mather, N. (2001). *Woodcock-Johnson III Tests of Achievement.* Itasca, IL: Riverside.

WorldNetDaily.com. (2005, October). School board bans religious holidays. Accessed March 2011 from *WorldNetDaily.com*, http://www.wnd.com/news/article.asp?ARTICLE_ID=47063

Worrell, F. (2005). Cultural variation within American families of African descent. In C. L. Frisby & C. R. Reynolds (Eds.), *Comprehensive handbook of multicultural school psychology* (pp. 137–172). Hoboken, NJ: Wiley.

Wright, B. (2005, September 21). *Katrina reveals environmental racism's deadly force.* Accessed September 2010 from New America Media, http://news.ncmonline.com/news/view_article .html?article_id=74fb2e18f6e1c829ae73181353442a61

Wright, J. (2008, April 28). Transcript of Jeremiah Wright's speech to NAACP. Accessed January 2010 from http://edition.cnn.com/2008/POLITICS/04/28/wright.transcript/index .html

Wright, J. P., Tibbetts, S. G., & Daigle, L. E. (2008). *Criminals in the making: Criminality across the life course.* Los Angeles, CA: Sage.

Wyrick, P. A. (2006). Gang prevention: How to make the "front end" of your anti-gang effort work. *United States Attorneys' Bulletin, 54,* 52–60.

Yoon, J. S., & Cheng, L. L. (2005). Cultural variation within East Asian American families. In C. L. Frisby & C. R. Reynolds (Eds.), *Comprehensive handbook of multicultural school psychology* (pp. 265–300). Hoboken, NJ: Wiley.

Zarate, M. E., & Conchas, G. Q. (2010). Contemporary and critical methodological shifts in research on Latino education. In E. G. Murillo, S. A. Villenas, R. T. Galván, J. S. Muñoz, C. Martínez, & M. Machado-Casas (Eds.), *Handbook of Latinos and education* (pp. 90–107). New York, NY: Routledge.

Zeaman, D., & House, B. J. (1979). A review of attention theory. In N. R. Ellis (Ed.), *Handbook of mental deficiency, psychological theory and research* (pp. 63–120). Hillsdale, NJ: Erlbaum.

Zeidner, M. (1998). *Test anxiety: The state of the art.* New York City, NY: Plenum.

Author Index

Subject Index